LÉON WALRAS, ELEMENTS OF THEORETICAL ECONOMICS

In his fourth edition of *Éléments d'économie politique pure* (1900), Léon Walras introduced the device of written pledges to eliminate path dependency: sellers of products and services write out commitments to supply certain quantities at suggested prices. He tried unsuccessfully to show thereby that no commodities are actually produced and supplied until a set of prices is found at which supply and demand are equal simultaneously in every market. This brought about very serious alterations to the character of the book. Unfortunately, these changes resulted in an incomplete, internally contradictory, and occasionally incoherent text. This translation, therefore, by two leading scholars of Léon Walras's work, Donald Walker and Jan van Daal, revisits the third edition of his seminal work, including his brilliant explanation of his mature comprehensive model, with all its richness derived from reality. Growing research indicates that it was this third edition that contained his best theoretical research, so a translation of this edition of the book is therefore now a necessity.

Donald A. Walker received a Ph.D. in Economics from Harvard University. He specializes in microeconomic theory and the history of neoclassical economic thought. Dr. Walker was the president of the History of Economics Society (1987–1988), named Distinguished Fellow of that Society (2006), editor of the *Journal of the History of Economic Thought* (1990–1998), and founder and first president of the International Walras Association (1997–2000). Among numerous other publications, he is the author of many articles on the writings of Léon Walras, and of *Walras's Market Models* (Cambridge University Press, 1996) and *Walrasian Economics* (Cambridge University Press, 2006).

Jan van Daal received a Ph.D. from Erasmus University in Rotterdam. He has researched and taught in the area of mathematical economics and published on demand systems, aggregation problems, and the theory and history of general economic equilibrium. Dr. van Daal specializes in research on the life and works of Léon Walras and has published, among other writings, *The Equilibrium Economics of Léon Walras* (with Albert Jolink, 1993), the translation of *Walras's Études d'économie appliquée* (2005), and the translation of *Walras's Études d'économie sociales* (with Donald Walker, 2010).

To future generations of economists, whose understanding of economic life and of the methods of economic theorizing will be enriched by their study of this immortal work

Léon Walras, Elements of Theoretical Economics

or *The Theory of Social Wealth*

Translated and edited by

DONALD A. WALKER

Indiana University of Pennsylvania

JAN VAN DAAL

Triangle, University of Lyons-2

CAMBRIDGE UNIVERSITY PRESS

CAMBRIDGE
UNIVERSITY PRESS

University Printing House, Cambridge CB2 8BS, United Kingdom

One Liberty Plaza, 20th Floor, New York, NY 10006, USA

477 Williamstown Road, Port Melbourne, VIC 3207, Australia

314-321, 3rd Floor, Plot 3, Splendor Forum, Jasola District Centre, New Delhi - 110025, India

79 Anson Road, #06-04/06, Singapore 079906

Cambridge University Press is part of the University of Cambridge.

It furthers the University's mission by disseminating knowledge in the pursuit of
education, learning and research at the highest international levels of excellence.

www.cambridge.org
Information on this title: www.cambridge.org/9781107651456

© Donald A. Walker and Jan van Daal 2014

First published 2014
First paperback edition 2019

A catalogue record for this publication is available from the British Library

Library of Congress Cataloging in Publication data
Walras, Léon, 1834–1910.
[Éléments d'économie politique pure. English]
Léon Walras, Elements of theoretical economics : or The theory of social wealth /
[translated and edited by] Donald A. Walker, Indiana University of Pennsylvania;
Jan van Daal, Triangle, University of Lyons-2
pages cm
Includes bibliographical references and index.
ISBN 978-1-107-06413-3 (hardback)
1. Economics. 2. Economics, Mathematical. I. Walker, Donald A.
(Donald Anthony), 1934– II. Daal, J. van (Jan), 1937– III. Title.
HB173.W2213 2014
330–dc23
2014020409

ISBN 978-1-107-06413-3 Hardback
ISBN 978-1-107-65145-6 Paperback

Contents

Translators' introduction

Léon Walras was the founder of the modern theory of general economic equilibrium.[1] He was born on December 16, 1834, in Evreux, France, and christened Marie Esprit Léon. He had an excellent education during the period 1844 to 1854, covering such subjects as logic, philosophy, ethics, history, physical sciences, chemistry, mechanics, elementary mathematics, geometry, and calculus. After his *lycée* education, however, he failed the entrance examinations for the École Polytechnique, and did not make high enough grades to be retained in the program at the École impériale des Mines. Pursuing his predominant interests, in 1856 he abandoned the plan of becoming an engineer, began the pursuit of a literary career, and in fact published a novel and a short story. Revealing, however, an interest that had been latent but that had become even stronger, he made a promise in 1858 to his father, Auguste Walras, to give up his literary pursuits and to devote himself totally to the continuation of his father's economic studies.

Four phases of his subsequent scientific career can be distinguished: (1) the beginnings, (2) high creativity, (3) maturity, (4) decline. We deal with these phases in section 1 of this introduction. In section 2, we pay attention to the fourth phase, explaining that the fourth edition (1900) of Walras's *Éléments d'économie politique pure*, composed during that phase, contains new elements that are not improvements, but, on the contrary, that spoil his previous work. In section 3, we argue that the second and third editions of the *Éléments* are Walras's best theoretical work. In fact, there is so much original and creative

---

[1] For a biography of Walras, see Dockès and Potier 2001.

ix

economic thought in these editions that has been neglected that we decided to prepare an English translation of the third edition.[2] In section 4, we explain that the third edition has an important place in the history of economic thought because many contemporaries and immediate followers of Walras took elements of the third edition that are not in the fourth as a basis of their research on general economic equilibrium. This constitutes another reason for our translation. In section 5, we make some remarks on translating in general and on translating Walras's writings in particular. We also discuss some aspects of Jaffé's translation of the fifth edition of the *Éléments*. A short conclusion follows in section 6. We then added four appendixes. Appendix A presents two tables that are relevant for our discussion in section 2. Appendix B deals with some of Walras's terminological idiosyncrasies regarding the factors of production. Appendix C contains a table of correspondence between the parts, lessons, and sections of edition 3 and editions 4 and 5. A table of the correspondence between the parts, lessons, and sections of all the editions of the *Éléments* has been provided by Jaffé in his translation (1954, pp. 559–63), and modified in Walker 1996, pp. 436–42; see also *ŒÉC*, vol. VIII, pp. 733–7.[3] Appendix D informs the reader about our editorial treatment of the translation.

Unlike his procedure in the first edition, Walras preceded the second and third editions of the *Éléments* with a nineteen-page presentation titled 'Des fonctions et de leur représentation géométrique. Théorie mathématique de la chute des corps'. His intention in doing so was to aid the reader to understand better the mathematics employed in his economic writings and to assert, in two sections, a parallelism of the results of the application of mathematics to physical sciences and their application to economic theory. We have not included this treatment of functions and of the law of gravity because it is an extraneous element bound in the books that contain the second or third editions but is not part of them, and it is not an exposition of economics. Walras placed it before the title page for Part I, and he numbered its sections separately from those of the book. He did not put it into the subsequent editions of the *Éléments*.

---

[2]   See below for the differences between these two editions.
[3]   *ŒÉC* stands for *Œuvres économiques complètes*, the collected works of Auguste and Léon Walras (1987–2005).

1. FOUR PHASES OF INTELLECTUAL ACTIVITY

The first phase. Walras's first phase of intellectual activity in regard to economic theory, beginning in 1859 and continuing until 1872, consisted largely of journalistic applications of his knowledge of existing theory but also included his study of social economics. Of course, Walras had to earn a living for himself and his family, so, during the years 1860 to 1870, he worked successively as a journalist, in a bank, in a railroad office, became managing director of a cooperative association bank, and worked for another bank. During this time, however, he began his lifelong study of economics. That was therefore a subject to which he devoted himself for many years, so it is not surprising that the degree of his technical sophistication and the character and quality of his theoretical work changed over time. His participation in 1860 in a conference on taxation in Lausanne (1861)[4] and his publication of a long examination of the economic doctrines of P.-J. Proudhon in that year (1860) – one that mainly set forth the ideas of his father, Auguste Walras – are examples of his early interest in economic topics. Among his ideas was the argument that the state should own all land on the grounds that it is the patrimony of the entire nation because it is not produced as the result of the activity of any economic agent. Its value is given to it by the growth of the value of its services, which depends upon the growth of population and of the economy, but its increased value would occur whether the land is owned privately or by the state. Walras also wrote many analyses of economic problems, notably contributing articles to the journals *La Presse*, *L'Indépendant de la Moselle*, *Journal des Économistes*, and *Le Travail*, and gave and published public lectures on his ideas about an ideal society (1868). Those writings can be seen to be his early efforts to adopt an analytical approach to the study of practical economic issues, an approach that he refined in later years. Moreover,

---

[4] A date without a name, sometimes followed by a page or section number, refers to Léon Walras's writings. See the references at the end of this introduction. Furthermore, in order to facilitate the comparison of the present translation with Jaffe's and with volume VIII of *ŒÉC*, we use section numbers to refer to places in one or another of the editions of the *Éléments*. Such a section number always refers to the edition of the *Éléments* under discussion. In this respect, our table C1 will be helpful.

at the start and again toward the end of the first phase of his career, Walras began to use mathematics in the construction of rudimentary models dealing with exchange (1860, 1869, 1871; see *ŒÉC*, vol. XI, pp. 315–409). He relates in his autobiography that the 'idea of creating mathematical economics, which I had announced in my letter offering my services to the Council of State of Vaud, never ceased to occupy my mind after 1860' (1965, vol. I, p. 5). He did not, however, have an adequate foundation in mathematics and lacked some of the concepts that he needed to establish the foundations of a theory of supply and demand and of the interrelationships of markets. Nothing that he wrote during the first phase of his career can be considered a valuable contribution to economic theory. On the other hand, some of his writings on moral philosophy, in particular his analysis of the human society (see above), are of enduring value and found a rightful place in his *Études d'économie sociale* (1898, chapters 2 and 3; 2010, pp. 19–113).

Nevertheless, Walras's early research made a valuable contribution to his career. His 1861 paper on taxation drew him to the attention of Louis Ruchonnet, a Swiss statesman who, nine years later, recommended successfully that Walras be offered an appointment at the Académie (subsequently Université) de Lausanne. Walras began his duties there as a professor without tenure in 1870, and the next year his appointment became permanent. His subsequent attempts to obtain a position in a French university were rebuffed because he lacked the necessary educational credentials and, moreover, was an exponent of mathematical economics, which was regarded unfavorably by the academic establishment. He therefore remained at Lausanne for his entire academic career, retiring because of bad health in 1892.

The second phase. Walras's second phase of theoretical activity, his period of high creativity and maximum theoretical prolificacy, spanned the period 1872 to 1877. It was during those years that he developed his initial comprehensive model of general equilibrium. By his comprehensive model is meant one that includes exchange, production, consumption, capital formation, credit, and money. He first presented it in four memoirs (1877a), the substance and much of the wording of which he put into the first edition of the *Éléments d'économie politique pure* (1874; 1877b). Walras published that edition in two installments, one in 1874 and the other in 1877. We chose not to translate the first edition because, although it is a brilliant expression of pure originality, containing many theoretical innovations, it needed alteration and development in a variety of important respects.

The third phase. Walras's third intellectual phase, that of his maturity as an economic theoretician, began around 1877 and was given full expression in the second edition of the *Éléments*, published in 1889. In that edition he presented his mature comprehensive model of general equilibration and equilibrium in a purely competitive economy. Walras reaffirmed his satisfaction with that presentation in a third edition published in 1896. In it he also reissued the introduction and the body of the second edition, eliminated four lessons (37–40 of the second edition) that deal with the applied theory of money, and added 29 pages of appendixes of material previously published during his period of maturity. Henceforward, when we refer to the third edition, we will evidently mean the contents of the second edition reissued, along with the indicated deletions and additions, as a third edition. We will return very shortly to our discussion of the third edition.

The fourth phase. Walras's fourth intellectual phase began about 1896. His output of theoretical and other work had begun to diminish long before that year, but soon afterwards his powers of concentration and analysis weakened rapidly, and the lessening of his productivity and creativity became more marked (see Appendix A to this introduction). His only new research after 1898 was the article 'Équations de la circulation' (1899) and some revisions to the *Éléments* that resulted in a fourth edition in 1900. Although the new material in the fourth edition totaled only 35 pages, it profoundly affected the character of that edition and of the subsequent history of general equilibrium theory, as will be seen shortly. The major changes in that edition were Walras's displacement of his 1889 theory of money by the text of the 1899 article, and the introduction of a sketch of a pricing process that was outlined in a note appended to the article. Subsequently, making a few inconsequential alterations, he produced a fifth edition, published posthumously (1926).

A final phase of Walras's life spanned the years from 1901 to his death in 1910. That could be viewed as a period of repose rather than an intellectual phase, for after 1900 he wrote not another word of theory and very little of anything else. Thus as a contributor to economic theory, he bloomed late – at the age of thirty-seven or thirty-eight – and faded early, writing less each decade after 1877, and writing little and adding even less of value after he was sixty, and nothing at all in the way of theoretical contributions during the last eleven years of his life, as has been demonstrated in a methodical and quantitative way (Walker 1999, 2006, pp. 183–92). He died on January 5, 1910, in Clarens, Switzerland, and the publication of the fifth edition was accomplished by his daughter Aline in 1926.

2. RESEARCH DURING THE FOURTH PHASE

Prior to issuing the fourth edition, Walras had been aware that the irrevocable disequilibrium transactions and disequilibrium production in his mature comprehensive model generated path dependency, which meant that the solutions to his systems of equations of general equilibrium were not the outcomes of the behavior of the model.[5] He wanted those equations to be valid reflections and expressions of the interrelationships and equilibrium of a model that included durable goods and inventories. He realized that a virtual adjustment process would make it possible to have such a model. By a virtual economic process is meant one that is acted out without any changes in real economic magnitudes. If the model were complete, the only changes would be in suggested prices and desired supplies and demands. There would be no transactions, production, consumption, savings, or any other non-pricing economic behavior in disequilibrium, and thus no changes in the amount of capital goods or other asset holdings, and thus no changes in supply and demand functions during the equilibrating process of changing suggested prices.

---

[5] He implied that it was a problem in 1889, in a revision of passages in the second edition, when he inserted the condition that exchange must be suspended if supply and demand are not equal (§ 42). He indicated in 1885, as a reaction to a comment made in 1883 by the mathematician Joseph Bertrand, that he had excluded non-virtual behavior from his model of exchange in order to eliminate path dependency (1896b, p. 352, n. 1; 2010, p. 250, n. 2; see also Walker 1996, pp. 95–100).

In 1899 he came to believe that that type of a model could be constructed by introducing the device of written pledges.[6] That was the content of the above-mentioned note published in 1899 and elaborated slightly in the fourth edition. Walras specified that sellers of products and services write out commitments[7] to supply certain quantities at suggested prices with no commodities actually produced and supplied until a set of prices is found at which supply and demand is equal simultaneously in every market (1926, §§ 207, 251). If that were true, the holdings of assets would be constants during the process of finding those prices, fulfilling the requirement that the holdings be constants in the equations of his model. The equilibrium prices would therefore be the solutions to his system of static equations of general equilibrium. The equilibrating changes of asset holdings, production, consumption, etc., would occur only at the equilibrium set of prices and would therefore leave those prices unchanged. The new set of magnitudes of stocks and flows would remain unchanged until some parametric change disrupted the equilibrium.

By thrusting the written pledges sketch into the fourth edition and retaining it in the fifth, Walras brought about very serious alterations of the character of the *Éléments*. He presented a text that has created much mischief by confusing the reader as to what Walras's theories are. In the first place, it became internally contradictory because in the majority of the pages of the fourth edition (and hence of the fifth) that deal with the question of the stability of equilibrium, Walras retained most of the depictions of the behavior of disequilibrium transactions and production that he had carefully developed in the third edition. That non-virtual behavior is incompatible with

---

[6] So named after the term *engagements écrits* used in French securities markets. Walras used the word '*bons*' for the pledges written out by would-be suppliers, meaning that the seller pledges himself to be good for the quantity he offers. Jaffé translated Walras's word as 'tickets'. Walras did not, however, use a French word for 'tickets' (*ticket, billet*), and in English a ticket has no features in common with his '*bons*' or written pledges. A ticket has its conditions printed on it; it is not generated or written on by its holder but is bought by him. It is used to be admitted to a form of transportation or an event, or to be represented in a lottery; or, in other senses, is a tag or label, a license, a political slate, or a document issued by a police officer for a traffic violation. Thus Jaffé's translation conflicts with Walras's terminology, and with French and English language and practice.

[7] Only the sellers make commitments; see below.

what he asserted to be true of the written pledges sketch. That is to say, Walras tried to construct a comprehensive model that is virtual because of the use of written pledges, but that has some markets that he asserted were of that type, some markets that he described as virtual without having written or oral pledges, and some markets that do not have written pledges and are non-virtual. In some passages he even described some commodities as being sold in written pledges and in other passages described those same commodities as being sold in non-virtual markets.[8] The sub-models of particular markets are incompatible with each other and with his system of equations of general equilibrium, which require that all the markets be virtual.

Second, the sketch in the treatise is incomplete, illogical, superficial, and incoherent. Walras made his last mention of it and its supposed results less than two thirds of the way through the text (1900, 1926, § 274), and then apparently lost interest in that idea, not referring to it again, neither in the subsequent 185 pages of the book nor anywhere else. He was unable to devise a complete model of a virtual market, which is why we call it a sketch rather than a model. It lacks a demand side because there are no potential demanders who make written or oral pledges to purchase commodities, so they have no way of expressing demands. Since there are no equations of demand in the sketch, there are more unknowns than independent equations. This crucial defect is present in every one of Walras's presentations of the written pledges sketch. Moreover, it lacks the institutions and market rules and physical features and technology that would be necessary for the functioning of a pricing mechanism. There is no way for prices to be determined and announced, that is, no means of collecting information from would-be suppliers, and no market demands which could be used in conjunction with supply pledges in order for there to be excess demands. Since there are no excess demands, there is no behavior or information to serve as the basis for changing prices either up or down. Would-be suppliers and demanders do not meet, so there are no markets. Equilibrium does not exist in the sketch and it has no stability properties.

---

[8] See Walker 1996, pp. 411–12.

Readers of Walras's fifth edition have unthinkingly added the missing demanders in their account of Walras's sketch, as did Jaffé when he asserted in what he believed was an explanatory note that 'the tickets issued *by buyers* of products as well as *by buyers* and sellers of services *are similarly worded*' (Walras 1954, p. 528, note [5]; emphasis added). Walras never wrote that buyers issue tickets. For example, he wrote that *suppliers* of new capital goods ('entrepreneurs') represent them with *bons* – he used that word for 'written pledges' with the thought that suppliers write out the amounts for which they are good – and that there are *suppliers* of services, namely 'landowners, workers, and capitalists representing similarly by *bons* the successive quantities of services at prices cried first at random...' (Walras 1926, § 251; emphasis added[9]). He did not mention buyers in those markets (in this case, the markets for newly constructed capital goods and services). Nevertheless, the innocent reader of Jaffé's translation finds that he represented Walras as writing that 'land-owners, workers and capitalists also use *tickets* to represent the successive quantities of *services* **which are offered and demanded** at prices first cried at random...' (Walras 1954, p. 282; boldface added to Jaffé's words; see the boldfaced passage in the preceding footnote). As has just been shown, Walras did not write the words in boldface; they were added by Jaffé. The 'landowners, workers, and capitalists' in Walras's sentence are service suppliers; he did not mention demanders of the services.

---

[9] The original French passage is:

Un certain taux du revenu net et certains prix des services étant criés, et certaines quantités de produits et de capitaux neufs étant fabriquées, si ce taux, ces prix et ces quantités ne sont pas taux, prix et quantités d'équilibre, il faut non seulement crier un autre taux et d'autres prix, mais fabriquer d'autres quantités de produits et de capitaux neufs.

Nous résoudrons cette première difficulté en supposant les entrepreneurs de capitaux neufs représenter par des *bons* certaines quantités successives de ces *produits* déterminées d'abord au hasard, puis en augmentation ou diminution suivant qu'il y aura excédent du prix de vente sur le prix de revient ou réciproquement, jusqu'à égalité de ces deux prix; **et les propriétaires fonciers, travailleurs et capitalistes représenter de même par des bons des quantités successives de services à des prix criés d'abord au hasard**, puis en hausse ou baisse suivant qu'il y aura excèdent de la demande sur l'offre du montant des capitaux neufs en numéraire, ou réciproquement, jusqu'à égalité de l'une et de l'autre (Walras 1926, pp. 259–60; boldface added).

Since a critique of the written pledges sketch is part of the rationale for our translation, it is relevant to remark upon yet another indication of Walras's incapacity to undertake sound modeling in the fifth edition. In the exposition just mentioned and similarly elsewhere, not only did he not equip demanders of services with pledges or even mention such participants, he did not represent changes of the prices of services as being a function of the supply and demand for them. Instead, he went on to assert that their 'prices cried first at random' are 'then raised or lowered according to whether there is an excess of demand over supply *of the amount of new capital goods...*' (1900, 1926, § 251; emphasis added; see the preceding footnote). That is, he asserted that prices of services are changed, not as a direct function of their excess demand, which actually does not exist, but as a direct and exclusive function of the excess demand *in another market*, namely the market for new capital goods, which is absurd. Compounding the confusion, he wrote in this, as in other circumstances, as though there is a single market for new capital goods, whereas there are many in reality and in his treatise, one for each kind.

Methodologically, Walras did not derive the features he attributes to the sketch from economic reality; what he describes as its outcomes are actually postulates that have no foundation in any conceivable institutional, technological, and behavioral phenomena. The material inserted into the fourth/fifth edition cannot be used in any empirical connection, no matter how the written pledges sketch is amended, because the real economy is not virtual. Most transactions and all production and consumption are irrevocable disequilibrium magnitudes, whereas none of the variables in the written pledges sketch are supposed to materialize in disequilibrium. Additionally, Walras's exposition of virtual behavior negatively affects the content of the theorization. It is disorganized, analytically confused, characterized by unclear definitions, badly arranged statements, lacunae, conflations of separate topics, contradictions, fragmentary constructions, long but elliptical sentences, rambling discourses, symbols and words crowded together in baffling sequences (Walker 1996, p. 400). Therefore, Walras's allegation that the behavior of the written pledges sketch eventuates in finding the set of equilibrium prices and quantities that are the solutions of his equations is not true. Even if the sketch is revised to enable demanders to make written pledges, its problems are so fundamental that it cannot be made into a function-ing system (see Walker 1996, pp. 379–95). It is defective in ways that cannot be rectified.

Some of the writings that Walras presented as a monetary theory are a mystery, centered as they are on incomprehensible equations.[10] The text of the 1899 article on circulation and money, which con-tained his last theory of money and which he inserted verbatim into the fourth edition of the *Éléments*, made no mention whatsoever of pledges, and the monetary behavior in it contradicts the character-istics that he wanted to be true of the sketch. There are many other theoretical mistakes in the few lines that he added in the fifth edition but an exposition of them would require extensive contextualization and detailed economic analysis and is best read, like the whole of this critique, in a careful extended discussion (see Walker 1996, chap-ters 17 and 18).

With all respect for the Master of Lausanne, we have to conclude that the chaotic collection of incompatible non-virtual and incom-plete written pledge markets does not constitute a functioning gen-eral equilibrium model. Of course, Walras stated that the sketch has an equilibrium (1900, 1926, §§ 207, 251, 274), but that is not true. His proof that equilibrium exists in each of his models is the same, namely that the number of independent equations and the number of unknowns are equal. That is not a proof regarding any economic model and especially not regarding the sketch because it has fewer equations than unknowns. The sketch is not sufficiently complete behaviorally, institutionally, and technologically to have an equilib-rium. It has no path of variables and therefore no stability proper-ties. It does not achieve Walras's objective of validating his system of equations.

By initiating the idea of a virtual general equilibrium model, however, Walras laid a basis for a subsequent type of modeling. Modifications of the written pledges sketch, themselves without institutional and technological foundations and based on implausible

---

[10] Its characteristics prompted Pascal Bridel, an authority on Walras's treatment of money, to exclaim that 'there is no genuine monetary theory' in the fourth edition (Bridel 1997, p. 133). For a discussion of the merits of some of Walras's monetary innovations in the fourth edition, see Van Daal and Jolink 1993, ch. 16, and Van Daal 1994.

assumptions, constitute a branch of modern purely competitive general equilibrium theory, characterized by extreme unreality that has led to a scientific dead end. 'Suffice it to say, general equilibrium theory...had a very large burden to bear. It proved unequal to this task. Such became clear in a spectacular series of impossibility results that might be called Sonnenschein-Mantel-Debreu theorems after its main promulgators' (Rizvi 2003, p. 384). Their work 'showed that formalist general equilibrium theory had reached a dead end: no general results beyond existence of equilibrium were possible' (ibid.). 'Strictly, the arbitrariness results put an end to neoclassical general equilibrium theory of the Arrow-Debreu-McKenzie variety' (ibid., p. 385), that is to say, the virtual line of purely competitive general equilibrium models that were the descendants of the written pledges sketch in Walras's fourth and fifth editions.

The *Éléments* has been translated into Japanese (1933, 1953, and 1983), Chinese (1966), Italian (1974), and Spanish (1987); these are all translations of the fifth edition of the *Éléments* (1926). The previous English translation of the *Éléments*, namely, William Jaffé's (Walras 1954), is also a translation of that edition. That has been the unique source from which English-reading economists derived their knowledge of the *Éléments*. It has not even crossed the minds of most of them that the last edition of the *Éléments* may not be his best and definitive work on the theory of general equilibrium. Jaffé's translation of it has therefore led to a virtually complete neglect of his mature comprehensive model and therefore to much misunderstanding and under-valuation of Walras's contributions.

3. WORK DONE DURING THE MATURE PHASE

Fortunately, there is a magnificent alternative edition of the *Éléments*, namely the third, published in 1896. In it Walras presented the thoughts of his period of intellectual maturity as a theoretician, lasting from 1877 to about the middle of the 1890s. The defects of the fifth edition and the scientific and historical value of the third explain why we have chosen to translate the latter. We have made Walras's best theoretical work accessible to those who do not read French but who read English. We hope thereby to end, for the Anglophone economist, the monopolization of his writings by Jaffé's translation and hence the domination of Walras's worst ideas in certain parts of his general equilibrium theory.

During the years after the publication in 1874 and 1877 of the two parts of the first edition of the *Éléments*, Walras altered, fleshed out, refined, and extended his concepts and theoretical tools, including the use of calculus, work that culminated in the third edition of the *Éléments*. He presented there his mature comprehensive model of general economic equilibration and equilibrium in a freely competitive economy, a reasonably complete, well-organized, and coherent exposition of a system containing many sub-models of aspects of economic behavior, woven into a seamless functioning whole. In that model, Walras not only expressed the belief that all economic phenomena are interrelated, which had been done by many economists before him, he also specified their interrelations, provided an account of their disequilibrium behavior, and described their conditions of equilibrium. Its various parts included models of consumers, workers, landlords, capitalists, and entrepreneurs, of exchange, production, capital formation and credit, a time-period analysis of monetary behavior, an analysis of arbitrage, an account and analysis of the operations of securities exchanges, and a treatment of economic growth. Walras included in his treatise his theory of monopoly and price fixing, and his analysis of taxation, and left his account of those matters unchanged in the fourth edition. Walras also added three brilliant and important appendixes to the third edition. He eliminated the third of these from the fourth/fifth edition, thus depriving the reader of the latter of that particular systematic treatment of the theory of marginal productivity; instead, he inserted some of the content of the appendix into the body of the text of the fourth and fifth editions of the *Éléments*. Fortunately, Jaffé provided his English translation of that appendix as an extra to his translation of the fifth edition of the *Éléments*.

Unlike the written pledges sketch, the mature model is logically valid in the important respect that the behavior it contains and its outcomes are generated by economic and social institutions, market procedures and rules, technologies, and other structural and behavioral underpinnings. That is not to say that its outcomes are the solutions to the system of static equations of general equilibrium, as far as concerns his models with capital formation.[11] They are not, so there is an important respect in which the model is not logical if it is taken to be inclusive of the equations; or, to put differently, the model and equations are incompatible. The equations are inconsistent with the non-virtual behavior of the system in disequilibrium and the consequent path dependency of any equilibrium that it may have. Although Walras did not try to find a system of dynamic equations and their solutions that could complete the model, he identified its variables, its characteristics that determine the directions of their movements in disequilibrium, and their qualitative behavior.[12]

There is a sharp contrast between the degree of realism in the third and the fifth editions. In the fifth, the written pledges sketch has no connection with economic reality. The characteristics Walras assumed it to have are simply figments of his imagination. In the third, he tried to make sure that his assumptions are connected to reality, although they are abstract and general. To do so, Walras drew from the economy of his day the economic elements that he considered important and put them into his model. For example, believing that the majority of real markets in the economy of his day were freely competitive, Walras assumed that that is true of all the markets in his general equilibrium model. He observed that there is irrevocable disequilibrium economic behavior in the real world, and he assumed that it occurred in his model. Likewise, he inferred from his experience the assumption that all economic variables are interdependent. He even stated (erroneously) that his equations could, in principle, be converted into empirical statements by using statistical research to obtain numerical values for their coefficients.

Three major questions that arise concerning a model of general equilibrium are the existence of equilibrium in it, the uniqueness of equilibrium, and the stability of equilibrium. Walras was the first to consider these questions with reference to that type of model, thereby

---

[11] One aspect of the written pledges device is that Walras's mature consumer commodities model, into which he introduced it, has no need of such a feature because the model is not path dependent (Walker 1996, ch. 7), and another is that in his subsequent models, which are path dependent, the device does not work.

[12] Like all the great theorists, Walras recognized the truth of Claude Bernard's maxim that 'The *qualitative* study of phenomena must necessarily precede their *quantitative* study' (quoted in Robert 2002, p. 2129).

initiating the central agenda of general equilibrium research during the one hundred years that followed the first edition of his *Éléments*. We give a brief account of his research on these matters to alert the reader to the remarkably rich content of what is to be found in the third edition.

The existence of general equilibrium. Walras indicated the conditions of a Walrasian equilibrium, that is to say, that the supply and demand are equal simultaneously for each good and service at positive prices. He counted the number of variables and the number of independent equations in his model, established that the two are equal, and concluded from that equality that he had proved that an equilibrium exists. His immediate successors used the same procedure and arrived at the same conclusion. In regard to the uniqueness of equilibrium, Walras studied only the case of a model in which two commodities are exchanged for each other, concluding that there could be multiple equilibria and that there could be an unstable equilibrium. In the case of exchange of many commodities, he believed that 'generally' multiple equilibria are not possible, but he did not offer a proof of that assertion.

The stability of the mature comprehensive model. Reference to the stability of a model is a brief way of referring to the way that the model functions in disequilibrium. A stable model moves from disequilibrium to equilibrium. That is the principal topic that Walras takes up in the third edition. He wrote that the economy moves toward equilibrium by a process of tatonnement; that is, by groping its way. In what follows we briefly point out the main facets of economic behavior regarding which Walras explained how tatonnement and other adjustment processes occur, thereby presenting analyses and descriptions that pulsate with economic life (see, for example, lesson 37).

After having identified the market participants, the market institutions, the firms, the goods, the services, the manner of operating of the entrepreneurs, etc., Walras modeled their interrelated behavior in disequilibrium and in equilibrium. The sequence of prices quoted by the buyers and sellers in each market and the consequent sequence of quantities produced, sold, and used, influences the set of equilibrium prices and quantities. Walras believed that the sequences move toward equilibrium; that is, that stability of equilibrium is 'probable'

(§ 213) in the purely hypothetical case of a model in which all commodities are non-durable and are used as soon as they are produced. There are no asset holdings, so supply and demand functions do not change during the equilibrating process. In a model in which durable goods are produced, he stated that its stability is 'evident' (§ 254). As is evident from his conclusions regarding the processes of tatonnement, which occupy a great deal of the *Éléments*, he was convinced that his mature comprehensive model is stable. The reader of this book will see that Walras argued that the stability is brought about principally by a number of non-virtual aspects of the disequilibrium adjustment process.

First, Walras analyzed *homo œconomicus*, showing that he engages in tatonnements, that is, in successive adjustments in disequilibrium of the quantities he purchases and consumes of different products, including savings instruments, in order to maximize his utility.

Second, the entrepreneur ('*l'entrepreneur qui tâtonne*' (Walras 1896a, p. 490; this book, Appendix III)) makes a series of adjustments of the quantities of inputs into the process of production in his firm in the mature model, as distinct from the written pledges sketch in which he has no functions of any kind and does not make an appearance. In the mature model, the entrepreneur undertakes non-virtual adjustments in order to come progressively closer to the minimum cost of production and finally to reach it, and to maximize the output made by a given combination of inputs.

A third aspect of tatonnement is the changing of prices. This is done following a rule that Walras drew from his observations of real markets, namely that the price of each commodity in disequilibrium is changed in the same direction as the sign of the market excess demand until the price that equates supply and demand is reached. Suppliers and demanders meet in markets. They do not know the market excess demand, but suppliers lower the price when they find that they do not receive orders to sell all that they wish at the prevailing price, and demanders raise the price when they find that they do not receive commitments to provide all the amounts they wish. It will be noted that the participants change prices, so there is no mention of an auctioneer. Walras departed from reality by assuming that on any given market day there are no transactions at disequilibrium prices, and that trade occurs only at the price at which supply and demand are equal. He asserted that that was a hypothesis that no reasonable scientist would hesitate to concede to the theoretician. In his model, after trade occurs, the traders in each market consider the prices that have been found for commodities other than their own and react to them, changing their desired supply and demand quantities. The market day prices at which trade occurs are disequilibrium ones from the point of view of the general economy if the first round of pricing has not led all markets to be simultaneously in equilibrium. Normally they do not immediately reach general equilibrium, so additional rounds of pricing and irrecovable transactions occur within each market. Walras presented a detailed account of the paths of the prices, that is to say, of the economic behavior underlying and being expressed in the price changes, thus explaining why the prices in the many markets tend to an equilibrium set.

Fourth, in accordance with the behavior of real markets, Walras modeled the tatonnements in production. If the price of a product exceeds its average cost, the entrepreneurs increase the quantity produced in order to make more profits. That leads to the increase of the prices of services used in its production. Since the supply of an output increases, its price falls. The difference between the price and average cost, namely the profit, therefore decreases. That aspect of the overall tatonnement continues until the equalization of the two magnitudes reduces profits and the increase of output to zero. If the average cost is less than the price, the reverse process occurs.

A fifth aspect of tatonnement, also performed by the entrepreneurs, is their activity of directing economic resources in disequilibrium toward economic activities that are profitable and away from those in which there are losses. That has the effect of lowering prices in the lines of economic activity in which output is increased, diminishing their profitability, and the reverse in those in which output is decreased. The reallocations of resources cease when profits and losses are zero in all lines of activity. The profits to which Walras referred in the mature comprehensive model are really made, whereas in a virtual model profits are not actually made in any state of the market.

A sixth aspect of the tatonnement process occurs in the formation of new capital. This occurs until eventually the ratio of the net revenue per unit of each type of capital good and its price are the same for all capital goods, the price being equal to its average cost.

This same ratio is the equilibrium rate of interest that makes the consumers' and entrepreneurs' aggregate demand for money equal to its aggregate supply.

Some other contributions. Among the many other economic processes that Walras identified and explained in the third edition is his brilliant non-virtual theory of money, a theory which he had the bad judgment to eliminate from the fourth/fifth edition, thus leading its readers (in both French and English versions) to be unaware of that remarkable achievement. He examined monetary expenditures by means of a non-virtual time-period analysis, tracing a series of adjustments of payments, of cash balances held by the participants in the economy, and of changes of rates of interest. He thus anticipated the work of J.M. Keynes and D.H. Robertson on these matters. His theory of entrepreneurial profits is the foundation of Continental thinking on that subject. He anticipated (§ 370) the heart of the treatment of product differentiation and price discrimination that E.H. Chamberlin subsequently presented in his theory of monopolistic competition. Walras was the first to deal with the problem of bimetallism by noting that, in the case of a gold and silver standard, the problem of the ratio of the value of the two metals is not completely determined economically, and that the legislator can intervene to determine arbitrarily one of the six unknowns or introduce in one way or another a sixth equation (lesson 34). The third edition shows that Walras had a perfect grasp of the static theory of the firm (§ 362 ff.). He also studied the implications in disequilibrium and in equilibrium of Walras's law, of the budget of the firm and of the consumer, and of the theorem of equivalent distributions of commodities.

4. THE PLACE OF THE SECOND/THIRD EDITION IN THE HISTORY OF ECONOMIC THOUGHT

Another reason for providing Anglophone students of the history of economic thought with our translation is that the second and third editions were important in that history. Those editions were responsible for the origins and lines of development of the non-virtual branch of purely competitive general equilibrium theory. The treatise we have translated is the one that taught Walras's contemporaries and immediate successors their general equilibrium theory and in many other specific respects influenced their work, providing their methodological and theoretical points of departure. Their starting point was naturally the mature comprehensive model because that model, with its irrevocable disequilibrium tatonnement processes and phenomena, is the one presented in the editions of the *Éléments* that they studied, Walras having not yet devised the written pledges sketch when they began to learn his theories. Moreover, readers of his *Études d'économie politique appliquée* and of his *Études d'économie sociale* naturally found that when he referred to his *Éléments* in those books, he always meant editions prior to the fourth – naturally, because the *Études*, being collections of already existing articles, were published before the year 1900.

Despite the publication of the written pledges sketch in 1899 and 1900, the influence of Walras's third edition, and in particular its elaboration of non-virtual disequilibrium behavior, continued to be manifested. Vilfredo Pareto learned the foundations of his work on general equilibrium from the second edition of the *Éléments*[13] and never mentioned the written pledges sketch. In the 1890s, he praised Walras's mature concept of tatonnement, and used it in his account of the process of economic movement toward equilibrium (Pareto 1896/1897, *1*, pp. 24–5, 45–6). He refined Walras's equations, declaring that in his own studies 'the dynamic equilibrium' is finally attained, and he tried to give a rigorous account of its stability (Pareto 1897, p. 492). Knut Wicksell was strongly influenced by Walras. He also owned the second edition of the *Éléments*, and, indeed, he wrote to Walras in 1893 that he had a rather complete collection of the latter's writings (1965, vol. II, p. 596). Wicksell was concerned with the real economy, just as Walras was. Most of Wicksell's expositions consist of verbal accounts of non-virtual economic behavior, but he also used Walras's mathematical method of symbolizing some of its features and discovering its interconnections and consequences. H.L. Moore referred on one occasion (Moore 1929, p. 107) to the fourth edition, but he never mentioned the written pledges sketch or any of its characteristics. On the contrary, he devoted his career to the study

---

[13] See Pareto's acknowledgement of receipt of the second edition of the *Éléments* that Walras sent him in 1891 (1965, vol. II, p. 465) and Irving Fisher's acknowledgement in 1896 of receipt of the third edition (1965, vol. II, p. 676).

of a non-virtual economy, namely, the real economy. He stated that Walras's *Éléments* correctly describes the interdependence of economic variables (ibid., p. 2), but he wanted to extend Walras's general equilibrium analysis to the study of economic cycles and economic growth (ibid., pp. 2, 4). He therefore tried not only to find empirical equations for a Walrasian model – necessarily a non-virtual one (ibid., p. 92) – but also dynamic ones in order to provide 'a realistic treatment of an actual, moving general equilibrium' (ibid., p. 106) that occurs in the 'real economic complex' (ibid., p. 110) – comments that could never be made about the written pledges sketch. His student, Henry Schultz, undertook econometric studies using modified versions of Walras's equations (Schultz 1929, 1932, 1933, 1935, 1938). Although Joseph Schumpeter, the forceful advocate of Walrasian general equilibrium theory, described (inaccurately) the written pledges sketch for the benefit of students of the history of economic thought (Schumpeter 1954, pp. 1008, 1014), in his own research he dealt with a non-virtual economy, completing a monumental theoretical and empirical study of business fluctuations (Schumpeter 1939). Moreover, the study of Walrasian non-virtual theoretical models continued after the work of those economists and continues today, and the many present-day computable general equilibrium models are lineal descendants of Walras's mature economic model (Walker 2011).

5. SOME REMARKS ON TRANSLATING WALRAS'S WRITINGS

Throughout this book, we translate Walras's term 'économie politique pure' as 'economic theory', 'économie politique' as 'economics', and 'économie sociale' as 'social economics'. In Walras's time, these terms were to some extent in use, as may be inferred from the fact that W.S. Jevons changed the term 'political economy' to 'economics' in the text of the second edition (1879) of his *Theory of Political Economy* (first edition 1871), while retaining the original title of the book (see the Preface to that edition). Alfred Marshall also used the latter term in his *Principles of Economics* and elsewhere. Walras sometimes used the term 'économie politique et sociale' to stress explicitly that he was talking about the whole field of economics; most frequently, we translate this also simply as 'economics'.

What we wrote about our translation of Walras's book *Elements of Social Economics* (2010) is equally true of the present volume. By adhering to the letter and spirit of Walras's text, we have conveyed the stylistic quality of his writing in his mature phase. That quality requires not only felicitous phrases but also precision and logical constructions. His sentences and sections are often long but nevertheless fulfill those requirements very well in most cases, so, as a rule, we have not broken them up into shorter units. Their length is part of his style, part of the way that he wished to present matters, so there is no justification for shortening them. Similarly, we retained Walras's conjunctions at the beginning of sentences to be faithful to his style. To do otherwise would also entail a distortion in other respects of what follows in those sentences.

The exceptions to that policy were made necessary by the differences between the grammatical structure of French and English. A sentence can be long, with a subject far removed from the object and its words from their antecedents, but it can, nevertheless, be clear in French because of the available ways of indicating features such as number, person, tense, and gender, whereas English, not being an inflected language to the degree that French is, and using different ways to achieve clarity, must sometimes be expressed or punctuated in a different way to convey the meaning and to lead the reader skillfully.

Going beyond the structure of Walras's sentences and sections to the sequence of topics in the chapters of his book and the structure of each chapter, readers will see that they also follow a logical design.

We have drawn upon our knowledge of nineteenth-century French as it is found in both literary and economic writings. Although language evolves and Walras wrote some parts of this book long ago, from the literary point of view – that is, considering his grammar, literary vocabulary, turns of phrase, expressions, freedom from regionalisms, etc. – his text gives, with some exceptions, the impression of having been written yesterday. From the economics point of view, however, in a few respects, the meaning of his economic terminology differs from the usage of the economists of his own times and from modern usage. Fortunately, he specified the unusual meaning that he wished to attach to terms such as *rente*, *bénéfice*, and *rareté*.[14]

---

[14] See also Appendix B below.

Sometimes, however, Walras did not make his meaning clear, perhaps because his thoughts were not clear. The translators of some foreign language writings choose to write English sentences that have a clear meaning even though the foreign language text does not have a clear meaning to a native speaker of that language who has an expert knowledge of the subject matter. The result is an English sentence that does not state what the original states. Similarly, some translators choose on occasion not to convey certain stylistic features of their author's writing. They depart from his or her style, on the grounds that conveying it faithfully detracts from the clarity of the statements in English. Those choices produce inaccurate or inferior translations.

We have been careful not to distort what Walras wrote. We convey his style faithfully as well as his meaning accurately. If his meaning in French is obscure, or logically faulty, or understandable but expressed in words that do not strictly make sense, we have rendered it that way in English. We have then mentioned in a note the difficulties of translation that we have encountered, reproducing the original French text, and offering any possibly worthwhile speculations on what his meaning, not perfectly expressed by him or not clear to us, may have been.

There are many pages of the third and fifth editions that are the same in French, so those same pages have been translated by both William Jaffé (1898–1980) and us. His efforts cannot be too strongly commended, but it is always possible to improve upon translations, and we believe that we have done that. Jaffé was only thirty-one when he began his translation and had been studying French for only a few years. We admire his boldness in taking up that project, and the tenacity that enabled him to achieve it.[15] Nevertheless, being much older than Jaffé was at the time of his translation, we were able to draw upon much more experience with reading, writing, speaking, and translating French. We were also able to draw upon knowledge of developments of economic theory since Jaffé's time, and specifically of general equilibrium theory. Moreover, Jaffé began his translation more than eighty years ago, since which time a great deal of research

---

[15] See Potier and Walker 2004, pp. 9–17 for more details on Jaffé himself, and for an explanation of his translation's long gestation period.

has been done on Walras's writings. Our understanding of the significance of certain words has changed in the light of theoretical debates, requiring improvements in the use of English terms to translate Walras's, and research has broadened and improved our knowledge of his intellectual background and of the economy and markets with which he was familiar and hence of his usage of words.

With all respect, we must observe that, on the literary side, Jaffé's translations are very frequently so free as to be hardly recognizable as what Walras wrote; on the technical economic side, his translations are in frequent need of correction. We will not present a list, which would be a long one, of all the respects in which our translation of those pages differs from Jaffé's, but we will draw the reader's attention to several crucial matters involving market behavior and economic subjects.

Walras wrote about 'partial ('partielle') demand' and 'partial supply', and 'total ('totale') demand' and 'total supply'. Using modern terminology, Jaffé translated 'partielle' and 'totale' as 'individual' and 'market' respectively. That was not justified. The translation of 'partielle' is 'partial', not 'individual'; the translation of 'totale' is 'total', not 'market'. Walras wanted to say 'partial' and to have a strong contrast of that by using 'total' for the sum of individual curves. The rationale for retaining Walras's terminology in the English version is exactly the same for the French version. We would not change the French in a new edition of the French version, so why would we change it in a translation of the original edition and use instead the modern French economic terms 'individuel' and 'de marché'? Of course we would not do that. If we were to reprint Adam Smith's *Wealth of Nations* or Ricardo's *Principles* in English would we change the text and use modern terminology? Of course not. That would be changing what Smith and Ricardo wrote, and changing the French *Éléments* in a reprint of it would be changing what Walras wrote. Subject to the qualification implied by the general principle enunciated below, in an English translation we must try to find the closest English equivalent in meaning to the words he used. The reader will then have a translation of what he meant, not of the terms he might have used if he had written one hundred years later. Otherwise, we would create an illegitimate hybrid, a cross between a translation of Walras's French for some of his writings and our modern terminology for others.

The cardinal principle of translation in application to Walras's work is that what a word or phrase meant to him must be translated to have that meaning to the modern reader. For example, 'partielle' meant 'partial' to him and 'totale' meant 'total'. If a word was not anachronistic to Walras, it must not be translated in such a way as to be an anachronism to the modern reader. This means that some of Walras's terms should not be translated literally, that they should not be translated in such a way as to be nonsensical or anachronistic to the modern Anglophone reader, unless Walras wrote nonsense or employed a word that he considered to be an anachronism. Let us consider the principle in application to the translation of the title of his treatise, the *Éléments d'économie politique pure*. Jaffé translated that as *Elements of Pure Economics*. There is no problem with the word '*Elements*'. In French and English in this connection it meant and it means 'the basic parts of a discipline'. Also, '*Economics*' is a good translation of Walras's '*économie politique*' because that nineteenth-century name meant 'economics' to a French economist, and the branch of knowledge to which Walras was referring was precisely what English-speaking economists called 'economics' in that century and today. The English term 'political economy' was used mainly before the last quarter of the nineteenth century, but it would not be a faithful translation of Walras's term because 'political economy' has a different meaning today than it did in the nineteenth century; that is, it now means the study of economic policy and normative economics, and is even, by some economists, used to imply a rejection of mainstream economic theory.

So how should '*économie politique pure*' be translated? Since '*économie politique*' is replaced, as Jaffé did and as we have done, by 'economics' on the grounds that the literal translation of the old term does not convey accurately to the modern reader what Walras meant, then, on the same grounds, 'pure' should be replaced. That word in the context of the French title was not anachronistic to Walras, but 'pure economics' is at best an anachronism today and is, strictly speaking, nonsense. It was not even commonly used in English economic literature and is not used today, except in Jaffé's title; rather, the use of the word 'pure' that used to be accepted long ago in connection with economic studies is illustrated by J.M. Keynes's work on money in 1930: he referred to 'the applied theory of money' and 'the *pure theory* of money', but he never wrote 'pure economics' because that was never good usage. Our choices for Walras's title are therefore evidently 'theoretical economics' or 'economic theory'. The deciding factor between those two choices is that Walras used '*économie politique appliquée*' to refer to 'applied economics', and *économie sociale* to refer to 'social economics', so his evident desire for symmetry in the titles of his books implies that we should translate '*économie politique pure*' as 'theoretical economics', which is unmistakably what he meant.

When Walras wrote 'offre' he meant 'supply'. Demanders make offers, just as sellers do, which is just one reason to be highly selective about when to translate 'offre' as 'offer' rather than as 'supply'. Jaffé nevertheless introduced confusion by generally translating 'offre' as 'offer' and 'courbe d'offre' as 'offer curve'. For example, in the last sentence of § 91 of Walras 1926 (§ 90 in this book), Walras wrote: 'Il s'ensuite que les courbes d'offre totale partent le plus souvent de l'origine'. Jaffé translated this as: 'It follows from this that aggregate offer curves often start at the origin' (Walras 1954, p. 136). Here Jaffé added yet an additional distraction by switching from translating 'totale' as 'market' to translating it as 'aggregate'. It is true that a market supply or demand function is an aggregate function, but to use the latter term immediately leads the reader to think of an economy-wide function. Putting that solecism aside, however, it should be pointed out that the major problem with Jaffé's sentence is that, in English economic literature, an 'offer curve' is not a supply curve. For the two-commodity case, which is precisely the case of the section under discussion, an offer curve has as its coordinates the amounts of each of the commodities that the trader would want to hold at each possible price. The trader wants to move to his offer curve along a line that goes from the point with his existing holdings as its coordinates to the point indicating his desired holdings. The price is the slope of that line, and the quantity that the trader wants to supply of the commodity is his desired holding of it minus his existing (pre-trade) holding of it. In contrast, in all cases in which Walras wrote 'courbe d'offre', he was dealing with a supply curve, that is, a curve that has the coordinates price and quantity desired.

As another example of translation practices, consider this passage: Walras wrote about 'la distinction entre les frais fixes et les frais variables dans les enterprises. Mais, puisque nous supposons les entrepreneurs ne faisant ni bénéfices ni pertes, nous pouvons bien les supposer aussi fabriquant des quantités égales de produits, auquel cas tous le frais de toute nature peuvent être considérés comme proportionnels' (Walras 1889, 1896, and this book, § 200). Jaffé translated the last word as 'variable', adding a note in which he maintained that George Stigler was in error to have translated the last word as 'proportional', that it should be translated as 'variable', although Stigler was rightly exasperated that Walras did not explain to what the expenses are proportional (Jaffé in Walras 1954, p. 527, n. [4]). As can be seen, in the previous sentence, Walras wrote 'frais variables'. How should that be translated? In French and English the adjective means 'things that vary in magnitude', so the answer is 'variable expenses'. Then, we ask the reader rhetorically: Did he not choose a different word in the next sentence? Did he not write 'proportionnels'? Yes. The words for 'variable' and 'proportional' are not synonyms in English or French; they are different words with different meanings, which is why Walras chose different words. He was not restating that expenses are variable; he was adding an assumption about the variable expenses, namely that they are not only variable but proportional. So the latter should not be translated as 'variable'. How should it be translated? In French, the word 'proportionnels' means 'grandeurs mesurables qui sont ou dont les mesures sont et restent dans des rapports égaux (formant une *proportion).* Qui est, reste en rapport avec, varie dans le même sens que (qqch.)'. (Robert 2002, p. 2095). Translated, that definition is: 'Measurable magnitudes that are or whose measures are and stay in the same ratios (forming a proportion). That which is, stays in a ratio with, varies in the same direction as (something)'. The English definition is the same, so the answer is that the translation of the French word is 'proportional'. Jaffé was wrong and Stigler was right. Jaffé once more displayed his propensity for putting in the word that he thinks Walras should have used, in this case based upon Jaffé's understanding of the economics of the firm, not a translation of the words Walras did use. The question remains as to what Walras thought the expenses are proportional. What results from and changes with variable expenses is output, so it seems clear to us that he meant that, in his special case, all kinds of expenses can be treated as proportional to output, but the reader, having been furnished with the correct translation, can make his or her own judgment on the matter.

A final example of the mischief created by faulty translations concerns Walras's account in the *Éléments* of how prices are changed. Once again, we are dealing with passages that are the same in the third and fourth/fifth editions and that were therefore translated by Jaffé as well as by us. Walras explained that in organized markets such as securities exchanges, the direct participants are 'agents de change, courtiers de commerce, crieurs' (1889/1896, and 1900/1926, § 41). The former two groups are representatives of buyers and sellers. As for the latter word, Jaffé correctly translated it as 'criers' in one place (Jaffé in Walras 1954, p. 84), and we did so consistently (§ 41), but then he went on to translate that same word as 'auctioneers' (Jaffé in Walras 1954, § 61; but see Walras 1889/1896, § 61, and 1900/1926, § 61), a momentous error that has mislead generations of readers into thinking that the markets in Walras's model are auction markets and that he assigned the function of changing prices in his model to an auctioneer. The French word for 'auctioneer' is 'commissaire-priseur', and the ordinary name for an auction is a 'vente aux enchères', neither of which expressions appear in the *Éléments*.[16]

In fact, the 'crieurs' to which Walras was referring had the responsibility, in his model and in real securities markets, with which he was very familiar, of learning the prices that the agents of the buyers and sellers were quoting, and of calling them out loudly so that all participants would know them. Criers did not suggest prices; they called out prices after they had been suggested (see references in Walker 2001, pp. 195–6). Jaffé then reinforced the impression of auctioneers being the instrument of price changes by translating sales 'à la criée' as 'by auction' (Jaffé in Walras 1954, p. 84). In fact, Walras wrote that the persons who are active with respect to 'sales and purchases *à la*

---

[16] Jaffé made the same mistake in his translation of another passage that appears in the fourth and fifth editions. Walras described a single firm that undertakes all production as 'un entrepreneur unique qui demanderait les services à l'enchère et offrirait les produits au rabais' (Walras 1900 or 1926, § 188, p. 194), that is, 'would demand services at higher prices and would offer products at lower prices'. Jaffé translated that as an entrepreneur who 'bought his services and sold his products by auction' (Walras 1954, p. 225), which is wrong since there cannot be an auction if there is only one buyer, and sellers in auctions do not lower their prices.

criée are agents such as trading agents, brokers, criers' (§ 41). As will be seen below, when he wanted to refer to an auction, he used the word 'encan'.

Auction markets are radically different from those that Walras discussed (see Walker 1996, pp. 84–9). In his accounts of reality and in his model, markets are structured so that 'value in exchange occurs naturally in the market as the result of *competition*. As buyers, the traders make *offers to buy at higher prices*, as sellers, they make *offers to sell at lower prices*, and their competition thus leads to a certain value in exchange that is sometimes rising, sometimes falling, sometimes stationary' (§ 41; emphasis in the original).[17] In an ordinary auction, however, they never suggest prices, the price is not lowered, and the auctioneer represents only a single seller and sells only a single unit or batch of the commodity; and, in a Dutch auction, they never suggest prices and the price is never raised.[18]

It is true that Walras wanted to mention an auction on one occasion in the third edition, and so he used words with that meaning ('*vente à l'encan*'). He did so in reference to a special case, but he did so incorrectly, that is, in contradiction to the features of the case. He assumed that the sellers 'offer the entire quantity of the new commodity at any price, namely the total quantity in existence. The particular form of bidding in this case is that of a sale by auction' (§ 151). He then went on, however, to describe traders' behavior that could not possibly take place in an auction. There is no auctioneer in his special case, and he illustrated it by a diagram of market supply and demand

---

[17] In writings other than the *Éléments*, Walras also stated this many times. For example, we find 'the demanders bidding prices up in the event of an excess of the quantity demanded over the quantity supplied, and the suppliers lowering prices in the event of an excess of the quantity supplied over the quantity demanded' (Walras 1892, Appendix I to this book).

[18] Engendered by Jaffé's misunderstanding, the strangely named 'auctioneer' of modern general equilibrium theory has emerged in the literature as a single entity functioning for the entire model economy, not acting like an auctioneer but rather suggesting the price in every market and raising or lowering it in accordance with the sign of the excess demand that is somehow totalized in each market and made clear to him by unspecifiable means. There is nothing remotely like that in any edition of Walras's treatise. Since there is no price changing mechanism in the written pledges model, Kenneth Arrow and F.H. Hahn (1971, pp. 305–6) invented the central auctioneer in the hopes of providing such a mechanism for their virtual model.

curves that show that if the price is lower than the equilibrium value, the quantity demanded exceeds the quantity supplied – and that if the price exceeds the equilibrium value, the excess demand is negative (Fig. 21). Unlike an auction, in the former event, no part of the stock is sold to those that quote the highest price, and in the latter event, the sellers progressively lower the price. Walras went on to remark that 'This very simple case is, in reality, very common', by which he surely meant that all of or almost all of the total stock being put on sale is common, but unless he wanted to contradict his many statements on the characteristics of freely competitive markets and price formation and tatonnement in them, he was not maintaining that it is very common for markets for products to be conducted as auctions by auctioneers.

We end this section by stressing once more that none of these remarks are intended to detract from the value of Jaffé's accomplishment in introducing the English-speaking reader to many of Walras's contributions in the *Éléments* nor from the greatness of Jaffé's other major work of Walrasian scholarship, the three-volume *Correspondence of Léon Walras* (Walras 1965), a vast treasure trove of information on neoclassical economic literature.

6. CONCLUSION

The essence of Walras's work is contained in four texts: the second/third and fourth/fifth editions of the *Éléments*, the *Études d'économie sociale* (1896, 1936), and the *Études d'économie politique appliquée* (1898, 1936). An English translation of the fifth edition was made in 1954; of the book on applied economics in 2005; and of the book on social economics in 2010. For 125 years, however, the finest of Walras's accomplishments, the second/third edition of the *Éléments*, has been available only in French. Finally, it too has been translated, revealing in English the scope, power, grand structure, and detail – in short, the sheer genius of his renderings of economic behavior. How it can happen that a work of genius is created is inexplicable, but that quality is unmistakable and eternal. The edition presented in this book is such a work, so we feel deep satisfaction that it has fallen to us to have the privilege of making it accessible to English-speaking scholars.

APPENDIX A: DATA ON WALRAS'S LIFE-CYCLE OF PRODUCTIVITY

Walras's phases of productivity are shown in the following tables (Walker 1999, 2006).

Table A1. *Walras's Productivity: Number of Pages Newly Published or Written*

	Economics				
	Theory	Other	Total	Other	Total
1858–1871	260	1,310	1,570	501	2,071
1872–1877	448	218	666	135	801
1878–1895	479	271	750	245	995
1896–1900	70	98	168	0	168
1901–1910	0	50	50	3	53

Table A2. *Walras's Productivity: Average Number of Pages Per Year*

	No. of Years	Economics				
		Theory	Other	Total	Other	Total
1858–1871	14	18.57	93.57	112.14	35.78	147.93
1872–1877	6	74.67	36.33	111.0	22.5	133.5
1878–1895	18	26.61	15.06	41.67	13.61	55.28
1896–1900	5	14.0	19.6	33.6	0	33.6
1901–1910	10	0	5.0	5.0	0.3	5.3

APPENDIX B: WALRAS'S TERMINOLOGY WITH REGARD TO THE FACTORS OF PRODUCTION

Walras distinguished three aspects of a capital good: the good itself, its services, and the price paid for its services. There are three types of capital goods, that is, goods that are durable and that give off their services over a period of productive use. First, there is land, the services of land, and rent. In our Table B1, we show that Walras defined the services of land ('services foncières') as 'rente foncière' or 'rente', not using the latter word to mean an amount of money or in-kind payment. For instance, land can be used as a meadow, it can support and nourish crops, buildings can be erected on it, it can be used as a garden, etc. By the expression 'produce of land' ('les produits de la terre'), Walras meant more specifically the things that are produced when the services of land are combined with other inputs, as, for example, when labor, fertilizer, machines, and tools are used on the land to produce corn, fruits, grass, flowers, tomatoes, etc. Walras therefore deals with the value of the in-kind services of land (the money value of 'la rente'), the value of the produce of land (the money value of 'les produits'), and the value of land (the money value of 'la terre'). In normal French and English usage, the rent of land, paid at the beginning of the rental period, is the present money value of the services of land for one year. That is the phenomenon that Walras called 'le prix de la rente', but sometimes inconsistently called simply 'la rente'.

Second, there is human capital, for which case Walras distinguished persons, the labor they perform, and the remuneration for the labor, in other words: workers, labor, and wages.

Third, there are 'capital goods properly speaking' (machines, buildings, etc.), the services of capital goods, and interest. In Walras's theory, individual owners of capital goods rent them out to the entrepreneurs, or, in other words, they sell the services of the capital goods to the entrepreneurs. Formulating abstract theory on the basis of this supposition is one thing; in practice, one cannot abstract so easily from the facts of life. There are indeed markets where capital good services, land services, or labor are offered by their owners and bought by the demanders, but capital goods properly speaking, like machines or factory buildings, are bought with money saved by individuals. They are almost never bought by these individuals and rented out by them to an entrepreneur. They prefer to lend their savings to an entrepreneur via an intermediary or financial instrument. He then buys or hires the capital good in question. If he borrows money to acquire the capital good, he pays interest, and at the agreed time repays the capitalist in money and not in kind. Hence, there are capitalists who own capital in the form of money that they lend. The word 'capital' may therefore have two different meanings: capital goods, such as tools, machinery, and factory buildings that are

Table B1. *Walras's terminology regarding capital and its services and prices*

Type of capital				Service in kind (sometimes called 'income')			Remuneration in money		
French	*English*	*Some Examples*	*Owners*	*French*	*English*	*Supply, Demand Symbols*	*French*	*English*	*Price Symbols*
Capitaux fanciers or terre	Landed capital or land	Agricultural land, forests, ground beneath buildings	Land owners	Rente or rente foncière or services fonciers	Land-services	$O_t, O_{t'} \dots$ $D_t, D_{t'} \dots$	Fermage	Rent (of land) or ground rent	$p_t, p_{t'} \dots$
Capitaux personnels or personnes	Personal capital or persons	Plumbers, teachers, cooks, judges, doctors, artists	Workers	Services personnels or travail	Services of persons or labor (work)	$O_p, O_{p'} \dots$ $D_p, D_{p'} \dots$	Salaire	Wages	$p_p, p_{p'} \dots$
Capitaux mobiliers or artificiels or proprements dits	Capital proper or artificial capital	Dwellings, factories, buildings, furniture, machines, tools, circulating capital, fixed capital	Capitalists or capital owners	Revenues mobiliers or services mobiliers or profits	Capital services or 'profits'	$O_k, O_{k'} \dots$ $D_k, D_{k'} \dots$	Intérêt	Interest payment or interest	$p_k, p_{k'} \dots$

used in productive processes, and capital in the form of money. If the money is lent out for a short term, it is generally used for commercial purposes, such as financing the production of the entrepreneur's stocks until they are sold; Walras speaks then of 'circulating capital'. If the money is lent out for a long term, for financing machinery, for instance, Walras speaks of 'fixed capital'. Of course, in his financial dealings the capitalist does not use the terms fixed capital or circulating capital; to him, capital means simply a certain amount of money, deposited in a bank or the money value of his financial assets, such as bonds and stocks.

The fourth type of durable productive agent in Walras's mature model is the entrepreneur. His or her entrepreneurial service is 'essentially that of demanding services and selling products' (Walras 1895 in Walras 1965, p. 629; Walker 1996, pp. 282–3), and the remuneration for that activity in disequilibrium is profit ('bénéfice'). Profit per unit of output is price minus average cost, so that type of income is positive or negative in disequilibrium in an industry when the rate of production and purchases are unequal and zero when they are equal.

All this is summarized and assembled in Table B1.

APPENDIX C. COLLATION OF EDITIONS 3 AND 4/5 OF THE *ÉLÉMENTS*

The third edition of *Éléments d'économie politique pure* is divided into 38 chapters ('lessons'), not including the three appendixes. Each chapter is subdivided into sections, of which, in total, there are 388. The fourth edition has 42 chapters, subdivided into 408 sections. In order to enable the reader to find those sections of the third edition, or what remains of them, that appear in editions 4/5, we have provided a table of correspondence between the latter and edition 3 in this appendix.

Italicized section numbers indicate that the parallelism with corresponding sections is found only in the general character of the subject matter. It has not been noted in the table that corresponding sections may have differences in the details of their wording, nor that they may have small insertions or suppressions.

Table C1. *Comparison of edition 3 with editions 4/5*

Edition 3		Edition 4/5	
§§	Lesson/*Part*	§§	Lesson/*Part*
	Part I		*Part I*
1–9	1	1–9	1
10–20	2	10–20	2
21–30	3	21–30	3
31–39	4	31–39	4
	Part II		*Part II*
40–48	5	40–48	5
49–61	6	49–61	6
62–70	7	62–70	7
71–80 } 81 } 8 82–83 }		71–80 } *81–82* } 8 83–84 }	
84–97	9	85–98	9
98–102	10	99–103	10
	Part II (ctnd)		*Part III*
103–115	11	104–116	11
116–120 } — } 12 121–128 }		117–121 } 122 } 12 123–130 }	
129–136	13	131–138	13
137–148	14	139–150	14
149 } 150–154 } 15		*151* } 152–156 } 15	
155–159 } 160 } 16		157–161 } 162–164 } 16	
	Part III		*Part IV*
161–173	17	165–177	17
174–184	18	178–188	18
185–195	19	189–199	19
196–202 } 203 } 20		200–206 } *207* } 20	
204 } 205–209 } 210 } 21 211–216 }		208 } 209–213 } *214* } 21 215–220 }	
217–226	22	221–230	22

Table C1. (*cont.*)

Edition 3		Edition 4/5	
§§	Lesson/*Part*	§§	Lesson/*Part*
	Part IV		*Part V*
227–229 ⎫		231–233 ⎫	
230 ⎬ 23		234 ⎬ 23	
231–237 ⎪		235–241 ⎪	
238–239 ⎭		242–243 ⎭	
240–242 ⎫		244–246 ⎫	
243–246 ⎬ 24		247–250 ⎬ 24	
247 ⎭		251 ⎭	
248–252 ⎫		252–256 ⎫	
253–254 ⎬ 25		257–258 ⎬ 25	
255 ⎪		259 ⎪	
256 ⎭		260 ⎭	
257–258 ⎫		261–262	26
259 ⎬ 26		263 ⎫	
260 ⎪		264 ⎬ 27	
261 ⎭		— ⎭	
— ⎫		265–267 ⎬ 28	
262–265 ⎪		268–271 ⎭	
⎬ 27			*Part VII*
266–267 ⎪		317–318 ⎬ 35	
268–271 ⎭		319–322 ⎭	
272–(274) ⎫		323–325 ⎫	
— ⎬ 28		326 ⎬ 36	
(274)–275 ⎪		327 ⎪	
276–283 ⎭		328–335 ⎭	
284–289	29	336–341	37
290–297	30	342–349	38
298–310	31	350–362	39
311–318	32	363–370	40
	Part V		*Part VI*
319–323 ⎬ 33		272–282 ⎬ 29–30	
324–325 ⎭		283 ⎭	
326–331	34	284–289	31
332–336 ⎫		290–294 ⎫	
337 ⎬ 35		295 ⎬ 32	
338–339 ⎭		296–297 ⎭	
340–344 ⎫		⎧ 298–302 ⎫ 33	
— ⎪		⎪ 303 ⎬	
345 ⎬ 36		⎨ 304 ⎭	
— ⎪		⎪ 305	
346–356 ⎭		⎩ 306–316	34

Table C1. (*cont.*)

	Edition 3		Edition 4/5
§§	Lesson/*Part*	§§	Lesson/*Part*
	Part VI		*Part VIII*
357–373	37	371–387	41
374–380	⎫	388–394	⎫
—	⎪	395	⎪
381–383	⎪	396–398	⎪
—	⎬ 38	399	⎬ 42
384–385	⎪	400–401	⎪
—	⎪	402–404	⎪
386–387	⎪	405–406	⎪
—	⎪	407	⎭
388	⎭	408	
Appendix I		Appendix I	
Appendix II		Appendix II	
Appendix III		—	

APPENDIX D. EDITORIAL TREATMENT OF THE TRANSLATION

Additions to the text, such as the first name of an author cited by Walras, appear between brackets. The footnotes with Arabic numbers in the main text are Walras's. The notes at the ends of the chapters, with Roman numbers, are our editorial notes. Symbols indicating quantities in the text or in the formulas and equations are always written in italics. Function symbols are written in roman font.

Our treatment of the graphs in *ETE* requires some more extensive explanation. Walras presented his graphs on separate plates at the end of his book; sometimes, he presented several graphs in one single figure. He did this in order to save space on the plates. In the third edition of *Éléments d'économie politique pure* the first four figures refer to an introductory mathematical exposition and therefore started the main text of the third edition with a figure numbered 5. There are five plates relating to the main text, with 23 figures, most of them with several quadrants within each figure, and with more than one curve on a given quadrant; and one plate with nine figures including 16 quadrants relating to the appendixes. Inspired by William Jaffé's

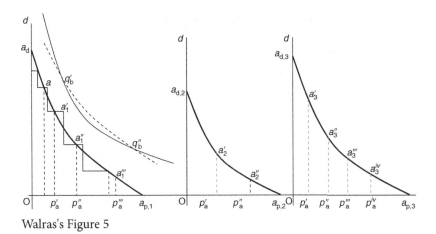

Walras's Figure 5

procedure, we split up the figures, and placed the graphs in their context. All the graphs in our translation have been drawn anew. We illustrate this matter with a discussion of Walras's Figure 5.

This figure is mentioned by Walras for the first time in the first sentence of § 51. We present as our Fig. 1 only the part of Walras's Fig. 5 that is relevant to the treatment of an individual in the first paragraph of section 51. This results in our Fig. 1. The subsequent paragraph of § 51 deals with the fact that the other participants in the exchange also have demand equations similar to those of individual 1. This means that for the latter paragraph only the second and the third graphs of Walras's Fig. 5 are relevant. Hence, we present those two graphs as our Fig. 2. In the last paragraph of section 53, Walras discusses discontinuous demand functions, in relation to which only a part of the first graph of his Fig. 5 is of importance. We therefore present only this part as our Fig. 4. Walras mentioned his Fig. 5 once more in § 71 of the text. There he discussed, in the two-goods case, the dependence of the demand for (A) on the quantity of (B) possessed. We therefore present, at the corresponding place of our translation, only a part of the left graph of Walras's Fig. 5, thus producing our Fig. 10, which we modified by presenting the shifted demand curve as a dashed line. Finally, Walras dealt a second time with this problem in § 89.

Sometimes he indicated a point in a figure by the same symbol as the one he used for a quantity. Therefore, we decided to indicate the

Table D1. *Correspondence between the figures of ETE and those of editions 3 and 5 of the Éléments*

ETE	Edition 3	Edition 5
–	1, 2, 3, 4*	–
1, 2	5	1
3	6	2
4	5	1
5, 6, 7, 8a, 8b, 9	6	2
10	5	1
11, 12, 13, 14, 15	7	3
16	8	4
–	9**	–
17	10	5
18, 19	12	7
20, 21	13	8
22	11	6
23	14	9
24	15	10
25, 26	18	13
27	19	14
28, 29	20	15
30, 31	21	17, 16,
32	23	18
33	22	19 (modified)
34	14	9
35	15	10
36	16	11
37	17	12
38, 39, 40	A1	20
41	A2	21
42	A3	22
43	A4	23
44	A5	24
45	A6	25
46	A7	26 (modified)
47	A8	27
48	A9	28

* These figures belong to the mathematical introduction added to the third edition. (Not inserted into the translation.)
** While preparing edition 3, Walras eliminated four lessons of the second edition, but he forgot to remove one of the graphs in those lessons.

points in his figures always in roman font in the text. We indicate the length of a segment by a bar above its identifying symbols.

For completeness' sake, we present a table of the correspondence of all the graphs of our translation of the third edition with those of the French editions 3 and 5.

Because Walras's first four figures belong to the mathematical introduction, his figures that relate to the text of the third edition begin with number 5.

References

Arrow, Kenneth, and F.H. Hahn, 1971, *General Competitive Analysis*, San Francisco: Holden-Day; Edinburgh: Oliver and Boyd.

Bertrand, Joseph, 1883, 'Review of *Théorie mathématique de la richesse sociale* par Léon Walras, professeur d'économie politique à l'Académie de Lausanne', *Journal des savants*, September, 504–8.

Bridel, Pascal, 1997, *Money and General Equilibrium Theory. From Walras to Pareto*, Cheltenham, UK, and Lyme, US (CT): Edward Elgar Publishing Ltd.

Bridel, Pascal and Elisabeth Huck, 2002, 'Yet another look at Walras's theory of tâtonnement', *Journal of the History of Economic Thought*, 9: 513–40.

Dockès, Pierre and Jean-Pierre Potier, 2001, *Léon Walras. Vie et œuvre économique*, Paris: Economica.

Jevons, Stanley W., 1879, *The Theory of Political Economy*, second edition, revised and enlarged, London: Macmillan.

Moore, Henry Ludwell, 1929, *Synthetic Economics*, New York: Macmillan.

Pareto, Vilfredo, 1897, 'The New Theories of Economics', *Journal of Political Economy*, 5: 485–502.

1896/1897, *Cours d'économie politique*, edited by G.H. Bousquet and G. Busino, Geneva: Librairie Droz, 1964.

Potier, Jean-Pierre and Donald A. Walker, 2004, *La correspondance entre Aline Walras et William Jaffé, et autres écrits*, Paris: Economica.

Rebeyrol, Antoine, 1999, 'Yet Another Look?', *Journal of the History of Economic Thought*, 9: 541–9.

Rizvi, S. Abu Turab, 2003, 'Postwar Neoclassical Microeconomics', in *A Companion to the History of Economic Thought*, edited by Warren J. Samuels, Jeff E. Biddle, and John B. Davis, Malden, MA, and Oxford, UK: Blackwell Publishing Ltd., 377–94.

Robert, Paul, 2002, *Le nouveau petit Robert; Dictionnaire alphabétique et analogique de la langue française*, Paris: Dictionnaires le Robert.

Schultz, Henry, 1929, 'Marginal Productivity and the Pricing Process', *Journal of Political Economy*, 37: 505–51.

1932, 'Marginal Productivity and the Lausanne School', *Economica*, 12: 285–96.

1933, 'Interrelations of Demand', *Journal of Political Economy*, 41: 468–512.

1935, 'Interrelations of Demand, Price and Income', *Journal of Political Economy*, 43: 433–81.

1938, *The Theory and Measurement of Demand*, University of Chicago Press.

Schumpeter, Joseph A. 1939, *Business Cycles. A Theoretical, Historical and Statistical Analysis of the Capitalist Process*, New York: McGraw-Hill.

1954, *History of Economic Analysis*, New York: Oxford University Press.

Van Daal, Jan, 1994, 'De la nature de la monnaie dans les modèles monétaires de l'équilibre général économique de Léon Walras', *Économies et Sociétés*, Série Œconomia, Histoire de la Pensée Économique, 20–21, 10–11: 115–132.

Van Daal, Jan and Albert Jolink, 1993, *The equilibrium economics of Léon Walras*, London: Routledge.

Walker, Donald A., 1996, *Walras's Market Models*, Cambridge University Press.

1999, 'Some comments on Léon Walras's health and productivity', *Journal of the History of Economic Thought*, 21: 437–48.

2001, 'A factual account of the functioning of the nineteenth-century Paris Bourse', *European Journal of the History of Economic Thought*, 9: 186–207.

2006, *Walrasian Economics*, Cambridge University Press.

2011, 'Non virtualité et virtualité dans les modèles d'équilibre économique général', in *Léon Walras et l'équilibre économique général. Recherches récentes*, edited by Roberto Baranzini, André Legris, and Ludovic Ragni, Paris: Economica, 233–60.

Walras, Auguste and Léon, 1987–2005, *Œuvres économiques complètes*; edited by Pierre Dockès, Pierre-Henri Goutte, Claude Hébert, Claude Mouchot, Jean-Pierre Potier, and Jean-Michel Servet, under the auspices of the Centre Auguste et Léon Walras, Paris: Economica. The following four volumes are in this series.

Walras, Léon. vol. VIII. *Éléments d'économie politique pure ou Théorie de la richesse sociale*, comparative edition; edited by Claude Mouchot, 1988.

vol. IX. *Éléments d'économie sociale (Théorie de la répartition de la richesse sociale)*, edited by Pierre Dockès, 1990 (translated into English 2010).

vol. X. *Études d'économie politique appliquée (Théorie de la production de la richesse sociale)*, edited by Jean-Pierre Potier, 1992 (translated into English 2005).

vol. XI. *Théorie mathématique de la richesse sociale et autres écrits d'économie pure*, edited by Claude Mouchot, 1993.

1860, *L'économie politique et la justice. Examen critique et réfutation des doctrines économiques de M. P.-J. Proudhon, précédés d'une Introduction à l'étude de la question sociale*, Paris: Librairie de Guillaumin & Cie.

1861, *Théorie critique de l'impôt, précédée de Souvenirs du Congrès de Lausanne*, Paris, Guillaumin et Cie.

1868, *Théorie générale de la société. Leçons publiques faites à Paris. Première série (1867–68)*, Paris: Guillaumin. (*ŒÉC* vol. IX: 9–173. English translation: Chs. 2 and 3 of Walras 2010.)

1874, *Éléments d'économie politique pure ou Théorie de la richesse sociale*, 1st edition, 1st part, Lausanne: Imprimerie L. Corbaz & Cie; Paris: Guillaumin & Cie; Bâle: H. Georg. (In: *ŒÉC*, vol. VIII.)

1877a, *Théorie mathématique de la richesse sociale. Quatre mémoires lus à l'Académie des sciences morales et politiques, à Paris, et à la Société Vaudoise des Sciences Naturelles, à Lausanne*, Paris: Guillaumin & Cie. (*ŒÉC*, vol. XI: 18–136.)

1877b, *Éléments d'économie politique pure*, 1st edition, 2nd part, Lausanne: Imprimerie L. Corbaz & Cie; Paris: Guillaumin & Cie; Bâle: H. Georg. (In: *ŒÉC*, vol. VIII.)

1889, *Éléments d'économie politique pure ou Théorie de la richesse sociale*, 2nd edition, *revue, corrigée et augmentée*, Lausanne, F. Rouge ; Paris: Guillaumin & Cie; Leipzig: Verlag von Duncker & Humblot. (In: *ŒÉC*, vol. VIII.)

1892, 'Théorie géométrique de la détermination des prix. De l'échange de produits et services entre eux. De l'échange d'épargnes contre capitaux neufs. *Recueil Inaugural de l'Université de Lausanne, Travaux des Facultés*. Lausanne, Imprimerie Ch. Viret-Genton.

1896a, *Éléments d'économie politique pure ou Théorie de la richesse sociale*. 3rd edition. Lausanne, F. Rouge ; Paris, F. Pichon; Leipzig: Verlag von Duncker & Humblot. (In: *ŒÉC*, vol. VIII.)

1896b, *Études d'économie sociale (Théorie de la répartition de la richesse sociale)*. Lausanne: F. Rouge; Paris: F. Pichon. (In: *ŒÉC*, vol. IX.)

1898, *Études d'économie politique appliquée (Théorie de la production de la richesse sociale)*. Lausanne: F. Rouge; Paris: F. Pichon. (In: *ŒÉC*, vol. X.)

1899, 'Équations de la circulation'. *Bulletin de la Société Vaudoise des Sciences Naturelles* 35, no. 132 (June 1899). (*ŒÉC*, vol. XI: 563–88.)

1926, *Éléments d'économie politique pure ou Théorie de la richesse sociale. Édition définitive revue et augmentée par l'auteur*, Paris: R. Pichon et R. Durand-Auzias; Lausanne: F. Rouge. This is the fifth edition of the *Eléments*. (In: *ŒÉC*, vol. VIII.)

1936a, *Études d'économie sociale (Théorie de la répartition de la richesse sociale). Édition définitive par les soins de Gaston Leduc*, 2nd edition. Lausanne: F. Rouge et Cie; Paris: R. Pichon et R. Durand-Auzias. (In: *ŒÉC*, vol. IX.)

1936b, *Études d'économie politique appliquée (Théorie de la production de la richesse sociale). Édition définitive par les soins de Gaston Leduc*, 2nd edition, Lausanne: F. Rouge et Cie; Paris: R. Pichon et R. Durand-Auzias. (In: *ŒÉC*, vol. X.)

1954, *Elements of Pure Economics or The Theory of Social Wealth*; translated by William Jaffé. Published for the American Economic Association and the Royal Economic Society, Homewood, IL: Richard D. Irwin; London: George Allen and Unwin Ltd.

1965, *Correspondence of Léon Walras and Related Papers*; edited and annotated by William Jaffé; published for the Royal Netherlands Academy of Sciences and Letters, Amsterdam: North-Holland Publishing Company, 3 vols.

2005, *Studies in Applied Economics Theory of the production of social wealth*; translated and introduced by Jan van Daal, 2 vols, London and New York: Routledge, Taylor & Francis Group. This is a translation into English of Walras 1936a.

2010, *Studies in Social Economics*; translated and introduced by Jan van Daal and Donald A. Walker, London and New York: Routledge, Taylor & Francis Group. This is a translation into English of Walras 1936b.

ÉLÉMENTS

D'ÉCONOMIE POLITIQUE

PURE

ou

THÉORIE DE LA RICHESSE SOCIALE

PAR

LÉON WALRAS

TROISIÈME ÉDITION

LAUSANNE

F. ROUGE, ÉDITEUR

Librairie de l'Université.

PARIS	LEIPZIG
F. PICHON, IMPRIMEUR-ÉDITEUR	VERLAG VON DUNCKER & HUMBLOT
Rue Soufflot, 24.	Dresdnerstrasse, 17.

1896

I

Preface to the second edition[1]

I wrote, in June 1874, at the beginning of the first part of the first edition of the present work, the lines that I would like now to reproduce:

I am in debt to the enlightened initiative of the Council of State of Vaud that created a chair of economics in the School of Law of the Academy of Lausanne in 1870, and instituted a competition to select an occupant of the chair. It is especially to the benevolent confidence in me of Mr. Louis Ruchonnet, who is head of the Department of Public Education and Worship and member of the Swiss National Council, and who, after having invited me to enter the competition for obtaining that chair, has not ceased to encourage me unsparingly since my occupancy of it, that I owe being able to begin the publication of a treatise on the elements of economics, arranged in accordance with a new plan, developed according to a novel method, and reaching conclusions that, I must state, will also differ on certain points from those of the present science.

This treatise is divided into three parts each forming a volume published in two fascicles. The books will be the following:

1st part: – ÉLÉMENTS D'ÉCONOMIE POLITIQUE PURE or *Théorie de la richesse sociale*.

---

[1] This third edition differs from the second only by the elimination of the four lessons on the applied theory of money mentioned on page lvi, and by the addition of three appendixes. – The second and the third parts, discussed on page liv, will be replaced by two volumes, *Études d'économie sociale* and *Études d'économie politique appliquée*. The applied theory of money will appear in the latter. I beg of my readers to be so kind as to accept this plan, which seems to me very nearly to achieve my œuvre more promptly, while relieving me of a task that I fear I am no longer capable of undertaking. (February 1896).

Part I. Object and divisions of economics. − Part II. Mathematical theory of exchange. − Part III. The numeraire[i] and money. − Part IV. Natural theory of the production and the consumption of wealth. Part V. Conditions and consequences of economic progress. − Part VI. Natural and necessary effects of the various modes of the economic organization of society.

2nd part: − *ÉLÉMENTS D'ÉCONOMIE POLITIQUE APPLIQUÉE* or *Théorie de la production agricole, industrielle et commercial de la richesse.*

3rd part: − *ÉLÉMENTS D'ÉCONOMIE SOCIALE* or *Théorie de la répartition de la richesse par la propriété et l'impôt.*

The first fascicle of the first volume is presented here. It contains a mathematical solution of the problem of the determination of equilibrium prices and also a scientific formulation of the law of supply and demand in the case of the exchange of any number of commodities for one another. I realize that the notations used there will at first appear a little complicated, but I beg the reader not to be discouraged by this complexity, which is inherent in the subject and which, besides, constitutes the only mathematical difficulty. This system of notation once understood, the system of economic phenomena is, in a way, also thereby understood.

This half-volume was completely written and almost completely printed, and I had already communicated the principle of the theory expounded in it to the Académie des sciences morales et politiques in Paris,[2] when, a month ago, my attention was drawn to a work on the same subject entitled *The Theory of Political Economy*, published in 1871 by Macmillan & Co. in London by Mr. W. Stanley Jevons, Professor of Political Economy at Manchester. That author applies, as I do, mathematical analysis to economic theory, especially to the theory of exchange; and, what is really remarkable, he bases the whole of that application on a fundamental formula that he calls the equation of exchange, and that is rigorously identical to the formula that serves as my point of departure and that I call the *condition of maximum satisfaction.*

Mr. Jevons is above all concerned with developing a general and philosophical exposition of the new method, and with laying down the foundations of its application to the theory of *exchange,* and to the theories of *labor, land services,* and *capital.* For my part, I have especially made an effort in the present half-volume to give a thorough exposition of the *mathematical theory of exchange.* It is only proper that I restore to Mr. Jevons the priority of his formula while retaining the right of priority for certain important deductions from it. I will not enumerate these points, which a competent public will be perfectly able to recognize. Let it suffice for me to say that, in my opinion,

---

[2] See the *Report* of the sessions and work of the Académie, January 1874, or the *Journal des Économistes*, April 1874.

the work of Mr. Jevons and my own, far from destroying each other, confirm, complement, and markedly enhance each other. That is my firm conviction, and I demonstrate it to be such by strongly recommending that eminent English economist's excellent book to everyone who is not familiar with it.

The second part of the first edition of my treatise was published in 1877. In it, I developed a theory of the determination of the prices of productive services (wages, rent, and interest) and a theory of the determination of the rate of net income very different from those of Jevons.[3]

In 1879, Jevons, then professor at University College, London, published the second edition of his *Theory of Political Economy*, and, in the preface of that edition (pp. XXXV–XLII), he partly conceded to Gossen, a German, the priority of discovering the starting-point of mathematical economics, which I had already conceded to Jevons, as indicated above. I consecrated to Gossen, in the *Journal des Économistes* for April and May 1885, an article titled 'Un économiste inconnu, Hermann-Henri Gossen' in which I presented information about his life and work, and made an effort to determine what remained as my own contribution after the work of my two predecessors. At the end of lesson 16, which concludes part II of this volume, the reader will find a section in which I return to this matter. It will be seen there that the importance of considering rareté[ii] in the theory of exchange was again discovered and stressed, independently of the three of us, by Mr. Carl Menger, professor of economics at the University of Vienna, and, I hope it will be understood, that, given these circumstances, I feel it necessary to state with precision the respects in which my second edition differs from the first.

---

[3] Part I of the first edition of the *Éléments d'économie politique pure* was summarized in two memoirs entitled: *Principe d'une théorie mathématique de l'échange* and *Équations de l'échange,* the first having been submitted to the Académie des sciences morales et politiques in Paris in August 1873, and the second to the Société Vaudoise des sciences naturelles at Lausanne in December 1875. Part II was summarized before its publication in two memoirs entitled: *Équations de la production* and *Équations de la capitalisation,* both submitted to the Société vaudoise des sciences naturelles, the first in January and February, and the second in July 1876. These four memoirs were translated into Italian as *Teoria matematica della ricchezza sociale* (Biblioteca dell'Economista, 1878) and in German as *Mathematische Theorie der Preisbestimmung der wirthschaftlichen Güter* (Stuttgart. Verlag von Ferdinand Enke, 1881).

Stocks of the first edition had been exhausted for several years; the publication of the second was delayed only by the studies that I had undertaken on the question of money.[4] In order to introduce the results of my research in the present edition, I have placed after the part on capital formation and credit the part on money, a part that, in the first edition, came immediately after the part on exchange. I put eight lessons into that part, numbered 33 to 40, of which four are on theory and four on applied economics. Among the first four, I included two lessons, numbered 34 and 35, that contain my theory of bimetallism. Moreover, in the other lesson on economic theory, regarding the solution of the problem of the value of money, I substituted, in place of the demonstration founded on the concept of the 'needed monetary circulation',[iii] which was an idea that I borrowed from the economists[iv] and used in the first edition of the *Éléments d'économie politique pure*, the demonstration, completed in the necessary way, based on the concept of a 'desired cash balance' that I used in the *Théorie de la monnaie*. Among the latter four lessons, I put two lessons, numbered 39 and 40, one with the critique of the doctrine of Cournot on the changes of absolute and relative value, which I took up from the part on exchange to introduce it in the part on money, and added to it the critique of Jevons's doctrine on the same subject, and the other with the conclusions of my new theory regarding the regularization of the variation of the value of money. In all these lessons on applied theory, I substituted in place of the system of gold coinage with divisible silver tokens of the first edition of the *Éléments* the system of gold coinage with divisible silver tokens and the regulatory silver tokens of the *Théorie*. If we leave on one side the four applied theory lessons, that perhaps should have been moved to the *Éléments d'économie politique appliquée*, we have, in the four lessons on economic theory, the solution of the fourth great problem that arises in economic theory after those of exchange, production, capital formation and credit: the problem of money.

---

[4] Some of these are studies in economic theory: – *Note sur le 15¹/₂ légal*; – *Théorie mathématique du bimétalisme*; – *De la fixité de valeur de l'étalon monétaire* (*Journal des Économists*, December 1876, May 1881, October 1882); they have been put into the present volume. The others, notably the *Théorie de la monnaie* (1886), which are studies in applied economics, will be found in the *Études d'économie politique appliquée*. (February 1896).

If I have enlarged considerably the part devoted to money, I have, on the other hand, made few important changes in the parts devoted to the three other problems. I have, in the part on exchange, added to the proof of the theorem of the maximum satisfaction[v] in the case of continuous utility curves, a proof for the case of discontinuous curves. I have improved upon several matters of detail in the solution of the equations of exchange, of production, of capital formation and of credit, while leaving it as it was in its overall presentation. I have established, in a new theorem, that the condition of equality of the rate of net income is also the condition of maximum utility for new capital goods. When I published my first edition, I had seen only one of the two problems of the maximization of utility relative to the services of new capital goods: that which presents itself with reference to the distribution by an individual of his income among his diverse wants, if it is assumed that the quantities of capital goods are given by the very nature of things or determined by chance. I call that, for short, the problem *of the maximization of satisfaction of wants*; it is solved mathematically by the proportionality of raretés to the prices of the services of the capital goods. However, in preparing the second edition, I became aware that there is a second problem: that which presents itself with reference to the distribution by a society of the excess of its income over its consumption among the diverse varieties of capital goods, when one seeks the determination of the quantities of new capital goods in view of the maximum of effective utility of their services. I call that the problem *of the maximum utility of new capital goods*; it is solved mathematically by the proportionality of the prices of the services to the prices of the goods, which is, subject to a single qualification, precisely the result to which free competition leads.

I have slightly modified the titles of my parts in order to mark better the order of the four problems of which I have spoken; and I have often melded two or three lessons into one, not thinking it more useful to deal, in the treatise, with the division of the course into very short lessons.

Finally, I have added a mathematical introduction in which I have given the necessary guidance for the reading of the volume. I have profited from the opportunity to give that guidance in regard to derivatives and definite integrals, which has enabled me to furnish from time to time the true formula for certain fundamental theorems and to demonstrate the theorem of the maximum utility of new capital goods. I preface my course at the Academy of Lausanne with an analogous introduction, and I find that a useful practice: it permits those of my students who wish to do so to follow me without difficulty. If the introduction that I provide here gains me a single attentive reader more, my trouble will not be unrewarded.

As a consequence of these modifications, the outline of the volume now appears as follows:

Functions and their geometrical representation. Mathematical theory of the law of gravity.

ÉLÉMENTS D'ÉCONOMIE POLITIQUE PURE, or *Théorie de la richesse sociale*.

Part I. Object and divisions of economics. – Part II. Theory of exchange. – Part III. Theory of production. – Part IV. Theory of capital formation and credit. – Part V. Theory of money. – Part VI. Price fixing, monopoly, and taxation.

However, the volume modified in this way is still the second edition of the volume of 1874–1877. By that I mean that my present doctrine is just the same as it was fifteen years ago. It can be summarized as follows.

Economic theory is essentially the theory of the determination of prices in a hypothetical regime of perfectly free competition. The ensemble of all things, material or immaterial, on which a price can be set because they are *scarce*, that is to say, are both *useful* and *limited in quantity*, constitutes *social wealth*. That is why economic theory is also the *theory of social wealth*.

Among the things that make up social wealth a distinction must be made between *capital goods*, or, *durable goods*, which can be used more than once, and *income goods*, or, *non-durable goods*, which cannot be used more than once. Capital goods comprise *land, personal faculties*, and *capital goods properly speaking*. Income goods comprise not only *consumers' goods* and *raw materials*, which are, for the most part, material things, but they also include, under the name of services, the successive uses of capital goods, services that are, in most instances, immaterial things. The services of capital goods that have a direct utility are put in the same class as consumers' goods under the name *consumers' services*; those services of capital goods that have only indirect utility are put in the same class as raw materials under the name *productive services*. That, in my opinion, is the key to all of economic theory. If the distinction between capital goods and income goods is neglected, and particularly if the immaterial services of capital goods are not put among social wealth along with material income, the possibility of a scientific theory of the determination of prices is precluded. If, on the other hand, the proposed distinction and classification are accepted, then it becomes possible to arrive successively, by means of the *theory of exchange*, at a determination of the prices of consumers' goods and services; by means of the *theory of production*, at a determination of the prices of raw materials and productive services; by means of the *theory of capital formation*, at a determination of the price of fixed capital goods; and, by means of the *theory of circulation*, at a determination of the prices of circulating capital goods. Here is how this is done.

First, let us imagine a market in which only consumers' goods and consumable services are bought and sold; that is to say, exchanged, the *sale of any service* being done by the *hiring out of a capital good*. The *prices* or the ratios of exchange of all these goods and services having been cried at random in terms of one of them selected as the numeraire, each party to the exchange *offers* at these prices those goods or services of which he thinks he has relatively too much, and he *demands* those articles or services of which he thinks he has relatively too little. The quantities of each item effectively demanded and supplied having thus been determined, the prices of those things for which the demand exceeds the supply are raised, and the prices of those things of which the supply exceeds the demand are lowered. At the new prices that are cried, each exchanger offers and demands new quantities. And again, prices are made to rise or fall until the demand and the supply of each good or service is equal. At that point, the prices are *current equilibrium prices* and exchange takes place.

The problem of production is posed by introducing into the problem of exchange the circumstance that consumers' goods are products resulting either from a combination of productive services alone or from the application of these services to raw materials. In order to take this circumstance into account, it is necessary to place the *landowners, workers,* and *capitalists,* who are sellers of services and buyers of consumable services and consumer goods, face to face with sellers of products and buyers of productive services and raw materials. Those sellers and buyers are entrepreneurs, who seek a profit by transforming productive services into products; that is to say, into raw materials that they sell to one another, or into consumer goods that they sell to the landowners, workers, and capitalists from whom they have bought productive services. In this connection, to better understand these phenomena, instead of thinking of one market, we can suppose there are two: a *market for services* on which services are offered exclusively by landowners, workers, and capitalists, and demanded as follows: the consumable services by the selfsame landowners, workers, and capitalists, and the productive services by the entrepreneurs; and a *market for products* on which these products are offered exclusively by entrepreneurs, and demanded as follows: the raw materials, by the selfsame entrepreneurs, and consumer goods by landowners, workers, and capitalists. On the two markets, at prices cried at random, the landowners, workers, and capitalists, in their capacity as consumers, offer services and demand consumable services and consumer goods in such a way as to obtain the largest possible sum total of utility, and the entrepreneurs, in their capacity as producers, offer products and demand productive services or raw materials in the course of increasing their output in the case of an excess of the price of the product over the average cost resulting from the productive services involved in their production; and they reduce their output, on the other hand, in the case of the excess of the average cost resulting from the productive services used over the price of the product. On each market, prices are raised in the case of an excess of the demand over the supply and are lowered in the case of the excess of supply over demand. The current equilibrium prices are those at which the demand and the supply of each service or product are equal and at which, moreover, the *price* of each product is equal to the *average cost* resulting from the productive services used.

In order to pose the problem of capital formation, it must be supposed that there are landowners, workers, and capitalists who *save*; that is to say, who, instead of demanding consumers' goods and services equal to the total value of the services they offer, demand *new capital goods* for part of that value. And, facing these creators of savings, it must be assumed that there are entrepreneurs who produce new capital goods in lieu of raw materials or consumers' goods.

A certain sum of savings being given on the one hand, and certain quantities of newly manufactured capital goods on the other hand, these savings and these new capital goods are exchanged against each other on a *market for new capital goods,* in conformity with the mechanism of bidding up and down, in proportion to the prices of the consumable or productive services of those goods determined by virtue of the theories of exchange and production. Hence, we have a certain rate of income, and for each capital good a certain selling price that is equal to the ratio of the price of its service to the rate of income. The entrepreneurs who produce new capital goods, like those who produce consumer goods, expand or contract their output according to whether the price exceeds the average cost or the average cost exceeds the price.

When the rate of income has been determined, we have not only the price of new capital goods but also the price of old capital goods: land, personal faculties, and already existing capital goods properly speaking, by dividing by that rate the prices of the services of old capital goods: rents, wages, and interest. We then have the prices of all the social wealth in numeraire, and it remains only to know, by the *theory of money,* what becomes of all these prices when the numeraire is also money.

But this whole theory is mathematical; that is to say, although the exposition can be made in ordinary language, the demonstration of the theory must be made mathematically. The demonstration rests wholly on the theory of exchange; and the theory of exchange can be summed up in its entirety in this double condition of market equilibrium: first, that of the obtaining by each exchanger of a maximum of utility, and, next, that of the equality of the quantity demanded and the quantity supplied of each commodity by all the exchangers. Only mathematics can make clear to us the condition of maximum utility. It does so by attributing to each exchanger, for each consumer good or consumable service, an equation or curve expressing the *intensity of the last want satisfied,* or rareté, as a decreasing function of the *quantity consumed,* and in enabling us to see that an exchanger will obtain the greatest possible total satisfaction of his wants if he demands and offers commodities in such quantities when certain prices are cried that the raretés of these commodities are proportional to their prices after exchange has taken place. And only mathematics can make clear to us why and how, not only in exchange but also in production and capital formation, current equilibrium prices are attained by raising the price of services, products, and new capital goods for which the demand exceeds the supply, and by lowering the price of those for which the supply exceeds the demand. Mathematics does this, first, by deducing from the rareté functions the functions that express the supply of services and the demand for the services, products, and new capital goods offered and demanded with a view to maximizing the satisfaction of wants; and then by uniting these equations to other equations that express the equality of the price and the average cost of products and new capital goods, and the equality of the rate of income for all the new capital goods; and finally by showing: 1° that the problems of exchange, production, and capital formation are determinate problems; that is to say, that the number of equations is exactly equal to the number of unknowns, and 2° that the mechanism of the raising and lowering of prices on the market, combined with the fact of the flow of entrepreneurs from enterprises showing a loss to enterprises showing a profit is nothing other than a mode of solution by tatonnement[vi] of the equations expressing these problems.

Such is the system of which I am now giving an exposition and a demonstration as careful and detailed as it has been possible for me to give them, but that I had already expounded and demonstrated in the four first memoirs of my *Théorie mathématique de la richesse sociale*, from 1873 to 1876, and in the first edition of my *Éléments d'économie politique pure*, in 1874 and 1877. I made it my duty, as soon as I had mastered the principle of the entire theory, to communicate it to the Académie des sciences morales et politiques in Paris; and accordingly I had written the first of the four above-mentioned memoirs, and I had given, at the same time, for the case of the exchange of two commodities in kind for each other, the solution of the problem of maximum satisfaction of wants for each exchanger given by the proportionality of the intensities of the last wants satisfied to the values in exchange, and the solution of the problem of the determination of the respective current prices of the two commodities by a rise in price when the demand exceeds supply and by a fall in price when the supply exceeds demand. The Académie received this paper in the least favorable and the most discouraging manner. I grieve for this learned body, and I dare say that after having had the double misfortune of crowning Canard and underrating Cournot, it would have done well, in its own interest, to seize the opportunity to establish its competence in the subject a little more brilliantly. But, so far as I am concerned, the bad reception by the Académie actually brought me good luck, for, from the double point of view of substance and form, the doctrine that I espoused fifteen years ago has since then traveled a considerable path.

The theory of exchange that recognizes the proportionality of prices to the *intensities of the last wants satisfied*, to the *Final Degrees of Utility*, to *Grenznutzen*, a theory conceived almost simultaneously by Jevons, Mr. Menger and myself, and which furnishes the foundation of the whole edifice, has become an accepted part of economics. I was able to cite, in the preface of my *Théorie de la monnaie*, some fifteen professors in the top ranked universities and higher education institutes of Europe and America who have been won over to it, and that list immediately became incomplete. I could draw up here another which would certainly also be incomplete. Suffice it for me to say that that theory is taught, as at Lausanne, in Cambridge, London, Edimbourg, Dublin, Utrecht, Leyden, Amsterdam, Louvain, Hanover, Würzburg, Vienna, Prague, Innsbruck, Montpellier, Bordeaux, Naples, and Boston.

But as soon as the principle of the theory of exchange had made its entrance into the science, it could not be long before the principle of the theory of production made its entrance also, and that has in fact happened. In the second edition of his *Theory of Political Economy*, Jevons recognized a point he had missed in the first edition, namely, that as soon as the *Final Degree of Utility* determined the prices of products, it determined also, because of that circumstance, the prices of the productive services, or the rent, wages, and interest, because, in a regime of free competition, the price of products and their average cost resulting from the services employed in producing them tends towards equality; and he said clearly, in May 1879, at the end of the preface to the second edition of his work, in ten very interesting pages (pp. xlviii–lvii), that he had to reject completely the formula of the English school, or at least that of the Ricardo-Mill school, and determine the price of productive services by the price of the products instead of determining the price of products by the price of productive services. The Austrian economists, who arrived spontaneously at the conception of *Grenznutzen* in the

theory of value in exchange, also took that idea to its logical consequence in the theory of production, and they introduced between the
value of *Producte* and the value of *Produktivmittel* exactly the same
relation that I myself introduced between the value of products and
the value of raw materials and productive services.[5]

There remains the theory of capital formation, on which Mr. Carl
Menger recently published an article titled *Zur Theorie des Kapitals*
in vol. XVII of the *Jahrbücher für Nationalokonomie und Statistik*.
Menger's views were completed by Mr. von Bœhm-Bawerk, professor at Innsbruck, in *Kapital und Kapitalzins*, in giving, after the first
part, which appeared in 1884: –*Geschichte und Kritik de Kapitalzins-
Theorieen*, the second part, which appeared at the beginning of the
present year: – *Positive Theorie des Kapitales*, in which he derives
the fact of the interest on capital from the difference between the
value of a present good and that of a future good.[6] I must state
plainly that here Mr. von Bœhm-Bawerk and I part company; and
explain briefly why I cannot accept his theory. But that is something I cannot do without formulating that theory mathematically,
or at least the theory of the determination of the rate of interest that
it implies.

It is necessary only to open the first treatise on business finance
that comes to hand to learn there that a thing worth A if it is delivered immediately will be worth today

$$A' = \frac{A}{(1+i)^n}$$

for future delivery n years hence, at an annual rate of interest i. But, to
base an economic theory of the determination of the rate of interest
on this formula, we must first be told how A is determined, and then
be shown the market on which i is deduced from A' in conformity
with the given equation. I have looked for such a market without

---

[5] In this regard, I should add the following work of Mr. Frédéric de Wieser's to the
references given at the end of my 16th lesson: *Der natürliche Werth* (1889).
[6] Mr. Menger's article and Mr. von Bœhm-Bawerk's book were very carefully
analyzed in the *Revue d'Économie Politique* (November–December 1888 and
March–April 1889).

finding it. And that is why I persist in deriving (abstracting from depreciation insurance) i from the equation

$$\frac{D_k p_k + D_{k'} p_{k'} + D_{k''} p_{k''} + \cdots}{i}$$

$$= F_e \left(p_t, p_p, p_k, p_{k'}, p_{k''}, \cdots, p_b, p_c, p_d, \cdots \right),$$

in which $p_k, p_{k'}, p_{k''}, \cdots$ are the prices of the services of the capital goods (K), (K'), (K'') $\cdots$ and are determined by the theories of exchange and production; $D_k, D_{k'}, D_{k''}, \cdots$ are the quantities manufactured of these new capital goods and are determined by the condition of equality between their price and their average cost of production or by the condition of uniformity of the rate of income, which is also the condition of their maximum utility, in which, finally, $F_e \left(p_t, p_p, p_k, p_{k'}, p_{k''}, \cdots, p_b, p_c, p_d, \cdots \right)$ is the amount of savings, determined by the comparison that each saver makes, at the current price of services and products, between the utility for him of a unit to be consumed immediately and the utility for him of i consumed year in and year out. The left-hand member of the above equation constitutes the supply of new capital goods in terms of numeraire, and is evidently a decreasing function of i. The right-hand member constitutes the demand for new capital goods in terms of numeraire, by either the savers themselves or entrepreneurs who borrow the savings in the form of money capital and is a successively increasing and decreasing function of i. Equality between the two sides of the equation is achieved by increasing or decreasing the price of new capital goods brought about by the fall or the rise of i, according as the demand is greater than the supply or the supply is greater than the demand. All attentive readers will recognize here that which happens on the market of the stock exchange when new capital goods represented by their titles to property are brought to be exchanged against savings at prices proportional to their incomes, according to the mechanism of the raising and lowering of prices, and will agree that my theory of capital formation, the whole of which, let me repeat, is based on the anterior theories of exchange and production, is just what a theory of this nature ought to be: the abstract expression and rational explanation of real phenomena. And in this respect, let me be permitted to remark how truly my theorem of maximum utility of new capital goods confirms my whole system of economic theory. Admittedly, it is no great discovery to have recognized that society realizes a gain in utility by withdrawing capital from an employment where it yields a low interest in order to invest it in an employment where it yields a higher interest; but it seems to me that to have demonstrated mathematically so plausible and even so evident a truth validates the definitions and analyses by which it was reached.

The mathematicians will be the judge of this; and, even at present, there are a few to whom I am ready to submit the cause I espouse. Soon after they appeared, Jevons's theory and my own were translated into Italian, as were the earlier efforts of Whewell and Cournot. Then, in Germany, Gossen's book, at first unnoticed, was added to the already known works of Thünen and Mangoldt. Since that time these books have appeared: Launhardt's *Mathematische Begründung der Volkswirthschaftslehre* (1885); in England, Edgeworth's *Mathematical Psychics* (1881), Wicksteed's *The Alphabet of Economic Science* (1888).[7] The school that will take form inspired by these writers will be very able to discern which system, among so many, should constitute the science. As for those economists who, without knowing mathematics, without even knowing what mathematics consists of, have decided that mathematics cannot possibly serve to clarify economic principles, they can go their way repeating that *'human liberty will never allow itself to be put into equations'* or that 'mathematics abstracts from the frictions *that are everything in the moral sciences'*, and other forcefully expressed niceties. They cannot prevent the theory of the determination of prices under free competition from being

---

[7] Among the works published subsequently, I should particularly mention, apart from the two works of Auspitz and Lieben and of Wicksteed with which my appendixes II and III are concerned, the following works: – Giovanni Rossi. *La Matematica applicata alla teoria della ricchezza sociale* (1889); – Maffeo Pantaleoni. *Principii di Economia pura* (1889); – Alfred Marshall. *Principles of Economics* (2nd ed. 1891); – Irving Fisher. *Mathematical Investigations in the Theory of Value and Prices* (1892); – Julius Lehr. *Grundbegriffe und Grundlagen der Volkswirtschaft* (1893); – Knut Wicksell. *Ueber Wert, Kapital und Rente nach den neueren nationalœkonomischen Theorien* (1893); – Vilfredo Pareto. *Cours d'économie politique professé à l'Université de Lausanne* (1896); – and the very numerous and very important articles by Messrs. Pareto and Barone published in the *Giornale degli Economisti* since 1892. (February 1896.)

a mathematical theory; and they will always have to face the alternative either of avoiding this discipline and of developing applied economics without having developed theoretical economics, or of approaching it without the necessary intellectual resources, and, in that case, of producing at the same time very bad economic theory and very bad mathematics. In my lesson 40, the samples of these theories that are mathematical, as are mine, will be found, which abstract from frictions as much and more than mine, and of which the only difference with mine is that I feel constrained always to have as many equations as there are unknowns in my problems, neither more nor less, while those gentlemen reserve themselves the right sometimes to determine a single unknown by means of two equations and sometimes to use a single equation to solve for two, three, and even four unknowns; and one doubts, I trust, that such a method can indefinitely be opposed to the one that wishes to make economic theory an exact science.

L.W.
Lausanne, May 1889.

Notes

i We have anglicized Walras's word '*numéraire*' throughout this book.

ii By this word, Walras meant 'marginal utility'. Although he was familiar with the latter term, he preferred the word that had been used, although with a less precise meaning, by his father. Since Walras preferred 'rareté', we have left it untranslated throughout the book.

iii It may be asked whether Walras's 'circulation à desservir' is the circulation of money necessary to effectuate transactions or the goods that need to be cleared off the market. His idea was that the demand for money is an amount of (for example) metallic currency necessary to make payments for the current amount of goods to change hands. The money itself circulates. The goods do not; even the units constituting 'circulating capital goods' do not circulate. The 'circulation à desservir' is 'la quantité du metal...employée à desservir la circulation monétaire' (ŒÉC p. 557 and see p. 558). It is the needed circulation of money that is served by the amount of currency in the system. It corresponds to the amount of money needed to satisfy the transactions demand for money. For a statement that is unhelpful because of its ambiguity, see Jaffé 1983, page 133.

iv Walras meant the Physiocrats.

v Walras wrote 'théorème de la satisfaction maxima'. He wrote 'maxima' and not 'maximum' because 'satisfaction' is a singular feminine noun and the pedantic editors of the *Revue scientifique*, in which he published this study, asked him to treat that adjective as a Latin one. Employing the normal English usage in economic literature, we translate his expression as 'theorem of maximum satisfaction'.

vi As is the practice now in English, the word '*tâtonnement*', which is a noun derived from the verb 'tâtonner', 'to grope' or 'to proceed by trial and error', has been anglicized.

THEORY OF SOCIAL WEALTH

PART I

OBJECT AND DIVISIONS OF ECONOMICS

LESSON 1

Adam Smith's and J.-B. Say's definitions

SUMMARY: – Two-fold objective assigned to economics: 1° To provide the people with an income or an abundant level of living; 2° To furnish the State or the community a sufficient income. First observation. Two goals, equally important, but neither of which is the object of a proper science. There is another point of view for economics. Second observation. Two operations equally important, but of a different character, one a matter of economic advantageousness and the other a matter of justice.

Economics envisaged as the simple exposition of the manner in which wealth is produced, distributed, and consumed. Naturalist point of view, permitting an easy refutation of socialism, but which is inaccurate if applied to the entire science. In regard to the production and distribution of wealth, humans are led to choose one or another combination, not on the grounds of what is most natural, but on the grounds of what is most useful or most equitable.

1. The first thing to be done at the beginning of a course or treatise on economics is to define the science, its object, divisions, nature, and limits. I have no thought of evading this obligation; but I must warn that it is longer and more difficult to fulfill than perhaps is supposed. We lack a definition of economics. Of all the definitions that have been proposed, not one has met with the general definitive acceptance that is the sign of truths acquired by science. I shall quote and criticize the most interesting of these definitions, and I shall try to provide one. In the course of this task, I shall find occasion to mention certain names, titles of books, and dates that should be known.

2. Quesnay and his disciples are the first important group of economists. They have a common doctrine; they form a school. They themselves call their doctrine *Physiocracy*; that is to say, the natural government of society; and that is why they are known today as Physiocrats. Apart from Quesnay, who wrote the *Tableau économique* (1758), the principal Physiocrats are Mercier de la Rivière, author of *L'ordre naturel et essentiel des sociétés politiques* (1767), Dupont de Nemours, author of *Physiocratie ou constitution naturelle du gouvernement le plus avantageux au genre humain* (1767–1768), the abbé Baudeau, and Le Trosne. Turgot is in a separate category. It can be seen from the titles of their works that the Physiocrats enlarged rather than narrowed the domain of the science. The theory of the natural government of society is not so much economics as it is social science. The term Physiocracy therefore implies too wide a definition.

3. Adam Smith in his *Inquiry into the Nature and Causes of the Wealth of Nations,* published in 1776, was the first to try, with remarkable success, to arrange the subjects of economics into an organized discipline. It was not, however, until the beginning of the introduction to Book IV of that work, a Book titled 'Of Systems of Economics', that it occurred to him to provide a definition of the science, and this is the one he gave: – 'Economics', he said, 'considered as a branch of the science of a statesman or legislator, proposes two distinct objects: first, to provide a plentiful revenue or subsistence for the people, or more properly to enable them to provide such a revenue or subsistence for themselves; and secondly, to supply the state or commonwealth with a revenue sufficient for the public services. It proposes to enrich both the people and the sovereign.' That definition, given by the person who has been called the father of economics, not at the beginning but towards the middle of his work, at a point at which he should have had a complete understanding of his subject, deserves careful consideration. It seems to me that it gives rise to two principal observations.

4. To provide a plentiful income for the people, to supply the State with a sufficient income, is assuredly a very important double-faceted goal, and if economics helps to achieve it, it renders us a signal service. But I do not see, however, that that constitutes the object of

a science properly speaking. Indeed the characteristic of a science properly speaking is the complete indifference to any consequences, advantageous or undesirable, of its attachment to the pursuit of pure truth. Thus when the geometer enunciates that an *equilateral triangle is at the same time equiangular*, and when the astronomer enunciates that *the planets move in an elliptical orbit of which the sun occupies one of the foci*, they are doing science properly speaking. It is possible that the first of these two truths, like the other truths of geometry, may lead to results that are valuable for carpentry, stone cutting, and every type of architecture or construction of houses; it is possible that the second truth and the entirety of astronomical truths may be of the greatest help to navigation; but neither the carpenter, nor the mason, nor the architect, nor the navigator, nor even those who work out the theories of carpentry, stone cutting, architecture, or navigation are scientists or do science in the true meaning of those words. Now, the two activities of which Adam Smith speaks are analogous, not to those of the geometer and the astronomer, but to those of the architect and the navigator. If, therefore, economics were what Adam Smith said, and if it were nothing else, it would certainly be a very interesting subject, but it would not be a science properly speaking. Thus it must be stated that economics is something other than what Adam Smith says. Before thinking of providing a plentiful revenue for the people, and before concerning itself with furnishing the State with an adequate income, the economist pursues and grasps purely scientific truths. That is what he does when he states, for example, that *the value of things tends to increase when the quantity demanded increases or when the quantity supplied decreases*, and that *this value tends to diminish in the two opposite cases*; that *the rate of interest falls in a progressive economy*; that *a tax levied on ground rent falls exclusively on the landowner without affecting the prices of agricultural products*. In all these cases, economists are doing pure science. Adam Smith himself did this. His disciples, Malthus and Ricardo, the former in his *Essay on the Principles of Population* (1798) and the latter in his *Principles of Political Economy and Taxation* (1817), did even more. Adam Smith's definition is therefore incomplete in that it fails to mention the aim of economics considered as a science strictly speaking. To say, in effect, that the objective of economics is to provide a plentiful income for the people and to furnish the State with an adequate income is like saying that the object of geometry is to build solid houses, and that the aim of astronomy is to navigate the seas safely. It is, in a word, to define a science in terms of its applications.

5. That first observation about Adam Smith's definition relates to the objective of the science; I have another, no less important, observation to make relative to its character.

To provide a plentiful income for the people and to furnish the State with a sufficient income are two equally important, equally delicate operations, but having a very different character. The first consists in providing agriculture, industry, and trade with various determinate conditions. According as these conditions are favorable or unfavorable, the agricultural, industrial, and commercial production will be plentiful or restricted. Thus, in past times it has been seen that industry suffered and stagnated under a regime of associations of artisans, guilds, regulations, and price fixing; it is seen today that under the opposite regime of freedom of work and of trade, industry grows and prospers. It was 'so much the worse' in the former case and 'it is all the better' in the second case; but, in each of them, it is only economic advantageousness that is frustrated or favored; it is not justice that is attained or respected. Matters are quite otherwise when it is a question of supplying the State with sufficient income. That case is, in effect, an operation that consists in deducting from individual incomes the amount necessary to provide the income of the community. But, according to whether the conditions are good or bad, it happens not only that the income of the State is sufficient or insufficient, it happens in addition that individuals are treated equitably or inequitably; equitably if each contributes his share, inequitably if some are sacrificed while others are privileged. Thus, there were formerly seen to be classes of society that were exempt from taxes that weighed exclusively on certain other classes. It is considered today that that was a flagrant injustice. Thus, to obtain a plentiful income for the people is a useful activity, and to furnish the State with a sufficient income is an equitable activity. Usefulness and equity, economic advantageousness and justice, are two very different orders of consideration, and it could be wished that A. Smith had made this difference clear by saying, for example, that the objective of economics is to indicate the conditions first for the production of a *plentiful* social income, and then for an *equitable* division of this income between individuals and the State. That definition would be better, but it would still leave out the truly scientific part of economics.

6. Jean-Baptiste Say, who, in chronological order, is, after Adam Smith, the most illustrious name in economics, said of his predecessor's definition: 'I would rather say that the objective of economics is to make known the means by which wealth is produced, distributed, and consumed.' And, indeed, his work, the first edition of which appeared in 1803, while the second, banned by the Consulate censorship, could not be published until after the fall of the First Empire, is titled *Traité d'économie politique, ou simple exposition de la manière dont se forment, se distribuent et se consomment les richesses.* This definition and the divisions that it establishes have been very generally approved and adopted by economists. It is surely those that one would be most tempted to consider as classic. But I ask permission not to side with that opinion, and to do so precisely on the grounds that have made them successful.

7. It is evident at first glance that J.-B. Say's definition is not only different from Adam Smith's, but that it is, in a certain sense, the complete opposite. While, if Adam Smith is to be believed, the whole of economics is an *art* rather than a *science* (§ 4), according to J.-B. Say, the whole of the science is a *natural* science. It seems, according to him, that the *production, distribution,* and *consumption* of wealth take place, if not completely independently, at least in a *manner* in some way independent of the human will, and that all of economics consists in a *simple exposition* of that manner.

What has seduced economists in this definition is precisely the appearance of a natural science that it gives to the whole of economics. That point of view, in fact, has singularly aided them in their fight against the socialists. Every plan of organization of work, every plan of organization of property was rejected by them a priori and, so to speak, without discussion, not as being contrary to economic advantageousness, nor as contrary to social justice, but simply as an artificial scheme designed to replace a natural scheme. And what is more, this naturalistic viewpoint was borrowed from the Physiocrats by J.-B. Say and was inspired by the formula: *Laissez faire, laissez passer* that summarizes their doctrine in regard to industrial and commercial activity. That is what earned the school of economists the epithet *fatalistic* given by Proudhon, and it is hard to believe, in fact, the point to which that school has pushed its consequences. It is necessary, in order to become aware of that, to read certain articles in the *Dictionnaire de l'économie politique,* such as Charles Coquelin's 'Concurrence', 'Économie politique' and 'Industrie', or Mr. Andre Cochut's 'Morale'; very meaningful passages are to be found in these articles.

Unfortunately, the indicated point of view is as false as it is convenient. If men were only a superior species of animal, were only bees undertaking instinctively their work and their habitual ways, it is certain that the exposition and explanation of social phenomena in general, and of the phenomena of production, distribution, and consumption of wealth in particular, would be a natural science that would not be, to speak accurately, other than a branch of natural history, the natural history of man following that of the bee. But matters are quite different. Man is a creature endowed with reason and freedom, capable of initiative and progress. In regard to the production and distribution of wealth, and generally in all matters of social organization, he has the choice between that which is good and that which is not, and increasingly turns from the latter to the former. Thus man has progressed from a system of guilds, trade regulations, and price fixing to a system of liberty of industry and commerce, to the system of *laisser faire* and *laisser passer,* from slavery to serfdom, from serfdom to the wage system. The more recent forms of organization are superior to the earlier forms not because they are more natural (both are artificial, and the newer one even more so than the older ones, because they appeared only subsequent to them), but because they are more in conformity with economic advantageousness and justice. It is only after a demonstration of this conformity that *laisser faire, laisser aller* must be adopted. And, if that can be demonstrated, it is on the grounds of being contrary to economic advantageousness and justice that socialist schemes should be rejected.

8. Inferior to Adam Smith's definition, which was only incomplete, J.-B. Say's is therefore incorrect. I add that the divisions of the subject

that follow from Say's definition are completely empirical. The theory of property and the theory of taxation, which are in reality only the two halves of the theory of the distribution of wealth among the people in human society, considered first in isolation as individuals and then collectively as the State, and which are both dependent so essentially on moral principles, are separated and rejected, the first, that of property, in the theory of production, and the other, that of taxation, in the theory of consumption, and are both elaborated exclusively from the economic point of view. The theory of value in exchange, which, on the contrary, has so clearly the character of a study of natural phenomena, is made part of the theory of distribution. It is true that his disciples interpret it as they please, using these arbitrary classifications, and, no less arbitrarily, some classify the theory of value in exchange under the theory of production while others classify the theory of property under the theory of distribution. That is the sort of economics that is done and taught today; but is it not justified to say that in that sort of economics there are only broken structures, of which just the façade remains, and that, given the existence of such a state of affairs, the right and the duty of the economist is to formulate carefully the philosophy of the science?

9. The defect of J.-B. Say's definition has nevertheless been glimpsed by some of his students, but they have not remedied it. Adolphe Blanqui wrote:

In Germany and France, economists have strayed furthest from the true field that today is generally assigned to economics. Some economists have attempted to make it a universal science; others have tried to restrict it to a narrow scope and popularized content. The struggle in France between these two extreme opinions turns upon the question whether economics should be considered as the statement of what is or as an agenda of what ought to be; that is to say, as a natural science or a moral science? We believe that it partakes of both characters.

It is in this way, an excellent means of condemning it, that Blanqui approves of J.-B. Say's definition.

Subsequent to Blanqui's writings, Joseph Garnier wrote that

economics is both a natural and a moral science; from these two points of view, it sets forth that which is and that which ought to be according to the natural course of things and in conformity with the idea of justice.

Consequently, Garnier proposes a modification of J.-B. Say's definition by making a slight addition to it by saying that

economics is the science of wealth; that is to say, the science that has as its
goal to determine how most rationally (naturally, equitably) wealth *is* and
ought to be produced, exchanged, distributed, and used in the interest of
individuals as well as in the interest of the whole society.

Garnier here makes a completely serious and truly praiseworthy
effort to get out of the rut in which his school is stuck. It is strange,
however, that he has not immediately recognized how the overlap-
ping amalgam that he proposes of two definitions melded into one is
bizarre and inconsistent. That is a curious example of a lack of philosophy that offsets and nullifies, in French economists, so many of
their intellectual qualities, the principal ones of which are clarity and
precision. How could economics be simultaneously a natural science
and a moral science? And what is one to make of such a science?
On the one hand, there would be a moral science with the aim of
determining how wealth *ought to be* most equitably distributed, and
on the other hand, there would be a natural science with the aim of
determining how wealth *is* most naturally produced. Moreover, the
latter would advantageously be replaced by an art, that of the abundant production of wealth. Taken all in all, J.-B. Say's definition leads
us back, as can be seen, to Adam Smith's (§ 5), and, in this entire
affair, the true natural science still escapes us.

  We shall undertake to seek it on our own account. We are going
to separate, if necessary, economics into a natural science, a moral
science, and an art. And to do so, as a preamble, we are going to distinguish between science, art, and ethics.

LESSON 2

Distinction between science, the arts, and ethics

SUMMARY: – The arts[i] advise, prescribe, direct; science observes, describes, explains. A different matter is the distinction between science and the arts; yet another matter is the distinction between theory and practice. The facts given by a science can throw light on several arts; an art can draw upon the information furnished by several sciences. These distinctions are excellent but insufficient.

Science, the study of facts. First distinction: *natural* facts, having their origin in the play of the forces of nature; *human* facts, drawing their source from the exercise of the will of man. Natural and human facts, the subjects of pure *science* (*science* properly speaking and *history*). Second distinction: human *industrial* facts, or the relations among persons and things; human *moral* facts, or the relations among persons. Industrial facts, the subject of applied science or of the *arts*. Ethical facts, the subject of moral science or of *ethics*.

10. Several years ago Charles Coquelin, author of a quite good *Traité du crédit et des banques*, and one of the most active and esteemed collaborators on the *Dictionnaire de l'économie politique*,[ii] declared in the article *Économie politique* that economics still needed to be defined. In support of this assertion, he cited the definitions of Adam Smith and J.-B. Say, to which I drew attention, and those of Sismondi, Storch, and Rossi, showing the differences that distinguished one from another, declaring that a decided preference had not been shown for any of them, and even establishing that their authors had been the first to fail to adhere to them in their own works. Charles Coquelin then very judiciously observes that before defining economics, it

should be asked whether it is a science or an art, and if it is not at the same time both, and that, before doing anything else, it is advisable to distinguish an art and a science. The considerations he raises on this subject are strikingly accurate, and since the question is still in the state in which he left it, nothing better can be done other than to reproduce them:

An art (he says) consists...of a series of precepts or rules to be followed; a science consists of knowledge of certain phenomena or relationships observed or revealed.... An art advises, prescribes, directs; science observes, describes, explains. When an astronomer observes and describes the course of the stars, he is practicing science; but when, after making his observations, he deduces from them rules applicable to navigation, he is practicing an art.... Thus, to observe and describe real phenomena is science; to lay down precepts, prescribe rules, that is art.

11. In a footnote the author adds an observation that succeeds in clarifying the distinction and that equally deserves to be reproduced here.

The very real distinction (he says) that we have made between science and arts has nothing in common with the one that, rightly or wrongly, is made between theory and practice. There are theories of the arts, as there are of science, and it is even only of the former can it be said that they are sometimes in opposition to practice. Arts lay down the rules, but they are general rules, and it is not unreasonable to suppose that these rules, however sound, may be in conflict with practice in certain particular cases. But it is not the same with science, which demands nothing, which recommends nothing, which prescribes nothing, which limits itself to observing and explaining. In what sense could science ever come to find itself in opposition to practice?

12. The arts and science having thus been distinguished, Coquelin indicates very clearly their respective roles and importance.

We are far (he says) from complaining or finding strange that men try to draw, from scientific truths that have been observed and are properly deduced, rules that are applicable to the conduct of human affairs. It is not a good thing for scientific truths to remain sterile, and the only way to use them is to deduce art from them. There are, we have already said, close relationships between science and the arts. Science lends its knowledge to the arts, it corrects its conduct, it clarifies and directs its path; without the help of science, the arts would only be groping their way, stumbling at each step.

On the other hand, it is the arts that make the truths that science has discovered useful, and that, without the arts would remain sterile. It is also almost always the principal motive of the work of science. Mankind rarely studies solely for the pleasure of having knowledge; he has, in general, a goal of usefulness for his work, and this goal can only be achieved by the arts.

13. But he insists, nonetheless, that a distinction must be maintained between science and the arts, in support of which he makes a final remark that is worthy of being mentioned.

It is all the more important (he says) to emphasize the distinction that we have just made, because if science and the arts often have a great number of points of contact, it is far from being the case that their rays and their circumferences are identical. The information furnished by a science can sometimes be used by many different arts. For example, geometry, or the science of space relations, illuminates or directs the work of the surveyor, the engineer, the artilleryman, the navigator, the ship-builder, the architect, etc. Chemistry comes to the aid of the pharmacist, just as it does to the dyer and to many industrial occupations. Who can say how many different arts make profitable use of the general knowledge of physics? Conversely, an art can make use of the information furnished by several sciences; and it is in this way, just to cite one example, that medicine, or the art of healing, consults the information contained in anatomy, physiology, chemistry, physics, botany, etc.

14. Charles Coquelin endeavors finally to make it understood how greatly the distinction between the arts and science would prove to have a felicitous and fruitful application in defining economics and in the classification of economic subject matter, and he adds:

Will we attempt…, from now on, to effectuate a more precise separation between science and the arts by giving them different names? No; it suffices for us to make the distinction clearly: time and a better understanding of the subject will do the rest.

That decision is surprising. It is strange that a writer, after having had such a sound idea, should thus deprive himself voluntarily of the pleasure and the honor that developing it would bring. But here is what is even more curious: whatever he may say, the author tries, in reality, to effectuate the separation between economic art and economic science in specifying the true objective of economics, and in that effort succeeds so little that, confusing the elements of the arts for those of science as a consequence of a conception of the world of industrial facts too imprinted with the naturalistic and Physiocratic point of view, for which I criticized J.-B. Say (§ 7) and from which his students cannot free themselves, far from dissipating the confusion that he himself identified, he even increases it. Certainly he does this when he wonders: *Is it wealth that is the object of economic science, or industry, the source of wealth?* and when he inquires *how is it that the subject matter of the study of economics has been specified to be wealth rather than human industry?* and what have been the *Consequences of this error;* and finally when he declares that *the defining Characteristic of economic science is* that *it is a branch of the natural history of mankind.* It is impossible to go any further astray after having taken the most detailed precautions against doing so.

15. This result would truly be such as to make it believed that the very idea of a distinction between the arts and science is not as appropriate to the affair as it appears to be. And yet this distinction is perfectly applicable to economics. It suffices to reflect for a moment, once having been alerted to the situation, to remain convinced, if we are free from partisan bias, that there is a theory of wealth; that is to say, of value in exchange, of exchange, a theory that is a science; and that there is a theory of the production of wealth, namely, a theory of agriculture, industry, and commerce, that is an art.[iii] However, it must be said immediately, if the distinction is valid, it is also incomplete because it does not take into account the distribution of wealth.

To convince ourselves of this immediately, let us recall Blanqui's observation that economics can be considered both as an *explanation of what is* and as *a program of what ought to be.* Now, what ought to be, ought to be the case either from the point of view of utility or of economic advantageousness, or from the point of view of equity or of justice. What ought to be from the point of view of economic advantageousness is the concern of applied science or art; while what ought to be from the point of view of justice is the concern of moral science or ethics. It is evident that what, above all, concerns Blanqui and Garnier is what ought to be from the point of view of justice, since they speak of economics considered as a moral science, of the idea of right and justice, of the manner in which wealth should most equitably be distributed (§ 9). It is evident that, by contrast, this point of view escapes Coquelin, and that in pointing out the distinction to be made between the arts and science, he fails to point out that which is to be made between the arts and ethics. Very well! Let us, for our part, not neglect anything. Let us take up the whole question again, and make the distinction in a rational, complete, and definitive manner.

16. We have to distinguish between science, the arts, and ethics. In other words, it is a question of sketching, necessarily very rapidly, the general philosophy of science in order to arrive at the particular philosophy of economics.

A truth long ago made clear by the Platonic philosophy is that science does not study bodies but the facts of which bodies are the theater. Bodies are temporary; facts endure. Facts, their relations and their laws, are the subject of all scientific study. Moreover, sciences can differ because of their subject matter, or the facts they study. Thus, in order to differentiate the sciences, we must differentiate the facts.

17. Now, first, the facts that are to be found in the world can be considered of two sorts: those that result from the play of the forces of nature, which are blind and inevitable; the others have their source in the exercise of the human will, a force that is perceptive and free. Facts of the first sort have nature for their theater and that is why we call them *natural* facts; facts of the second sort have humanity for their theater, and that is why we call them *human* facts. Alongside the many blind and inevitable forces, there is in the universe a force that is self-conscious and controls itself: it is the will of man. Perhaps this force does not know itself and does not have control of itself as completely as it supposes. That is something that only the study of that force can discover. For the moment, it does not matter: the essential thing is that it knows itself and controls itself, at least within certain limits, and that makes a profound difference between the effects of that force and the effects of other forces. It is clear that, in regard to the effects of natural forces, nothing else can be done other than to recognize them, to describe them, to explain them, and then to guide them. That is clear, because the natural forces are not conscious of their actions, and even less are they able to act in any other way than

they do, and since the human will, on the contrary, is conscious of its acts and can act in several ways. The effects of the natural forces will therefore be the subject matter of what is called *pure natural science* or *science* properly speaking. The effects of the human will be the subject matter, first, of a field of study that will be called *pure moral science* or *history,* and, second, of a field of study that will be called by some other name, be it the arts, be it ethics, as we will shortly see. Thus, Charles Coquelin's distinction between science and the arts (§ 10) is justified. An art 'advises, prescribes, and directs', because of the circumstances that it has as its subject matter the facts that have their source in the exercise of the will of man, and that the will of man being, at least up to a certain point, a force that is perceptive and free, there are grounds for advising it, for prescribing such and such conduct for it, for guiding it. Science 'observes, describes, explains', because of the circumstances that it deals with facts that have their origin in the play of natural forces, and that the natural forces being blind and inevitable, there is nothing else to do in regard to them other than to observe them and to describe them and to explain their effects.

18. We thus find, not empirically as Coquelin did, but methodically through considering the perceptiveness[iv] and freedom of the human will, the distinction between science and the arts. The present concern is to find the distinction between the arts and ethics. The same consideration of the perceptiveness and the freedom of the human will, or at least the consideration of a consequence of that fact, is going to furnish us the principle of that distinction through furnishing us the principle that divides human facts into two categories.

The fact of the perceptiveness and freedom of the human will divides all the beings in the universe into two great classes: *persons* and *things.* Any being that does not have self-awareness and control of itself is a thing. Any being that has self-awareness and control of itself is a person. Man has self-awareness; he has control of himself; he is a person. Only man is a person; minerals, plants, animals are things.

The aims of things are rationally subordinate to the aims of persons. A thing does not have awareness of itself, does not have control of itself, is not responsible for pursuing its aims, for the fulfillment of its destiny. Equally incapable of vice and of virtue, it is always completely innocent; it can be likened to a pure mechanism. Matters are this way, in that regard, for animals as they are for minerals and vegetation: an animal's instinct is no more than a blind and inevitable force, like all other natural forces. A person, on the other hand, just because he is conscious of himself and controls himself, is responsible for fulfilling his destiny; he will be meritorious if he achieves it, faulty in the contrary case. He has, therefore, unlimited faculties, unlimited latitude to *subordinate* the aims of things to his own aim. This faculty, this latitude, in all its length and breadth, is endowed with a particular character: it is a moral power, it is a right. This is the basis of the right of persons over things.

But while the aims of all things are under the dominion of the aims of all persons, on the other hand, no person's aim is ever subordinated to the aim of any other person. If there were only one man in the world, he would be master of everything. But that is not the case, and all those who are here, each being a person just like everyone, are equally responsible for the pursuit of their ends and for the pursuit of their aims, for the fulfillment of their destiny. All these aims, all these destinies have to be *coordinated* with each other. That is the origin of the reciprocity of rights and duties among persons.

19. In accordance with those considerations, it is seen that a fundamental distinction must be made between human facts. It is necessary to distinguish, on the one hand, those that result from the will, from the activity of man acting in the realm of natural forces, otherwise known as the relations between persons and things. And it is necessary to distinguish, on the other hand, those that result from the will, from the activity of man acting in the realm of the will, from the activity of other men, otherwise known as the relations among persons. The laws of these two classes of facts are essentially different. The objective of the human will acting in the realm of natural forces, the goal of the relations among persons and things, is the subordination of the aims of things to the aims of persons. The objective of the human will acting in the realm of the will of other men, the goal of the relations among persons, is the coordination with each other of the destinies of persons.

Marking, as is proper, this distinction by defining the phenomena, I call the ensemble of facts of the first category *industry,* and the ensemble of facts of the second category *institutions.* The theory of industry will be called *applied science* or *art;* the theory of institutions will be called *moral science* or *ethics.*

In order, consequently, that a fact belong to the category of industry, and that the theory of that fact be some art or another, it is necessary and sufficient that the fact, having its origin in the exercise of the human will, be a relationship between persons and things intended to subordinate the aims of things to the aims of persons. You can reconsider all the examples of the arts that have been cited and you will recognize that they all display that character. Thus, architecture, shipbuilding, navigation, that have been mentioned, signalize wood and stone as materials used in the construction of houses, wood and iron for shipbuilding, hemp as the material used for rope-making, for the means of trimming sails, for setting them, and for maneuvering them. The sea supports the vessels, the wind fills the sails, the skies and the stars point the way to the navigator.

And in order that a fact belong to the category of institutions, and in order that the theory of this phenomenon be a branch of ethics, it is necessary and sufficient that this fact, having always its origin in the exercise of the human will, consist of relationships among persons intended to coordinate the destinies of the persons. So, for example, in regard to marriage or the family, it is ethics that determines the role and position of husband and wife, of parents and children.

20. Such, then, are science, the arts, and ethics. Their respective *criteria* are *truth, usefulness* or economic advantageousness, and *goodness* or justice. Now, is there, in a comprehensive study of social wealth and of the facts related to it, the material for only one or for two of those kinds of intellectual investigations, or for all three? That is what we shall see in the next lesson in the course of analyzing the idea of wealth.

Notes

i Walras uses the terms 'the arts' and 'art', in the context of this lesson, to refer to activities such as architecture, metallurgy, agronomy, sculpture, and the other examples given in sections 13 and 19 below.

ii Charles Coquelin and Gilbert-Umbert Guillaumin, *Dictionnaire de l'économie politique*, third edition, Paris, Guillaumin, 1864.

iii Theory is not an art, but agriculture, industry, and commerce are. Below, however, he writes: 'The theory of industry will be called *applied science* or *art*'.

iv Walras's word 'clairvoyance' has the English equivalent with the same spelling. The primary meaning of 'clairvoyance' in English is 'the power to perceive things that are out of the natural range of human senses', like the knowledge of a medium or a gypsy fortune teller. The word 'clairvoyant' has a strong supernatural connotation to Anglophones. That is also a special, psychological, meaning of the French word. The secondary meaning of the English word is: 'Acute intuitive insight or acute perceptiveness'. Walras did not mean 'acute intuitive insight', which verges upon the paranormal definition. Moreover, 'far-seeing' is open to too many different interpretations. Walras did not use the word in those senses, so we should not translate the French 'clairvoyant' by the English 'clairvoyant'. The primary and non-paranormal meaning of 'clairvoyance' in French is: 'Vue exacte, claire et lucide des choses; acuité, discernement, finesse, flair, lucidité, perspicacité. *Analyser la situation avec clairvoyance. Rien n'échappe à sa clairvoyance*'. Clairvoyant is defined as 'Qui a de la clairvoyance. *Esprit clairvoyant;* fin, intelligent, lucide, pénétrant, perspicace, sagace. *D'un œil clairvoyant*' (Robert 2002, p. 449). The French to English dictionary translation of 'clairvoyance' is: 'of a person, clear-sightedness, perceptiveness; of the mind: perceptiveness'. In the light of the foregoing, it becomes clear that Walras's 'clairvoyance' should be translated as 'perceptiveness' or 'discernment'.

LESSON 3

Social wealth. Triple consequences of scarcity. The fact of value in exchange and of economic theory

SUMMARY: – Social wealth, the totality of all scarce things; that is to say, 1° *useful*, and 2° *limited in quantity*. Scientific rareté. Only scarce things and all scarce things are 1° *appropriable*, 2° *valuable and exchangeable*, 3° *producible industrially* or *multipliable*. Economics: theory of value in exchange, theory of industry, theory of property.

The fact of *value in exchange*. Brought about in the market. 'The value of wheat is 24 francs per hectoliter.' Natural fact. Mathematical fact. Equation $5v_b = 600v_a$. Value in exchange, a measurable magnitude; theory of exchange and of value in exchange, or theory of social wealth, a *physico-mathematical* science. The rational method. The algebraic language.

21. By *social wealth*, I mean the totality of material or immaterial things (the materiality or immateriality of a thing does not in any respect matter here) that are *scarce*; that is to say that, on the one hand, are useful to us, and that, on the other hand, are available for our use only *in limited quantity*.

This definition is important; I am going to make its terminology clear.

I say that things are useful whenever they can serve for any use, whenever they can be applied to any want and permit its satisfaction. It is therefore not necessary to be occupied here with the fine distinctions by which utility is classified, in ordinary conversation, along with what is agreeable and between what is necessary and what is superfluous. Necessary, useful, agreeable, and superfluous, all those conditions amount for us only to degrees of being more or less useful.

Furthermore, neither is it necessary to take account here of the morality or immorality of any need to which a useful thing can be applied and that it can satisfy. Whether a substance is sought by a doctor to cure a sick person, or by a murderer to poison his family are very serious matters from some points of view, but a matter totally indifferent from ours. To us, the substance is useful in both cases, and may even be more so in the latter case than in the former.

I say that things are available to us only in a limited quantity from the moment that they do not exist in a quantity such that each of us has enough of it available when it is wanted to satisfy fully the need that he has of it. There are a certain number of things in this world that, when they are not totally absent, are available to us in unlimited quantities. Such are atmospheric air, the light and heat of the sun when it is shining, the water in lakes and rivers, that exist in such quantities that no one need have an insufficiency of them, everyone taking as much as he wishes. These things, that are useful, are generally not scarce and are not part of social wealth; in exceptional cases they can become scarce, and then they become part of that wealth.

22. It can be seen from that what the meaning here is of the words *scarce* and *rareté*.[i] It is a scientific meaning like that of the word *velocity* in mechanics and *heat* in physics. For the mathematician and the physicist, velocity is not opposed to slowness, nor heat to cold, as is done in ordinary language: to the mathematician, slowness is only less speed; to the physicist, cold is only less heat. A body, in the language of science, has velocity as soon as it moves and heat as soon as it has any temperature. Similarly here, scarcity and abundance are not in opposition to each other: however abundant it may be, a thing is scarce, in economics, the moment that it is useful and limited in quantity, exactly as a body has velocity, in mechanics, as soon as it moves a certain distance in a certain length of time. Does this mean that rareté is a ratio of utility to quantity, or the utility per unit of quantity, in the way that velocity is the ratio of distance traveled to the time taken to travel it, or the distance traveled per unit of time? This is a point on which we will not take a position at the moment, for we must come back to it later. Now, the fact that the limitation in the quantity of useful things makes them scarce has three consequences.

23. 1° Useful things limited in quantity are *appropriable*. Useless things are not appropriated: no one thinks of appropriating things that cannot serve any purpose. Things that are useful but that exist in unlimited quantities are also not appropriable. In the first place, they are not controllable by force or seizable; much as one might like to take them out of the common domain, one cannot do so because of their quantity. And as for putting aside a small fraction of such a thing but leaving the greater part at the disposition of everyone, what would be the good of that? To extract a profit from it? But who would demand it, since everyone will always be able to have it freely? To use it oneself? But what good would it do to have a stock of it if one is sure of always having it at will? Why have a store of atmospheric air (I mean in ordinary circumstances), since you will not have the occasion to give it to anyone and since you yourself, when you feel the need to breathe, have only to open your mouth to do so? Contrariwise, useful things that exist only in limited quantity are appropriable and appropriated. First, they are controllable by force or seizable: it is physically possible for a certain number of individuals to acquire the existing quantity of such a thing, to store it, to put it, so to speak, under lock and key, in such a way that none is left in the public domain. And there is, for these individuals, a double advantage to doing that. In the first place, they assure for themselves a provision of those things, they bring about the possibility of using them themselves, of applying them to the satisfaction of their own needs. In the second place, they reserve for themselves also the ability, if they are unwilling or unable to consume directly more than a part of their supply, to obtain for themselves, by exchange of the surplus, other utilities that are limited in quantity that they will consume instead of the original ones. But this leads us to a different fact. Let us limit ourselves to remarking, for the moment, that *appropriation* (and consequently *property*, that is appropriation that is legitimate or in conformity with justice) is applicable only to social wealth and applicable to all social wealth.

24. 2° Useful things limited in quantity are *valuable and exchangeable*, as we have just briefly noted. Once scarce things have been appropriated (and only scarce things are, and all of them are) there is established among all these things a relationship consisting in

the circumstance that, independently of their direct utility, each of them acquires, as a special property, the faculty of being exchangeable against the others in such and such a determinate ratio. If a person possesses any one of these scarce things, he can, by giving it up, obtain in exchange any other scarce thing that he lacks. If he does not possess it, he cannot obtain it except on the condition of giving up in exchange some other scarce thing that he possesses. And if he does not, and has nothing to give in exchange, he will be unable to obtain what he lacks. Such is the fact of *value in exchange*, that, like the fact of the appropriation of property, applies only to social wealth, and like that fact, applies to all social wealth.

25. 3° Useful things limited in quantity are *industrially producible* or *multipliable*. I mean by this that it is advantageous to produce them and to multiply their quantity as much as possible by means of regular and systematic efforts. There are, in the world, useless things (without speaking of those that are even harmful), such as weeds and animals that are of no use; we concern ourselves with them only to seek attentively to discover in them some property that will make them pass from the category of useless things into the category of useful ones. There are useful things that are unlimited in quantity; we do well to concern ourselves with making use of them, but obviously not with increasing their quantity. Finally, there are useful things that are limited in quantity, scarce things; clearly, only the latter can be the subject of studies and activities having the goal of rendering their quantity less limited than it is, and clearly, furthermore, all of the latter can and must be the subject of such studies and such activities. Therefore, if we call, as we have done, social wealth the totality of scarce things, we can also state that *industrial production* or *industry*, also applies only to social wealth and that it applies also to all social wealth.

26. *Value in exchange*, *industry*, and *property* are, then, the three general facts, the three series or groups of particular facts that result from the limitation in quantity of useful things or the scarcity of things, the three facts that make up the whole of social wealth and of which only social wealth is the theater. Now we can appreciate how vague, imprecise, and unphilosophical, perhaps even wrong, it is to say, as, for example, did Rossi in starting his work on economics, that he

was proposing to study social wealth. And, from what point of view would you study it? Is it from the point of view of *value in exchange,* that is, from the point of view of the phenomena of purchase and sale to which it is subject? Is it from the point of view of *industrial production*; that is to say, from the point of view of the conditions that favor or hinder the increase of its quantity? Is it from the point of view of *property,* the object of which is social wealth, that is to say, from the point of view of the conditions that render the appropriation of social wealth legitimate or illegitimate? We have to take a position. And above all, you must sedulously avoid studying these three points of view at the same time or any two of them simultaneously; for there is nothing more different from each other than they are, as will be seen.

27. We have seen a priori how scarce things, once appropriated, acquire value in exchange (§ 24). We need only to open our eyes to recognize a posteriori, among the class of general facts, the fact of exchange.

Given the way that we are constituted, we daily make, as a series of special acts, transactions; that is to say, sales and purchases. Some among us sell land or the use of land or the fruits of the land; some, houses, or the use of houses; some, industrial products or merchandise that they have acquired wholesale and that they sell at retail; some, consultations, legal services, works of art, days or hours of labor. All, in return, receive money. With the money thus obtained, we buy at one moment bread, wine, and meat; at another, clothes; at another, shelter; at another, furniture, jewels, horses, carriages; at another, raw materials or labor; at another, merchandise; at another, houses, land; at another, stocks or bonds of various businesses.

The transactions are carried on in the market. The place where exchanges of a special kind are made is considered a special market. We say: the European market, the French market, the Parisian market; Le Havre is a market for cotton, and Bordeaux is a market for wine; the covered central markets are markets for fruit and vegetables, for wheat and cereals; the stock exchange is a market for industrial securities.

Let us consider the wheat market, and supposing that, at a given moment, we see that five hectoliters of wheat are being exchanged for

120 francs, or, for 600 grams of silver 0·900 fine, we say: 'Wheat is worth 24 francs a hectoliter.' That manifests the fact of value in exchange.

28. Wheat is worth 24 francs a hectoliter. We notice first of all that this fact has the character of a *natural* fact. The value of wheat in silver, or this price of wheat, does not result from either the will of the buyer or the will of the seller, or from an agreement between the two. The seller would very much like to sell at a higher price; he cannot do so, because the wheat *is not worth more,* and because if he did not want to sell at that price, the buyer would find close by a certain number of sellers willing to do so. The buyer would ask for nothing better than to buy at a lower price; but he finds that impossible because the wheat *is not worth less,* and because, if he did not want to buy at this price, the seller would find close by a certain number of buyers willing to agree to it.

The fact of value in exchange is therefore a natural fact, natural in its origin, natural in its manifestations and in its fundamental being. If wheat and silver have *value,* it is because they are scarce; that is to say, are useful and limited in quantity, two natural circumstances. And if wheat and silver have a *particular value* with respect to each other, it is because they are, respectively more or less scarce; that is to say, more or less useful and more or less limited in quantity, again two natural circumstances, the same as are mentioned above.

This does not mean that we have no influence on prices. Because gravity is a natural fact and obeys natural laws, it does not follow that we can never do anything but watch its action. We can either resist it or let it operate freely, as we please, but we cannot change its character and its laws. We do not command it, as has been said, except in obeying it. It is the same with respect to value. In regard to wheat, for example, we could raise its price by destroying part of its supply; we could lower the price by eating, instead of wheat, rice, potatoes, or some other foodstuff. We could even decree that wheat will sell for 20 francs instead of 24 francs a hectoliter. In the first case, we would act upon the causes of the fact of value to substitute one natural value for another natural value. In the second case, we would act upon the fact itself by substituting an artificial value for a natural one. But we could not prevent, in the one case or in the other, that, certain circumstances of supply and consumption being given, that, in a word, certain conditions of scarcity being given, they naturally result in or tend to result in a certain value.

29. Wheat is worth 24 francs a hectoliter. We notice now that this fact is *mathematical* in character as well. The value of wheat in terms of money, or the price of wheat, was 22 or 23 francs yesterday; not long ago it was 23 francs 50 centimes or 23 francs 75 centimes; in a little while it will be 24 francs 25 centimes or 24 francs 50 centimes; tomorrow it will be 25 or 26 francs; but today, and for the time being, it is 24 francs, *neither more nor less*. This fact has so clearly the character of a mathematical fact that I am immediately going to express it by an equation and thereby give it its true expression.

The hectoliter being taken as the unit of measure of the quantity of wheat, and the gram as the unit of measure of the quantiy of silver, we can state rigorously that, if 5 hectoliters of wheat are exchanged for 600 grams of silver, it is true that '5 hectoliters of wheat are equivalent to 600 grams of silver', or that 'the *value in exchange* of 5 hectoliters of wheat *equals* the *value in exchange* of 600 grams of silver', or finally, that '5 times the value in exchange of 1 hectoliter of wheat *equals* 600 times the value in exchange of 1 gram of silver'.

Consequently, letting v_b be the value in exchange of 1 hectoliter of wheat, and v_a be the value in exchange of 1 gram of silver 0·900 fine, we have the equation

$$5v_b = 600v_a,$$

or, dividing both sides of the equation by 5,

$$v_b = 120v_a. \qquad [1]$$

If it is agreed, as we have assumed to be the case on the market that we have taken as an example, to choose as a unit of measure of value, not the value in exchange of 1 gram of silver, but the value in exchange of 5 grams of silver 0·900 fine, namely a *franc*; that is to say, if we set

$$5v_a = 1\,franc,$$

it follows that

$$v_b = 24\,francs \qquad [2]$$

But, in form [1] or in form [2] the equation is nonetheless, in either case, the exact translation of the following statement and, I will say, the scientific expression of this fact: 'Wheat is worth 24 francs a hectoliter'.

30. Value in exchange is thus a magnitude, and, we now see, is measurable. And if the object of mathematics in general is to deal with magnitudes of this kind, it is certain that there is a branch of mathematics, forgotten thus far by mathematicians, and still undeveloped, namely the theory of exchange.

I do not say I have already stressed suficiently, that this science is the whole of economics. Forces and velocities are also measurable magnitudes, and the mathematical theory of forces and velocities is not the whole of mechanics. It is nevertheless certain that pure mechanics must precede applied mechanics. Similarly, there is *economic theory*, which must precede *applied economics*, and economic theory is a physico-mathematical science. This assertion is new and will seem strange; but I have just proved it, and I will prove it even more convincingly in the following discussion.

If economic theory, or the theory of value in exchange and of exchange; that is, the theory of social wealth considered in itself, is a physico-mathematical science like mechanics or hydrodynamics, it should not be afraid to employ the methods and language of mathematics.

The mathematical method is not an *experimental* method; it is the *rational* method. Do the natural sciences properly speaking restrict themselves purely and simply to describing nature and not go beyond experience? I leave it to the natural scientists the task of answering this question. What is sure, is that the physico-mathematical sciences, like the mathematical sciences properly speaking, do go beyond experience as soon as they have borrowed their type concepts from it. They abstract from these real types ideal types that they define, and on the basis of these definitions they construct a priori the whole framework of their theorems and proofs. They re-enter after that into experience not to confirm but to apply their conclusions. Everyone knows perfectly well, no matter how little geometry they have studied, that the radii of a circumference are not equal to each other and that the sum of the three angles of a triangle is not equal to the sum of two right angles, except in an abstract and ideal circumference and triangle. Reality does not confirm these definitions and proofs; it permits only a fruitful application of them. To follow this same method, economic theory must borrow from experience the real types of exchange, supply, demand, market, capital, income, productive services, products, etc. From these real types, economic theory must abstract ideal types by defining them, and conduct its reasoning on the latter, not returning to reality until the science is completed, and with a view to practical applications. We will thus have, in an ideal market, ideal prices that will be in a rigorous relationship to ideal demand and supply. And so on. Will these pure truths have frequent applications? To be sure, it would be the right of the scholar to pursue science for its own sake, just as it is the right of the geometer (which, in fact, he exercises every day) to study the most singular properties of the most bizarre forms, if they are curious. But it will be seen that these truths of economic theory furnish solutions of the most important, debated, and least clarified problems of applied and social economics.

As to language, why persist in using everyday language to express matters in a very difficult and very incorrect way, as Ricardo always does and as John Stuart Mill repeatedly does in his *Principles of Political Economy*, when matters can be stated in mathematical language in far fewer words and in a much more exact and clear fashion?

Note

i Walras defined 'rareté' in the introduction to the second edition of the *Éléments*, page XI above.

LESSON 4

The fact of industry and applied economics.
The fact of property and social economics

SUMMARY: – The fact of *industry*. *Direct* utility; *indirect* utility. Multiplication of utilities. Transformation of indirect utilities into direct utilities. Double sequence of industrial operations: 1° *technical* operations, 2° *economic* operations resulting from the division of labor. The fact of industrial economic production, a human and not a natural fact; an industrial and not an ethical fact. Theory of the production of social wealth, an *applied* science.

The fact of *appropriation*, a human and not a natural fact. Nature creates appropriability; men do the appropriation. An ethical and not an industrial fact. *Property*, legitimate appropriation. Communism and individualism. Theory of the distribution of social wealth, a *moral* science. The question of the relationships between ethics and economics.

31. Only useful things that are limited in quantity can be produced by industry; they are all industrially producible (§ 25). And, in fact, it is certain that industry is undertaken only to produce scarce things and that it endeavors to produce all things that are scarce.

This fact of industrial production now needs to be described somewhat more precisely. Useful things that are limited in quantity, besides suffering from the drawback (for such it is) of this limitation, sometimes have another: that of not being of *direct* utility but only of an *indirect* utility. The fleece of a sheep is unquestionably a useful thing, but before it can be applied to the satisfaction of a need, namely our need for clothing, it must undergo two preliminary industrial operations, one of which converts the wool into cloth, and the other of which converts the cloth into clothing. One has to reflect only for a moment to convince oneself that the number of things that are limited in quantity that are useful but have only an indirect utility is very large. From that it follows that industrial production has a twofold aim: first, to increase the number of useful things that do not exist in unlimited quantities, and, second, to transform indirect utilities into direct utilities.

This specifies clearly the object of industry that we initially defined in a very general fashion as the totality of relations between persons and things designed to subordinate the purposes of things to the purposes of persons. It is certain that man enters into relationships with all things in order to make use of them, but it is also certain that the constant aim of these contacts is the multiplication and transformation of social wealth.

32. This twofold aim is pursued by human kind by means of two very distinct classes of operations.

> 1° The first of these two classes of industrial operations is composed of industrial operations properly speaking or *technical* operations. Thus agriculture increases the number of plants and animals that are used for food and clothing; extractive industries increase the quantity of minerals that we use to make instruments and tools; manufacturing industries transform textile fibers into linen, woolen and cotton fabrics, and minerals into all kinds of machines; engineering industries construct factories, railways. Assuredly, these operations have the well defined character of relationships between persons and things, having the purpose of subordinating the purposes of things to the purposes of persons, as well as the purpose, more circumscribed and more specific, of multiplying and transforming social wealth. They thus constitute a first class of industrial facts forming the subject of a first group of applied sciences or arts, namely the *technical arts.*
> 2° The second class of operations comprises those that are related to the *economic* organization of industry properly speaking.

In fact, the first class of operations of which we have just spoken would constitute the whole of industry and would be the objective of all the arts, except that that completeness requires the essential fact that we encounter here, the fact of man's physiological aptitude for the *division of labor.* If the destinies of all men were independent from the point of view of the satisfaction of their wants, each of us would have to pursue our objectives in isolation, by increasing, as he saw fit, the quantity of useful things that do not exist in unlimited quantity and by transforming indirect utilities into direct utilities as it suited him. Each of us would have to be in turn his own plough-man, spinner, baker, tailor. Our condition would thus approach that of animals, because industry properly speaking, technical industry, would be insignificant without the developments that it owes to the division of labor. Nevertheless, it is conceivable that this first form of industry might still exist up to a point. But what could not exist to any degree would be, for example, economic industrial production.

Matters are not as we have just temporarily assumed. Not only does man possess a physiological aptitude for the division of labor, but, as we will see, this aptitude is the very condition of his existence and his subsistence. Instead of being independent, the destinies of all men are tied together from the point of view of the satisfaction of their wants. This, however, is not the place to examine the nature and origin of the division of labor; for the present, we are limiting our-selves to noting the existence of this fact, just as we have noted the fact of the freedom and of the moral personality of mankind. The fact exists, and it consists in the circumstance that in place of multiplying scarce things by ourselves for our own use, of transforming indirect into direct utilities only to the extent to which we are individually concerned, we split up this task into specialized occupations. Some of us are ploughmen by specialty and nothing but ploughmen, others are spinners by specialty and nothing but spinners, and so forth. That constitutes, we say, the division of labor. That is a fact the existence of which springs into sight at a first glance at the nature of society. And it is that fact alone that engenders industrial economic production.

33. Two problems result from that circumstance.

It is necessary, first, that in the case of the division of labor, as is also true in the absence of the division of labor, industrial production of the social wealth must be not only *abundant*, but also properly *proportioned*. It is necessary to avoid producing too much of some scarce things while producing too little of others. It is also neces-sary to avoid converting some indirect utilities into direct utilities on too large a scale while converting others in insufficient quantity.

If each of us were simultaneously his own farmer, his own manufacturer, and his own engineer, he would engage in each trade to just the extent and in just such a manner as he saw fit. But if the occupations are specialized, there must not be, for example, an abundance of manufacturers while there is an insufficiency of farmers, etc.

It is necessary, second, that, in the case of the division of labor, as is also true in its absence, the distribution of social wealth among men in the society be *equitable*. There should not be moral disorder any more than there should be economic disorder. If each of us produced everything that he consumes and consumed only what he produces, not only would he adjust his production to his consumption needs but his consumption would also be determined by the extent of his production. Well then! It must not be that, thanks to the specialization of occupations, some of us, who have produced little, consume a lot, while others, who have produced a great deal, consume little.

We understand that these two problems are important, and we also understand the direction taken by the various solutions that have been devised for them. The object of the guild system was, clearly, to provide for the condition of proper apportionment in production. The system of freedom of industry and of commerce, or, as it is called, the system of *laisser faire, laisser passer* is claimed to have best harmonized the condition of proportionality with the condition of abundance. We will decide whether that is so. Before that system, those of slavery and serfdom had the obvious disadvantage of forcing some classes of the community to work for the benefit of other classes. Our present system of property and taxation is claimed to have put a complete end to this exploitation of man by man. We will see if that is so.

34. As for the present, we have only one thing to do, and that is to recognize the two questions, and, after having defined their objective, to identify their character. It is absolutely impossible for us, whatever Charles Coquelin and the economists of his school may say, to attribute the character of a natural science to the question of the production of social wealth, any more than to the question of its distribution. The will of man is free to influence the production as well as the distribution of social wealth, with the qualification that in the second case, the will of man should be guided by

considerations of justice, and in the first case, it should be guided by considerations of economic advantageousness. Moreover, technical production and economic production, as we have defined them, are not unlike in essence. There is, in fact, no difference of fundamental nature between the fact of industrial technique and the fact of economic production that we have defined. The two facts support each other and are interconnected, each being complementary to the other. They are both human facts and not natural facts; they are both, moreover, industrial and not ethical facts, because they both consist of relationships among persons and things in order to subordinate the purposes of things to the purposes of persons.

The theory of the economic production of social wealth, that is, of the organization of industry under the division of labor, is therefore an applied science. That is why we will call it *applied economics*.

35. We have seen that only useful things limited in quantity are appropriable, and that they are all appropriable (§ 23). We have only to look around us to recognize that these things are the only ones that are appropriated and that they are all appropriated. Useless things are disregarded; things that are useful but unlimited in quantity are also relegated to the common domain; but scarce things are taken out of the common domain and are no longer at the disposition of the first-comer.

The appropriation of scarce things or of social wealth is a human fact and not a natural fact: it has its origin in the exercise of the human will and in human activity and not in the activity of natural forces.

Without a doubt, it does not depend on us that useful things unlimited in quantity are appropriable; it does not depend on us that useful things limited in quantity are not appropriable. But once the natural conditions of appropriation are fulfilled, it depends on us that the appropriation be made in one way rather than in another. Obviously, that does not depend on each of us individually but on all of us taken collectively. It is a human fact that has its origin not in the individual will of each man, but in the collective activity of society as a whole. In fact, human initiative has always acted, still acts, and will always act upon the fact of appropriation to modify it to suit its own purpose. In early societies, the appropriation of things by persons in a system of division of labor, otherwise known as the distribution of social wealth among men in society, was effectuated by force, cunning, and luck, although not, however, in ways totally outside of rational conditions. The boldest, the strongest, the cleverest, the luckiest obtained the majority, the others had what was left over, that is, nothing or very little. But in regard to property as in regard to the government, the human race has always patiently progressed from the initial disorder of facts towards the ultimate order of principles. To summarize, nature creates only appropriability; humans do the appropriation.

36. The appropriation of things by persons or the distribution of social wealth among men in society is, furthermore, an ethical and not an industrial fact. It is a person-to-person relationship.

Most certainly, we enter into a relationship with scarce things in order to appropriate them, and often we succeed in achieving the appropriation only after long and persistent efforts. But this point of view, which is the one of which we have just spoken, is no longer the one that occupies us at present. For the time being, we will consider the fact of the distribution of social wealth in itself and independently of both preparatory circumstances and natural conditions. I explain myself by an example.

I assume there is a tribe of savages and a deer in a forest. The deer is a useful thing limited in quantity and hence subject to appropriation. This point once having been made, nothing more needs to be said about it. Moreover, before the deer can be appropriated in the proper sense, it has to be hunted and killed. Neither do I consider the second side of the question, namely the point of view of the hunt that is to be studied at the same time as the necessity of dressing the deer and cooking it or the point of view of cookery. Abstraction made from these aspects of man's relation to the deer, there is another question that arises, namely that of knowing, when the deer is still in the forest, or when it is dead, who will own it. It is the fact of appropriation thus envisaged that is of concern, and it is the fact of appropriation thus envisaged that constitutes a relationship of persons to persons. We need only take one step further into the question to convince ourselves of this. 'It will be owned', says one of the young and active members of the tribe, 'by the person who kills it. If you are too lazy or if your aim is not good enough, so much the worse for you!' An older, weaker member replies: 'No! The deer belongs to all of us to be shared equally. If there is only one deer in the forest, and you happen to be the first to catch sight of it, that is no reason why the rest of us should go without food.' The fact is essentially moral, as can be seen, and is a question of justice or of the coordination of the destinies of persons.

37. Thus the mode of appropriation depends on our decisions, and according to whether those decisions are good or bad, the mode of appropriation will be good or bad. If good, it will have coordinated destinies among persons; it will have satisfied justice; if bad, it will have subordinated the destinies of some persons to the destinies of others; it will have sanctioned injustice. What mode of appropriation is good and just? What mode of appropriation is recommended by reason of its being compatible with the requirements of the moral personality? That is the problem of property. Property is equitable and rational appropriation, legitimate appropriation. Appropriation is a fact pure and simple; property is a legitimate fact and a right. Between the fact and the right, there is the place for ethical theory. This is an essential point and one that must not be misunderstood. To find fault with the natural conditions of appropriation, to ennumerate the different ways in which men have distributed social wealth in all places and at all times, that is nothing. To criticize all these various systems of distribution from the standpoint of justice that derives from the moral personality of man, from the point of view of equality and inequality; to say in what respects they were always defective and still are, to indicate the only good system, that is everything.

38. Ever since there has been social wealth and humans in societies, the question of the distribution of social wealth among men in society has been debated. It has always been debated on these grounds, which are the true ones, and on which it should continue to be debated. Among all the systems of distribution that have been developed, there are two that are renowned, that have had for their champions the two greatest minds of antiquity, Plato and Aristotle: they are communism and individualism. Now, what do these systems say? — 'Goods,' communism says, 'ought to be appropriated collectively. Nature has given them to all men, and not only to those that exist today, but also to those who will exist in the future. To divide them among individuals

is to alienate the patrimony of the community and of future generations; it is to expose those born after this division to finding themselves robbed of the resources that Providence had prepared for them;
it is to hinder their pursuit of their goals and the fulfillment of their
destiny.' — 'The goods', individualism replies, 'should be appropriated
individually. Nature has made men unequal in virtue and talent. To
compel those who are industrious, who are capable, who are thrifty to
make available for common use the fruits of their labor and of their
saving is to rob them for the benefit of those who are lazy, incom-
petent, and wasteful; it is to relieve all men of responsibility for the
pursuit, whether good or bad, of their goals and for the fulfillment,
whether moral or immoral, of their destinies.' I stop there. Which is
right, communism or individualism? Are they not both wrong and
right at the same time? We do not need to decide this difference of
opinion here, and I do not want to add anything, for the moment,
whether it be a judgment or only a more developed exposition of
these doctrines. I only wanted to make clear what exactly the problem
of property is considered in the broadest and most complete manner.
Now, this object consists essentially in establishing the relations of
persons to persons in regard to the appropriation of social wealth in
view of the coordination of the destinies of persons in relation to each
other, in conformity with reason and justice. The fact of appropriation is therefore essentially an ethical fact; the theory of property is
therefore essentially an ethical science. *Jus est suum cuique tribuere*—
justice consists in rendering to each that which is due to him; if ever
a science has had the objective of rendering to each that which is due
to him, if ever a science consequently has had justice as its objective,
it is surely that of the distribution of social wealth, or, as we will call
it, *social economics*.

39. There is, however, a difficulty here that I do not want to conceal.
   The theory of property fixes and determines the relations between
men considered as moral persons in regard to the appropriation of
social wealth, or the conditions of the equitable distribution of social
wealth among men in society. The theory of industry fixes and determines those relations between things and men considered as workers devoted to specialized occupations, relations having the purpose
of increasing and transforming social wealth, or, the conditions of

an abundant production of social wealth among men in society. The first conditions are ethical conditions that will be deduced from the point of view of justice. The others are economic conditions that will be deduced from the point of view of economic advantageousness. But they are both social conditions, prescriptions for the organization of society. Now, will these two orders of consideration be in conflict with each other, or will they lend themselves to being mutually supportive? If, for example, the theory of property and the theory of industry both repudiate slavery or communism, that will be well; but assume that while one of these theories prohibits slavery or advocates communism in the name of justice, the other advocates slavery or prohibits communism in the name of economic advantageousness, there would be disagreement and a contradiction between ethical science and applied science. Is such a contradiction possible, and, if it arises, what should be done about it?

We will meet this problem again and give it the attention it merits. It is the question of the relation of ethics to economics that was vigorously debated by Proudhon and Bastiat around 1848. Proudhon, in his *Contradictions économiques*, argued that there is a conflict between justice and economic advantageousness. Bastiat, in his *Harmonies économiques*, maintained the opposite thesis. I think, for my part, that neither proved his point, and I will take up Bastiat's thesis and defend it in a different way. However that may be, if the question exists, it must be solved, and not suppressed by confusing two distinct sciences with each other: the theory of property, which is an ethical science, and the theory of industry, which is an applied science.

PART II

THEORY OF EXCHANGE

LESSON 5

The market and competition. The problem of the exchange of two commodities for each other

SUMMARY: – *Social wealth*, the totality of valuable and exchangeable things. *Value in exchange*, the property that things have of being obtained and given up for one another in certain proportions. A *market*, a place where exchanges are made. Analysis of the mechanism of commerce. The securities market. *Effective demand and supply*. Equality of supply and demand[i] *current stationary price*. Demand greater than supply, *price increase*. Supply greater than demand, *price decrease*.

Commodities (A) and (B). Equation $mv_a = nv_b$. Prix p_a and p_b. Effective demands and supplies D_a, O_a, D_b, O_b. Theorem $O_b = D_a p_a$ $O_a = D_b p_b$. Demand, the principal fact; supply, the accessorial fact. Theorem $\dfrac{D_a}{O_a} = \dfrac{O_b}{D_b}$. Hypothesis of the equality of supply and demand, or of equilibrium. Hypothesis of the inequality of supply and demand. The increase or the decrease of the price causes the demand to decrease or increase. What about the supply?

40. In our general preliminary considerations (§ 21), we defined social wealth as the totality of all things, material or immaterial, that are scarce; that is to say, that are both useful and limited in quantity, and we have shown that all scarce things and only such things have value and are exchangeable. Here we will proceed otherwise. We will define *social wealth* as being the totality of all things, material or immaterial, that are valuable and exchangeable, and we will show

that all valuable and exchangeable things, and only those things, are useful and at the same time limited in quantity. We went, in the first case, from cause to effect; we will go, in the second case, from effect to cause. It is clear that, provided we establish the linkage between the two facts of scarcity and value in exchange, we are free to proceed as we wish. Now, I think that in a methodical study of any general fact like value in exchange, the examination of its nature should precede a search for its origin.

41. *Value in exchange* is the property certain things have of not being obtained or given up freely, but of being *bought* and *sold*, received and given up in return for other things in certain quantitative proportions. The buyer of a thing is the seller of what he gives in exchange. The seller of a thing is the buyer of what he receives in exchange for it. In other words, every exchange of two things, one for the other, is composed of a double purchase and a double sale.

Things that are valuable and exchangeable are also called *commodities*. The *market* is a place where commodities are exchanged. The fact of value in exchange occurs in the market, and so it is to the market that we must go to study value in exchange.

Value in exchange left to itself occurs naturally in the market under the regime of *competition*. As buyers, the traders make *offers to buy at higher prices*; as sellers, they make *offers to sell at lower prices*, and their competition thus leads to a certain value in exchange that is sometimes rising, sometimes falling, sometimes stationary. Depending upon whether the competition functions more or less well, the value in exchange is determined in a more or less precise manner. The markets that are best organized in regard to competition are those in which purchases and sales are made by the crying out of prices, through the intermediation of agents such as floor traders, commercial agents, criers, who centralize transactions in such a way that no transaction takes place without the conditions being announced and known and without the sellers being able to lower their prices and buyers to raise them. This is the manner of functioning of stock exchanges, commercial markets, grain markets, fish markets, etc. Alongside these markets, there are others in which competition, although less well organized, nevertheless functions in a fairly effective and satisfactory manner; examples are the markets for fruits and vegetables, for fowl. The streets of a town in which there are stores, and the shops of bakers, butchers, grocers, tailors, shoemakers, are markets in which competition is somewhat more defective, but where, however, it makes itself very adequately felt. It is similarly incontestable that competition presides in the determination of the value of doctors' and lawyers' consultations, of musicians' and singers' recitals, etc. In short, the world can be considered as a vast general market composed of various special markets in which social wealth is sold and bought, and our concern is to recognize the laws according to which these sales and purchases tend to be made of their own accord. In that endeavor, we will always assume a market perfectly organized under the regime of competition, just as in pure mechanics we initially assume that machines are frictionless.

42. Let us therefore see how competition works in a well-organized market, and to do so, let us go into the stock exchange of a large capital market like Paris or London. What is bought and sold, in such places, are parts of certain very important kinds of social wealth represented by their certificates: fractions of State and municipal loans, shares of railways, canals, metals factories, etc. At first, upon entering such an exchange, we hear only a confused clamor, we are aware only of chaotic movement; but, once we are informed of what is happening, the noise and activity are perfectly explained.

Let us take, for example, the trading activities in 3% French government bonds on the Paris Bourse,[ii] separating them from all other operations.

The three per cent is, as is said in market terminology, quoted at 60 francs. Agents who have received some orders to sell at 60 francs *or less* offer a certain quantity of 3 per cent government bonds, that is, a certain number of bonds each yielding 3 francs annually payable by the French State, at a price of 60 francs. We will call an offer made in that way of a definite amount of a commodity at a definite price an *effective supply*. On the other hand, the agents who have received orders to buy at 60 francs *or more* will demand a certain quantity of 3% government bonds at a price of 60 francs. We will call that demand for a certain amount of a commodity at a certain price an *effective demand*.

We now have to make three suppositions in accordance with whether the demand is *equal to, greater than,* or *less than* the supply.

First Hypothesis. The quantity demanded at 60 francs is equal to the quantity offered at that price. Each agent, on either the buying or the selling side, finds exactly his *counterpart* in another agent who is a buyer or a seller. Exchange takes place. The price of 60 francs is maintained; there is a *stationary state* or *equilibrium* of the market.

Second Hypothesis. The agents with orders to buy no longer find their counterpart, which proves that the quantity of 3% bonds demanded at a price of 60 francs is greater than the quantity offered at that price. Theoretically, trading must be suspended. Those among them who have orders to buy at 60 francs 5 centimes *or more* will be demanders at that price. They raise the price.

Two results follow from that increase: first, buyers at 60 francs, who are no longer buyers at 60 francs 5 centimes, withdraw; second, sellers at 60 francs 5 centimes, who were not sellers at 60 francs, come forward. These buyers and sellers submit their orders if they have not already done so. Thus, for a twofold reason, the difference between effective demand and effective supply is reduced. If the equality is restored, the *rise in price* stops at that level; otherwise, the price continues to go up from 60 francs 5 centimes to 60 francs 10 centimes, and from 60 francs 10 centimes to 60 francs 15 centimes, until equality of supply and demand is reestablished. There is then a new stationary state at a higher price.

Third Hypothesis. Agents with orders to sell can no longer find their counterpart, which indicates that the quantity of 3% bonds offered at a price of 60 francs is greater than the quantity demanded at that price. Trading is suspended. Those among them who have orders to sell at 59 francs 95 centimes *or less* make offers at that price. They lower the price.

Two results follow: first, the withdrawal of sellers at 60 francs who are no longer sellers at 59 francs 95 centimes; second, the coming forward of buyers at 59 francs 95 centimes who were no longer buyers at 60 francs. Reduction of the difference between supply and demand. The price *falls,* if necessary, from 59 francs 95 centimes to 59 francs 90 centimes, and from 59 francs 90 centimes to 59 francs

85 centimes, until equality between supply and demand is restored. At that time, a new equilibrium is found at a lower price.

Suppose that the same operation that is made in that way in the market for 3% French government bonds is made at the same time in the markets for the bonds of all countries: English, Italian, Spanish, Turkish, Egyptian; for the stocks and bonds issued by railways, ports, canals, mines, gas works, other factories, banks, credit institutions, by conventional variations of 5 centimes, 25 centimes, 1 franc 25 centimes, 5 francs, 25 francs, according to the value of the securities; and suppose that besides operations of sale and purchase on cash terms, there are operations of sale and purchase of *futures*, some *firm* and others *optional,* then the tumult of the Bourse becomes a veritable concert in which everyone plays his part.

43. We are going to study value in exchange that occurs under the indicated competitive conditions. Economists have, generally speaking, been wrong to consider it much too exclusively as it takes place in exceptional circumstances. They talk to us always only about diamonds, Raphael's paintings, and recitals given by fashionable tenors and sopranos. A certain Mr. De Quincey, quoted by John Stuart Mill, assumes that two individuals are crossing Lake Superior in a steam boat. One owns a music box; the other, who is 'making his way to an uninhabited region 800 miles from civilization', suddenly realizes that in leaving London he forgot to buy one of those instruments that have 'the magic power of calming the agitations of his soul'; and he buys the music box from the first individual at the last possible moment that a sale can be made, at a price of 60 guineas. Of course, the theory should take account of all these special cases; the general laws of the market should apply to the diamond market, the market for Raphael's paintings, and to the market for tenors and sopranos. They should even apply to a market, that, like the one Mr. De Quincey imagines, is constituted of a single buyer, of a single seller, and of a single item, and in which there is only one minute in which to make the exchange. But sound logic demands that we consider general before special cases, and not the special case before the general case, as would be done by a physicist who, in order to observe the sun, carefully chooses an overcast time instead of taking advantage of a cloudless sky.

44. To give a preliminary idea of the fact of exchange and the mechanism of competition, I have taken the example of buying and selling securities for gold and silver on the Bourse. But those securities are a very special kind of commodity, and the intervention of money in trading is also a special fact, the study of which will be postponed until later, and not interwoven, at the outset, with the general fact of value in exchange. Let us, therefore, retrace our steps, and, to give our observations a scientific character, let us take any two commodities, say oats and wheat, or, designate them even more abstractly as (A) and (B).[iii] I put the letters A and B in parentheses in order not to lose sight of the fact that they do not represent *quantities,* which are the only category of things susceptible of being used in equations, but instead represent kinds, species, or, as would be said in philosophical terms, *essences.*

Let us now imagine a market on one side of which some people arrive holding the commodity (A), and who would like to exchange part of it in order to procure commodity (B); and on the other side people who have the commodity (B) and would like to give up some of it in order to procure commodity (A). Since there must be an initial basis for the bidding, we shall suppose that an agent offers to give up n units of (B) for m units of (A) in accordance with, for example, the closing rate of exchange on the preceding day, and in accordance with the equation of exchange

$$mv_a = nv_b$$

in which v_a is the value in exchange of one unit of (A) and v_b is the value in exchange of one unit of (B), using the notation already indicated (§ 29).

In naming in general the ratios between values in exchange *prices,* or the relative values in exchange, in designating in general by p_b the price of (B) in terms of (A), and by p_a the price of (A) in terms of (B), and in designating, in the present case, by μ and $1/\mu$ the quotients of the ratios $\dfrac{m}{n}$ and $\dfrac{n}{m}$, we obtain from the first equation

$$\frac{v_b}{v_a} = p_b = \frac{m}{n} = \mu,$$

$$\frac{v_a}{v_b} = p_a = \frac{n}{m} = \frac{1}{\mu}$$

and, moreover, we obtain from the last two equations

$$p_b = \frac{1}{p_a} \qquad p_a = \frac{1}{p_b}$$

Thus: – *Prices, or ratios of values, are equal to the inverse ratios of the quantities exchanged.*

They are reciprocals of each other.

If (A) is oats and (B) is wheat, and an agent offered to exchange 5 hectoliters of wheat for 10 hectoliters of oats, then the price proposed for wheat in terms of oats would be 2, and that of oats in terms of wheat would be 1/2. Similarly, there is always a double sale and a double purchase in every transaction, just as there is also always a double price. That invariable reciprocity is the most important circumstance that must be recognized in the fact of exchange, and the employment of algebraic symbols is above all invaluable because it displays that condition as clearly as possible. It has also the merit, as is seen, of permitting a clear and precise formulation of general propositions. That is why we will continue to use them.

45. Let D_a, O_a, D_b, and O_b be the effective demand for and supply of commodities (A) and (B) at their respective prices $p_a = \frac{1}{\mu}$ and $p_b = \mu$. There is an essential relationship between the quantities demanded and supplied and prices that must be indicated first of all.

Effective demand and effective supply are, as we have seen, the demand and the supply of a given quantity of a commodity at a given price. Consequently, to say that a quantity D_a of (A) is demanded at the price p_a is, *ipso facto*, to say that a quantity O_b of (B) equal to $D_a p_a$, is being offered. Thus, to say, for example, that there is a demand for 200 hectoliters of oats at the price 1/2 in terms of wheat is to say that there is a supply of 100 hectoliters of wheat. In general, therefore, there is, between D_a, p_a and O_b, the equation

$$O_b = D_a p_a.$$

Similarly, to say that a quantity O_a of (A) is offered at the price p_a is, *ipso facto*, to say that a quantity D_b of (B), equal to $O_a p_a$ is being demanded. Thus, to say, for example, that 150 hectoliters of oats are being offered at the price of 1/2 in terms of wheat is to say that 75 hectoliters of wheat are demanded. In general, therefore, there is, between O_a, p_a and D_b, the equation

$$D_b = O_a p_a$$

It could be proved, similarly, that there are, between D_b, O_b, p_b, O_a and D_a, the equations:

$$O_a = D_b p_b$$

$$D_a = O_b p_b,$$

if it were not that the proof would be redundant because these two equations result from the two previous ones together with the equation $p_a p_b = 1$.

Thus: – *The effective demand for or supply of one commodity in exchange for another is equal to the effective supply of or demand for the second commodity multiplied by its price in terms of the first.*

It can be seen that two of the four quantities D_a, O_a, D_b and O_b will determine the other two. We will assume until further notice that it is the quantities supplied, O_b and O_a, that are determined by the quantities demanded, D_a and D_b, and not that the quantities demanded result from the quantities supplied. Indeed, when two commodities are exchanged for each other in kind, demand ought to be considered as the principal fact, and supply as an accessory fact. We do not supply goods just in order to supply; we only supply because we cannot demand goods without supplying some; supply is only a consequence of demand. We will therefore content ourselves with the indirect relationship between supply and price, and not seek for a direct relationship except between demand and price. At prices p_a and p_b, the demands are D_a and D_b, from which result the supplies $O_a = D_b p_b$ and $O_b = D_a p_a$.

46. That having been said, letting

$$D_a = \alpha O_a$$

we have three hypotheses to make according to whether we have $\alpha = 1$, $\alpha > 1$, or $\alpha < 1$. But, let us first state one last theorem.

If we substitute in the above equation the two values of D_a and O_a given by the equations

$$D_a = O_b p_b$$

$$O_a = D_b p_b$$

there results

$$O_b = \alpha D_b$$

Thus: – *Given two commodities, the ratio of the effective demand of either one of them to its effective supply is equal to the ratio of the effective supply of the other to its effective demand.*

This theorem may be deduced as follows:

$$D_a = O_b p_b$$

$$D_b = O_a p_a$$

$$D_a D_b = O_a O_b$$

or, similarly,

$$O_a = D_b p_b$$

$$O_b = D_a p_a$$

$$O_a O_b = D_a D_b$$

so that we have, in either way,

$$\frac{O_b}{D_b} = \frac{D_a}{O_a} = \alpha$$

We know, therefore, that if the effective demand for and effective supply of (A) are equal, the effective supply of and effective demand for (B) will also be equal; that if the effective demand for (A) is greater than its effective supply, then the effective supply of (B) will be proportionately greater than its effective demand; that, finally, if the effective supply of (A) is greater than its effective demand, then the effective demand for (B) will be proportionately greater than its effective supply. That is the meaning of the above-stated theorem.

47. Now assume that $\alpha = 1, D_a = O_a$, and $O_b = D_b$, the quantities demanded and supplied of the two commodities (A) and (B) at their respective prices $p_a = \dfrac{1}{\mu}$ and $p_b = \mu$ are equal: each buyer or seller finding his exact counterpart in a seller or buyer. The market is in equilibrium. At the equilibrium prices $\dfrac{1}{\mu}$ and μ, the quantity $D_a = O_a$ of (A) is exchanged for the quantity $O_b = D_b$ of (B), and, the market day having ended, the owners of the two commodities go their own way.

48. But assume that $\alpha \gtrless 1, D_a \gtrless O_a$, and $O_b \gtrless D_b$.

The first idea that occurs is to repeat purely and simply the reasoning that we followed about the stock exchange in regard to government bonds. That would be a very serious error. In the stock exchange, we had buyers and sellers of government bonds, that is, of securities the value of which depend both on their particular yield and on the general rate of return on capital. As we will see later, a rise in the price of government bonds can only decrease the demand for them and increase their supply; a fall could only increase the demand for them and decrease their supply. Here, we have traders of (A) and (B) that we assume to be two commodities that are of direct utility and are the only commodities on the market. That circumstance alters everything.

Unquestionably, it will always be necessary to raise p_a (or lower p_b), if D_a is greater than O_a, or, contrariwise, to raise p_b (or lower p_a) if D_b is greater than O_b. There is also no doubt, in regard to demand, that our previous reasoning is correct. When the price increases, the demand cannot increase; it can only decrease. And when the price decreases, the demand cannot decrease, it can only increase. Thus, a rise in p_a, which will be a fall in p_b, can only decrease D_a and increase D_b; on the other hand, a rise in p_b, which will be a fall in p_a, can only decrease D_b and increase D_a. But what will happen to O_a and O_b? It is impossible to say. O_a is equal to the product of D_b multiplied by p_b. Now, if one of these two factors, say p_b, decreases or increases, the other factor, D_b, must increase or decrease as a result. Likewise, O_b is equal to the product of D_a multiplied by p_a. Now, according as p_a increases or decreases, D_a must decrease or increase as a result. How consequently can we know if we are moving toward equilibrium?

Notes

i   Being faithful to Walras's textual terminology, neither here nor elsewhere do we write 'quantity supplied' and 'quantity demanded' unless he specifically used that terminology. He used the Marshallian terminology occasionally, but he had his own terminology, explaining in §§ 42 and 45 that he calls a quantity supplied, that is, a specific amount at a specific price, 'an effective supply', and a quantity demanded, that is, a specific amount at a specific price, 'an effective demand'. In any event, it is clear from the context when he meant specific quantities as distinct from the entire supply or demand function.

ii   The meaning of the word 'Bourse' in French is 'a public market on which stocks, or bonds, or both; or commodities, or services, are traded'. Walras used the word 'Bourse' here in conjunction with the word 'Paris', thus referring to the institution with those two words as its name, a market on which stocks and bonds are traded. He also used the word, without explicitly using the word 'Paris' but in obvious reference to the Paris Bourse, when he dealt with French government bonds, and in that and in similar instances we have retained his word 'Bourse'. Elsewhere he used the word 'Bourse', always capitalized as is the French custom, to refer to a securities exchange in any town, and in those instances we have translated 'Bourse' as 'stock exchange'.

iii   Oats is 'Avoine' in French, and wheat is 'Blé'.

LESSON 6

Curves of effective demand and effective supply

SUMMARY: – Fact of the decrease of effective demand caused by the increase of the price. Curves or equations of partial demand as a function of the price. Curves or equations of total demand. Demand curves are also supply curves. Hyperbolas of the existing quantity. Intermediate position of demand curves between the coordinate axes and the hyperbolas of the existing quantity.

Solution of the problem of the exchange of two commodities for each other. Geometric solution by inscription under the demand curves of rectangles with reciprocal bases and ordinates that are inversely equal to their surfaces. Algebraic solution. Combination of the two solutions by the construction of supply curves as a function of prices. Law of effective supply and demand, or of the determination of equilibrium prices.

49. Since we will assume that there is only an indirect or mediate relation between price and effective supply, and that the direct and immediate relation is between price and effective demand, it is the latter that we must study.

We consider, for this purpose, one of the holders of wheat. This individual has wheat, but he has no oats; he wants to retain a certain quantity of wheat for himself, and to give up a certain quantity of it in exchange for oats for his horses. As for the respective quantities that he will retain and give up, they depend on the price of oats and on the quantity of oats that he will demand having regard to its price. How does this happen? That is what must be seen. Very well, at a price of zero (if he has to give zero hectoliters of wheat for one hectoliter of oats; in other words, if oats are free), our man will demand all the oats he wants; that is to say, enough for all the horses he owns and even for all those he could own on the assumption that it costs nothing to feed horses. He will not have to give up any wheat at all in exchange. At the successive prices, 1/1000, 1/100, 1/10, 1/5, 1/2, ⋯ (if 1/1000, 1/100, 1/10, 1/5, 1/2, ⋯ hectoliters of wheat have to be given up for one hectoliter of oats), he will progressively reduce his demand. At the prices 1, 2, 5, 10, ⋯ (if 1, 2, 5, 10, ⋯ hectoliters of wheat have to be given up to obtain one hectoliter of oats), he will reduce his demand even more. At the same time, the quantity of wheat that he offers in exchange will always equal the quantity of oats he demands multiplied by the price of oats. Finally, at some more or less high price, for example, at a price of 100 (if 100 hectoliters of wheat have to be given up for 1 hectoliter of oats), our man will not demand any oats at all, because, at that price, he will no longer be able or will not want to feed a single horse. It is clear, besides, that at that point, he will no longer offer any wheat in exchange. It is therefore truly the case that, in that process, the effective demand for oats diminishes as the price increases: it begins at a certain quantity at a zero price, and ends up at a zero quantity at a certain price. As for the corresponding effective supply of wheat, it starts at zero, increases, attains at least one maximum, then decreases and returns to zero.

50. All the holders of wheat, and not only all the holders of wheat on one side of the market, but all the holders of oats on the other side, have dispositions to trade that are not the same, but are analogous. And, in a general fashion, all holders of any commodity whatsoever who go to the market to exchange a certain quantity of that commodity for a certain quantity of whatever other commodity go there with certain virtual or effective *dispositions to buy or sell* that are susceptible of a rigorous determination.

A holder (1) of a quantity q_b of commodity (B), as we hereby specify in passing from concrete examples to algebraic notation, comes to the market to exchange a quantity o_b of (B), in return for a quantity d_a of (A) in conformity with the equation of exchange

$$d_a v_a = o_b v_b,$$

and he leaves the market carrying away a quantity d_a of (A) and a quantity $y = q_b - o_b = q_b - d_a \dfrac{v_a}{v_b}$ of (B). In one way or another, between the quantities q_b, $\dfrac{v_a}{v_b}$ or p_a, d_a, and y, there is always the relation

$$q_b = y + d_a p_a.$$

Our man knows what amount q_b is. He does not know, before arriving at the market, what $\dfrac{v_a}{v_b}$ or p_a will be; but he is certain that he will learn it as soon as he arrives, and that, this value of p_a once being known, he must immediately decide upon a certain value of d_a, from which value, by virtue of the above equation, y will finally be determined.

If our man goes to the market in person, he can leave his dispositions to buy or sell for the time being in the virtual state and not effective; that is to say, he may not determine what his demand d_a will be until the price p_a is known. Those dispositions nevertheless exist. But if he were prevented from going to the market himself, or if, for one reason or another, he had to have his trades made by a friend or give his orders to an agent, he would have to anticipate all the possible values of p_a from zero to infinity and determine accordingly all the corresponding values of d_a, expressing them in one way or another. Now, all persons at all familiar with mathematics know that there are two ways of representing the expression mathematically.

51. Consider two coordinate axes, as drawn in Fig. 1 a horizontal *price axis*, Op, and a vertical *demand axis*, Od. On the price axis, beginning at the origin O, I mark off the lengths $\overline{\mathrm{Op_a'}}$, $\overline{\mathrm{Op_a''}}$, $\overline{\mathrm{Op_a'''}}$, $\cdots$ representing various possible prices of oats in terms of wheat, or of (A) in terms of (B). On the other axis, beginning at the same origin O, I mark off the length $\overline{\mathrm{Oa_{d,1}}}$ representing the quantity of oats or (A) that our holder of wheat or (B) will demand at the price zero. On lines

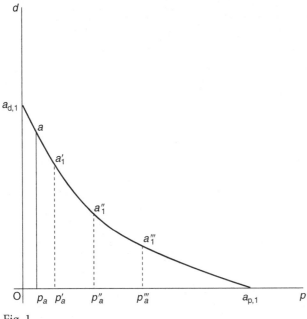

Fig. 1

drawn through the points P'_a, P''_a, $\cdots$ parallel to the vertical demand axis, I lay off the lengths $\overline{p'_a a'_1}$, $\overline{p''_a a''_1}$, $\cdots$, corresponding to the quantities of oats or (A) that will be demanded at the prices p'_a, p''_a, $\cdots$ respectively. The length $\overline{Oa_{p,1}}$ represents the price at which our holder of wheat or (B) will not demand any oats or (A).

That being done, the dispositions to trade of holder (1) of commodity (B) are expressed either geometrically by the curve $a_{d,1}a_{p,1}$ drawn through the points $a_{d,1}$, a'_1, a''_1, $\cdots$, $a_{p,1}$, or algebraically by the equation $d_a = f_{a,1}(p_a)$ of this curve. The curve $a_{d,1}a_{p,1}$ and the equation $d_a = f_{a,1}(p_a)$ are empirical. In the same way, we would obtain the curves $a_{d,2}a_{p,2}$, $a_{d,3}a_{p,3}$, $\cdots$ or their equations $d_a = f_{a,2}(p_a)$, $d_a = f_{a,3}(p_a)$, $\cdots$ (Fig. 2), expressing geometrically or algebraically the dispositions to trade of all the other holders of (B), individuals (2), (3), $\cdots$.

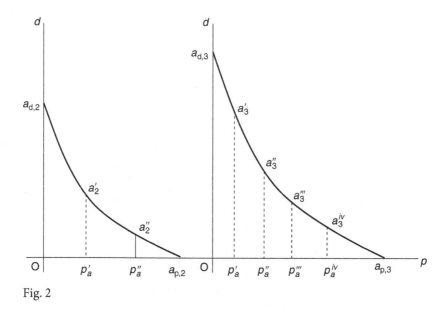

Fig. 2

52. If we now add together all the partial curves $a_{d,1}a_{p,1}$, $a_{d,2}a_{p,2}$, $a_{d,3}a_{p,3}$, ⋯ by joining all the ordinates with the same abscissa, we obtain a total curve A_dA_p (Fig. 3), representing geometrically the dispositions to trade of all the holders of (B). If we then sum up all the partial equations, we obtain a total equation

$$D_a = f_{a,1}(p_a) + f_{a,2}(p_a) + f_{a,3}(p_a) + \cdots = F_a(p_a)$$

expressing those dispositions algebraically. That is the *demand curve* or the *demand equation* for (A) in exchange for (B) as a function of the price of (A) in terms of (B). Similarly, we could derive the demand curve or the demand equation of (B) in exchange for (A) as a function of the price of (B) in terms of (A).

Nothing indicates that the partial curves or partial equations, $a_{d,1}a_{p,1}$ or $d_a = f_{a,1}(p_a)$, and the other ones, are *continuous*; that is to say, that an infinitesimally small increase in p_a produces an infinitesimally small decrease in d_a. On the contrary, these functions are often discontinuous. In the case of oats, for example, it is certain that our first holder of wheat will reduce his demand for wheat not

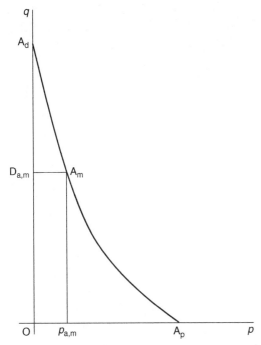

Fig. 3

along with the rise of the price but in an intermittent way each time he decides to have one horse less in his stable. His partial demand curve will therefore, in reality, have the form of the stepped path passing through the point a (Fig. 4). The same will be true of all the others. And nevertheless the total demand curve A_dA_p (Fig. 3) can, by virtue of the so-called *law of large numbers*, be considered for all practical purposes as continuous. In fact, when a very small increase in price occurs, at least one of the holders of (B), *out of the large number of them*, reaches the point of being obliged to do without one horse, and there will also occur a very small diminution in the total demand.

53. In these conditions, the curve A_dA_p therefore gives the quantity of (A) effectively demanded as a function of the price of (A). For example, at the price $p_{a,m}$, represented by the abscissa $\overline{Op_{a,m}}$ of the point A_m, the effective demand is $D_{a,m}$, represented by the ordinate

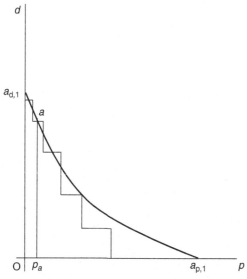

Fig. 4

$\overline{\text{OD}}_{a,m}$ of the same point A_m. Moreover, when the effective demand for (A) in exchange for (B) is $D_{a,m}$ at the price $p_{a,m}$, the effective supply of (B) in exchange for (A) is, in consequence, $O_{b,m} = D_{a,m}p_{a,m}$ (§ 45), represented by the area of the rectangle $\text{OD}_{a,m}A_mP_{a,m}$ with a base of $\overline{\text{Op}}_{a,m}$ and a height $\overline{\text{Od}}_{a,m}$. Thus the curve A_dA_p shows both the demand for (A) and the supply of (B) as a function of the price of (A) in terms of (B). Similarly, the curve B_dB_p of Fig. 5 shows both the demand for (B) and the supply of (A) as a function of the price of (B) in terms of (A).

54. Let $Q_b{}^i$ be the total quantity of (B) existing in the market in the hands of holders of (B), and let an equilateral hyperbola [with equation] $xy = Q_b$, with the axes as asymptotes, be drawn through the point Q_b. Let the line $p_{a,m}A_m$ be extended until it meets the hyperbola at the point Q_b, and let the line βQ_b be drawn parallel to the x axis, i.e., the price axis. The surface Q_b of the rectangle $O\beta Q_b P_{a,m}$ represents the total quantity of (B) brought to the market; $D_{a,m}$ multiplied by

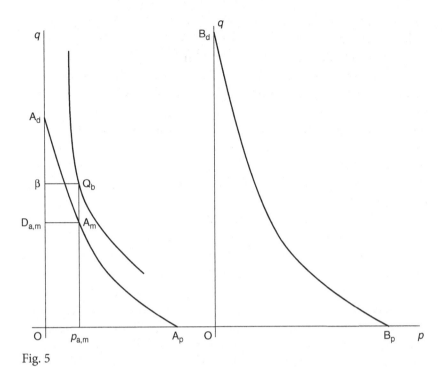

Fig. 5

$p_{a,m}$ is the area of the rectangle $OD_{a,m}A_mP_{a,m}$ representing that part of the total quantity of (B) that is given up in exchange for (A) at the price $p_{a,m}$; and, consequently, $Y = Q_b - D_{a,m}p_{a,m}$, the area of the rectangle $D_{a,m}\beta Q_b A_m$, that is $Q_b - D_{a,m}p_{a,m}$, represents the part that would be withheld from the market and kept by the holders at the price $p_{a,m}$. Now, in any case, there will always be, between the quantities Q_b, p_a, D_a and Y, the relation

$$Q_b = Y + D_a p_a.$$

Thus, [the hyperbola with equation] $xy = Q_b$, or the curve passing through the point Q_b, is the *hyperbola of the existing quantity* of (B), and $A_d A_p$ is the curve that separates the part of (B) that is exchanged for (A) and the part that is withheld from sale depending on the prices of (A) in terms of (B). Naturally, the same general relationship could be found between the curve $B_d B_p$ and the hyperbola of the existing quantity of (A), the equation of which would be $xy = Q_a$.

55. Demand curves are, therefore, enclosed in the quantity hyperbolas. It can also be said that generally those curves meet the coordinate axes and are not asymptotic to them.

They generally intersect their demand axes. In fact, the quantity of any commodity demanded by an individual at a zero price is generally finite. If oats were free, some individuals would perhaps have dozens or hundreds of horses; but they would not have an infinite number of them and consequently would not demand an infinite quantity of oats. Now, the sum total of the demands at the price zero being the sum of finite quantities, it would itself be a finite quantity.

They usually intersect the price axis. In fact, it can generally be assumed that there is a price high enough, though not infinite, at which any commodity is no longer demanded by anyone even in an infinitely small quantity. We cannot, however, make any absolute statement about this matter. It is perfectly possible for a case to occur in which commodity (B) is offered *at each possible price*, either in the total amount existing or in part, and in which case the demand curve A_dA_p will coincide, totally or in part, with the hyperbola passing through Q_b or with some other interior hyperbola. That is why, so as not to prejudge anything, we will consider demand curves as being susceptible of taking all the positions between the coordinate axes and the hyperbolas of the existing quantity.

56. We now know completely the direct and immediate relationship that links the effective demand for a commodity to its price in terms of another commodity, or, at least, we know the nature of the relationship and we have conceived a mathematical expression for it.

Thus, for the commodity (A), this relationship can be expressed geometrically by the curve A_dA_p, or algebraically by the equation (§ 52) of that curve

$$D_a = F_a(p_a).$$

For the commodity (B), it can be expressed geometrically by the curve B_dB_p, or algebraically by the equation of that curve

$$D_b = F_b(p_b).$$

Moreover, we also know the nature of the indirect and mediate relationship that exists between the effective supply of one commodity offered in exchange for another and the price of the other commodity in terms of the first, and we have conceived a mathematical expression for this relationship.

For the commodity (A), the relationship in question would be expressed geometrically by a series of rectangles inscribed within the curve B_dB_p, or algebraically by the equation (§ 53)

$$O_a = D_b p_b = F_b(p_b)p_b.$$

For the commodity (B), the relationship would be expressed geometrically by a series of rectangles inscribed within the curve A_dA_p, or algebraically by the equation

$$O_b = D_a p_a = F_a(p_a)p_a.$$

Nothing is easier than to deduce from the latter expressions those of the relationship that links the effective supply of each commodity to its price in terms of the other commodity. It is only necessary to replace, in the last two equations, the price p_b by $\dfrac{1}{p_a}$ and the price p_a by $\dfrac{1}{p_b}$ in virtue of the relationship $p_a p_b = 1$. It then results that

$$O_a = F_b\left(\frac{1}{p_a}\right)\frac{1}{p_a}, \qquad O_b = F_a\left(\frac{1}{p_b}\right)\frac{1}{p_b}.$$

With all these elements, we are in a position to solve mathematically the general problem of the exchange of two commodities for each other, which consists, *being given two commodities, (A) and (B), and the demand curve of each in terms of the other, or the equations of these curves,* in *determining their respective equilibrium prices.*

57. Geometrically, the problem consists in inscribing within the two curves A_dA_p and B_dB_p [of Fig. 6] two rectangles with reciprocal bases, OD_aAp_a and OD_bBp_b respectively, such that their heights are

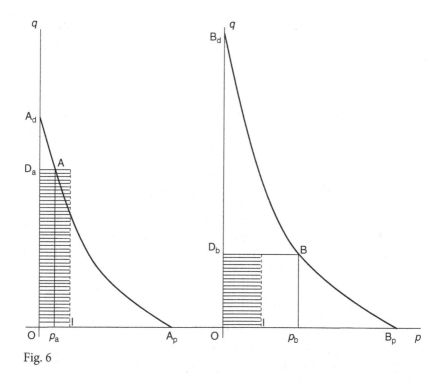

Fig. 6

so related that the height of the first, $\overline{OD_a}$, is equal to the area of the second, $\overline{OD_b} \times \overline{Op_b}$, and that, conversely, the height of the second, $\overline{OD_b}$, is equal to the area of the first, $\overline{OD_a} \times \overline{Op_a}$. The bases of these two rectangles, $\overline{Op_a}$ and $\overline{Op_b}$, represent equilibrium prices, since, at these respective prices, the demand for (A), represented by the height $\overline{OD_a}$, equals the supply of (A) represented by the area $\overline{OD_b} \times \overline{Op_b}$, and the demand for (B), represented by the height $\overline{OD_b}$, equals the supply of (B) represented by the area $\overline{OD_a} \times \overline{Op_a}$ (§ 47).

The expression of which I made use: *the height of either rectangle is equal to the area of the other*, is not homogeneous.[ii] But homogeneity in these circumstances is not necessary for the reason that the condition that the bases be reciprocals of each other implies the determination of the common unit $\overline{OI}$ that was used in the construction of both curves. It could also be said, if even more clarity is desired, that the height of each rectangle should contain the unit of length as many times as the other rectangle contains the unit of area; or, putting it yet another way, that the area of each rectangle should be equal to the area of a rectangle constructed with the same height as the other rectangle and a base of one unit. It follows, moreover, under the given conditions of the problem, that the bases of the two rectangles are inversely equal to the ratio of the heights and directly equal to the ratio of the areas.

58. Algebraically, the problem consists in finding the two roots p_a and p_b, of the two equations

$$F_a(p_a) = F_b(p_b)p_b, \qquad p_a p_b = 1;$$

or the two roots, p_a and p_b, of the two equations

$$F_b(p_b)p_a = F_b(p_b), \qquad p_a p_b = 1;$$

or, finally, the two [respective] roots p_a and p_b, of the two [respective] equations

$$F_a(p_a) = F_b\left(\frac{1}{p_a}\right)\frac{1}{p_a},$$

indicating that $D_a = O_a$, and

$$F_a\left(\frac{1}{p_b}\right)\frac{1}{p_b} = F_b(p_b),$$

indicating that $O_b = D_b$.

59. The two methods, furthermore, may be combined into a single one. We already have the curves

$$D_a = F_a(p_a), \qquad D_b = F_b(p_b);$$

these are the curves A_dA_p and B_dB_p. Let us construct the curves

$$O_a = F_b\left(\frac{1}{p_a}\right)\frac{1}{p_a}, \qquad O_b = F_a\left(\frac{1}{p_b}\right)\frac{1}{p_b};$$

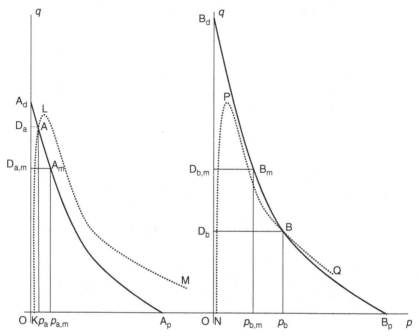

Fig. 7

these will be the curves KLM and NPQ (Fig. 7), the intersection of which with the first pair, at the points A and B, will furnish precisely the rectangles that were mentioned above.

It is easy to take cognizance of the meaning of the curves KLM and NPQ that are drawn as dotted curves in the figure, and of the manner of their construction.

The first, KLM, is a *supply curve* of (A), no longer identified by means of the demand curve of (B), which gave the supply of (A) as a function of p_b as the areas of inscribed rectangles constructed on the coordinate axes, but distinct from it and giving that same supply of (A) by the length of the ordinates as a function of p_a.

The curve starts from an ordinate of zero at an infinitely high price of (A) in terms of (B), corresponding to an infinitesimally small price of (B) in terms of (A); that is to say, KLM is asymptotic to the price axis. The curve rises as it approaches the origin, with each fall in the price of (A) in terms of (B) corresponding to a rise in the price of (B) in terms of (A). It reaches its maximum at the point L, the abscissa of which represents a price of (A) in terms of (B), the inverse of $p_{b,m}$, the price of (B) in terms of (A), measured by the abscissa $\overline{Op_{b,m}}$ of the point B_m, at which the rectangle inscribed within B_dB_p is a maximum. Then the curve falls as it approaches the origin until its ordinate becomes zero again at a price of (A) in terms of (B) represented by the length $\overline{OK}$, the inverse of the price of (B) in terms of (A) measured by the abscissa $\overline{OB_p}$ of the point B_p where the curve B_dB_p meets the price axis.

Similarly, the second curve, NPQ, is the supply curve of (B), no longer derived from the demand curve of (A), which gave the supply of (B) as a function of p_a as the areas of inscribed rectangles constructed on the coordinate axes, but distinct from it and giving the supply of (B) by the lengths of the ordinates as a function of p_b.

That curve, NPQ, starts from an ordinate of zero at an infinitely high price of (B) in terms of (A), corresponding to an infinitesimally small price of (A) in terms of (B); that is to say, it is asymptotic to the price axis. It rises as it moves toward the origin, with each fall in the price of (B) in terms of (A) corresponding to a rise in the price of (A) in terms of (B). It reaches a maximum at the point P, the abscissa of which represents a price of (B) in terms of (A), the inverse of the price $p_{b,m}$ of (A) in terms of (B), measured by the abscissa $\overline{Op_{a,m}}$ of the point A_m at which the rectangle inscribed within A_dA_p is a maximum. Then the curve falls as it approaches the origin until it returns to zero at a price of (B) in terms of (A), represented by the length $\overline{ON}$, this price being the reciprocal of the price of (A) in terms of (B) measured by the abscissa $\overline{OA_p}$ of the point A_p at which the curve A_dA_p meets the price axis.

It goes without saying that the shapes of the curves KLM and NPQ are essentially related to the shapes of B_dB_p and A_dA_p respectively. If the latter curves were assumed to be different, the former would also be entirely different. At all events, under the given conditions that we have assumed, the curve B_dB_p, while falling from left to right, *after* having passed the maximum point B_m, meets the dotted curve NPQ at the point at which that curve rises *from zero to its maximum* P; and, consequently, the curve A_dA_p while also falling, *before* passing through the maximum point A_m, meets the dotted curve KLM at the point at which it falls *from its maximum* L *to zero*.[iii]

60. Now, after all that has been noted, it is evident that if the two curves A_dA_p and KLM intersect at the point A, *on the right* or *on the left* of this point, alternatively, the curve A_dA_p lies *below* or *above* the curve KLM; and that, similarly, if the two curves B_dB_p and NPQ intersect at the point B, *to the right* or *to the left* of this point, alternatively, the curve B_dB_p is *above* or *below* the curve NPQ.

Thus, since the prices $p_a = \dfrac{1}{\mu}$ and $p_b = \mu$ are, by hypothesis, those at which $D_a = O_a$ and $D_b = O_b$, it follows that at all prices of (A) in terms of (B) higher than p_a, corresponding to prices of (B) in terms of (A) lower than p_b, we will have at the same time $O_a > D_a$ and $D_b > O_b$. And, conversely, at all prices of (A) in terms of (B) lower than p_a, corresponding to prices of (B) in terms of (A) higher than p_b, we will have at the same time $D_a > O_a$ and $O_b > D_b$. In the first case, the equilibrium price could only be reached by an increase in p_b, which would be a decrease in p_a. In the second case, equilibrium price could only be reached by an increase in p_a, which would be a decrease in p_b.

This leads us to formulate in the following terms *the law of effective supply and effective demand*, or *the law of the determination of equilibrium prices* in the case of the exchange of two commodities for each other: — *Given two commodities, for the market to be in equilibrium with respect to those commodities, or for the price of either commodity to be stationary in terms of the other, it is necessary and sufficient that the effective demand for each of these two commodities be equal to its effective supply. When this equality does not obtain, it is necessary, in order to arrive at the equilibrium price, for there to be a rise in the price of the commodity for which the effective demand is greater than the effective supply, and a fall in the price of the one for which the effective supply is greater than the effective demand.*

That is the law that we might have been tempted to formulate immediately after our study of the Bourse (§ 42); but a rigorous demonstration was necessary (§ 48).

61. It is clearly seen now what the mechanism of competition in the market is: it is the practical solution, reached through raising and lowering of prices, of the problem of exchange for which we have furnished the theoretical and mathematical solution. It must

furthermore be understood that we have no intention of substituting one solution for the other. The practical solution has a rapidity and reliability that leaves nothing to be desired. It can be seen, on big markets that function even without agents or criers, that the current equilibrium price is determined in a few minutes, and considerable quantities of merchandise are exchanged at that price in half or three quarters of an hour. By contrast, the theoretical solution would be, in almost all cases, completely impractical.[iv] It follows that to speak to us about the difficulty of establishing the empirical curves of exchange or their equations would be to make a very strange objection. The advantage there may be, in certain cases, of constructing, totally or partially, the demand curve or the supply curve of a given commodity, and the possibility or impossibility of doing so, is a question that we defer entirely. For the moment, we are studying the problem of exchange in general, and the pure and simple concept of curves of exchange is sufficient and at the same time indispensable.

Notes

i   That is, a magnitude numerically equal to the area of the rectangle of $O\beta Q_b P_{a,m}$ of Fig. 5.

ii In the sense that the one is a length and the other is an area.

iii This is from the perspective of looking from right to left.

iv Walras here is indicating that in the theoretical model on a market day, all of the exchanges on a given day take place at the price at which supply and demand are equal. In real competitive markets, however, he indicates that there are exchanges at disequilibrium prices as the market moves toward equilibrium; but, he goes on to explain, a price is quickly found at which supply and demand are equal, and, although all trade does not occur at that price, 'considerable quantities' are exchanged at it. Moreover, the trading at the price that equates current demand and supply goes on for a relatively long period of real time.

LESSON 7

Discussion of the solution of the problem of exchange of two commodities for each other

SUMMARY: – Discussion restricted to the case of supply curves that are continuous and have a single maximum. The supply curves do not intersect the demand curves; no equilibrium price. The supply curves intersect the demand curves in three points; three equilibrium prices. Two stable equilibrium prices; one unstable equilibrium price. One of the two demand curves coincides with the hyperbola of the existing quantity. Both of them coincide.

62. To summarize: given two commodities (A) and (B) for which the relationships between the effective demand and the price are established by the equations

$$D_a = F_a(p_a), \quad D_b = F_b(p_b),$$

the equilibrium price is given by the equation

$$D_a v_a = D_b v_b$$

that is to say, replacing D_a and D_b with their values, by the equation

$$F_a(p_a)v_a = F_b(p_b)v_b,$$

which can be written in the form

$$F_a(p_a) = F_b\left(\frac{1}{p_a}\right)\frac{1}{p_a},$$

68

or in the form

$$F_a\left(\frac{1}{p_b}\right)\frac{1}{p_b}=F_b\left(p_b\right),$$

according to whether we wish to solve for p_a or p_b. The first of these two forms states that $D_a = O_a$; the second states that $O_b = D_b$.

We have solved the equation in its two forms (§ 59) by the intersection of the curves

$$D_a = F_a\left(p_a\right), \qquad O_a = F_b\left(\frac{1}{p_a}\right)\frac{1}{p_a}$$

and of the curves

$$O_b = F_a\left(\frac{1}{p_b}\right)\frac{1}{p_b}, \qquad D_b = F_b\left(p_b\right);$$

but this solution requires further discussion.

63. We will not discuss it for all possible cases, which would be much too lengthy and, moreover, premature, but only for the fairly simple general case portrayed in our figure [Fig. 7 of the preceding chapter]. In this figure, we assumed that the curves A_dA_p and B_dB_p are continuous, and have only one maximum for the rectangles with coordinates (p_a, D_a) and (p_b, D_b), between [respectively] the point at which $D_a = \overline{OA_d}$ and $p_a = 0$, and the point at which $p_a = \overline{OA_p}$ and $D_a = 0$, and between the point at which $D_b = \overline{OB_d}$ and $p_b = 0$, and the point at which $p_b = \overline{OB_p}$ and $D_b = 0$. We need, furthermore, consider only that portion of each of these curves that falls within the first quadrant, and, regarding that portion, the part that lies between the points A_d and A_p, and between the points B_d and B_p. This very evidently follows from the very nature of the fact of exchange. Given that hypothesis, KLM and NPQ are continuous curves, and have only one maximum

of the ordinates. Now, even in this case, thus defined and limited, there is material for an interesting discussion.

64. We have been reasoning as if A_dA_p and KLM, on the one hand, and as if B_dB_p and NPQ, on the other, intersect respectively at only one point A and only one point B. But first of all, we must note that these curves may have no point of intersection at all. If, for example, B_dB_p ended up on the price axis at a point that lies to the left of the point N, it would not intersect the curve NPQ. In that case, furthermore, the curve KLM would itself leave the price axis at a point situated beyond the point A_p and it would not be intersected by the curve A_dA_p. There would be no solution.

There is nothing surprising about this eventuality. It corresponds to the case in which no holder of (B) is willing to give $\overline{OA_p}$ of (B) for 1 of (A), that is, 1 of (B) for $\dfrac{1}{OA_p}$ $[= \overline{ON}]$ of (A), while, on the other hand, no holder of (A) is willing to give $\dfrac{1}{OA_p}$ of (A) for 1 of (B), that is, 1 of (A) for $\overline{OA_p}$ of (B). It is obvious that, in this case, the offers to buy and sell would not result in any transactions on the market. If there were a price of (A) in terms of (B) less than $\overline{OA_p}$ corresponding to some price of (B) in terms of (A) greater than $\dfrac{1}{OA_p}$, there would be plenty of demanders of (A) offering (B) in exchange, but there would be no demanders of (B) in exchange for (A). And, if there were a price of (B) in terms of (A) below $\dfrac{1}{OA_p}$, corresponding to some price of (A) in terms of (B) higher than A_p, there would be plenty of demanders of (B) who are suppliers of (A), but there would be no demanders of (A) who are suppliers of (B).

65. Now, after the case in which the curves of demand and the curves of supply have only one point of intersection, and the case in which they have no point of intersection, a careful examination of the form

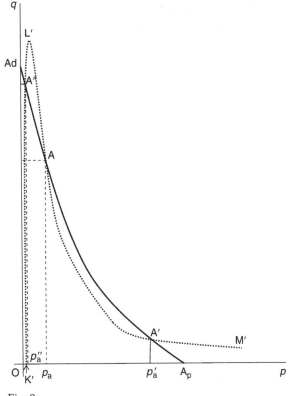

Fig. 8a

of the curves reveals the case in which there would be several points of intersection. If, for example [Fig. 8a and Fig. 8b], the two commodities (A) and (B) were such that, the demand for (A) in terms of (B) continuing to be represented by the curve A_dA_p, the demand for (B) in terms of (A) was represented by the curve $B'_dB'_p$, that curve $B'_dB'_p$ would be intersected by the curve NPQ at the three points B, B', and B''. In this case, the supply curve of (A) for (B), KLM, would be replaced by the curve K'L'M', which would itself intersect the curve A_dA_p at the three points A, A', and A'', the point A corresponding to the point B, the point A' to the point B', and the point A'' to the point B''. There would thus be three different solutions to the problem of exchange of two commodities (A) and (B) for each other since there would be three systems each with two rectangles

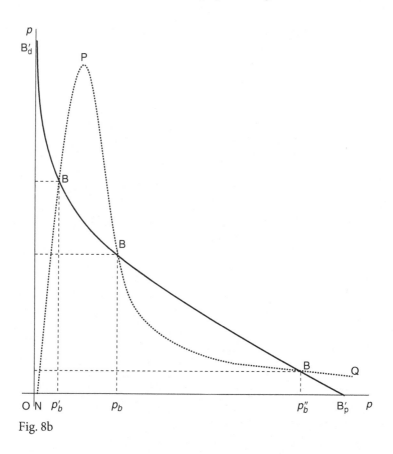

Fig. 8b

with reciprocal bases, inscribed within the curves $A_d A_p$ and $B'_d B'_p$, and each having heights that would be inversely equal to their areas. But do these three solutions have the same importance?

66. Among the three systems, if we first examine those that relate to the points A' and B' and A" and B", we find ourselves in conditions identical to those of the system relative to the points A and B in the case of a unique solution (§ 60). To the *right* or to the *left* of the point A', where the two curves $A_d A_p$ and K'L'M' intersect, the curve $A_d A_p$ is *below* or *above* the curve K'L'M'; and similarly, to the *right* or to the *left* of the point B', where the two curves $B'_d B'_p$ and NPQ intersect, the curve $B'_d B'_p$ is *below* or *above* the curve NPQ. To the *right* or

to the *left* of the point A″, the curve $A_d A_p$ is *below* or *above* the curve K′L′M′; and, similarly again, to the *right* or to the *left* of the point B″, the curve $B'_d B'_p$ is *below* or *above* the curve NPQ.

In the two cases, *beyond* the point of equilibrium, *the supply of the commodity in question is greater than the demand for it*, which must result in a *fall* in price, that is, in a return to the point of equilibrium. In the two cases, to the *left* of the point of equilibrium, *the demand for the commodity in question is greater than the supply*, which must result in a *rise* in price, that is, in a movement towards the point of equilibrium. We can therefore exactly compare that equilibrium to that of a suspended body whose center of gravity lies directly on a vertical line beneath the point of suspension, so that the center of gravity, if displaced from its vertical position, would automatically return to its original position simply by the force of gravity. That is a *stable* equilibrium.

67. The same does not hold regarding the points A and B of Fig. 8a and 8b. The curve $A_d A_p$ lies *above* the curve K′L′M′ to the *right*, and below the curve K′L′M′ to the *left* of the point A. Likewise, the curve $B'_d B'_p$ lies *above* the curve NPQ to the *right*, and *below* the curve NPQ to the *left* of the point B. Hence, in this case, to the *right* of the point of equilibrium, *the demand for the commodity is greater than its supply*, which must lead to a *rise* in the price, that is, to a movement away from the point of equilibrium. And, in this case, to the *left* of the point of equilibrium, *the supply of the commodity is greater than the demand for it*, which must lead to a *fall* in the price, that is, to a movement again away from the point of equilibrium. This equilibrium is therefore exactly comparable to that of a body that has a point of suspension lying on a vertical line directly beneath the center of gravity, so that if this center of gravity leaves the vertical line, the body moves further and further away, not restoring its position, and solely through the force of gravity it places itself below the point of suspension. That sort of equilibrium is *unstable*.

68. In reality, only the systems A′, B′ and A″, B″ give solutions to the problem, and the system A, B marks only the point of separation and the limit of the field respectively of each of the two solutions. To the

right of $p_b = \mu$, the price of (B) in terms of (A) tends to move toward the equilibrium price p_b'' which is the abscissa of the point B'; to the left of p_b, it tends toward the price p_b', which is the abscissa of the point B'. Correlatively, to the left of $p_a = \dfrac{1}{\mu}$, the price of (A) in terms of (B) tends toward the equilibrium price p_a'', which is the abscissa of the point A''; while to the right of p_a it tends toward the price p_a', which is the abscissa of the point A'.

This eventuality corresponds, as is easily seen, to the case in which it happens, because of the nature of the two commodities, that a relatively large quantity of (A), which is demanded at a relatively low price of (A) in terms of (B), can have the same value as a relatively small quantity of (B) demanded at a relatively high price of (B) in terms of (A), and at the same time that a relatively small quantity of (A), which is demanded at a relatively high price of (A) in terms of (B), can have the same value as a relatively large quantity of (B) demanded at a relatively low price of (B) in terms of (A). Then, according to whether the pricing starts at a low price of (A) in terms of (B) corresponding to a high price of (B) in terms of (A), or at a low price of (B) in terms of (A) corresponding to a high price of (A) in terms of (B), it will eventuate in the first or the second of the two equilibria. We are forced to recognize that eventuality as being theoretically possible for two commodities that are exchanged for each other; we will see later if it is still possible for several commodities that are exchanged for one another with the intervention of money.

69. Thus far we have assumed, in all our discussion, that the demand curves A_dA_p, B_dB_p, and $B'_dB'_p$ intersect both the coordinate axes. Without departing from the given conditions of our general hypothesis, it is appropriate to examine the extreme case in which the demand curves, by coinciding with the hyperbola of the existing quantity, would be asymptotic to these axes.

For example, if A_dA_p coincided with the hyperbola $D_a p_a = Q_b$, all of the commodity (B) being offered at each price, the equation

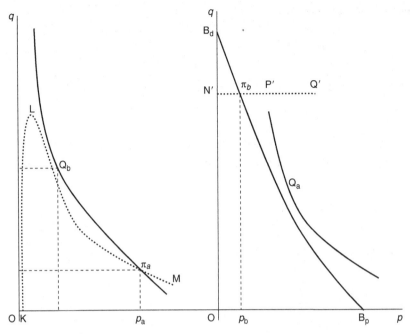

Fig. 9

$$F_a(p_a) = F_b\left(\frac{1}{p_a}\right)\frac{1}{p_a}$$

would become

$$Q_b \frac{1}{p_a} = F_b\left(\frac{1}{p_a}\right)\frac{1}{p_a},$$

which represents the intersection at π_a of the curve passing through the point Q_b and the curve KLM (Fig. 9). I am abstracting from the solution given by the equation $\dfrac{1}{p_a} = 0$ or $p_a = \infty$.

The equation

$$F_a\left(\frac{1}{p_b}\right)\frac{1}{p_b} = F_b(p_b)$$

would then become

$$Q_b = F_b(p_b),$$

which represents the intersection at π_b of the curve $B_d B_p$ and a straight line $N'P'Q'$ lying parallel to the price axis at a distance $\overline{ON'} = Q_b$.

70. Finally, if all of both commodities were offered at each possible price, we would have at the same time

$$Q_b \frac{1}{p_a} = Q_a, \qquad Q_b = Q_a \frac{1}{p_b}$$

which would give, for the respective values of p_a and p_b,

$$p_a = \frac{Q_b}{Q_a}, \qquad p_b = \frac{Q_a}{Q_b}.$$

Thus, in this last case, the two commodities would be exchanged for each other purely and simply in the inverse ratio of the existing quantities; that is to say, the exchange would take place according to the equation

$$Q_a v_a = Q_b v_b.$$

And, moreover, as is very easily seen, that equality of the existing quantities and the quantities exchanged would then represent the equality of the effective supply and the demand for both the commodities.

LESSON 8

Utility or want curves. The theorem of
maximum satisfaction

SUMMARY: – Circumstance that determines the intercept on the quantity axis of the partial demand curves: *extensive utility*. Circumstance that determines their slope and intercept on the price axis: *intensive utility*. Influence of the *quantity possessed*. Hypothesis of a unit of measurement of utility or want. Construction of the curves of utility or want. They are curves of *effective utility* and of *rareté* as functions of the *quantity possessed*.

Exchange takes place in order to maximize satisfaction of wants. The exchange of a quantity o_b of (B) for a quantity d_a of (A), after which the ratio of the rareté of (A) to the rareté of (B) is equal to the price p_a, is advantageous. This exchange is more advantageous than any other exchange of two quantities smaller or greater than o_b and d_a. Hence, maximum satisfaction of wants occurs when the ratio of the raretés is equal to the price. Equation of the demand curve deduced from the condition of maximum satisfaction. The case of discontinuous want curves.

71. Our study of the nature of the fact of exchange up to this point makes possible the study of the cause of the fact of value in exchange. If it is true that prices or ratios of values result mathematically from demand curves, then to know the causes and primary conditions of the determination and variation of prices, it is necessary to study the causes and primary conditions of the establishment and variation of demand curves.

Let us, therefore, return to the partial demand curves,[i] and take, for example, the curve $a_{d,1}a_{p,1}$ (Fig. 10) or its equation $d_a = f_{a,1}(p_a)$

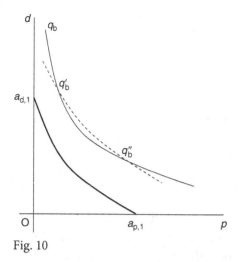

Fig. 10

($ 51), expressing respectively geometrically or algebraically the dispositions of holder (1) of (B) to buy (A); and let us first consider the circumstance that determines the position of the point $a_{d,1}$ where

the curve leaves the demand axis. The length $\overline{Oa_{d,1}}$ represents the quantity of (A) effectively demanded by that individual at a zero price; that is to say, it represents the quantity he would consume if the commodity were free. Now, upon what does this quantity generally depend? On the utility of the commodity, or at least on a certain kind of utility of the commodity that we will call *extensive* utility because this type of wealth satisfies wants that are more or less extensive or numerous, because more or fewer men experience them, or because those who experience them do so in a greater or lesser proportion, because, in a word, abstracting from any sacrifice that has to be made to obtain them, the commodity would be consumed in a greater or lesser quantity. This first circumstance is simple or absolute in the respect that the extensive utility of (A) influences only the demand curves of (A) and not the demand curves of (B), and, similarly, the extensive utility of (B) influences only the demand curves of (B) and not the demand curves of (A). Furthermore, extensive utility is a mathematical fact in that *the quantity demanded at a zero price* is a measurable quantity.

72. But extensive utility is not the whole of utility; it is only one of its constituent elements. There is another which reveals itself if we turn our attention to the circumstance that determines the slope of the curve $a_{d,1}a_{p,1}$, and consequently the position of the point $a_{p,1}$ where the curve ends up on the price axis. The slope of the curve is nothing other than the ratio of two quantities: the increase in price and the decrease in demand caused by that increase. Now, upon what does this ratio generally depend? It is again the utility of the commodity, but another sort of utility that we will call *intensive* utility because this type of wealth satisfies wants that are more or less intense or urgent, either because the wants exist, despite their dearness, in a more or less great number of men, or because they exist more or less in those who experience them, because, in a word, the greatness of the sacrifice that has to be made to obtain them has a greater or lesser influence upon the quantity of the commodity consumed. Unlike the first attribute of utility, this second circumstance is complex or relative in the respect that the slopes of the demand curves for (A) depend not only on the intensive utility of (A) but also on the intensive utility of (B), just as the slopes of the demand curves for (B) depend not only on the intensive utility of (B) but also on the intensive utility of (A). Thus the slope of the demand curves defined as *the limit of the ratio of a decrease of demand to the increase of the price*, which would be a mathematical circumstance very easy to determine, presents us with a more or less complex relationship between the intensive utility of the two commodities.

73. There is, moreover, another circumstance that also influences the slope of the curve $a_{d,1}a_{p,1}$ of the demand for (A): that is the quantity q_b of commodity (B) being in the possession of individual (1), who is a holder of this commodity. Generally, the partial demand curves are below the partial quantity hyperbolas, just like the curves of total demand are below the hyperbolas of total quantities. If, therefore, the partial quantity hyperbola changes while moving toward or away from the origin of the coordinate axes, the partial demand curve will vary in the same way, just as it would also do as a result of a variation

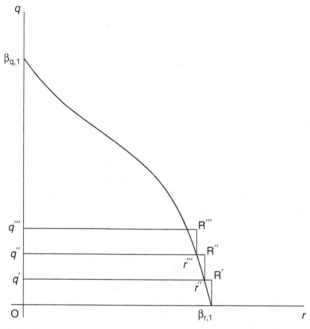

Fig. 11

of the intensive utilities. In both cases, the figure depicts this necessary behavior faithfully.

74. This analysis is incomplete; and it seems impossible, at first glance, to pursue it further, because of the fact that absolute intensive utility eludes us because it has no direct or measurable relationship to space or time, unlike extensive utility and the quantity of a commodity possessed. So be it! This difficulty is not insurmountable. Let us assume that the relationship exists, and we will be able to give an exact and mathematical account of the respective influences on prices of extensive utility, intensive utility, and the quantity possessed.

I therefore assume that there is a standard of measurement of wants or intensive utility, common not only to similar units of the same kind of wealth but also to different units of various kinds of wealth. Accordingly, let there be [Fig. 11] two coordinate axes, one vertical, Oq, and the other horizontal, Or. On the former, Oq, starting at the point O, I mark off the successive lengths, $\overline{Oq'}, \overline{q'q''}, \overline{q''q'''}, \ldots$, which represent the units of (B) that holder (1) would successively consume if he had those units at his disposition. But all these successive units have, for holder (1), an intensive utility that is decreasing after the first unit, namely the one that satisfies the most urgent want, until the least urgent want is satisfied, after which satiation is reached; and the question arises of how to state this decrease mathematically. If commodity (B) is naturally consumed in whole units, like pieces of furniture or articles of clothing, I mark off on the horizontal axis Or, and, on lines drawn parallel to this axis through the points q', q'', $\cdots$, the lengths $\overline{O\beta_{r,1}}, \overline{q'r''}, \overline{q''r'''}, \cdots$, which represent respectively the *intensive utilities* of each of the successive units consumed. I form the rectangles $Oq'R'\beta_{r,1}, q'q''R''r'', q''q'''R'''r''', \cdots$, and obtain the curve $\beta_{r,1}R'r''R''r'''R''' \cdots$. This curve is discontinuous. If, on the other hand, commodity (B) could be consumed in infinitely small amounts, like food, the intensive utility would diminish not only from one unit to the next but also from the first to the last fraction of each unit, and the discontinuous curve $\beta_{r,1}R'r''R''r'''R''' \cdots$ would change into the continuous curve $\beta_{r,1} r'r''' \cdots \beta_{q,1}$.[ii] Similarly, I could obtain the curve $\alpha_{r,1}\alpha_{q,1}$ for the commodity (A). In the case of continuity, as in the case of discontinuity, I assume that the intensive utilities are decreasing from the intensity of the utility of the first unit or fraction of a unit consumed down to the intensity of the utility of the last unit or fraction of a unit consumed.

The lengths $\overline{O\beta_{q,1}}$ and $\overline{O\alpha_{q,1}}$ (Fig. 12) represent the *extensive utilities* that the commodities (B) and (A) yield for holder (1), or the extent of the wants that holder (1) has for the commodities (B) and (A). The areas $O\beta_{q,1}\beta_{r,1}$ and $O\alpha_{q,1}\alpha_{r,1}$ represent the *virtual utilities* of the commodities (B) and (A) for the same holder, or the sum of the wants that the holder has, in extension and in intensity, for the same commodities. The curves $\alpha_{r,1}\alpha_{q,1}$ and $\beta_{r,1}\beta_{q,1}$ are therefore holder (1)'s *utility curves* or *want curves* for the commodities (A) and (B). But this is not all; in addition, they have a double character.

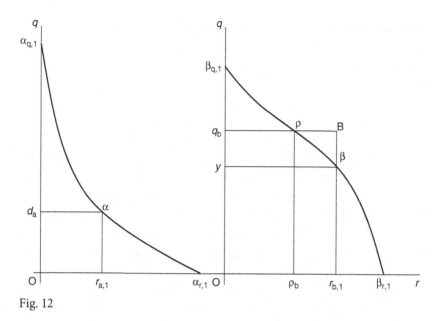

Fig. 12

75. In calling the sum total of wants satisfied, extensively and intensively, by a *quantity consumed* of a commodity its *effective utility*, the curve $\beta_{r,1}\beta_{q,1}$ would be the curve of effective utility as a function of the quantity of (B) consumed by our individual. Thus (Fig. 12), for a quantity q_b of (B) consumed represented by the length $\overline{Oq_b}$, the effective utility would be represented by the area $Oq_b\rho\beta_{r,1}$. And, in calling the intensity of the last want satisfied by any given *quantity consumed* of a commodity its *rareté*, the curve $\beta_{r,1}\beta_{q,1}$ would be the rareté curve for the same individual as a function of the quantity consumed of (B). Thus, if he consumes a quantity q_b of (B), represented by the length $\overline{Oq_b}$, the rareté would be ρ_b, represented by the length $q_b\rho = \overline{O\rho_b}$. The curve $\alpha_{r,1}\alpha_{q,1}$ would be, similarly, the curve of effective utility and of rareté, as a function of the quantity of (A) consumed. That is why I can also call the two axes of coordinates the *rareté axis* and the *quantity axis*. It must be stated, I repeat, that rareté increases as the quantity possessed decreases, and reciprocally.

Analytically, the raretés being given as functions of the quantities consumed by the equations $r = \varphi_{a,1}(q)$ and $r = \varphi_{b,1}(q)$, then the

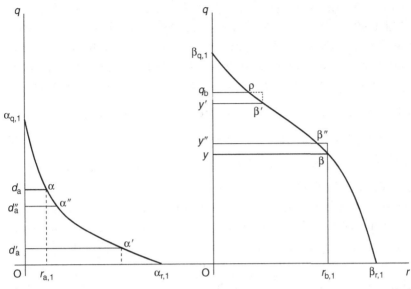

Fig. 13

effective utilities would be given by the definite integrals from 0 to of these functions: $\int_0^q \varphi_{a,1}(q)dq$ and $\int_0^q \varphi_{b,1}(q)dq$.

All that being specified, the extensive and intensive utility of commodity (A) for holder (1) of (B) being represented geometrically by the continuous curve $\alpha_{r,1}\alpha_{q,1}$, and algebraically by the equation of this curve $r = \varphi_{a,1}(q)$; the extensive and intensive utility of commodity (B) for this same holder being represented geometrically by the continuous curve $\beta_{r,1}\beta_{q,1}$ and algebraically by the equation of this curve, $r = \varphi_{b,1}(q)$; moreover, the quantity q_b, represented by the length $\overline{Oq_b}$, being the initial quantity of (B) that holder (1) possesses, let us see if we can specify what his demand for (A) will be at any given price.

76. Because of the way in which our want curves are established and the characteristics we have recognized that they have in constructing them, it follows that if holder (1) reserved all of his q_b units of (B) for his own consumption, he would satisfy a sum total of wants

represented by the area $Oq_b\rho\beta_{r,1}$. This is not, however, what that individual will generally do, because, generally, he will be able to satisfy a larger sum total of wants by consuming only part of his commodity and by exchanging the surplus for a certain quantity of (A) at the current price. If, for example [Fig. 13], at a price p_a of (A) in terms of (B) he keeps only y units of (B) represented by $\overline{Oy}$, and exchanges the surplus $o_b = q_b - y$, represented by $\overline{yq_b}$ for d_a units of (A), represented by $\overline{Od_a}$, he will be able to satisfy a sum total of wants represented by the two areas, $Oy\beta\beta_{r,1}$ and $Od_a\alpha\alpha_{r,1}$, a sum that could be greater than the previous one. Assuming that he undertakes the exchange in such a way as to satisfy the greatest possible sum total of wants, it is certain that, p_a being given, d_a is determined by the condition that the sum of the two areas $Oy\beta\beta_{r,1}$ and $Od_a\alpha\alpha_{r,1}$ is a maximum. What is that condition? I say that it is that the ratio of the intensities $r_{a,1}$ and $r_{b,1}$ of the last wants satisfied by the quantities d_a and y, or of the raretés after the exchange, is equal to the price p_a.

77. We assume that this condition is fulfilled; then we have the two equations

$$o_b = q_b - y = d_a p_a,$$

$$r_{a,1} = p_a r_{b,1}.$$

Eliminating p_a, we obtain

$$d_a r_{a,1} = o_b r_{b,1}$$

or, replacing d_a, o_b, $r_{a,1}$ and $r_{b,1}$ by the lengths by which they are represented in Fig. 13, namely $\overline{Od_a}$, $\overline{q_b y}$, $\overline{d_a \alpha}$ and $\overline{y\beta}$, we obtain

$$\overline{Od_a} \times \overline{d_a \alpha} = \overline{q_b y} \times \overline{y\beta}.$$

Thus the areas of the two rectangles $Od_a\alpha r_{a,1}$ and $yq_b B\beta$ are equal.[iii] But, by virtue of the nature of the curves $\alpha_{r,1}\alpha_{q,1}$ and $\beta_{r,1}\beta_{q,1}$ we have, on the one hand

$$\text{area Od}_a \alpha \alpha_{r,1} > \overline{\text{Od}_a} \times \overline{\text{d}_a \alpha}$$

and on the other hand,

$$\overline{q_b y} \times \overline{y \beta} > \text{area } y q_b \rho \beta.$$

Therefore, we have

$$\text{area Od}_a \alpha \alpha_{r,1} > \text{area } y q_b \rho \beta.$$

Thus the exchange of a quantity o_b of (B) for a quantity d_a of (A) is advantageous for our holder of (B), because the area of the satisfaction he acquires thereby is greater than the area of satisfaction he relinquishes. This, however, is not sufficient, and it must now be shown that that exchange is more advantageous for our holder than any other exchange of a quantity of (B) smaller or greater than o_b in return for a quantity of (A) smaller or greater than d_a.

78. To do this, let us represent the entire exchange that has been made of o_b of (B) for d_a of (A) as being composed of s successive equal partial exchanges. In selling successively s times $\frac{o_b}{s}$ of (B), and buying successively s times $\frac{d_a}{s}$ of (A), in accordance with the equation of exchange

$$\frac{o_b}{s} = \frac{d_a}{s} p_a,$$

our individual has decreased the rareté of (A) and increased the rareté of (B). It is in this way that the ratio of these raretés, which started out by being higher than the price p_a, becomes equal to this price. Now, I say, first, that under these conditions all the partial exchanges have been advantageous, although less and less advantageous from the first to the sth.

Indeed, let $\overline{\text{Od}_a'}$ and $\overline{q_b y'}$ be two lengths measured along Od_a and $q_b y$ respectively, the first above the point O, the other below the point

q_b, the former representing the quantity $\dfrac{d_a}{s}$ of (A), the latter representing the quantity $\dfrac{o_b}{s}$ of (B), these being the quantities exchanged in the first partial exchange. This first exchange having been made, the ratio of the decreased raretés is still, by hypothesis, greater than the price, and we have, calling these raretés r_a and r_b,

$$r_a > p_a r_b,$$

which gives, by virtue of the preceding equation,

$$\frac{d_a}{s} r_a > \frac{o_b}{s} r_b,$$

that is, in replacing $\dfrac{d_a}{s}$, $\dfrac{o_b}{s}$, r_a, and r_b by the lengths $\overline{Od_a'}$, $\overline{q_b y'}$, $\overline{d_a' \alpha'}$, and $\overline{y'\beta'}$, which represent them geometrically,

$$\overline{Od_a'} \times \overline{d_a' \alpha'} > \overline{q_b y'} \times \overline{y'\beta'}.$$

But, by virtue of the want curves we have, on the one hand,

$$\text{area } Od_a' \alpha' \, \alpha_{r,1} > \overline{Od_a'} \times \overline{d_a' \alpha'},$$

and on the other hand,

$$\overline{q_b y'} \times \overline{y'\beta'} > \text{area } y' q_b \rho \beta'.$$

We therefore have a fortiori

$$\text{area } Od_a' \alpha' \alpha_{r,1} > y' q_b \rho \beta'.$$

Therefore, the first exchange of $\frac{o_b}{s}$ of (B) for $\frac{d_a}{s}$ of (A) has been advantageous. It can be shown similarly that the following $s - 2$ exchanges, successively effectuated, have been advantageous, because the ratio of the raretés after each exchange, though diminishing, was still, by hypothesis, greater than the price. It is, for example, evident that the advantage diminishes with the related diminution of the ratios of the raretés.

Now let the length $\overline{d_a d_a''}$ be drawn directly below the point d_a and the length $\overline{yy''}$ be drawn directly above the point y. These represent the same quantities exchanged in the last partial exchange, $\frac{d_a}{s}$ of (A) and $\frac{o_b}{s}$ of (B). This last exchange having been made, the ratio of the smaller raretés is, by hypothesis, equal to the price, and we have

$$r_{a,1} = p_a r_{b,1},$$

which, by virtue of the equation of exchange, gives

$$\frac{d_a}{s} r_{a,1} = \frac{o_b}{s} r_{b,1},$$

that is to say, replacing $\frac{d_a}{s}$, $\frac{o_b}{s}$, $r_{a,1}$, and $r_{b,1}$ by the lengths $\overline{d_a d_a''}$, $\overline{yy''}$, $\overline{d_a \alpha}$, and $\overline{y\beta}$ that represent them, we obtain

$$\overline{d_a d_a''} \times \overline{d_a \alpha} = \overline{yy''} \times \overline{y\beta}.$$

But, by virtue of the nature of the want curves, we have, on the one hand,

$$\text{area } d_a'' d_a \alpha \alpha'' > \overline{d_a d_a''} \times \overline{d_a \alpha}$$

and on the other hand,

$$\overline{yy''} \times \overline{y\beta} > \text{area } yy''\beta''\beta.$$

We therefore have

$$\text{area } d_a''d_a\alpha\alpha'' > \text{area } yy''\beta''\beta.$$

Thus, the last exchange of $\dfrac{o_b}{s}$ of (B) for $\dfrac{d_a}{s}$ of (A) has still been advantageous. Since, moreover, we can assume s to be as large as we wish, it is therefore certain that all of the partial exchanges, without exception, including the last one however small it may be, have been advantageous, although less and less advantageous from the first to the sth exchange. Consequently, holder (1) of (B) should not supply a quantity of (B) less than o_b nor demand a quantity of (A) less than d_a.

79. We could demonstrate in the same way that there would not be supplied a quantity of (B) greater than o_b or demanded a quantity of (A) greater than d_a, because all the partial exchanges without exception, including the first, however small it may be, that would be made in excess of that limit would be disadvantageous, and increasingly disadvantageous. But this demonstration logically takes its place within the one we have just made. In fact, in continuing to diminish the rareté of (A) and to increase the rareté of (B) by the exchange of any quantity of (B) for a quantity of (A) of equal value, after the limit constituted by the equality of the ratio of the raretés with the price p_a has been reached, we arrive at the inequality

$$r_a < p_a r_b,$$

which can be put into the form

$$r_b > p_b r_a.$$

Now, in virtue of the demonstration that has been presented, it is certain that, in these conditions, maximum satisfaction would be more closely approached by exchanging additional quantities of (A) for additional quantities of (B), until the limit

$$r_{b,1} = p_b r_{a,1}$$

has been attained; that is,

$$r_{a,1} = p_a r_{b,1}.$$

80. o_b of (B) and d_a of (A), neither more nor less, will be the quantities of (B) and of (A) respectively that will be supplied and demanded by holder (1) at the price p_a of (A) in terms of (B), if these quantities are the ones for which the relation $r_{a,1} = p_a r_{b,1}$ holds good.

In general: *Given two commodities in a market, the maximum satisfaction of wants, or maximum effective utility, is achieved, for each holder, when the ratio of the intensities of the last wants satisfied, or the ratio of their raretés, is equal to the price. Until this equality has been reached, it is advantageous for the exchanger to sell the commodity the rareté of which is smaller than its price multiplied by the rareté of the other commodity, and to buy the other commodity the rareté of which is greater than its price multiplied by the rareté of the first.*

It can therefore be advantageous for the exchanger to offer all of one of the two commodities that he holds and not to demand any of the other. We will return to this matter presently.

81. If, in the equation

$$r_{a,1} = p_a r_{b,1},$$

we replace $r_{a,1}$ and $r_{b,1}$ by their values, then we get

$$\varphi_{a,1}(d_a) = p_a \varphi_{b,1}(y) = p_a \varphi_{b,1}(q_b - o_a) = p_a \varphi_{b,1}(q_b - d_a p_a).$$

That equation gives d_a as a function of p_a. If we assume the equation to be solved for the first of the two variables, the equation takes the form

$$d_a = f_{a,1}(p_a).$$

This is precisely the equation of curve $a_{d,1}a_{p,1}$ of holder (1)'s demand for (A) in exchange for (B). That equation would therefore be mathematically determinable if the equations $r = \varphi_{a,1}(q)$ and $r = \varphi_{b,1}(q)$ were themselves determinable; it is because they are not determinable that the equation $d_a = f_{a,1}(p_a)$ is empirical.

That is the way to solve this problem: *Given two commodities (A) and (B) and the utility or want curves of each exchanger for these two commodities, or the equations for these curves, and given the initial stock that each exchanger possesses, determine their demand curves, or their equations.* It is instructive to present the formula of this solution in accordance with usual notation of the infinitesimal calculus.

$\varphi_{a,1}(q)$ and $\varphi_{b,1}(q)$ being the decreasing raretés of (A) and (B) for holder (1) of (B) as a function of the quantities consumed, the definite integrals $\int_0^q \varphi_{a,1}(q)dq$ and $\int_0^q \varphi_{a,1}(q)dq$ are, as we have noted (§ 75), the *effective utilities* of those commodities for that holder as a function of the same commodities consumed. After the exchange of $o_b = d_a p_a$ of (B) for d_a of (A), at a price p_a of (A) in terms of (B); that is to say, with the quantities d_a of (A) and $q_b - o_b = q_b - d_a p_a$ of (B), the total effective utility of the two commodities of the holder in question is

$$\int_0^{d_a} \varphi_{a,1}(q)dq + \int_0^{q_b - d_a p_a} \varphi_{b,1}(q)dq.$$

And this total effective utility attains its maximum when its derivative with respect to d_a is zero, that is, when

$$\varphi_{a,1}(d_a) - p_a \varphi_{b,1}(q_b - d_a p_a) = 0,$$

or when

$$\varphi_{a,1}(d_a) = p_a \varphi_{b,1}(q_b - d_a p_a).^{\text{iv}}$$

82. Our demonstration assumes that the want curves are continuous; it is appropriate to examine the cases in which, among those curves, there are curves that are discontinuous. To be precise, there are three of these cases: one is the exchange of a commodity with a continuous curve for a commodity with a discontinuous curve; the second is the exchange of a commodity with a discontinuous curve for a commodity with a continuous curve; and the third is that of a commodity with a discontinuous curve for a commodity with a discontinuous curve. But, as we will see later, inasmuch as we choose a commodity to whose value we relate the values of all the others and with which all the others are purchased, and that can and must have a continuous want curve, it is permissible to restrict ourselves to the first case.

As before, let $\beta_{r,1}\beta_{q,1}$ (Fig. 14) be the utility curve of (B) for the holder (1) of (B), and q_b the quantity of (B) that he owns. And let a step-wise curve passing through the points **a** and **a'''** be the utility curve of (A) for that exchanger. The commodity (A) is purchased only in whole units, and p_a being its price in (B), the commodity (B) is sold only in quantities equal to p_a. If the lengths $\overline{d_a d_a''}$ and $\overline{d_a d_a'''}$ represent the last unit bought and the first unit not bought of (A), and if the lengths $\overline{yy''}$ and $\overline{yy'''}$ represent the last quantity sold and the first quantity not sold of (B), when the exchanger has arrived at maximum satisfaction, two inequalities will obtain: area

$$yy''\beta''\beta < \overline{d_a a}^{\text{v}}$$

and

$$\text{area} \, yy'''\beta'''\beta > \overline{d_a''' a'''}.$$

Designating by m'' and m''' two lengths, the first intermediate between $\overline{y\beta}$ and $\overline{y''\beta''}$, the other between $\overline{y\beta}$ and $\overline{y''\beta''}$, such that in multiplying them by $\overline{yy''} = \overline{yy'''} = p_a$ we obtain two areas $yy''\beta''\beta$ and $yy'''\beta'''\beta$, which will be the average intensities of utility of the last quantity sold and of the first quantity unsold of (B); we can set forth

Theory of exchange

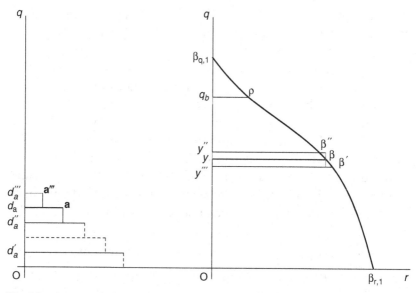

Fig. 14

the two inequalities, which, taken together, determine the demand d_a for (A), in the form

$$\overline{d_a a} = p_a m'' + \varepsilon'',$$

$$\overline{d_a''' a} = p_a m''' - \varepsilon'''.$$

From these two equations, it is easy to obtain

$$\frac{\overline{d_a a} + \overline{d_a''' a}}{m'' + m'''} = p_a + \frac{\varepsilon'' - \varepsilon'''}{m'' + m'''}.$$

Now, $m'' + m'''$ is a magnitude very close to $2\overline{y}\beta$, and $\dfrac{\varepsilon'' - \varepsilon'''}{m'' + m'''}$ is a fairly small magnitude. It therefore does not take much for it to be true that

$$\frac{\overline{d_a a} + \overline{d_a''' a'''}}{2} = p_a.$$

Thus, in the case of the exchange of a commodity that has a want curve that is continuous for a commodity that has a want curve that is discontinuous, when maximum satisfaction has been attained, what is (at least approximately) equal to the price is not the ratio of the intensities of the last wants satisfied of the two commodities, but *the ratio of the average of the intensities of the last want satisfied and of the first want not satisfied of the commodity that is bought to the intensity of the last want satisfied of the commodity that is sold* is (at least approximately) *equal to the price*.

We said approximately; because not only is it possible that the product $p_a \times \overline{y\beta}$ of the price of (A) in terms of (B) by the intensity of the last want satisfied of (B) is not equal to the average of the intensities of the last want satisfied and of the first want unsatisfied of (A), but it can even be greater or lesser than each of those two quantities. In fact, it is necessarily true that

$$\text{area } yy''\beta''\beta < p_a \times \overline{y\beta}$$

and

$$\overline{d_a a} > \text{area } yy''\beta''\beta;$$

but it is not necessarily true that

$$\overline{d_a a} > p_a \times \overline{y\beta}$$

and if, on the contrary,

$$\overline{d_a a} < p_a \times \overline{y\beta}$$

then $\overline{d_a a}$ and $\overline{d_a'''a'''}$, which is $< \overline{d_a a}$, will both be less than $p_a \times \overline{y\beta}$. Similarly, it is necessarily true that

$$\text{area } yy'''\beta'''\beta < p_a \times \overline{y\beta}$$

and that

$$\overline{d_a'''a'''} < \text{area } yy'''\beta'''\beta;$$

but it is not necessarily true that

$$\overline{d_a'''a'''} < p_a \times \overline{y\beta};$$

and if, on the contrary,

$$\overline{d_a'''a'''} > p_a \times \overline{y\beta},$$

then $\overline{d_a'''a'''}$ and $\overline{d_a a}$, which is $> \overline{d_a'''a'''}$, will both be greater than $p_a \times \overline{y\beta}$.

83. Let us consider again the two inequalities

$$\text{area } yy''\beta''\beta < \overline{d_a a}$$

$$\text{area } yy'''\beta'''\beta > \overline{d_a'''a'''}.$$

When p_a decreases, the left-hand sides of these inequalities decrease. The first inequality is not changed; but there comes a point at which the sign of the second inequality changes and d_a increases by at least one unit. When p_a increases, the two first members of the inequalities increase. The second inequality is not changed, but there comes a point at which the sign of the first inequality changes and d_a decreases by at least one unit. The demand curve for (A) is thus both descending and discontinuous.

Analytically, any price p_a of (A) in terms of (B) being cried, according as our individual demands 1, 2, $\cdots$ units of (A) corresponding to wants with intensities $r_1, r_2, \cdots$, thereby obtaining effective utilities of (A) measured by the same magnitudes $r_1, r_2, \cdots,$ will keep the quantities $q_b - p_a,\ q_b - 2p_a,\ \cdots$ of (B) and give up the effective utilities of (B) that are measured by the numerical integrals

$$\int_{q_b - p_a}^{q_b} \varphi_{b,1}(q) dq,\ \int_{q_b - 2p_a}^{q_b - p_a} \varphi_{b,1}(q) dq,\ \cdots.$$ And the demand d_a that will yield

maximum satisfaction will be determined by these two inequalities taken together:

$$\int_{q_b - d_a p_a}^{q_b - (d_a - 1) p_a} \varphi_{b,1}(q) dq < r_{d_a},$$

$$\int_{q_b - (d_{a+1}) p_a}^{q_b - d_a p_a} \varphi_{b,1}(q) dq < r_{d_a + 1}.$$

That is how d_a could be determined mathematically for all values of p_a, and it would be possible to construct the descending and discontinuous demand curve for (A) in terms of (B) as a function of the price.

Notes

i In modern economic language, we use the terms 'individual demand' and 'market demand', but Walras used the terms 'demande partielle' and 'demande totale'. Properly translated, those expressions are obviously 'partial demand' and 'total demand'. Walras's 'total demand' is the demands of all the traders in a specific market aggregated together, and, of course, must not be confused with an economy-wide aggregate curve used in modern macroeconomics.

ii Walras's use of the words 'discontinuous' and 'continuous' in the last two sentences is confusing. He means to say that the 'step function' $\beta_{r,1}$ R'r"R'"r"R''' $\cdots$ changes into the 'smooth function' $\beta_{r,1}$ r"r''' $\cdots \beta_{r,1}$. In fact, in the latter case, he certainly had in mind the notion of a differentiable function.

iii Walras did not indicate the point B in Fig. 13, but in Fig. 12 it is clear which point is intended.

iv It was only in the fourth edition that Walras continued at this place with the examination of the second derivative of the above equation, namely

$$\varphi'_{a,1}(d_a) + p_a^2 \varphi'_{b,1}(q_b - d_a p_a).$$

This second derivative is negative because the derivatives of the functions φ are assumed to be negative.

v In fact, this is a comparison of an area with a length, a procedure repeated in the equations below. Walras wants to say that the area in the left-hand member is less than the area of the rectangle with $\overline{d_a a}$ as horizontal side and $\overline{d_a d''_a}$ as vertical side. The length of the latter is 1.

LESSON 9

Discussion of demand curves. General formula for the mathematical solution of the problem of exchange of two commodities for each other

SUMMARY: – Demand at a zero price, demand then being equal to the extensive utility. Price at which there is no demand for (A). Price at which the supply of (B) is equal to the quantity possessed. Condition of supply equal to the quantity possessed: intersections of the quantity possessed and the demand curve; the hyperbola is the demand curve between the points of intersection. Decrease of the quantity possessed. Increase.

The general case is that of a holder of both commodities. Two equations or curves of partial effective demand. The equation or curve of demand for each commodity is also the equation or curve of supply of the same commodity as a function of the price. General system of equations of the dispositions to buy or sell commodities in the case of the exchange of two commodities for each other; solution of the equations.

84. Since the equation of partial demand

$$d_a = f_{a,1}(p_a)$$

is nothing other than the equation

$$\varphi_{a,1}(d_a) = p_a \varphi_{b,1}(q_b - d_a p_a),$$

which is assumed to be solved with respect to d_a, we can discuss it as it appears in the latter form.

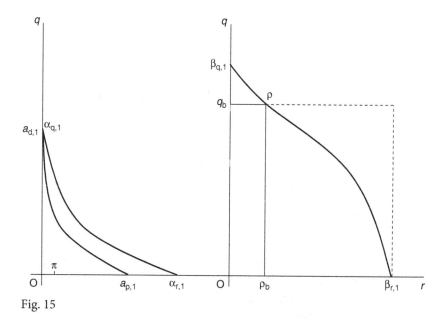

Fig. 15

First let $p_a = 0$; the equation then reduces to

$$\varphi_{a,1}(d_a) = 0$$

the root of which is $d_a = \alpha_{q,1} = \overline{Oa_{d,1}}$ [Fig. 15].

Therefore: – *Given two commodities in a market, when the price of one of them is zero, the quantity of that commodity demanded by each holder of the other will equal the quantity necessary for the satisfaction of all his wants for it, or, to the extensive utility.*

This must be the case (§ 71). The curve $a_{d,1}a_{p,1}$ starts at the point $\alpha_{q,1}$.

85. Let us now assume that in the demand equation $d_a = 0$; we then obtain

$$\varphi_{a,1}(0) = p_a\varphi_{b,1}(q_b),$$

the root of which equation is

$$p_a = \frac{\varphi_{a,1}(0)}{\varphi_{b,1}(q_b)} = \frac{\alpha_{r,1}}{\rho_b} = \overline{\mathrm{Oa}}_{p,1}.$$

Therefore: – *The quantity demanded of one of the two commodities by a holder of the other commodity becomes zero when the price of the commodity demanded is equal to or greater than the ratio of the intensity of his maximum want for it to the intensity of the last want that can be satisfied by the quantity possessed of the commodity supplied.*

This, too, must be the case, since now the last amount of (B) that holder (1) consumes, for example $\frac{o_b}{s}$, yields him the satisfaction

$\frac{o_b}{s}\rho_b$, while this same amount of (B), if exchanged for $\frac{d_a}{s}$ of (A) at

the price p_a, would yield him only the satisfaction

$$\frac{d_a}{s} = \frac{o_b}{s}\frac{\alpha_{r,1}}{p_a},$$

which is equal to or less than $\frac{o_b}{s}\rho_b$.

86. After having noted the price condition that is necessary in order that our holder (1) of (B) does not demand any of (A), let us see how to express the price condition that is necessary for our holder not to retain any of (B). The equation must be stated that

$$\varphi_{a,1}(d_a) = p_a\varphi_{b,1}(q_b - d_a p_a), \qquad [1]$$

$$d_a p_a = q_b. \qquad [2]$$

It then becomes

$$\varphi_{a,1}(d_a) = p_a\varphi_{b,1}(0), \qquad [3]$$

the root of which is $p_a = \dfrac{\varphi_{a,1}(d_a)}{\varphi_{b,1}(0)} = \dfrac{\rho_a}{\beta_{r,1}}.$

Therefore: – *The quantity of one of the two commodities supplied by a holder of that commodity is equal to the quantity of it that he possesses when the price of the commodity he demands in exchange is equal to or less than the ratio of the intensity of the last want that can be satisfied by that commodity to the intensity of the maximum want satisfied by the commodity supplied.*

This is, again, what must be the case because the first amount of (B) consumed by holder (1), for example, $\dfrac{O_b}{s}$, yields him no more than

$\dfrac{O_b}{s}\beta_{r,1}$ in satisfaction, whereas this same batch of (B), exchanged

for $\dfrac{d_a}{s}$ of (A) at the price p_a, would yield him a satisfaction $\dfrac{d_a}{s}\,p_a =$

$\dfrac{O_b}{s}\dfrac{p_a}{p_a}$ equal to or greater than $\dfrac{O_b}{s}\beta_{r,1}$.

87. In multiplying the two equations [2] and [3], member for member, and dividing both sides by p_a so as to eliminate the latter quantity, we obtain

$$d_a\varphi_{a,1}(d_a)=q_b\varphi_{b,1}(0),$$

or, replacing q_b, and $\varphi_{b,1}(0)$ by the lengths which represent them [in Fig. 15], namely $\overline{Oq_b}$ and $\overline{O\beta_{r,1}}$, we obtain

$$d_a\varphi_{a,1}(d_a)=\overline{Oq_b}\times\overline{O\beta_{r,1}}.$$

This equation is an equation of condition that can be expressed in these terms: – *In order that the supply of one of the two commodities can equal the quantity possessed of that commodity, it is necessary that there can be inscribed within the want curve of the commodity to be demanded a rectangle with an area equal to the area of a rectangle whose height is the quantity possessed of the commodity to be supplied and whose base is the intensity of the maximum want for that commodity.*

Now, this condition is not always fulfilled; notably, it is not fulfilled in our example. We could, however, replace that condition with another. The system of equations [1] and [2] represents the intersection of the hyperbola of the quantity possessed of (B) $d_a p_a = q_b$, with the partial demand curve for (A), $d_a = f_{a,1}(p_a)$. These two curves do not always meet; notably, they do not meet in the particular case of our holder.

88. This observation leads to another very important one. Assume that the equation of condition was satisfied and that the demand curve [the dashed curve in Fig. 10] met the hyperbola of the quantity possessed at the points q_b' and q_b''. The supply of (B) would be equal to the quantity possessed, q_b, at prices represented by the abscissas of the points q_b' and q_b''. It would also be equal at the intermediate prices. It seems, according to the combination of the equations or the curves, that, at the intermediate prices the supply of (B) must have been greater than q_b, the quantity possessed of (B). But since a holder cannot supply more than the quantity he has, it is obviously necessary to introduce the restriction that $q_b - d_a p_a$ cannot be a negative quantity, which can be done by stating the condition in these terms: – *In order that the supply of one of the two commodities be equal to the quantity possessed, the hyperbola of the quantity possessed and the demand curve of the other commodity must meet. Between the points of intersection, the hyperbola of the quantity possessed is the demand curve.*

89. If, the curves $\alpha_{r,1}\alpha_{q,1}$ and $\beta_{r,1}\beta_{q,1}$ (Fig. 15) being invariant, q_b happens to decrease, ρ_b increases, and consequently $\dfrac{\alpha_{r,1}}{\rho_b} = \overline{Oa_{p,1}}$

decreases. When $q_b = 0$, then $\rho_b = \beta_r$, and the ratio $\dfrac{\alpha_{r,1}}{\rho_b}$ becomes

identical with $\dfrac{\alpha_{r,1}}{\beta_{r,1}} = \overline{O\pi}$. Then the demand curve $a_{d,1}a_{p,1}$ coincides

with the segments $a_{d,1}O\pi$ of the coordinate axes.

Therefore: – *The utility of the two commodities being invariant for a holder of one of them, if the quantity possessed of that commodity happens to decrease, the point of intersection of the demand curve for the other commodity and the price axis approaches the origin of the* coordinate axes. When the quantity possessed is zero, the demand curve coincides with the part of the coordinate axes formed, on the demand axis, by the extensive utility of the commodity that will be demanded, and, on the price axis, by a length equal to the ratio of the maximum intensities of wants of the two commodities that will be demanded and supplied.

90. But contrariwise, if q_b happens to increase, ρ_b decreases and consequently $\dfrac{\alpha_{r,1}}{\rho_b} = \overline{Oa_{p,1}}$ increases. When $q_b = \beta_{q,1}$, then $\beta_b = 0$, and the ratio $\dfrac{\alpha_{r,1}}{\rho_b}$ becomes infinitely great. The distance of the point $a_{p,1}$ from the point O then becomes infinite.

　　Therefore: – *The utility of the two commodities being invariant for a holder of one of them, if the quantity possessed of that commodity happens to increase, the point of intersection of the demand curve for the first commodity and the price axis moves away from the origin of the coordinate axes. As soon as the quantity possessed becomes equal to its extensive utility, the demand curve becomes asymptotic to the price axis.*

　　It is perfectly clear that this must be the case. It can be seen, moreover, how truly we were right not to say anything prematurely about the form of the total demand curves (§ 55). We can now affirm that they always intersect the demand axis, no commodity having an infinite total extensive utility. But with respect to their being asymptotic to the price axis, it must be considered an ordinary and frequent fact, since it occurs as soon as, among the holders of a commodity, a single one of them owns a sufficient quantity of it to satisfy all his wants for it. It follows that total supply curves[i] most often start at the origin.

91. We have always assumed up to this point that all our exchangers were holders of only one commodity, either commodity (A) or commodity (B). It is necessary, however, to take account of the case in which an individual is a holder of the two commodities (A) and (B), and to express mathematically that individual's dispositions to trade. It is all the more necessary to do so in order to take full account of the possibilities, because the second case is the general case, from which

the first case is derived by assuming that one of the two quantities possessed is zero. We did not introduce it at the beginning of our study because of the complication that that would have introduced into our analysis, and we wanted to avoid consideration of the special case. But the theorem of maximum satisfaction permits us now to treat it in a simple and easy fashion.

Let us assume, therefore, that holder (1) of (B), having the same wants for (A) and (B) as before expressed by the two equations $r = \varphi_{a,1}(q)$ and $r = \varphi_{b,1}(q)$ of the want curves $\alpha_{r,1}\alpha_{q,1}$ and $\beta_{r,1}\beta_{q,1}$, instead of coming to the market with no (A) and a quantity q_b of (B) represented by $\overline{Oq_b}$ [Fig. 15], comes with a quantity $q_{a,1}$ of (A) represented by $\overline{Oq_{a,1}}$, and a quantity $q_{b,1}$ of (B) represented by $\overline{Oq_{b,1}}$ [Fig. 16]; and we will see how to express his demand for (B) and his demand for (A) as functions of the prices p_b and p_a.

If, at a price p_b of (B) in terms of (A), represented by the length $\overline{q_{b,1}p_b}$, he demands a quantity d_b of (B), represented by the length $\overline{q_{b,1}d_b}$, he will have to supply a quantity o_a of (A), represented by the length $\overline{q_{a,1}o_a}$, such that there obtains, between p_b, d_b, and o_a, the equation

$$o_a = d_b p_b.$$

Then, the intensity of the last want satisfied by (B) being r_b, represented by the length $\overline{d_b\beta}$, and the intensity of the last want satisfied by (A) being r_a, represented by the length $\overline{o_a\alpha}$, we have, by virtue of the theorem of maximum satisfaction (§ 80),

$$r_b = p_b r_a,$$

or, in replacing r_b and r_a by their values,

$$\varphi_{b,1}(q_{b,1} + d_b) = p_b\varphi_{a,1}(q_{a,1} - o_a) = p_b\varphi_{b,1}(q_{a,1} - d_b p_b), \qquad [1]$$

the equation of the demand curve of (B), $b_{d,1}b_{p,1}$, as a function of the price of (B) in terms of (A), referred to the axes $q_{b,1}q$ and $q_{b,1}p$.

Likewise, if, at a price p_a of (A) in terms of (B), our man demands a quantity d_a of (A), he will have to supply a quantity o_b of (B) such that there obtains, between p_a, d_a, and o_b, the equation

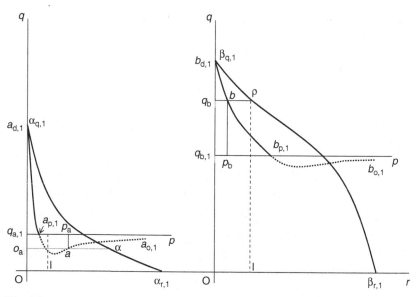

Fig. 16

$$o_b = d_a p_a.$$

Then, the intensity of the last want satisfied by (A) being r_a, and the intensity of the last want satisfied by (B) being r_b, we have

$$\varphi_{a,1}\left(q_{a,1}+d_a\right)= p_a\varphi_{b,1}\left(q_{b,1}-o_b\right)= p_a\varphi_{b,1}\left(q_{b,1}-d_a p_a\right), \qquad [2]$$

the equation of the demand curve of (A), $a_{d,1}a_{p,1}$, as a function of the price of (A) in terms of (B), referred to the axes $q_{a,1}q$ and $q_{a,1}p$.

92. The discussion of the two equations [1] and [2] for the various cases of demand at a zero price, of the price at which demand is zero, of when the quantity supplied equals the quantity possessed, of the decrease or increase of the quantities possessed, would be completely analogous to the preceding discussion. Therefore I will not present such a discussion, except regarding a special point that it is essential to establish.

If, in equation [1], $d_b = 0$, that equation becomes

$$\varphi_{b,1}\left(q_{b,1}\right)= p_b\varphi_{a,1}\left(q_{a,1}\right).$$

Since it is always true that $p_a p_b = 1$, that equation can be written in the form

$$\varphi_{a,1}(q_{a,1}) = p_a \varphi_{b,1}(q_{b,1}),$$

which would be the form we would obtain by setting $d_a = 0$ in equation [2].

Therefore: – *If the demand for one of the two commodities is zero at a certain price, the demand for the other commodity is also zero at the corresponding price.*[ii]

93. That proposition is only a corollary of a more general theorem.

To transform equation [1] of the demand for (B) as a function of the price of (B) in terms of (A) into an equation of the supply of (A) as a function of the price of (A) in terms of (B), it would suffice to replace d_b by $o_a p_a$ and p_b by $\dfrac{1}{p_a}$. It would therefore become

$$\varphi_{a,1}(q_{a,1} - o_a) = p_a \varphi_{b,1}(q_{b,1} + o_a p_a),$$

which is nothing other than equation [2] in which d_a is replaced by $-o_a$. In consequence, equation [2] of the demand for (A) is the equation of the supply of (A) for negative values of d_a. We could demonstrate similarly that equation [1] for the demand for (B) becomes an equation of the supply of (B) for negative values of d_b. Now, prices being essentially positive, when d_b is *positive*, $o_a = d_b p_b$ is positive, and consequently $d_a = -o_a$ is *negative*; and when d_b is *negative*, $o_a = d_b p_b$ is negative, and consequently $d_a = -o_a$ is *positive*. We could demonstrate similarly that, when d_a is *positive*, d_b is *negative*, and when d_a is *negative*, d_b is *positive*.

Therefore: – *If the demand for one of the two commodities is positive at a given price, the demand for the other is negative; that is to say, its supply is positive at the corresponding price.*

And, in fact, a holder of the two commodities can only demand one of them by offering the other in exchange, and reciprocally. It follows from this that if he neither demands nor supplies any quantity of one of these commodities, he neither supplies nor demands any of the other. This, as is very easily seen, is the case in which, the ratio of the raretés of the two commodities being equal to the price, the real maximum utility is realized.

94. The curves [in Fig. 16] from $a_{d,1}$ to $a_{p,1}$ and from $b_{d,1}$ to $b_{p,1}$ are, therefore, demand curves, the [abscissas of the] points $a_{p,1}$ and $b_{p,1}$ being reciprocals. The curves from $a_{p,1}$ to $a_{o,1}$ and from $b_{p,1}$ to $b_{o,1}$ that are dotted and lie below the axes $q_{a,1}p$ and $q_{b,1}p$ in the diagram, are supply curves. Taken together and referred to the Or axis, each of them is a curve of the total quantity retained and obtained of each of the two commodities as a function of the price. Each has a minimum corresponding to the maximum quantity supplied in exchange for the other commodity.

95. To sum up, if, more simply, we designate by x_1 and y_1 the positive or negative quantities of commodities (A) and (B) that exchanger (1), having regard to the price, will add to the quantities $q_{a,1}$ and $q_{b,1}$ that he possesses, the dispositions to trade of that individual will result in the equation of exchange and the equation of maximum satisfaction, namely

$$x_1 v_a + y_1 v_b = 0,$$

and

$$\frac{\varphi_{a,1}(q_{a,1} + x_1)}{\varphi_{b,1}(q_{b,1} + y_1)} = \frac{v_a}{v_b},$$

from which we can eliminate y_1 and solve for x_1 as a function of p_a, and eliminate x_1 and solve for y_1 as a function of p_b. The formulas obtained in this way,

$$\varphi_{a,1}(q_{a,1} + x_1) = p_a \varphi_{b,1}(q_{b,1} - x_1 p_a),$$

and

$$\varphi_{b,1}\left(q_{b,1}+y_1\right)=p_b\varphi_{a,1}\left(q_{a,1}-y_1p_b\right),$$

are general formulas that we have only to suitably develop in order to express the dispositions to trade in the case of the exchange of several commodities for one another.

It is essential to note that for such values of p_a as will render any negative x_1 numerically larger than $q_{a,1}$, the first of the above two equations must be replaced by $x_1=-q_{a,1}$, and in that case the value of y_1 would be given by the equation $y_1p_b=-q_{a,1}$; and that, similarly, for such values of p_b as will render any negative y_1 numerically greater than $q_{b,1}$, the second of these equations must be replaced by $y_1=-q_{b,1}$, and in that case the value of x_1 would be given by $x_1p_a=q_{b,1}$.

96. These equations, solved for x_1 and y_1 and properly arranged so as to satisfy the above-mentioned restrictions, would take the form

$$x_1=f_{a,1}\left(p_a\right),\qquad y_1=f_{b,1}\left(p_b\right).$$

Similarly, to express the dispositions to trade of exchangers (2), (3), $\cdots$, we would have

$$x_2=f_{a,2}\left(p_a\right),\qquad y_2=f_{b,2}\left(p_b\right).$$

$$x_3=f_{a,3}\left(p_a\right),\qquad y_3=f_{b,3}\left(p_b\right).$$

$$\vdots\qquad\qquad\vdots$$

And the equality of the effective supply and of the effective demand of each of the two commodities (A) and (B) would be expressed by either one of the following equations:

$$X=f_{a,1}\left(p_a\right)+f_{a,2}\left(p_a\right)+f_{a,3}\left(p_a\right)+\cdots=F_a\left(p_a\right)=0,$$

$$Y=f_{b,1}\left(p_b\right)+f_{b,2}\left(p_b\right)+f_{b,3}\left(p_b\right)+\cdots=F_b\left(p_b\right)=0.$$

For example, we could derive p_a from the first equation and p_b from the equation

$$p_a p_b = 1;$$

and this value of p_b would necessarily satisfy the second equation because obviously

$$Xv_a + Yv_b = 0,$$

from which it follows that, if for a certain value of p_a, $F_a(p_a) = 0$, then for the corresponding value of p_b we have $F_b(p_b) = 0$.

This solution is analytical. We could present it geometrically. The sum of the positive xs would yield the demand curve of (A), and the sum of the positive ys the demand curve of (B). From these two demand curves, the two supply curves of the two commodities can be deduced, which are nothing other than the sums of the negative xs and the negative ys taken positively. The intersection of these two curves would determine the current prices.

97. That would be the mathematical solution. The solution in the marketplace would be effectuated in the following manner:

Any two prices that are reciprocals of each other, p_a and p_b, being cried, $x_1, x_2, x_3, \cdots\ y_1, y_2, y_3, \cdots$ would be mutually determined without mathematics, but nevertheless in conformity with the condition of maximum satisfaction. X and Y would be determined under the same condition. If $X = 0$, then also $Y = 0$, and the prices would be equilibrium prices. But generally $X \gtrless 0$, and consequently $Y \gtrless 0$. The first inequality can be put into the form

$$D_a \gtrless O_a$$

in which D_a designates the sum of the positive xs and Q the sum of the negative xs taken positively. Then it is a question of bringing D_a and O_a into equality.

In regard to D_a, this quantity is positive when $p_a = 0$; it decreases indefinitely if p_a increases; and it is zero for a certain value of p_a somewhere between zero and infinity. As for O_a, that quantity is zero when $p_a = 0$, and even for certain positive values of p_a; then it increases if p_a increases, but not indefinitely: it passes through at least one maximum and then decreases if p_a continues to increase; and it is zero if $p_a = \infty$. In these conditions, and if D_a does not fall to zero before O_a ceases to be zero, in which case there is no solution, there exists at least one value of p_a at which O_a and D_a are equal. To find this value, it is necessary to increase p_a if $D_a > O_a$, and decrease p_a if $D_a < O_a$. We recognize the law of effective supply and demand.

Notes

i   Jaffé translated these words as 'offer curves', a mistake that he repeated systematically. See the translators' introduction for a discussion of this matter.

ii By 'the corresponding price' Walras meant the price of the other commodity in terms of the first.

LESSON 10

Rareté, or the cause of value in exchange

SUMMARY: – Analytic definition of the exchange of two commodities for each other. Proportionality of values in exchange to raretés. Qualification relative to the case of discontinuity of want curves. Qualification relative to the case of zero demand, and of supply equal to the quantity possessed. Rareté, the cause of value in exchange. Value in exchange, a relative fact; rareté, an absolute fact. There are only individual raretés. Average rareté. Variation of the prices of two commodities, each in terms of the other; four causes of variation; possibility of verifying these causes. Law of the variation of equilibrium prices.

98. After due consideration, it becomes clear that the utility curves and the quantities possessed are the necessary and sufficient elements for the determination of current or equilibrium prices. From these elements, there result mathematically, in the first place, the curves of partial and total demand, because of the fact that each holder tries to obtain the greatest possible satisfaction of his wants. And from these partial and total demand curves, there result mathematically, in the second place, the current or equilibrium prices, because of the fact that there can be only one price in the market, that at which total effective demand equals total effective supply; otherwise stated, because each must receive in proportion to what he gives, or must give in proportion to what he receives.

Thus: – *The exchange of two commodities for each other in a freely competitive market is an operation by which all holders of either one, or of both, of the two commodities can obtain the greatest satisfaction of their wants consistent with the condition of giving the commodity that they sell and receiving the commodity that they buy in a common and identical proportion.*

The principal object of the theory of social wealth is to generalize this proposition by showing that it applies to the exchange of several commodities for one another just as it does to the exchange of two commodities for each other, and that it applies to free competition in production just as it does to exchange. The principal object of the theory of production of social wealth is to trace its consequences by showing how the rule of organization of agriculture, manufacturing, and commerce is deduced from it. We can say, therefore, that it contains the germ of all theoretical and applied economics.

99. v_a and v_b being the values in exchange of commodities (A) and (B), the ratios of which constitute the current equilibrium prices, $r_{a,1}, r_{b,1}, r_{a,2}, r_{b,2}, r_{a,3}, r_{b,3}, \cdots$ being the raretés of these commodities, or, the intensities of the last wants satisfied for holders (1), (2), (3), $\cdots$ after the exchange, we have, by virtue of the theorem of maximum satisfaction, for holder (1),

$$\frac{r_{a,1}}{r_{b,1}} = p_a, \qquad \frac{r_{b,1}}{r_{a,1}} = p_b;$$

for holder (2),

$$\frac{r_{a,2}}{r_{b,2}} = p_a, \qquad \frac{r_{b,2}}{r_{a,2}} = p_b;$$

for holder (3),

$$\frac{r_{a,3}}{r_{b,3}} = p_a, \qquad \frac{r_{b,3}}{r_{a,3}} = p_b;$$

and so on. We have, therefore,

$$p_a = \frac{r_{a,1}}{r_{b,1}} = \frac{r_{a,2}}{r_{b,2}} = \frac{r_{a,3}}{r_{b,3}} = \cdots$$

$$p_b = \frac{r_{b,1}}{r_{a,1}} = \frac{r_{b,2}}{r_{a,2}} = \frac{r_{b,3}}{r_{a,3}} = \cdots$$

which can also be expressed in this way:

$$v_a : v_b$$

$$:: r_{a,1} : r_{b,1}$$

$$:: r_{a,2} : r_{b,2}$$

$$:: r_{a,3} : r_{b,3}$$

$$\vdots$$

It should be noted that, if it is a question of commodities that are naturally consumed in whole units and that have discontinuous utility curves, we will have to put into the tables of raretés, underlining them in order to make them distinguishable, proportional terms that would be, we have seen (§ 82), very close, not to the intensities of the last wants satisfied, but to the averages of the intensities of the last wants satisfied and of the first wants unsatisfied.

It is also possible that one of the two terms may be missing one or several of the ratios of the raretés. Thus, it can happen, for example, that at the price p_a holder (2) does not demand (A); then there would be no rareté of (A) for holder (2) because it would not satisfy any want for him, and the term $r_{a,2}$ would have to be replaced by $p_a r_{b,2}$, which would be greater than the intensity of the first want for (A) that this holder experiences (§ 85). It can also happen, for example, that holder (3), at the price p_a, demands all the (A) he can get at any possible price; that is to say, becomes a supplier of the quantity he possesses of (B); then there would be no rareté of (B) for him, because it would not satisfy any want for him, and the term $r_{b,3}$ would have to be replaced by a term $p_b r_{a,3}$ greater than the intensity $\beta_{r,3}$ of the first want for (B) that this holder experiences (§ 87). We could agree to introduce the terms $p_a r_{b,2}$ and $p_b r_{a,3}$ into the above tables, putting them in parentheses, which would revert to defining rareté as the intensity of the last want that *is* or that *could have been* satisfied.

Subject to those two reservations, we may set forth the following proposition:

Current prices or equilibrium prices are equal to the ratios of the raretés.

In other words:

Values in exchange are proportional to the raretés.

100. We have arrived here, in regard to the exchange of two commodities for each other, at the goal we set for ourselves at the beginning of this mathematical theory of exchange (§ 40), namely to arrive at rareté by beginning with value in exchange, instead of arriving at value in exchange by beginning with rareté as we did in the first part devoted to the object and divisions of economics. In fact, rareté as we present it here, that is to say, the intensity of the last want satisfied, is precisely rareté as we have defined it earlier (§ 21) by the double condition of utility and limitation in quantity. There could not be a last want satisfied if there were no want; that is to say, if a commodity had neither extensive nor intensive utility, if it were *useless*. And the intensity of the last want satisfied would be zero if the commodity, having a utility curve, existed in a quantity greater than the extensive utility, as would be the case, for example, if it were *unlimited in quantity*. Our present rareté is therefore the same as our former rareté. The only additional aspects are that it is conceived to be a measurable magnitude, and that value in exchange not only necessarily follows and accompanies it but also is measured by it. Now, if it is certain that rareté and value in exchange are two concomitant and proportional phenomena, it is certain that rareté is the cause of value in exchange.

Value in exchange is a *relative* fact; rareté is an absolute fact. If, of the two commodities, (A) and (B), one of them became useless, or, though remaining useful, became unlimited in quantity, it would no longer be scarce and would no longer have value in exchange. In this case, the other commodity would also cease to have value in exchange, but it would not cease to be scarce; it would even be more scarce or less scarce, it would have such and such a determinate rareté, for each of the holders of the commodity.

I say, 'for each of the holders of this commodity'. And, in fact, it is essential to state once more: there is no such thing as *the rareté* of commodity (A) or of commodity (B), no such thing either, consequently, as the ratio of the rareté of (A) to the rareté of (B), or as the ratio of the rareté of (B) to the rareté of (A); there are rather the raretés of the commodity (A) or the commodity (B) for holders (1), (2), (3), ⋯ of these two commodities, and the ratios of the raretés of (A) to the raretés of (B), or of the ratios of the raretés of (B) to the raretés of (A) for those holders. Rareté, it can be said, is *personal.* It is only with respect to such and such an individual that we can define rareté by rigorously establishing the parallelism of, on the one hand, *rareté, effective utility,* and *quantity possessed,* and, on the other hand, *velocity, distance traveled,* and *time taken* to travel it. Thus, *the derivative of effective utility with respect to the quantity possessed* is defined exactly as velocity is defined: *the derivative of distance traveled with respect to the time taken to travel it.*

If we wanted to define something that we might call *the* rareté of commodity (A) or of commodity (B), it would be necessary to take the *average* rareté, which would be the arithmetical average of the raretés of each of those commodities for each of the exchangers after trading, a conception that would be no more extraordinary than that of the average height or average longevity in a given country and that could be useful in certain cases. These average raretés would themselves be proportional to the values in exchange.

101. It is the right of the theorist to assume that the determinants of prices are invariant during the period he specifies in his formulation of the law of the establishment of equilibrium prices. But it is his duty, once this operation has been completed, to remember that the determinants of prices are essentially variable, and consequently to formulate the law of the variation of equilibrium prices. This now remains to be done here. And, furthermore, the first operation leads immediately to the second. Indeed, the determinants of the establishment of prices are also the determinants of the variation of prices. These determinants of the establishment of prices are the utilities of the commodities and the quantities possessed of the commodities. These forces are, therefore, the primary causes and conditions of the variation of prices.

Let us assume that, in the same market where (A) and (B) were traded initially at the above-mentioned current prices, $\dfrac{1}{\mu}$ of (A) in terms of (B) and μ of (B) in terms of (A), that trading now takes place at the different current prices $\dfrac{1}{\mu'}$ of (A) in terms of (B) and μ' of (B) in terms of (A); then we can state that this change in price is the result of one of the following four causes, or of several of them, or even of all of them:

1. A change in the utility of commodity (A);
2. A change in the quantity of that commodity possessed by one or several holders;
3. A change in the utility of commodity (B);
4. A change in the quantity of that commodity possessed by one or several holders.

These circumstances are absolute and could be identified if necessary. Practically, this identification could prove to be more or less difficult; but nothing obliges us to declare it theoretically impossible. An investigation in which all the exchangers would be interrogated successively regarding the determinants of their partial demand curves would clarify the matter. One can even conceive of a case in which the primary cause of a variation of a price imposes itself in one way or other on the attention of the observer. For example, if it is assumed that a rise in price from μ to μ' occurs at the same time as the discovery of a remarkable property of commodity (B), or of an accident that would have partially destroyed the supply of that commodity, we could not have done otherwise than to associate one or the other of those two events with the rise in price. Now, it is clear that the association that one makes, sometimes despite oneself, is not impossible in fact, and that is how the investigation of the primary causes and conditions of variations in prices is conducted.

102. Let it be assumed that equilibrium is established and that the exchangers possess the quantities of (A) and (B) that, at the reciprocal prices $\dfrac{1}{\mu}$ of (A) in terms of (B) and μ of (B) in terms of (A), yield

them maximum satisfaction. This condition is fulfilled because of the equality of the ratios of the raretés to the prices; it no longer holds true if that equality ceases to exist. Let us see, then, how variations in utility and in the quantity possessed disturb the state of maximum satisfaction and what the consequences of the disturbance are.

As for the variations in utility, they can occur in very diverse ways: there may be an increase in intensive utility and a decrease in extensive utility or vice versa, etc. We must, therefore, take some care as to how we enunciate general propositions in this respect. That is why we will reserve the expressions *increase in utility* and *decrease in utility* for shifts in the want curve that have the result of increasing or decreasing the intensity of the last want satisfied, or, the rareté, after exchange occurs. This being understood, we assume an increase in the utility of (B); that is to say, a shift in the want curve of (B) resulting in an increase in the rareté of (B) for certain parties. These individuals will no longer obtain maximum satisfaction. On the contrary, they will find it to their advantage to demand (B) by offering some of their (A) at the current reciprocal prices $\frac{1}{\mu}$ and μ. Therefore, since the supply was equal to the demand for each of the two commodities at the prices $\frac{1}{\mu}$ and μ, there will now be, at these prices, an excess of demand over supply of (B) and an excess of supply over demand of (A). The result will be a rise in p_b and a fall in p_a. But there will no longer be a maximum of satisfaction for the other exchangers. On the contrary, it will be advantageous for them, at a price of (B) in terms of (A) greater than μ and at a price of (A) in terms of (B) less than $\frac{1}{\mu}$, to supply (B) and demand (A). Equilibrium will be re-established when, at a price of (B) higher than μ and at a price of (A) lower than $\frac{1}{\mu}$, the demand and supply of the two commodities are equated. Thus an increase in the utility of (B) for our individuals will have had the result of an elevation of the price of (B).

A decrease in the utility of (B) would obviously have had the result of a reduction of the price of (B).

It is sufficient to look at the want curves to see that an increase in the quantity possessed results in a decrease in rareté, and that a decrease in the quantity possessed results in an increase in rareté. Moreover, we have just seen that as rareté decreases or increases, price decreases or increases. Consequently, the effects of changes in the quantity possessed are purely and simply the opposite of the effects of changes in utility, and we can now enunciate the law we have been looking for in the following terms:

– *Two commodities being given in a state of equilibrium in a market, if, all other things being equal, the utility of one of these two commodities increases or decreases for one or more of the exchangers, the value of that commodity in relation to the value of the other, or, its price, increases or decreases.*

If, all other things being equal, the quantity of one of the two commodities possessed by one or more holders increases or decreases, the price of that commodity decreases or increases.

We remark, before going beyond this subject, that, although the change of prices necessarily indicates a variation in the determinants of the prices, on the other hand, constancy of the prices does not necessarily indicate constancy of the determinants of these prices. In fact, we can, without another demonstration, also enunciate the following double proposition:

– *Two commodities being given, if the utility and the quantity of one of these two commodities possessed by one or more exchangers or holders vary in such a way that their raretés do not change, then the value of this commodity with respect to the value of the other, or, its price, does not vary.*

If the utility and the quantity of the two commodities possessed by one or more exchangers or holders vary in such a way that the ratios of their raretés do not vary, then the prices of the two commodities do not vary.

LESSON 11

The problem of the exchange of several commodities for one another. Theorem of general equilibrium

SUMMARY: – Generalization of the notations regarding the case of the exchange of two commodities for each other. Exchange of three commodities for one another. Equations of partial demand and total demand. Equations of exchange. Exchange of m commodities for one another. Demand equations. The mathematical solution of the problem of the exchange of several commodities for one another is always possible algebraically, but not geometrically.

Conditions of general economic equilibrium. The hypothesis of $p_{c,b} = \alpha \dfrac{p_{c,a}}{p_{b,a}}$ with $\alpha > 1$. Arbitrages (B, A, C), (A, C, B), (C, B, A). Decrease of $p_{c,b}$. Decrease of $p_{c,a}$. Assume $\alpha < 1$. Inverse operations and results. General equilibrium equations. Substitution of the equations of equality of the demand and supply for each commodity against all the others together in place of the equations of equality of the supply and demand for each commodity for each of the others separately.

103. It is now a question of passing from the study of the exchange of two commodities (A) and (B) to the study of several commodities (A), (B), (C), (D), $\cdots$ for one another. To do this, it will suffice that we generalize appropriately our formulas, first making the replacements in the case in which the exchangers are holders of only one commodity.

Henceforth, we shall denote by $D_{a,b}$ the effective demand of (A) in terms of (B), by $p_{a,b}$ the price of (A) in terms of (B), by $D_{b,a}$ the effective demand of (B) in terms of (A), and by $p_{b,a}$ the price of (B)

118

in terms of (A). For the four unknowns $D_{a,b}$, $D_{b,a}$, $p_{a,b}$, $p_{b,a}$ we have two equations of effective demand:

$$D_{a,b} = F_{a,b}(p_{a,b}),$$

$$D_{b,a} = F_{b,a}(p_{b,a}),$$

and two equations of equality of effective supply and demand:

$$D_{b,a} = D_{a,b}p_{a,b},$$

$$D_{a,b} = D_{b,a}p_{b,a}$$

We know that the first two equations can be represented geometrically by two curves, and the last two by inscribing in these curves two rectangles with bases that are inversely equal to the ratio of their heights and directly equal to the ratio of their surfaces (§ 57).[i]

104. Let us now pass from the case of two commodities (A) and (B) to the case of three commodities (A), (B) and (C). To that end, we will depict a market where, from one side, enter people who own commodity (A) and who are ready to give up a part of it to obtain (B), and a part to obtain (C); from another side, people arrive who own commodity (B) and who are ready to give up a part of it to obtain (A), and a part to obtain (C); from another side, finally, people arrive who own commodity (C) and who are ready to give up a part of it to obtain (A), and a part to obtain (B).

That having been posited, selecting from all those people, an owner of (B), for instance, and developing our preceding reasoning accordingly, we will see, here too, that this individual's dispositions to bid can be rigorously determined.

Indeed, each owner of a quantity q_b of commodity (B) who comes to the market to exchange a certain quantity $o_{b,a}$ of this commodity for a quantity $d_{a,b}$ of commodity (A), in accordance with the equation of exchange

$$d_{a,b}v_a = o_{b,a}v_b,$$

and a certain quantity $o_{b,c}$ of this same commodity for a quantity $d_{c,b}$ of commodity (C) in accordance with the equation of exchange

$$d_{c,b}v_c = o_{b,c}v_b,$$

will come back from the market with a quantity $d_{a,b}$ of (A), a quantity $d_{c,b}$ of (C), and a quantity

$$y = q_a - o_{b,a} - o_{b,c} = q_b - d_{a,b}\frac{v_a}{v_b} - d_{c,b}\frac{v_c}{v_b}$$

of (B). In any case, between the quantities q_b, $\dfrac{v_a}{v_b}$ or $p_{a,b}$, d_a, $\dfrac{v_c}{v_b}$ or $p_{c,b}$, $d_{c,b}$, and y there will always be the relationship

$$q_b = y + d_{a,b}p_{a,b} + d_{c,b}p_{c,b}.$$

Our individual does not know, before having entered the market, what $\dfrac{v_a}{v_b}$ or $p_{a,b}$ and $\dfrac{v_c}{v_b}$ or $p_{c,b}$ will be; but he is sure that he will know them as soon as he enters into the market, and that, these values of $p_{a,b}$ and $p_{c,b}$ being known, he will accept, as a result, a value of $d_{a,b}$ and a value of $d_{c,b}$, from which finally will result a certain value of y in accordance with the above equation. Most certainly, we are forced to recognize that $d_{a,b}$ cannot be determined without knowing $p_{c,b}$ in addition to $p_{a,b}$, nor can we determine $d_{c,b}$ without knowing $p_{a,b}$ in addition to $p_{c,b}$. But we are also forced to accept that, $p_{a,b}$ and $p_{c,b}$ being known, $d_{a,b}$ and $d_{c,b}$ can be determined because of that very circumstance.

105. Now, here again, nothing is simpler than expressing mathematically the direct relation of $d_{a,b}$ and $d_{c,b}$, that is, the effective demand of (A) and (C) in terms of (B), with $p_{a,b}$ and $p_{c,b}$, that is, with the price of these commodities. This relation, corresponding to the dispositions to bid of our individual, will be completely expressed by the

two equations $d_{a,b} = f_{a,b}(p_{a,b}, p_{c,b})$ and $d_{c,b} = f_{c,b}(p_{a,b}, p_{c,b})$. We would obtain in the same way the equations expressing the dispositions to bid of all the other holders of (B); and, finally, by purely and simply adding these partial demand equations, we would obtain the two equations of total demand:

$$D_{a,b} = F_{a,b}(p_{a,b}, p_{c,b}),$$

$$D_{c,b} = F_{c,b}(p_{a,b}, p_{c,b}),$$

expressing the dispositions to bid of all the holders of (B).

Likewise, we would have the two equations of total demand:

$$D_{a,c} = F_{a,c}(p_{a,c}, p_{b,c}),$$

$$D_{b,c} = F_{b,c}(p_{a,c}, p_{b,c}),$$

expressing the dispositions to bid of all the holders of (C).

Finally, we would likewise have the two equations of total demand:

$$D_{b,a} = F_{b,a}(p_{b,a}, p_{c,a}),$$

$$D_{c,a} = F_{c,a}(p_{b,a}, p_{c,a}),$$

expressing the dispositions to bid of all the holders of (A).

106. Moreover, we have the two equations of exchange

$$D_{b,a} = D_{a,b}p_{a,b}, D_{b,c} = D_{c,b}p_{c,b},$$

of (B) for (A) and (C).

We have the two equations of exchange

$$D_{c,a} = D_{a,c}p_{a,c}, D_{c,b} = D_{b,c}p_{b,c}$$

of (C) for (A) and (B).

Finally, we have the two equations of exchange

$$D_{a,b} = D_{b,a} p_{b,a}, D_{a,c} = D_{c,a} p_{c,a}$$

of (A) for (B) and (C).

Hence, we have in all 12 equations in the 12 unknowns that are the 6 prices of the three commodities in terms of one another, and the 6 total quantities of the three commodities exchanged for one another.

107. Let there now be m commodities (A), (B), (C), (D), $\cdots$ in a market; it is clear that by virtue of reasoning exactly the same as was developed for the case of two commodities and for the case of three commodities, and that is unnecessary to repeat once more, we can set forth the $m - 1$ equations of effective demand of (B), (C), (D), $\cdots$ in terms of (A):

$$D_{b,a} = F_{b,a} \left(p_{b,a}, p_{c,a}, p_{d,a}, \cdots \right),$$

$$D_{c,a} = F_{c,a} \left(p_{b,a}, p_{c,a}, p_{d,a}, \cdots \right),$$

$$D_{d,a} = F_{d,a} \left(p_{b,a}, p_{c,a}, p_{d,a}, \cdots \right)$$

$$\vdots$$

the $m - 1$ equations of effective demand of (A), (C), (D), $\cdots$ in terms of (B):

$$D_{a,b} = F_{a,b} \left(p_{a,b}, p_{c,b}, p_{d,b}, \cdots \right),$$

$$D_{c,b} = F_{c,b} \left(p_{a,b}, p_{c,b}, p_{d,b}, \cdots \right),$$

$$D_{d,b} = F_{d,b} \left(p_{a,b}, p_{c,b}, p_{d,b}, \cdots \right),$$

$$\vdots$$

the $m - 1$ equations of effective demand of (A), (B), (D), $\cdots$ in terms of (C):

$$D_{a,c} = F_{a,c} \left(p_{a,c}, p_{b,c}, p_{d,c}, \cdots \right),$$

$$D_{b,c} = F_{b,c}\left(p_{a,c}, p_{b,c}, p_{d,c}, \cdots\right),$$

$$D_{d,c} = F_{d,c}\left(p_{a,c}, p_{b,c}, p_{d,c}, \cdots\right),$$

$$\vdots$$

the $m - 1$ equations of effective demand of (A), (B), (C), $\cdots$ in terms of (D):

$$D_{a,d} = F_{a,d}\left(p_{a,d}, p_{b,d}, p_{c,d}, \cdots\right),$$

$$D_{b,d} = F_{b,d}\left(p_{a,d}, p_{b,d}, p_{c,d}, \cdots\right),$$

$$D_{c,d} = F_{c,d}\left(p_{a,d}, p_{b,d}, p_{c,d}, \cdots\right),$$

$$\vdots$$

and so forth; hence, in all $m(m - 1)$ equations.

108. Furthermore, it is obvious that without further explanation we can set forth the $m - 1$ equations of exchange of (A) for (B), (C), (D), $\cdots$

$$D_{a,b} = D_{b,a}p_{b,a}, D_{a,c} = D_{c,a}p_{c,a}, \quad D_{a,d} = D_{d,a}p_{d,a}, \quad \cdots,$$

the $m - 1$ equations of exchange of (B) for (A), (C), (D), $\cdots$

$$D_{b,a} = D_{a,b}p_{a,b}, D_{b,c} = D_{c,b}p_{c,b}, \quad D_{b,d} = D_{d,b}p_{d,b}, \quad \cdots,$$

the $m - 1$ equations of exchange of (C) for (A), (B), (D), $\cdots$

$$D_{c,a} = D_{a,c}p_{a,c}, D_{c,b} = D_{b,c}p_{b,c}, \quad D_{c,d} = D_{d,c}p_{d,c}, \quad \cdots,$$

the $m - 1$ equations of exchange of (D) for (A), (B), (C), $\cdots$

$$D_{d,a} = D_{a,d}p_{a,d}, D_{d,b} = D_{b,d}p_{b,d}, \quad D_{d,c} = D_{c,d}p_{c,d}, \quad \cdots,$$

and so forth; hence, in all $m(m - 1)$ equations.

These $m(m - 1)$ equations of exchange form, together with the $m(m - 1)$ equations of effective demand, a system of in all $2m(m - 1)$ equations. Now, we have precisely $2m(m - 1)$ unknowns; indeed, for the m commodities exchanged for one another there are $m(m - 1)$ prices and $m(m - 1)$ quantities exchanged in all.

109. In the special case of the exchange of two goods for each other, and in that of the exchange of three goods for one another, the problem can be solved either geometrically or algebraically, because, in those two cases the demand functions can themselves be represented geometrically. In the first case, the demand functions are functions of one variable and therefore can be represented by two curves. In the second case, these functions are functions of two variables and therefore can be represented by six surfaces. A simple inscription of rectangles under the two curves, in the first case, and an inscription of rectangles under the curves that can be obtained by the intersection of the surfaces by planes, in the second case, thus gives us the geometrical solution of the problem.

In the general case, on the contrary, the demand functions are functions of $m - 1$ variables that cannot be represented in three-dimensional space. That is why, in this case, the problem can be considered as amenable to being posed and solved mathematically, but not geometrically. Let us recall, moreover, that we do not have to do here with posing and solving the problem in reality in any given case, but only of conceiving scientifically the nature of the problem that presents itself and is solved empirically in the market. Now, from this point of view, the algebraic solution is not only just as valuable as the geometric one, but it may even be said that in adopting the analytical form, we adopt the general and scientific form par excellence.

110. The problem of the exchange of several commodities against one another seems to be solved. However, it is only half solved. Under the conditions defined above, we would undoubtedly, in the market, have a certain equilibrium of the prices of the commodities taken two at a time; but this would be only an imperfect equilibrium. The perfect or *general market equilibrium occurs only if the prices of any two commodities in terms of each other are equal to the ratio of the price of each one in terms of any third commodity.* This has to be demonstrated. To

do so, from all the commodities we take three, (A), (B) and (C), for example; we assume that the price $p_{c,b}$ is greater than the ratio of the prices $p_{c,a}$ and $p_{b,a}$, and let us see what will happen.

We will imagine, to fix our ideas, that the place that serves as the market for the exchange of all the commodities (A), (B), (C), (D), $\cdots$ for one another be divided in just as many parts as there are exchanges of two commodities for each other, hence into $\dfrac{m(m-1)}{2}$ special markets indicated by signboards on which are mentioned the names of the commodities that are exchanged and the exchange prices determined by means of the equations above. Hence: – 'Exchange of (A) for (B) and of (B) for (A) at prices $p_{a,b}$ and $p_{b,a}$.' – 'Exchange of (A) for (C) and of (C) for (A) at prices $p_{a,c}$ and $p_{c,a}$.' – 'Exchange of (B) for (C) and of (B) for (C) at prices $p_{b,c}$ and $p_{c,b}$.' – Having posited this, if each holder of (A) who wants (B) and (C) exchanged his (A) for (B) and (C) only in the first two special markets mentioned above, if each holder of (B) who wants (A) and (C) exchanged his (B) for (A) and (C) only in the first and the third special market, and if each holder of (C) who wants (A) and (B) exchanged his (C) for (A) and (B) only in the last two special markets, the equilibrium would be maintained as it is. But is to easy to show that neither the holders of (A), nor those of (B), nor those of (C) will adopt this method of exchange; they will proceed in quite another way, which will be more advantageous to them.

111. Let us therefore assume that

$$p_{c,b} = \alpha \frac{p_{c,a}}{p_{b,a}},$$

hence

$$\frac{p_{c,b} p_{b,a} p_{a,c}}{\alpha} = 1,$$

α being, first of all, greater than 1.

From this equation, it follows that the true price of (C) in terms of (B) is not $p_{c,b}$, but $\dfrac{p_{c,b}}{\alpha}$, because with $\dfrac{p_{c,b}}{\alpha}$ of (B) we have $\dfrac{p_{c,b}p_{b,a}}{\alpha}$ of (A), at the price $p_{b,a} = \dfrac{1}{p_{a,b}}$ of (A) in terms of (B) in the market (A, B);

and for $\dfrac{p_{c,b}p_{b,a}}{\alpha}$ of (A) we have $\dfrac{p_{c,b}p_{b,a}p_{a,c}}{\alpha} = 1$ of (C) at the price

$p_{c,a} = \dfrac{1}{p_{a,c}}$ of (C) in terms of (A) in the market (A, C).

It follows also that the true price of (B) in terms of (A) is not $p_{b,a}$, but $\dfrac{p_{b,a}}{\alpha}$, because with $\dfrac{p_{b,a}}{\alpha}$ of (A) we have $\dfrac{p_{b,a}p_{a,c}}{\alpha}$ of (C), at the price

$p_{c,a} = \dfrac{1}{p_{a,c}}$ of (C) in terms of (A) in the market (A, C); and for $\dfrac{p_{b,a}p_{a,c}}{\alpha}$

of (C) we have $\dfrac{p_{b,a}p_{a,c}p_{c,b}}{\alpha} = 1$ of (B) at the price $p_{b,c} = \dfrac{1}{p_{c,b}}$ of (B) in

terms of (C) in the market (B, C).

Finally, it follows also that the true price of (A) in terms of (C) is not $p_{a,c}$, but $\dfrac{p_{a,c}}{\alpha}$, because with $\dfrac{p_{a,c}}{\alpha}$ of (C) we have $\dfrac{p_{a,c}p_{c,b}}{\alpha}$ of (B), at

the price $p_{b,c} = \dfrac{1}{p_{c,b}}$ of (B) in terms of (C) in the market (B, C); and

for $\dfrac{p_{a,c}p_{c,b}}{\alpha}$ of (B) we have $\dfrac{p_{a,c}p_{c,b}p_{b,a}}{\alpha} = 1$ of (A) at the price $p_{a,b} = \dfrac{1}{p_{b,a}}$ of (A) in terms of (B) in the market (A, B).

112. Taking concrete numbers to clarify this point, we assume that $p_{c,b} = 4$, $p_{c,a} = 6$, $p_{b,a} = 2$; this yields $\alpha = 1.33$.

It follows from the equation[ii]

$$\frac{4 \times 2 \times \dfrac{1}{6}}{1.33} = 1,$$

that the true price of (C) in terms of (B) is not 4, but $\dfrac{4}{1.33} = 3$, because

with 3 of (B) we have $3 \times 2 = 6$ of (A), at the price of $\dfrac{1}{2}$ of (A) in terms

of (B) in the market (A, B); and for 6 of (A) we have $6 \times \dfrac{1}{6} = 1$ of (C)

at the price of 6 of (C) in terms of (A) in the market (A, C).

It follows also that the true price of (B) in terms of (A) is not 2, but

$\dfrac{2}{1.33} = 1.50$, because with 1.50 of (A) we have $1.50 \times \dfrac{1}{6} = \dfrac{1}{4}$ of (C), at

the price 6 of (C) in terms of (A) in the market (A, C); and for $\dfrac{1}{4}$ of

(C) we have $\dfrac{1}{4} \times 4 = 1$ of (B) at the price of $\dfrac{1}{4}$ of (B) in terms of (C) in

the market (B, C).

Finally, it follows also that the true price of (A) in terms of (C) is

not $\dfrac{1}{6}$, but $\dfrac{1}{6 \times 1.33} = \dfrac{1}{8}$, because with $\dfrac{1}{8}$ of (C) we have $\dfrac{1}{8} \times 4$ of (B), at

the price of $\dfrac{1}{4}$ of (B) in terms of (C) in the market (B, C); and for $\dfrac{1}{2}$

of (B) we have $\dfrac{1}{2} \times 2 = 1$ of (A) at the price of $\dfrac{1}{2}$ of (A) in terms of (B)

in the market (A, B).

113. The holders of (A), of (B), of (C) obviously will not hesitate to substitute commodities in this way: the first group, indirect exchange of (A) for (C) and of (C) for (B) instead of direct exchange of (A) for (B); the second group, indirect exchange of (B) for (A) and of (A) for (C) instead of direct exchange of (B) for (C); the third group, indirect exchange of (C) for (B) and of (B) for (A) instead of direct exchange of (C) for (A). This indirect exchange is called *arbitrage*. As for the savings they will obtain in this way, they will distribute them over their needs just as they please, by giving themselves a supplement of this or that commodity to procure the greatest possible total satisfaction. We could have shown that the condition for this maximum would be that the ratios of the intensities of the last needs be equal to

the real prices resulting from this arbitrage. However, without entering into these considerations, it suffices for us to remark that this supplementary demand will take place, just as the principal demand: for the holders of (A), by exchanging (A) for (C) and (C) for (B), but never (A) for (B); for the holders of (B), by exchanging (B) for (A) and (A) for (C), but never (B) for (C); for the holders of (C), by exchanging (C) for (B) and (B) for (A), but never (C) for (A). Hence, in the market (A, B), there will always be demand for (A) and supply of (B), but no demand for (B) and no supply of (A); hence $p_{b,a}$ will decrease. In the market (A, C) there will always be a demand for (C) and a supply of (A), but no demand for (C) or supply of (A); hence $p_{c,a}$ will increase. In the market (B, C) there will always be a demand for (B) and a supply of (C), but no demand for (C) or supply of (B); hence $p_{c,b}$ will decrease.

114. It is clear that, in the case where $p_{c,b} > \dfrac{p_{c,a}}{p_{b,a}}$, the market equilibrium is not definitive or general, and that arbitrages take place resulting in a decrease of $p_{c,b}$, an increase of $p_{c,a}$, and a decrease of $p_{b,a}$. At the same time, it is clear that in the case that $p_{c,b} < \dfrac{p_{c,a}}{p_{b,a}}$, there will be arbitrage in the market with as a result an increase of $p_{c,b}$, a decrease of $p_{c,a}$ and an increase of $p_{b,a}$. Indeed, we would then have

$$p_{c,b} = \alpha \frac{p_{c,a}}{p_{b,a}},$$

hence

$$\alpha p_{b,c} p_{c,a} p_{a,b} = 1,$$

with $\alpha < 1$; from this, it would follow that the true price of (B) in terms of (C) would be $\alpha p_{b,c}$, if (C) is exchanged for (A) and (A) for (B), that the true price of (A) in terms of (B) would be $\alpha p_{a,b}$, if (B) is exchanged for (C) and (C) for (A); and that the true price of (C) in terms of (A) would be $\alpha p_{c,a}$, if (A) is exchanged for (B) and (B) for (C). Moreover, it is quite clear that what has been said about the prices of (A), (B), and (C) can also be said about the prices of any three commodities. If, therefore, it is desired that arbitrage not take place and that the equilibrium of the commodities two by two in the market be general, the condition must be introduced that the price of one of any two commodities in terms of the other must be equal to the ratio of the price of the one to the price of the other, in terms of any arbitrary third commodity; that is to say, that the following equations must be added:

$$p_{a,b} = \frac{1}{p_{b,a}}, \quad p_{c,b} = \frac{p_{c,a}}{p_{b,a}}, \quad p_{d,b} = \frac{p_{d,a}}{p_{b,a}}, \cdots$$

$$p_{a,c} = \frac{1}{p_{c,a}}, \quad p_{b,c} = \frac{p_{b,a}}{p_{c,a}}, \quad p_{d,c} = \frac{p_{d,a}}{p_{c,a}}, \cdots$$

$$p_{a,d} = \frac{1}{p_{d,a}}, \quad p_{b,d} = \frac{p_{b,a}}{p_{d,a}}, \quad p_{c,d} = \frac{p_{c,a}}{p_{d,a}}, \cdots$$

$$\vdots$$

and so forth; consequently comprising in all $(m-1)(m-1)$ equilibrium equations containing implicitly $\dfrac{m(m-1)}{2}$ equations expressing the reciprocity of the prices.

The commodity in terms of which the prices of all the others are expressed is the *numeraire*.

115. Clearly, this introduction of $(m-1)(m-1)$ conditions requires that our preceding system of demand equations and equations of exchange be diminished by the same number of equations. This is exactly what happens in the case of a substitution in place of special markets of one general market by means of the substitution in place of the equations of exchange, expressing the equality of the demand for and supply of each commodity in exchange for each of the other ones separately, of the following equations of exchange expressing the equality of the demand for and supply of each commodity in exchange for all the other commodities:

$$D_{a,b} + D_{a,c} + D_{a,d} + \cdots = D_{b,a}P_{b,a} + D_{c,a}P_{c,a} + D_{d,a}P_{d,a} + \cdots$$

$$D_{b,a} + D_{b,c} + D_{b,d} + \cdots = D_{a,b}P_{a,b} + D_{c,b}P_{c,b} + D_{d,b}P_{d,b} + \cdots$$

$$D_{c,a} + D_{c,b} + D_{c,d} + \cdots = D_{a,c}P_{a,c} + D_{b,c}P_{b,c} + D_{d,c}P_{d,c} + \cdots$$

$$D_{d,a} + D_{d,b} + D_{d,c} + \cdots = D_{a,d}P_{a,b} + D_{b,d}P_{b,d} + D_{c,d}P_{c,d} + \cdots$$

$$\vdots$$

and so forth, hence m equations. However, these m equations can be reduced to $m - 1$ equations. Indeed, if we introduce in these equations the values of the prices obtained from the equations of general equilibrium, and indicate more simply the prices of (B), (C), (D), $\cdots$ in terms of (A) by $p_b, p_c, p_d, \cdots$, they become:

$$D_{a,b} + D_{a,c} + D_{a,d} + \cdots = D_{b,a}p_b + D_{c,a}p_c + D_{d,a}p_d + \cdots$$

$$D_{b,a} + D_{b,c} + D_{b,d} + \cdots = D_{a,b}\frac{1}{p_b} + D_{c,b}\frac{p_c}{p_b} + D_{d,b}\frac{p_d}{p_b} + \cdots$$

$$D_{c,a} + D_{c,b} + D_{c,d} + \cdots = D_{a,c}\frac{1}{p_c} + D_{b,c}\frac{p_b}{p_c} + D_{d,c}\frac{p_d}{p_c} + \cdots$$

$$D_{d,a} + D_{d,b} + D_{d,c} + \cdots = D_{a,d}\frac{1}{p_d} + D_{b,d}\frac{p_b}{p_d} + D_{c,d}\frac{p_c}{p_d} + \cdots$$

$$\vdots$$

If, then, we add the last $m - 1$, after having multiplied the two members of the first [of these $m - 1$ equations] by p_b, the second by p_c, the third by p_d, and so forth, and having eliminated on both sides the identical terms, we come back to the first equation of the system. This first one can therefore be neglected and the system reduced to the $m - 1$ subsequent equations. These remain then $m - 1$ equations of exchange that, combined with $m(m - 1)$ demand equations and the $(m-1)(m-1)$ equations of general equilibrium, form in all $2m(m - 1)$ equations whose roots are the $m(m - 1)$ prices of the commodities in one another and the $m(m - 1)$ total quantities of the commodities exchanged for one another. It is in this way, the demand equations being given, that the prices result mathematically from them. It remains only to demonstrate, and this is the essential point, that this selfsame problem of exchange of which we just have furnished the theoretical solution is also the problem that is solved practically in the market by the mechanism of free competition. However, before carrying out this demonstration, we will move on to the case in which the exchangers to the exchange are holders of several commodities, which is the general case, a simple and easy treatment of which is enabled by the theorem of maximum satisfaction.

Notes

i   This is the literal translation of a nonsensical sentence in which Walras vainly tried to summarize what he said correctly in § 57.

ii Walras should have written 'equality'.

General formula of the mathematical solution of the problem of the exchange of several commodities for one another. Law of the determination of the prices of the commodities

SUMMARY: – The general case of holders of several commodities. Equation of the equivalence of quantities demanded and quantities supplied. Equations of maximum satisfaction. Equations of partial demand and supply. Condition of supply equal to the quantity possessed. The system of $m - 1$ equations of the equality of total demand and total supply.

Exchange of several commodities for one another on the market. Price that is cried: price in numeraire implying general equilibrium. Determination without calculation of partial supply and demand in accordance with the condition of maximum satisfaction. Inequality of total supply and demand. Variation of total supply and demand in accordance with the variation of the price between zero and infinity. It is necessary to increase prices when demand is greater than supply and decrease them when supply is greater than demand.

116. In the case of the exchange of an arbitrary number of commodities, similar to the case of the exchange of two commodities for each other, the equations of partial effective demand are determined mathematically by the condition of the maximum satisfaction of wants. What then is this condition? It is, as always, that the ratio of the raretés of the two commodities be equal to the price of the one in terms of the other; otherwise an advantageous exchange between the two exchangers would still be possible (§ 80). If the exchangers

in the exchange are holders of only a single commodity, and, bearing in mind allowing arbitrage to take place, if $m(m-1)$ prices of the m commodities are cried two by two not subject to the condition of general equilibrium, maximum satisfaction will be achieved, for each exchanger, when the ratios of the raretés of the commodities demanded to the rareté of the commodity of which he is a holder are equal, not to the cried prices, but to the true prices obtained by arbitrage. But if the exchangers are holders of several commodities, and if, on the contrary, in order to prevent arbitrage from occurring, the $m-1$ prices of $m-1$ of the commodities are cried in terms of the mth, taken as numeraire, it being understood that the price of one of any two commodities in terms of the other will be equal to the ratio of the price of the one commodity to the price of the other in numeraire, it is obvious that maximum satisfaction will occur for each exchanger when the ratios of the raretés of the commodities other than the numeraire and the rareté of the numeraire commodity are equal to the cried prices.

117. Let therefore exchanger (1) be the holder of $q_{a,1}$ of (A), $q_{b,1}$ of (B), $q_{c,1}$ of (C), $q_{d,1}$ of (D), $\cdots$. Let $r = \varphi_{a,1}(q)$, $r = \varphi_{b,1}(q)$, $r = \varphi_{c,1}(q)$, $r = \varphi_{d,1}(q)$, $\cdots$ be the equations of utility or want for the commodities (A), (B), (C), (D), $\cdots$ for this exchanger. Let $p_b, p_c, p_d, \cdots$ be the respective prices of the commodities (B), (C), (D), $\cdots$ in terms of (A). And let $x_1, y_1, z_1, w_1, \cdots$ be the respective quantities of (A), (B), (C), (D), $\cdots$ that exchanger (1) will add to the quantities $q_{a,1}, q_{b,1}, q_{c,1}, q_{d,1}, \cdots$ that he has in possession at prices $p_b, p_c, p_d, \cdots$. The quantities $x_1, y_1, z_1, w_1, \cdots$ can be positive, representing then quantities demanded; and they can be negative, representing quantities supplied. Since our exchanger can only demand certain commodities under the condition of offering certain other commodities in equivalent quantities, it is certain that among the quantities $x_1, y_1, z_1, w_1, \cdots$ some are positive and others are negative, and that, generally speaking, we have between all these quantities the equation

$$x_1 + y_1 p_b + z_1 p_c + w_1 p_d + \cdots = 0.$$

Assuming in addition that maximum satisfaction prevails, we have between these same quantities the system of equations

$$\varphi_{b,1}\left(q_{b,1}+y_1\right)= p_b\varphi_{a,1}\left(q_{a,1}+x_1\right),$$

$$\varphi_{c,1}\left(q_{c,1}+z_1\right)= p_c\varphi_{a,1}\left(q_{a,1}+x_1\right),$$

$$\varphi_{d,1}\left(q_{d,1}+w_1\right)= p_d\varphi_{a,1}\left(q_{a,1}+x_1\right),$$

$$\vdots$$

hence $m-1$ equations that form with the preceding one a system of m equations, of which one can eliminate successively $m-1$ of the unknowns $x_1, y_1, z_1, w_1, \cdots$ such that remains only one equation representing the mth as a function of $p_b, p_c, p_d, \cdots$. In this way, we will have the following equations of demand for and supply of (B), (C), (D), $\cdots$ for exchanger (1):

$$y_1 = f_{b,1}(p_b, p_c, p_d, \ldots)$$

$$z_1 = f_{c,1}(p_b, p_c, p_d, \ldots)$$

$$w_1 = f_{d,1}\left(p_b, p_c, p_d, \ldots\right)$$

$$\vdots$$

where the demand for or the supply of (A) is furnished by the equation

$$x_1 = -\left(y_1 p_b + z_1 p_c + w_1 p_d + \cdots\right).$$

Likewise, we will have the following equations of demand for and supply of (B), (C), (D), $\cdots$ for exchangers (2), (3), $\cdots$:

$$y_2 = f_{b,2}(p_b, p_c, p_d, ...)$$

$$z_2 = f_{c,2}(p_b, p_c, p_d, ...)$$

$$w_2 = f_{d,2}(p_b, p_c, p_d, ...)$$

$$\vdots$$

$$y_3 = f_{b,3}(p_b, p_c, p_d, ...)$$

$$z_3 = f_{c,3}(p_b, p_c, p_d, ...)$$

$$w_3 = f_{d,3}(p_b, p_c, p_d, ...)$$

$$\vdots$$

and so forth, where the demand for or the supply of (A) for these same exchangers is furnished by the equations

$$x_2 = -(y_2 p_b + z_2 p_c + w_2 p_d + \cdots)$$

$$x_3 = -(y_3 p_b + z_3 p_c + w_3 p_d + \cdots)$$

$$\vdots$$

In this way, the dispositions to bid of all the exchangers to the exchange would be deduced for each of them from his utility of the various commodities and the quantities of the commodities possessed by him. However, before proceeding further, a very important observation must be made.

118. It is possible that y_1 becomes negative for certain prices $p_b, p_c, p_d, \cdots$: this is the case in which exchanger (1) supplies

commodity (B) instead of demanding it. It is even possible that y_1 becomes equal to $-q_{b,1}$: this is the case in which the exchanger does not keep commodity (B) for himself. Introducing this value of y_1 into the $m-1$ equations of maximum satisfaction, they become

$$\varphi_{b,1}(0) = p_b \varphi_{a,1}(q_{a,1} + x_1),$$

$$\varphi_{c,1}(q_{c,1} + z_1) = p_c \varphi_{a,1}(q_{a,1} + x_1),$$

$$\varphi_{d,1}(q_{d,1} + w_1) = p_d \varphi_{a,1}(q_{a,1} + x_1),$$

$$\vdots$$

And, eliminating $p_b, p_c, p_d, \cdots$ from these equations and from the equation

$$x_1 + z_1 p_c + w_1 p_d + \cdots = q_{b,1} p_b,$$

we obtain the equation

$$x_1 \varphi_{a,1}(q_{b,1} + x_1) + z_1 \varphi_{c,1}(q_{c,1} + z_1)$$
$$+ w_1 \varphi_{d,1}(q_{d,1} + w_1) + \cdots = q_{b,1} \varphi_{b,1}(0).$$

This equation is a condition that can be translated into these words: – *In order that the supply of one of the commodities can be equal to the quantity possessed of the commodity,[i] it must be possible to inscribe, in the portion of the area of the want curves of the commodities that are demanded that is above the portion representing the wants satisfied by the quantity possessed, rectangles the sum of which is equal in its area to the rectangle that has as its height the quantity possessed of the commodity supplied, and as its base the intensity of the maximum want for the commodity.*

This condition may or may not be fulfilled. If it is, exchanger (1)'s supply of (B) will be, in certain cases, equal to the quantity $q_{b,1}$ of which he is the holder. Moreover, the supply can never be greater than this quantity. It is therefore essential to notice that, for all the values $p_b, p_c, p_d, \cdots$ that would make y_1 more negative than $-q_{b,1}$ in the demand or supply equation of (B), this equation should be replaced by the equation $y_1 = -q_{b,1}$.

119. However, this is not all. First, the same observation is applicable to the equations of demand and supply for (C), (D), $\cdots$ for values of $p_b, p_c, p_d, \cdots$ that make $z_1, w_1, \cdots$ more negative than $-q_{c,1}, -q_{d,1}, \cdots$. Then, and exactly in the case in which these equations would have to be replaced by the equations $z_1 q_{c,1}, w_1 = -q_{d,1}, \cdots$, the equation of demand or supply of (B) would have to be modified accordingly.

Hence, in the case of $z_1 = -q_{c,1}$, for instance, the system of equations that has to furnish the demand for or the supply of (B) for exchanger (1) would be the following

$$x_1 + y_1 p_b + w_1 p_d + \cdots = q_{c,1} p_c,$$

$$\varphi_{b,1}(q_{b,1} + y_1) = p_b \varphi_{a,1}(q_{a,1} + x_1),$$

$$\varphi_{d,1}(q_{d,1} + w_1) = p_b \varphi_{a,1}(q_{a,1} + x_1),$$

$$\vdots$$

hence, in all $m - 1$ equations from which we can eliminate the $m - 2$ unknowns such as $x_1, w_1, \cdots$ so that only one equation remains giving y_1 as a function of $p_b, p_c, p_d, \cdots$. Likewise in the case $w_1 = -q_{d,1}$, and so forth. Likewise, finally, this will be understood without it being necessary to insist upon it more, if not only the supply of a single one of the commodities (C), (D), $\cdots$, but of two, three, four, $\cdots$ and generally of several of them, were equal to the quantity possessed.

120. We have said nothing about the equation of demand or supply of the numeraire commodity (A) which has a particular form. It is obvious, firstly, that, for the values of $p_b, p_c, p_d, \cdots$ that make x_1 more

negative than $-q_{a,1}$, this equation, too, will have to be replaced by the equation $x_1 = -q_{a,1}$, and, furthermore, that in this case the system of equations that must furnish the demand for or the supply of (B) for exchanger (1) will be the following:

$$y_1 p_b + z_1 p_c + w_1 p_d + \cdots = q_{a,1},$$

$$p_b \varphi_{c,1}\left(q_{c,1} + z_1\right) = p_c \varphi_{b,1}\left(q_{b,1} + y_1\right),$$

$$p_b \varphi_{d,1}\left(q_{d,1} + w_1\right) = p_d \varphi_{b,1}\left(q_{b,1} + y_1\right),$$

$$\vdots$$

hence, again, $m - 1$ equations from which we can assume that the $m - 2$ unknowns $z_1, w_1, \cdots$ have been eliminated successively so that only one equation remains giving y_1 as a function of $p_b, p_c, p_d, \cdots$.

121. The demand and supply equations for (A), (B), (C), (D), $\cdots$ for the exchangers (1), (2), (3), $\cdots$ now having been properly established, by hypothesis, to meet the foregoing restrictions, let us now denote by X, Y, Z, W, $\cdots$ the sums $x_1 + x_2 + x_3 + \cdots$, $y_1 + y_2 + y_3 + \cdots$, $z_1 + z_2 + z_3 + \cdots$, $w_1 + w_2 + w_3 + \cdots$, and by F_b, F_c, F_d, $\cdots$ the sums of the functions $f_{b,1}, f_{b,2}, f_{b,3}, \cdots, f_{c,1}, f_{c,2}, f_{c,3}, \cdots, f_{d,1}, f_{d,2}, f_{d,3}, \cdots$. The condition of equality of supply and demand for the commodities (A), (B), (C), (D), $\cdots$ being expressed, in the general case we are now dealing with, by the equations $X = 0$, $Y = 0$, $Z = 0$, $W = 0$, $\cdots$, we have, for the determination of the current equilibrium prices, the equations

$$F_b\left(p_b, p_c, p_d, \cdots\right) = 0,$$

$$F_c\left(p_b, p_c, p_d, \cdots\right) = 0,$$

$$F_d\left(p_b, p_c, p_d, \cdots\right) = 0,$$

$$\vdots$$

hence $m - 1$ equations. Furthermore, it is obvious that, $p_b, p_c, p_d, \cdots$ being essentially positive, if these $m - 1$ equations are fulfilled, that is to say, if we have $Y = 0$, $Z = 0$, $W = 0$, $\cdots$, we have also

$$X = -\left(Yp_b + Zp_c + Wp_d\right) = 0.$$

122. In this way, the $m - 1$ prices of the $m - 1$ commodities in terms of the mth taken as the numeraire will be determined mathematically by the threefold condition: 1° that each exchanger obtains maximum satisfaction of his wants, the ratios of the raretés being equal to the prices;[ii] 2° that everyone must receive in proportion to what he gives or must give in proportion to what he receives there being for each commodity only one price in terms of the numeraire, the one for which total effective demand equals total effective supply; 3° that arbitrage will not take place, the equilibrium price of the one in terms of the other of two commodities being equal to the ratio of the equilibrium price of each of them in terms of any third commodity, that is, to the inverse ratio of the equilibrium prices of any third commodity in terms of each of them. Let us see now how this same problem of the exchange of several commodities for one another, for which we just have found the theoretical solution, is also the problem that is solved empirically in the market by the mechanism of competition.

123. To begin with, by adopting a numeraire in the market, we have in fact reduced the $m(m - 1)$ prices of the m commodities the one in terms of the other to $m - 1$ prices of $m - 1$ of them in terms of the mth. The latter is the numeraire; and, as for the $(m - 1)(m - 1)$ prices of the other commodities in one another, these are assumed to be equal to the ratios of the prices of the commodities in numeraire in accordance with the condition of general equilibrium. Let $p_b', p_c', p_d', \cdots$ be $m - 1$ prices of (B), (C), (D), $\cdots$ in terms of (A) cried in this way, at random. At these prices so cried, each exchanger determines his demand or his supply of (A), (B), (C), (D), $\cdots$. This takes place after reflection, without calculation, but exactly as if it were done by calculation in accordance with the system of equations of equivalence of the quantities demanded and supplied and of maximum satisfaction under the agreed upon restrictions. Let $x_1', x_2', x_3', \cdots$, $y_1', y_2', y_3', \cdots$, $z_1', z_2', z_3', \cdots$, $w_1', w_2', w_3', \cdots$, positive or negative, be the partial demands or supplies corresponding to the prices $p_b', p_c', p_d', \cdots$. If the total demand

and supply relating to each commodity were equal; that is to say, if we immediately had $Y' = 0$, $Z' = 0$, $W' = 0$, $\cdots$ and, consequently, $X' = 0$, exchange would take place at these prices, and the problem would be solved. However, generally total demand and total supply for each commodity will be unequal, that is to say, $Y' \gtrless 0$, $Z' \gtrless 0$, $W' \gtrless 0, \cdots$, and, consequently, $X' \gtrless 0$. What will people do in the market in this case? If demand is greater than supply, they will increase the price of the commodity in numeraire; if supply is greater than demand, they will lower the price. What must therefore be proved to establish that the theoretical solution and the one in the market are identical? The answer is simply that raising and lowering prices is a method of solving by tatonnement the system of equations of equality of demand and supply.

124. Let us recall that we have the equation

$$X' + Y'p'_b + Z'p'_c + Wp'_d + \cdots = 0.$$

Denoting the sum of the positive x, y, z, w, $\cdots$ by $D'_a, D'_b, D'_c, D'_d, \cdots$ and the sum of the negative x, y, z, w, $\cdots$ by $O'_a, O'_b, O'_c, O'_d, \cdots$ all corresponding with the prices $p'_b, p'_c, p'_d, \cdots$, the equation above can be put into the form

$$D'_a - O'_a + (D'_b - O'_b)p'_b + \left(D'_c - O'_c\right)p'_c + (D'_d - O'_d)p'_d + \cdots = 0,$$

and we observe that, $p'_b, p'_c, p'_d, \cdots$ being positive by their very nature, if, among the quantities $X' = D'_a - O'_a$, $Y' = D'_b - O'_b$, $Z' = D'_c - O'_c$, $W' = D'_d - O'_d$, $\cdots$, some are positive, the rest must be negative,[iii] and vice versa. That is to say, that at prices $p'_b, p'_c, p'_d, \cdots$ the total demand of certain commodities is superior to the supply, and the supply of other commodities is superior to their demand, and vice versa.

125. Let us now take the function

$$F_b(p'_b, p'_c, p'_d, \cdots) \gtrless 0,$$

and let us write it in the form

$$\Delta_b(p'_b, p'_c, p'_d, \cdots) \gtreqless \Omega_b(p'_b, p'_c, p'_d, \cdots),$$

the function Δ_b representing the sum of the positive ys, hence D_b, and the function Ω_b the sum of the negative ys taken as positive, hence O_b. Let us abstract from $p'_c, p'_d, \cdots$, supposing these prices as predetermined, and let us find out how the price p_b has to be varied between 0 and infinity so that the demand for (B) becomes equal to its supply. We do not know the function F_b, nor the functions Δ_b and Ω_b, but from the very nature of the fact of exchange, as we have studied it, we can deduce with respect to these functions sufficient information to be sure that, in the operation under consideration, p_b will meet with a value, if it exists, that will make F_b pass through zero, or will bring about equality of Δ_b and Ω_b.

126. With regard to, first, the function Δ_b of the demand for (B) in exchange for (A), (B), (D), $\cdots$, we can say that it is positive for $p_b = 0$; that is to say, for prices of (B) that are zero in terms of (A), (C), (D), $\cdots$. Indeed, at these prices, the total effective demand for (B) equals the excess of total extensive utility over the total quantity possessed, and this excess will be positive if commodity (B) is scarce and is part of social wealth. If p_b increases and, with it, all the prices of (B) in terms of (A), (C), (D), $\cdots$ in proportion, the function will decrease, since it is a sum of decreasing functions. Then, indeed, the commodity (B) will become more and more expensive compared with the commodities (A), (C), (D), $\cdots$; now, it cannot happen, under this hypothesis, and, moreover, all other things being unchanged, that its demand increases: it can only decrease. What is more, we can, in any event, assume that there is a value of p_b, that is to say, prices of (B) in terms of (A), (C), (D), $\cdots$, so high, possibly infinite, that the demand for (B) is zero.

With regard to the function Ω_b of the supply of (B) for (A), (C), (D), $\cdots$, we can say that it is zero for $p_b = 0$, and possibly even for certain positive values of p_b; that is to say, for zero or even positive prices of (B) in terms of (A), (C), (D), $\cdots$. Indeed, just as we can assume that there are prices of (B) in terms of (A), (C), (D), $\cdots$ so high that its demand is zero, we can also assume that there are prices of (A), (C), (D), $\cdots$ in terms of (B) so high that their demand is zero, in which case the supply of (B) is zero. If p_b increases, and, with it all prices of (B) in terms of (A), (C), (D), $\cdots$ proportionally, the function Ω_b will be successively increasing and decreasing because it is a sum of functions that are successively increasing and decreasing. Then, indeed, the commodities (A), (C), (D), $\cdots$ will become less and less expensive compared with the commodity (B), and the demand for these commodities will materialize at the same time as the supply of (B) that accompanies them. However, the supply does not increase indefinitely; it will pass through at least one maximum, which cannot be superior to the total quantity possessed, and become zero again if p_b tends to infinity; that is to say, if (A), (C), (D), $\cdots$ are free commodities.

127. Under these conditions, and provided that D_b does not become zero before O_b ceases to be so, in which case there is no solution, there exists a certain value of p_b for which O_b and D_b are equal. In order to find this value, we must increase p_b' if, at the price p_b', we have $Y' > 0$, hence $D_b' > O_b'$, and decrease p_b' if, at the price p_b', we have $Y' < 0$, hence $O_b' > D_b'$. In this way, we get the equation

$$F_b(p_b'', p_c', p_d', \cdots) = 0.$$

Having carried out this operation, the function

$$F_c(p_b', p_c', p_d', \cdots) \gtreqless 0$$

has become

$$F_c(p_b'', p_c', p_d', \cdots) \gtreqless 0;$$

but we can obtain the equation

$$F_c(p_b'', p_c'', p_d', \ldots) = 0$$

by increasing or decreasing p_c' in accordance with whether we have, at the price p_c', either $Z' > 0$, hence $D_c' > O_c'$, or $Z' < 0$, hence $O_c' > D_c'$.

Similarly, we get the equation

$$F_c(p_b'', p_c'', p_d'', \ldots) = 0;\text{ iv}$$

and so forth.

128. Having carried out all these operations, we have

$$F_b(p_b'', p_c'', p_d'', \cdots) \gtrless 0,\text{ v}$$

and it must be demonstrated that this function is closer to zero than the original basic one

$$F_b(p_b', p_c', p_d', \ldots) \gtrless 0.$$

Now, this will appear probable[vi] if it is recognized that the change of p_b' to p_b'' that has brought the latter inequality into equality has had effects that are direct and, at least as far as concerns the demand for (B), all in the same direction, whereas the change of p_c' into p_c'', of p_d' into p_d'', and so forth, which have changed the latter from equality into the inequality, have had indirect effects and, at least as far as concerns the demand for (B), in opposite directions, and has cancelled out each other to a certain degree. For this reason, the system of new prices $p_b'', p_c'', p_d'', \cdots$ is closer to equilibrium than the old system of prices $p_b', p_c', p_d', \cdots$, and we have only to continue in the same way to approach equilibrium more and more closely.

So, we have arrived at the following formulation of the law of the determination of the equilibrium prices in the case of exchange of several commodities for one another by means of a numeraire: – *Given several commodities, the exchange of which takes place by means of a numeraire, for the market to be in equilibrium, or for stationary prices of all these commodities, it is necessary and sufficient that at these prices the effective demand for each commodity is equal to its effective supply. When this equality does not exist, it is necessary, in order to bring about equilibrium, to increase the price of the commodities for which the effective demand is greater than the effective supply, and decrease the price of the commodities for which the effective supply is greater than the effective demand.*

Notes

i To make a correct assertion, Walras should have inserted at this place: 'and when no other commodities are supplied, i.e., when all the other commodities are demanded'.

ii Walras meant 'the ratios of the raretés being equal to the ratios of the prices'.

iii Strictly speaking, Walras should have written 'at least one of the rest should be negative'.

iv The other prices in this function have only one prime.

v Now all the prices in the functions have a double prime.

vi Regarding the stability, Walras wrote 'certain' in the first edition of the *Éléments*.

LESSON 13

Law of the variation of the prices of the commodities

SUMMARY: – Analytical definition of the exchange of several commodities for one another. Identity of the ratio of the rareté of any two commodities for all the exchangers in the state of general equilibrium. Proportionality of the exchange values to the raretés. Reservation regarding the case of discontinuity of the want curves. Reservation regarding the case of zero demand, or of supply equal to the quantity possessed. Average raretés. Undetermined and arbitrary terms of value in exchange. Variation in the prices because of variation in the utility and the quantity. Unchanging prices and simultaneous variation of utility and of quantity. On the *law* known as the *law of supply and demand*.

129. From the preceding considerations, it is quite obvious that, for several commodities as for two, the necessary and sufficient elements for the determination of the current prices, or equilibrium prices, are the exchangers' equations of utility or want of the commodities, equations that can always be represented by curves, and the quantities of the commodities possessed by their holders. From these constituent elements result mathematically: 1° the partial and total demand and supply equations, and 2° the current, or equilibrium, prices. To the conditions of maximum satisfaction, on the one hand, and unity of the prices of whatever two commodities, with equality of total supply and demand of the one in terms of the other, on the other hand, we have only to add here the condition of general equilibrium of the prices.

Hence: – *Exchange of several commodities for one another in a market governed by free competition is an operation by means of*

145

which all the holders, either of one, or of several, or of all of these commodities, can obtain the greatest satisfaction of their needs compatible with the condition that not only are two arbitrary commodities exchanged in a common, identical proportion, but that, moreover, these two commodities can be exchanged for an arbitrary third one in accordance with two proportions, the ratio of which is equal to the first one.

130. If prices have been cried in terms of the numeraire, the condition of general economic equilibrium has been fulfilled *ipso facto*. Otherwise, it would have been brought about by arbitrage. It is useful to be aware of the exact result of these operations.

Let trader (1) be a holder of (A), trader (2) a holder of (B), trader (3) a holder of (C); let $r_{a,1}, r_{b,1}, r_{c,1}, r_{d,1}, \cdots, r_{a,2}, r_{b,2}, r_{c,2}, r_{d,2}, \cdots, r_{a,3}, r_{b,3}, r_{c,3}, r_{d,3}, \cdots$ be the raretés of the commodities (A), (B), (C), (D), $\cdots$ for these three traders, and, for the time being, let these raretés be variable, depending on the variable prices. Under the hypothesis that arbitrage does not occur, the condition of maximum satisfaction can be expressed as follows:

$$p_{b,a} = \frac{r_{b,1}}{r_{a,1}}, \qquad p_{c,a} = \frac{r_{c,1}}{r_{a,1}}, \qquad p_{d,a} = \frac{r_{d,1}}{r_{a,1}}, \cdots$$

$$p_{a,b} = \frac{r_{a,2}}{r_{b,2}}, \qquad p_{c,b} = \frac{r_{c,2}}{r_{b,2}}, \qquad p_{d,b} = \frac{r_{d,2}}{r_{b,2}}, \cdots$$

$$p_{a,c} = \frac{r_{a,3}}{r_{c,3}}, \qquad p_{b,c} = \frac{r_{b,3}}{r_{c,3}}, \qquad p_{d,c} = \frac{r_{d,3}}{r_{c,3}}, \cdots.$$

Let us now assume that arbitrage is possible, and let us consider only the three commodities (A), (B) and (C), and the traders (1), (2) and (3). Before the arbitrage, we had already, by virtue of the reciprocity of the prices:

$$\frac{r_{b,1}}{r_{a,1}} = p_{b,a} = \frac{1}{p_{a,b}} = \frac{r_{b,2}}{r_{a,2}},$$

$$\frac{r_{c,1}}{r_{a,1}} = p_{c,a} = \frac{1}{p_{a,c}} = \frac{r_{c,3}}{r_{a,3}},$$

$$\frac{r_{c,2}}{r_{b,2}} = p_{c,b} = \frac{1}{p_{b,c}} = \frac{r_{c,3}}{r_{b,3}}.$$

Moreover, we have, after the arbitrage, by virtue of the general equilibrium:

$$\frac{r_{b,2}}{r_{a,2}} = p_{b,a} = \frac{p_{b,c}}{p_{a,c}} = \frac{r_{b,3}}{r_{a,3}},$$

$$\frac{r_{c,1}}{r_{a,1}} = p_{c,a} = \frac{p_{c,b}}{p_{a,b}} = \frac{r_{c,2}}{r_{a,2}},$$

$$\frac{r_{c,2}}{r_{b,2}} = p_{c,b} = \frac{p_{c,a}}{p_{b,a}} = \frac{r_{c,1}}{r_{b,1}}.$$

If it is noted that the reasoning concerning the three commodities (A), (B) and (C), and the traders (1), (2) and (3) can be extended to all commodities and all traders, it can be seen that: – *When the market is in a state of general equilibrium, the ratio of the raretés of two arbitrary commodities, equal to the price of the one in terms of the other, is the same for all the holders of these two commodities.*

131. If $v_a, v_b, v_c, v_d, \cdots$ are the exchange values of the commodities (A), (B), (C), (D), $\cdots$, and if $r_{a,1}, r_{b,1}, r_{c,1}, r_{d,1}, \cdots, r_{a,2}, r_{b,2}, r_{c,2}, r_{d,2}, \cdots, r_{a,3}, r_{b,3}, r_{c,3}, r_{d,3}, \cdots$ are the raretés of these commodities for the traders (1), (2), (3), $\cdots$ after the exchange, we have then:

$$p_b = \frac{r_{b,1}}{r_{a,1}} = \frac{r_{b,2}}{r_{a,2}} = \frac{r_{b,3}}{r_{a,3}} = \cdots$$

$$p_c = \frac{r_{c,1}}{r_{a,1}} = \frac{r_{c,2}}{r_{a,2}} = \frac{r_{c,3}}{r_{a,3}} = \cdots$$

$$p_d = \frac{r_{d,1}}{r_{a,1}} = \frac{r_{d,2}}{r_{a,2}} = \frac{r_{d,3}}{r_{a,3}} = \cdots$$

$$\vdots$$

which can also be expressed in this way:

$$v_a : v_b : v_c : v_d : \cdots$$

$$:: r_{a,1} : r_{b,1} : r_{c,1} : r_{d,1} : \cdots$$

$$:: r_{a,2} : r_{b,2} : r_{c,2} : r_{d,2} : \cdots$$

$$:: r_{a,3} : r_{b,3} : r_{c,3} : r_{d,3} : \cdots$$

$$\vdots$$

In setting forth and solving the equations of exchange, we have until now considered only the case of commodities that can be consumed in infinitely small quantities, and that have utility curves or want curves that are continuous. But we have also to give attention to the cases of commodities that are by their nature consumed in integral units, having utility or want curves that are discontinuous. These cases are numerous. Cases in point are those of furniture, articles of clothing, etc. There is always a substantial difference of intensity between the first bed, a first piece of clothing, a first hat, a first pair of shoes, and that of a second article of the same type, and also between the utility of a second object and that of a third one, etc. This difference is sometimes even substantial. Thus, a first pair of crutches for a lame person, a first pair of glasses for a short-sighted person, a first violin for a professional musician, are, so to speak, indispensible; a second pair of crutches or glasses, or a second violin are, in a way, superfluous. In all these cases it would be necessary, for several commodities as for two, to put into the tables of rareté, underlining them, proportional terms that would be very close to the average of the last wants satisfied and the first wants unsatisfied.

Moreover, here too it is possible that one or several terms are lacking among the raretés of a given trader. This happens every time that a trader, not being a holder of a certain commodity, will not be a demander of it at the current price, or, being a holder, will be a supplier of all of it that he possesses. The rich persons are those whose last wants satisfied are numerous and of little intensity, and the poor persons, on the contrary, are those whose last wants satisfied are few and intense. And here also, for the case of several commodities as for the case of two, we will have to put into the above tables, putting them within parentheses, the terms that would be obtained by taking the price of the commodity not consumed in terms of any other commodity that is consumed and multiplying that price by the rareté of the latter.

Under this double reservation, we can state the following proposition:

– *The values in exchange are proportional to the raretés.*

132. Let, on the one hand, (A), (B) and (D) be commodities that can be consumed in infinitely small quantities; and let, consequently, $\alpha_{r,1}\alpha_{q,1}$, $\alpha_{r,2}\alpha_{q,2}$, $\alpha_{r,3}\alpha_{q,3}$, $\beta_{r,1}\beta_{q,1}$, $\beta_{r,2}\beta_{q,2}$, $\beta_{r,3}\beta_{q,3}$, $\delta_{r,1}\delta_{q,1}$, $\delta_{r,2}\delta_{q,2}$, $\delta_{r,3}\delta_{q,3}$ (Fig. 17) be the continuous utility or want curves of the these commodities for the traders (1), (2), (3). Let, on the other hand, (C) be a commodity that is, because of its nature, consumed in unit quantities, and let, consequently, $\gamma_{r,1}\gamma_{q,1}$, $\gamma_{r,2}\gamma_{q,2}$, $\gamma_{r,3}\gamma_{q,3}$,$\cdots$ be the discontinuous utility or want curves of this commodity for the traders (1), (2), (3), $\cdots$. Let the prices of (B), (C), and (D) in terms of (A) be 2, 2.5 and 0.5.

In the example of our figure, trader (1) is a rich man who consumes (A), (B), (C), and (D) in quantities 7, 8, 7, and 6, and who obtains the small raretés 2, 4, 6 and 1, procuring a very considerable total amount of effective utility represented by [the sum of] the surfaces $Oq_{a,1}r_{a,1}\alpha_{r,1}$, $Oq_{b,1}r_{b,1}\beta_{r,1}$, $Oq_{c,1}r_{c,1}\gamma_{r,1}$, $Oq_{d,1}r_{d,1}\delta_{r,1}$. The raretés of (A), (B), and (D), namely 2, 4 and 1, are strictly proportional to the prices 1, 2 and 0.5. The rareté of (C), 6, should be replaced by the underlined number 5 = 2 × 2.5, intermediate between the intensity 6 of the last want satisfied and the intensity 4 of the first want not satisfied of (C). Trader (2) is a poor man who consumes (A) and (D) in quantities 3 and 2 and obtains the large raretés 6 and 3, procuring a insignificant total amount of effective utility represented by the surfaces $Oq_{a,2}r_{a,2}\alpha_{r,2}$ and $Oq_{d,2}r_{d,2}\delta_{r,2}$; he abstains from consuming (C) or (D) because the amounts 12 = 6 × 2 and 15 = 6 × 2.5, that should

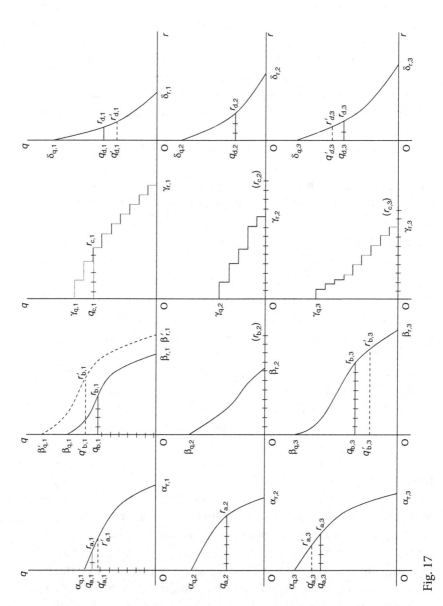

Fig. 17

have been put into the series of raretés, exceed the intensities 8 and 11 of the first wants to be satisfied of these commodities. And, trader (3) is simply a wealthy man who consumes (A), (B) and (D) in quantities 5, 4 and 3 and obtains the moderate raretés 4, 8 and 2, procuring an unexceptional total amount of effective utility represented by the surfaces $Oq_{a,3}r_{a,3}\alpha_{r,3}, Oq_{b,3}r_{b,3}\beta_{r,3}, Oq_{d,3}r_{d,3}\delta_{r,3}$, but who does without (C) because the amount $10 = 4 \times 2.5$, that should have been put into the series of raretés, exceeds 8, the intensity of the first want for this commodity to be satisfied. Putting these proportional amounts corresponding to virtual, non-effective raretés between parenthesis, we obtain the equilibrium table:

	1	:	2	:	2.5	:	0.5
::	2	:	4	:	5	:	1
::	6	:	(12)	:	(15)	:	3
::	4	:	8	:	(10)	:	2

133. The ratios of the average raretés will be, as we know, the same as that of the individual raretés. In determining the averages, we must take account only of the underlined proportional numbers and the ones between parentheses. Under these conditions, and denoting the average raretés of (A), (B), (C), (D), $\cdots$ by $R_a, R_b, R_c, R_d, \cdots$, we can substitute for the equations

$$p_b = \frac{v_b}{v_a}, \quad p_c = \frac{v_c}{v_a}, \quad p_d = \frac{v_d}{v_a}, \cdots$$

the equations

$$p_b = \frac{R_b}{R_a}, \quad p_c = \frac{R_c}{R_a}, \quad p_d = \frac{R_d}{R_a}, \cdots.$$

134. The fact of value in exchange, which is such a complicated fact, in particular in the case of several commodities, finally appears here in its true character. What are $v_a, v_b, v_c, v_d, \cdots$? Absolutely nothing other than undetermined and arbitrary terms regarding which only the ratio represent the common and identical ratio of all the commodities for all the traders in the state of general equilibrium in the

market; of the raretés and, consequently, regarding which only their ratios two by two, equal to the ratios two by two of the raretés of any trader, can be given a numerical expression. So, value in exchange remains an essentially relative fact, always having its cause in rareté, which alone is an absolute fact. As before, however, just as there is no more for each trader than m raretés of the m commodities, there is, in a market in the state of general equilibrium, no more than m undetermined terms of value in exchange of these commodities, of which the combination two by two gives the $m(m-1)$ prices of these commodities in terms of one another. This circumstance permits, in certain cases, the arbitrary terms themselves to be brought into the calculations, instead of their ratios. One would even be tempted to go a little further and benefit from this circumstance by stating that in a state of general equilibrium, *each commodity has only one exchange value with respect to all other commodities in the market.* But this way of putting it would perhaps point too much into the direction of absolute value; it is better to express the fact being considered here by using the terms of the theorem of general equilibrium (§ 110) or the analytical definition of exchange (§ 129).

135. The utilities and the quantities possessed being always the causes and the initial conditions of the determination of the prices, they are also by this very fact always the causes and the initial conditions for the variations of these prices.

Assume equilibrium is established and let the several traders be in possession of certain quantities of (A), (B), (C), (D), ⋯ that, at the prices $p_b, p_c, p_d, \cdots$ of (B), (C), (D), ⋯ in terms of (A), give them maximum satisfaction. Furthermore, let us reserve the expressions *increase in utility* and *decrease in utility* to denote shifts of the want curve that have as a result an increase or decrease in the intensity of the last want satisfied, or the rareté after the exchange. And, this being well understood, let us assume there is an increase in the utility of (B); that is to say, a shift of the want curve of (B) resulting in an increase in the rareté of (B) for certain traders. There is no longer maximum satisfaction for these individuals. On the contrary, at the prices $p_b, p_c, p_d, \cdots$, it is advantageous for them to demand (B) in exchange for (A), (C), (D), ⋯. Hence, where there existed equality of demand and supply for all the commodities (A), (B), (C), (D), ⋯, there will be now, at these prices, an excess of the demand for (B) over its supply and an excess of the supply of (A), (C), (D), $\cdots$ over the demand for these goods, resulting in a rise of the price of (B). But then there will no longer be maximum satisfaction for the other traders. On the contrary, it will be advantageous for them, at a price of (B) in terms of (A) superior to p_b, to offer (B) and demand (A), (C), (D). The equilibrium will be re-established when demand and supply for all the commodities will be equal. So, the increase in the utility of (B) for our traders will have had for result an increase in the price of (B). It can also result in price changes for (C), (D), $\cdots$. However, first, this second result will be less important than the first if the goods other than (B) are numerous in the market, and if, consequently, the quantity of each of them exchanged for (B) is very small. Second, moreover, nothing indicates whether these changes of the prices of (C), (D), will be price increases or price decreases, nor even if they have taken place, as one can convince himself by studying the situation of the raretés when the new equilibrium is established after the complementary exchange. In this operation, the ratios of the raretés of (B) to those of (A) will have necessarily increased for all traders: they will have increased by the increase in the raretés of (B) and the decrease in the raretés of (A) for those whose utility of (B) did not increase and who have sold (B) and bought (A), (C), (D), $\cdots$, and they will have increased by the increase in the raretés of (A) and the greater increase in the raretés of (B) for those traders for whom the utility of (B) has increased and who have bought (B) and sold (A), (C), (D), $\cdots$. As far as regards the ratios of the raretés of (C), (D), $\cdots$ to the raretés of (A), some will have increased, others decreased, and others, finally, will have remained unchanged; consequently, among the prices of (C), (D), $\cdots$ some will have increased, others will have decreased, and others will have remained stationary. To sum up, it should be noticed that the raretés of (B) have increased for all traders in the sense that the average rareté has increased, whereas the raretés of (A), (C), (D), $\cdots$ have increased for some and decreased for others in such a way that the average rareté has scarcely changed. If one so wishes, the above phenomena for a trader of each category can be represented graphically. In Fig. 17, for instance, the utility of (B) having increased for trader (1), that trader has bought (B) and sold (A) and (D); trader (2)'s position did not change; and trader (3) has sold (B) and bought (A) and (D). These are the results of increase in the utility of (B); obviously, a decrease in this utility would have had the opposite results; that is to say, a fall of the price of (B) and hardly appreciable changes of the prices of (C), (D), ⋯.

We only have to look to the want curves to see that an increase in the quantity possessed will result in a decrease in the rareté, and that a decrease of the quantity possessed will result in an increase in the rareté. Moreover, as we have seen above, when the rareté decreases or increases, the price will decrease or increase. Thus, the effects of the variation in the quantity possessed are purely and simply the opposite of those of the variation in the utility, and we can state the law that we seek as follows:

– *Given several commodities in a state of general equilibrium in a market with a numeraire as intermediary, if, everything else remaining the same, the utility of one of these commodities increases or decreases for one or more traders, then the price of this commodity in numeraire increases or decreases.*

If, everything else remaining the same, the quantity of one of these commodities increases or decreases for one or more traders, then the price of this commodity increases or decreases.

We observe that whereas the variation in the prices indicates necessarily a variation in the elements of these prices, the persistence of these prices does not necessarily imply the persistence of the elements of the prices. Indeed, we can, without further demonstration, state the following twofold proposition:

– *Several commodities being given, if the utility and the quantity of one of these commodities for one or more of the traders or holders vary such that the raretés do not change, the price of this commodity remains unchanged.*

If the utility and the quantity of all the commodities for one or more traders or holders vary such that the ratios of the raretés do not change, the prices will remain unchanged.

136. This is *the law of the variation of the equilibrium prices*; uniting it with the *law of the determination of the equilibrium prices* (§ 128), we obtain the scientific formulation of what is called in economics THE LAW OF SUPPLY AND DEMAND, a fundamental law, but one that until now has been formulated only in meaningless or erroneous expressions.

Thus, it is sometimes said: 'The price of things is determined by the ratio of supply to demand', aiming in particular at the determination of the prices; and sometimes: 'The price of things varies directly with demand and indirectly with supply', thus aiming rather at the variation of prices. However, in the first place, in order to give these two expressions, which really state the same thing, any meaning, it would be necessary to define supply and demand. And then, whether supply be defined by effective supply or by the quantity possessed or existing, and demand defined by effective demand, or by utility, be it extensive, intensive, or virtual, if one means the word proportion in the mathematical sense of a quotient, it is certain that the price is no more the ratio of demand to supply than it is the ratio of supply to demand, and does no more vary directly with demand and inversely with supply than it varies directly with supply and inversely with demand. I therefore take the liberty of remarking that, until now, the fundamental law of economics has not only never been demonstrated, but has never even been formulated correctly. And I permit myself to add that, to provide the formulation and the demonstration of the law in question, or of the two laws of which it is composed, it was necessary to define effective supply and effective demand, and to study the relation of effective supply and effective demand with the price, to define rareté, and also to study the relation of rareté to the price, all being things that it is impossible to do without having recourse to the language, the method, and the principles of mathematics. From this it follows, to sum it all up, that the mathematical form is, for economic theory, not only a possible form, but the necessary and indispensable form. I think, moreover, that this is a point with respect to which none of the readers who have followed me up to this point could have retained the least doubt.

LESSON 14

Theorem of equivalent redistributions. Choice of a standard of measurement and of a medium of exchange

SUMMARY: – Redistribution of commodities among traders. Condition of equivalence of quantities possessed. Condition of equality of total quantities existing. Partial demand and supply in accordance with the condition of maximum satisfaction. The quantities demanded and the quantities supplied by each exchanger are always equivalent. Total demand and total supply for each commodity are always equal. Hence, the current prices do not change under the two conditions of the equivalence of the quantities possessed and the equality of the total quantities. Necessity of the two conditions.

Numeraire, Standard, Change of standard. Rational statement of the price; popularized statement. Twofold error of the popular statement: 1° the value of the standard is not fixed and invariable; 2° there is nothing that can be the value of the standard. The standard is not the value of a certain quantity of the numeraire, but is this quantity itself. Measurement of value and of wealth by means of the numeraire. Money. Exchange of wealth by means of money.

137. The commodities (A), (B), (C), (D), $\cdots$ possessed respectively by the traders (1), (2), (3), $\cdots$ in quantities $q_{a,1}, q_{b,1}, q_{c,1}, q_{d,1}, \cdots$, $q_{a,2}, q_{b,2}, q_{c,2}, q_{d,2}, \cdots$, $q_{a,3}, q_{b,3}, q_{c,3}, q_{d,3}, \cdots$ are respectively the total quantities

$$Q_a = q_{a,1} + q_{a,2} + q_{a,3} + \cdots$$

$$Q_b = q_{b,1} + q_{b,2} + q_{b,3} + \cdots$$

$$Q_c = q_{c,1} + q_{c,2} + q_{c,3} + \cdots$$

$$Q_d = q_{d,1} + q_{d,2} + q_{d,3} + \cdots$$

$$\vdots$$

And, under these conditions of quantity possessed together with the conditions of virtual utility determined by the utility or want equations, these commodities are exchanged for one another at the general equilibrium prices $p_b, p_c, p_d, \cdots$.

Let us now assume that these same commodities (A), (B), (C), (D), $\cdots$ are redistributed among the traders (1), (2), (3), $\cdots$ in a different way but in such a way, however, that for each trader the amounts of the new quantities, $q'_{a,1}, q'_{b,1}, q'_{c,1}, q'_{d,1}, \cdots,\ q'_{a,2}, q'_{b,2}, q'_{c,2}, q'_{d,2}, \cdots,$ $q'_{a,3}, q'_{b,3}, q'_{c,3}, q'_{d,3}, \cdots$ are equivalent to the original quantities; that is to say, in such a way that

$$q_{a,1} + q_{b,1}p_b + q_{c,1}p_c + q_{d,1}p_d + \cdots = q'_{a,1} + q'_{b,1}p_b + q'_{c,1}p_c + q'_{d,1}p_d + \cdots$$

$$q_{a,2} + q_{b,2}p_b + q_{c,2}p_c + q_{d,2}p_d + \cdots = q'_{a,2} + q'_{b,2}p_b + q'_{c,2}p_c + q'_{d,2}p_d + \cdots \quad [1]$$

$$q_{a,3} + q_{b,3}p_b + q_{c,3}p_c + q_{d,3}p_d + \cdots = q'_{a,3} + q'_{b,3}p_b + q'_{c,3}p_c + q'_{d,3}p_d + \cdots$$

$$\vdots$$

Assume, moreover, that the total quantities in existence do not vary, or that the commodities (A), (B), (C), (D), $\cdots$ are the total quantities

$$Q_a = q'_{a,1} + q'_{a,2} + q'_{a,3} + \cdots$$

$$Q_b = q'_{b,1} + q'_{b,2} + q'_{b,3} + \cdots$$

$$Q_c = q'_{c,1} + q'_{c,2} + q'_{c,3} + \cdots \quad [2]$$

$$Q_d = q'_{d,1} + q'_{d,2} + q'_{d,3} + \cdots$$

$$\vdots$$

I say that under these new conditions of quantity possessed, together with the old conditions of virtual utility, the prices $p_b, p_c, p_d, \cdots$ still are, theoretically and practically, the equilibrium prices.

138. Let us select trader (1) out of all of them and assume that at these prices he acquires the quantities, respectively, $x_1', y_1', z_1', w_1', \cdots$ of the commodities (A), (B), (C), (D), $\cdots$ so that he has in all the quantities

$$q_{a,1}' + x_1' = q_{a,1} + x_1$$

$$q_{c,1}' + y_1' = q_{b,1} + y_1$$

$$q_{c,1}' + z_1' = q_{c,1} + z_1 \qquad\qquad [3]$$

$$q_{d,1}' + w_1' = q_{d,1} + w_1$$

$$\vdots$$

In this way, this trader will obtain maximum satisfaction of his wants because the following system of equations is obviously satisfied:

$$\varphi_{b,1}(q_{b,1}' + y_1') = p_b \varphi_{a,1}(q_{a,1}' + x_1')$$

$$\varphi_{c,1}(q_{c,1}' + z') = p_c \varphi_{a,1}(q_{a,1}' + x_1')$$

$$\varphi_{d,1}\left(q_{d,1}' + w_1'\right) = p_d \varphi_{a,1}(q_{a,1}' + x_1')$$

$$\vdots$$

The traders (2), (3), $\cdots$ would also obtain maximum satisfaction of their wants if they would have acquired, at the prices indicated above, quantities $x_2', y_2', z_2', w_2', \cdots, x_3', y_3', z_3', w_3', \cdots$ such that in all they would have the quantities

$$q_{a,2}' + x_2' = q_{a,2} + x_2$$

$$q_{b,2}' + y_2' = q_{b,2} + y_2$$

$$q'_{c,2} + z'_2 = q_{c,2} + z_2 \qquad\qquad [3]$$

$$q'_{d,2} + w'_2 = q_{d,2} + w_2$$

$$\vdots$$

$$q'_{a,3} + x'_3 = q_{a,3} + x_3$$

$$q'_{b,3} + y'_3 = q_{b,3} + y_3$$

$$q'_{c,3} + z'_3 = q_{c,3} + z_3 \qquad\qquad [3]$$

$$q'_{d,3} + w'_3 = q_{d,3} + w_3$$

$$\vdots$$

and so forth.

It remains only to demonstrate that 1°, under the assumed conditions, these traders can demand and supply the above quantities, and that 2°, under the same conditions, the total effective demand of each commodity is equal to its total effective supply.

139. Now, first we have, because of system [1],

$$q_{a,1} - q'_{a,1} + \left(q_{b,1} - q'_{b,1}\right)p_b + \left(q_{c,1} - q'_{c,1}\right)p_c + \left(q_{d,1} - q'_{d,1}\right)p_d + \cdots = 0;$$

this equation can, by virtue of system [3], be put into the form

$$x'_1 - x_1 + \left(y'_1 - y_1\right)p_b + \left(z'_1 - z_1\right)p_c + \left(w'_1 - w_1\right)p_d + \cdots = 0.$$

And, since we have

$$x_1 + y_1 p_b + z_1 p_c + w_1 p_d + \cdots = 0,$$

we have also

$$x'_1 + y'_1 p_b + z'_1 p_c + w'_1 p_d + \cdots = 0.$$

Further we have, for the same reason,

$$x_2' + y_2' p_b + z_2' p_c + w_2' p_d + \cdots = 0,$$

$$x_3' + y_3' p_b + z_3' p_c + w_3' p_d + \cdots = 0,$$

$$\vdots$$

Consequently, the sum of the quantities of the commodities (A), (B), (C), (D), $\cdots$ demanded by the traders (1), (2), (3), $\cdots$ is equivalent, under the conditions defined above, to the sum of the quantities of these commodities supplied by these traders.

140. On the other hand, we have, by suitably adding the equations of the system [3],

$$x_1' + x_2' + x_3' + \cdots = q_{a,1} + q_{a,2} + q_{a,3} +$$
$$\cdots - \left(q_{a,1}' + q_{a,2}' + q_{a,3}' + \cdots \right) + x_1 + x_2 + x_3 + \cdots.$$

And, since we already have

$$X = x_1 + x_2 + x_3 + \cdots = 0,$$

and

$$q_{a,1}' + q_{a,2}' + q_{a,3}' + \cdots = q_{a,1} + q_{a,2} + q_{a,3} + \cdots,$$

we have therefore also

$$X' = x_1' + x_2' + x_3' + \cdots = 0.$$

Similarly, we have likewise

$$Y' = y_1' + y_2' + y_3' + \cdots = 0,$$

$$Z' = z_1' + z_2' + z_3' + \cdots = 0,$$

$$W' = w_1' + w_2' + w_3' + \cdots = 0,$$

$$\vdots$$

and, consequently, total effective demand and total effective supply for each commodity are equal.

141. The prices $p_b, p_c, p_d, \cdots$ are thus the theoretical equilibrium prices, after, just as before the change of the distribution. And, since the mechanism of competition in the market is nothing other than the practical determination of the calculated prices, it follows that: – *Given several commodities in a market in a state of general equilibrium, the current prices of these commodities do not change if the respective quantities are redistributed among the traders in any way whatsoever but provided that the sum of the quantities possessed by each of the traders remains always equivalent.*

142. During the entire course of this demonstration, we have assumed that $Q_a, Q_b, Q_c, Q_d, \cdots$ do not change. Consequently, if the quantities of the commodities (A), (B), (C), (D), $\cdots$ in the possession of a trader, trader (1), for example, vary more or less within the limits imposed by the condition of equivalence, then it is evident that the quantity of these commodities in the possession of one or more other traders, traders (2) or (3), for example, would vary less or more within the same limits in order that the condition of fixedness of total quantities be fulfilled. It is certain that if these commodities exist in large quantities in the market, and if the traders themselves are present in large numbers, the variation between the limits of the condition of equivalence of the quantities in possession of a single trader without the corresponding change of the quantities in possession of the other traders would not have any perceptible influence on the prices and could be considered as not changing anything in the particular situation of our trader or in the general situation of the market. Here we have an application of the law of great numbers of which we can make good use in some cases. But here we want to remain within the domain of mathematical rigor; and to be able to assert that the prices do not change at all, we must assume that the two conditions, equivalence of the quantities possessed and constancy of the total quantities, are fulfilled.

143. The theorem of the general equilibrium of the market can be stated in the following terms:

– *In the state of general equilibrium of the market the m(m – 1)*
prices that regulate the exchange of m commodities taken two at a time
are implicitly determined by the m – 1 prices that regulate the exchange
with the mth commodity of any of the m – 1 commodities chosen from
the m commodities.

So, in the state of general equilibrium, we can define the situation
in the market completely by relating the values of all the commodities to the value of one of them. This latter commodity is called the
numeraire, and a unit of it is called the *standard*. Assuming the values
of (A), (B), (C), (D), $\cdots$ thus related to the value of (A), we have the
series of prices:

$$p_{a,a} = 1, \quad p_{b,a} = \mu, \quad p_{c,a} = \pi, \quad p_{d,a} = \rho, \cdots.$$

If, instead of relating the values to (A)'s, we had related them to the
value of (B), we would have had the series of prices

$$p_{a,b} = \frac{1}{\mu}, \quad p_{b,b} = \frac{\mu}{\mu}, \quad p_{c,b} = \frac{\pi}{\mu}, \quad p_{d,b} = \frac{\rho}{\mu}, \cdots.$$

Hence: – *In order to pass from one numeraire to another, it suffices*
to divide the prices expressed in terms of the first of these two numerai-
res by the price of the new standard expressed in the old numeraire.

144. In this system, let (A) be silver, and let a half-decagram of 9/10
fine silver be its unit; let (B) be wheat, and let the hectoliter be its unit
of quantity. The fact that, in the market in the state of general equilibrium, a hectoliter of wheat will be exchanged currently for 24 half-
decagrams of silver of 9/10 fine will be expressed by the equation

$$p_{b,a} = 24,$$

which should be stated thusly: – 'The price of wheat in silver is 24,'
or, if we wish to mention the quantity units: – 'The price of a hectoliter of wheat is 24 half-decagrams of silver 9/10 fine,' or, differently:
'A hectoliter of wheat is worth 24 half-decagrams of silver 9/10 fine.'
Between this statement and the one that we have used in our general considerations (§ 29) about practical usage and that is conceived

thusly – 'Wheat is worth 24 francs per hectoliter', there is a difference consisting in the substitution of the word *francs* for the words *half-decagrams of silver 9/10 fine*. This difference needs to be discussed meticulously.

The word *franc*, is, in the thought of many people, analogous to the words, *meter, gram, liter*, etc. Now, the word *meter* expresses two things: first, it expresses the length of a certain fraction of the terrestrial meridian, and, second, it expresses a fixed and invariable unit of *length*. Likewise, the word *gram* expresses two things: first, the weight of a certain quantity of distilled water at its maximum density, and, second, a fixed and invariable unit of *weight*. Likewise for the *liter* in regard to *capacity*. The same applies also, in the eyes of ordinary persons, to the word *franc*. This word expresses two things: first, the value of a certain quantity of silver, and second, a fixed and invariable unit of *value*.

Two points have to be distinguished regarding those opinions on the matter: 1° that the word *franc* expresses the value of the half-decagram of silver 9/10 fine; 2° that this value, taken as the unit, is fixed and invariable. The second point represents nothing more than a gross error that is not shared by any economist. Each person, however little he has occupied himself with economics, admits that there is the essential difference between the *meter* and the *franc* that the meter is a fixed and invariable unit of length, whereas the franc is a unit of value that is neither fixed nor invariable, but that, on the contrary, changes and varies from one place to another, from one time to another, because of circumstances that are more or less agreed upon. It is therefore not worth the trouble of losing any time refuting the point in question.

However, this second point set aside, there remains the first one, namely that the franc is the value of a half-decagram of silver 9/10 fine, like the meter is the length of the ten-millionth part of the quarter of the terrestrial meridian. The franc, say the economists who subscribe to this point of view, is a variable measure, but it is a measure. If all lengths, without exception, were in a continuous movement of change, because of contraction or dilation of matter, we could measure them only within certain limits, but we could still measure them within these limits. Well, as we know, all values vary in a continuous movement of change: that forbids us to compare them between one point and another, between one time and another, but not to compare them or to measure at a given point, or at a given time. We will measure them under those conditions.

In this system, (A) being silver, the half-decagram 9/10 fine of silver being the unit of silver, and (B) being wheat, the hectoliter being the unit quantity of wheat, it is thought to be possible to posit the equation

$$v_a = 1 \, franc,$$

and then the fact that, in the market, 1 hectoliter of wheat is currently exchanged for 24 half-decagrams of silver 9/10 fine can be expressed by the equation

$$v_b = 24 \, francs,$$

which can be expressed as follows: 'Wheat is worth 24 francs per hectoliter.'

However, this second point is an error, just as is the first one; and, in neither this respect nor in the other is there any analogy between value on the one hand, and length, weight, capacity on the other. When I measure a given length, the length of a façade, for instance, there are three things: the length of the façade, the length of the ten-millionth part of a quarter of the terrestrial meridian, and the ratio of the first length to the second one, which is the façade's measurement. In order that there be an analogy and that I can, at a given point, at a given time, measure similarly a given value, the value of a hectoliter of wheat, for instance, there must be three things: the value of the hectoliter of wheat, the value of the half-decagram of silver 9/10 fine, and the ratio of the first value to the second one, which is the measurement of the value of the hectoliter of wheat. Now, two of these three things do not exist, the first and the second; only the third exists. Our analysis has perfectly well demonstrated that value is an essentially relative thing. Undoubtedly, behind relative value there is something absolute, namely the intensities of the last wants satisfied, or the raretés. But these raretés, which are absolute and not relative, are subjective or personal and not at all part of external reality or objective. They are within us, and not within the things. It is therefore impossible to substitute them for the values in exchange. From this follows that there is nothing that is either the rareté or the *value of a half-decagram of silver 9/10 fine*, and the word *franc* is a word for a thing that does not exist. J.-B. Say clearly perceived this truth, one which our science must always keep in mind.

145. It does not follow from this that we are unable to measure value and wealth; it follows only that our standard of measure must be a certain quantity of a certain commodity, and not the value of that quantity of the commodity.

As always, let (A) be the numeraire, and let the unit quantity of (A) be the standard of measure. Regarding the values, they measure themselves, because their ratios appear directly as the inverse ratios of the quantities of commodities exchanged. In this way, the ratios of the values of (B), (C), (D), $\cdots$ to the value of (A) appear directly in numbers of units of (A) exchanged for 1 of (B), 1 of (C), 1 of (D), $\cdots$; that is to say, in the prices of (B), (C), (D), $\cdots$ in terms of (A).

Under these circumstances, let $Q_{a,1}$ be the quantity of (A) equivalent to the total amount of the quantities (A), (B), (C), (D), $\cdots$ in possession of trader (1), so that we have, designating the prices of (B), (C), (D), $\cdots$ in terms of (A) simply by $p_b, p_c, p_d, \cdots$,

$$Q_{a,1} = q_{a,1} + q_{b,1}p_b + q_{c,1}p_c + q_{d,1}p_d + \cdots.$$

By virtue of the theorem of equivalent redistributions, we can vary $q_{a,1}, q_{b,1}, q_{c,1}, q_{d,1}, \cdots$. Provided that the new quantities satisfy the equation above (together with the condition of the equality of the total quantities of the commodities), they permit trader (1) always to obtain in the market, at the prices $p_b, p_c, p_d, \cdots$, quantities of (A), (B), (C), (D), $\cdots$ that yield him, at these prices, maximum satisfaction. $Q_{a,1}$, representing all these different quantities, and also the quantities of maximum satisfaction, is therefore the quantity of wealth possessed by trader (1).

Let, under the same conditions,

$$Q_{a,2} = q_{a,2} + q_{b,2}p_b + q_{c,2}p_c + q_{d,2}p_d + \cdots$$

$$Q_{a,3} = q_{a,3} + q_{b,3}p_b + q_{c,3}p_c + q_{d,3}p_d + \cdots$$

$$\vdots$$

$Q_{a,2}, Q_{a,3}, \cdots$ will be the quantities of wealth possessed by traders (2), (3), $\cdots$. These quantities are comparable to $Q_{a,1}$ and are comparable to one another, being composed of units of the same kind of commodity.

Let, finally, $Q_a, Q_b, Q_c, Q_d, \cdots$ be the total quantities of (A), (B), (C), (D), $\cdots$ existing in the market, and let

$$\mathbf{Q}_a = Q_{a,1} + Q_{a,2} + Q_{a,3} + \cdots$$

$$= Q_a + Q_b p_b + Q_c p_c + Q_d p_d + \cdots.$$

$\mathbf{Q}_a$ will be the total existing quantity of wealth in the market; and this quantity is comparable to $Q_{a,1}, Q_{a,2}, Q_{a,3}, \cdots$ and to $Q_a, Q_b p_b, Q_c p_c, Q_d p_d, \cdots$.

146. That is the true role of the instrument of measurement of value and wealth. But, generally, the same commodity that serves as numeraire serves also as *money* and plays the role of medium of exchange. The numeraire standard thus becomes a money standard. These are the two functions that, even when both being operative, are distinct; after having explained the first function, we must also explain the second.

Let (A) still be the commodity designated to serve as medium of exchange. Let, as before, $p_b = \mu, p_c = \pi, p_d = \rho, \cdots$. At these prices of general equilibrium correspond, by virtue of the condition of maximum satisfaction, the quantities effectively demanded that are equal to the quantities effectively supplied: $M, P, R, \cdots, N, F, H, \cdots, Q, G, K, \cdots, S, J, L, \cdots$ of the commodities (A), (B), (C), (D), $\cdots$. And, under the hypothesis of direct exchange, this exchange will take place in accordance with the equations

$$Nv_b = Mv_a, \quad Qv_c = Pv_a, \quad Sv_d = Rv_a, \cdots,$$

$$Gv_c = Fv_b, \quad Jv_d = Hv_b, \quad Lv_d = Kv_c, \cdots.$$

147. But, given the hypothesis of the intervention of money, which is unquestionably the hypothesis that conforms to reality, things are different. Let (A) be silver, (B) wheat, (C) coffee, etc. In reality, the

producer of wheat sells his wheat for silver, and the producer of coffee acts likewise; with the silver thus received, the one buys coffee and the other buys wheat. That is what we assume here. The holders of (A) will become intermediaries because of the fact that they hold the money commodity. The holders of (B) will sell to them, at the price μ, all the wheat they want to sell, only under the condition of buying from them, at prices π, ρ, $\cdots$, all the (C), (D), $\cdots$ they want to buy. These transactions can be expressed by the equations

$$\left(N + F + H + \cdots\right)v_b = (M + F\mu + H\mu + \cdots)v_a$$

$$\left(F\mu = G\pi\right)v_a = Gv_c, \quad \left(H\mu = J\rho\right)v_a = Jv_d \cdots.$$

The holders of (C), (D), $\cdots$ will carry out analogous transactions, which can be expressed by the equations

$$\left(Q + G + K + \cdots\right)v_c = (P + G\pi + K\pi + \cdots)v_a.$$

$$(G\pi = F\mu)v_a = Fv_b, \quad (\kappa\pi = L\rho)v_a = Lv_d \cdots$$

$$\left(S + J + L + \cdots\right)v_d = (R + J\rho + L\rho + \cdots)v_a$$

$$\left(J\rho = H\mu\right)v_b = Hv_b, \quad \left(L\rho = K\pi\right)v_a = Kv_c \cdots.$$

148. We are assuming here that the purchases and resales of (A) as intermediary take place in such a way that the price of that commodity will not be influenced at all. In reality, the use of a commodity as money does have a certain influence that we will study later on. But, subject to this qualification, we see that there exists a perfect analogy between the intervention of money and the intervention of a numeraire. Likewise, just as from the two equations

$$\frac{v_b}{v_a} = \mu, \quad \frac{v_c}{v_a} = \pi,$$

we derive

$$\frac{v_c}{v_a} = \frac{\pi}{\mu},$$

similarly, from the two equations

$$\left(F\mu = G\pi\right)v_a = Gv_c, \quad \left(G\pi = F\mu\right)v_a = Fv_b,$$

we derive

$$Gv_c = Fv_b.$$

Thus, just as we pass, when we so desire, from the indirect price to the direct price by making abstraction from the numeraire, we can also pass, when we so desire, from indirect exchange to direct exchange by making abstraction from money.

LESSON 15

Purchase curves and sales curves.
Price curves

SUMMARY: – The case of several commodities reduced to the case of two commodities. General equilibrium among (A), (C), (D), ···. Introduction of (B). Partial demand curves for (A), (C), (D), ··· in terms of (B). Partial demand curves for (B) in terms of A), (C), (D), ···. The case of a holder of (A), (C), (D), ··· and of (B). Purchase curves and sales curves. Condition of proportional reduction. The case of the supply of (B) equal to the total quantity existing. Price curves. Purchase curves and sales curves can be derived from the equations of exchange.

149. The adoption of a commodity as numeraire and money has as a result the simplification of the determination of the current general equilibrium prices by reducing the case of the exchange of several commodities for one another to the case of the exchange of two commodities for each other. That is the simplification that we have to study now, which is all the more necessary because in adopting the hypothesis of the use of a numeraire and of money, we approach more and more closely the reality of things.

Let (A) therefore be the numeraire and money. Let now, on the one hand, $P', R', \cdots, Q', K', \cdots, S', L', \cdots$ be quantities of the commodities (A), (C), (D), ··· effectively demanded and equal to the quantities effectively supplied, and exchanged or lent for one another at the general equilibrium prices $p_c = \pi$, $p_d = \rho$, ··· of (C), (D), ··· in terms of (A), in accordance with the equations

$$\left(Q' + K' + \cdots\right)v_c = (P' + K'\pi + \cdots)v_a$$

$$\left(K'\pi = L'\rho\right)v_a = L'v_d\cdots$$

$$\left(S' + L' + \cdots\right)v_d = (R' + L'\rho + \cdots)v_a$$

$$\left(L'\rho = K'\pi\right)v_a = K'v_c\cdots$$

And, on the other hand, let commodity (B) be available in the market for exchange for (A), (C), (D), $\cdots$.

Having posited this, let us consider a holder of (B), selected from all holders. If, at price p_b of (B) in terms of (A), corresponding to a price $\dfrac{1}{p_b}$ of (A) in terms of (B), this holder supplies a quantity o_b of (B), he will receive in exchange a quantity $d_a = o_b p_b$ of (A); and, knowing, moreover, the prices of (C), (D), $\cdots$ in terms of (A), he can decide with full knowledge of the facts how to distribute this quantity of (A) among (A), (C), (D), $\cdots$. In other words, knowing the determined prices π, ρ, $\cdots$, he is only ignorant of the undetermined price p_b; but he can make all possible hypotheses about this price, and, for each of these hypotheses, express his disposition to bid, either by means of a supply curve of (B) as a function of p_b, or by a demand curve $a_d a_p$ of (A) as a function of $\dfrac{1}{p_b}$ (Fig. 18).

It is in this way that things take place in reality. A new commodity being introduced into the market, the holders of that commodity determine their supply in accordance with its price, deciding on both what quantity of it they want to give up and what quantity of the other commodities they want to acquire.

On the other hand, let us consider a holder of (A), (C), (D), $\cdots$, selected from among all holders. If, at a price p_b of (B) in terms of (A), this holder demands a quantity d_b of (B), he must give in exchange a quantity of (A), (C), (D), $\cdots$ equivalent to $o_a = d_b p_b$; and, knowing, moreover, the prices of (C), (D), $\cdots$ in terms of (A), he can decide, with full knowledge of the circumstances, how to distribute this quantity of (A) among (A), (C), (D), $\cdots$. In other words, knowing the determined prices π, ρ, $\cdots$, he is only ignorant of the undetermined price p_b; but he can make all possible hypotheses about this

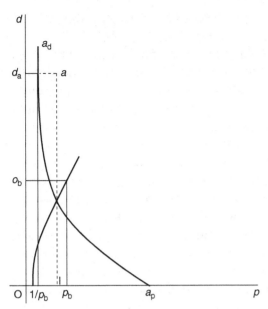

Fig. 18

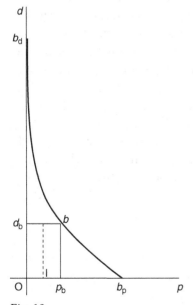

Fig. 19

price, and, for each of these hypotheses, express his disposition to bid by a demand curve $b_d b_p$ as a function of p_b (Fig. 19).

In this case also, things take place in just that way in reality. When a new commodity is introduced into the market, the holders of the other commodities determine their demand for that commodity in accordance with its price, deciding at the same time what quantity they want to acquire of it and what quantity they want to give up of the other commodities.

We have not spoken about the case in which a trader would be at the same time a holder of (B) and of (A), (C), (D), ⋯. But this case, too, is provided for in the theory of the exchange of two commodities for each other. Such a trader would have to produce two curves: a demand curve for (A) or a supply curve for (B) at certain prices, and a demand curve for (B) or a supply curve of (A) at reciprocal prices (§ 93). These two curves would be added to the preceding ones.

The partial demand curves, being added, will give the total demand curves $A_d A_p$, $B_d B_p$ (Fig. 20). From the demand curve $A_d A_p$ for (A), the supply curve NP of (B) can be derived, which could, moreover, also be obtained directly by adding vertically the partial supply curves of this commodity. The curve $B_d B_p$, which is the demand curve for (B) in numeraire, can be called the *purchase curve*; and the curve NP, which is the supply curve of (B) offered for numeraire, can be called the *sales curve*. The intersection of these two curves at point B will determine the price $p_b = \mu$.

150. But will this first determination be definitive? Here a question appears that did not exist regarding the exchange of two commodities for each other. In the general equilibrium existing before the introduction of (B) in the market, we had, between the prices $\pi, \rho, \cdots$ and the quantities to be exchanged at these prices $P', Q', R', S', K', L', \cdots$ the relations

$$P' = Q'\pi, \quad R' = S'\rho, \quad K'\pi = L'\rho, \cdots.$$

In order that this equilibrium will obtain after the introduction of (B) we must have, between the prices $\mu, \pi, \rho, \cdots$ and the quantities $M, N, P, Q, R, S, F, G, H, J, K, L, \cdots$ (§ 146), not only the relations

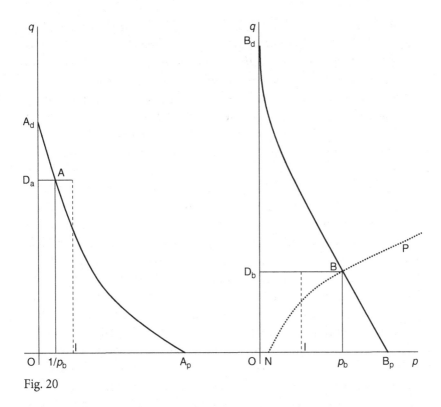

Fig. 20

$$M = N\mu, \quad F\mu = G\pi, \quad H\mu = J\rho, \cdots$$

that we have in actuality, in accordance with the way in which μ has been determined, but we must also have the equations

$$P = Q\pi, \quad R = S\rho, \quad K\pi = L\rho, \cdots.$$

Now, comparing these latter equations with the former, we readily obtain

$$\frac{P}{Q} = \frac{P'}{S'}, \quad \frac{R}{S} = \frac{R'}{S'}, \quad \frac{K}{L} = \frac{K'}{L'}, \cdots.$$

Hence: – *When a new commodity is introduced in a market in the state of general equilibrium, and when the price of this commodity is determined by the equality of its demand in numeraire and its supply for numeraire, in order that the general equilibrium will not be disturbed and the determined price be definitive, the reciprocal demands or supplies of the old commodities must be proportional, before and after the introduction of the new commodity into the market.*

This condition will almost never be completely fulfilled, no more in the case of the appearance of a new commodity than in the case of a price increase of one of the old commodities. As a result, the demand for and the supply of (B) at the price π being equal, the demand for and the supply of (A), (C), (D), $\cdots$ at the prices π, ρ, $\cdots$ will have become unequal. We then find ourselves in the general case, that is to say, we find that we have to increase the price of the commodities the demand for which is superior to their supply, and to decrease the price of the commodities the supply of which is superior to their demand (§ 128). In this way, we arrive at a state of general equilibrium in which the price of (B) will be a little different from μ.

Not only will the condition in question hardly ever be completely fulfilled; but one may even assume a case in which the commodity (B), able to play the role and take the place of some other commodity (C) or (D), will cause a considerable fall in the price of the latter. This can be seen every day. However, if we put aside this special case and assume the commodity (B) is a commodity in a class of its own, or if we consider, among the commodities that were previously on the market, only those with which commodity (B) is not in any appreciable degree of competition, we readily recognize that, if the commodities are numerous and present in considerable quantities, the price μ resulting from the purchase curve and the sales curve of (B), determined as has been described above, will be approximately a definitive price. Indeed, in this case, the portions of (A), (C), (D), $\cdots$ set aside to constitute the supply of these commodities for (B) will be very small fractions of each of these numerous commodities, and even smaller in a relative sense, that is, when considered relative to the quantity of each of them; therefore, those portions cannot perceptibly change the original proportions of their exchange with all the other commodities.

151. There is a special case of the problem that occupies us that is extremely simple and that deserves special consideration: that is the case in which all the holders of the new commodity that appears on

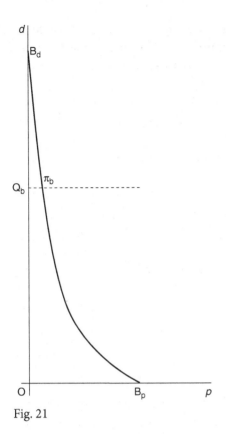

Fig. 21

the market, be they holders of only this commodity (B), or of the old commodities also, offer the entire quantity of the new commodity at any price, namely the total quantity in existence. The particular form of bidding in this case is that of a sale by auction, provided it is assumed that the total amount of the commodity is offered at once. Mathematically, the current price is then determined by the intersection (Fig. 21) at π_b of the purchase curve B_dB_p with the straight line parallel to the price axis through the point Q_b such that the distance $\overline{OQ_b}$ is equal to the existing quantity of (B). This parallel line is then the sales curve. This very simple case is, in reality, very common for the reason that most commodities are products, and that, generally, the producers put on sale the total quantity of their products or keep for themselves only an insignificant fraction. In these conditions, the purchase curve has a very remarkable character: it becomes a *curve of the price* as a function of the total quantity in existence, since its abscissas give the price of the commodity as a function of the total quantity in existence represented by its ordinates.

152. Instead of assuming that the original equilibrium established among (A), (C), (D), ⋯ and then introducing (B) and determining p_b, we could have assumed there is equilibrium between (A), (B), (D), ⋯ and then introducing (C) and determining p_c, or between (A), (B), (C), ⋯ and then introducing (D) and determining p_d, and so forth. Consequently, each commodity can be considered as having a purchase curve that becomes, moreover, a price curve if we assume that supply is equal to the total quantity in existence and if, by virtue of the law of the great numbers, we abstract from the condition of proportionality of demand and supply before and after. The general equation of this curve considered as purchase curve would be $D = F(p)$; the general equation of this same curve considered as the price curve would be $Q = F(p)$, so

$$p = \mathfrak{F}(Q),$$

if we assume the equation is solved with respect to the price. The purchase curve is exactly the one posited a priori by Cournot in his *Recherches sur les principles mathématique de la théorie des richesses* (1838) and that he calls the equation of the demand or of sales.[i] The curve lends itself to many applications.

153. The sales and purchase curves can be related to the equations of exchange in the following way.

Let (A) be the numeraire. And let, on the one hand, the commodities (A), (C), (D), ⋯ be exchanged or be ready to be exchanged for one another at the established general equilibrium prices $p_c = \pi$, $p_d = \rho$, ⋯ of (C), (D), ⋯ in terms of (A). And, on the other hand, let the commodity (B) come onto the market to be exchanged for the commodities (A), (C), (D), ⋯.

Theoretically, the appearance of (B) would have necessitated a new establishment of the system of equations of exchange (§ 121) with the introduction of a new variable p_b and an additional equation

$$F_b(p_b, p_c, p_d, \cdots) = 0$$

that by designating, as we did before (§§ 125, 126), the sum of the positive ys by a function Δ_b, hence D_b, and, the sum of the negative ys by a function Ω_b, hence O_b, we can put into the form

$$\Delta_b(p_b, p_c, p_d, \cdots) = \Omega_b(p_b, p_c, p_d, \cdots).$$

However, if we abstract from the variations in the prices and the effective demands and supplies already determined, by considering them as constants, the first member of the equation

$$\Delta_b(p_b, \pi, \rho, \cdots),$$

is a decreasing function of the single variable p_b, and can be represented geometrically by a purchase curve $B_d B_p$ (Fig. 20), and the second member,

$$\Omega_b(p_b, \pi, \rho, \cdots),$$

is a successively increasing and decreasing function from zero to zero of the same single variable p_b, that can be represented geometrically by a sales curve NP. The intersection of the two curves $B_d B_p$ and NP in B will determine, at least approximately, the price $p_b = \mu$.

We will use the same procedure to connect the price curves with the equations of production.

154. Let us, before finishing, make an interesting observation regarding a point discussed earlier. When the commodities in the market are numerous, the sales curve of each of them, even though it does not coincide exactly with the parallel of the total quantity in existence, will evidently approach it very closely, with the result that ordinarily[ii] there are not, in the case of the exchange of several commodities for one another, several current possible equilibrium prices, contrary to what happens in the case of the exchange of two commodities for each other (§ 68).

Notes

i   Translated, in 1897, by Nathaniel T. Bacon, with the title *Researches into the Principles of the Theory of Wealth*. The equation $D = F(p)$ in question can be found on page 47. Cournot, however, does not discuss the inverse of F, as Walras does.

ii This is an important section. Jaffé mistakenly translated 'généralement' as 'in general', giving the impression that Walras meant 'always; without exception'. In fact, it appears that he was leaving open the possibility that there may be several possible equilibria in the multi-commodity case. 'Generally' in English in this context means 'ordinarily' or 'in most cases'. That is also what 'généralement' means in French, as witness this dictionary definition: 'Généralement ♦ Dans la plupart des cas, le plus souvent. ⇒ habituellement, ordinairement (cf. En général). *Généralement, cela se passe ainsi.*' Walras did not use the words 'en général' here, contrary to Jaffé's implication, but even if he had, he would not necessarily, in French, have been stating 'in every case': 'EN GÉNÉRAL: *Parler en général,* abstraction faite des cas spéciaux. « *c'est l'homme en général et non tel homme qu'ils représentent* » (Taine). – Dans la plupart des cas, le plus souvent. ⇒ communément, généralement. *C'est en général ce qui arrive*' (Robert 2002, p. 1172).

LESSON 16

Exposition and refutation of Adam Smith's
and J.-B. Say's doctrines of the origin of value
in exchange

SUMMARY: – Three principal solutions of the problem of the origin of value. Doctrine of A. Smith, or, of *labor*. This doctrine is limited to stating that only labor has value; it does not in any way explain why labor has value, nor, consequently, from whence in general the value of things arises. Doctrine of J.-B. Say, or, of *utility*. Utility is a necessary condition of value, but not a sufficient one. Doctrine of rareté. Gossen's condition of maximum satisfaction: the maximum utility to which it refers is not the one achieved by free competition. Jevons's equations of exchange: they are applicable only to the case of two exchangers.

155. There are, in the science of economics, three principal solutions to the problem of the origin of value. The first is that of Adam Smith, Ricardo, and McCulloch; it is, it could be said, the English solution: it finds the origin of value in *labor*. This solution is too narrow and it denies that there is value in things that, in fact, do have it. The second is that of Condillac and J.-B. Say; it is, it could be said, the French solution: it finds the origin of value in *utility*. This solution is too broad and it finds value in things that do not, in fact, have it. Finally, the third, which is the right one, is the one espoused by Burlamaqui and my father, A.-A. Walras: it finds the origin of value in *rareté*.

156. Adam Smith formulated his doctrine in the following terms in Book I, Chapter V of the *Wealth of Nations:*

The real price of everything, what everything really costs to the man who wants to acquire it, is the toil and trouble of acquiring it. What everything

179

is really worth to the man who has acquired it, and who wants to dispose of it or exchange it for something else, is the toil and trouble which it can save to himself, and which it can impose upon other people. What is bought with money or with goods is purchased just as much by labour as what we acquire by the toil of our own body. That money or those goods indeed save us this toil. They contain the value of a certain quantity of labour which we exchange for what is supposed at the time to contain the value of an equal quantity. Labour was the first price, the original purchase-money that was paid for all things. It was not by gold or by silver, but by labour, that all the wealth of the world was originally purchased; and its value, to those who possess it, and who want to exchange it for some new productions, is precisely equal to the quantity of labour which it can enable them to purchase or command.[1]

This theory has generally not been well refuted. It consists essentially in the assertion that all things that have value and that are exchanged are labor in one form or another; that labor, in a word, constitutes by itself alone all of social wealth. Whereupon Adam Smith is instructed that there are certain things that have value and that are exchanged that are not the result of labor, and that there are things other than labor that are part of social wealth. But that answer is badly reasoned. Whether labor is by itself the entirety of social wealth, or is simply one species of it, is something that we do not yet know and that, in fact, is of little importance. In either case, why is labor worth anything and why is labor exchanged? That is the question before us, and that is the question that A. Smith neither asked nor answered. Now, if labor has value and is exchanged, it is because it is both useful and limited in quantity, because it is scarce (§ 100). Value, thus, comes from rareté, and all things that are scarce, whether or not there are such things other than labor, that have value, and that are exchangeable like labor. Therefore, the theory that finds the origin of value in labor is less a theory that is too narrow than a theory that is completely vacuous; it is certainly an incorrect declaration, but it is above all a statement that is unfounded.

157. As for the second solution, here are the words in which J.-B. Say formulated it:

---

[1] A. Smith. *Wealth of Nations*, bk. 1, ch. V.

Why does the utility of a thing make it have value?
Because the utility that it has makes it desirable and prompts men to make sacrifices to possess it. No one will give anything in exchange to have something that is good for nothing; but everyone will give a certain quantity of the things he possesses (a certain amount of silver money, for example) in order to obtain the thing for which he feels the need. That is what makes it have value.[2]

Here is at least an attempted demonstration, albeit, it must be admitted, a poor one. 'The utility of a thing makes it desirable'. Certainly! 'It prompts men to make sacrifices to possess it.' Well, that depends, for it will only prompt men to make sacrifices if they cannot get the thing in any other way. 'No one will give anything in exchange to have something that is good for nothing.' No doubt! 'But everyone will give a certain quantity of the things he possesses in order to obtain the thing for which he feels the need.' On one condition: namely, that he cannot get it without giving something in exchange. Utility, therefore, is not sufficient to create value: in addition it is necessary that the useful thing does not exist in unlimited quantities, that it is scarce. This reasoning is confirmed by facts. The air we breathe, the wind that fills the sails at sea or turns windmills on land, the sun that gives us light and heat and ripens our harvests and fruits, water and steam from heated water, and many other forces of nature are useful, even indispensable. And yet they have no value. Why? Because they are unlimited in quantity, because each of us can obtain all he wants of them, whenever they are present at all, without giving up anything or making any sacrifice in return.

Condillac and J.-B. Say both met with this objection on the path they followed. They each answered it in very different ways. Condillac considered air, light, and water very useful things, and he undertook to demonstrate to us that they really cost us something. What would that be? The effort necessary to use them. For Condillac, the act of breathing, the act of opening one's eyes to see the light, the act of stooping to take the water from a river are the sacrifices that we pay for these goods. This puerile argument has been cited more often than would be thought possible; but that does not make it a better argument. It is, in effect, evident that if we call these actions

---

[2] J.-B. Say, *Catéchisme d'économie politique.* Ch. II.

economic sacrifices, we shall have to find another word for the sacrifice associated with value properly so called; because when I go for meat to the butcher's or for a suit to the tailor's, I make an effort or a sacrifice in acquiring these items, but I also make another very special one, namely that of taking out of my pocket a certain sum of money for the merchant.

J.-B. Say regards the matter in a different way. Air, sunlight, the water of streams and rivers are useful, according to him, and, in consequence, are valuable. They are, indeed, so useful, so necessary, so indispensable that their value is great, immense, infinite. And that is precisely why we get them for nothing. We do not pay for them, because we could never pay what they are worth. The explanation is ingenious; unfortunately, there are cases in which air, light, water are paid for; that occurs when, in exceptional circumstances, they are scarce.

158. We have been able to find, without too much trouble, in A. Smith and J.-B. Say, two characteristic passages; but it must be said that in reality these authors have only touched the surface of the question of the origin of value in exchange and that neither of them limited themselves to the inadequate theories that we have mentioned. A few lines after the ones we have quoted, J.-B. Say turns his utility theory into one of labor; elsewhere he seems to come around to one of scarcity. As for Adam Smith, he fortunately contradicted himself by placing land, like labor, among social wealth. Only Bastiat undertook to systematize the English theory, and accepted, and tried to persuade others to accept, consequences that are very contrary to the reality of the facts.

159. Finally, there remains the theory of rareté, enunciated by Burlamaqui in the following excellent manner:

> The foundations of inherent and intrinsic price are, firstly, the capacity that things have to serve our wants, our convenience, or pleasures of life; in a word, their *utility* and their *scarcity*.
> I say firstly their utility, by which I mean not only real utility, but also utility that is only arbitrary or imaginary, like that of precious stones; and because of this circumstance it is commonly said that a thing that is of no use has no price.

But utility alone, be it ever so real, does not suffice to give a price to things; their *scarcity* must also be considered; that is to say, the difficulty of procuring these things, and the fact that no one can easily obtain as much as he wants of them.

Need alone is very far from determining the price of a thing; we usually see that those things that are the most necessary to human life are the cheapest, like ordinary water.

Scarcity alone is also not sufficient to give price to things; they must also be of some use.

Just as these circumstances are the true foundations of the price of things, it is also these same circumstances combined in different ways that cause the price to rise or fall.

If a thing goes out of fashion, or if fewer people care for it, it will become cheap, however dear it may have been before. On the other hand, as soon as an ordinary thing, that costs little or nothing, becomes scarce, it immediately begins to have a price and sometimes becomes even very dear, as happens, for example, to water in arid regions or sometimes during a siege or during a sea voyage, etc.

In a word, all the special circumstances that cause a thing to have a high price can be shown to be related to their scarcity. Such special circumstances are the difficulty of making the thing, its intricacy, the reputation of the artisan.

We can subsume under the same reason what we call the *sentimental* or *affective price* when, because of some special circumstance, we value a thing we possess more highly than the price that is ordinarily paid for it; for example, if it has served to save us from a great danger, if it is a souvenir of some remarkable event, if it is a mark of honor, etc.[3]

That is the doctrine of scarcity. Abbé Genovesi taught it at Naples in the middle of the eighteenth century, and Nassau W. Senior at Oxford about 1830. But it was really my father who introduced it into economics, by presenting it in a special way with all the necessary developments, and by defending it against all the opposing doctrines, in his book titled *De la nature de la richesse et de l'origine de la valeur*.[i] No one could have done that better than my father did in that book using the resources of ordinary logic, and, to advance matters a bit further, it is necessary to use the techniques of mathematical analysis, as I have done.

---

[3] [J.J.] Burlamaqui. *Éléments du droit naturel.* Part 3. Ch. XI.

160.[4] But I am not the only one to have had recourse to those techniques to achieve the same goal. Others have done it before me: the first was a German, Hermann-Heinrich Gossen, in a work titled *Entwiekelung der Gesetze des menschlichen Verkehrs, und der daraus fliessenden Regeln für menschlichen Handeln,* published in 1854; then an Englishman, William Stanley Jevons, in a work titled *Theory of Political Economy,* the first edition of which appeared in 1871 and the second in 1879. Both Gossen and Jevons, the latter without having any knowledge of the work of the former, postulated the decreasing utility or want curve; and Gossen deduced mathematically from it the condition of maximum utility, while Jevons deduced mathematically the equations of exchange.

Gossen stated the condition of maximum utility in these terms: – *The two commodities must, after exchange, be so divided between the two exchangers that the last atom received of each commodity has the same value for each exchanger* (p. 85). To translate this statement into our formulas, we shall call the two commodities (A) and (B), and the two exchangers (1) and (2). Let $r = \varphi_{a,1}(q)$ and $r = \varphi_{b,1}(q)$ be the equations of the utility curves of commodities (A) and (B) for exchanger (1), and $r = \varphi_{a,2}(q)$ and $r = \varphi_{b,2}(q)$ be the corresponding equations for exchanger (2). Let q_a be the quantity of (A) possessed by exchanger (1) and q_b be the quantity of (B) possessed by exchanger (2); and let d_a and d_b be the quantities of (A) and (B) to be exchanged. Under these conditions, Gossen's wording can be translated by the two equations

$$\varphi_{a,1}(q_a - d_a) = \varphi_{a,2}(d_a)$$

$$\varphi_{b,1}(d_b) = \varphi_{b,2}(q_b - d_b)$$

that determine d_a and d_b for exchangers (1) and (2). Now, it is very obvious that the maximum utility attained in this way is not the relative maximum utility of free competition, compatible with the condition that all exchangers give and receive the two commodities in a

---

[4] I repeat, to prevent any misunderstanding, that I added this section to the second edition of my book, and that if I did not cite, in the first edition in 1874, the three works mentioned here that appeared before mine, it was because I was completely ignorant of their existence.

common and identical proportion, but rather an absolute maximum that takes no account of the condition of a single price.

As for Jevons, he formulated his equations of exchange as follows: – *The ratio of exchange of the two commodities will be the inverse of the ratio of the final degrees of utility of the quantities of commodity available for consumption after the exchange* (Ed. 2, p. 103). Letting (A) and (B) be the two commodities, (1) and (2) the two exchangers, φ_1 and ψ_1 the letters for the utility functions of (A) and (B) for exchanger (1), φ_2 and ψ_2 the corresponding letters for exchanger (2), a the quantity of (A) possessed by exchanger (I), and b the quantity of (B) possessed by exchanger (2), and x and y the quantities of (A) and (B) to be exchanged, Jevons translated his own wording into the two equations

$$\frac{\varphi_1(a-x)}{\psi_1 y} = \frac{y}{x} = \frac{\varphi_2 x}{\psi_2(b-y)},^{\text{ii}}$$

which, in our system of notation recalled above, would become

$$\frac{\varphi_{a,1}(q_a - d_a)}{\varphi_{b,1}(d_b)} = \frac{d_a}{d_b} = \frac{\varphi_{a,2}(d_a)}{\varphi_{b,2}(q_b - d_b)}$$

and would serve to determine d_a and d_b. This formula differs from ours in two respects. In the first place, the *prices* that are the inverse ratios of the quantities of the commodities exchanged are replaced by the *ratios of exchange* that are the direct ratios of these quantities and that are always furnished by the two terms, d_a and d_b. In the second place, the problem is considered as being resolved with the case of two exchangers. The author simply reserved the right to consider each of these exchangers (*trading bodies*) as being made up of a group of individuals, for example, of all the inhabitants of a continent, of all the manufacturers in a certain industry of a given country (p. 95). But he himself recognized that in making such a hypothesis, he left the terrain of reality to place himself on that of *fictitious means* (p. 97). As for us, wanting to remain on the former, we cannot accept Jevons's formula as valid except for the limited case where only two individuals are present. For this limited case, Jevons's formula is identical to ours, except for his substitution of quantities exchanged in place of prices. It remains therefore to introduce the general case in which any number of individuals come together to exchange, first, two commodities for each other, and then in which any number of commodities are exchanged for one another. That is what Jevons did not do, and it is precisely what he was prohibited from doing by his attachment to the unfortunate idea of taking the quantities exchanged as the unknowns of the problem instead of the prices.

I have criticized only a special point of the doctrine of my predecessors. I should add immediately that Gossen's conception of the intensity of the last want satisfied, under the name *Werth des letzten Atoms* and by Jevons under the name *Final Degree of Utility*, enabled them to clarify other important points, and that their works should be read with the greatest care by economists who are desirous of working on the definitive construction of economic theory.

At the same time that Jevons first published his *Theory of Political Economy*, that is, in 1871 and 1872, Mr. Carl Menger, Professor at the University of Vienna, published his *Grundsätze der Volkswirthschaftslehre*, which is a third work that preceded mine in which the foundations of the new theory of exchange are set forth in an independent and original manner. Mr. Menger developed, as we did, the utility theory, in setting forth the law of the decrease of wants with the quantity consumed, for the purpose of drawing the theory of exchange from it. He followed the deductive method, but was opposed to following the mathematical method, although he made use, if not of functions or curves, at least of arithmetical tables to express either utility or demand. This makes it impossible for me to comment upon his theory in a few lines as I did for Gossen and Jevons. I shall only say that he and the authors that followed his teachings, like Professor Frederic de Wieser, of Prague, in his work *Ueber den Ursprung und die Hauptgesetze des wirthschaftlichen Werthes* (1894) and Professor Eugène von Bœhm-Bawerk, in his *Grundzüge der Theorie des wirtschaftlichen Güterwerts* (1886), seem to me to deprive themselves of a precious and even indispensible resource by refusing a straightforward use of the method and language of mathematics in treating an essentially mathematical subject. Nevertheless, I will add that with the imperfect method and language that they employ, they have perhaps more firmly grasped the problem of exchange than did Gossen and Jevons. What is sure is that they have at least succeeded in bringing the theory of scarcity, or, as they say, of *Grenznutzen* (final utility), sharply to the attention of economists in Germany. This theory is now being developed in economic science and has a very promising future. I have drawn from it, as has been seen, the theory of the determination of the prices of commodities. I am going to draw from it, as will be seen: 1° the theory of the simultaneous determination of the prices of products and the prices of land services, personal services, and capital services, and 2° the theory of the determination of the rate of net income and, as a consequence, of landed capital, personal capital, and capital goods.

Notes

i   Paris, Johanneau, 1831.
ii The notations $\psi_1 y$ and $\varphi_2 x$ were already antiquated in Jevon's own time. Now we write $\psi_1(y)$ and $\varphi_2(x)$.

PART III

THEORY OF PRODUCTION

LESSON 17

Capital and income. The three services

SUMMARY: – Commodities considered as *products*. Having obtained the law of supply and demand, we now seek the law of costs of production, or, of average cost. *Capital goods*, a type of social wealth used more than once; *income*, a kind of social wealth that is used only once. Capital goods and income considered as to their nature or as to their purpose, material or immaterial. The flow of services of capital are incomes. *Consumable* services; *productive* services.

Land and *its services*, or, *landed capital* and its services. *Persons* and *labor*, or, personal capital and its services. *Capital goods* properly speaking and '*profits*'[i] or, *movable*[ii] capital and its services. Incomes. Land, a type of capital existing in approximately constant quantity. Persons, a type of capital that disappears and reappears independently of trends of consumption and industrial production. Capital goods properly speaking, a type of capital produced [as a function of economic conditions]. Having obtained the prices of products, we now seek the prices of productive services.

161. However complicated an order of phenomena may be, and the order of economic phenomena is surely that to a high degree, there is always a means of studying it scientifically provided that the rule that prescribes going from the simple to the complex is observed. I have followed that rule in constructing the mathematical theory of exchange, by passing from the exchange of two commodities for each other to the exchange of any number of commodities for each other with the intervention of a numeraire. In doing so, I left out of consideration the fact that commodities are *products* resulting from

191

the combination of productive factors such as land, men, and capital goods. The moment has come to introduce and pose, after the problem of the mathematical determination of the prices of products, that of the mathematical determination of the prices of productive services. The solving of the former problem and of the equations of exchange brought us to the scientific formula of the *law of supply and demand*. The solving of the latter problem and of the equations of production will bring us to the scientific formula of the *law of the cost of production*, or, of *average cost*. Thus I found the two great laws of economics; except that, rather than putting them in competition and in opposition to one another in the matter of the determination of prices, I made them each play their part by basing on the first the determination of the prices of products, and on the second the determination of the prices of productive services. It is certain, as economists have recognized, and – I hope will be believed – as has not completely escaped me, that in a certain normal and ideal state, the price of commodities is equal to their average cost. In that state, the state of equilibrium of exchange and of production, a bottle of wine that sells for 5 francs cost to produce 2 francs in rent, 2 francs in wages, and 1 franc in interest. It remains to be seen whether it is because 2 francs were paid out in rent, 2 francs in wages, and 1 franc in interest that this bottle of wine sells for 5 francs, or whether it is because the bottle sells for 5 francs that 2 francs were paid out in rent, 2 francs in wages, and 1 franc in interest. It remains to determine, in a word, if it is, as has been maintained, the prices of productive services that determine the prices of products, or if it is not rather the prices of products, determined, as we have seen, by virtue of the law of supply and demand, that determine the prices of productive services by virtue of the law of costs of production, or, of average cost. That is the subject that we are going to examine.

162. There are three productive services. When they refer to these factors, authors most frequently employ the terms *land*, *labor*, and *capital*. But these names are not sufficiently rigorous to serve as a basis for rational deductions. *Labor* is the service of personal faculties or of *persons*; it is necessary, therefore, to place alongside it, not land and capital, but *land services* or the services of *land*, and *capital good services* or the services of *capital goods*. Since I use these

terms in a way not exactly different from but a little narrower than is ordinarily done, I must define them carefully. To this end, I must first introduce the definition of capital and of income.

163. I call *capital* in general, as my father did in his *Théorie de la richesse sociale* (1849), all forms of social wealth that are not used up at all or are used up only after a period of time, i.e., every utility limited in quantity that outlasts the first use made of it; in a word, that is used more than once: a house, a piece of furniture. And I call *income* all kinds of social wealth that are used up immediately, every scarce thing that no longer exists after the first service that it yields; in brief, that is usable only once: bread, meat. Among these incomes are included, alongside items privately consumed, the raw materials of agriculture and industry: seeds, textile fibers, etc. The duration in question here is not, in effect, material duration, but the duration of usefulness or economic duration. Textile fibers still continue to exist materially in the cloth; but they have disappeared as primary materials, and cannot serve a second time in the same capacity. On the other hand, buildings and machines are capital goods, not income. I add that while certain kinds of social wealth are naturally capital and other kinds are naturally income, there is also a large number of kinds that are either capital or income depending upon how they are used or the service required of them. Trees, for example, are capital when they bear fruit, but are income when they are cut down for fuel or lumber. Animals, too, are capital when they work or give milk or eggs, but are income when they are slaughtered for food. It is always the case that, whether by nature or by purpose, each useful thing limited in quantity, each scarce thing, either serves more than once or serves only once, and is, in consequence, either capital or income.

When we speak of people who consume their capital, we mean that they first exchange their capital for income and that they consume the income. Similarly to capitalize their income, they must exchange it for capital goods.

Capital must not be confused with *stocks*, which are sums of income prepared in advance for consumption. Wine in the cellar, wood in the woodshed are stocks. Minerals, stones in mines and quarries are also accumulations of income and not of capital. After a little reflection, it is impossible to make a mistake on this matter.

164. Since we have called social wealth the ensemble of material or immaterial things that are scarce; that is to say, are both useful and limited in quantity (§ 21), we hardly need to say that the capital and income into which we are dividing that same social wealth are themselves either material or immaterial. The materiality or immateriality is unimportant to us in either case. We will see presently how capital engenders income; we will then also see that material capital may very well engender immaterial income, and immaterial capital engender material income. I mention this fact now because it lends support to the distinction that has been made between capital and income.

165. It is of the essence of capital to give birth to income; and it is of the essence of income to be given birth, directly or indirectly, by capital. Here is how this happens. Capital, by definition, outlasts the first use made of it; several successive uses are therefore made of it; the flow of these uses is evidently a flow of incomes. A piece of land will grow our crops every year; a house will shelter us, in winter as in summer, from inclemencies of the weather; this fecundity of land, this shelter provided by the house constitutes their annual income. A worker is active in the workshop every day; a lawyer, a doctor see clients daily; that work, those consultations are the daily incomes produced by those individuals. It is the same regarding the incomes of machines, instruments, tools, furniture, and clothing. The thought of many writers is obscure and confused as a result of failing to consider capital and its incomes separately.

In order to distinguish them, we will give the name of *services* to those incomes that consist of the uses made of capital. There are two sorts of them. There are those that are used up without being changed in the course of either private or public consumption: examples of these services are the shelter of the house, the consultation of the lawyer, of the doctor, the use of furniture, clothing. These we will call *consumable* services. And there are those that are transformed by means of agriculture, industry, or commerce into incomes or capital; that is to say, into *products*: examples of these services are the fertility of the soil, the labor of the workman, the use of machines, instruments, tools. These we will call *productive* services. This distinction corresponds closely to the distinction made by most authors between *unproductive* and *reproductive* consumption. The distinction will presently be made clearer. Moreover, the question to be studied here especially is the transformation of productive services into products.

166. By means of the definition of capital and income, we can start by dividing the whole of social wealth into four main categories, three of which are categories of capital, and one of which is the category of income.

We put land into the first category: land used for parks and gardens, public and private; land that produces trees and all sorts of vegetal matter for nourishing man and animals: fruits, vegetables, cereals, fodder; land that supports homes or public buildings, offices, factories, workshops, or shops; land used for means of transportation: roads, highways, public squares, canals, railways. All this land is truly capital. The garden and the park, bare during the winter, will grow green again and have blossoms again in the summer; the land that was productive this season will be productive again in the next season; that which has supported a house or factory this year will support it again the following year; we will use the street and the road in the coming year as in the year past. Thus the land outlasts the first use that is made of it, and the succession of its uses constitutes its income. The enjoyment of a walk and the view is the income of the park or the garden; the productive power is the income from land that is used; the site made available for buildings is the income from land so used; the facilitation of moving from one place to another is the income from streets and roads. Thus we have our first category of capital, *landed capital* or *land*, capable of furnishing income, namely *land income*, which we will also call *land services*.

167. We place *persons* into the second category: those who do nothing other than travel and seek amusement; and those who serve other persons: coachmen, cooks, valets, maids; public officials in the service of the State, such as administrators, judges, military persons; male and female workers in agriculture, industry, and commerce; men engaged in the liberal professions, such as lawyers, doctors, artists. All these persons are truly capital. The idler who has lounged about today will lounge about tomorrow; the blacksmith

who has just finished his day will finish many more; the lawyer who leaves the courtroom will come back to plead again. Thus, persons still exist after rendering their first service, and the series of services they render constitutes their income. The pleasure enjoyed by the idler, the task performed by the artisan, the pleading of the lawyer are the incomes of these people. We have therefore a second category of capital, *personal capital* or *persons*, capable of furnishing their incomes, their *incomes* or *personal services*, which we will also call *labor*.

168. We now place into the third category all the remaining assets that are capital assets and that are neither land nor persons: homes in either town or country, public buildings; business buildings, factories, workshops, shops, constructions of all kinds, considered, of course, apart from the ground on which they stand; trees and plants of all sorts; animals; furniture, clothes, pictures, statues, carriages, jewelry; machines, instruments, tools. We assume that all these things are not income, but are capital itself productive of income. The house that shelters me now can shelter me for a long time to come; my paintings, my jewelry are always at my disposal; the train and its freight cars that today have brought passengers and goods from a neighboring town, will return tomorrow along the same tracks, with other passengers and other goods. Moreover, the shelter provided by a house, the decorative effect of paintings and jewels, the transportation furnished by the train and its freight cars are the incomes from the capital goods. Thus we have a third category of capital, *movable capital goods* or *capital goods properly speaking*, ready to provide incomes, the *incomes* or *movable services* that we will also call '*profits*'.

169. All of capital being accounted for by our first three categories of social wealth, in the fourth category there are only incomes: *things that are consumed*[iii] such as wheat, flour, bread, meat, wine, beer, vegetables, fruit, fuels for lighting and for the warmth of consumers; *raw materials* such as fertilizers, seeds, metals, lumber, textiles, cloth, fuel for lighting and heat in businesses, all things destined to disappear as raw materials in order to reappear as products.

170. We see that land, persons, and capital goods properly speaking are capital; the services of land, the services of persons, or labor, the services of capital goods properly speaking, are incomes. It is necessary, therefore, in order to be exact and precise, to recognize as productive services three sorts of capital and incomes: the capital and income of land, of persons, and of capital goods properly speaking; namely land and land services, persons and labor, and capital goods properly speaking and 'profits'.[iv] In this corrected form, the current classifications can be accepted. They are now based on the nature of things.

Land is *natural* capital and not artificial or produced. It is also *unconsumable* capital; it is not destroyed by usage or destroyed by accidents. There is, however, some landed capital that has been artificially produced by putting soil over rock surfaces, by fertilizing land, by draining marshes; and there is also some that is destroyed as a result of earthquakes, the flow of rivers, or torrents. But such cases are small in number; and we can, with few exceptions, consider landed capital as capital that is not consumed and as capital that is not produced. Each of those two circumstances has an importance of its own; but it is above all their coexistence that gives landed capital its own and special character. It results from those circumstances, in fact, that the quantity of land is, if not a quantity rigorously constant, at least a quantity only slightly variable; that, as a result, the quantity of land can be very considerable in a primitive society, but, on the contrary, very limited in an advanced society, relatively to the quantity of persons and to the quantity of capital goods properly speaking; that, in consequence, land can be, and we will see that it is in reality, not scarce and has no value in the former case, and has a high degree of scarcity and value in the latter case.

171. Persons, like land, are also *natural* capital, but they are *consumable capital; that is to say, destructible by use or by accidents.* They disappear, but they reappear, through the process of reproduction. Thus their quantity, far from being constant, is susceptible of indefinite increase under certain conditions. Regarding them, we must make an observation. In saying that persons are natural capital and that they reappear through reproduction, we are taking account of the principle of social ethics that is more and more generally accepted

that persons should not be bought and sold like things, and that they cannot be produced in farms or in stud farms like cattle or horses. On those grounds, it might be thought of no use to include them in a theory of the determination of prices. But, first, although personal capital is not bought and sold, personal income, i.e., labor, is supplied and demanded every day in markets, and therefore personal capital can, and often must, at least be evaluated. And, second, we are not afraid of recalling that economic theory is, after all, based upon making complete abstraction from the point of view of justice as well as of economic advantageousness, and upon considering personal capital, like land and movable capital, exclusively from the point of view of value in exchange. We will therefore continue to speak of the price of labor and even of the price of persons, without taking any position either for or against slavery.

172. Capital goods properly speaking are *artificial* capital or *products* and are *consumable* capital. It is, perhaps, possible to cite some examples of capital assets, other than land and persons, that are natural assets: certain trees, certain animals; but hardly any can be found that are inconsumable. They are destroyed and perish, like persons; but, also like persons, they reappear, not as a result of natural reproduction, but as a result of economic production. Their quantity, like that of persons, is, therefore, susceptible of an indefinite increase under given conditions. We have again an observation to make regarding them. Capital goods are always associated with land in industry, particularly in agricultural industry. It should be clearly understood, however, that when we speak of land, we consider it apart from dwellings or office buildings, from enclosing or supporting walls, from irrigation and drainage systems, in a word, from all capital goods properly speaking, and, with all the more reason, apart from fertilizers, seeds, unharvested crops, in short, apart from all the incomes that accompany them; and that it is exclusively the services of land thus considered that we call land services, reserving the name of 'profits' for the services rendered by capital goods properly speaking that are associated with land.

The above characteristics of social wealth have a significance that not only explains but justifies the distinction between land, persons, and capital goods properly speaking. It has to be said, however, that this significance will become evident principally in social economics, and, regarding the matters that are the concern of economic theory, in the part devoted to the study of the conditions and consequences of economic progress. In all this, the only circumstance that the analysis will assume will be that the landed capital, personal capital, and movable capital are capital and not income.

173. That said, we still have to inquire why and how it happens that, in an economic society governed by a regime of free competition in regard to production as in regard to exchange, there are, for the services of land, for the services of personal faculties (or labor), for the services of capital goods properly speaking (or 'profits'), equilibrium prices that are mathematical quantities; we have to formulate the system of equations of which rent, wages, and interest are the roots. The importance of this study is not fully evident unless it is remembered that in current economic theory there are at present five or ten theories of rent, which amounts precisely to saying that there is no theory of rent, no more than there are theories of wages or of interest.

Notes

i   When the word 'profits' is used in Walras's special sense, namely as the services of capital goods properly speaking, it will be put in quotation marks. Otherwise, it will have the conventional modern meaning of the excess of revenue over costs.

ii   Walras uses the adjective 'mobilier' in a special sense. We have translated that word as 'movable', which is correct, but it must be remembered that 'capitaux mobiliers' include all goods other than land that produce products or services. This broad definition therefore places houses and trees, for example, in the category of movable capital goods. They can be moved, although only with difficulty. Moreover, to underscore the fact that Walras intended his definitions to identify a principal characteristic of most particular cases, land, which he differentiates from movable capital goods, can, in many cases, be moved in the sense that earth and stones can be moved from one location to another.

iii   The examples Walras gives in this section of 'Objets de consommation', or consumption goods, are only ones that have physical mass, unlike services. 'Goods', as distinct from services, are 'commodities that are tangible, usually movable, and generally not consumed at the same time as they are produced'. Like 'investment goods', there are 'consumer goods' or 'consumption goods'. Some authors write 'consumers' goods' or even 'consumer's goods', but those are abuses of language, just as writing 'investors' goods' would be. The commodity name is not possessive. A consumption good is not used directly to make other goods; it is what it is, whether possessed by a consumer or stored in a warehouse or shop or on display in a shop.

iv This is badly written. Walras contradicts his definitions and usage by writing that capital is a service. It is perhaps best to understand his sentence in this way: 'It is necessary, therefore, in order to be exact and precise, to recognize as *the elements of production* three sorts of capital and *their* incomes: the capital and income of land, of persons, and of capital goods properly speaking; namely land and land services, persons and labor, and capital goods properly speaking and "profits"'. The italicized words are ours.

LESSON 18

Elements and mechanism of production

SUMMARY: – 1, 2, and 3: Capital that yields consumable services: landed capital, personal capital, and movable capital goods; 3, 4, and 5: Capital that yields productive services: landed capital, personal capital, and movable capital goods; 7: New movable capital goods; 8: Consumer goods; 9: Raw materials; 10: New income commodities; 11, 12, and 13: Circulating money and savings. Abstraction from new movable capital goods, new income commodities, stocks of consumer goods and raw materials, and money. Production of income and of movable capital goods by capital that yields productive services.

Only capital goods can be hired out. The hiring out of capital is the sale of its service. *Landowners; workers; capitalists. Entrepreneurs. The market for services: rent, wages, interest. The market for products.* The two markets, while distinct from each other, are related. The equilibrium of production preassumes the equilibrium of exchange on the two markets and the equality of the price of the products to their average cost, the entrepreneurs not making either *profit* or *loss*.

174. Just as, in taking up the problem of the mathematical determination of the prices of products, we had to define with precision the mechanism of free competition as regards exchange, in taking up the problem of the mathematical definition of the prices of productive services, we must similarly carefully examine the facts and experience, asking them to provide an accurate notion of the mechanism of free competition as regards production. Now, if, for the needs of this analysis, we assume the process of economic production in a

given country to be momentarily halted, we can, in combining the distinction between consumable services and productive services (§ 165) with the enumeration of capital and income (§§ 166, 167, 168, 169), classify the elements of that process under the following 13 headings.

We have, in regard to capital, the following:

1, 2, and 3: *Landed capital, personal capital,* and *movable capital* productive of consumer services; that is to say, of income directly consumed either by the owners of these different types of capital themselves or by those who acquire the income derived from them, be they individuals, or communities, or the State. Thus we have, as landed capital: parks and gardens; ground supporting houses or public buildings; streets, roads, public squares; – as personal capital: idle persons, servants, government workers; – as movable capital goods: houses, public buildings; trees, plants and domestic animals; furniture, clothes, art objects, luxury goods.

4, 5, and 6: *Landed capital, personal capital* and *movable capital goods* yielding productive services; that is to say, income commodities transformable into products through agriculture, industry, or trade. Thus, as landed capital: farm land, ground supporting office buildings, factories, workshops, or shops; – as personal capital: wage-earners, professional men; – as movable capital goods: farm buildings, factories, workshops, stores; fruit-bearing trees and plants; work animals; machines, instruments, tools.

7: *New movable capital goods* unproductive of income for the moment, held for sale by their producers in the form of such products: houses and buildings newly constructed for sale; plants, animals, furniture, clothes, art objects, luxury goods, machines, instruments, tools in warehouses or on display in shops.

We have, in regard to income, the following:

8: Stocks of *income goods* consisting of *consumer goods* held by consumers. Thus: bread, meat, wine, vegetables, fruit, oils, and firewood.

9: Stocks of *income goods* consisting of *raw materials* held by producers. Thus: fertilizers, seeds, metals, lumber, textiles fiber, cloth in bolts, industrial fuels.

10: *New income goods* consisting of *consumer goods* and *raw materials* held for sale by their producers. Thus: bread at the baker's, meat at the butcher's; metals, lumber, textile fibers, bolts of cloth in warehouses or on display in shops.

Finally, we have, with respect to money:

11, 12, and 13: *Transactions balances of money* held by consumers; *transactions balances of money* held by producers; *money savings.*

It can be seen without difficulty that we obtain our first six headings by introducing into the discussion of each of the three kinds of capital the distinction between capital yielding consumable services and capital yielding productive services; the seventh by putting aside capital goods properly speaking that are not productive of income; the eighth, ninth, and tenth, on the one hand, and the eleventh, twelfth, and thirteenth, on the other, by similarly introducing the distinction between income goods and money. We place money in a separate category, apart from capital and income, because of the mixed role it plays in production. From the point of view of society, money is capital, since it is used in society more than once for making payments; from the point of view of individuals, it is income, because they can use it only once, since they no longer have it after it has served once to make a payment.

175. We have assumed that the process of economic production is halted for a moment. Now let us assume it is set in motion again.

Among the items classified under the first six headings, land, which is unconsumable, will not be destroyed nor perish; men will die and men will be born in accordance with the rhythm of population changes, independently of fluctuations in agricultural, industrial, and commercial production, although not, however, as we will see, without any relation with economic production; capital goods properly speaking, which is destructible by usage, and can perish in accidents, will be used up or will disappear, but is replaced by the new capital goods properly speaking classified under the seventh heading. Thus, the quantity of the latter will be reduced in those ways, but will be restored by production. We can, in order to simplify the given conditions of the problem and with the proviso of returning later to the matter, abstract from the seventh heading, and assume that the new movable capital goods pass into the third and sixth categories as soon as they are produced.

The items classified under the eighth and ninth headings, consumer goods and raw materials, which are immediately consumable income goods, will be consumed, but will be replaced by the new income goods classified under the tenth heading. Thus, the quantity of the latter will consequently decrease, but will be restored by production. We can again abstract from the tenth category by assuming that the new income goods pass, as soon as they are produced, into the eighth and ninth categories. We may even abstract from the eighth and ninth categories by assuming that consumer goods and raw materials are consumed as soon as they are produced, without previously being stored.

Money will intervene in exchanges. At each moment, part of circulating money will be absorbed by savings, and part of money savings will be injected back into circulation by credit. If we abstract from the fact of saving, we can abstract from money saving. We will see presently that we can also abstract from circulating money.

176. In summary, what are consumed are the consumable services immediately reproduced by the landed capital, personal capital, and movable capital goods classified under headings 1, 2, and 3, and the consumable income goods, unfinished consumer goods, and raw materials, immediately reproduced by the landed capital, personal capital, and movable capital goods classified under headings 4, 5, and 6. Income, by definition, does not exist after the first service that it renders. When its service is required of it, it is going to perish; in technical terms, it is going to be *consumed*. Bread and meat will be eaten; wine will be drunk; oil and wood will be burned; fertilizers and seeds will be put in the soil; metals, lumber, and textile fibers will be processed, fuels will be used up. But no sooner will these income goods disappear than they will reappear as a result of the functioning of capital. Capital, by definition, outlasts the first use made of it. When they are put to the successive services for which they are designed, they will render them; technically speaking, they will *produce*. Farm land will be

cultivated; ground will support businesses; workers will work in those businesses; they will use their machines, instruments, and tools. In short, landed capital, personal capital, and movable capital goods will render their land services, their personal services, and their capital good services; and, from a combination of these land services, these personal services, and these capital good services, agriculture, industry, and commerce will draw new income goods to replace the income goods consumed.

177. But even that is not enough to exhaust the subject, because, as well as the consumer goods and the raw materials that are consumed immediately, there are various kinds of capital goods properly speaking that are consumed slowly. Houses and buildings depreciate, furniture, clothes, art objects, and luxury goods wear out. The same is true of farm buildings, machines, instruments, and tools. All these capital goods are depreciated more or less rapidly by usage; they are also all subject to destruction in a sudden and unpredictable manner by unforeseeable accidents. Consequently, it is not enough that the landed capital, personal capital, and movable capital goods under headings (4), (5), and (6) produce new income; it is also necessary that they produce new movable capital goods in replacement of the movable capital goods used up, new movable capital goods in replacement of movable capital goods accidentally destroyed, and even, if possible, new movable capital goods to increase the quantity of existing movable capital goods. And, in that respect, we can already point to one of the traits of economic progress. Let us assume, in effect, that at the end of a certain period of time we again halt for a moment, as we have already done, the process of economic production, and that we find an enlarged quantity of movable capital goods. That would be a sign of a progressive state. Thus, one of the traits of economic progress consists of an increase of the quantity of movable capital goods. Since our following part will be specially consecrated to the study of the conditions and consequences of economic progress, we can reserve for later study the question of the production of new capital goods and restrict ourselves for the moment to that of the production of new income goods: consumer goods, and raw materials.

178. The production of consumable income and of movable capital goods by productive capital is accomplished by the functioning of the latter, not in isolation but always in combination with other factors of production. Even in agriculture, where the role of landed capital is preponderant, the products are composed not only of land services, but also of labor and capital good services. And even in manufacturing, where, by contrast, the role of capital goods is predominant, rent enters into the composition of products along with labor and capital good services. Perhaps without exception, in order to produce anything, it is necessary to have land, even if only to provide support under the feet of the worker, personal faculties, and some kind of tool, which is capital. The cooperation of land, man, and capital is therefore the very essence of economic production. It is this collaboration that now requires clear definition; but the distinction between capital and income, which has enabled us to classify the factors of production (§ 174), is also going to enable us to summarize its mechanism.

179. Income, simply because it does not outlast the first service that it yields, can only be *sold* or *given away*. It cannot be hired out, at least not in kind. How can bread or meat be hired out? A capital good, on the contrary, simply because it outlasts the first use that is made of it, can be *hired out*, either for a consideration or free of charge. Thus, a house, a piece of furniture can be sold or given away, and it can also be rented. And what is the reason for the latter action? It is to procure the enjoyment of the service for the renter. *The hiring out of a capital good is the alienation of the service of that capital good.* Fundamental definition, based entirely on the distinction between capital and income, and without which the theory of production and the theory of credit are impossible. The renting out of a capital good for a payment is the sale of its service, and letting it out for nothing is the gift of its service. In fact, it is by being rented out for a payment that items of landed capital, personal capital, and movable capital goods classified under headings 4, 5, and 6 are combined for production.

180. Let us call the owner of land a *landowner*, whomever he may be, the owner of personal faculties a *worker*, and the owner of capital goods properly speaking a *capitalist*. And now, let us call a fourth

person an *entrepreneur*, entirely distinct from the preceding, and whose distinctive role is to lease land from the landowner, personal faculties from the worker, and capital from the capitalist, and to combine the three productive services in agriculture, industry, or commerce. It is undoubtedly true that, in real life, the same individual can assume concurrently two or three of the above-defined roles, or even assume concurrently all four of them, and that the diversity of these combinations engenders the diversity of types of enterprises; but it is equally certain that he then fulfills two, three, or four distinct roles. From the scientific point of view, we must therefore distinguish these roles, and avoid both the error of the English economists who identify the entrepreneur with the capitalist, and that of a certain number of French economists that make the entrepreneur a worker by considering him as specially charged with the work of direction of the firm.

181. That having been set forth, we must, as a consequence of this first conception of the role of the entrepreneur, conceive of two distinct markets.

The first is the *market for services*. There landowners, workers, and capitalists meet as sellers and entrepreneurs as buyers of productive services, that is, of land services, labor, and capital good services. Alongside the entrepreneurs who buy land services, labor, and capital good services as productive services, are also found, on the market for services, landowners, workers, and capitalists who buy land service, labor, and capital good services as consumable services. We will introduce them at an appropriate time; for the moment, we must concentrate on the study of the purchase of services as productive services. These productive services are exchanged in accordance with the mechanism of free competition with the intervention of a numeraire (§ 42). For each of them a price is cried in terms of the numeraire; if, at the price cried in that way, the effective demand exceeds the effective supply, the entrepreneurs bid against one another and the price rises; if the effective supply exceeds the effective demand, the landowners, workers, and capitalists underbid one another, and the price falls. The current price is the one for which effective supply and demand are equal.

The current contract price of land services in numeraire, determined in the manner discussed, we will call *rent*.

The current contract price of labor in numeraire, determined in advance in the manner discussed, will be called *wages*.

The current price of capital good services in numeraire, will be called *interest*.

That is how, thanks to the distinction between capital and income, and to the definition of the entrepreneur, we immediately identify productive services, a market for these services, effective supply and demand, and finally, as a result of supply and demand, a current price. We will see later on, the fruitless efforts made by French or English economists to determine rent, wages, and interest; that is to say, the price of productive services, without markets for these services.

182. The other market is the *market for products*. There the entrepreneurs gather as sellers, and the landowners, workers, and capitalists as buyers of products. These products are also exchanged in accordance with the mechanism of free competition with the aid of a numeraire. For each of them a price is cried in terms of the numeraire; if, at the price cried in this way, the effective demand exceeds the effective supply, the landowners, workers, and capitalists will bid against one another and the price rises; if the effective supply exceeds the effective demand, the entrepreneurs will underbid each other, and the price falls. The current price is the one at which the effective demand and supply are equal.

That is how we identify, in this connection, a market, supply and demand, and a current price of products.

183. These concepts, it should be noted attentively, are in exact conformity with the facts, with observation, with experience. In fact, thanks to the intervention of money, the two markets, one for services and the other for products, are perfectly distinct in the real world just as they are in regard to science. And, on each of them, sales and purchases take place in accordance with the mechanism of raising and lowering the price. Go to a shoemaker to buy a pair of shoes; it is the entrepreneur that hands over the product and who receives the money: the transaction takes place on the market for products. If more of the products are demanded than supplied, another consumer will outbid you; if more products are supplied than demanded, another producer will underbid your shoemaker. On one side of you,

a worker sets his price for making a pair of shoes; it is the entrepreneur who obtains the productive service and who pays the money: the transaction takes place on the market for services. If more labor is demanded than supplied, another entrepreneur will outbid the shoemaker; and if more is supplied than demanded, another workman will offer his services at a lower price. Although these two markets are distinct, they are, nevertheless, closely related to each other; for it is with the money that they have received for their productive services on the first market that the landowners, workers, and capitalists go as consumers to the second market to buy products; and it is with the money they have received for their products in the second one that the entrepreneurs go as producers to the first market to buy productive services.

184. The state of equilibrium in production, implicitly containing the state of equilibrium in exchange, is now easy to define. First, it is the one in which the effective supply and demand for productive services are equal, in which there is a stationary current price in the market for these services. Second, it is the one in which the effective supply and demand for products are equal, and in which there is a stationary current price in the products market. Finally, it is the one in which the price of products is equal to the average cost of the productive services that are used. The two first conditions relate specifically to the equilibrium in exchange; the third is specific to the equilibrium of production.

That state of equilibrium in production is, like the state of equilibrium in exchange, an ideal and not a real state. It never happens in the real world that the prices of products are absolutely equal to the average cost of the productive services that enter into them, no more than it ever happens that the effective supply and demand of productive services or of products are absolutely equal. But it is the normal state in the sense that it is the one towards which things spontaneously tend in a regime of free competition in production as well as in exchange. In this regime, in fact, if the price of a product exceeds the average cost in certain firms, which constitutes a *profit*, entrepreneurs flow towards this branch of production or increase their output, which increases the quantity of the product; they lower the price, and reduce the excess; and, if, in certain enterprises, the average cost exceeds the price, which constitutes a *loss*, entrepreneurs leave this branch of production or decrease their output, which decreases the quantity of products; in fact they raise the price and once again reduce the difference. Let us note in passing that we find here, in the desire to avoid losses and to make profits, the determining reason for the demand for productive services and the supply of products by the entrepreneurs, just as we have already found, in the desire to obtain the maximum satisfaction of wants, the determining reason for the supply of productive services and the demand for products by the landowners, workers, and capitalists. Let us add that in the state of equilibrium of exchange and of production, we can, as we have observed (§ 175), make abstraction if not from the numeraire at least from money, the landowners, workers, and capitalists receiving and the entrepreneurs giving a certain quantity of products under the name of rent, wages, and interest in exchange for a certain quantity of productive services under the name of land services, labor, and capital good services. We can even, in that state, make abstraction from the intervention of the entrepreneur, and consider not only the productive services as being exchanged for products and products as being exchanged for productive services, but, when all is said and done, even consider the productive services as being exchanged for each other. Bastiat and his disciples truly said, as we have, that in the last analysis services are exchanged for services; but they meant to speak only of personal services, whereas for our part, we are speaking of the services of land, persons, and movable capital goods.

Thus, in the state of equilibrium in production, the entrepreneurs make neither profit nor loss. They make their living not as entrepreneurs, but as landowners, workers, or capitalists in their own firms or in others. In my opinion, to have rational bookkeeping, an entrepreneur who owns the land that he cultivates or occupies, who participates in the management of his firm, who has his own funds invested in the business, ought to charge his business with his general expenses and credit it with the rent, wages, and interest calculated at the market rate for productive services, by means of which he earns a living, without his making, as an entrepreneur, either profit or loss. And, in fact, is it not evident that if he gets for his productive services, in his own business, a higher or lower price than he can get elsewhere, the difference is a profit or a loss?

LESSON 19

The entrepreneur. Business accounting and inventory

SUMMARY: – Capital goods properly speaking are lent not in kind, but in money. *Credit. Fixed capital; circulating capital. Cash* account: *debit; credit; balance.* Origin and purpose of till cash. *Capital* account. *Fixed capital* account or *expenses of fixed assets. Circulating capital* account (*Stock* and *General Expenses*). The principle of double entry bookkeeping. *Assets; liabilities. Ledger; journal.*

Credit to Capital account; debit to Expenses of establishment of the enterprise; debit to Stock; debit to general Expenses; credit to Stock. Balance of general Expenses by debit to Stock; balance of Stock by credit or debit to *Profit* and *loss.* Balance sheet. Complications: 1. Detail of entries; 2. *Debtor clients*; 3. *Accounts receivable*; 4. *Bank accounts*; 5. *Creditor suppliers*; 6. *Bills payable*; 7. *Inventory.*

185. The entrepreneur is therefore the person (an individual or a corporate entity) who buys raw materials from other entrepreneurs, then obtains land from landowners by payment of a rent, hires the personal faculties of workers by payment of wages, borrows capital from capitalists by payment of interest, and, finally, having applied certain productive services to the raw materials, sells the resulting products for his own account. The agricultural entrepreneur buys seed, fertilizers, and unfattened livestock; he rents land, farm buildings, farm implements, hires workers, harvesters, farm hands; and he sells agricultural crops and fattened livestock. The industrial entrepreneur buys textile fibers, crude metals; he rents factories, workshops, machines, tools; employs spinners, metal workers, mechanics;

211

and he sells his made products: fabrics, metallic goods. The commercial entrepreneur buys merchandise wholesale; he rents warehouses, shops, employs clerks, traveling salesmen; and he sells his goods at retail. When these entrepreneurs sell their products or merchandise at a price higher than the cost of the raw materials, rent, wages, and interest, they make a profit; in the contrary case, they incur a loss. That is the alternative that characterizes the role of the entrepreneur.

186. Taken together with our table of elements of production (§ 174), that definition explains the table and justifies it.

The capital goods classified under the first, second, and third headings, which are the capital goods that yield consumable services, are those found in the hands of landowners, workers, or capitalists, in their capacity as consumers. The capital goods classified under the fourth, fifth, and sixth headings, that is, the capital goods that yield productive services, are those found in the hands of entrepreneurs. Thus, it is always possible to tell whether a service is a consumable service or a productive service. For example, the land services of public parks, the work of public officials, and the capital good services of public edifices are not productive services but consumable services, because the State is not an entrepreneur trying to sell products at a price at least equal to their average cost, but a consumer that is substituted, through taxation, for landowners, workers, and capitalists, and that buys services and products in their place.

Similarly, among income commodities, those classified under the eighth heading are in the hands of consumers; and those classified under the ninth heading are in the hands of entrepreneurs. But this is the place for a very important observation.

Landed capital and personal capital are hired in kind. The landowner rents out his land and the worker hires out his personal faculties for a year, for a month, for a day, and they regain them at the end of the contracted period. Movable capital goods, apart from buildings and a few kinds of furnishings or tools, are hired out not in kind, but in money. The capitalist accumulates his capital by successive savings and lends money to the entrepreneur for a given period; the entrepreneur converts this money into capital goods properly speaking and, at the expiration of the contract, he returns the money to the capitalist. That operation constitutes *credit*. The result is that the income goods consisting of raw materials, classified under the ninth heading, and the movable capital goods classified under the sixth heading, can be part of the capital borrowed by the entrepreneur. The name *fixed capital* or *expenses of fixed assets* is given to movable capital goods; it is the ensemble of all those things that are used more than once in production. The name *circulating* or *working capital* is used to designate raw materials along with the capital goods classified under the seventh heading and the new income goods classified under the tenth heading; it is the ensemble of all those things that are not used more than once in production.

The circulating money classified under the eleventh heading is in the hands of consumers; money classified under the twelfth heading forms part of the circulating capital of entrepreneurs. The savings classified under the thirteenth heading is in the hands of consumers and represents exactly the excess of income over consumption.

187. The profit or loss position of an entrepreneur results at any moment from the situation in his books and the state of his raw materials and products in inventory. Hence this is the time to explain the business methods of accounting and inventorying. These methods, derived from ordinary practice, will be found completely in accord with the preceding conceptions, proving that our theory of production is well-founded on the nature of things. I shall first explain in a few words the principles of double entry bookkeeping.

188. As an entrepreneur I have, first, a till into which I put money when I receive it, and from which I take cash when I need it for my expenses. There is thus, coming from the outside into the till and going from the till to the outside, a double flow of money: a flow of money received and a flow of money paid out. It is clear, moreover, that the quantity of money in my till at any given moment is always equal to the difference between the quantity of money put in and the quantity of money paid out, neither more nor less. As a general rule, there is never found in the till any money other than that which has been put there minus that which has been taken out. That being stated, if I take a blank page in an account book and head it *Cash*; if I enter, in a column on one side of the page, on the left, for example, the various amounts that I have successively put into my till; if I enter

in a similar column on the other side of the page, the right side in this case, the amounts that I have successively taken out, then the difference between the total on the left and the total on the right must always represent exactly the total amount of cash in the till. These two totals may be equal, or their difference zero, as happens when the till is empty; but the right-hand total can never be greater than the left. The two columns taken together make up what is called the *Cash account*; the total on the left is usually called the *debit*, while that on the right is called the *credit* balance of the Cash account; the difference between the two, positive or zero but never negative, is called the *balance* of the Cash account.

189. Up to this point we see nothing resembling double entry book-keeping; but we will now see its nature.

The money that enters my till comes from capitalists who have lent it to me or from consumers who have bought products from me, and the money that leaves my till will be transformed either into fixed capital or working capital. Now, I am assuming that whenever I enter on the debit side of my Cash account an amount put into my till, I always wish to record where it comes from, and that, similarly, when I enter on the credit side of my Cash account an amount taken out of my till, I always wish to record where it is going. Let us see how I do this. For instance, the first money that I am going to put into my till is a sum lent to me by my friend named Martin to whom I promise repayment in installments over a period of two or three years. How shall I indicate that this sum comes from Martin? Very simply. After the entry to the debit of Cash, I write these words: *To Capitalist* or *To Martin*. But if I am going to do this properly, I cannot stop there. I take another blank page in my account book and I write at the top: *Capitalist* or *Martin*; and then, immediately after entering the amount on the debit side of the page of the Cash account, that is, on the left side of the page, I write the same amount on the credit or right side of the page of Capitalist's or Martin's account; and, immediately before the notation of this sum to the credit of the Capitalist or Martin account, I write these words: *By Cash*. That much, then, is done. One can guess that there is another step that is now to be taken, namely the one to be taken when, in the contrary case, instead of putting money into the till, I take it out to pay an installment on what I owe to my capitalist Martin. I enter this sum to the credit of my Cash account with the notation: *By Capitalist* or *By Martin*, and at the same time I debit it to Martin's account with the notation: *To Cash*. Consequently, just as the debit balance of the *Cash account* at all times furnishes information concerning the cash I have on hand, so also the credit balance of Martin's account always keeps me informed on another matter that I must constantly keep in mind, namely that of knowing the amount of money I still owe to my capitalist Martin.

It is the same for the other sums that I withdraw from or put into my till. If, for example, I take out cash in order to install a machine in my workshop, since that machine is part of what we have called fixed capital, the amount of which I must be in a position to ascertain rapidly at all times, I open an account: *Fixed Assets*, and I then enter the sum withdrawn to the credit of Cash with the notation: *By Fixed Assets*, and to the debit of Fixed Assets with the notation: *To Cash*. I deal in the same way with items of working capital. If I take money to buy raw materials or merchandise wholesale, or to pay my rent or my workers, that is, generally speaking, to pay rent, wages, and interest, I will enter it to the credit of Cash and to the debit of *Working Capital*. And if I put into my till the money earned from the sale of my products, I will enter the sum to the debit of the Cash account and to the credit of the Working Capital account. In current accounting practice, the Working Capital account is replaced by two others: a *Merchandise* account that is charged with raw materials and merchandise purchased wholesale, and a *General Expenses* account that is charged with rent, wages, and interest. We can, if we find it of interest, make this subdivision or any other in even greater detail; but, as we will shortly see, all these special accounts, by which the general Working Capital account will be replaced, must be reunited when the inventory is made.

That is double entry bookkeeping, the cardinal principle of which is *never to enter a sum to the debit or credit of an account without simultaneously entering the amount to the credit or debit of some other account*; from which it follows that the total of the debit balances or *assets* is always equal to the total of the credit balances or *liabilities*. The book that contains entries made in the order of accounts, and secondarily in the order of dates, is called the *Ledger*. It is accompanied by another record containing the same entries in the order of

their dates, and secondarily in the order of accounts, known as the
Journal.

190. A Cash account, that is sometimes debited and sometimes credited; a Capitalist liability account that may be divided into as many
sub-accounts as there are capitalists that lend money; a Fixed Assets
account that is generally debited; a Working Capital account that
is sometimes debited and sometimes credited: those are the four
accounts essential for any enterprise. The debit side of the Fixed
Assets account represents the total money value of the fixed capital,
and the debit side of the Working Capital account represents the
total money value of the unrealized circulating capital. A question
much discussed these days is whether the double entry bookkeeping
that we have described above is or is not as suitable for use in agriculture as it is in industry, commerce, and banking. That amounts
to asking whether or not agriculture is an industry that consists in
applying land services, labor, and capital good services to raw materials in order to obtain products. If so, and that most certainly is the
case, then unquestionably double entry bookkeeping can be used in
agricultural enterprises just as well as in industrial, commercial, and
financial enterprises, and if people have not yet succeeded in so using
it, that is only because they do not know how to create the various
accounts on a rational basis. We have here a striking example of the
way in which theory and practice ought to be of help to one another;
for it is certain that industrial practice, expressed through accounting, can successfully serve to establish the theory of production, and
it is equally certain that that theory, once established, can serve no
less felicitously to express agricultural practice through accounting.

191. We now have to expound the method of making business inventories and how an entrepreneur's profit or loss position is established.
The best way of doing this will be to take an example that conforms
to the usages and terminology of current accounting.

I am now an entrepreneur in the business of cabinet making. I
started with 3,000 francs that I saved and 7,000 francs lent to me by
relatives and friends who were interested in me and had confidence
in me. These persons and I signed a private agreement in accordance
with which they committed themselves to lend me their 7,000 francs

for ten years, and I pledged to pay them 5 per cent annual interest. They thus became my *silent partners*, while I am my own silent partner and ought to pay myself 5 per cent interest on my 3,000 francs. When I put the 10,000 francs into my till, I debited that amount to my *Cash* account and credited 10,000 francs to my *Capitalist* account. If the silent partners did not pay the whole sum to me immediately, or if they did not all pay at the same time, I would have had to open separate accounts A, B, C, etc.

Having done this, I rented a plot of ground for 500 francs a year, on which I had a workshop built that I equipped with machines, work-benches, and lathes. That cost me 5,000 francs that I paid in cash. Upon withdrawing the 5,000 francs from my till, I credited the Cash account 5,000 francs and debited my *Fixed Assets* account 5,000 francs.

Then I bought lumber, cloth, etc., for 2,000 francs; and, in consequence, I credited this amount to the Cash account, and debited the *Merchandise* account 2,000 francs.

In addition, I paid out 500 francs for interest on the capital that I invested, 500 francs for the rent of my land, and 2,000 francs for wages. I credited the Cash account 3,000 francs and debited the *General Expenses* account 3,000 francs.

But, all these expenses having been made, I had pieces of carpentry and furniture that clients had ordered and that I delivered. I sold them for 6,000 francs cash; and, in putting the 6,000 francs into my till, I debited the Cash account 6,000 francs and credited the Merchandise account 6,000 francs.

192. At this point in time, I make my inventory. And, in order to simplify as much as possible, I assume that I no longer have any merchandise, or raw materials, or products, in stock. I have no more merchandise, and nevertheless the Merchandise account is not balanced. It owes the Cash account 2,000 francs, and it has been credited 6,000 francs from the Cash account. The difference is 4,000 francs. From where does this come? The answer is very clear: from my selling my merchandise for more than I paid for it. In fact, that is what I ought to have done: I bought lumber, cloth, raw materials, and I sold pieces of carpentry, furniture, and other finely carved products. Now, it is clear that, in the price of the finished goods, I must recover not

only the price of the raw materials, but also, first of all, the cost of the labor as well as the sum of my overhead expenses, and, secondly, a certain profit. Thus, that difference of 4,000 francs covers my general expenses of 3,000 francs, and leaves me a profit of 1,000 francs. That is why I first balance the General Expenses account by debiting the Merchandise account, and then balance the Merchandise account, which must be balanced because there is no longer any merchandise in storage, by crediting 1,000 francs to a *Profit and Loss* account that appears among the liabilities. This Profit and Loss account would appear among the assets as a debit balance, if I had made a loss.

193. All that being finished, my accounts balance in the following way:

The Cash account has received 16,000 francs and has furnished 10,000 francs. It has a debit balance of 6,000 francs.

The Capitalist account has furnished 10,000 francs. It has a credit balance of 10,000 francs.

The Fixed Assets account has received 5,000 francs. It has a debit balance of 5,000 francs.

The Merchandise account has received with 6,000 francs and credited with 6,000 francs. It is balanced.

The General Expenses account has received 3,000 francs and has provided 3,000 francs. It is balanced.

The Profit and Loss account has furnished 1,000 francs. It has a credit balance, of 1,000 francs.

And, to summarize, my Balance Sheet is as follows:

ASSETS (composed of all accounts with a debit balance)

Cash account	6,000 Fr.
Fixed Assets	5,000 Fr.
Total	11,000 Fr.

LIABILITIES (composed of all accounts with a credit balance)

Capitalist	10,000 Fr.
Profit and Loss	1,000 Fr.
Same total	11,000 Fr.

I have earned 1,000 francs, and begin the new accounting period with a capital of 11,000 francs instead of 10,000, that is, with 5,000 francs of fixed capital and 6,000 francs of working capital.

194. We have simplified as much as possible. But, in practice, there are certain complications that must be noted.

(1) The entries are neither found nor made in whole amounts, but always piecemeal. It is not all at once but rather in several amounts that I paid 5,000 francs for fixed capital, 2,000 francs for merchandise, 3,000 francs for general expenses, and when I sold 6,000 francs worth of merchandise.

(2) I do not usually sell for cash, but on credit. And when I sell on credit to customers L, M, and N, instead of crediting the Merchandise account and debiting the Cash account, I credit Merchandise and debit Messrs. *L, M,* and *N*; and later, when they pay, I credit the accounts of L, M, and N and debit the Cash account. I therefore normally have a certain number of *Customers'* Debtor accounts.

(3) That is not all. The clients L, M, and N, after being debtors on my books for a certain time, do not usually settle their accounts in cash, but either with promissory notes that they make payable to me, or with bills of exchange that I draw on them and that they accept. And then, when I receive those documents, instead of crediting L, M, and N with offsetting debits to Cash, I credit their accounts by debiting a *Bills Receivable* account, except that I credit Bills Receivable by debiting the Cash account when I receive the payment. I have therefore, under normal conditions, a Bills Receivable account (or *Portfolio* account) with a debit balance. This account is analogous to the Cash account, inasmuch as the difference between the debit and the credit sides always corresponds exactly to the total of the notes and bills of exchange in my portfolio.

(4) There is still more. Generally, I do not take possession of my bills, but I negotiate them with a banker who discounts them before maturity. And when I negotiate bills in this way, instead of crediting Bills Receivable by debiting Cash, I credit Bills Receivable by debiting my *Bank* account, except that I credit my Bank account by debiting my Cash account when my banker remits the funds. The discount, which is interest, is naturally entered as a debit to General Expenses.

(5) I do not generally buy for cash, but on credit. And when I buy on credit from suppliers X, Y, and Z, instead of debiting the Merchandise account by crediting Cash, I debit Merchandise by crediting the accounts of X, Y, and Z, except that I debit X, Y, and Z by crediting the Cash account when I pay them. I have, therefore, normally, a certain number of *Suppliers'* Creditor accounts.

(6) Here again, after having sums credited on the books for a certain time period, I generally do not settle up with my suppliers X, Y, and Z in cash, but with promissory notes that I make payable to them or with bills of exchange that they draw on me and that I accept. And then, when I deliver these documents to my creditors, instead of debiting X, Y, and Z by crediting Cash, I debit them by crediting a *Bills Payable* account, except that I debit Bills Payable by crediting Cash when I pay these notes and bills. Thus, I also have, normally, a credit account under Bills Payable.

(7) Finally, it never happens that I do not have sufficient merchandise, be it raw materials or products, in stock at the time of the inventory. That would create, at the end of each accounting period, a totally unfortunate and pointless interruption of operations. On the contrary, as I sell furniture, I constantly purchase lumber, cloth. This is the merchandise of which I make an inventory. I always balance General Expenses by debiting to Merchandise; but instead of balancing the Merchandise account, I simply balance it by using the Profit and Loss account in such a way as to leave the Merchandise account with a debit balance exactly equal to the inventoried merchandise. Here is how that is done. M_d and M_c being the debit and credit of the Merchandise account; F the debit balance of the General Expenses account, I the money value of the Inventory, it is necessary that I add, in the case of there being a profit, to $M_d + F$ on the debit side of my Merchandise account, a sum P such that

$$\left(M_d + F + P\right) - M_c = I,$$

the Merchandise account remaining with a debit balance of I, and the Profit and Loss account having a credit balance of P; or that, in case of a loss, I add to M_c of the Merchandise account an amount P such that

$$\left(M_d + F\right) - \left(M_c + P\right) = I,$$

the Merchandise account always having a debit balance of I, and the Profit and Loss account then having a debit balance of P. These two sums are given by the single equation

$$M_d + F - I \pm P = M_c,$$

which may be directly deduced from the consideration that the sum of the expenditures on raw materials, plus the general expenses paid, minus the unused raw materials and the products in stock, plus or minus the profit or loss, is equal to the sum realized from the sale of products.

In accordance with this, to make up the Assets statement, the Customers' Debtor accounts, the Bills Receivable, the Bank account, and the Merchandise Inventory are added to Cash and to Fixed Assets; and, to make up the Liabilities statement, the Suppliers' Creditor accounts and the Bills Payable account are added to the Capitalist account and the Profit and Loss account. With these additions, we have the ordinary balance sheet of an industrial enterprise. Balance sheets of agricultural, commercial, and financial enterprises would be completely analogous.

195. We have seen how, in principle, an entrepreneur can find out at any moment by means of an inventory whether he is making a profit or a loss. Our definitions being established theoretically and in reference to practice, we are now going to assume that our entrepreneurs make neither profit nor loss; we are going, as we said (§ 179), to abstract from the entrepreneurs' working capital in the form of raw materials, new capital goods, new income goods, and cash on hand, as well as from the consumers' working capital in the form of accumulations of income goods, circulating money, and savings; and we are going to show how the current prices of products and of services are mathematically determined in a state of equilibrium.

LESSON 20

Equations of production

SUMMARY: – Utility of products and services; quantities in possession. Equation of the equivalence of the quantities of services supplied and the quantities of products demanded; equations of maximum satisfaction; individual supply equations for services and individual demand equations for products. Equations [1] of total supply of services. Equations [2] of total demand for products. Equations [3] of equality of supply of and demand for services. Equations [4] of equality of the price and the average cost of the products. Constancy of the production coefficients. Raw materials.

196. Let us therefore now go back to the services classified under the first six headings (§ 174) that will remain, after all the simplifications we have pointed out, the essential data of the problem; and let these services of land be of the kinds (T), (T'), (T''), ⋯, of labor of persons of the kinds (P), (P'), (P''), and of capital goods of the kinds (K), (K'), (K''), ⋯. We assume that these services are valued by means of the following two metrics: 1° the natural or artificial quantity of the capital good, the hectare of land, the person, and the capital good itself, and 2° the unit of time, the day, for instance. So, we will have certain quantities of days of land services from a hectare of this or that land, certain quantities of days from this or that person, certain quantities of days of services from this or that capital good. Let the number of these services be n.

By means of the services thusly defined, we can manufacture products of the kinds (A), (B), (C), (D), ⋯. This production can take place either directly, or with a prior production of raw materials; that is to say, either by combining some land services, labor, and capital goods services, or by applying land services, labor and capital goods services to raw materials; but we will see that the second case can be reduced to the first one. Let the number of products that can be produced in this way be *m*.

197. For every individual, the products have a utility that we may express by a utility function of the form $r = \varphi(q)$ (§ 75). The services themselves, however, have a direct utility for each individual. And not only can a person, as he wishes, either rent out, or keep for himself the whole or a part of the services of his land, his personal faculties, and his capital goods properly speaking, but, if he wishes to do so, may, moreover, purchase land services, labor, or capital good services not as an entrepreneur to transform them into products, but as a consumer to use them directly; that is to say, not as productive services but as consumable services. We have accounted for this by placing in a separate category, distinguished from the services classified under the headings 4, 5 and 6, those that are classified under the three first headings (§ 174). The services are therefore also commodities whose utility for each individual can be expressed by a utility or want equation of the form $r = \varphi(q)$.

Having said this, let an individual be in the possession of q_t of (T), q_p of (P), q_k of (K), $\cdots$. And let $r = \varphi_t(q), r = \varphi_p(q), r = \varphi_k(q), \cdots$, $r = \varphi_a(q), r = \varphi_b(q), r = \varphi_c(q), r = \varphi_d(q), \cdots$ be the utility or want equations for this individual. Let $p_t, p_p, p_k, \cdots, p_b, p_c, p_d, \cdots$ be the current prices of the services and the products, measured in (A). Let $o_t, o_p, o_k, \cdots$ be the quantities effectively supplied of the services at these prices, which may be positive and therefore representing quantities supplied, but which also may be negative and therefore representing quantities demanded. Let, finally, $d_a, d_b, d_c, d_d, \cdots$ be the quantities effectively demanded of the products at these same equilibrium prices. Abstracting, till the following part [Part V], from depreciation of existing capital goods and their insurance, as well as from the creation of savings with a view to the creation of new capital goods properly speaking, we have first between these quantities and prices the equation

$$o_t p_t + o_p p_p + o_k p_k + \cdots = d_a + d_b p_b + d_c p_c + d_d p_d + \cdots$$

Because of the condition of maximum satisfaction (§ 80) that determines obviously the positive or negative supply of services and the demand for products, we have, moreover, between these same prices and these same quantities, the equations

$$\varphi_t \left(q_t - o_t \right) = p_t \varphi_a (d_a),$$

$$\varphi_p \left(q_p - o_p \right) = p_p \varphi_a (d_a),$$

$$\varphi_k \left(q_k - o_k \right) = p_k \varphi_a (d_a),$$

$$\vdots$$

$$\varphi_b \left(d_b \right) = p_b \varphi_a (d_a),$$

$$\varphi_c \left(d_c \right) = p_c \varphi_a (d_a),$$

$$\varphi_d \left(d_d \right) = p_d \varphi_a (d_a),$$

$$\vdots$$

hence $n + m - 1$ equations that form with the preceding one a system of $n + m$ equations of which one can eliminate successively $n + m - 1$ of the unknowns $o_t, o_p, o_k, \cdots, d_a, d_b, d_c, d_d, \cdots$ such that there will only remain one equation yielding the $n + m^{\text{th}}$ one as function of the prices $p_t, p_p, p_k, \cdots, p_b, p_c, p_d, \cdots$. We would then have the following equations of supply of or demand for (T), (P), (K), $\cdots$

$$o_t = f_t (p_t, p_p, p_k, \cdots, p_b, p_c, p_d, \cdots),$$

$$o_p = f_p (p_t, p_p, p_k, \cdots, p_b, p_c, p_d, \cdots),$$

$$o_k = f_k (p_t, p_p, p_k, \cdots, p_b, p_c, p_d, \cdots),$$

$$\vdots$$

and the following equations of demand for (B), (C), (D), $\cdots$

$$d_b = f_b(p_t, p_p, p_k, \cdots, p_b, p_c, p_d, \cdots),$$

$$d_c = f_c(p_t, p_p, p_k, \cdots, p_b, p_c, p_d, \cdots),$$

$$d_d = f_d(p_t, p_p, p_k, \cdots, p_b, p_c, p_d, \cdots),$$

$$\vdots$$

The demand for (A) would be given by the equation

$$d_a = o_t p_t + o_p p_p + o_k p_k + \cdots - (d_b p_b + d_c p_c + d_d p_d + \cdots).$$

198. Likewise, we would have the individual demand or supply equations of the services and the individual demand equations of the products for all the other possessors of services. Now, denoting by $O_t, O_p, O_k, \cdots$ the total quantities supplied of the services, namely the excesses of the positive $o_t, o_p, o_k, \cdots$ over the negative $o_t, o_p, o_k, \cdots$, by $D_a, D_b, D_c, D_d, \cdots$ the total quantities demanded of products, and by $F_t, F_p, F_k, \cdots, F_b, F_c, F_d, \cdots$ the sums of the functions $f_t, f_p, f_k, \cdots, f_b, f_c, f_d, \cdots$, we would already have, in order to determine the quantities we seek, and subject to the reservation that the functions satisfy the restrictions relating to the case in which a quantity supplied equals the total quantity possessed, like those in the theory of exchange ([Part III] §§ 118, 119, 120), the following system of n equations of total supply of services:

$$O_t = F_t(p_t, p_p, p_k, \cdots, p_b, p_c, p_d, \cdots),$$

$$O_p = F_p(p_t, p_p, p_k, \cdots, p_b, p_c, p_d, \cdots), \qquad [1]$$

$$O_k = F_k(p_t, p_p, p_k, \cdots, p_b, p_c, p_d, \cdots),$$

$$\vdots$$

and the following system of m equations of total demand for products:

$$D_b = F_b(p_t, p_p, p_k, \cdots, p_b, p_c, p_d, \cdots),$$

$$D_c = F_c(p_t, p_p, p_k, \cdots, p_b, p_c, p_d, \cdots),$$

$$D_d = F_d(p_t, p_p, p_k, \cdots, p_b, p_c, p_d, \cdots), \tag{2}$$

$$\vdots$$

$$D_a = O_t p_t + O_p p_p + O_k p_k + \cdots - (D_b p_b + D_c p_c + D_d p_d + \cdots);$$

hence, in total *m* + *n* equations.

199. Moreover, let, $a_t, a_p, a_k, \cdots, b_t, b_p, b_k, \cdots, c_t, c_p, c_k, \cdots, d_t, d_p, d_k, \cdots$ be the *coefficients of production*; that is to say, the respective quantities of productive services (T), (P), (K), $\cdots$ that enter into the production of one unit of each of the products (A), (B), (C), (D), $\cdots$; we would then have further, for the determination of the quantities searched for, the following two systems:

$$a_t D_a + b_t D_b + c_t D_c + d_t D_b + \cdots = O_t,$$

$$a_p D_a + b_p D_b + c_p D_c + d_p D_b + \cdots = O_p, \tag{3}$$

$$a_k D_a + b_k D_b + c_k D_c + d_k D_b + \cdots = O_k,$$

$$\vdots$$

hence *n* equations expressing that *the quantities of employed productive services are equal to the quantities effectively supplied*;

$$a_t p_t + a_p p_p + a_k p_k + \cdots = 1,$$

$$b_t p_t + b_p p_p + b_k p_k + \cdots = p_b,$$

$$c_t p_t + c_p p_p + c_k p_k + \cdots = p_c, \tag{4}$$

$$d_t p_t + d_p p_p + d_k p_k + \cdots = p_d,$$

$$\vdots$$

hence *m* equations expressing that *the prices of the products are equal to their average costs in terms of productive services*.

200. As can be seen, we assume that the coefficients $a_t, a_p, a_k, \cdots, b_t,$ $b_p, b_k, \cdots, c_t, c_p, c_k, \cdots, d_t, d_p, d_k, \cdots$ are fixed a priori. In reality that is not the case: in the production of a product, more or less productive services can be used; more or less land services, for example, on the condition of using less or more other productive services, less or more capital good services or labor, for example. The respective quantities of the productive services that enter thus into the making of a unit of each of the products are determined only after the prices of the productive services are determined, by the condition that the average cost of the products be minimized. It would be easy to express this condition by a system of as many equations as there are production coefficients to be determined. For the time being, we abstract from that procedure by assuming that the above coefficients are included in the given data and not among the unknowns of the problem.

In making this assumption, we are neglecting another circumstance, that of the distinction between the fixed expenses and the variable expenses in the firms. However, since we are assuming that the entrepreneurs do not make profits or losses, we can also assume that they manufacture equal quantities of products, in which case all the expenses of whatever kind may be considered as proportional.[i]

201. As we have said above, we will reduce the case of the application of productive services to raw materials to the case of combining land services, labor, and capital good services with each other. This is how we must proceed, because the raw materials themselves are products obtained either by the combination of quantities of productive services with each other, or by the application of productive services to other raw materials of which one could say the same thing, and so forth.

A unit of product (B), for example, being obtained by applying the quantities β_t of (T), β_p of (P), β_k of (K), $\cdots$, and the quantity β_m of the raw material (M), the average cost p_b of (B) is given by the equation

$$p_b = \beta_t p_t + \beta_p p_p + \beta_k p_k + \cdots + \beta_m p_m,$$

where p_m is the average cost of (M). The raw material (M), however, being itself a product of which a unit is obtained by the combination of m_t of (T), m_p of (P), m_k of (K), $\cdots$, has average cost p_m given by the equation

$$p_m = m_t p_t + m_p p_p + m_k p_k + \cdots$$

Substituting this value of p_m in the preceding equation, we obtain

$$p_b = (\beta_t + \beta_m m_t) p_t + \left(\beta_p + \beta_m m_p\right) p_m + (\beta_k + \beta_{mk} m_k) p_k + \cdots$$

This equation is none other than the second one of system [4] if one sets

$$\beta_t + \beta_m m_t = b_t, \; \beta_p + \beta_m m_p = b_p, \; \beta_k + \beta_m m_k = b_k, \cdots.$$

It is immediately seen what would have to be done if the raw material (M) were to be obtained, not by the combination of productive services with each other, but by the application of productive services to whatever other raw material.

202. Thus we have a total of $2m + 2n$ equations. But these $2m + 2n$ equations can be reduced to $2m + 2n - 1$. Indeed, if we multiply the two members of the n equations of system [3] by p_t, p_p, p_k, $\cdots$, and the two members of the m equations of the system [4] with D_a, D_b, D_c, D_d, $\cdots$, respectively, and if we add separately the equations of each system, then we arrive at two total equations of which the first members are identical, and this results in equality of the two second members:

$$O_t p_t + O_p p_p + O_k p_k + \cdots = D_a + D_b p_b + D_c p_c + D_d p_d + \cdots,$$

which is nothing other than the mth equation of system [2]. Hence we can, if we wish so, keep this one and skip, for instance, the first one of system [4], or vice versa. However, there are $2m + 2n - 1$ equations to determine $2m + 2n - 1$ variables in the state of equilibrium, and these are: 1. the n total quantities of services supplied, 2. the n prices of these quantities, 3. the m total quantities of products demanded, and 4. the $m - 1$ the $m - 1$ of $m - 1$ of these products expressed in the mth. The only thing we still have to show, as far as concerns the equilibrium of production just as it concerned that of exchange, is that this same problem, whose theoretical solution we have presented, is also the one that solves itself automatically in the market by means of the mechanism of free competition.

203. The problem is to arrive at the equilibrium of production in the same way as we arrived at the equilibrium of exchange; that is to say, assuming that the data of the problem do not change during the whole time of duration of our tatonnements, apart from the assumption later that these data will vary with a view to the study of the effects of these variations. However, with respect to the tatonnement in matters of production, a problem arises that did not occur in exchange. In exchange, commodities do not undergo quantity changes. When a price is cried, and when effective supply and demand at that price are not equal, another price is cried which entails other amounts of effective supply and demand. In production, productive services are transformed into products. If certain prices of services have been cried and certain quantities of products made, and if these prices and these quantities are not equilibrium prices and quantities, it is not only necessary to cry other prices, but also manufacture other quantities of products.

Accepting this necessity, we must assume that, for every reprise of the tatonnement, our entrepreneurs will find, in the country, landowners, workers, and capitalists who possess the same quantities of services and have the same wants for services and products. A reprise of the tatonnement will consist of the following. At prices in the first instance cried at random, and then raised or lowered in accordance with circumstances, the entrepreneurs borrow from the landowners, workers, and capitalists the quantities of services necessary for the production of certain quantities of products determined in first instance at random, and then increased or decreased in accordance with the circumstances. Then they sell these products in the market for products, in accordance with the mechanism of free competition, to these landowners, workers and capitalists, who are still in the possession of the same quantities of services[ii] and still have the same wants for products and services. The tatonnement will be finished when the entrepreneurs will obtain, in exchange for the products they have made, from the landowners, workers, and capitalists exactly the quantities of land services, labor, and capital good services they owe these landowners, workers, and capitalists, and that they will have used in making products; with the result that the entrepreneurs will be able either to settle their debts and end their activity, or, instead, continue indefinitely producing the amounts that, from then onwards, satisfy the market, provided that no variations occur in the data; that is to say, in the quantities of services possessed and in the utilities of the services and products.

Notes

i   See Appendix I, first footnote of § 8. See also the discussion of this section in the translators' introduction.

ii This is because Walras assumed that, in the model of production, the capital goods are constant in amount during the process of equilibration; they are not used up in any degree. That is how it is possible for the services of capital goods controlled by the participants in the model to be the same amounts from one reprise of the tatonnement to the next. That is also part of the features of the model of production that make its equilibrium independent of the path followed by the variables.

LESSON 21

Solution of the equations of production. Law of the determination of the prices of products and services

SUMMARY: – Assumption that the entrepreneurs commit themselves to return productive services in equivalent quantities. Prices of productive services cried at random. Average costs of the products. Random quantities of products made. Prices of the products. Profits or losses of the entrepreneurs. Tatonnement with a view to equality of price and average cost of the products. Demand for the numeraire product. Equality of the average cost of the numeraire product to unity is necessary for the equilibrium of production.

Assumption that the entrepreneurs commit themselves to return productive services in equal quantities. Effective supply of and demand for services. Quantities demanded by the entrepreneurs; quantities demanded by the consumers. Variations in demand and supply in accordance with variations of the price between zero and infinity. Tatonnement with a view to equality to unity of the average cost of the numeraire product. The law of the determination of the equilibrium prices of products and services.

204. Let us, therefore, come to the market, and assume that there are n prices of productive services $p'_t, p'_p, p'_k, \cdots$ and m quantities $\Omega_a, \Omega_b, \Omega_c, \Omega_d, \cdots$ of products to be made, all determined at random. In order to have a better grasp on the operations that will follow, we split them into two phases by means of the following double hypothesis. First, we assume that the entrepreneurs producing (A), (B), (C), (D), $\cdots$ buy productive services (T), (P), (K), $\cdots$ while committing themselves to return at a later time quantities of these services that are not equal, but simply equivalent, and so we determine the

quantities $\Omega_a, \Omega_b, \Omega_c, \Omega_d, \cdots$ such that the entrepreneurs make neither profits nor losses. Then we assume that the entrepreneurs commit themselves to providing later on quantities that not only have the same value, but that are equal to the quantities bought, and so we determine the quantities $p'_t, p'_p, p'_k, \cdots$ [i] such that effective demand for and supply of services are equal. We can see quite clearly how this procedure abstracts, if not from the numeraire, at least from money.

It may perhaps be useful to make the observation that, with our data and under the conditions we have imposed, we are assuming that the capital goods properly speaking are rented in kind. Nevertheless, we have explained (§ 186) that, in reality, the capital goods are lent in money, because the capitalist has formed his capital by means of saving. However, later on we will consider both the creation of capital goods and their lending in the form of money.

205. From the prices $p'_t, p'_p, p'_k, \cdots$ of (T), (P), (K), $\cdots$, randomly determined as has already been said, result the average costs $p'_a, p'_b, p'_c, p'_d \cdots$, in accordance with the equations

$$p'_a = a_t p'_t + a_p p'_p + a_k p'_k + \cdots$$

$$p'_b = b_t p'_t + b_p p'_p + b_k p'_k + \cdots$$

$$p'_c = c_t p'_t + c_p p'_p + c_k p'_k + \cdots$$

$$p'_d = d_t p'_t + d_p p'_p + d_k p'_k + \cdots$$

$$\vdots$$

It will be noticed that we could have determined, if we wished, $p'_t, p'_p, p'_k, \cdots$ such that $p'_a = 1$. We will benefit from this omission at the right moment, and we will show later on that the average cost of the numeraire commodity automatically tends to be equal to unity in a regime of free competition. For the moment, we will reason as though the average cost of (A) is greater or less than its price, or equal to it.

Moreover, the quantities $\Omega_a, \Omega_b, \Omega_c, \Omega_d, \cdots$ of (A), (B), (C), (D), $\cdots$ require quantities $\Delta_t, \Delta_p, \Delta_k, \cdots$ of (T), (P), (K), $\cdots$ in accordance with the equations

$$\Delta_t = a_t \Omega_a + b_t \Omega_b + c_t \Omega_c + d_t \Omega_d + \cdots$$

$$\Delta_p = a_p \Omega_a + b_p \Omega_b + c_p \Omega_c + d_p \Omega_d + \cdots$$

$$\Delta_k = a_k \Omega_a + b_k \Omega_b + c_k \Omega_c + d_k \Omega_d + \cdots$$

$$\vdots$$

Then being brought to the market, the quantities $\Omega_a, \Omega_b, \Omega_c, \Omega_d, \cdots$ will be sold by the entrepreneurs in accordance with the mechanism of free competition. Let us first consider the selling conditions for the products (B), (C), (D), $\cdots$. Then we will consider the conditions for the sale of the product (A), which serves as numeraire.

206. The quantities $\Omega_b, \Omega_c, \Omega_d, \cdots$ of (B), (C), (D), $\cdots$ will be sold at prices $\pi_b, \pi_c, \pi_d, \cdots$ in accordance with the equations

$$\Omega_b = F_b(p'_t, p'_p, p'_k, \cdots, \pi_b, \pi_c, \pi_d, \cdots)$$

$$\Omega_c = F_c(p'_t, p'_p, p'_k, \cdots, \pi_b, \pi_c, \pi_d, \cdots)$$

$$\Omega_d = F_d(p'_t, p'_p, p'_k, \cdots, \pi_b, \pi_c, \pi_d, \cdots)$$

$$\vdots$$

Indeed, since free competition is the market rule, the products will be sold in conformance with the triple condition: 1° maximum satisfaction of wants, 2° uniformity of prices of both products and services, and, 3° general equilibrium (§ 122). Now, the above-mentioned system has $m - 1$ equations with $m - 1$ unknowns, thus fulfilling those three conditions precisely.

Consequently, and because the prices $\pi_b, \pi_c, \pi_d, \cdots$ are generally different from the average costs $p'_b, p'_c, p'_d, \cdots$, the entrepreneurs producing (B), (C), (D), $\cdots$ will make profits or losses that can be expressed by the differences

$$\Omega_b(\pi_b - p'_b), \quad \Omega_c(\pi_c - p'_c), \quad \Omega_d(\pi_d - p'_d), \cdots.$$

However, we see immediately that if $\Omega_b, \Omega_c, \Omega_d, \cdots$ are functions of $\pi_b, \pi_c, \pi_d, \cdots$, these latter magnitudes are, by this very fact, functions of the former, and that, consequently, by means of appropriate modifications, we will bring the prices of these products into equality with their average costs.

207. We do not know the functions F_b, F_c, F_d, $\cdots$, but from the very nature of exchange it follows that these functions are increasing or decreasing at decreasing or increasing values of, respectively, p_b, p_c, p_d, and so on. Hence, if, for example, $\pi_b > p'_b$, then we could decrease π_b by increasing Ω_b; and if, for example, $\pi_b < p'_b$, we could increase π_b by decreasing Ω_b. Likewise, if, $\pi_c \gtrless p'_c$, $\pi_d \gtrless p'_d$, $\cdots$, we could decrease or increase π_c, π_d, $\cdots$ by increasing or decreasing Ω_c, Ω_d, $\cdots$.

Let $\Omega'_b, \Omega'_c, \Omega'_d, \cdots$ be the quantities to be made of (B), (C), (D), $\cdots$ and for which

$$\Omega'_b = F_b(p'_t, p'_p, p'_k, \cdots, p'_b, \pi_c, \pi_d, \cdots)$$

$$\Omega'_c = F_c(p'_t, p'_p, p'_k, \cdots, \pi_b, p'_c, \pi_d, \cdots)$$

$$\Omega'_d = F_d(p'_t, p'_p, p'_k, \cdots, \pi_b, \pi_c, p'_d, \cdots)$$

$$\vdots$$

These quantities are substituted for $\Omega_b, \Omega_c, \Omega_d, \cdots$ in the tatonnement and then brought to the market where they will be sold in accordance with the mechanism of free competition at prices $\pi'_b, \pi'_c, \pi'_d, \cdots$ in accordance with the equations

$$\Omega'_b = F_b(p'_t, p'_p, p'_k, \cdots, \pi'_b, \pi'_c, \pi'_d, \cdots)$$

$$\Omega'_c = F_c(p'_t, p'_p, p'_k, \cdots, \pi'_b, \pi'_c, \pi'_d, \cdots)$$

$$\Omega'_d = F_d(p'_t, p'_p, p'_k, \cdots, \pi'_b, \pi'_c, \pi'_d, \cdots)$$

$$\vdots$$

and what we must explain is that π'_b, π'_c, π'_d are closer to equality with p'_b, p'_c, p'_d than were $\pi_b, \pi_c, \pi_d, \cdots$.

208. Under the conditions of the tatonnement that we are carrying out at this moment, the prices of the services have been fixed and do not change. Each exchanger in the exchange has therefore always the same income measured in numeraire

$$r = q_t p'_t + q_p p'_p + q_k p'_k + \cdots,$$

and this income has to be divided between the consumption of services and the consumption of products in accordance with the equation

$$(q_t - o_t) p'_t + (q_p - o_p) p'_p + (q_k - o_k) p'_k + \cdots + d_a + d_b p_b$$
$$+ d_c p_c + d_d p_d + \cdots = r.$$

As a consequence of the production of certain quantities of the goods (B), (C), (D), $\cdots$, certain prices of them are determined, and if the quantity of one of the products, say (B), were to increase or decrease,[ii] the first thing to do, to establish a new equilibrium, would be to increase or to decrease the demand for (B) of all the exchangers in such a way as to decrease or increase the raretés by a common and identical proportion, and at the same time to decrease or increase the price of (B) in the same proportion. This can be called a first-order consequence because it has an important effect on the price of (B). After this adjustment, equilibrium would have been restored if, for each exchanger, the amount spent on the consumption of (B), $d_b p_b$, remained unchanged. However, in all cases, that is, in case of either an increase or in case of a decrease of the quantity of (B) produced, this amount has undoubtedly increased for certain individuals and decreased for others. This means that the former would have to sell a part of all their goods, which tends to lower the prices, and the latter would have to buy all those goods, which tends to raise the prices. This now would be a second-order consequence, being of minor importance as far as the prices of (B), (C), (D), $\cdots$ are concerned for the following three reasons: 1° the variation in the amount to be spent on the consumption of (B), $d_b p_b$, is limited by the fact that the two factors d_b and p_b vary in opposite directions; 2° this variation, which leads to a sale and a purchase of all goods, would, because of this very fact, entail the sale and purchase of only very small amounts of each of them; and 3° the effects of the sales and of the purchases would counteract each other.

What has just been said about the consequences of the change of the quantity made of (B), could be said of the consequences of the changes of the quantities made of (C), (D), $\cdots$. Hence, it is certain that the change in the quantity made of each product has had a direct effect on the price of this product, entirely in the same direction, whereas the changes in the quantities produced of the other products, assuming that they all act in the same direction, have had only indirect effects on the price of the product in question, these effects being exercised in one direction by some commodities and in the opposite direction for others and offsetting each other to a certain degree. Consequently, the system of new quantities produced and of their prices is nearer to equilibrium than its predecessor, and, it is necessary only to continue the tatonnement in order to approach the equilibrium more and more closely.

In that way, we arrive at the determination of certain quantities $D_b', D_c', D_d', \cdots$ of (B), (C), (D), $\cdots$ that require quantities $D_t', D_p', D_k', \cdots$ of (T), (P), (K), $\cdots$ in accordance with the following equations:

$$D_t' = a_t \Omega_a + b_t D_b' + c_t D_c' + d_t D_d' + \cdots$$

$$D_p' = a_p \Omega_a + b_p D_b' + c_p D_c' + d_p D_d' + \cdots$$

$$D_k' = a_k \Omega_a + b_k D_b' + c_k D_c' + d_k D_d' + \cdots$$

$$\vdots$$

and these products are sold at prices $p_b', p_c', p_d', \cdots$ in accordance with the equations

$$D_b' = F_b(p_t', p_p', p_k', \cdots, p_b', p_c', p_d', \cdots)$$

$$D_c' = F_c(p_t', p_p', p_k', \cdots, p_b', p_c', p_d', \cdots)$$

$$D'_d = F_d(p'_t, p'_p, p'_k, \cdots, p'_b, p'_c, p'_d, \cdots)$$

$$\vdots$$

The entrepreneurs would not make profits or suffer losses on these quantities of (B), (C), (D), $\cdots$.

Now, this tatonnement is precisely what takes place automatically in the markets for products under the regime of free competition, when the entrepreneurs flow toward or turn away from firms according to whether profits or losses are to be made in them (§ 184).

209. To the prices $p'_b, p'_c, p'_d, \cdots$ equal to the average costs, correspond the quantities effectively demanded $D'_b, D'_c, D'_d, \cdots$ of (B), (C), (D), $\cdots$ and the quantities effectively supplied $O'_t, O'_p, O'_k, \cdots$ of (T), (P), (K), $\cdots$, in accordance with the equations of total supply

$$O'_t = F_t(p'_t, p'_p, p'_k, \cdots, p'_b, p'_c, p'_d, \cdots)$$

$$O'_p = F_p(p'_t, p'_p, p'_k, \cdots, p'_b, p'_c, p'_d, \cdots)$$

$$O'_k = F_k(p'_t, p'_p, p'_k, \cdots, p'_b, p'_c, p'_d, \cdots)$$

$$\vdots$$

that form, together with the equations of total demand for products, a system of equations of exchange fulfilling these three conditions: maximum satisfaction, uniformity of prices, and general equilibrium.

Then, there is also an effective demand for D'_a for (A) determined by the equation

$$D'_a = O'_t p'_t + O'_p p'_p + O'_k p'_k + \cdots - (D'_b p'_b + D'_c p'_c + D'_d p'_d + \cdots).$$

What is more, we derive from the two systems of equations, one of which expresses the average costs of the products as functions of the prices of the production factors (§ 205), and the other the quantities of productive services demanded as functions of the quantities produced (§ 208), by multiplying the m equations of the first system by $\Omega_a, D'_b, D'_c, D'_d, \cdots$, respectively, multiplying the n equations of the second one by $p'_t, p'_p, p'_k, \cdots$, respectively, adding the two systems thus obtained, and observing that the two second members of the two additions are identical, the following equation

$$\Omega_a p'_a = D'_t p'_t + D'_p p'_p + D'_k p'_k + \cdots - \left(D'_b p'_b + D'_c p'_c + D'_d p'_d + \cdots\right).$$

Consequently, we have also

$$D'_a - \Omega_a p'_a = (O'_t p'_t - D'_t p'_t) + (O'_p p'_p - D'_p p'_p) + (O'_k p'_k - D'_k p'_k) + \cdots.$$

The quantity produced of the good (A) is still only determined at random; it should likewise be determined such that the entrepreneurs do not make profits or losses. It is obvious, then, that the average cost of the numeraire must be equal to the price. This is what will take place if we had taken care to posit from the beginning

$$p'_a = a_t p'_t + a_p p'_p + a_k p'_k + \cdots = 1.$$

Without this equation, equilibrium is impossible. Moreover, assuming that it is satisfied, there will be equilibrium if $D'_a, D'_b, D'_c \cdots$ are determined as above. Indeed, the quantities of services of production factors owed to the capitalists by the entrepreneurs and the quantities to be received by them in exchange of their products will be equivalent, since, p'_a being equal to 1, neither the entrepreneurs producing (A) nor those producing (B), (C), (D), $\cdots$, will make profits or losses. So, we have

$$(O'_t p'_t - D'_t p'_t) + (O'_p p'_p - D'_p p'_p) + (O'_k p'_k - D'_k p'_k) + \cdots = 0,$$

and, consequently, also

$$D'_a = \Omega_a p'_a = \Omega_a.$$

Hence, in fact, when the price of the services has been fixed so that the average cost of the numeraire good becomes equal to unity, it will suffice, to obtain the partial equilibrium we are seeking, to determine, just as we said, $D'_a, D'_b, D'_c \cdots$ such the entrepreneurs producing (B), (C), (D), $\cdots$ make neither profits nor losses. The quantity D'_a demanded of (A) will be quite naturally the quantity Ω_a made at random. Then, the first condition will be satisfied, namely that the entrepreneurs take on the commitment to return the productive services in quantities that are not equal but simply equivalent to the quantities they have borrowed. In other words, all the equations of production will then be satisfied, except, however, those of the system $[1]^{iii}$ of equations of total supply of services.

210. Nevertheless, like the other systems, this one must be satisfied as well. In other words, it is not enough that the quantities of productive services borrowed and returned be equivalent; they must be equal, since these same quantities must be used in the fabrication of the products.[iv] Hence the moment has come to close, as it were, the production circle by the introduction of the condition, conforming to reality, that the products are exchanged for the same quantities of services as those entering into their production.

The condition of equality just mentioned will be satisfied if we have

$$D'_t = O'_t, \; D'_p = O'_p, \; D'_k = O'_k, \cdots.$$

In general, however, we have

$$D'_t \gtreqless O'_t, \; D'_p \gtreqless O'_p, \; D'_k \gtreqless O'_k, \cdots.$$

Observe, $p'_t, p'_p, p'_k, \cdots$ being essentially positive, that when we have made $p'_a = 1$ and $\Omega_a = D'_a$, if there are certain quantities among $D'_t - O'_t, D'_p - O'_p, D'_k - O'_k, \cdots$ that are positive, the other ones must be negative, and conversely.

211. The function O'_t can be written in the form $U - u$, where the function U represents the sum of the positive o_t's, that is of the quantities effectively supplied of the service (T), and the function u the sum of the negative o_t's, that is of the quantities effectively demanded of this service, not by the entrepreneurs for the production of (A), (B), (C), (D), $\cdots$ but by the consumers as a commodity; that is to say,

not as a productive service but as a consumable service. Hence, the inequality $D'_t \gtreqless O'_t$ can be written in the form

$$a_t D'_a + b_t D'_b + c_t D'_c + d_t D'_d + \cdots + u \gtreqless U.$$

Let us assume that D'_a does not vary; that is to say, that the entrepreneurs producing (A) always make the same quantities, irrespective of the variations of $p'_t, p'_p, p'_k, \cdots$ and, accordingly, of the average cost p'_a. The variable terms $b_t D'_b, c_t D'_c, d_t D'_d, \cdots$ of the first member of the inequality above are decreasing functions of $p_b, p_c, p_d, \cdots$ and, consequently, of p'_t, since these average costs themselves are increasing functions of p'_t. The variable term u, too, is a decreasing function of p'_t, Hence, if p'_t augments from zero to infinity and if $p'_p, p'_k, \cdots$ do not change, $D'_t + u$ will decrease from a certain value onwards to zero.

Regarding the single term U of the second member, it is equal to zero if p_t is equal to zero and even perhaps for certain positive values of p_t; this will be the case if the values of the various products in proportion to the value of the service (T) are so high that the demand for these products by the owners of this service is zero. If the price p_t increases, the function U is initially increasing. The products will then become less expensive in relation to the price of the service (T), and the demand for the products will be greater than zero and increase simultaneously with the supply of the service. The supply, however, will not increase indefinitely. It passes through at least one maximum, which will not be superior to the total quantity Q_t possessed; then it will decrease to zero if the price tends to infinity, namely if (A), (B), (C), (D), $\cdots$ have become free. Hence, if p_t increases from zero to infinity, U passes from zero, increases, then decreases and will become zero again.

212. Under these conditions, and provided that $D'_t + u$ does not become zero before U starts increasing, in which case there will be no solution, there will be a value of p_t, greater or less than p'_t according to whether $D'_t + u$ is greater or less than U, for which the effective supply of and demand for (T) are equal. Let this price be p''_t; let $\pi''_b, \pi''_c, \pi''_d, \cdots$ be the prices, equal to the average costs, of (B), (C), (D), $\cdots$;[v]

and let $\varOmega_t''$ be the corresponding supply of (T), equal to its demand. Then we have

$$\varOmega_t''= F_t\,(p_t'',p_p',p_k',\cdots,\pi_b'',\pi_c'',\pi_d'',\cdots).$$

After this operation, the function

$$O_p' = F_p(p_t',p_p',p_k',\cdots,p_b',p_c',p_d',\cdots)$$

has become

$$\varOmega_p''= F_p\,(p_t'',p_p',p_k',\cdots,\pi_b'',\pi_c'',\pi_d'',\cdots),$$

and this supply of the service (P) is greater or less than its demand. There is, however, a certain value of p_p for which effective supply and demand are equal that can be found in the same way as the one used to find p_t''. Let this value be p_p''; let π_b''', π_c''', π_d''', $\cdots$ be the prices, equal to the average costs, of (B), (C), (D), $\cdots$;[v] and let $\varOmega_p'''$ be the corresponding supply of (P), equal to its demand. Then we have

$$\varOmega_p'''= F_p(p_t'',p_p'',p_k',\cdots,\pi_b''',\pi_c''',\pi_d''',\cdots).$$

Likewise, we obtain

$$\varOmega_k^{iv} = F_t\left(p_t'',p_p'',p_k'',\cdots,\pi_b^{iv},\pi_c^{iv},\pi_d^{iv},\cdots\right),$$

and so forth.

213. When all these operations have come to an end, we have

$$O_t''= F_t\left(p_t'',p_p'',p_k'',\cdots,p_b'',p_c'',p_d'',\cdots\right),$$

and it has to be established that this supply O_t'' is closer to the demand D_t'' than the supply O_t' was to the demand D_t'. Now, this seems probable[vi] if one observes that the variation from p_t' to p_t'' that brought supply and demand to equality had its effect [directly on (T)] just in one direction, whereas the changes of p_p', p_k', $\cdots$ into p_p'', p_k'', $\cdots$, which disturbed this equality had indirect effects in opposite directions on the demand for (T), and therefore compensated each other up to a certain point. The system of the new prices $p_t'', p_p'', p_k'', \cdots$ is therefore nearer to the equilibrium prices than the system $p_t', p_p', p_k', \cdots$, and we have only to continue in the same way in order to get closer and closer to equilibrium.

Now, this tatonnement occurs naturally in the market for services under the regime of free competition, since, under this regime, the price of the services is raised when demand is superior to supply, and lowered when supply is superior to demand.

214. Assume equilibrium has been obtained. We have then the product prices

$$p_a'' = a_t p_t'' + a_p p_p'' + a_k p_k'' + \cdots$$

$$p_b'' = b_t p_t'' + b_p p_p'' + b_k p_k'' + \cdots$$

$$p_c'' = c_t p_t'' + c_p p_p'' + c_k p_k'' + \cdots$$

$$p_d'' = d_t p_t'' + d_p p_p'' + d_k p_k'' + \cdots$$

$$\vdots$$

and, on the other hand, we have quantities of productive services demanded

$$D_t'' = a_t D_a' + b_t D_b'' + c_t D_c'' + d_t D_d'' + \cdots$$

$$D_p'' = a_p D_a' + b_p D_b'' + c_p D_c'' + d_p D_d'' + \cdots$$

$$D_k'' = a_k D_a' + b_k D_b'' + c_k D_c'' + d_k D_d'' + \cdots$$

$$\vdots$$

where the quantities $D_b'', D_c'', d_k D_d'', \cdots$ satisfy also the equations of the demand for the products (B), (C), (D), $\cdots$, and the quantities $D_t'' = O_t'', D_p'' = O_p'', D_k'' = O_k'', \cdots$ satisfy the equations of the supply of services (T), (P), (K), $\cdots$, in which $p_t'', p_p'', p_k'', \cdots, p_b'', p_c'', p_d'', \cdots$ are the independent variables. From these two systems, we can deduce the equation

$$D_a' p_a'' = D_t'' p_t'' + D_p'' p_p'' + D_k'' p_k'' + \cdots - \left(D_b'' p_b'' + D_c'' p_c'' + D_d'' p_d'' + \cdots \right).$$

A quantity D_a'' of (A) is then demanded in accordance with the following equation

$$D_a'' = O_t'' p_t'' + O_p'' p_p'' + O_k'' p_k'' + \cdots - \left(D_b'' p_b'' + D_c'' p_c'' + D_d'' p_d'' + \cdots \right).$$

Since $D_t'' = O_t''$, $D_p'' = O_p''$, $D_k'' = O_k''$, $\cdots$, we have therefore

$$D_a'' = D_a' p_a''.$$

By this, we see that all the equations of the problem are satisfied with the exception of the equation of the average cost of the numeraire good, from which would follow the equality of the supply and demand, or the equation of the demand for this same numeraire good, from which would follow the equality of the price and the average cost, hence being equal to unity. Therefore, if we had by chance $p_a'' = 1$, we would have also $D_a'' = D_a'$, or if we had by chance $D_a'' = D_a'$, we would have $p_a'' = 1$. But, generally, after the change of the prices $p_t', p_p', p_k', \cdots$ into $p_t'', p_p'', p_k'', \cdots$, brought about as described above, we will have

$$p_a'' \gtrless 1,$$

and, consequently

$$D_a'' \gtrless D_a'.$$

215. To finish, still by tatonnement, the solution of the general system of the equations of production, we have to determine $p_t'', p_p'', p_k'', \cdots$ in accordance with the equation

$$a_t p_t''' + a_p p_p''' + a_k p_k''' + \cdots = p_a''' = 1,$$

that is to say, by making $p_t''' \lesseqgtr p_t''$, $p_p''' \lesseqgtr p_p''$, $p_k''' \lesseqgtr p_k''$, $\cdots$ depending on whether we have $p_a'' \gtrless 1$.

Starting from this point, we will first arrive, during the first stage, in the market for products, at a determination of D_a''' in accordance with the equation

$$D_a''' = O_t'''p_t''' + O_p'''p_p''' + O_k'''p_k''' + \cdots - \left(D_b'''p_b''' + D_c'''p_c''' + D_d'''p_d''' + \cdots \right),$$

[§ 209] and then, during the second stage, in the market for services, at a determination of D_a^{iv} in accordance with the equation

$$D_a^{iv} = D_a'''p_a^{iv}.$$

It must now be established that p_a^{iv} is closer to unity than p_a''. This will seem probable if one realizes that in the case that, for instance, p_a'' was > 1, we would have had $p_b'''<p_b''$, $p_c'''<p_c''$, $p_d'''<p_d''$, $\cdots$, and, consequently $D_b'''>D_b''$, $D_c'''>D_c''$, $D_c'''>D_c''$, $\cdots$, which means also $D_a'''<D_a''$. Hence, $p_a'''=1$, when changing into p_a^{iv}, has increased because of the increase of the demand for (B), (C), (D), $\cdots$, and decreased because of the decrease of the demand for (A). In the case that p_a'' would have been < 1, $p_a'''=1$, when changing into p_a^{iv}, has decreased because of the decrease of the demand for (B), (C), (D), $\cdots$ and increased because of the increase of the demand for (A). In both cases, these tendencies are opposite, and therefore p_a will probably move less far from unity under the influence of these tendencies than it moved towards unity under the influence of the decrease or the increase of p_t, p_p, p_k, $\cdots$. Furthermore, when we continue in the same way, p_a will more and more closely approach unity. If we assume unity will be obtained with $p_a^{iv} = 1$, we also have $D_a^{iv} = D_a'''$, and the problem is completely solved.

Now, the tatonnement we just described still takes place under the regime of free competition. In fact, when we have

$$D_a'' = D_a'p_a'',$$

the producers of (A) owe $D_a'p_a''$. If they sell the quantity D_a'' of (A) demanded at the price 1, they will make a profit $D_a' - D_a'' = D_a'\left(1 - p_a''\right)$. This difference is a profit in the proper sense if $p_a''<1$ and $D_a' > D_a''$. But then the producers of (A) will expand their production, which will increase p_t'', p_p'', p_k'', $\cdots$ and, consequently, p_a'', which will get nearer to unity. This difference is a loss if $p_a'' > 1$ and $D_a' < D_a''$. But then the producers of (A) will contract their production, which will lower $p_t'', p_p'', p_k'', \cdots$ and, consequently, p_a'', which will get nearer to unity. Observe that the entrepreneurs producing (A) are free to avoid this situation by not producing at all when the average cost of the numeraire good is superior to its price; that is to say, to unity, which puts them in a position of unavoidable loss, and will only resume production when the average cost is less than or equal to unity. Whatever may be the case, after all, the entrepreneurs producing (A), just like those producing (B), (C), (D), $\cdots$, only have to expand, as they do indeed, their production in the case of an excess of the price over the average cost, and to restrict their production in the case of an excess of the average cost over the price. In the market for services, in the first case, they raise the prices of the services; in the second case, they lower them. In both cases, they tend to bring about equilibrium.

216. Combining all the elements of this demonstration, we arrive at the following formulation of the law of the determination of the equilibrium prices in exchange and production: – *If several services are given with which several products can be manufactured, and if these services are exchanged for their products with a numeraire as intermediary, for there to be market equilibrium, or, stationary prices in numeraire for all these services and all these products, it is necessary and sufficient: 1° for each service and each product, effective demand is equal to effective supply at these prices; 2° the prices of the products are equal to their average costs in terms of the services. When this double equality is not fulfilled, it is necessary, to arrive at the first one, to raise the prices of the services and products of which the effective demand is superior to their effective supply, and to lower the prices of those of which the effective supply is superior to the effective demand; and, to arrive at the second one, to increase the quantity of the products of which the price is superior to their average cost, and to decrease the quantities of the products of which the average cost is superior to their price.*

This is *the law of the determination of the equilibrium prices* in exchange and production; joined, as we shall do below, with the *law of the variation of the equilibrium prices,* properly generalized, we will have the scientific formulation of the double LAW OF SUPPLY AND DEMAND AND OF AVERAGE COST.

Notes

i Of course, Walras meant prices and not quantities. From the fourth edition onwards, he simply omitted the words 'the quantities'.

ii Walras meant that the produced quantity Ω'_b may (and probably will) differ from the randomly chosen quantity Ω_b.

iii See lesson 20.

iv In this section, it will become clear that it did not matter whether Walras had put $p'_a = a_t p'_t + a_p p'_p + a_k p'_k + \cdots = 1$ or not.

v These prices are obtained in the same way as $\pi'_b, \pi'_c, \pi'_d, \cdots$ in § 207 above.

vi Here he wrote 'certain' in the first edition.

LESSON 22

The principle of free competition. Law of the variation of the prices of products and services. Price curves

SUMMARY: – Analytical definition of free competition in exchange and production. The fact or the concept of free competition becomes a principle. The demonstration of *laisser-faire laisser-passer* has been lacking. Unacknowledged exceptions: public services; natural and necessary monopolies; distribution of social wealth. Proportionality of the exchange values of services to the raretés. Law of the variation of the equilibrium prices of products and services. Purchase and sales curves of a service. Price curve of a product.

217. From the demonstration given in lesson 21, it results that free competition in production; that is to say, the freedom of entrepreneurs to increase their output in the case of making profits and to restrict it in the case of making losses, combined with free competition in exchange; that is to say, the freedom of landowners, workers, and capitalists and entrepreneurs to buy and to sell services and products, by bidding up and lowering prices, is certainly the solution in practice of the equations of lesson 20. Now, if we go back to these equations and to the conditions on which they are based, we see that

– *Production and exchange in a market ruled by free competition is an operation through which services can be combined into products of the kinds and quantities that give greatest possible satisfaction of wants within the limits imposed by the condition that each service as well as each product has only a single price in the market.*

218. It is now, finally, that the importance of the scientific treatment of economic theory will perhaps be properly acknowledged. Taking this

point of view of pure science, we have to accept, and we have accepted until now, free competition only as a fact, or even only as a hypothesis; for it was of little importance to have recognized it: it was sufficient, when necessary, to have been able to conceive it. Under these conditions, we study the nature, the causes, and the consequences of free competition. As it now happens, these consequences come down to obtaining, within certain limits, the maximum of utility. Hence, free competition becomes a principle of economic advantageousness, or a rule the application of which we only have to pursue meticulously in agriculture, industry, and commerce. In this way, the conclusion of pure science brings us to the doorway of applied science. Observe how certain objections to our method automatically vanish here. We are told in the first place: – 'One of the elements of price determination under free competition is human freedom, the decisions of which cannot be calculated.' Well, we have never attempted to calculate the decisions of human liberty; we have only attempted to express its effects by means of mathematics. In our theory, each exchanger can be assumed to establish his utility or want curves as he pleases. These curves once determined, we show how the prices result from them under a hypothetical regime of absolute free competition. – 'Exactly,' they then say to us, 'absolute free competition is only a hypothesis. In reality, free competition is impeded by an infinity of disturbing factors. It is therefore of no interest whatsoever, except out of curiosity, to study free competition in itself without considering these disturbing elements, which cannot be represented by any formula.' The pointlessness of this objection is obvious. Assuming that there is no further progress of science that will allow us to introduce the disturbing elements in the equations of production and exchange, which is perhaps an imprudent assumption and certainly a useless one, does not mean that these equations, as we have developed them, do not lead us, in spite of everything, to the general and superior rule of freedom of exchange and production. That freedom procures, within certain limits, the maximum of utility; the causes that disturb it are therefore hindrances to that maximum; and, whatever those causes may be, they must be suppressed insofar as is possible.

219. All in all, this is what the economists already said when recommending their *laisser faire, laisser passer*. Unfortunately, it must be

said: until now, the economists did not so much demonstrate their *laisser faire, laisser aller* as maintain it against the socialists, traditional and modern, who, in their turn, advocated state intervention, without proving it either. I feel that by expressing myself in this way I am going to ruffle some sensitivities. Nevertheless, I will at least be permitted to ask: – How would the economists have demonstrated that the results of free competition were good and advantageous if they did not know exactly what those results are? And how would they have known those results since they have not established the definitions nor formulated the laws that relate to them and that establish them? That is a priori reasoning. Here is some a posteriori reasoning. When a principle is scientifically established, the first thing that can be done, as a consequence, is to detect the cases in which it is applicable and those in which it is not. And, vice versa, the fact that the economists often have extended it beyond its true range, would undoubtedly be a good proof that the principle of free concurrence has not been demonstrated. Thus, for example, as far as we are concerned, our demonstration of the principle of free competition is based, firstly, on the appreciation of the utility of the services and products by the consumer. It assumes, therefore, that there is a fundamental distinction between individual wants, or private utility, which the consumer is able to appreciate, and social wants, or public utility, which is appreciated in quite another way. Hence the principle of free competition, applicable to the production of things of individual interest, is not applicable to the production of things of public interest. However, are there not economists who fall into this error of wanting to submit public services to free competition by putting them in the hands of private industry? Another example. Our demonstration is based, secondly, on leveling the price and the average cost of products. It assumes therefore the possibility of the flow of entrepreneurs toward enterprises where profits are made and of the turning away from enterprises in which entrepreneurs are making losses. Hence, the principle of free competition is also not necessarily applicable to the production of things that are produced by a natural and necessary monopoly. However, are there not economists who talk to us every day about free competition in regard to monopolized industries? A final observation, of the highest importance, to close this point. Our demonstration of free competition, while giving a prominent place to the question of utility, leaves the question of justice completely aside; this is because it restricts itself to showing how a certain distribution of products results from a certain distribution of services, and questions about this latter distribution remain unanswered. However, are there not economists who, not satisfied by exaggerating *laisser passer, laisser aller* in matters of industry, still apply it, completely irrelevantly, to matters of property? These are the dangers of using the verbal method in place of the scientific method. People maintain both what is true and what is false; in this respect, there is also no lack of people who deny both what is true and what is false. And science stops, perpetually tugged in opposite directions by the adversaries, who are, those on one side as well as those on the other, both right and wrong.

220. If $v_t, v_p, v_k, \cdots$ are the values in exchange of the services (T), (P), (K), $\cdots$, the ratios of which to the value in exchange v_a of the product (A) constituting the prices of these services, and if $r_{t,1}, r_{p,1}, r_{k,1}, \cdots$, $r_{t,2}, r_{p,2}, r_{k,2}, \cdots$, $r_{t,3}, r_{p,3}, r_{k,3}, \cdots$ are the raretés of these services or the intensities of the last wants satisfied, after exchange, for the individuals (1), (2), (3), $\cdots$ who have kept or acquired them for direct consumption, then we have to complete the representation of general equilibrium (§ 131) as follows:

$$v_a \ : \ v_b \ : \ v_c \ : \ v_d \ : \ \cdots \ : \ v_t \ : \ v_p \ : \ v_k \ : \ \cdots$$

$$:: \ r_{a,1} \ : \ r_{b,1} \ : \ r_{c,1} \ : \ r_{d,1} \ : \ \cdots \ : \ r_{t,1} \ : \ r_{p,1} \ : \ v_{r,1} \ : \ \cdots$$

$$:: \ r_{a,2} \ : \ r_{b,2} \ : \ r_{c,2} \ : \ r_{d,2} \ : \ \cdots \ : \ r_{t,2} \ : \ r_{p,2} \ : \ v_{r,1} \ : \ \cdots$$

$$:: \ r_{a,3} \ : \ r_{b,3} \ : \ r_{c,3} \ : \ r_{d,3} \ : \ \cdots \ : \ r_{t,3} \ : \ r_{p,3} \ : \ v_{r,3} \ : \ \cdots$$

$$\vdots$$

The land services, labor, and capital good services that are consumed directly can be consumed either in infinitely small quantities measured over time, or in quantities corresponding with units of measurement of land, persons, and capital goods proper. There may therefore be reason to inscribe in the relevant parts of the above scheme underlined quantities of rareté that are more or less between the intensities of the last wants satisfied and the first one not satisfied. Furthermore, it is always possible, for services as well as for products, that we have to enter in parentheses raretés that are higher than the first want satisfied. Subject to these two reservations, the proposition [of § 131] can be extended to products and services as follows: – *Values in exchange are proportional to the raretés.*

221. Let (T), (P), and (K) be land services, personal services, and capital good services that can be consumed in infinitesimally small quantities, and let $\tau_{r,1}\tau_{q,1}$, $\tau_{r,2}\tau_{q,2}$, $\tau_{r,3}\tau_{q,3}$, $\pi_{r,1}\pi_{r,1}$, $\pi_{r,2}\pi_{q,2}$, $\pi_{r,3}\pi_{q,3}$, $\kappa_{r,1}\kappa_{q,1}$, $\kappa_{r,2}\kappa_{q,2}$, $\kappa_{r,3}\kappa_{q,3}$ (Fig. 22) be the continuous utility curves, or want curves, of these services for the exchangers (1), (2), (3) in the exchange. Let the prices of (T), (P), (K) in (A) be 0.76, 2.16, and 1.50.

In the example of our figure, exchanger (1) and exchanger (3) consume all three services: one of the exchangers consumes quantities 7, 9, and 5 to arrive at raretés 1.50, 4.33, and 3; the other consumes quantities 3, 1, and 2, to arrive at raretés 3, 8.66, and 6. As far as concerns exchanger (3), he consumes quantity 1 of land services to arrive at rareté 4.50, but he does without labor and capital good services because the magnitudes 13 and 9 of his raretés exceed the intensities 9 and 6 of the first wants of these services satisfied. We therefore have the equilibrium scheme:

	0.754	:	2.16^{i}	:	1.50
::	1.50	:	4.33	:	3.00
::	4.50	:	(13)	:	(9)
::	3.00	:	8.66	:	6.

222. Denoting by R_t, R_p, R_k the average raretés of (T), (P), and (K), and on condition of taking account of the underlined magnitudes and those between parentheses in computing these averages, we could put

$$p_t = \frac{R_t}{R_a}, \quad p_p = \frac{R_p}{R_a}, \quad p_k = \frac{R_k}{R_a}$$

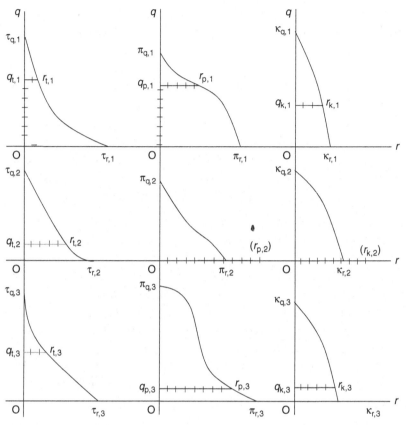

Fig. 22

223. We may also generalize the law of the variation of the prices (§ 135), expressing it in the following terms:

– *Let several products or services be given and be in a state of equilibrium in a market where exchange takes place through the intervention of a numeraire, then, all other things remaining unchanged, if the utility of one of these products or services increases or decreases[ii] for one or for several of the exchangers, the price of this product or service decreases or increases.*

If, all other things remaining unchanged, the quantity possessed by one or by several of the exchangers of one of these products or services increases or decreases, the price of this product or service decreases or increases.

– *Several products or services being given, if the utility and the quantity possessed by one of these products or services for one or more exchangers change in such a way that the raretés do not change, the price of this product or service will not change.*

If the utility and the quantity of all the products and services possessed by one or several exchangers change in such a way that the ratios of the raretés do not change, the prices of these products and services do not change.

To this we may add two other propositions:

– *If, all other things remaining unchanged, the quantity of a service possessed by one or more individuals increases or decreases,* the effective supply of this product by these individuals increasing or decreasing in the market for services, and, consequently, the price decreasing or increasing, *the price of the products in the production of which this service is used, decreases or increases.*

If, all other things remaining unchanged, the utility of a product to one or more of the consumers increases or decreases, effective demand of these consumers for this product increasing or decreasing in the market for the products, and, consequently, the price increasing or decreasing, *the price of the services used in making this product increases or decreases.*

224. In lesson 15, we introduced (§ 149) the *purchase curves* and the *sales curves*; that is to say, the curves of demand in numeraire and the curves of supply to acquire numeraire regarding commodities assumed to be newly arrived one by one in an exchange market in a situation of general equilibrium. Then we transformed the purchase curves (§ 151) into *price curves* by assuming supply equal to the quantity possessed. We must come back to this concept to complete it for the case of services and products.

225. Let, therefore, (A) be the numeraire. And let, on the one hand, the services (P), (K), $\cdots$ and the products (A), (B), (C), (D), $\cdots$ be exchanged or ready to be exchanged at prices $p'_p, p'_k, \cdots, p'_b, p'_c, p'_d, \cdots$, determined by general equilibrium, and let, on the other hand, the very recently discovered and appropriated service (T) be introduced into the market to be incorporated into the mechanism of exchange and production.

Theoretically, the appearance of (T) would require reestablishing the four systems of equations of production (§§ 198–9) with the introduction of two new unknowns p_t and O_t, and two additional equations, one of the demand for (T):

$$a_t D_a + b_t D_b + c_t D_c + d_t D_d + \cdots = O_t$$

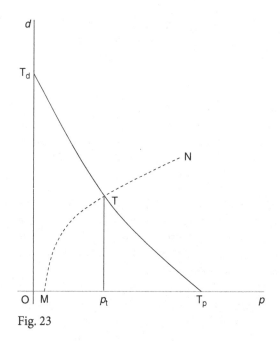

Fig. 23

and the other of the supply of (T):

$$O_t = F_t(p_t, p_p, p_k, \cdots, p_b, p_c, p_d, \cdots)$$

We can reduce these equations to one single equation by designing, as we have done in § 211, the sum of the positive o_t's by U and of the negative o_t's by u:

$$a_t D_a + b_t D_b + c_t D_c + d_t D_d + \cdots + u = U$$

However, if we abstract from the changes of the other prices and the other effective demands and supplies, and consider them as constants, the first member of this equation is a decreasing function of p_t that can be represented geometrically by a *purchase curve* $T_d T_p$ (Fig. 23), and the second member is a function of the same variable p_t that is successively increasing and decreasing from zero to zero and that can be represented by a *sales curve* MN. The intersection of the two curves in T determines the price p_t.

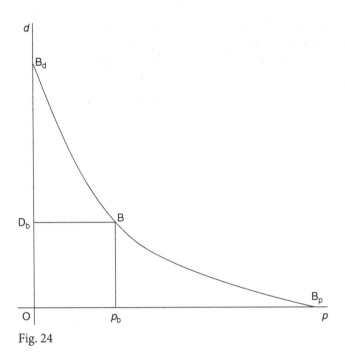

Fig. 24

226. Let (A) still be the numeraire. And let, on the one hand, the services (T), (P), (K), ⋯ and the products (A), (C), (D), ⋯ be exchanged or ready to be exchanged for one another at general equilibrium prices $p'_t, p'_p, p'_k, \cdots, p'_c, p'_d, \cdots$, and, on the other hand, let the product (B), the production of which has just been discovered and brought into the public domain, be introduced into the market to be incorporated into the mechanism of exchange and production.

Theoretically, the appearance of (B) would require restating the systems of equations of production with the introduction of two new unknown variables p_b and D_b, and two additional equations, one of the demand for (B):

$$D_b = F_b(p_t, p_p, p_k, \cdots, p_b, p_c, p_d, \cdots)$$

and the other of the average cost of (B):

$$b_t p_t + b_p p_p + b_k p_k + \cdots = p_b$$

However, if we abstract from the changes of the other prices and the other effective demands and supplies, and consider them as constants, D_b is a decreasing function of a single variable that can be represented geometrically by a *price curve* B_dB_p (Fig. 24). Thus, we are led back to the geometrical expression we had already furnished [§§ 152–3].

Notes

i   The exact entries of this column are 2.16, 4.32, (12.96), and 8.64.
ii Walras meant upward and downward shifts of curves like those in Figure 22.

PART IV

THEORY OF CAPITAL FORMATION
AND CREDIT

LESSON 23

Gross and net income. The rate of net income. The excess of income over consumption

SUMMARY: – The prices of capital depend on the prices of the services. Destruction of capital goods by usage, *depreciation premium*. Accidental destruction, *insurance premium*. *Gross* income minus these two premiums is *net* income. The prices of capital goods are proportional to their net incomes. The common ratio of the net incomes of the capital goods to their prices is the *rate of net income*. Hypothesis about the production and the supply of new productive capital goods. The prices of existing capital goods are the same as those of new capital goods, equal to the average cost of the latter. The lending of money saving, or credit, and the demand for new capital goods by the entrepreneurs.

Land: inconsumable, natural capital goods; their quantities are given. Persons, consumable natural capital goods; their quantities are also given. Capital goods properly speaking: consumable artificial capital goods; their quantities are unknowns. Equations of the average costs and of the prices of new capital goods properly speaking. Income and consumption. Equality, positive excess; zero or negative excess. Positive excess equal, less than, or greater than the amount of depreciation plus insurance. Equations of partial excess. Equations of total excess of income over consumption and of the total price of new capital goods properly speaking.

227. The existence of landed incomes, personal incomes, and incomes from capital goods properly speaking, (T), (T′), (T″), ⋯, (P), (P′), (P″), ⋯, (K), (K′), (K″), ⋯ assumes the existence of landed capital, personal capital, and capital goods properly speaking each of the

same type. We have determined the prices of these incomes, but we have not yet determined the prices of the capital goods generating the incomes in the form of uses or services. The problem regarding this determination is the third great problem of the mathematical theory of social wealth: it is the one we are going to tackle in this fourth part.

For us, there can be no prices other than market prices. Consequently, just as we have considered markets for products and services for the determination of the prices of products and the prices of services, we must, for the determination of the prices of capital goods, consider a market that we will call the *market for capital goods*, in which the capital goods will be bought and sold. The products are demanded because of their utility; the services are demanded because of their utility and the prices of the products that they serve to produce. Why are capital goods demanded? Because of their land services, labor, and 'profits', but above all because of the rent, wages, and interest they yield.[i] Undoubtedly, one can buy a capital good with the intention of consuming its services as well as with the intention of selling these services, but the latter point of view should be considered as the most important one as far as the purchase of capital goods is concerned, for otherwise a person would restrict himself to buying the service, that is, to hiring the capital good. A person who buys a house to live in himself has to be decomposed by us into two individuals, one of whom makes an investment of funds and the other of whom consumes directly the service of his capital good. We have already discussed the latter individual; now we are going to deal with the first.

228. The prices of the capital goods therefore depend essentially on the prices of their services, that is to say, on their *incomes*. Here, it can be seen, we limit the meaning of the word *income*, making it express the price of the service and not the service itself, just as it is the object of consumption and the raw material thereof. Moreover, this price consists of three completely distinct elements.

First, the different existing capital goods do not all wear out by usage with the same rapidity. Consequently, while having a given income, a more or less expensive capital good will be bought depending on whether it will be used up less or more quickly.

Second, different capital goods are not equally susceptible to perishing in a sudden and unforeseen manner because of an accident. Consequently, while having a given income, a more or less expensive capital good will be bought depending on whether it will have less or more chance of perishing accidentally.

Indeed, nothing is easier than to take these two circumstances into account mathematically.

With respect to the first element, we only have to assume that the amount of its annual income be set apart, proportional to the price of the capital good, that is needed either to maintain the capital as it was when new, or to replace it when used up. This is called the *depreciation* of capital. The amount to be set apart, the *depreciation premium*, will vary from one capital good to another; but once set apart, all the capital goods will become rigorously identical with respect to wear and tear by usage, since all have been made, in a sense, indestructible.

It is the same with respect to the second circumstance: we only have to assume that the amount, proportional to the price of the capital good, be set apart that is needed to contribute to the reconstitution of all similar capital goods that yearly perish by accidents. This is what is called the *insurance* of capital. The amount to be set apart, the *insurance premium*, will likewise vary from one capital good to another; but once set apart, all the capital goods will become rigorously identical with respect to accidental perishing, since all have been made, in a sense, imperishable.

Let P be the price of a capital good. Let p be the price of its service, including the depreciation premium and the insurance premium; that is the *gross* income. Let μP be the fraction of this income representing the depreciation premium, and vP the insurance premium. What remains from gross income after the deduction of these two premiums, i.e. $\pi = p - (\mu + v)P$, is *net* income.

229. We can now understand the difference in gross income of capital goods of the same value, or, in other words, the difference in value of capital goods yielding the same gross income. But it is understood as well, no doubt, that the values of the capital goods are rigorously proportional to their net incomes. This would at least be the case in a certain normal and ideal state that will be the state of equilibrium in

the market for capital goods. In this state, the ratio $\dfrac{p-(\mu+v)P}{P}$, or the *rate of net income*, is the same for all capital goods. Let this ratio be i; when we have determined it, we will have determined the price of all landed capital, personal capital, and movable capital goods, by virtue of the equation

$$p-(\mu+v)P = iP$$

or

$$P = \frac{p}{i+\mu+v}.$$

230. We would not have, with only the data we have now at our disposal, the elements of this determination. Until now, we have assumed that there are quantities of land, personal faculties and capital properly speaking that are determined, and that the landowners, workers, and capitalists exchange the services of these capital goods, with the exception of the fraction of the services they consume directly. Under these conditions, the sale and purchase of capital goods could not occur; for the capital goods could only be exchanged against each other in proportion to their net incomes, and this operation, that theoretically would not have any purpose, would not furnish any price in numeraire if the numeraire were not a capital good itself, this numeraire being a product or a service having a rareté that can be related to the raretés of the other products and services, as it must be for the establishment of equilibrium of production to be possible. In order to have supply, demand, and prices of capital goods, the concept of a stationary economic state must be replaced by that of a progressive economic state. We must assume there are entrepreneurs who, instead of manufacturing consumer goods, produce new capital goods. Moreover, we must assume there are landowners, workers, and capitalists who, having bought consumable products and services for an amount less than the amount of their income, are in the position to buy these new capital goods by means of the difference.

With these new facts, we have all the elements for the solution of the problem, if we remember that the new capital goods are products whose prices are subject to the law of costs of production. Indeed, in the state of equilibrium, the price of these new capital goods must be equal to their average cost; and, on the other hand, the price of the already existing capital goods must be equal to the price of the new capital goods. So, if we know the average cost of the new capital goods, we will know the price of the new or existing capital goods, and, consequently, the rate of net income. Here, just as elsewhere, we have to express this state of equilibrium mathematically, and we have to show how it actualizes itself in the market. Before this, however, we must mention an important circumstance whose introduction we have postponed (§ 204) until now.

231. In reality, land and personal faculties are only hired in kind; capital goods properly speaking are generally hired in money in the market for services. The capitalist builds up his capital by saving money; he lends the money to the entrepreneur, who, at the expiration of the loan, repays him the money. This operation is called *credit*. From this it follows that it is the entrepreneurs, producers of products, who demand the new capital goods in the markets, and not the capitalists, the creators of savings. However, it is evident that, theoretically, it is immaterial to the capitalist whether he lends a new or existing capital good or the money price of the capital good, and immaterial to the entrepreneur which of these alternatives he chooses: it is only from the practical point of view that lending money is highly preferable to the capitalist. Let us only observe that we should not confuse the market for capital goods, which is the market where capital goods are bought and sold, with the capital market, where money capital is hired, and which is only an annex of the market for services. We will meet these two distinct markets in the course of our demonstration. Let us also observe that, since we are abstracting from money, from now onwards we must speak of *numeraire* capital, and not of *money* capital.

232. Except in a few cases, that could easily taken into account, but with which it is of no use to complicate our formulas, land is a natural capital good, and not an artificial, produced good. The price of

land has no influence on its quantity, and its quantity does not react on its price. Furthermore, except in a few cases of which we say the same as above, land is an indestructible, imperishable capital good: there is no need to set apart from its income a depreciation premium or an insurance premium. From these two observations, it follows that the quantities of the several types of land are always given and are not unknown variables in our problem, and that, regarding their prices, they will simply be equal to the quotients of their gross incomes divided by the rate of net income, once we have determined the latter, in accordance with the equation $P_t = \dfrac{p_t}{i}$.

233. Man's personal faculties are natural capital goods, too. Their quantities do not depend on the rise and fall of industrial production, but on the fluctuations of the population. On the other hand, they are destructible, perishable capital goods whose depreciation and insurance may be considered as being provided for by reproduction, and by maintenance, education, and instruction of the wives and children of the workers. Hence, the quantities of personal faculties remain given, too, and are not unknown variables in our problem, and as for their prices, if we want to know them, they will simply be equal to the quotients of their net incomes divided by the rate of net income, as given by the equation $P_p = \dfrac{\pi_p}{i}$.

234. Capital goods properly speaking are artificial capital goods; they are products; their price is subject to the law of production costs. If their price is greater than their average cost, the quantity produced will increase and the price will decrease; if their price is less than their average cost, the quantity produced will decrease and the price will increase. In the state of equilibrium, the price and the average cost are equal. So, let there be l types of capital goods (K), (K'), (K''), $\cdots$ and let $P_k, P_{k'}, P_{k''}, \cdots$ be their respective prices. If $p_t, \cdots, p_p, \cdots, p_k, p_{k'}, p_{k''}, \cdots$ are, respectively, the prices of the types of services (T), $\cdots$, (P), $\cdots$, (K), (K'), (K''), $\cdots$, and if $k_t, \cdots, k_p, \cdots, k_k, k_{k'}, k_{k''}, \cdots$, $k'_t, \cdots, k'_p, \cdots, k'_k, k'_{k'}, k'_{k''}, \cdots, k''_t, \cdots, k''_p, \cdots, k''_k, k''_{k'}, k''_{k''}, \cdots$ are the respective

quantities of these services that enter into the production of one unit of (K), of (K'), of (K''), $\cdots$, we obtain the following l equations:

$$k_t p_t + \cdots + k_p p_p + \cdots + k_k p_k + k_{k'} p_{k'} + k_{k''} p_{k''} + \cdots = P_k$$

$$k_t' p_t + \cdots + k_p' p_p + \cdots + k_k' p_k + k_{k'}' p_{k'} + k_{k''}' p_{k''} + \cdots = P_{k'}$$

$$k_t'' p_t + \cdots + k_p'' p_p + \cdots + k_k'' p_k + k_{k'}'' p_{k'} + k_{k''}'' p_{k''} + \cdots = P_{k''}$$

$$\vdots$$

Furthermore, capital goods properly speaking are destructible and perishable capital; we must therefore set apart from their income a depreciation premium and an insurance premium. Let $\mu_k P_k, \mu_{k'} P_{k'}, \mu_{k''} P_{k''}, \cdots, v_k P_k, v_{k'} P_{k'}, v_{k''} P_{k''}, \cdots$ be the fractions to set apart from the gross incomes $p_k, p_{k'}, p_{k''}, \cdots$, of the capital goods (K), (K'), (K''), $\cdots$. The prices of these capital goods will be equal to the quotients of their net incomes divided by the rate of net income, hence the quotients of their gross incomes divided by the sum of these three rates: the rate of net income, the rate of depreciation, and the rate of insurance:

$$P_k = \frac{\pi_k}{i} = \frac{p_k}{1 + \mu_k + v_k},$$

$$P_{k'} = \frac{\pi_{k'}}{i} = \frac{p_{k'}}{1 + \mu_{k'} + v_{k'}},$$

$$P_{k''} = \frac{\pi_{k''}}{i} = \frac{p_{k''}}{1 + \mu_{k''} + v_{k''}},$$

$$\vdots$$

235. Let now an individual possess quantities q_t of (T), $\cdots$, q_p of (P), $\cdots$, q_k of (K), $\cdots$, $q_{k'}$ of (K'), $\cdots$, $q_{k''}$ of (K''), $\cdots$ At prices $p_t, \cdots, p_p, \cdots, p_k, p_{k'}, p_{k''}, \cdots$ of the services and prices $P_t, \cdots, P_p, \cdots, P_k, P_{k'}, P_{k''}, \cdots$ of the capital goods, his income is

$$q_t p_t + \cdots + q_p p_p + \cdots + q_k p_k + \cdots + q_{k'} p_{k'} + \cdots + q_{k''} p_{k''} + \cdots$$

and his capital

$$q_t P_t + \cdots + q_p P_p + \cdots + q_k P_k + \cdots + q_{k'} P_{k'} + \cdots + q_{k''} P_{k''} + \cdots.$$

If this individual cedes quantities, positive or negative, of (T), $\cdots$, (P), $\cdots$, (K), (K'), (K''), $\cdots$, equivalent to

$$o_t p_t, \cdots, o_p p_p, \cdots, o_k p_k, \cdots, o_{k'} p_{k'}, \cdots, o_{k''} p_{k''}, \cdots$$

he consumes quantities of them that are worth

$$(q_t - o_t)p_t + \cdots + (q_p - o_p)p_p + \cdots + (q_k - o_k)p_k + \cdots +$$
$$(q_{k'} - o_{k'})p_{k'} + \cdots$$
$$+(q_{k''} - o_{k''})p_{k''} + \cdots$$

In addition, he will consume respective quantities of the products (A), (B), (C), (D), $\cdots$ equivalent to

$$d_a, d_b p_b, d_c p_c, d_d p_d, \cdots$$

236. It is possible that our individual demands products (A), (B), (C), (D), $\cdots$ for a value equal to that of the services he supplies, in accordance with the following equation:

$$o_t p_t + \cdots + o_p p_p + \cdots + o_k p_k + \cdots + o_{k'} p_{k'} + \cdots + o_{k''} p_{k''} + \cdots =$$
$$d_a + d_b p_b + d_c p_c + d_d p_d + \cdots.$$

But it is also possible that there will be an *excess* of the value of the productive services supplied over the value of the products demanded

$$e = o_t p_t + \cdots + o_p p_p + \cdots + o_k p_k + \cdots + o_{k'} p_{k'} + \cdots + o_{k''} p_{k''} + \cdots$$
$$-(d_a + d_b p_b + d_c p_c + d_d p_d + \cdots).$$

Adding and subtracting

$$r = q_t p_t + \cdots + q_p p_p + \cdots + q_k p_k + \cdots + q_{k'} p_{k'} + \cdots + q_{k''} p_{k''} + \cdots$$

in the second member yields

$$e = r - \left[(q_t - o_t)p_t + \cdots + \left(q_p - o_p\right)p_p + \cdots + \right.$$
$$\left(q_k - o_k\right)p_k + \cdots + \left(q_{k'} - o_{k'}\right)p_{k'} + \cdots + \left(q_{k''} - o_{k''}\right)p_{k''} + \cdots +$$
$$\left. d_a + d_b p_b + d_c p_c + d_d p_d + \cdots \right].$$

And hence: – *The excess of the value of the services supplied over the value of the consumable products demanded is also equal to the excess of income over consumption.*

This excess can be negative; that is to say, that it can turn into an excess of consumption over income. We must then assume that our individual not only sells all the services he does not consume himself, but also a part of his capital goods. This is called 'consuming his capital'. This negative excess can even be greater than the total value of the capital goods

$$q_t P_t + \cdots + q_p P_p + \cdots + q_k P_k + q_{k'} P_{k'} + q_{k''} P_{k''} + \cdots.$$

In this case, our individual consumes the capital of others as well as his own.

237. The definitions having been made, three cases present themselves:

1° The positive excess is equal to the sum needed for covering depreciation and insurance of the capital goods of the types (K), (K'), (K''), $\cdots$; we have then

$$e = q_k P_k (\mu_k + \nu_k) + q_{k'} P_{k'} (\mu_{k'} + \nu_{k'}) + \cdots + q_{k''} P_{k''} (\mu_{k''} + \nu_{k''}) + \cdots,$$

and our person limits himself purely and simply to maintaining the quantity of capital goods properly speaking in his possession, without increasing or decreasing them.

2° The excess, positive, zero, or negative, is less than the sum of depreciation and insurance; we have then

$$e < q_k P_k (\mu_k + \nu_k) + q_{k'} P_{k'} (\mu_{k'} + \nu_{k'}) + \cdots + q_{k''} P_{k''} (\mu_{k''} + \nu_{k''}) + \cdots,$$

and our person really consumes a part of his capital goods properly speaking, which, by lack of provision of depreciation and insurance, will no longer, when he uses them in the future, be fully the same amounts he possessed, since they will partly be used up and partly be destroyed by accidents.

3° The positive excess is greater than the sum of depreciation and insurance; we have then

$$e > q_k P_k (\mu_k + v_k) + q_{k'} P_{k'} (\mu_{k'} + v_{k'}) + \cdots + q_{k''} P_{k''} (\mu_{k''} + v_{k''}) + \cdots,$$

and our person increases the quantities of his capital goods, demanding the production of new capital goods properly speaking instead of consumable products. He *saves.*

Hence: – *Savings are the positive difference between the excess of income over consumption and the sum of depreciation and insurance of the capital goods properly speaking.*

Whether the individual in question purely and simply provides for the depreciation and insurance of his capital goods properly speaking, or eats into his capital partly or totally, or saves, in each case he demands the production of more or less quantities of consumable products instead of new capital goods properly speaking, or of new capital goods properly speaking instead of consumable products. This is why we will consider the positive, zero, or negative excess of income over consumption as an element to introduce now into our system of equations of production in order to deduce from it the system of the equations of capital formation. It will be understood that true saving occurs only if the excess is not only positive, but also greater than the sum of depreciation plus insurance of existing capital goods properly speaking.

238. Reasoning as in the case of exchange, we ask, singling out a particular individual: – On what will the excess of his income over his consumption depend? And we answer: – On the prices of the services, the prices of the consumable products, and the prices of the capital goods. Instead of the prices of the capital goods, we can introduce the rate of net income into our equations, for the sake of simplicity. It is certain that if our individual does not know the prices $p_t, \cdots, p_p, \cdots, p_k, p_{k'}, p_{k''}, \cdots, p_b, p_c, p_d, \cdots$ and i, he cannot arrive at the determination of his supply of services, nor his demand for consumable products, nor his demand for new capital goods properly speaking. But it is also certain that, once these prices and i are known, he

possesses all the necessary elements for this operation, and that, particularly, his readiness to save can be expressed mathematically in the most explicit way by means of an equation of the form:

$$e = f_e\left(p_t, \cdots, p_p, \cdots, p_k, p_{k'}, p_{k''}, \cdots, p_b, p_c, p_d, \cdots, i\right),$$

expressing the *excess* of income over consumption e as a function of the prices of the services and consumable products $p_t, \cdots, p_p, \cdots, p_k, p_{k'}, p_{k''}, \cdots, p_b, p_c, p_d, \cdots$ and of the rate of net income i.

We posit this savings equation empirically, just as we have posited, initially, the equation of effective demand. It is perhaps desirable to investigate the constituent mathematical elements of the savings function, just as we investigated them for the effective demand function. Evidently it would be necessary for this investigation to consider utility from a new point of view, and to differentiate *present* utility and *future* utility. We are not going to undertake this research, and we will leave the savings function with its empirical character; we do not do so with the pretension in any respect that it is impossible to trace its basic elements, but because that operation does not seem to be necessary for the moment. It will be enough for us to lay down as a fact that this function is successively increasing and decreasing for increasing values of i, because the supply of services in exchange for new capital goods does not, any more than does their supply in exchange for consumable products, increase indefinitely with the quantity of new capital goods desired, but tends to become zero again when the price becomes infinitely high; that is to say, when one can obtain an extremely high supplement of income with a minimal amount of savings.

Let the aggregate of the individual saving functions be indicated by F_e, and the sum of the individual excess quantities, from now onwards always assumed to be positive, by E; then we have the equation

$$E = F_e\left(p_t, \cdots, p_p, \cdots, p_k, p_{k'}, p_{k''}, \cdots, p_b, p_c, p_d, \cdots, i\right).$$

And let $D_k, D_{k'}, D_{k''}, \cdots$ denote the respective quantities produced of new capital goods properly speaking (K), (K′), (K″), $\cdots$; then we have the equation:

$$D_k P_k + D_{k'} P_{k'} + D_{k''} P_{k''} + \cdots = E.$$

239. In this way, we have, finally, $2l + 2$ equations for the determination of the l quantities produced of new capital goods properly speaking, the l prices of these capital goods (which are, of course, also the prices of capital goods properly speaking that already exist), the total excess of income over consumption to be capitalized, and the rate of net income, hence just as many equations as unknowns. It is evident at first sight that, after reducing our $2l + 1$ equations to $l + 1$ by the quite easy elimination of $P_{k'}, P_{k''}, \cdots$ and E, we have the following l equations of equality of the average cost and the price of new capital goods:

$$k_t p_t + \cdots + k_p p_p + \cdots + k_k p_k + k_{k'} p_{k'} + k_{k''} p_{k''} + \cdots = \frac{p_k}{1 + \mu_k + v_k}$$

$$k'_t p_t + \cdots + k'_p p_p + \cdots + k'_k p_k + k'_{k'} p_{k'} + k'_{k''} p_{k''} + \cdots = \frac{p_{k'}}{1 + \mu_{k'} + v_{k'}}$$

$$k''_t p_t + \cdots + k''_p p_p + \cdots + k''_k p_k + k''_{k'} p_{k'} + k''_{k''} p_{k''} + \cdots = \frac{p_{k''}}{1 + \mu_{k''} + v_{k''}}$$

$$\vdots$$

to determine the l quantities of new capital goods $D_k, D_{k'}, D_{k''}, \cdots$ to be produced, and the following equation of equality of the value of new capital and the excess of income over consumption

$$D_k \frac{p_k}{1 + \mu_k + v_k} + D_{k'} \frac{p_{k'}}{1 + \mu_{k'} + v_{k'}} + D_{k''} \frac{p_{k''}}{1 + \mu_{k''} + v_{k''}} + \cdots$$

$$= F_e \left(p_t, \cdots, p_p, \cdots, p_k, p_{k'}, p_{k''}, \cdots, p_b, p_c, p_d, \cdots, i \right)$$

to determine the rate i of net income. And if we also eliminated i, we would have a system of l equations of the distribution of the total excess of income over consumption among the l types of capital formation, in such a way that shows that the ratio of net income to the average cost would be the same for all capital goods, just as we would, in the cases of exchange (§ 117) and production (§ 197), have respectively systems of n and of $n + m$ equations of the distribution of an amount of wealth or income in the possession of an individual among his m and $n + m$ types of needs respectively, showing that the ratio of the rareté to the price would be the same for all commodities. This condition of equality of the ratios of the raretés to the prices of the services and the products is the condition for maximum effective utility for each exchanger, inasmuch as, if it is not fulfilled for any two commodities, it is advantageous to demand less of the one with the lower ratio and more of the one with the higher ratio. I will show later that the condition of the equality of the ratios of the net incomes to the prices of the new capital goods is, subject to a particular qualification, the condition for the maximum of effective utility for all the exchangers, inasmuch as, if it is not fulfilled for any two capital goods, it is advantageous to make less of the one for which the ratio is smaller and more of the one for which the ratio is greater. In all cases, we could carry out, by means of the $l + 1$ above equations, the determination of our $l + 1$ unknown variables, and from these we could then deduce the prices of the new capital goods and the total amount of savings, subject to sole condition that we abstract from changes in the quantities of products to be produced and in the prices of the products and services brought about by saving and capital formation. However, we want to try to encompass the economic mechanism in its entirety; and this is why, in spite of the complication of the notation (which is, after all, only an inconvenience that is just as trifling as it is inevitable), we are going to bring the $2m + 2n + 1$ equations of production and $2l + 2$ of capital formation and credit together into a single system.

Note

i   Obviously, when Walras refers to 'capital goods' without qualification in the first part of this section and frequently elsewhere in this lesson he means all three types of capital. In this lesson, he also uses that same term to refer to capital goods properly speaking but fails to add the latter two qualifying words. The reader has to pay attention to the context to determine his meaning. This poses no difficulty in the cases in which he uses the symbol 'K' and states that it refers to a 'capital good' without the qualifying words.

LESSON 24

Equations of capital formation and credit

SUMMARY: – Equation [1] of the total excess of income over consumption. Equations of equivalence between the quantities of services supplied and the quantities of products and new capital goods demanded; equations of maximum satisfaction; equations of partial supply of services and partial demand for products and new capital goods. Equations [2] of total supply of services; Equations [3] of total demand for products. Equations [4] of equality of supply of and demand for services. Equations [5] and [6] of equality of the prices and the average costs of products and new capital goods. Equation [7] of equality of the total amount of new capital goods and the total excess of income over consumption. Equations [8] of the prices of new capital goods.

240. First, we have the equation

$$F_e\left(p_t,\cdots,p_p,\cdots,p_k,p_{k'},p_{k''},\cdots,p_b,p_c,p_d,\cdots,i\right),\tag{1}$$

or one equation for the excess of income over consumption.

241. Furthermore, we have for any individual, the equation of exchange of services for capital goods, consumable products, and consumable services

$$o_t p_t + \cdots + o_p p_p + \cdots + o_k p_k + o_{k'} p_{k'} + o_{k''} p_{k''} + \cdots$$
$$= f_e\left(p_t,\cdots,p_p,\cdots,p_k,p_{k'},p_{k''},\cdots,p_b,p_c,p_d,\cdots,i\right)$$
$$+ d_a + d_b p_b + d_c p_c + d_d p_d + \cdots.$$

Moreover, the condition of maximum satisfaction (§ 80), which is always the condition determining the positive or negative supply of services and the demand for consumable products, yields the following equations between the quantities supplied, the quantities demanded, and the prices

$$\varphi_t \left(q_t - o_t \right) = p_t \varphi_a (d_a)$$

$$\vdots$$

$$\varphi_p \left(q_p - o_p \right) = p_p \varphi_a (d_a)$$

$$\vdots$$

$$\varphi_k \left(q_k - o_k \right) = p_k \varphi_a (d_a)$$

$$\varphi_{k'} \left(q_{k'} - o_{k'} \right) = p_{k'} \varphi_a (d_a)$$

$$\varphi_{k''} \left(q_{k''} - o_{k''} \right) = p_{k''} \varphi_a (d_a)$$

$$\vdots$$

$$\varphi_b \left(d_b \right) = p_b \varphi_a (d_a)$$

$$\varphi_c \left(d_c \right) = p_c \varphi_a (d_a)$$

$$\varphi_d \left(d_d \right) = p_d \varphi_a (d_a)$$

$$\vdots$$

hence $n + m - 1$ equations that form, with the foregoing one, a system of $n + m$ equations by means of which we can obtain, by successive eliminations, the n equations of positive or negative supply of (T), $\cdots$, (P), $\cdots$, (K), (K'), (K''), $\cdots$

$$o_t = f_t \left(p_t, \cdots, p_p, \cdots, p_k, p_{k'}, p_{k''}, \cdots, p_b, p_c, p_d, \cdots, i \right)$$

$$\vdots$$

$$o_p = f_p\left(p_t, \cdots, p_p, \cdots, p_k, p_{k'}, p_{k''}, \cdots, p_b, p_c, p_d, \cdots, i\right)$$

$$\vdots$$

$$o_k = f_k\left(p_t, \cdots, p_p, \cdots, p_k, p_{k'}, p_{k''}, \cdots, p_b, p_c, p_d, \cdots, i\right)$$

$$o_{k'} = f_{k'}\left(p_t, \cdots, p_p, \cdots, p_k, p_{k'}, p_{k''}, \cdots, p_b, p_c, p_d, \cdots, i\right)$$

$$o_{k''} = f_{k''}\left(p_t, \cdots, p_p, \cdots, p_k, p_{k'}, p_{k''}, \cdots, p_b, p_c, p_d, \cdots, i\right)$$

$$\vdots$$

and the $m - 1$ equations of the demand for (B), (C), (D), $\cdots$

$$d_b = f_b\left(p_t, \cdots, p_p, \cdots, p_k, p_{k'}, p_{k''}, \cdots, p_b, p_c, p_d, \cdots, i\right)$$

$$d_c = f_c\left(p_t, \cdots, p_p, \cdots, p_k, p_{k'}, p_{k''}, \cdots, p_b, p_c, p_d, \cdots, i\right)$$

$$d_d = f_d\left(p_t, \cdots, p_p, \cdots, p_k, p_{k'}, p_{k''}, \cdots, p_b, p_c, p_d, \cdots, i\right)$$

$$\vdots$$

the demand for (A) being furnished, without elimination, by the exchange equation

$$d_a = o_t p_t + \cdots + o_p p_p + \cdots + o_k p_k + o_{k'} p_{k'} + o_{k''} p_{k''} + \cdots$$
$$-f_e\left(p_t, \cdots, p_p, \cdots, p_k, p_{k'}, p_{k''}, \cdots, p_b, p_c, p_d, \cdots, i\right)$$
$$+d_b p_b + d_c p_c + d_d p_d + \cdots.$$

242. Likewise, we can obtain the equations of partial supply of services and the partial demand for products for all the other holders of services. And, while keeping the adopted notation, we will finally have the following system of n equations of total supply of services

$$O_t = F_t\left(p_t, \cdots, p_p, \cdots, p_k, p_{k'}, p_{k''}, \cdots, p_b, p_c, p_d, \cdots, i\right)$$

$$\vdots$$

$$O_p = F_p\left(p_t, \cdots, p_p, \cdots, p_k, p_{k'}, p_{k''}, \cdots, p_b, p_c, p_d, \cdots, i\right)$$

$$\vdots$$

$$O_k = F_k\left(p_t, \cdots, p_p, \cdots, p_k, p_{k'}, p_{k''}, \cdots, p_b, p_c, p_d, \cdots, i\right) \qquad [2]$$

$$O_{k'} = F_{k'}\left(p_t, \cdots, p_p, \cdots, p_k, p_{k'}, p_{k''}, \cdots, p_b, p_c, p_d, \cdots, i\right)$$

$$O_{k''} = F_{k''}\left(p_t, \cdots, p_p, \cdots, p_k, p_{k'}, p_{k''}, \cdots, p_b, p_c, p_d, \cdots, i\right)$$

$$\vdots$$

and the following system of m equations of the total demand for products

$$D_b = F_b\left(p_t, \cdots, p_p, \cdots, p_k, p_{k'}, p_{k''}, \cdots, p_b, p_c, p_d, \cdots, i\right)$$

$$D_c = F_c\left(p_t, \cdots, p_p, \cdots, p_k, p_{k'}, p_{k''}, \cdots, p_b, p_c, p_d, \cdots, i\right)$$

$$D_d = F_d\left(p_t, \cdots, p_p, \cdots, p_k, p_{k'}, p_{k''}, \cdots, p_b, p_c, p_d, \cdots, i\right) \qquad [3]$$

$$\vdots$$

$$D_a = O_t p_t + \cdots + O_p p_p + \cdots + O_k p_k + O_{k'} p_{k'} + O_{k''} p_{k''} + \cdots$$

$$-F_e\left(p_t, \cdots, p_p, \cdots, p_k, p_{k'}, p_{k''}, \cdots, p_b, p_c, p_d, \cdots, i\right) + D_b p_b + D_c p_c + D_d p_d + \cdots.$$

243. If $a_t, b_t, c_t, d_t, \cdots, \quad k_t, k'_t, k''_t, \cdots, \quad a_p, b_p, c_p, d_p, \cdots, \quad k_p, k'_p, k''_p, \cdots,$ $a_k, b_k, c_k, d_k, \cdots, \quad k_k, k'_k, k''_k, \cdots, \quad a_{k'}, b_{k'}, c_{k'}, d_{k'}, \cdots, \quad k_{k'}, k''_{k'}, k''_{k'}, \cdots,$ $a_{k''}, b_{k''}, c_{k''}, d_{k''}, \cdots, \quad k_{k''}, k'_{k''}, k''_{k''}, \cdots$

are the respective quantities, still assumed to be constants, of productive services (T), $\cdots$, (P), $\cdots$, (K), (K''), (K''), $\cdots$ needed for the
production of one unit of each of the products (A), (B), (C), (D), $\cdots$
and of each of the capital goods (K), (K'), (K''), $\cdots$, we would have the
three systems of equations:

$$a_t D_a + b_t D_b + c_t D_c + d_t D_d + \cdots + k_t D_k + k_t' D_{k'} + k_t'' D_{k''} + \cdots = O_t$$

$$a_p D_a + b_p D_b + c_p D_c + d_p D_d + \cdots + k_p D_k + k_p' D_{k'} + k_p'' D_{k''} + \cdots = O_p$$

$$a_k D_a + b_k D_b + c_k D_c + d_k D_d + \cdots + k_k D_k + k_k' D_{k'} + k_k'' D_{k''} + \cdots = O_k \quad [4]$$

$$a_{k'} D_a + b_{k'} D_b + c_{k'} D_c + d_{k'} D_d + \cdots + k_{k'} D_k + k_{k'}' D_{k'} + k_{k'}'' D_{k''} + \cdots = O_{k'}$$

$$a_{k''} D_a + b_{k''} D_b + c_{k''} D_c + d_{k''} D_d + \cdots + k_{k''} D_k + k_{k''}' D_{k'} + k_{k''}'' D_{k''} + \cdots = O_{k''}$$

$$\vdots$$

namely n equations stating that *the quantities of productive services
used are equal to the quantities effectively supplied;*

$$a_t p_t + \cdots + a_p p_p + \cdots + a_k p_k + a_{k'} p_{k'} + a_{k''} p_{k''} + \cdots = 1$$

$$b_t p_t + \cdots + b_p p_p + \cdots + b_k p_k + b_{k'} p_{k'} + b_{k''} p_{k''} + \cdots = p_b$$

$$c_t p_t + \cdots + c_p p_p + \cdots + c_k p_k + c_{k'} p_{k'} + c_{k''} p_{k''} + \cdots = p_c \quad [5]$$

$$d_t p_t + \cdots + d_p p_p + \cdots + d_k p_k + d_{k'} p_{k'} + d_{k''} p_{k''} + \cdots = p_d$$

$$\vdots$$

namely m equations stating that *the prices of the products are equal to
their average costs;*

$$k_t p_t + \cdots + k_p p_p + \cdots + k_k p_k + k_{k'} p_{k'} + k_{k''} p_{k''} + \cdots = P_k$$

$$k_t' p_t + \cdots + k_p' p_p + \cdots + k_k' p_k + k_{k'}' p_{k'} + k_{k''}' p_{k''} + \cdots = P_{k'} \quad [6]$$

$$k_t'' p_t + \cdots + k_p'' p_p + \cdots + k_k'' p_k + k_{k'}'' p_{k'} + k_{k''}'' p_{k''} + \cdots = P_{k''}$$

$$\vdots$$

namely *l* equations stating that *the prices of the new capital goods are equal to their average costs* (§ 238).

244. Now, we have the equation expressing the equality between the value of the new capital goods and the total excess of income over consumption (§ 234):

$$D_k P_k + D_{k'} P_{k'} + D_{k''} P_{k''} + \cdots = E \tag{7}$$

that is, an equation of exchange of the total excess of income over consumption exchanged for the newly produced capital goods (§ 238).

245. Finally, we have the equations

$$P_k = \frac{p_k}{1 + \mu_k + v_k}$$

$$P_{k'} = \frac{p_{k'}}{1 + \mu_{k'} + v_{k'}} \tag{8}$$

$$P_{k'} = \frac{p_{k''}}{1 + \mu_{k''} + v_{k''}}$$

$$\vdots$$

namely a system of *l* equations expressing the *equality of the rate of net income* for all capital goods properly speaking (§ 234).

246. Recapitulating, we have in total $2n + 2m + 2l + 2$ equations. But these $2n + 2m + 2l + 2$ equations can be reduced to $2n + 2m + 2l + 1$. Indeed, multiplying the two members of the *n* equations of system [4] by $p_t, \cdots, p_p, \cdots, p_k, p_{k'}, p_{k''}, \cdots$ respectively, and multiplying the two members of the $m + n$ equations of systems [5] and [6] by $D_a, D_b, D_c, D_d, \cdots, D_k, D_{k'}, D_{k''}, \cdots$, respectively, and adding the equations of each system separately, we obtain two equations whose first members are identical, yielding the following equation between the second members

$$O_t p_t + \cdots + O_p p_p + \cdots + O_k p_k + O_{k'} p_{k'} + O_{k''} p_{k''} + \cdots =$$

$$D_a + D_b p_b + D_c p_c + D_d p_d + \cdots + D_k p_k + D_{k'} p_{k'} + D_{k''} p_{k''} + \cdots.$$

By virtue of the mth equation of system [3], we have

$$O_t p_t + \cdots + O_p p_p + \cdots + O_k p_k + O_{k'} p_{k'} + O_{k''} p_{k''} + \cdots =$$

$$D_a + D_b p_b + D_c p_c + D_d p_d + \cdots + E.$$

Consequently, we have also

$$D_k p_k + D_{k'} p_{k'} + D_{k''} p_{k''} + \cdots = E$$

an equation that is nothing other than equation [7]. We have therefore the choice of keeping this one and removing either the mth equation of system [3] or the first of system [5], or the reverse. In any case, there will remain $2n + 2m + 2l + 1$ equations to determine precisely $2n + 2m + 2l + 1$ unknowns, which are: 1°, the n total quantities of services supplied; 2° the n prices of these services; 3° the m total quantities of the products demanded; 4° the $m - 1$ prices of $m - 1$ of these products measured in the mth one; 5° the amount of the total excess of income over consumption; 6° the l quantities produced of new capital goods; 7° the l prices of these capital goods, and, 8° the rate of net income. However, we still have to show that this problem formulated here theoretically is also the one that is solved practically in the market by the mechanism of free competition.

247. It is always a question of arriving at the equilibrium of capital formation in the same way as we arrived at the equilibrium of exchange and the equilibrium of production, that is to say, in assuming that the data of the problem do not change during the whole time of duration of our tatonnements, apart from assuming later that these data are variables, in order to study the effects of their variations. Moreover, in capital formation, there is a transformation of services into new capital goods, just as in production there is a transformation of services into products. A certain rate of net income and certain prices of the services being cried, and certain quantities of products and

new capital goods being produced, if that rate, these prices, and these quantities are not the equilibrium rate, prices, and quantities, not only must another rate and other prices be cried, but also must other quantities of products and new capital goods be produced. Accepting this necessity, we must assume that, for each reprise of the tatonne-ment, our entrepreneur making products or new capital goods will find, somewhere in the country, landowners, workers, and capitalists possessing the same quantities of services, having the same needs of services and products, and the same preferences for saving. A reprise of tatonnement will consist in the following, as far as con-cerns capital formation envisaged separately. At a rate of net income being cried at random initially, and revised subsequently upwards or downwards in accordance with circumstances, the entrepreneurs in capital goods industries will produce certain quantities of new cap-ital goods determined initially at random, and revised subsequently upwards or downwards in accordance with the circumstances. Then they will enter the market for capital goods to sell these new cap-ital goods in accordance with the mechanism of free competition; that is to say, at a price equal to their net income divided by the rate of net income (§ 234). The tatonnement will be finished when, at the rate of net income cried and with these quantities of new capital goods produced, 1° the total amount of the excess of income over consumption will be equal to the total amount of new capital goods, and 2° the price of new capital goods will be equal to their average cost. Production and capital formation will then be able to continue, but, of course, with the changes resulting from the existence of the new capital goods.

LESSON 25

Solution of the equations of capital formation and credit. Law of the determination of the rate of net income

SUMMARY: – Rate of net income and quantities to be produced of new capital goods determined randomly. Prices of the services brought about by tatonnement subject to conditions of equality of price and average cost of the products and equality of supply and demand of the services. Tatonnement in such a way as to result in equality of supply and demand of new capital goods. The market for numeraire capital. Price of new capital goods equal to the quotients of the gross incomes and the sum of three rates, namely of net income, of depreciation, and of insurance; profit or loss for the entrepreneurs. How the average costs and the prices of new capital goods are functions of the quantities produced. Tatonnement in such a way as to result in equality of the price and the average cost of new capital goods. Law of the establishment of the rate of net income.

248. Let us therefore come to the market and assume that a certain rate of net income i' has been determined randomly there, and l quantities $D'_k, D'_{k'}, D'_{k''}, \cdots$ of new capital goods to be produced, plus n prices of services, plus m quantities of products to be produced. Since we have given the solution of the problem of production, we know how we can, by various tatonnements brought into operation precisely by the mechanism of free competition, lead the prices of the services to the values $p'_t, \cdots, p'_p, \cdots, p'_k, p'_{k'}, p'_{k''}, \cdots$, determining m values of the average cost of products by means of the equations

$$p'_a = a_t p'_t + \cdots + a_p p'_p + \cdots + a_k p'_k + a_{k'} p'_{k'} + a_{k''} p'_{k''} + \cdots$$
$$p'_b = b_t p'_t + \cdots + b_p p'_p + \cdots + b_k p'_k + b_{k'} p'_{k'} + b_{k''} p'_{k''} + \cdots$$
$$p'_c = c_t p'_t + \cdots + c_p p'_p + \cdots + c_k p'_k + c_{k'} p'_{k'} + c_{k''} p'_{k''} + \cdots$$
$$p'_d = d_t p'_t + \cdots + d_p p'_p + \cdots + d_k p'_k + d_{k'} p'_{k'} + d_{k''} p'_{k''} + \cdots$$
$$\vdots$$

in such a way that, these n prices of the services and these m prices of the products being given, we obtain:

1° A total excess of net income over consumption

$$E' = F_e(p'_t, \cdots, p'_p, \cdots, p'_k, p'_{k'}, p'_{k''}, \cdots, p'_b, p'_c, p'_d, \cdots, i');$$

2° n quantities of services supplied

$$O'_t = F_t(p'_t, \cdots, p'_p, \cdots, p'_k, p'_{k'}, p'_{k''}, \cdots, p'_b, p'_c, p'_d, \cdots, i')$$
$$\vdots$$
$$O'_p = F_p(p'_t, \cdots, p'_p, \cdots, p'_k, p'_{k'}, p'_{k''}, \cdots, p'_b, p'_c, p'_d, \cdots, i')$$
$$\vdots$$
$$O'_k = F_k(p'_t, \cdots, p'_p, \cdots, p'_k, p'_{k'}, p'_{k''}, \cdots, p'_b, p'_c, p'_d, \cdots, i')$$
$$O'_{k'} = F_{k'}(p'_t, \cdots, p'_p, \cdots, p'_k, p'_{k'}, p'_{k''}, \cdots, p'_b, p'_c, p'_d, \cdots, i')$$
$$O'_{k''} = F_{k''}(p'_t, \cdots, p'_p, \cdots, p'_k, p'_{k'}, p'_{k''}, \cdots, p'_b, p'_c, p'_d, \cdots, i')$$
$$\vdots$$

3° $m - 1$ quantities of the products (B), (C), (D), $\cdots$ demanded

$$D'_b = F_b(p'_t, \cdots, p'_p, \cdots, p'_k, p'_{k'}, p'_{k''}, \cdots, p'_b, p'_c, p'_d, \cdots, i')$$
$$D'_c = F_c(p'_t, \cdots, p'_p, \cdots, p'_k, p'_{k'}, p'_{k''}, \cdots, p'_b, p'_c, p'_d, \cdots, i')$$
$$D'_d = F_d(p'_t, \cdots, p'_p, \cdots, p'_k, p'_{k'}, p'_{k''}, \cdots, p'_b, p'_c, p'_d, \cdots, i')$$
$$\vdots$$

These quantities and this excess, joined with the randomly determined quantities $[D'_k, D'_{k'}, D'_{k''}, \cdots]$ of new capital goods and the equally randomly determined quantity $[\Omega_a]$ of product (A) to be produced will satisfy the equations

$$a_t \Omega_a + b_t D'_b + c_t D'_c + d_t D'_d + \cdots + k_t D'_k + k'_t D'_{k'} + k''_t D'_{k''} + \cdots = O'_t$$

$$\vdots$$

$$a_p \Omega_a + b_p D'_b + c_p D'_c + d_p D'_d + \cdots + k_p D'_k + k'_p D'_{k'} + k''_p D'_{k''} + \cdots = O'_p$$

$$\vdots$$

$$a_k \Omega_a + b_k D'_b + c_k D'_c + d_k D'_d + \cdots + k_k D'_k + k'_k D'_{k'} + k''_k D'_{k''} + \cdots = O'_k$$

$$a_{k'} \Omega_a + b_{k'} D'_b + c_{k'} D'_c + d_{k'} D'_d + \cdots + k_{k'} D'_k + k'_{k'} D'_{k'} + k''_{k'} D'_{k''} + \cdots = O'_{k'}$$

$$a_{k''} \Omega_a + b_{k''} D'_b + c_{k''} D'_c + d_{k''} D'_d + \cdots + k_{k''} D'_k + k'_{k''} D'_{k'} + k''_{k''} D'_{k''} \cdots = O'_{k'}$$

$$\vdots$$

The values $p'_t, \cdots, p'_p, \cdots, p'_k, p'_{k'}, p'_{k''}, \cdots$ of the prices of the services determine, in addition to the values of the average costs of the products, the values of the average cost of the new capital goods:

$$P'_k = k_t p'_t + \cdots + k_p p'_p + \cdots + k_k p'_k + k_{k'} p'_{k'} + k_{k''} p'_{k''} + \cdots$$

$$P'_{k'} = k'_t p'_t + \cdots + k'_p p'_p + \cdots + k'_k p'_k + k'_{k'} p'_{k'} + k'_{k''} p'_{k''} + \cdots$$

$$P'_{k''} = k''_t p'_t + \cdots + k''_p p'_p + \cdots + k''_k p'_k + k''_{k'} p'_{k'} + k''_{k''} p'_{k''} + \cdots$$

$$\vdots$$

Moreover, multiplying, on the one hand, the $m + l$ equations expressing the equality of[i] the m average costs of the products[ii] and the l average costs indicated above of the new capital goods, respectively by $\Omega_a, D'_b, D'_c, D'_d, \cdots D'_k, D'_{k'}, D'_{k''}, \cdots$, and, on the other hand, multiplying the n equations expressing equality of supply and demand of the services respectively, by $p'_t, \cdots, p'_p, \cdots, p'_k, p'_{k'}, p'_{k''}, \cdots$, adding separately the two systems of equations thus obtained, and observing that the second member of the first sum and the first member of the second one are identical, we obtain the following equation:

$$\Omega_a p_a' + D_b' p_b' + D_c' p_c' + D_d' p_d' + \cdots + D_k' P_k' + D_{k'}' p_{k'}' + D_{k''}' p_{k''}' + \cdots =$$
$$O_t' P_t' + \cdots + O_p' P_p' + \cdots + O_k' P_k' + O_{k'}' p_{k'}' + O_{k''}' p_{k''}' + \cdots.$$

Now, there is also a quantity D_a' of (A) demanded in accordance with the following equation:[iii]

$$D_a' + D_b' p_b' + D_c' p_c' + D_d' p_d' + \cdots + E' = O_t' p_t' + \cdots + O_p' p_p' + \cdots +$$
$$O_k' P_k' + O_{k'}' p_{k'}' + O_{k''}' p_{k''}' + \cdots.$$

We have then also

$$\Omega_a p_a' + D_k' P_k' + D_{k'}' p_{k'}' + D_{k''}' p_{k''}' + \cdots = D_a' + E';$$

that is to say, that in this state, which we could call a preliminary equilibrium, the aggregate cost of the product serving as the numeraire and that of the new capital goods is necessarily equal to the demand for the numeraire plus the excess of income over consumption. Thus, at this moment, we have satisfied the equations of the system [5] except the first, and satisfied [2], and satisfied [3] except the mth, and satisfied [4], [1], and [6], and we only have to satisfy the first equation of system [5], the mth equation of system [3], and the equations of the systems [7] and [8], in such a way that if we had by chance

$$D_k' P_k' + D_{k'}' p_{k'}' + D_{k''}' p_{k''}' + \cdots = E'$$

and

$$P_k' = \frac{p_k'}{i' + \mu_k + v_k}$$

$$P_{k'}' = \frac{p_{k'}'}{i' + \mu_{k'} + v_{k'}}$$

$$P_{k''}' = \frac{p_{k''}'}{i' + \mu_{k'} + v_{k''}}$$

$$\vdots$$

we would have by those very conditions

$$\Omega_a p'_a = D'_a$$

and then we would have only to carry out the last tatonnement of production that must bring about both equality of the average cost of the numeraire to unity and equality of its effective supply to its effective demand in order to solve the problem in its entirety. However, generally we have

$$D'_k P'_k + D'_{k'} p'_{k'} + D'_{k''} p'_{k''} + \cdots \gtrless E'$$

and

$$P'_k \gtrless \frac{p'_k}{i' + \mu_k + v_k}$$

$$P'_{k'} \gtrless \frac{p'_{k'}}{i' + \mu_{k'} + v_{k'}}$$

$$P'_{k''} \gtrless \frac{p'_{k''}}{i' + \mu_{k''} + v_{k''}}$$

$$\vdots$$

and we must change these inequalities into equalities by means of tatonnements that act on the quantities $i', D'_k, D'_{k'}, D'_{k''}, \cdots$ that are still determined randomly. This is above all the objective of the problem that concerns us.

249. Let us first consider the inequality

$$D'_k \frac{p'_k}{i' + \mu_k + v_k} + D'_{k'} \frac{p'_{k'}}{i' + \mu_{k'} + v_{k'}} + D'_{k''} \frac{p'_{k''}}{i' + \mu_{k''} + v_{k''}} + \cdots$$
$$\gtrless F_e(p'_t, \cdots, p'_p, \cdots, p'_k, p'_{k'}, p'_{k''}, \cdots, p'_b, p'_c, p'_d, \cdots, i')$$

and let us try to change it into an equality. The first member of that inequality is a decreasing function of i. And, with regard to the other member, although we do not know the function F_e, we know that it is a function of i that is successively increasing from zero and decreasing to zero. This being so, we see immediately that, to change the inequality to equality, we must decrease or increase i' in accordance with whether the first member is lesser than or greater than the second.

Let i'' be the value for which we have

$$D'_k \frac{p'_k}{i'' + \mu_k + \nu_k} + D'_{k'} \frac{p'_{k'}}{i'' + \mu_{k'} + \nu_{k'}} + D'_{k''} \frac{p'_{k''}}{i'' + \mu_{k''} + \nu_{k''}} + \cdots$$
$$= F_e \left(p'_t, \cdots, p'_p, \cdots, p'_k, p'_{k'}, p'_{k''}, \cdots, p'_b, p'_c, p'_d, \cdots, i'' \right).$$

If we substitute i'' for i' in the tatonnement, then we arrive, as a result of its reprise, at the inequality

$$D'_k \frac{p''_k}{i'' + \mu_k + \nu_k} + D'_{k'} \frac{p''_{k'}}{i'' + \mu_{k'} + \nu_{k'}} + D'_{k''} \frac{p''_{k''}}{i'' + \mu_{k''} + \nu_{k''}} + \cdots$$
$$\gtrless F_e \left(p''_t, \cdots, p''_p, \cdots, p''_k, p''_{k'}, p''_{k''}, \cdots, p''_b, p''_c, p''_d, \cdots, i'' \right),$$

and we must now show that the two members of this inequality are closer to being equal than the two members of the preceding inequality.

250. Subject to conditions of the present tatonnement, the quantities to be produced of the numeraire product (A) and of the new capital goods (K), (K'), (K''), $\cdots$ are fixed and do not change. Consequently, we always have to reserve for their production the following quantity of service (T):

$$a_t \Omega_a + K'_t = a_t \Omega + k_t D'_k + k'_t D'_{k'} + k''_t D'_{k''} + \cdots$$

where K'_t is the quantity of (T) reserved for the production of the new capital goods; and we can distribute the remaining quantity between consumption in the form of services and consumption in the form of products, in accordance with the following formula:

$$b_t D_t + c_t D_c + d_t D_d + \cdots + S_t = Q_t - (a_t \Omega_a + K'_t)$$

where Q_t is the total quantity of service (T) and S_t the quantity directly consumed. The other services are treated similarly.

The substitution of i'' for i' in the tatonnement has led to equality of the total amount of new capital goods and the total excess of income over consumption because of changes in these two quantities that can be considered as a first-order effect of the change of the rate of net income. But there is a second-order effect to be examined. If the total excess of income over consumption has increased or decreased at the prices $p'_t, \cdots, p'_p, \cdots, p'_k, p'_{k'}, p'_{k''}, \cdots, p'_b, p'_c, p'_d, \cdots$, the amount of consumption will first tend to decrease or increase; and, since the total quantities of consumable and productive services remain the same, all their prices, that are equal to the ratios of the raretés that have remained nearly constant of the commodities (T), $\cdots$, (P), $\cdots$, (K), (K'), (K''), $\cdots$, (B), (C), (D), $\cdots$ to the rareté of the commodity (A) demanded that have increased or decreased, fall or rise. It remains to understand what will be the effect of this decrease or increase on the new amount of new capital goods and on the total amount of excess of income over consumption. The first quantity will decrease or increase because it is an increasing function of the prices $p'_k, p'_{k'}, p'_{k''}, \cdots$ Regarding the second quantity, this will also decrease or increase because the amount of income decreases or increases with decreasing or increasing prices, and, as a result, the amount of consumption and that of capital formation must both decrease or increase. Because the total amount of new capital formation and the excess of income over consumption both change into the same direction, the change of prices from $p'_t, \cdots, p'_p, \cdots, p'_k, p'_{k'}, p'_{k''}, \cdots, p'_b, p'_c, p'_d, \cdots$, to $p''_t, \cdots, p''_p, \cdots, p''_k, p''_{k'}, p''_{k''}, \cdots, p''_b, p''_c, p''_d, \cdots$ will have moved them less far from equality than the change from i' into i'' will have led them to move in the direction of equality. The system of the new rate of net income and of the new prices is therefore closer to equilibrium than the preceding one, and it is necessary only to continue the tatonnement to approach it still more closely.

In this way, we would arrive at the equality

$$D'_k \frac{p'''_{k}}{i''' + \mu_k + v_k} + D'_{k'} \frac{p'''_{k'}}{i''' + \mu_{k'} + v_{k'}} + D'_{k''} \frac{p'''_{k''}}{i''' + \mu_{k''} + v_{k''}} + \cdots$$

$$= F_e\left(p'''_t, \cdots, p'''_p, \cdots, p'''_k, p'''_{k'}, p'''_{k''}, \cdots, p'''_b, p'''_c, p'''_d, \cdots, i''' \right).$$

Now, the indicated tatonnement is exactly the one that happens in the market for capital goods, where the new capital goods are sold in accordance with the mechanism of bidding up prices and lowering them in proportion to their net incomes (§ 234); that is to say, when the amount of net income of the new capital goods is exchanged for the amount of the excess of income over consumption in accordance with the equation

$$D_k \pi_k + D_{k'} \pi_{k'} + D_{k''} \pi_{k''} + \cdots$$

$$= i F_e \left(p_t, \cdots, p_p, \cdots, p_k, p_{k'}, p_{k''}, \cdots, p_b, p_c, p_d, \cdots, i \right),$$

where i represents the rate of net income, and $\dfrac{1}{i}$ the *price of a unit of net income.*

251. Instead of assuming that the creators of the excess of income over consumption go in person to the market for capital goods in order to buy new capital goods that they subsequently hire out in the market for services to the entrepreneurs engaged in production, we now assume that the savers lend a part of the amount in numeraire of these capital goods to those entrepreneurs, and that the latter, instead of the savers, go to the market for capital goods to buy the new capital goods. In that market, nothing will change other than that the demand for new capital goods will be exercised by the entrepreneurs engaged in production in place of being exercised by the creators of savings. And, consequently, the rate of net income will be determined there in the way we have indicated, except that in place of the market for services there will, for the hiring out of new capital goods, in part be substituted a *market for* numeraire *capital* in which there will be determined the price of numeraire capital, to be called *rate of interest.* Now, it is obvious that this rate of interest, if it is determined in accordance with the mechanism of bidding up prices and lowering them and the law of supply and demand, cannot differ at all from the rate of net income that we determined above. Indeed, if it were higher, it would be more advantageous for the creators of the excess to lend their capital in the form of numeraire in the market for numeraire capital, rather than to hire it out in kind in the market for

services, and would, consequently move from the latter market to the former; whereas it would be advantageous for the entrepreneurs, on the contrary, to hire capital in kind in the market for services rather than to borrow it in the form of numeraire in the market for numeraire capital, moving, consequently, from the second to the first market. Thus, the effective supply of numeraire capital increasing and its demand decreasing, the rate of interest would decrease. And if the rate of interest were lower than the rate of net income, the inverse phenomenon would take place, and, consequently, the effective supply of numeraire capital decreasing and its demand increasing, the rate of interest would increase. In this way, the rate of interest, which is the ratio of net profit[iv] to the price of movable capital, reveals itself, of course, in the market for numeraire capital; that is to say, in the banking system; but in reality it is determined as the rate of net income, which is the common ratio of the net price of a service to the price of the corresponding landed, personal, or movable capital, in the capital goods market, that is to say, in the stock market. We see here clearly that the key to the whole theory of capital is to be found in this elimination of lending capital *in numeraire* and the exclusive consideration of lending capital *in kind*. Since the market for numeraire capital is only of practical interest and not of theoretical importance, we leave it aside and go back to the market for capital goods to find there the equilibrium price of new capital goods.

252. Now, at the prices $p_k''', p_{k'}''', p_{k''}''', \cdots$ of their services, the new capital goods (K), (K'), (K''), $\cdots$ will be sold at the prices

$$\Pi_k = \frac{p_k'''}{i''' + \mu_k + \nu_k}$$

$$\Pi_{k'} = \frac{p_{k'}'''}{i''' + \mu_{k'} + \nu_{k'}}$$

$$\Pi_{k''} = \frac{p_{k''}'''}{i''' + \mu_{k''} + \nu_{k'}}$$

$$\vdots$$

So, $\Pi_k, \Pi_{k'}, \Pi_{k''}, \cdots$ are the prices of new capital goods, where $P_k''', P_{k'}''', P_{k''}''', \cdots$ are their average costs. These prices and average costs being in general unequal, the entrepreneurs of new capital will make profits or losses expressed by the differences

$$D_k'(\Pi_k - P_k'''), \; D_{k'}'(\Pi_{k'} - P_{k'}'''), \; D_{k''}'(\Pi_{k''} - P_{k''}'''), \cdots.$$

It is not immediately clear, in the case of inequality of the prices and the average costs, how, by modifying the quantities $D_k', D_{k'}', D_{k''}'', \cdots$, we can bring the prices Π_k and P_k''', $\Pi_{k'}$ and $P_{k'}'''$, $\Pi_{k''}$ and $P_{k''}'''$, $\cdots$ to equality. This is due to the fact that we do not see immediately that these prices and average costs are functions of the quantities of new capital goods produced. But this circumstance is easy to make apparent.

Let us go back to the various systems of equations of capital formation as these have been posited in the preceding section. Assume that we have introduced the values of $p_b, p_c, p_d, \cdots$ given by the equations of system [5] into the equations of the systems [1], [2], and [3], and that then we introduce the values of $O_t, O_p, \cdots, O_k, O_{k'}O_{k''}, \cdots$ and those of $D_a, D_b, D_c, D_d, \cdots$ given by the modified systems [2] and [3] into the equations of system [4]; this system would then be a system of n equations in $n + l + 1$ unknowns, namely the n prices $p_t, \cdots, p_p, \cdots, p_k, p_{k'}, p_{k''}, \cdots$ of the productive services, the l quantities of new capital goods $D_k, D_{k'}, D_{k''}, \cdots$ produced, and rate of net income i. Considering the $l + 1$ latter quantities as given and only the former n as unknowns, and assuming that we have successively eliminated $n - 1$ of these unknowns, we would finally obtain n equations of the following form, giving the prices of the services as functions of the quantities of new capital goods to be produced and the rate of net income:

$$p_t = \mathfrak{F}_t\left(D_k, D_{k'}, D_{k''}, \cdots, i\right)$$
$$\vdots$$
$$p_p = \mathfrak{F}_p(D_k, D_{k'}, D_{k''}, \cdots, i)$$
$$\vdots$$

$$p_k = \mathfrak{F}_k\left(D_k, D_{k'}, D_{k''}, \cdots, i\right)$$

$$p_{k'} = \mathfrak{F}_{k'}\left(D_k, D_{k'}, D_{k''}, \cdots, i\right)$$

$$p_{k''} = \mathfrak{F}_{k''}\left(D_k, D_{k'}, D_{k''}, \cdots, i\right)$$

$$\vdots$$

After that, assuming that we have introduced the values of $p_t, \cdots, p_p, \cdots, p_k, p_{k'}, p_{k''}, \cdots$ given by these equations into those of systems [6] and [8], we would have finally two systems of l equations each, of which the one gives the average costs and the other the prices of new capital goods as functions of the quantities of new capital goods to be produced and of the rate of net income.

253. As we said above, we do not know the equations that give us $p_t, \cdots, p_p, \cdots, p_k, p_{k'}, p_{k''}, \cdots$ as functions of $D_k, D_{k'}, D_{k''}, \cdots$ and i. However, it follows quite explicitly from the laws of the variation of the prices of the services that we have developed, that, given the inequalities

$$k_t p_t''' + \cdots + k_p p_p''' + \cdots + k_k p_k''' + k_{k'} p_{k'}''' + k_{k''} p_{k''}''' + \cdots \gtreqless \frac{p_k'''}{i''' + \mu_k + v_k}$$

$$k_t' p_t''' + \cdots + k_p' p_p''' + \cdots + k_k' p_k''' + k_{k'}' p_{k'}''' + k_{k''}' p_{k''}''' + \cdots \gtreqless \frac{p_{k'}'''}{i''' + \mu_{k'} + v_{k'}}$$

$$k_t'' p_t''' + \cdots + k_p'' p_p''' + \cdots + k_k'' p_k''' + k_{k'}'' p_{k'}''' + k_{k''}'' p_{k''}''' + \cdots \gtreqless \frac{p_{k''}'''}{i''' + \mu_{k''} + v_{k''}}$$

$$\vdots ,$$

if we increase or decrease the quantity D_k we increase or decrease somewhat, on the one hand, the price of all the services that enter into the production of the capital good (K); that is to say, we increase or decrease considerably the average cost of this capital good expressed by the first member of the first inequality given above, whereas, on the other hand, we decrease or increase considerably the price of the service of the type of capital good (K); that is to say, we decrease or increase considerably the price of the capital good of this type as expressed by the second member of this same inequality. So, the first member of the inequality is an increasing function and the second member is a decreasing function of the quantity of capital good (K) produced. Consequently, assuming, for example, $P_k''' > \Pi_k$, we could decrease P_k''' and increase Π_k by decreasing D_k'; on the contrary, if $P_k''' < \Pi_k$, we could increase P_k''' and decrease Π_k by increasing D_k'. Likewise, assuming $P_{k'}'' \gtrless \Pi_{k'}$, we could decrease or increase $P_{k'}'''$ and increase or decrease $\Pi_{k'}$ by decreasing or increasing $D_{k'}'$. Likewise, if $P_{k''}''' \gtrless \Pi_{k''}$, we could decrease or increase $P_{k''}'''$ and increase or decrease $\Pi_{k''}$ by decreasing or increasing $D_{k''}'$, and so forth.

Let Δ_k be the quantity of capital good (K) to be produced that, substituted for D_k' in the functions $\mathfrak{F}_t, \cdots, \mathfrak{F}_p, \cdots, \mathfrak{F}_k, \cdots, \mathfrak{F}_k, \mathfrak{F}_{k'}, \mathfrak{F}_{k''}, \cdots$, will change the first inequality [above] to equality; let $\Delta_{k'}$ be the quantity of capital good (K') to be produced that, substituted for $D_{k'}'$ in the functions $\mathfrak{F}_t, \cdots, \mathfrak{F}_p, \cdots, \mathfrak{F}_k, \mathfrak{F}_{k'}, \mathfrak{F}_{k''}, \cdots$ will change the second inequality to equality; let $\Delta_{k''}$ be the quantity of capital good (K'') to be produced that, substituted for $D_{k''}'$ in the same functions will change the third inequality to equality; and so forth. These quantities $\Delta_k, \Delta_{k'}, \Delta_{k''}, \cdots$ also substituted for $D_k', D_{k'}', D_{k''}' \cdots$, in the general tatonnement, then brought onto the market for capital goods and sold there in accordance with the mechanism of free competition, would be sold at prices that differ from the average costs, but would be closer to equality than the preceding prices were with respect to the preceding average costs. This is, at least, what must be established, even for the case in which the changes of the quantities to be produced would be all in the same direction.

254. Let us assume that these changes are all increases of the quantities produced. The substitution of Δ_k for D_k' would have changed the first inequality to equality by an increase of $p_t, \cdots, p_p, \cdots, p_{k'}, p_{k''}, \cdots$ and a decrease of the price p_k. The substitution of $\Delta_{k'}'$ for $D_{k'}'$, which then occurs, would have produced an increase of $p_t, \cdots, p_p, \cdots, p_k, p_{k''}, \cdots$ and a decrease of the price $p_{k'}$. Then the substitution of $\Delta_{k''}'$ for D_k' would have produced an increase of $p_t, \cdots, p_p, \cdots, p_k, p_{k'}, \cdots$ and a decrease of the price $p_{k''}$. And so forth. The equality of the average

cost and the price of (K) would therefore have been disturbed by an increase of the prices $p_t, \cdots, p_p, \cdots, p_k, \cdots$ and by a decrease of the prices $p_{k'}, p_{k''}, \cdots$ The average cost would have been considerably increased by the increase of the former prices, and at the same time decreased somewhat by the decrease of the latter prices. The price would have been increased by the increase of p_k. Now, subject to these conditions, it is evident that the price and the average cost of capital goods (K) would not have been much displaced from equality by the increases in the quantities produced of (K′), (K″), ... We would reason in the same way in the case of a general decrease of the quantities produced.

What has been said about the effect of the variations of the quantities produced of (K′), (K″), ... on the price and the average cost of (K), could be said about the effect of the variations of the quantities produced of (K), (K″), ... on the price and the average cost of (K′), the effect of the variations of the quantities produced of (K), (K′), ... on the price and the average cost of (K″), and so forth. Subject to these conditions, there is reason to believe that the change of the quantity produced of each new capital good has brought the price and the average cost of this capital nearer to equality than the changes of the quantities produced of the other new capital goods have displaced them from equality. The system of the new quantities to be produced and the new prices and average costs of new capital goods is therefore nearer to equilibrium than the preceding one, and we only have to continue the tatonnement in order to approach it more and more.

Combining this tatonnement with the preceding ones, we would determine certain quantities D_k'', $D_{k'}''$, $D_{k''}''$, ... such that we would have

$$k_t p_t^{iv} + \cdots + k_p p_p^{iv} + \cdots + k_k p_k^{iv} + k_{k'} p_{k'}^{iv} + k_{k''} p_{k''}^{iv} + \cdots = \frac{p_k^{iv}}{i^{iv} + \mu_k + v_k}$$

$$k_t' p_t^{iv} + \cdots + k_p' p_p^{iv} + \cdots + k_k' p_k^{iv} + k_{k'}' p_{k'}^{iv} + k_{k''}' p_{k''}^{iv} + \cdots = \frac{p_{k'}^{iv}}{i^{iv} + \mu_{k'} + v_{k'}}$$

$$k_t'' p_t^{iv} + \cdots + k_p'' p_p^{iv} + \cdots + k_k'' p_k^{iv} + k_{k'}'' p_{k'}^{iv} + k_{k''}'' p_{k''}^{iv} + \cdots = \frac{p_{k''}^{iv}}{i^{iv} + \mu_{k''} + v_{k''}}$$

$$\vdots$$

and the equations of system [8] would be satisfied.

Now, this tatonnement is precisely the one that takes place automatically in the market for products, subject to regime of free competition, when the entrepreneurs manufacturing new capital goods, just like the entrepreneurs manufacturing other products, flow toward the enterprises or turn away from them according to whether profits or losses are made in them.

255. After having carried out this tatonnement, we have, as we have seen (§248), calling p_a^{iv} the average cost and D_a^{iv} the effective demand for (A),

$$\Omega_a p_a^{iv} = D_a^{iv}$$

and there remains only to carry out the well-known tatonnement that leads simultaneously to the equality of the average cost of (A) to unity, and equality of its effective supply and effective demand (§ 215).

256. Bringing together all the elements of our demonstration, we formulate thusly the law of the establishment of the equilibrium prices of new capital goods by the determination of the rate of net income:

– *Given several services from the price of which it is possible to deduct an excess of income over consumption that will be transformed into new capital goods properly speaking, and that are exchanged for various consumable products and for various new capital goods with a numeraire as intermediary, then it is sufficient and necessary for equilibrium in the market for these capital goods, or stationary prices in numeraire of all new capital goods, that: 1° at the prices determined by the ratio of the net incomes and the common rate of net income, the effective demand for these new capital goods be equal to their effective supply, and, 2° the price of these new capital goods be equal to their average cost. When this double equality does not exist, it is necessary, to arrive at the first equality, to raise the prices by decreasing the rate of net income if effective demand is greater than effective supply and to lower the prices by increasing the rate of net income if effective supply is greater than effective demand; and, to arrive at the second equality, it is necessary to increase the quantity of new capital goods of which the price is greater than the average cost and to decrease the quantity of those of which the average cost is greater than the price.*

Since the new capital goods properly speaking are nothing other than products, and since the condition of equality of their price to their average cost is an element of the principle of their cost of production, it turns out that the principal result of this study is the determination of the rate of net income in the market for those capital goods, in accordance with the law of supply and demand. Before finishing, let us make two remarks on these two points.

Let us first remark, with regard to the determination of the prices of the new capital goods properly speaking, that the entrepreneurs who make these products, knowing beforehand the prices of the services and the rate of net income, knowing beforehand the average cost and the price of their products, find themselves, theoretically, in the same position as the entrepreneurs producing the numeraire commodity, who are free not to produce except in the case of profits and to refrain from production in the case of losses (§ 211).

Let us, in what follows, remember with regard to the rate of net income, that this rate having been determined, the rate of interest, which is the price of hiring numeraire capital, is determined, too, and has only to manifest itself in the market for this numeraire capital (§ 247). And let us remark that, from the moment that fixed capital is hired in the form of numeraire, nothing prevents that circulating capital be hired in the same form and at the same price (abstraction made of certain circumstances that are of practical but not theoretical importance), since it makes absolutely no difference to the capitalist who lends numeraire if the borrowing entrepreneur transforms this numeraire into machines, instruments, tools or in raw materials in inventory and manufactured products on display for sale. In this way, the problem of hiring capital is completely solved by the determination of the rate of net income.

Notes

i   Walras inserted the words 'the equality of' in editions 2 and 3, and suppressed them in editions 4 and 5. The insertion appears to be a mistake because he does not say to what the prices are equal. He probably meant the equality of average cost to the price of each product.

ii   He meant the system of equations at the top of page 282.

iii   See the last equation of system [3] of lesson 24.

iv   This is an example of Walras using the word *profit* in the conventional sense, i.e., as revenue minus cost, inconsistently with his definition of it as the services of capital goods properly speaking.

v   The three dots at the end of $p_t, \cdots, p_p, \cdots, p_k, \cdots$ appear here to be an error by Walras. He should have written $p_t, \cdots, p_p, \cdots, p_k$.

LESSON 26

Theorem of the maximum utility of new
capital goods. Law of the variation of the rate
of net income

SUMMARY: – There is maximum satisfaction of the needs of an
exchanger when he has distributed his income among his diverse
types of needs in such a way that the ratios of the raretés of the services and the products to their prices are equal. There is maximum
effective utility of new capital of which the services are consumable by a society when the excess of its income over consumption
has been distributed among the diverse varieties of capital formation in such a way that the ratios of the gross incomes to the prices
of the capital goods are equal. There is maximum effective utility
of new capital goods that render productive services if the same
condition is fulfilled. Analytical definition of free competition in
matters of capital formation and credit. Law of the establishment
of the variation in the rate of net income subject to the hypothesis
of a constant excess of income over consumption.

257. I have promised (§ 239) to demonstrate that using the excess
of income over consumption in such a way that the ratios of the net
incomes to the prices of the new capital goods are equal is, subject
to a certain reservation, the condition for maximum effective utility
of the services of these new capital goods, just as using individual
incomes in such a way that the ratios of the raretés of the services
and products to the prices are equal is the condition for maximum
effective utility of these services and products. The time has come to
demonstrate these propositions.

Let $\delta_t, \cdots, \delta_p, \cdots, \delta_k, \delta_{k'}, \delta_{k''}, \cdots, \delta_a, \delta_b, \delta_c, \delta_d, \cdots$ be quantities to
keep or to buy, by an exchanger, of services (T), (P), (K), (K'),
(K''), $\cdots$ and of products (A), (B), (C), (D), $\cdots$ at prices

297

$p_t, \cdots, p_p, \cdots, p_k, p_{k'}, p_{k''}, \cdots, p_b, p_c, p_d, \cdots$ of the services and products in terms of (A) such that

$$\delta_t p_t + \cdots + \delta_p p_p + \cdots + \delta_k p_k + \delta_{k'} p_{k'} + \delta_{k''} p_{k'''} + \cdots$$
$$+\delta_a + \delta_b p_b + \delta_c p_c + \delta_d p_d + \cdots = s,$$

where s is the income to allocate, by this individual, among his needs of the n types of services and m types of products.

Moreover, let

$$u = \Phi_t(q), \cdots, u = \Phi_p(q), \cdots, u = \Phi_k(q), u = \Phi_{k'}(q),$$
$$u = \Phi_{k''}(q), \cdots,$$
$$u = \Phi_a(q), \cdots, u = \Phi_b(q), \cdots, u = \Phi_c(q), \cdots, u = \Phi_d(q), \cdots$$

be the equations expressing the effective utilities of the services (T), (P), (K), (K'), (K''), $\cdots$ and of products (A), (B), (C), (D), $\cdots$ for this individual as functions of the quantities consumed. The derivatives of these functions being essentially decreasing, there will be maximum of effective utility, for our individual, when the differential increments of the quantities consumed of each commodity are equal, since, if one assumes any two of these increments unequal, it will be advantageous to demand less of the commodity of which the differential increment is less and to demand more of the commodity for which it is greater. The condition of the maximum satisfaction of wants can therefore be expressed by the equation system

$$\Phi_t'(\delta)\partial\delta_t = \cdots = \Phi_p'(\delta)\partial\delta_p = \cdots =$$

$$\Phi_k'(\delta)\partial\delta_k = \Phi_{k'}'(\delta)\partial\delta_{k'} = \Phi_{k''}'(\delta)\partial\delta_{k''} = \cdots =$$

$$\Phi_a'(\delta)\partial\delta_a = \Phi_b'(\delta)\partial\delta_b = \Phi_c'(\delta)\partial\delta_c = \Phi_d'(\delta)\partial\delta_d = \cdots$$

Now, on the one hand, the derivatives of the effective utility functions with respect to the quantities consumed are nothing other than the raretés; and, on the other hand, from the point of view of the distribution by an individual of a certain income over the diverse types of wants, the differentials of these quantities consumed are inversely proportional to the prices, which are themselves the inverse ratios of the quantities of commodities exchanged in accordance with the equations

$$p_t \partial \delta_t = \cdots = p_p \partial \delta_p = \cdots =$$

$$p_k \partial \delta_k = p_{k'} \partial \delta_{k'} = p_{k''} \partial \delta_{k''} = \cdots =$$

$$\partial \delta_a = p_b \partial \delta_b = p_c \partial \delta_c = p_d \partial \delta_d = \cdots$$

The above system can therefore be replaced by this one:

$$\frac{r_t}{p_t} = \cdots = \frac{r_p}{p_t} = \cdots = \frac{r_k}{p_k} = \frac{r_{k'}}{p_{k'}} = \frac{r_{k'}}{p_{k''}} = \cdots$$

$$= \frac{r_a}{1} = \frac{r_b}{p_b} = \frac{r_c}{p_c} = \frac{r_d}{p_d} = \cdots$$

258. Now, initially making abstraction from the services of new capital goods used as productive services; that is to say, initially assuming that all those capital services are used as consumable services, let

$$D_k = \delta_{k,1} + \delta_{k,2} + \delta_{k,3} + \cdots$$

$$D_{k'} = \delta_{k',1} + \delta_{k',2} + \delta_{k',3} + \cdots$$

$$D_{k''} = \delta_{k'',1} + \delta_{k'',2} + \delta_{k'',3} + \cdots$$

$$\vdots$$

be quantities that are both the *quantities of capital services* (K), (K′), (K″), $\cdots$ *consumed* by exchangers (1), (2), (3), at prices $p_k, p_{k'}, p_{k''}, \cdots$ respectively of these capital services in terms of (A), and the *quantities produced of new capital goods* (K), (K′), (K″), $\cdots$ to be kept by their owners or borrowed by consumers. Further, let $P_k, P_{k'}, P_{k''}, \cdots$ be the prices of the capital goods, such that we have

$$D_k P_k + D_{k'} P_{k'} + D_{k''} P_{k''} + \cdots = E,$$

where E is the excess of total income over total consumption, to be distributed by the society among the l types of new capital goods.

Let, moreover,

$$u = \Phi_{k,1}(q), \quad u = \Phi_{k',1}(q), \quad u = \Phi_{k'',1}(q), \cdots$$

be the equations expressing the effective utilities of the capital services (K), (K′), (K″), $\cdots$ to trader (1) as functions of the *quantities consumed of these services* or of the *quantities produced of these capital goods*. The derivatives of these functions being strictly decreasing, there will be a maximum of effective utility, for our exchanger, when the differential increments of the quantities produced of each of the new capital goods are equal, since, if one assumes that any two of these increments are unequal, it will be advantageous to produce less of the capital good of which the differential increment is less and to produce more of the capital good the increment of which is greater. The condition of maximum utility of the new capital goods for exchanger (1) can therefore be expressed by the equation system

$$\Phi'_k\left(\delta k_{k,1}\right) d\delta_{k,1} = \Phi'_{k'}\left(\delta_{k',1}\right) d\delta_{k',1} = \Phi'_{k''}\left(\delta_{k'',1}\right) d\delta_{k'',1} = \cdots$$

Now, on the one hand, the derivatives of the effective utility functions with respect to the quantities produced of each of the new capital goods, which are also the derivatives of these function with respect to the quantities of each of the capital services, are nothing other than the raretés, which are directly proportional to the prices $p_k, p_{k'}, p_{p'}, \cdots$ in accordance with the equations

$$\frac{r_{k,1}}{p_k} = \frac{r_{k',1}}{p_{k'}} = \frac{r_{k'',1}}{p_{k''}} = \cdots.$$

On the other hand, from the point of view that concerns us at present, namely of the problem of the allocation by a society of a certain excess of income over consumption among the diverse varieties of capital formation, the differentials of the quantities produced of the various capital goods are inversely proportional to the prices $P_k, P_{k'}, P_{k''}, \cdots$ of these capital goods in accordance with the equations

$$P_k d\delta_{k,1} = P_{k'} \delta_{k',1} d\delta_{k',1} = P_{k''} \partial \delta_{k'',1} = \cdots$$

We can therefore replace the system above by the following

$$\frac{p_k}{P_k} = \frac{p_{k'}}{P_{k'}} = \frac{p_{k''}}{P_{k''}} = \cdots,$$

which expresses also the condition of maximum effective utility of the new capital goods for the exchangers (2), (3), $\cdots$.

This demonstration does not say anything about the duration of the enjoyment of the service, and does not need to say anything about it. According to whether the duration is a year, a month, or a day, the ratio $\dfrac{p}{P}$ will be the annual, monthly, or daily rate of net income. We have always considered up to this point that the rate is an annual one.

The demonstration also does not take into account the depreciation and insurance of the capital goods; in other words, it assumes that these capital goods are indestructible and imperishable, or that their depreciation and insurance are paid for voluntarily by the owners at their own expense. If we wished now to introduce the condition that the depreciation and insurance are paid for by the consumers of the services, we must, while leaving the maximum satisfaction to be established by the proportionality of the raretés of the capital good services to their prices, add to the average cost of each capital-good unit the sum necessary to provide, at the rate of net income for the capital good, the amount of the depreciation and insurance. If this were the case, then, instead of being inversely proportional to the prices $P_k, P_{k'}, P_{k''}, \cdots$, in accordance with the equations

$$P_k d\delta_{k,1} = P_{k'} d\delta_{k',1} = P_{k''} d\delta_{k'',1} = \cdots,$$

the differentials of the quantities produced of the diverse capital goods would be inversely proportional to the sums

$$P_k + \frac{\mu_k + v_k}{i_k}, \quad P_{k'} + \frac{\mu_{k'} + v_{k'}}{i_{k'}}, \quad P_{k''} + \frac{\mu_{k''} + v_{k''}}{i_{k''}},$$

hence to the products

$$\frac{p_k}{\pi_k} P_k, \quad \frac{p_{k'}}{\pi_{k'}} P_{k'}, \quad \frac{p_{k''}}{\pi_{k''}} P_{k''}, \cdots$$

in accordance with the equations

$$\frac{p_k}{\pi_k} P_k d_{k,1} = \frac{p_{k'}}{\pi_{k'}} P_{k'} d_{k'1} = \frac{p_{k''}}{\pi_{k''}} P_{k''} d_{k'',1} = \cdots,$$

which would yield, finally, as the condition for the maximum utility of new capital goods

$$\frac{\pi_k}{P_k} = \frac{\pi_{k'}}{P_{k'}} = \frac{\pi_{k''}}{P_{k''}} = \cdots$$

259. In the preceding section, we have assumed that the new capital goods were destined to generate consumable capital services. Now we must assume that the new capital goods are destined to generate productive services; that is to say, services that are not directly consumed, but are used in the production of products, and see, in this case, what the condition for a maximum is.

Therefore, finally, let

$$\Delta_a = \delta_{a,1} + \delta_{a,2} + \delta_{a,3} + \cdots$$

$$\Delta_b = \delta_{b,1} + \delta_{b,2} + \delta_{b,3} + \cdots$$

$$\Delta_c = \delta_{c,1} + \delta_{c,2} + \delta_{c,3} + \cdots$$

$$\Delta_d = \delta_{d,1} + \delta_{d,2} + \delta_{d,3} + \cdots$$

$$\vdots$$

be the quantities of products (A), (B), (C), (D), $\cdots$ consumed respectively by the exchangers (1), (2), (3), $\cdots$ at prices $p_b, p_c, p_d, \cdots$ of (B), (C), (D), $\cdots$ in terms of (A). Let, as before, $a_t, \cdots, a_p, \cdots, a_k, a_{k'}, a_{k''}, \cdots,$ $b_t, \cdots, b_p, \cdots, b_k, b_{k'}, b_{k''}, \cdots,$ $c_t, \cdots, c_p, \cdots, c_k, c_{k'}, c_{k''}, \cdots,$ $d_t, \cdots, d_p, \cdots, d_k,$ $d_{k'}, d_{k''}, \cdots$ be the coefficients of production; that is to say, the respective quantities of (T), (P), (K), (K'), (K''), $\cdots$ used in the production of each of the products (A), (B), (C), (D), $\cdots$, and therefore let

$$D_k = a_k \Delta_a + b_k \Delta_b + c_k \Delta_c + d_k \Delta_d + \cdots$$

$$D_{k'} = a_{k'} \Delta_a + b_{k'} \Delta_b + c_{k'} \Delta_c + d_{k'} \Delta_d + \cdots$$

$$D_{k''} = a_{k''} \Delta_a + b_{k''} \Delta_b + c_{k''} \Delta_c + d_{k''} \Delta_d + \cdots$$

$$\vdots$$

be quantities that are both *quantities of capital services* (K), (K'), (K''), $\cdots$ *used*, respectively, for producing (A), (B), (C), (D), $\cdots$ and the *quantities of newly produced capital goods* (K), (K'), (K''), $\cdots$ to be borrowed by the producers. And let $P_k, P_{k'}, P_{k''}, \cdots$, as always, be the prices of these capital goods. Thus, we have

$$D_k P_k + D_{k'} P_{k'} + D_{k'} P_{k''} + \cdots = E,$$

E being as always the total excess of income over consumption to be distributed by the society among the l types of new capital.

Moreover, let

$$u = \Phi_{a,1}(q), \quad u = \Phi_{b,1}(q), \quad u = \Phi_{c,1}(q), \quad u = \Phi_{d,1}(q), \cdots$$

be the equations that express the effective utilities of the products (A), (B), (C), (D), $\cdots$ for exchanger (1) as functions of the quantities consumed of these products equal to the quotients of, on the one hand, the *quantities of capital services used*, or the quantities of capital goods produced, and, on the other hand, the coefficients of production. The derivatives of the functions Φ being essentially decreasing, there will be maximum effective utility of new capital goods for our exchanger when the sums of the individual differential increments with respect to the quantities produced of each of these new capital goods will be equal, since, if any two of these sums are assumed to be unequal, then it will be advantageous to produce less of the capital good of which the sum of the individual differential increments is less and produce more of the capital good for which this sum is greater. The only problem that arises here is that instead of the differential increments relating to the quantities of each of these new capital goods presenting themselves separately from each other, we find them mixed together in the sum of the differential increments of utility relating to the quantities of products consumed, from which we have to disentangle them.

The sum of the differential increments relating to the quantities consumed of the products is the following:

$$\Phi'_{a,1}\left(\delta_{a,1}\right)d\delta_{a,1} + \Phi'_{b,1}\left(\delta_{b,1}\right)d\delta_{b,1} + \Phi'_{c,1}\left(\delta_{c,1}\right)d\delta_{c,1} +$$
$$\Phi'_{d,1}\left(\delta_{d,1}\right)d\delta_{d,1} + \cdots$$

Now, on the one hand, the derivatives of the utility functions with respect to the quantities consumed are nothing other than the raretés, which are directly proportional to prices $1, p_b, p_c, p_d, \cdots$ of the products in accordance with the equations

$$\frac{r_{a,1}}{1} = \frac{r_{b,1}}{p_b} = \frac{r_{c,1}}{p_c} = \frac{r_{d,1}}{p_d} = \cdots,$$

and these prices of the products are equal to their average costs in accordance with the equations

$$1 = a_t p_t + \cdots + a_p p_p + \cdots + a_k p_k + a_{k'} p_{k'} + a_{k''} p_{k''} + \cdots$$

$$p_b = b_t p_t + \cdots + b_p p_p + \cdots + b_k p_k + b_{k'} p_{k'} + b_{k''} p_{k''} + \cdots$$

$$p_c = c_t p_t + \cdots + c_p p_p + \cdots + c_k p_k + c_{k'} p_{k'} + c_{k''} p_{k''} + \cdots$$

$$p_d = d_t p_t + \cdots + d_p p_p + \cdots + d_k p_k + d_{k'} p_{k'} + d_{k''} p_{k''} + \cdots$$

$$\vdots$$

from which follows that all these derivatives can be decomposed into parts that are directly proportional to the expenses of production in rent, wages, and interest, and, in particular, into the coefficients of production multiplied by the prices of the capital services $p_k, p_{k'}, p_{k''}, \cdots$ And, on the other hand, differentials of the quantities of products consumed can be replaced by the quotients of the differentials of the quantities of capital services used up in the production of these products (which, here, are also the differentials of the quantities produced of each of the new capital goods) divided by the coefficients of production, in accordance with the equations

$$d\delta_{a,1} = \frac{d\delta_{k,1,a}}{a_k} = \frac{d\delta_{k',1,a}}{a_{k'}} = \frac{d\delta_{k'',1,a}}{a_{k''}} = \cdots$$

$$d\delta_{b,1} = \frac{d\delta_{k,1,b}}{b_k} = \frac{d\delta_{k',1,b}}{b_{k'}} = \frac{d\delta_{k'',1,b}}{b_{k''}} = \cdots$$

$$d\delta_{c,1} = \frac{d\delta_{k,1,c}}{c_k} = \frac{d\delta_{k'1,c}}{c_{k'}} = \frac{d\delta_{k'',1,c}}{c_{k''}} = \cdots$$

$$d\delta_{d,1} = \frac{d\delta_{k,1,d}}{d_k} = \frac{d\delta_{k',1,d}}{d_{k'}} = \frac{d\delta_{k'',1,d}}{d_{k''}} = \cdots$$

$$\vdots$$

Moreover, from the point of view of the problem of the distribution by a society of a certain excess of income over consumption among the various capital goods, these differentials of the quantities produced of each of the new capital goods are equal for each capital good, in accordance with the equations

$$\delta_{k,1,a} = \delta_{k,1,b} = \delta_{k,1,c} = \delta_{k,1,d} = \cdots = \delta_{k,1}$$

$$\delta_{k',1,a} = \delta_{k',1,b} = \delta_{k',1,c} = \delta_{k',1,d} = \cdots = \delta_{k',1}$$

$$\delta_{k'',1,a} = \delta_{k'',1,b} = \delta_{k'',1,c} = \delta_{k'',1,d} = \cdots = \delta_{k'',1}$$

$$\vdots$$

and inversely proportional to the prices of the capital goods in accordance with the equations

$$P_k d\delta_{k,1} = P_{k'} d\delta_{k',1} = P_{k''} d\delta_{k'',1} = \cdots$$

from which it follows, from the point of view of the problem with which we are dealing, that the differentials of the quantities of products consumed are inversely proportional to the coefficients of production multiplied by the prices of capital goods $P_k, P_{k'}, P_{k''}, \cdots$

The differentials of individual effective utility with respect to the quantities produced of each of the new capital goods (K), (K'), (K''), $\cdots$ for individual (1) are therefore for each of the commodities (A), (B), (C), (D), $\cdots$ directly proportional to the products of the coefficients of production and the prices of the capital goods; and the condition for maximum utility of new capital goods for this individual can be expressed by the system of equations

$$\frac{a_k p_k}{a_k P_k} + \frac{b_k p_k}{b_k P_k} + \frac{c_k p_k}{c_k P_k} + \frac{d_k p_k}{d_k P_k} + \cdots =$$

$$\frac{a_{k'} p_{k'}}{a_{k'} P_{k'}} + \frac{b_{k'} p_{k'}}{b_{k'} P_{k'}} + \frac{c_{k'} p_{k'}}{c_{k'} P_{k'}} + \frac{d_{k'} p_{k'}}{d_{k'} P_{k'}} + \cdots =$$

$$\frac{a_{k'} p_{k'}}{a_{k'} P_{k'}} + \frac{b_{k'} p_{k'}}{b_{k'} P_k} + \frac{c_{k'} p_{k'}}{c_{k'} P_{k'}} + \frac{d_{k'} p_{k'}}{d_{k'} P_{k'}} + \cdots =$$

$$\vdots$$

which likewise express the condition of maximum effective utility of new capital goods for the exchangers (2), (3), ⋯

That being the case, the equality of the sums of the partial differential increments relating to the quantities produced of each new capital good that constitutes the condition of maximum effective utility of the services of the new capital goods, in the case in which they are destined to render productive capital services and not consumable services, can always be expressed by the system of equations

$$\frac{p_k}{P_k} = \frac{p_{k'}}{P_{k'}} = \frac{p_{k''}}{P_{k''}} = \cdots,$$

Hence, it is certain that: – *Whether the excess of income over consumption is transformed into capital goods rendering consumable services, or into capital goods rendering productive services, there will be maximum effective utility of the services of the new capital goods, for the society, when the ratio of the price of the capital service to the price of the capital good, or the rate of net income, is the same for all the capital goods.*

260. The system that we have introduced into our equations of capital formation and credit:

$$\frac{\pi_k}{P_k} = \frac{\pi_{k'}}{P_{k'}} = \frac{\pi_{k''}}{P_{k''}} = \cdots$$

differs from the preceding one by the substitution of net incomes for gross incomes. Consequently and, moreover, from our demonstration that free competition in matters of the creation of new capital constitutes the solution by tatonnement of the equations of capital formation and credit as we have posited them, it results that:

– *Capital formation in a market characterized by the regime of free competition is an operation by means of which the excess of income over consumption can be transformed into new capital goods properly speaking of a nature and in quantities such that they generate the greatest possible satisfaction of wants within the limits of the condition that all the capital goods in the market earn the same rate of net income; in other words, that the depreciation and insurance of the capital goods properly speaking are paid by the consumer of the capital services and not by the owner of the capital goods.*

Maximum effective utility on the one hand; singularity of price on the other, be it of the products in the market for products, be it of the services in the market for services, be it of the net incomes in the market for capital goods: such is in all cases the double condition in accordance with which the world of economic matters is organized, just as gravity being directly proportional to the mass and inversely proportional to the square of the distances is the double condition in accordance with which the world of astronomic movements automatically regulates itself. In both cases, a formula of two lines contains the whole science, and provides the explanation of a countless number of specific facts.

Furthermore, an important truth that economists have stated, but not proved, is finally established, in spite of the denials by socialists, namely that free competition is, under certain conditions and within certain limits, a self-activating and self-regulating mechanism of transformation of savings into capital properly speaking, as well as of transformation of services into products. And so, in matters of capital formation and credit as well as in matters of exchange and production, the conclusion of economic theory provides us the starting point for applied economics. In the one case as in the other, this conclusion moreover shows us clearly the task that social economics has to fulfill. Free competition in matters of exchange and production provides maximum utility of products and services subject to the reservation that there is only a single and unique exchange rate for all the services and all the products for all the exchangers. Free competition in capital formation and credit provides the maximum utility of new capital goods subject to the reservation that there is only a single and same ratio of net interest to capital for all the creators of savings. Are these reservations just? That is for the moral theory of the distribution of social wealth to say: and, only after having done so, the economic theory of the production of social wealth will be able to pursue boldly in detail the application of the principle of free competition in agriculture, industry, commerce, banking, and speculation.

261. The quantities $D_k, D_{k'}, D_{k''}, \cdots$ to be produced of the new capital goods (K), (K'), (K''), $\cdots$ being determined exactly in this way by the system of equations

$$\frac{\pi_k}{P_k} = \frac{\pi_{k'}}{P_{k'}} = \frac{\pi_{k''}}{P_{k''}} = \cdots,$$

the rate of net income is exactly determined by the equation

$$i = \frac{D_k \pi_k + D_{k'} \pi_{k'} + D_{k''} \pi_{k''} + \cdots}{E}$$

If we then abstract from the fact that the excess of income over consumption, *E*, is itself a function of the rate of net income, *i*, and if we assume it to be given by the nature of things, we can state the very simple law of the establishment and the variation of the rate of net income:

– *The rate of net income is equal to the ratio of the total net income of new capital goods to the total excess of income over consumption.*

If, all other things remaining unchanged, the net income of one or several types of capital goods increases or decreases, the rate of net income increases or decreases.

If the excess of income over consumption increases or decreases, the rate of net income decreases or increases.

LESSON 27

Laws of the determination and variation of the prices of capital goods. The permanent market

SUMMARY: – Equations of the prices of existing movable capital, of land, and of personal faculties. Law of the establishment and the variation of these capital goods. These prices are nominal prices. Reasons for the purchase and sale of capital goods: *speculations* on new capital goods and on existing capital goods. The *Bourse.* Bidding up or lowering of the price there will always decrease or increase demand and increase or decrease supply.

Mathematical expression for circulating capital: *consumption working capital*; *production working capital.* Division of the excess of income over consumption into fixed capital and circulating capital. Periodically annual market: $T = 80$ billion, $P = 50$ billion, $K = 60$ billion; $t = 2$ billion, $p = 5$ billion, $k = 3$ billion; $C = 40$ billion, $C' = 20$ billion. Circulating capital as a proportion of the annual production. Consumption and reproduction of circulating capital. The permanent market; oscillations toward equilibrium; *crises.*

262. The rate of net income and the prices of new capital goods having been determined, it remains to determine the prices of the existing capital goods: landed, personal, and movable.

The prices of existing movable capital goods are equal to those of new movable capital goods and are established in a capital market in accordance with the equations [8]

$$ P_k = \frac{p_k}{i + \mu_k + \nu_k}, \quad P_{k'} = \frac{p_{k'}}{i + \mu_{k'} + \nu_{k'}}, \quad P_{k''} = \frac{p_{k''}}{i + \mu_{k''} + \nu_{k''}}, \cdots $$

The prices of land and of personal faculties are established, in the same market: the prices of land in accordance with the equations

$$P_t = \frac{p_t}{i}, \quad P_{t'} = \frac{p_{t'}}{i}, \quad P_{t''} = \frac{p_{t''}}{i}, \cdots$$

and those of personal faculties in accordance with the equations

$$P_p = \frac{p_p}{i + \mu_p + v_p}, \quad P_{p'} = \frac{p_{p'}}{i + \mu_{p'} + v_{p'}}, \quad P_{p''} = \frac{p_{p''}}{i + \mu_{p''} + v_{p''}}, \cdots$$

Now, from the simple inspection of these three systems of equations, we easily derive the following laws of the establishment and variation of the prices of capital goods:

– *The equilibrium prices of the capital goods in terms of the numeraire in the market of these capital goods are equal to the ratios of the prices of net income to the rate of net income.*

If, all other things remaining unchanged, the price of the gross income of a capital good increases or decreases, the price of the capital good increases or decreases.

If the rate of depreciation or the insurance premium increases or decreases, the price of the capital good decreases or increases.

If, all other things remaining unchanged, the rate of net income increases or decreases, the prices of all capital goods decrease or increase.

263. It is essential, however, to note that the prices thus obtained are, in a way, nominal prices; that is to say, established without exchange occurring. If in the market for products the equilibrium price is established, the exchange of these products takes place immediately; in the market for capital goods, on the contrary, exchange does not necessarily take place under the rational and ideal conditions we have introduced. Undoubtedly, prices in terms of numeraire have been determined; but, looking more closely to the matter, we see that these prices come down, at last, to a single price, namely the price of a unit of net income in terms of numeraire. If the rate of net income i is equal, for instance, to 3/100, 2.5/100, 2/100, $\cdots$, the price in numeraire of a capital good having a net income equal to 1 will be $1/i$, equal to 33.33, 40, 50, $\cdots$ However, given all this, what

motivation is there to exchange net income for net income, to sell, for example, a house that yields a net rent of 2,500 francs at a price of 100,000 francs, in order to purchase at the price of 100,000 francs a piece of land yielding 2,500 francs of rent? This exchange of capital goods for each other makes no more sense than the exchange of a commodity for the same commodity. For these sales and purchases to take place in a capital goods market, we must borrow from reality and experience some essential circumstances. So, we must take into consideration that, in addition to the people who have an excess of their income over their consumption, and who are able to buy capital goods, there are, as we have already said (§ 236), people who have an excess of their consumption over their income, and have to sell capital goods. We must also bear in mind that the net income of new capital goods is not as well known as that of existing capital goods, that it may be greater or smaller, that it is, in a word, more uncertain. From this it results that the creators of savings, who are in general prudent and circumspect, do not hand over their savings in exchange for new capital goods but rather in exchange for existing capital goods; and then it is the owners of these existing capital goods who, with the proceeds, invest in new capital goods. In our course in applied economics we will have to study especially the role of these *speculators*, who intervene in this way to *evaluate* new capital goods. Further, it should be observed that the price of capital goods not only varies because of unexpected changes, but also because of expected changes in either gross income, or in the depreciation rate or insurance premium, and that, concerning the expected changes especially, the evaluations differ from individual to individual. Hence, many people sell capital goods whose net income they fear, rightly or wrongly, will decrease, to buy other capital goods that they expect, rightly or wrongly, to have an increase in net income. That is another type of speculation that we will have to study together with the type we mentioned above. Moreover, the exchange of new or existing capital, once decided, will take place in accordance with the mechanism of free competition and the law of supply and demand.

264. Of the three equation systems of the capital market, there is one that has a particular importance: the one relating to movable capital goods. Indeed, the identical character of the gross and net income

of land eliminates a two-fold cause of variation in their price: that of changes of the rate of depreciation and that of changes of insurance premiums. Regarding personal faculties, they are not sold or bought because slavery is not allowed. There remain, therefore, capital goods properly speaking, whose gross income is generally far from unchanging, and for which the depreciation rates and insurance premiums are as changeable as are the factors on which they depend: the chances of deterioration due to usage and of accidental demolishment; the price of those capital goods is, consequently, very changeable, and they are daily sold and bought for the sake of speculation. Thus, just as there is reason, in the market for services, to distinguish the market for hiring capital properly speaking from the markets for hiring land and personal faculties, there is reason, regarding the capital goods market, to distinguish the market for movable capital goods from the market for landed capital and for personal capital. This market for movable capital is the *Bourse*, which we visited at the beginning of this course in economic theory, to look there for the description of the mechanism of free competition in exchange (§ 42), and that we subsequently neglected until the present after having successively taken account of all the complications of exchange, production, capital formation, and credit. We have, in the equation system [8], the means of discussing all the price variations that can occur in it. If capital good (K) is a railway, and p_k is a sum to be received annually as dividend, the price P_k of the shares of this railway company in terms of numeraire will change with the variations, unexpected or not, in this dividend. If the capital good (K') is a capital good lent to a factory or to the state, and $v_{k'}$ is a premium corresponding with the risk of collapse of the factory or the nation, the price $P_{k'}$ of the obligations of the factory or the state will change with the variations, unexpected or not, in these risks. Moreover, these price variations will often be purely nominal or, at least, will occur almost without transferring securities.

265. If the price P_k is increased indefinitely, it tends to become progressively greater than the ratio of its net income to the rate of net income; and, consequently, the demand for capital good (K) is decreased indefinitely. At the same time, the supply of the same capital good is increased indefinitely, because its owners, by exchanging

it for other capital goods, will be able to procure for themselves a growing income. The reverse results would occur in the case of indefinite decreases of the price of capital good (K). That is how, in the Bourse, bidding up or lowering the price will always decrease or increase the demand and increase or decrease the supply, which does not take place, as we have seen (§§ 48, 59, 97, 126, 211), in the markets of products and services.

266. We remember that we have made abstraction from the elements of production identified under the headings 7, 8, 9, 10, 11, 12, 13 (§ 175). It is not, for us, of pressing interest to find out how the respective quantities of capital goods, income, and money included under these varied headings are determined, and without any inconvenience, we can consider them as resulting, in a certain economic situation, from the nature of the things; that is to say, from the very conditions of production and consumption, except that we will return later to this subject in a special part on money. But, after this simplification, it is worthwhile to notice the effects of the creation of a greater or lesser fund of working capital in either consumption or production.

We still assume a market for exchange and production in which certain productive services are transformed into products, fixed capital, and, finally, into circulating capital. With respect to the latter, let $d_a, d_b, d_c, d_d, \cdots$ be the quantities of (A), (B), (C), (D), $\cdots$ in the hands of consumers destined for consumption; let d'_a, d''_a be the quantities of (A) in the hands of the consumers constituting circulating money and savings; let $p_b, p_c, p_d, \cdots$ be the prices of (B), (C), (D), $\cdots$ in terms of (A). There will then be a *fund of working capital for consumption*

$$c = d_a + d'_a + d''_a + d_b p_b + d_c p_c + d_d p_d + \cdots.$$

Furthermore, let $\delta_k, \delta_{k'}, \delta_{k''}, \cdots, \delta_a, \delta_b, \delta_c, \delta_d, \cdots, \delta_m, \delta_{m'}, \delta_{m''}, \cdots, \delta'_m,$ $\delta'_{m'}, \delta'_{m'}, \cdots$ be the quantities of (K), (K'), (K''), $\cdots$, (A), (B), (C), (D), $\cdots$ and (M), (M'), (M''), $\cdots$ as new capital goods and income and as stocks of raw materials in the hands of the entrepreneurs; let δ'_a be their quantity of (A) held as circulating money; and let $P_k, P_{k'}, P_{k''}, \cdots, p_m, p_{m'}, p_{m''}, \cdots$ be the prices of (K), (K'), (K''), $\cdots$ and (M), (M'), (M''), $\cdots$ in terms of (A). There will then be a *fund of working capital for production*

$$\kappa = \delta_k P_k + \delta_{k'} P_{k'} + \delta_{k''} P_{k''} +$$

$$+\delta_a + \delta_a' + \delta_b p_b + \delta_c p_c + \delta_d p_d +$$

$$+\left(\delta_m + \delta_m'\right) p_m + \left(\delta_{m'} + \delta_{m'}'\right) p_{m'} + \left(\delta_{m''} + \delta_{m''}'\right) p_{m''} + \cdots$$

The totality of these two funds of working capital, $c + \kappa$, will form the society's circulating capital C'. Moreover, if $Q_k, Q_{k'}, Q_{k''}, \cdots$ are the quantities of (K), (K′), (K″), capital goods properly speaking in the hands of the consumers or the producers destined to render consumption or productive services, there will be fixed capital valued at

$$C = Q_k P_k + Q_{k'} P_{k'} + Q_{k''} P_{k''} + \cdots$$

and the totality of circulating capital and this fixed capital, $C' + C$, will form the total capital K of the society that, theoretically, can be considered as being lent and borrowed in the market for numeraire capital at the interest rate i equal to the rate of net income (§ 256).

267. We do not introduce the quantities d_a, d_a', d_a'', δ_a, δ_a', $d_b, \delta_b, d_c, \delta_c, d_d, \delta_d, \cdots, \delta_k$, $\delta_{k'}, \delta_{k'}, \cdots$ in the equations of production and capital formation in addition to the quantities $D_a, D_b, D_c, D_d, \cdots, D_k, D_{k'}, D_{k''}, \cdots$ to which they are added, all the more so as there is nothing more simple and easy than to assume the former magnitudes are included in the latter. It will be sufficient for us to observe that it follows quite obviously from the equations of production and capital formation that any increase of the quantities $D_a, D_b, D_c, D_d, \cdots$ with a view to the creation of circulating capital will require a decrease of the quantities $D_k, D_{k'}, D_{k''}, \cdots$ because of the reduction of fixed capital, and that, conversely, each reduction of the quantity of circulating capital will permit an increase in the quantity of fixed capital.

268. Having said all that, and having restored all the accessory phenomena from which we abstracted, we pass from the hypothesis of a market that is held continuously, to that of a market that is held periodically, we could say once per day, we will say rather once per year to take better account of the renewal of the seasons. And, to make the

general system of economic phenomena completely understandable, we pass at the same time from abstract figures to concrete figures.

Assume that there is a country with about 25 to 30 million inhabitants that has land with a total value of $T = 80$ billion, persons valued at $P = 50$ billion, and fixed and circulating capital; that is to say, capital goods properly speaking and incomes having a total value of $K = 60$ billion. The rate of net income is $i = 2.5/100$; the land yields an annual rent of 2 billion; the persons earn a gross personal income of 5 billion, of which 1,250 million is net income and 3 750 million is depreciation and insurance premiums that they spend on the subsistence, the upbringing, and the instruction of their families (§ 233); the capital goods properly speaking yield a gross income of $k = 3$ billons, of which 1,500 million is net income and 1,500 million is depreciation and insurance premiums, used by the capitalists to buy new capital goods properly speaking, in addition to the new capital goods properly speaking that could be bought by these same capitalists or by landowners and workers by means of their savings properly speaking.

Assume that 32 billion of landed capital render consumable services, and 48 billion render productive services; that 14 billion of personal capital render consumable services, and 36 billion render productive services; that total capital is divided into 40 billion of fixed capital and 20 billion of circulating capital; that 12 billion of the fixed capital render consumable services, and 28 billion render productive services; that 4 billion of circulating capital is in the hands of the consumers, namely 2 billion of stocks of consumable products and 2 billion in the form of circulating money and savings, and that 16 billion are in the hands of the entrepreneurs, namely 4 billion as new capital, 4 billion as stocks of raw materials, 6 billion as new income goods, and 2 billion as circulating money. We thus readily encounter our 13 headings of the elements of production (§ 174).

269. It is quite understandable that there is a certain ratio between the figure for circulating capital and the figures for annual production and consumption. It may be that for an annual production and consumption of 10 billion there has to be 100 billion worth of business, that is, of transactions: the entrepreneurs do not only sell to consumers, they sell raw materials and commodities at wholesale to

each other. Now, to do a certain amount of business, each entrepreneur needs some working capital. The ratio of the fund of working capital to the total amount of business differs, however, for each type of production. There are certain agricultural products, like wine, the production of which takes a whole year: for these goods, the fund of working capital must be equal to the total annual turnover. There are certain commercial products, like fruits and vegetables, that are bought wholesale in the morning and sold at retail during the day: for these products, the fund of working capital is only one three hundredth of the total turnover. We have to use an average. Assuming a turnover of 100 billion and an amount of circulating capital of 20 billion means that we have assumed an average period of production of one fifth of a year.

270. We must properly understand that the total sum $T + P + K$ = 190 billion represents without exception all the social wealth of the country, in capital and income, and that the symbols t, p, k represent nothing other than the proportions in which the land, the personal faculties, and the fixed and circulating capital contribute to production, and also in which the landowners, the workers, and the capitalists share in the consumption of the annual income $t + p + k$ = 10 billion. This annual income of 10 billion consists of 3 billion of land services, personal capital, and 'profits' that are directly consumed either by the owners of the landed capital, personal faculties, and movable capital, or by the purchasers of the land services, labor, and 'profits', be they either private persons or the state; the other 7 billion of annual income consists of land services, labor, and capital good services to be transformed into products by agriculture, industry, or commerce. We may assume, if we wish, that of the 10 billion of annual income, 8 billion of are consumed and 2 billion are capitalized, of which 1,500 million are used for depreciation and insurance of existing capital goods properly speaking, and 500 million for the creation of new capital goods properly speaking.

271. Finally, in order to approach closer and closer to the reality of things, we must still pass from the hypothesis of a periodic annual market to the hypothesis of a permanent market. For this, we imagine

now that both the yearly production and the yearly consumption to which we have given numbers above are spread over all the days of the year. The 2 billion of stocks of consumable products, the 4 billion of new capital goods, the 4 billion of stocks of raw materials, and the 6 billion of new income are thus like as many stems that are incessantly cut at their ends. At each hour, each minute, a fraction of these varied components of the fund of working capital disappears and reappears. Personal capital, capital goods properly speaking, and money likewise disappear and reappear, but much less rapidly. Only landed capital escapes from this renewal. This is the permanent market, always tending to equilibrium without ever arriving there, because it can only move there by means of tatonnements, and before the tatonnements are finished they start anew, on a new basis, all the data of the problem, such as the quantities possessed, the utilities of the products and services, the coefficients of production, the excess of income over consumption, the fund of working capital required, etc., having changed. In this respect, the market is like a lake agitated by the wind; the water is always seeking its equilibrium without ever attaining it. There are, however, days when the surface of the lake is nearly horizontal; but there are none in which the effective supply of services and products equals their effective demand and the prices of the products are equal to their average costs in terms of productive services. The diversion of productive services from enterprises where losses are incurred toward enterprises that make profits takes places in many ways, of which the use of credit is a principal one, but, in all cases, in slow ways. It may happen, and in reality it does frequently, that sometimes the price continually remains above the average cost and that the increase of production cannot stop the price increase, and that sometimes a fall of the price, following upon that rise, suddenly changes the average cost from being below to being above the level of the price, and forces the entrepreneurs to reverse their course. For example, just as the lake is sometimes profoundly agitated by the storm, so also is the market sometimes violently perturbed by *crises*, which are sudden and general disturbances of equilibrium. We will study these crises, and we will see that we would be better able to suppress or prevent them if we had a better understanding of the conditions of the ideal equilibrium of exchange and production.

LESSON 28

Increase of the quantity of products. Laws of the general variation of prices in a progressive society

SUMMARY: – The possibility of a decrease in the coefficients of the use of land services due to an increase of the coefficients of the use of capital good services allows for indefinite progress; that is to say, the indefinite decrease of the raretés for an indefinitely growing population. Production function: *technical* progress because of a change of the nature of this function; *economic* progress because of a change of the value of the variables in this function. Condition for progress: increase in the amount of capital goods properly speaking that precedes and exceeds the increase in the numbers of persons. Malthus's theory of population and subsistence.

The prices of the products do not vary. Hypothesis of a society where the quantity of land has not changed, but the number of persons has doubled, and in which the amount of capital goods properly speaking has at least doubled. The disturbed equilibrium will be reestablished by an increase in rent and a decrease in interest. The rate of net income decreases. Consequently, the prices of capital goods do not change; those of personal faculties and of land increase.

272. It is hardly necessary to say that the principle of the proportionality of the values of products and services to their raretés, in a state of general equilibrium of the market (§ 220), and the law of variations in the equilibrium prices, because of variations in the raretés due to either variations in the utilities or in the quantities possessed (§ 223), remain completely valid after as well as before the solution of the equations of capital formation. But, on the other hand, the fact, which we observed when stating these equations (§§ 232–4), that the

quantity of land does not increase along with the possible increase in the number of persons and the amount of capital goods properly speaking, in a society that saves and creates capital, has extremely important consequences that we still have to formulate in laws that are among the most important ones for the completion of the theory of the establishment of prices in terms of numeraire. The *laws* are those *of the variation of prices in a progressive economy.*

273. We have included among the data and not among the unknowns of the problem the coefficients of production $a_t, b_t, c_t, d_t, \cdots,$ $k_t, k_t', k_t'', \cdots$ $a_p, b_p, c_p, d_p, \cdots, k_p, k_p', k_p'' \cdots,$ $a_k, b_k, c_k, d_k, \cdots, k_k, k_k', k_k'', \cdots,$ $a_{k'}, b_{k'}, c_{k'}, d_{k'}, \cdots, k_{k'}, k_{k'}', k_{k'}'', \cdots$ $a_{k''}, b_{k''}, c_{k''}, d_{k''}, \cdots,$ $k_{k''}, k_{k''}', k_{k''}'', \cdots$ or the respective quantities of each of the productive services (T), (P), (K), $\cdots$ (K'), (K''), $\cdots$ that are used in the manufacture of each of the products (A), (B), (C), (D), $\cdots$ and of each of the new capital goods properly speaking (K), (K'), (K''), $\cdots$ We have explained (§ 200) why we allowed ourselves to consider for the time being these quantities as determined a priori, all the while stating that they are not. Indeed, they are not, neither with respect to their value nor with respect to their nature. This circumstance is decisive; it has far-reaching consequences.

If we always needed fixed quantities of land services of type (T) for manufacturing one unit of (A), of (B), of (C), of (D), $\cdots$ of (K), of (K'), of (K''), $\cdots$ the multiplication[i] of these products and these new capital goods would be limited in an absolute sense by the existing quantity Q_t of land of this type. If, for example, 1/10 of the annual services of a hectare of land were always needed for the production of one hectoliter of wheat, or, to put it otherwise, if a hectare of land could never produce more than 10 hectoliters per year, the multiplication of wheat would be limited in an absolute sense by the existing quantity of land suitable for the cultivation of wheat. However, everybody knows that the situation is different. Due to the substitution of the system of letting land lie fallow in place of the system of crop rotation, due to the use of fertilizers like guano, of machines that work deeper into the ground or work more efficiently, of seeding machines, a hectare of land can produce annually a greater and greater number of hectoliters of wheat. Furthermore, ordinarily, in manufacturing products and new capital goods, we can use smaller and smaller quantities of land services, provided that greater and greater quantities of the services of capital goods properly speaking are used. Therefore, indefinite progress is possible.

Progress cannot consist in anything other than the decrease in the raretés or the intensities of the last wants satisfied by the products in a growing population. Hence, whether progress is possible or not depends on whether multiplication of the products is possible or not. If multiplication of products is possible only within certain limits, progress would be possible only within certain limits. The raretés could not decrease below a certain point, the population remaining constant; or the population could not grow above a certain point, the raretés remaining constant, or the raretés could not decrease below a certain point, the population itself growing up to a certain point. If the multiplication of the products is indefinitely possible, indefinite progress is possible. Now, indefinite multiplication of the products is possible because of the possibility of more and more, but never total, substitution in production of capital good 'profits'[ii] in place of land services. Two cases have to be distinguished. The case in which only the coefficients of production of land services diminish, and in which there is an increase in those of the use of 'profits'. We call this *economic* progress. And there is the case in which the very nature of these coefficients of production changes because of the use of different productive services and the abandonment of certain others. We call this *technical* progress. But since this distinction is essential, it will be good to clarify it mathematically.

274. Assume there is a commodity (B) the production of one unit of which requires respectively the quantities $b_t, b_p, b_k, \cdots$ of the productive services (T), (P), (K), $\cdots$; its average cost is therefore

$$p_b = b_t p_t + b_p p_p + b_k p_k + \cdots$$

To say, as we have done, that in manufacturing a product we can use more or less of such and such productive services, more or less land services, for example, under the condition of using less or more of such and such other productive services, less or more 'profits' or labor, for instance, is the same as saying that the coefficients of production $b_t, b_p, b_k, \cdots$ are variables connected with each other by an equation

$$\varphi\left(b_t, b_p, b_k, \cdots\right) = 0 \text{ iii}$$

such that when one of the coefficients, b_t, is decreasing, one of the other coefficients, $b_p, b_k, \cdots$, is increasing. And to say, as we have also done, that the respective quantities of each of the productive services that are used in the manufacture of a unit of any of the products are determined only after the determination of the prices of the productive services, by the condition that the average cost be a minimum, is the same as saying, the implicit function above being solved successively for each of its variables or expressed successively in its explicit forms

$$b_t = \vartheta\left(b_p, b_k, \cdots\right), \quad b_p = \psi\left(b_k, b_k, \cdots\right), \quad b_k = \chi\left(b_t, b_p, \cdots\right),$$

that the unknown variables $b_t, b_p, b_k, \cdots$ are determined by the condition that

$$p_b = \vartheta\left(b_p, b_k, \cdots\right)p_t + \psi\left(b_k, b_k, \cdots\right)p_p + \chi\left(b_t, b_p, \cdots\right)p_k + \cdots$$

be minimized. It is this condition that we said, finally, would be easy to represent by a system of as many equations as there are unknowns to be determined. We will not furnish here this expression any more than we did in the theory of production; indeed, we will only state that from now onwards when the production function changes, we always have a case of technical progress brought about by science, and that when, without any change in the production function, the coefficients of the use of land services are decreasing and those of the use of 'profits' are increasing, we always have a case of economic progress brought about by saving. In reality, those two forms of progress occur together; it can happen that the production function changes and that, simultaneously, the coefficients of production of land services decrease and those of capital good services increase. But here we abstract from technical progress and consider only economic progress; that is to say, assuming the production function to be determined, we will study the conditions of decreasing the coefficients of production of land services by means of increasing those of the use of 'profits'.

275. That condition is evident. The quantity of land does not increase in the progressive state; and precisely for that reason it is a question of obtaining more products with the same, or more or less the same, total quantity of land services. Since population growth is assumed by the very definition of progress, the number of persons increases; hence, it is certain that there is a supplement of labor that is by its nature proportional to the supplement of products to be obtained. So, what remains to be desired? That the amount of capital goods increases to such a degree that the necessary supplement of 'profits' will be furnished. Under the assumption of pure and simple economic progress, this supplement would be quite substantial: indeed it would not be sufficient for it to be proportional to the supplement of products to be obtained; it must also compensate for the absence of a proportional supplement of land services, and, moreover, it must also permit a supplement of products more than proportional to the population growth to be obtained, because of the decrease of the raretés. Furthermore, it is obvious that the capital goods must be created by savings before their services can be used. Consequently: – *Progress consisting in the decrease in the raretés of the products[iv] with the increase in the number of persons is, in spite of the fact that the quantity of land does not increase, possible due to the increase in the amount of capital goods properly speaking, subject to the essential condition that the increase in the amount of capital goods properly speaking precedes and exceeds the increase in the number of persons.* We have good reason to present here the controversial theory of Malthus on population and subsistence.

276. As we know, this theory is contained in its entirety in the following passages of Malthus's book:[1,v]

It may safely be pronounced, therefore, that population, when unchecked, goes on doubling itself every twenty-five years, or increases in a geometrical ratio.

It may be fairly pronounced, therefore, that, considering the present average state of the earth, the means of subsistence, under circumstances the most favorable to human industry, could not possibly be made to increase faster than in an arithmetical ratio.

---

[1] [Thomas] Malthus, *An Essay on the Principle of Population*, Book I, Chapter I.

[Taking the whole earth, instead of this island, emigration would of course be excluded; and, supposing the present population equal to a thousand millions,] the human species would increase as the numbers, 1, 2, 4, 8, 16, 32, 64, 128, 256, and subsistence as 1, 2, 3, 4, 5, 6, 7, 8, 9. In two centuries the population would be to the means of subsistence as 256 to 9; in three centuries as 4096 to 13, and in two thousand years the difference would be almost incalculable.

The first of these two propositions is not absolutely rigorous. It is obvious that, from one generation to the other, population growth tends to take place, abstraction made from the means of subsistence, or takes place, where the means are not lacking, according to a geometric series, the ratio of which is equal to half the number of a woman's children that survive her. Malthus assumes this number to be equal to four, the population doubling from generation to generation. This is an estimate that is less than rather than greater than is true in reality, because mankind does not escape the law, well known nowadays, according to which all sorts of plants and animals tend to perpetuate themselves by a rapid and considerable multiplication. The consequences deduced by Darwin from this fact are contested, but the fact itself is not.

The second quotation is far from having the same validity. Malthus made no distinction between technical and economic progress. But he seems to be equally speculative in asserting that the increase in the quantity of means of subsistence resulting, on the one hand, from the discovery of wheat or of potatoes, from the invention of machines, or from the improvement of credit, or, on the other hand, from the increase resulting from the growth of capital, takes place according to an arithmetic sequence with a difference equal to one. Such kinds of assertions are not based on reason or experience, and it is infinitely better to restrict oneself to saying that the increase in the amount of subsistence resulting both from technical progress and from economic progress takes place according to a less rapid progression than that of population growth.

277. A society in which nearly all the land is cultivated, and where it is only possible to produce some landed capital artificially by spreading fertile earth over rocks, fertilizing moors, or draining swamps (§ 170) is therefore, and after all, like the situation of an individual

who has a certain income and who consumes a certain part of it. If this individual keeps his consumption below his income, and capitalizes the excess, he increases his income more and more and can increase his consumption more and more; but if he raises his consumption all at once above his income, he goes headlong to his ruination. Likewise, if a society first develops its capital, its population can later grow indefinitely; but otherwise, it will fall straightaway into misery and starvation. And the latter will be the case as long as the labor of personal faculties is not the only productive factor in agriculture and industry, and as long as more 'profits' must be used in order to use less land services. We do not start out with that proposition, as will be seen later, in order to go along with Malthus as far as maintaining the thesis that social reforms are hardly of importance; but neither can we deny him the credit of having made apparent a very important proposition in economic theory. The late Jules Duval exclaimed one day, sitting beside me at the Economics Society of Paris: 'How is that? You are delighted when a calf is born, but you are not when a human being is born!' Just as we made him see then, we now point to the fact that, between the two cases, there is the difference between having an additional dish on the table and having an additional guest at the table. All reservations having been made about the desirability of the consequences of the application of Malthus's theory, we must nevertheless admit that the two cases are not entirely the same thing.

278. We have discussed at length, without having arrived at any serious and definitive conclusion in one direction or the other, the question whether the price of products would increase or decrease in a progressive society. Here is how we have to answer this question. What necessarily decreases in a progressive society is the raretés (§ 270^{vi}). Regarding the prices, which are the ratios of these raretés to the raretés of the numeraire good, they will remain unchanged if, as there is no reason not to assume, at the same time as the raretés of all the products other than the numeraire good decrease, the raretés of the numeraire also decrease proportionally. They will decrease only if the raretés of the numeraire good do not change. Only under the condition of this hypothesis that the raretés of the numeraire good do not change, may we say that *in a progressive society, the prices*

of products will decrease. J.-B. Say subscribed to the proposition as stated, while, however, confessing that he was unable to prove it. His remarkable sagacity served him well on this point, just as on several others; he was only lacking a more powerful method of research: for, as can be seen, the explication of the question here under discussion rests entirely on a complete mathematical analysis of the phenomenon of the establishment and of the variation of the prices.

279. Having said this regarding the prices of products, let us now proceed to the prices of services.

To fix our ideas, and to study the effects of progress while keeping all other things equal as far as possible, let us assume there is a society like the one that we have considered until now, in which a certain number of individuals, having certain utility or want curves, possess certain amounts of capital: land, personal faculties, and capital properly speaking, the number of which would, at a given time, be doubled by progress. It is obvious that, if a second society, in all aspects identical to the first one, were to be purely and simply added to the first one, the prices of the services would not change, nor those of the products. This results mathematically from the equations of production. But such a hypothesis is not in accordance with the experientially derived idea of progress. What we must assume is that, to form the new society, every individual in the original society be succeeded after some time by two other individuals each possessing, before the process of production and exchange starts:

1° The same utility or want curves;

2° Half of the same land;

3° An equal amount of the same personal faculties;

4° Such a proportionally greater amount of the same capital goods properly speaking as is necessary to allow the entrepreneurs to produce, with the same quantity of land, and with twice the quantity of personal faculties and labor, at least double the quantity of each of the products.

In this way, each member of the original society would have been replaced by two members of the new society who, after the process of production and exchange, can consume directly:

1° Half of the same land services;

2° An equal quantity of the same labor performed by personal faculties;

3° A proportionally much greater amount of the same 'profits' of capital goods properly speaking;

4° An at least equal quantity of the same products.

280. In these conditions, general equilibrium would not exist in the market for the new society at the same prices as those in the original society. It is immediately apparent that, of the two series of ratios of the raretés of the land services directly consumed to the raretés of the numeraire good, and those of the 'profits' directly consumed to the raretés of the numeraire good, the first ratios are very much greater, and the second very much less than the original prices of these land services and these 'profits', that is, to the rents and to interest. There would be an immediate effective demand for land services and an effective supply of 'profits' to be consumed directly: an increase of rent and a decrease of interest. That is certain; but it is easy to show that, if we assume that these increases in the price of the land services and decreases in the price of the 'profits' are effectuated without delay, general equilibrium is, if not entirely reestablished, at least well on the way to being reestablished.

If rent has increased and interest decreased, there will be very nearly maximum satisfaction as far as regards directly consumed land services and directly consumed 'profits'. Moreover, there is maximum satisfaction as far as regards directly consumed labor services. Hence, there is equilibrium, or close to it, with respect to the prices of services.

The entrepreneurs that make products pay higher land rent, but they use less land services in the manufacture of the products. They pay less interest, but they use more 'profits' in the manufacture of the products. Hence the average costs of the products are almost exactly the same and are equal, or almost exactly equal, to their prices.

The landowners, workers, and capitalists, as consumers, sell less land services, but they sell them for higher prices. They sell more 'profits', but they sell them more cheaply. So, they have almost exactly the same income, and can obtain, or very nearly obtain, at least an equal quantity of the same products at the same prices that match their average costs.

And finally, since the various ratios of the raretés of the products, which have decreased somewhat, to the raretés of the numeraire good, which also have decreased somewhat, are still equal to the price, there will be very nearly maximum satisfaction regarding the products, and equilibrium, or close to it, at the prices of these products.

This demonstration suffices to allow us to state: – *In a progressive society, the price of labor, or wages, does not change markedly, the price of land services, or rent, increases markedly, and the price of 'profit', or interest, decreases markedly.*

281. The capital goods properly speaking are products. If we take into account that, because of this reason, their price, equal to their average cost, does not vary, whereas the price of 'profits', or interest, decreases markedly, we infer: – *In a progressive society, the rate of net income decreases markedly.*

282. The rate of net income is thus given by the ratio of net interest to the price of capital goods properly speaking. Once this has been obtained, we obtain the price of the personal faculties and of the land services by dividing the net wage and the rent by this rate of net revenue. And because the wages do not change markedly and rent increases markedly, it follows that: – *In a progressive society, the price of personal faculties increases in proportion to the decrease of the rate of net income, and the price of land increases both in proportion to the decrease of the rate of net income and in proportion to the increase of rent.*

283. I will show very shortly how the triple theory of rent, wages, and interest that is implicitly comprised in the theory, explained just above, of the determination of the price of the services, is in accordance with the current theories or differs from them. Concerning only the theory of land services or of rent, I want to note immediately how one can see, in the theory here explained, that the value of land services comes into existence in a society as a result of the same causes that make that value increase, and increases by the same causes as

those that bring it into existence. This value is always proportional to the raretés, or the intensities of the last wants satisfied of the land services directly consumed. In a society that has just passed from the hunting and fishing stage to the pastoral or agricultural stage, everyone finds as much free land and land services as they want, not only for agriculture but also for building a dwelling and making a garden. The raretés and, therefore, the value of land services and land are zero. On the contrary, in a society having reached the industrial and commercial stage, people live in very large houses, and the parks gradually disappear. The raretés and, therefore, the value of the land services and land are substantial. The economists who, like Carey and Bastiat, have taken upon themselves to convince us that we are not paying rent while buying agricultural or other products should prove to us that we have as much free land as we want for our houses and our gardens, situated where we want to live, of course, not in the solitudes of Africa or America; but they do not give that proof, and will never give it. The truth is that the more and more considerable growth of the value of land services or rent, occurring, what is more, without necessarily leading to the increase of the value of the products, is, together with the growth of the amount of capital and of the population, the essential characteristic of economic progress, and that in making this truth apparent, economic theory throws no less light on social economics than it throws, in other respects, on applied economics.

Notes

i   By this term, Walras denoted the increase of this year's production of commodities and capital goods in comparison with that of the preceding year.

ii In the previous section, Walras wrote 'quantités...de profit de capitaux proprement dits'. The reader will remember that *profit* in Walras's French or 'profits' within quotation marks in English is Walras's term for the services of capital goods properly speaking. When we have not put the word *profit* in quotation marks, it is our translation of Walras's word 'bénéfice', which means revenue minus cost. To use his distracting word 'profit' as little as possible, we correctly translated the words opening this note as 'quantities...of services of capital goods properly speaking'. Walras defined 'capitaux' without qualification as all three kinds of capital – land, human capital, and capital properly speaking. However, repeatedly in this lesson, he wrote simply 'capitaux' without qualification but did not mean it in the sense he had defined it. Thus, in the example to which this note relates, he wrote about the substitution of the 'profit de capitaux à la rente', but he was referring to capital goods properly speaking. Evidently he felt he did not need to add 'properly speaking' because he had preceded the words with the French word *profit*, which, to him, means the services of only capital goods properly speaking, and because he immediately used the contrasting term *rente*, which, to him, is the services of land; and we followed the same reasoning and procedure in our translation. In short, we would have misled the reader if we had translated his words 'profit de capitaux' literally as 'the services of capital goods', because he was not referring to all three types of capital; but since he did not write 'capitaux proprement dits' we could not insert the latter three words in the English translation.

iii   Below, Walras calls this 'the production function'.

iv   This has to be interpreted as saying: 'decrease in the raretés of the products consumed by individuals, by the people, etc.'

v   Second edition, 1803. The citations are taken from a reprint from the seventh edition (1872), published by Dent, London/Melbourne/Toronto, Everyman's Library, 1973, pages 8 (the first two citations) and 10 (the third citation). It is unknown which edition Walras used. There is a French translation of the first edition, published in 1805, and one of the second edition, published in 1823. From the wording of Walras's transcription of the French translation of the passages above, we infer that he was using the latter translation.

vi   This is an error. Walras should have written § 273.

Critique of the doctrine of the Physiocrats

SUMMARY: – The *Tableau économique*. The *productive* class; the class of *proprietors*, the *sterile* class. The industrial class produces all it consumes; it is not unproductive; the Physiocrats are wrong to believe that wealth consists only of material goods. The industrial class produces, like the agricultural class, a net product that can provide for a class of proprietors. The industrial class makes, like the agricultural class, initial capital investments. The *Tableau économique* does not contain a theory of the determination of the prices of products and services.

284. The sketch of the economic life of a society we gave in lesson 27 by means of concrete numbers is called an economic table. There is at least one analogous table, the *Tableau économique*, that is famous in the history of economics. That is Dr. Quesnay's, ordered by King Louis the 15th and printed in 1758 at the palace of Versailles under his very eyes. It is the table in which the Physiocratic doctrine was summarized. No copy of this publication is known to exist; we can find only an *Analyse du Tableau économique* in Dupont de Nemours's volume titled *Physiocratie*, published in 1768, and an 'Explication du Tableau économique à Madame de ***', by the priest Baudeau in the *Éphémerides du citoyen* of the same year. This 'Explication' was reprinted separately in 1770. It has been reproduced, with the *Analyse*, in the *Collection des principaux économistes* published by Guillaumin.

285. The *Analyse* starts as follows:

The nation is divided into three classes of citizens: the *productive class*, the *class of proprietors*, and the *sterile class*.

The *productive class* is the one that renews, by the cultivation of the land, the annual wealth of the nation, that advances the expenses of agricultural labor, and that pays the yearly incomes of the owners of the land. The duties of this class include all the labor and all the expenditures that have to be made until the first sale of the output: it is through this sale that we know the value of the annual production of the wealth of the nation.

The *class of proprietors* consists of the sovereign, the landowners, and the persons having the right to levy certain special taxes in kind.[i] This class subsists on the income or *net product* of agriculture, paid to it annually by the productive class, after deducting from this annual reproduction of wealth the funds needed for repaying the annual advances, and for the maintenance of the productive resources.

The *sterile class* is formed by all the citizens that perform other services and other labor than that used in agriculture, and whose expenses are paid by the productive class and by the class of proprietors, who themselves draw their incomes from the productive class.[1]

To clarify this by means of a concrete example, the Physiocrats assumed there is a kingdom with an area of 130 million French acres[ii] and 30 million people.

In this country, the productive class, or agricultural class own, under the name *original advances*, 10 billion worth of initial fixed capital, and under the name *annual advances*, 2 billion of circulating capital. Provided with these funds, they draw from their land 5 billion of products per year, consisting of 4 billion of foodstuff and 1 billion of raw materials for industrial purposes. From this they hand over 2 billion of foodstuff as income to the class of proprietors; they keep 2 billion for themselves to replenish their circulating capital; and they give 1 billion of raw material to the sterile class in exchange for 1 billion of manufactured products, which constitutes the interest and maintenance of their original advances. To summarize: the 3 billion worth of agricultural and industrial products that are kept by the productive class constitute the *revenues* of that class.

---

[1] *Collection des principaux économistes*. Vol. II. *Physiocrates* [édition 1846], page 58.

The class of proprietors receives annually, as we just have seen, 2 billion of income in the form of foodstuff from the productive class. They keep 1 billion for themselves, and they exchange the other billion with the sterile class for manufactured objects.

The sterile class, or industrial class, own, under the name *advances*, as circulating capital, a fund of 1 billion in raw materials. Thus provided, they transform the raw materials into industrial products that they divide into three parts: 1 billion that, as was said above, they exchange with the productive class for 1 billion of raw materials with which they replenish their advances, 1 billion that they exchange with the class of owners of property, as also has been said above, against 1 billion of foodstuff, and, finally, a third part, on which the Physiocrats did not explain themselves clearly, that the proprietors apparently retain for themselves, and that apparently must be evaluated at 1 billion like the two other parts.

286. The first and most important criticism of the *Tableau économique* concerns the conception of the role of the sterile class, namely the industrial and commercial class. The Physiocrats repeated many times that in calling this class *sterile* they did not want to say that it is *useless*, but only that it is *unproductive* in the sense that it consumes everything that it produces and leaves no net product. Let us accept for a moment that it is true that the industrial and commercial class does not leave any product utilizable for the support of a class of proprietors; even then the name would be badly chosen. This class that consumes all that it produces, is also a class that produces all that it consumes. Why conceal the reality of the facts by saying that they neither produce nor consume?

When we try to go discover the reason for this way of thinking of the Physiocrats, we recognize that, for them, the idea of wealth was essentially linked to the idea of materiality. 4 billion of foodstuff and 1 billion of industrial raw materials; that was, in their view, the amount of wealth, produced, and consumed each year, produced in its entirety by the agricultural class, and divided among the three classes and consumed by them in the following amounts: 2 billion of foodstuff by the agricultural class, 1 billion by the class of proprietors, 1 billion by the industrial class; and raw materials in the amount of one third of a billion for each of the three classes. Having this point of view, they had to consider the agricultural class as being the productive class par excellence, sustaining the class of proprietors and the industrial and commercial class. However, it is precisely this point of view that is erroneous.

The name social wealth should be given to everything, material or immaterial, that is valuable and that is exchanged; and since, according to the Physiocrats themselves, the labor applied to the raw material by the industrial class makes possible that these raw materials, purchased for 1 billion, are resold for 3 billion, we can say that this so-called sterile class produces and consumes annually 2 billion of social wealth: it produces 2 billion of labor, and consumes 1 billion of agricultural products and 1 billion of industrial products. From this follows that the total annual production in this country is in reality 7 billion and not 5 billion.

287. Let us now go further. Is it true that the industrial and commercial class produces exclusively what it consumes or consumes entirely what it produces, without leaving a net product that can be used as income for the class of proprietors? Not at all. Industry and commerce do not use the land in the same way as agriculture does, but they nevertheless make a certain use of it. One cannot practice industry or commerce somewhere between heaven and earth; it must be undertaken somewhere on terra firma. Now, just as agriculture can sustain, by means of landed income, the class of proprietors that lives in the countryside, industry and commerce can similarly sustain by means of landed income the class of proprietors that lives in the cities. So, why did the Physiocrats not identify this income from the land in the cities, which is a real net product of industry and commerce? Obviously because it is an immaterial income.

288. This is therefore a first point regarding the similarity between the industrial class and the agricultural class. Here is another. Quesnay endows his productive class with two kinds of capital: an original endowment of fixed capital, and annual advances of circulating capital, but he gives the sterile class only advances in raw materials. Why is this? Is the loom less indispensable to the industrialist than the plow to the farmer? Is the workshop less necessary for the former than the barn for the latter? No, of course not; but because the service

of the plow transforms itself into wheat, which is a material thing, whereas the service of the loom transforms itself in a manner that is immaterial, identification of the existence of the latter service was forgotten.[iii]

289. If we introduce this point of view of immaterial production, with all its consequences, into the doctrine of the Physiocrats, we see without difficulty how we could arrive, from their conception of the three classes, the productive class, the class of proprietors, and the sterile class, at our own conception of the three categories, land-owners, workers, and capitalists. However, this having been done, we must still introduce agricultural, industrial, and commercial entre-preneurs, the markets of products, the market for services, etc., etc., in order to have a system of economic theory that is sufficiently com-plete and satisfactory.

There is, indeed, another very serious fault in the Physiocratic doctrine that we have to point out: namely that they do not actually furnish any theory of prices, whether of the prices of products, or of the prices of services. Neither Quesnay, nor his disciples, explain how the incomes of the productive class and the sterile class, and the net product constituting the income of the class of proprietors, are determined. That determination remains completely arbitrary in the *Tableau économique*. The Physiocrats have been wrongly criti-cized for their use of concrete numbers to make their theory more comprehensible. It is certain, however, that they have mixed up the quantities they were free to choose arbitrarily with those that they needed to deduce from the former; in a word, they have mixed up the data and the unknowns of the problem. The *Tableau économique* does not contain a theory of the determination of rent, nor of wages, nor of interest. In a complete treatise, there must, in particular, be an examination of these three points, and most notably of the question of whether the net product is or is not the interest yielded by the advances in agriculture. Likewise, there should be a critique of the Physiocratic ideas about the circulating capital of the productive and sterile classes, as well as of their ideas on the role of money. We would thus be led to reproach them for quite a number of imperfections, which did not, however, prevent them from being not only the first, but also the only school of economists that, in France, had an theory of economics that is original and in which, amidst its errors, appear insights of an extraordinary profoundness and accuracy.

Notes

i The French word Walras used for such a person is 'décimateur'. The décimateurs had the right to levy the so-called 'dîme', a tax in kind during the Ancien Régime, levied by the Church on agricultural products. The tax is more or less comparable to the tithes in England. Walras uses the word 'décimateur' to indicate such a person.

ii Walras used the word 'arpent'. The 'arpent' of the Ancien Régime measured 5,107 square meters, about half a hectare.

iii Walras meant that the loom does not produce a new thing, but only changes the way the yarn is treated; that is, it is made into cloth.

Exposition and refutation of the English theory of the prices of products

SUMMARY: – Fundamental distinction between products the quantity of which cannot be increased, and those the quantity of which can be increased without limit. There are no products the quantity of which can be increased without limit. There is no amount of the expenses of production that can determine the price of the products. Reaction of the price of productive services on the price of the products: the case of services that do not exist any longer; the case of specific services; the case of nonspecific services. The two latter cases are not opposites. A third category of products: confusion between immediate multiplication and progressive multiplication.

290. To arrive at a theory of rent, wages, and interest, the English School has made efforts that have been much more widely followed and are much more serious than those of the various schools that, in France, have succeeded the Physiocrats, and the critical study of those efforts is absolutely necessary. We will devote this and the following two lessons to it.

Ricardo wrote

There are some commodities, the value of which is determined by their scarcity alone. No labour can increase the quantity of such goods, and therefore their value cannot be lowered by an increased supply. Some rare statues and pictures, scarce books and coins, wines of a peculiar quality, which can be made only from grapes grown on a particular soil, of which there is a very limited quantity, are all of this description. Their value is wholly independent of the quantity of labour originally necessary to produce them, and varies with the varying wealth and inclinations of those who are desirous to possess them.

These commodities, however, form a very small part of the mass of commodities daily exchanged in the market. By far the greatest part of those goods which are the objects of desire, are procured by labour; and they may be multiplied, not in one country alone, but in many, almost without any assignable limit, if we are disposed to bestow the labour necessary to obtain them.[1]

It is quite remarkable, and it shows more than anything else the steady and continuous development and the persistence of the doctrine of the English School, that J.S. Mill, half a century after Ricardo, expresses himself in exactly the same terms.

There are things of which it is physically impossible to increase the quantity beyond certain narrow limits. Such are those wines which can be grown only in peculiar circumstances of soil, climate, and exposure. Such also are ancient sculptures; pictures by old masters; rare books or coins, or other articles of antiquarian curiosity. Among such may also be reckoned houses and building-ground, in a town of definite extent (such as Venice, or any fortified town where fortifications are necessary to security); the most desirable sites in any town whatever; houses and parks peculiarly favoured by natural beauty, in places where that advantage is uncommon. Potentially, all land whatever is a commodity of this class; and might be practically so in countries fully occupied and cultivated.

But there is another category (embracing the majority of all things that are bought and sold), in which the obstacle to attainment consists only in the labour and expense requisite to produce the commodity. Without a certain labour and expense it cannot be had: but when any one is willing to incur these, there needs be no limit to the multiplication of the product.[2]

This fundamental distinction can, as can be seen, be reduced to a division of products into two categories: a small number of products the quantity of which cannot be increased, and a large number of products that can be multiplied without limit. Having posited this, and leaving the first category aside in order to deal exclusively with the second, the English economists declare that, concerning this category, the amount of expenses of production determines the price of

---

[1] [David] Ricardo, *The Principles of Political Economy and Taxation.* Chapter I. [Third edition, 1821. The quotation has been taken from a reprint published by Dent, London/Melbourne/Toronto, Everyman's Library, 1973, page 6].

[2] J.S. Mill, *Principles of Political Economy.* [Ninth edition (1885), edited by W.J. Ashley, new impression, 1923, London/New York/Toronto: Longman, Green and Co.], book III, chapter II, § 2 [p. 444].

the products. If they had restricted themselves to dividing the products into two categories, and to stating, regarding the second type of goods, that their price tends to equality with the amount of expenses of production under the regime of free competition, there would be nothing more to say about it; but to say that the products of the second category can be multiplied without limit, and that there is, for these goods, a certain amount of expenses of production that determines their price, those are two errors that it is essential to refute.

291. There are no products that can be multiplied without limit. All the things that form part of social wealth: land, personal faculties, capital goods properly speaking, income of any kind, exist only in limited quantities. Among those things, land and personal faculties are natural wealth; capital goods properly speaking and incomes are artificial wealth; they are products that have passed through the mechanism of production. In some of them, land services predominate: this is the case with respect to fruits or wild animals, surface ores, and mineral water. In some other products, it is labor: this is the case with respect to lawyers' or doctors' consultations, to professors' lectures, to singing and dancing. In most cases, land services, labor, and 'profits' will be used all together. From this follows that all things that belong to social wealth are either land, or personal faculties, or products of land services and of the labor of personal faculties. Well, Mill admits that land exists only in limited quantity; if we make him observe that the same is the case with respect to personal faculties, how could he continue to maintain that products can be multiplied without limit?

292. Nor is there an amount of expenses of production that, itself being determinate, consequently determines the price of the products. The price of the products is determined on the market for products as a function of their utility and their quantity; there is no need to consider other conditions; they are necessary and sufficient. It does not matter whether the products have cost more or less than their price. If they have cost more, too bad for the entrepreneurs: they suffer a loss; if they have cost less, so much the better for the entrepreneurs: they make a profit. Far from it being true that it is the average cost of the products in terms of productive services that determines

their price, it is rather their price that determines their average cost in terms of productive services. Indeed, the price of the productive services is determined in the market for services as a function of the supply by the landowners, the workers, and the capitalists, and the demand for the services by the entrepreneurs. And this demand, on what does it depend? Precisely, on the prices of the products. With respect to the products whose average cost is more than the price, the entrepreneurs reduce their demand for productive services, and the price of these services decreases. With respect to the products whose average cost is less, the demand by the entrepreneurs is increased, and the price of the productive services increases. Such is the inter-linked character of the phenomena, and it is inaccurate to conceive of it in another way.

293. Now, can there not be a reaction of the price of productive services on the price of the products? Yes, undoubtedly, but only by a reaction on their quantity. And to study this reaction on the price we must divide the various possible cases into groups according to the ease or the difficulty of their reaction on the quantity of the products.

First, there is the case of the productive services that no longer exist: – '[R]are statues and pictures, scarce books and coins', mentioned by Ricardo [p. 6]; – '[A]ncient sculptures; pictures by old masters; rare books or coins, or other articles of antiquarian curiosity', Mill said [III, II, § 2]. The productive services no longer existing in these cases, we cannot say that they have any value and that their value can react on the quantity and the value of the products. Even according to Ricardo and Mill, the value of these products therefore results exclusively from the law of supply and demand.

294. Then there is the case of special productive services: – Ricardo's 'wines of an exquisite quality, which can be made only from grapes grown on a particular soil, of which there is a very limited quantity' [p. 6]; Mill's 'wines which can be grown only in peculiar circumstances of soil, climate, and exposure', and his 'houses and building-ground, in a town of definite extent (such as Venice, or any fortified town where fortifications are necessary to security); the most desirable sites in any town whatever; houses and parks peculiarly favored by

natural beauty, in places where that advantage is uncommon' [III, II, § 2]. What do we discover when we look closely into this case? The productive services are still existing; they are not monopolized; that is to say, they are not owned by a single person, but they are specific to the products. Other lands can yield other fruit, but not grapes, or if so, not the same kind of grapes. Other land can be used for houses or parks, but not houses and parks with the same views. That is why these productive services are not afraid of competition. An increase in their price cannot attract similar services because similar services do not exist. When the price of the products increases, the price of the productive services will rise accordingly, without any possible reaction on the quantity and the price of the products. Had Ricardo's and Mill's classification been a little more systematic, they would have cited some examples of personal services no less specialized than the land services they mentioned: those of living artists, singers, eminent doctors and surgeons. But let us now, at last, consider the case they have in mind.

295. This is the case of productive services that are not specialized. This is, it is true, the most frequent case. There are certain productive services that do not have specific applicability, and these are the most numerous. With respect to these productive services, it suffices to see what happens in the examples referred to by Ricardo and Mill, and in examples that can be added to theirs. Alongside the land that produces grapes of exceptional quality, there is land that produces grapes of standard quality. Alongside the land used for the production of wine, there is land used for the production of wheat, forage, and vegetables. Now, land producing wheat can also produce barley, hops, clover, or rape; land producing cabbage can also produce lettuce. We must therefore observe that some specificity will always be found, within wider limits but nevertheless within certain limits: wheat needs the soil of plains, dry and light; forage needs valley land, dense and humid. But it is above all for labor that being specialized is perhaps the exceptional case, and being unspecialized the normal case. Alongside the man who has a tenor voice or the legs of an acrobat, the eyes of a painter, or the ear of a musician, there is a crowd of people able to do the most diverse things because they are less capable of doing this or that particular task. A man who has

been educated to be a lawyer would often have also been able to be an administrator; but certainly a man who has become a carpenter could undoubtedly have also been able to be a locksmith. What do most people want information about when choosing a profession? Precisely the amount of the wages that can be earned in it; that is to say, the value of the productive services in that profession. Therefore, there are unspecialized services that, contrary to the specialized productive services, have reason to fear competitors. An increase in the prices of the unspecialized productive services can attract into the productive activity other similar productive services that exist in more or less considerable amounts. When the price of the products increases, the price of the productive services will increase, but only temporarily; for there will be an increase in the quantity of productive services and an increase in the quantity of products. Only a lesser increase in the price of the productive services in general and of the products in general will remain. We could argue similarly in the case of a decrease, instead of an increase, in the price of the unspecialized productive services.

296. Hence, in reality, the two cases distinguished by Ricardo and Mill are not completely opposites. In both cases, there is a natural tendency for the price of the products and the price of the productive services to be related. In both cases, an increase or decrease of the quantities of the products causes an increase or decrease in the quantities of the productive services. However, in the first case, the increase or decrease in the price of the productive services is a terminal result, without reaction on the price and the quantity of the products. In the second case, on the contrary, the increase or decrease of the productive services that results from the original increase or decrease of the products is a temporary occurrence that has as a first consequence an inflow or outflow of similar productive services, and has as a permanent consequence a general rise or fall in the price of productive services of the same kind and a rise or fall equally general, although smaller than the original rise or fall, in the price of all the products in the production of which these services compete. What the increase or decrease loses in intensity, it gains in its extent. Neither in the one case, nor in the other, is the price of the products determined by the amount of their expenses of production. And,

above all, neither in the one, nor in the other case, is there anything that looks like Ricardo's multiplication 'almost without any assignable limit'[i] or Mill's 'no limit to the multiplication.'[ii] After having introduced his first category, Mill adds: 'Potentially, all land whatever is a commodity of this class.'[iii] Undoubtedly; and, moreover, virtually all personal faculties could also be classified in that way. But after that, what remains in the second category? Nothing. Thus the fundamental distinction of the English school has none of the validity that its authors attribute to it.

297. Mill continues:

There is a third case, intermediate between the two preceding, and rather more complex, which I shall at present merely indicate, but the importance of which in political economy is extremely great. There are commodities which can be multiplied to an indefinite extent by labour and expenditure, but not by a fixed amount of labour and expenditure. Only a limited quantity can be produced at a given cost: if more is wanted, it must be produced at a greater cost. To this class, as has been often repeated, agricultural produce belongs; and generally all the rude produce of the earth.[3]

Here, without informing us, and without being aware of it, the author ends his considerations of the case of the multiplication of the products at a given time and with a given quantity of productive services, and begins to consider the case of the multiplication of products from period to period and by means of a growing quantity of productive services. And it is the circumstance that, among all the productive services, land services cannot be increased in quantity that leads him to form his third category of things: 'agricultural produce ... and generally all the rude produce of the earth'. In proceeding in this way, the famous logician, following his habitual procedure, of which he will give us shortly another very remarkable example, mixes up two quite different questions, that of the establishment of the prices of the products, and that of the variation of these prices in a progressive society. Without following him at the moment on that terrain, where we will soon meet him again when dealing with the

---

[3] J.S. Mill, *Principles of Political Economy*. [Ninth edition (1885), edited by W.J. Ashley, new impression, 1923, London/New York/Toronto: Longman, Green and Co, book III, ch. II, § 2, p. 445.]

theory of rent, we will restrict ourselves to maintaining that the commodities of his third category cannot be multiplied infinitely, no more than those of his second, and that the commodities of his second category, no more than those of his third, cannot even be multiplied in finite quantity, at a certain time and with a certain quantity of productive services, at the cost of fixed amounts of labor and expense, or, at least, at a fixed amount of expense, which, let it be said in passing, is not at all the same thing as a fixed quantity of labor.

Notes

i Fifth section of Chapter 1.
ii Book III, Chapter II, § 2.
iii Book III, Chapter II, § 4.

LESSON 31

Exposition and refutation of the English
theory of rent

SUMMARY: – 'The rent which any land will yield, is the excess of its produce beyond what would be returned to the same capital if employed on the worst land in cultivation. Rent is also the difference between the income from a capital and the capital employed in the most unfavorable circumstances.' Geometrical presentation of the theory: areas showing the net product of different land; areas showing the net product of the same land. Having the character of infinitesimals: curves of net product and of the rate of profit. Algebraic expression: the net product function and the rate of profit function.

'The rent is the excess of the net product over interest.' Composition of the net product. Composition of the capital used. Rectification of the theory: 'The rent is the excess of the net products over the wages and interest.' The English doctrine, saying that total products is a non-proportionally increasing function of capital used expressed in numeraire, assumes, without motivation, that the prices of personal services and movable capital services are predetermined and constant; this hypothesis implies increasing prices of the products. Moreover, the unwarranted assumption is made that only one type of land services is needed for the manufacture of the products.

298. The theory of land services or of rent of the English School is a theory presented for the first time, it seems, at the end of the last century by Dr Anderson,[i] expounded again at the beginning of this century by Sir Edward West[ii] and by Malthus,[iii] popularized by, in particular, Ricardo, whose name it bears, clarified by James Mill[iv]

and by McCulloch,[v] reproduced by John Stuart Mill, and still taught nowadays by almost all English economists. Here is how Ricardo presented it:

> Thus suppose land – No. 1, 2, 3, – to yield, with an equal employment of capital and labour, a net produce of 100, 90, and 80 quarters of corn. In a new country, where there is an abundance of fertile land compared with the population, and where therefore it is only necessary to cultivate No. 1, the whole net produce will belong to the cultivator, and will be the profits of the stock which he advances. As soon as population had so far increased as to make it necessary to cultivate No. 2, from which ninety quarters only can be obtained after supporting the labourers, rent would commence on No. 1; for either there must be two rates of profit on agricultural capital, or ten quarters, or the value of ten quarters must be withdrawn from the produce of No. 1, for some other purpose. Whether the proprietor of the land, or any other person, cultivated No. 1, these ten quarters would equally constitute rent; for the cultivator of No. 2 would get the same result with his capital, whether he cultivated No. 1, paying ten quarters for rent, or continued to cultivate No. 2, paying no rent. In the same manner it might be shown that when No. 3 is brought into cultivation, the rent of No. 2 must be ten quarters, or the value of ten quarters, whilst the rent of No. 1 would rise to twenty quarters; for the cultivator of No. 3 would have the same profits whether he paid twenty quarters for the rent of No. 1, ten quarters for the rent of No. 2, or cultivated No. 3 free of all rent.[1]

That is a first part of the demonstration that J.S. Mill formulated in this theorem: – Rent is the difference between the income of the land that produces it and that of the worst land in cultivation.[2,vi] However, in Ricardo's work the theory is immediately completed in the following way:

> 299. It often, and, indeed, commonly happens, that before No. 2, 3, 4, or 5, or the inferior lands are cultivated, capital can be employed more productively on those lands which are already in cultivation. It may perhaps be found, that by doubling the original capital employed on No. 1, though the produce will not be doubled, will not be increased by 100 quarters, it may be increased by eighty-five quarters, and that this quantity exceeds what could be obtained by employing the same capital, on land No. 3.

---

[1] [David] Ricardo, *The Principles of Political Economy and Taxation*. [Third edition, 1821. Reprint, London, J. M. Dent and Sons, 1948, ch. II, pp. 35–6].

[2] J.S. Mill, *Principles d'economie politique*; Book II, ch. XVI, § 3.

In such case, capital will be preferably employed on the old land, and will equally create a rent; for rent is always the difference between the produce obtained by the employment of two equal quantities of capital and labour. If, with a capital of £1,000, a tenant obtain 100 quarters of wheat from his land, and by the employment of a second capital of £1,000, he obtain a further return of eighty-five, his landlord would have the power at the expiration of his lease, of obliging him to pay fifteen quarters, or an equivalent value, for additional rent; for there cannot be two rates of profit. If he is satisfied with a diminution of fifteen quarters in the return for his second £1,000, it is because no employment more profitable can be found for it. The common rate of profit would be in that proportion, and if the original tenant refused, some other person would be found willing to give all which exceeded that rate of profit to the owner of the land from which he derived it.

In this case, as well as in the other, the capital last employed pays no rent. For the greater productive powers of the first £1,000, fifteen quarters is paid for rent, for the employment of the second £1,000 no rent whatever is paid. If a third £1,000 be employed on the same land, with a return of seventy-five quarters, rent will then be paid for the second £1,000, and will be equal to the difference between the produce of these two, or ten quarters; and at the same time the rent of the first £1,000 will rise from fifteen to twenty-five quarters; while the last £1,000 will pay no rent whatever.[3]

That is the second part of Ricardo's demonstration, also formulated by J.S. Mill in this second theorem: – Rent is also the difference between the income that a capital investment yields and the income of a similar capital employed in the most unfavorable circumstances.[4,vii]

300. This theory is a mathematical theory that must be expressed in mathematics before discussing it; for this is the only way to grasp it.

Let there be, therefore, two coordinate axes: a horizontal axis Ox (Fig. 25) and three vertical axes Oy. On the horizontal axis, we measure, starting in point O, lengths $\overline{Ox'_1}$, $\overline{Ox'_2}$, and $\overline{Ox'_3}$ corresponding to equal employments of capital on, respectively, lands 1, 2, and 3, employments regarding which Ricardo does not explicitly say, in the

---

[3] [David] Ricardo, *The Principles of Political Economy and Taxation*, ch. II, [pp. 36–7].

[4] J.S. Mill, idem, Book II, ch. XVI, § 4.

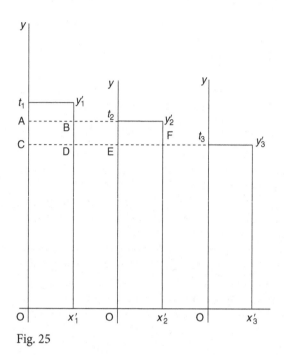

Fig. 25

first part of his demonstration, how they are evaluated nor what is their value, but that he assumes, in the second part of his demonstration, on the contrary, to be explicitly evaluated in terms of numeraire and that their value is £1,000. On the vertical axes, we measure, starting at the points O, the lengths, $\overline{Ot_1}$, $\overline{Ot_2}$, and $\overline{Ot_3}$ such that we will have three rectangles, $Ot_1y_1'x_1'$, $Ot_2y_2'x_2'$ and, $Ot_3y_3'x_3'$, with these lengths as height and the lengths $\overline{Ox_1'}$, $\overline{Ox_2'}$, and $\overline{Ox_3'}$ as basis; the areas of these rectangles represent quantities corresponding to the net products of the lands 1, 2, and 3, that Ricardo assumes are evaluated in units of products amounting to 100, 90, and 80 quarters. Having said this, the first part of his demonstration amounts to saying that, because there cannot be two different profit rates in agriculture, when land n° 2 has to be cultivated, there will be paid, for the lease of land n° 1, a rent equal to the difference of the areas of the first two rectangles, namely the area $At_1y_1'B$ corresponding to 10 quarters; and, when land n° 3 has to be cultivated, there will be

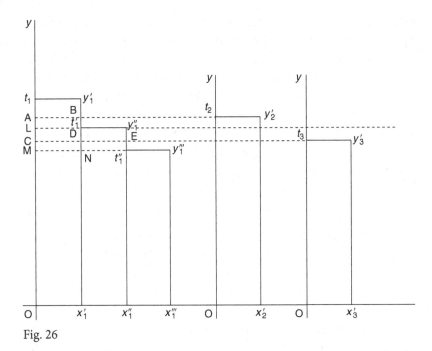

Fig. 26

paid, for the lease of land n° 1, a rent equal to the difference of the areas of the first rectangle and the third one, namely the area $Ct_1y_1'D$ corresponding to 20 quarters; and there must be paid, for the lease of land n° 2, a rent equal to the difference of the areas of the second rectangle and the third one, namely the area $Et_2y_2'F$ corresponding to 10 quarters, no rent being paid for the lease of land n° 3.

301. Now (Fig. 26), starting from the point O, let us also measure on the horizontal axis, extending the length $\overline{Ox_1'}$, lengths $\overline{x_1'x_1''}$ and $\overline{x_1''x_1'''}$ corresponding to employments of £1,000 of capital, successively invested in land n° 1. On the parallels $x_1'y_1'$ and $x_1''y_1''$ to the vertical axis, going through the points x_1' and x_1'' we measure, starting at these points, the lengths, $\overline{x_1't_1'}$ and $\overline{x_1''t_1''}$ such that we will have two rectangles, $x_1't_1'y_1'x_1''$ and $x_1''t_1''y_1''x_1'''$ with these lengths as height and the lengths $\overline{x_1'x_1''}$ and $\overline{x_1''x_1'''}$ as bases; the areas of these rectangles represent quantities corresponding to the net products of the successive employments of

amounts of land n° 1, evaluated as before in units of products amounting to 85 and 75 quarters. Having posited this, the second part of his demonstration amounts to saying that, because there cannot be two different profit rates in agriculture, when a second employment of £1,000 of capital has to be made on land n° 1, after having taken into use land n° 2 but before land n° 3 has been taken into use, there must be paid, because of the use of the first capital outlay of £1,000, a rent equal to the difference of the two rectangles $Ot_1y_1'x_1'$ and $x_1't_1'y_1''x_1''$, namely the area $Lt_1y_1't_1'$ corresponding to 15 quarters; and, when one has to use a third capital outlay of £1,000 on land n° 1, there must be paid, because of the use of the first capital outlay of £1,000, a rent equal to the difference of the two rectangles $Ot_1y_1'x_1'$ and $x_1''t_1''y_1'''x_1'''$, namely the area $Mt_1y_1'N$, corresponding to 25 quarters; and, because of the use of the second capital outlay of £1,000, there must be paid a rent equal to the difference of the two rectangles $x_1't_1'y_1''x_1''$ and $x_1''t_1''y_1'''x_1'''$ namely the area $Nt_1'y_1''t_1''$, corresponding to 10 quarters; thus, all in all, there will be paid for the lease of land n° 1 a rent represented by the two areas $Mt_1y_1'N$ and $Nt_1'y_1''t_1''$, namely by the area $Mt_1y_1't_1'y_1''t_1''$ corresponding to 35 quarters.

302. However, once the theory is thus put into mathematical form, one thing makes itself immediately apparent: namely that what Ricardo says about equal employments of capital successively used either on different land, or on the same land must be said, be it true or not, not only of employments of £1,000, but likewise of employments of £100, employments of £10, employments of £1; in short, if the rate of production is, for each piece of land, a decreasing function of the amount of capital employed, there is no reason not to assume that if capital increases by an infinitely small quantity, the rate of production must decrease by an infinitely small quantity. Of course, matters may be otherwise; however, until we have been shown that this last case is the general case or the exception, not by arbitrary assumptions but by observations drawn from experience, we are entitled to use the former case in our theoretical reasoning. Consequently, to represent the fact of the decrease in question, we must substitute the discontinuous curves such as $t_1y_1't_1'y_1''t_1''y_1'''\cdots$ by the continuous curves T_1T_1', T_2T_2', T_3T_3', $\cdots$

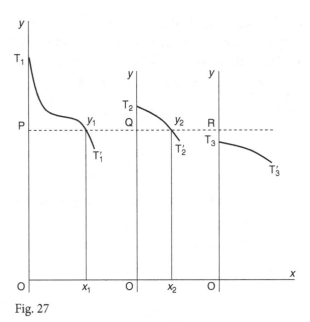

Fig. 27

(Fig. 27), constructed such that, the capital used on land n° 1 being represented by the length $\overline{Ox_1}$, the net product in units of product is represented by the area $OT_1y_1x_1$; that, the capital used on land n° 2 being represented by the length $\overline{Ox_2}$, the net product in units of product is represented by the area $OT_2y_2x_2$; and so forth. Then, the observation that there cannot be two different profit rates of capital in agriculture will require that the areas of the rectangles OPy_1x_1 and OQy_2x_2, representing in terms of units of product the profits in question on land n° 1, n° 2, ⋯ are proportional to their bases Ox_1, Ox_2, ⋯, or, putting it otherwise, the heights $x_1\,y_1$, $x_2\,y_2$, ⋯ representing the rate of profit in terms of units of product, that is to say, the rate of production, must be equal. And, consequently, the portions of the areas PT_1y_1, QT_2y_2, ⋯ that are above the horizontal line PQR represent, in terms of units of product, the rents of the lands n° 1 and n° 2, whereas the land n° 3 does not yield any rent, because, as assumed in our figure, the horizontal line PQR does not meet the curve T_3T_3'.

303. Algebraically, let $h_1, h_2, h_3, \cdots$ be the amounts of net product of land n° 1, n° 2, n° 3, $\cdots$, or the excesses of the total quantity of units of product over the quantity of these units necessary to pay the wages; let $x_1, x_2, x_3, \cdots$ be the amounts in numeraire of the capital goods used; t be the rate of interest expressed in units of product. The rents $r_1, r_2, r_3, \cdots$, expressed in the same way, are then furnished, according to the English doctrine, by

$$r_1 = h_1 - x_1 t, \; r_2 = h_2 - x_2 t, \; r_3 = h_3 - x_3 t, \cdots \qquad [1]$$

Between the net products and the capital goods used there is the relation

$$h_1 = F_1(x_1), \; h_2 = F_2(x_2), \; h_3 = F_3(x_3), \cdots \qquad [2]$$

and if we define

$$\phi_1(x) = F_1'(x), \; \phi_2(x) = F_2'(x), \; \phi_3(x) = F_3'(x), \cdots,$$

there are between the rate of interest and the capital goods used the relations

$$t = \phi_1(x_1) = \phi_2(x_2) = \phi_3(x_3) = \cdots \qquad [3]$$

These two kinds of relations are also represented by curves like $T_1 T_1'$, $T_2 T_2'$, $T_3 T_3'$, $\cdots$ in which the variable x corresponds to the abscissa, the function t to the ordinates, and the function h to the areas.

Attentive inspection of the above equations makes it clear that, for m pieces of land, there are $3m + 1$ unknowns and only $3m$ equations. Another equation is needed. Interpreting as faithfully as possible Ricardo's theory and conforming to the preceding analogues (§§ 117, 197, 239), we can posit the following:

$$x_1 + x_2 + x_3 + \cdots = X. \qquad [4]$$

According to Ricardo, it appears that there is, in a country, a certain amount of capital, always increasing, with which one can obtain a quantity of output always increasing, although not proportionally, so as to feed an always increasing population. This capital is determinate at a given moment; we call it X, and we allocate it among the various types of land such that the rate of production is the same for all the pieces of land.

The equations [3], assumed to be solved for x, take the form

$$x_1 = \psi_1(t), \quad x_2 = \psi_2(t), \quad x_3 = \psi_3(t), \cdots,$$

and t is then given by the modified equation [4]

$$\psi_1(t) + \psi_2(t) + \psi_3(t) + \cdots = X.$$

t being determined, $x_1, x_2, x_3, \cdots$ are determined by means of the modified equations [3]. The lands for which $\varphi(0) < t$ are not cultivated; only those for which $\varphi(0) > t$ are. $x_1, x_2, x_3, \cdots$ being determined, $h_1, h_2, h_3, \cdots$ can be found by means of equations [2]. And then $r_1, r_2, r_3, \cdots$ are determined by equations [1]. Hence, in the last analysis, rent depends on the capital of a country and is determined independently of wages and interest as well as of the prices of the products. That is the essence of the English theory of rent.

304. The necessity of presenting Ricardo's reasoning in terms of infinitesimals is so evident that, albeit without ceasing to discuss it in ordinary language, certain authors have done so, showing that the definitive form we have given it is certainly the true form of the English theory of rent. Therefore, we will adhere to it in the discussion, without giving attention to the imperfections in its explication or deduction resulting, in Ricardo's and Mill's work, from the use of a rudimentary form; without, for example, showing how Mill's first theorem, which assumes essentially that cultivated land of the worst quality does not yield rent, is basically incorrect, and, moreover, in formal contradiction with the second theorem. This error disappears, indeed, in the mathematical theory; and the simple inspection of the figure shows that the worst land cultivated yields a rent, at least in general and apart from the exceptional case of a discontinuous production curve that would be intersected precisely

at its starting point by the horizontal line representing the rate of production.

305. Let us again take up the general equation

$$r = h - xt;$$

and, following the notation we have frequently used and with which the reader must be familiar, let (B) be the product in question, p_b its price, (T) the type of land on which it is cultivated, H the total number of units obtained per hectare, and, consequently, $b_t = \dfrac{1}{H}$ the production coefficient of product (B) for productive service (T), p_t the rent, and i the rate of net income in numeraire. As we have seen, r and t are, respectively, the rent and the rate of interest expressed in units of product; they can be replaced by the values $\dfrac{p_t}{p_b}$ and $\dfrac{i}{p_b}$ in the equation above, which then becomes

$$\frac{p_t}{p_b} = h - x\frac{i}{p_b}.$$

Let, moreover, (P), (P′), (P″), ⋯ be the types of personal capital or persons whose services enter likewise into the manufacture of the product (B), let $b_p, b_{p'}, b_{p''}, \cdots$ be the coefficients of production, $p_p, p_{p'}, p_{p''}, \cdots$ the prices of the personal incomes or the wages, $P_p, P_{p'}, P_{p''}, \cdots$ the prices of personal capitals in numeraire; the net product in units of output, h, as introduced by Ricardo, is exactly equal to

$$H - \frac{H}{p_b}\left(b_p p_p + b_{p'} p_p + b_{p''} p_{p''} + \cdots\right),$$

hence, making abstraction from depreciation and insurance, taking account of which would be easy but would make the formula a little more complicated, is exactly equal to,

$$H - \frac{Hi}{p_b}\left(b_p P_p + b_{p'} P_{p'} + b_{p''} P_{p''} + \cdots\right).$$

Let, finally, (K), (K'), (K''), $\cdots$ be the types of movable capital or capital goods properly speaking the services of which are used in the manufacture of product (B), and $b_k, b_{k'}, b_{k''}, \cdots$ the coefficients of production, $p_k, p_{k'}, p_{k''}, \cdots$ the prices of the services of movable income, or profit, and $P_p, P_{p'}, P_{p''}, \cdots$ the prices of the capital in numeraire. The amount in numeraire of capital used, x, as introduced by Ricardo, is exactly equal to

$$H\left(b_k P_k + b_{p'} P_{p'} + b_{p''} P_{p''} + \cdots\right),$$

hence, abstraction made from depreciation and insurance, is exactly equal to

$$\frac{H}{i}\left(b_k p_k + b_{k'} p_{k'} + b_{k''} p_{k''} + \cdots\right).$$

306. Now, having said this, there is obviously a preliminary correction that we may justifiably make to the equation that we want to discuss, without touching on Ricardo's theory otherwise than to give it the greatest possible exactitude: that is, to bring the prices of the persons (P), (P'), (P''), $\cdots$ and those of the capital goods properly speaking (K), (K'), (K''), $\cdots$ together in order to get the total use of capital, either movable or personal, into the term x; for it is certain that there is only one wage rate, as there is only one rate of interest, and that, moreover this wage rate is exactly equal to the interest rate, so that in our theory we can and must reason at the same time in terms of the one and of the other, as has been done also by some English economists. This rectification having been made, the net product h is subsumed within the total product H, and the capital used becomes definitively

$$x = H\left(b_p P_p + b_{p'} P_{p'} + b_{p''} P_{p''} + \cdots + b_k P_k + b_{k'} P_{k'} + b_{k''} P_{k''} + \cdots\right)$$
$$= \frac{H}{i}\left(b_p p_p + b_{p'} p_{p'} + b_{p''} p_{p''} + \cdots + b_k p_k + b_{k'} p_{k'} + b_{k''} p_{k''} + \cdots\right).$$

307. These are the H and the x that will be functions of each other and that will be represented, the one, by the areas and, the other, by the abscissa of the curves TT. And now, having transformed the indeterminate function $F(x)$ into a determinate function, nothing is easier than finding out whether the term H is a non-proportionally increasing function of the term x, hence, in other words, whether the curves TT are decreasing. Indeed, solving the value of H from the latter equations, we will have

$$H = \frac{x}{b_p P_p + b_{p'} P_{p'} + b_{p''} P_{p''} + \cdots + b_k P_k + b_{k'} P_{k'} + b_{k''} P_{k''} + \cdots}$$
$$= \frac{xi}{b_p P_p + b_{p'} P_{p'} + b_{p''} P_{p''} + \cdots + b_k P_k + b_{k'} P_{k'} + b_{k''} P_{k''} + \cdots}.$$

Now, it is a fact of experience that, by associating increasing amounts of personal services and movable capital good services with landed capital, proportionally increasing quantities of product are not obtained; if so, we could obtain from a hectare of land, or even from a smaller area, an indefinite quantity of products by applying an indefinite amount of personal services and movable capital good services. Hence, in exact terms, we may say, as we did before (§ 274), that the $b_p, b_{p'}, b_{p''}, \cdots, b_k, b_{k'}, b_{k''}, \cdots$ are not constant magnitudes, but decreasing functions of b_t; that is to say, increasing functions of H. But Ricardo and the English economists say quite another thing. They say that by employing increasing amounts of personal services and movable capital good services on a piece of land, we do not obtain output in quantities that are proportionally increasing; and the employments of capital of which they speak are evaluated in numeraire. To make this assertion identical to the preceding one, we must assume that employments that are equal with respect to the quantity of numeraire in which they are expressed are also equal with respect to the quantity of personal services and movable capital good services that they represent, for otherwise, and if we assume that equal quantities of numeraire correspond to more than equal quantities of productive services, nothing would stop us from conceiving the product as being proportional to the employment of capital. In precise terms, in order to be able to say that H is a non-proportionally increasing function of x, not only at a certain given time, but also at different times, we must assume that $P_p, P_{p'}, P_{p''}, \cdots,$ $P_k, P_{k'}, P_{k''}, \cdots, i$ and, consequently, $p_p, p_{p'}, p_{p''}, \cdots, p_k, p_{k'}, p_{k''}, \cdots, i$, are not only determinate at a certain time, but are also constant from one time to another.

If we reread Ricardo's exposition, we can see that this twofold assumption is implicitly in it, if not explicitly, from the beginning to end. Obviously, Ricardo could not maintain that the product obtained depends on the capital used irrespective of the way, however absurd, in which this employment is applied. Consequently, for him, the employments of capital applied, either simultaneously or successively, either on the same land or on different pieces of land, represent certain determinate quantities of certain determinate types of capital. These employments always amount to £1,000; hence the prices of capital are determined and constant. However, considering everything, the product depends on the nature and the quantity of the productive services, and not on the nature and the quantities of the capital goods. Accordingly, we must admit that, for Ricardo, to the employment of certain determinate quantities of determinate types of capital goods there corresponds the employment of certain determinate quantities of certain determinate services. The employments of capital goods always amount to £1,000; if the rate of interest is 5 per cent, the employment of the services will always be £50; hence the prices of the services are determinate and constant.

308. This hypothesis has serious consequences, and it is important to point them out. It is the one that led Ricardo to base the existence, the emergence, and the development of rent on the fact of growing expensiveness of products. For him, indeed, it is the average cost that

determines the price. On the other hand, as we just saw, the determinate and constant expenditure necessary to obtain the net product amounts to £50. If we must add to the cultivation of land n° 1, where £50 of expenditure yield 100 quarters of net product, the cultivation of land n° 2, where £50 of expenditure yield 90 quarters, the average cost, and, consequently, the price will increase from 50/100 to 50/90. Or, if, in the cultivation of land n° 1, we must add to the first expenditure of £50, yielding 100 quarters of net product, another £50 yielding 85 quarters of net product, the average cost, which is also the price, will increase from 50/100 to 50/85. In the mathematical exposition of Ricardo's theory we presented above, we add the expense of wages to the interest cost; but the result is the same. Indeed, the price p_b of the product is equal to either the ratio of the total cost composed of rent, wages, and interest, $p_t + xi$, to the quantity H of product, or the ratio of the cost of rent p_t to the rent r in terms of units of product, or, finally the ratio of the cost of wages and interest, xi, to the wages and interest per unit of product, xt; that is to say, as a result, to the ratio i/t. Now, abstraction made of the variations in i, this ratio increases indefinitely because of decrease of t, which is the basis of the theory. From this it results, all things considered, that the rent in terms of numeraire increases for two reasons in the course of time; first, because of the increase r in the number of units of products that corresponds to it, and, second, because of the increase of the price p_b of the product. This consequence has been accurately perceived and accepted by Ricardo; it forms the subject of a special note at the end of his chapter 'On Rent'.

309. Hence, the English theory of land services can determine their price and demonstrate that it is a surplus value only given the twofold condition that it assumes the prices of personal capital and of movable capital goods, the rate of net income, and, as a consequence, the prices of personal services and of movable capital good services, to be determined and constant. We will see in the two[viii] following lessons that the English School determines neither wages nor interest; but, for the time being, we can grant them the hypothesis of such a determination. We cannot, for example, grant the School a priori the hypothesis of fixedness of the prices of productive services. From this follows that the curves or equations giving the product as a function

of the capital used do not have any value for the purpose of comparing rent at different instants of time for successive employments of capital, or for the purpose of stating the law of variation in rent in a progressive society; and they can, at the very most, serve only to determine purely and simply the rent at a given instant of time in relation to simultaneous employments of capital, or to state the law of the establishment of rent. Only within these limits can we make use of the curves in question. The prices $p_p, p'_p, p''_p, \cdots, p_k, p'_k, p''_k, \cdots$ being then assumed to be determined, rent will be determined in units of product by the equation

$$\frac{p_t}{p_b} = H - \frac{H}{p_b}\left(b_p p_p + b_{p'} p_{p'} + b_{p''} p_{p''} + \cdots + b_k p_k + b_{k'} p_{k'} + b_{k''} p_{k''} + \cdots\right)$$

and in numeraire by

$$p_t = H p_b - H\left(b_p p_p + b_{p'} p_{p'} + b_{p''} p_{p''} + \cdots + b_k p_k + b_{k'} p_{k'} + b_{k''} p_{k''} + \cdots\right).$$

So, to sum up, by the introduction of the curves $T_1 T'_1$, $T_2 T'_2$, $T_3 T'_3$, $\cdots$ (an introduction that should be allowed only subject to the preceding reservation and to another more serious condition that will follow), the English School introduces as best as it can, in the general problem of the determination of the prices, a number of equations equal to that of the unknowns, which are the rents in terms of units of product. And the problem thus put theoretically is solved practically by the competition of the entrepreneurs. Having done this, it remains to determine, on the other hand, these unknowns: wages, the remuneration of the capital services, and the rate of interest, in terms of numeraire. After that, the rate of production will be determined, as has been said above (§ 303), in relation to the amount of capital that is available; the price of the products will be determined by the ratio of the rate of net income to the rate of production, and, finally, the rent in terms of numeraire can be determined by multiplying the rent in terms of units of product by the price of the products. Hence, in this way, the English School would have succeeded well in establishing that *rent does not form part of the expenses of production*, if there were not a last difficulty that we have to point out and because of which its theory of rent will definitively fail.

310. Replacing H by $\dfrac{1}{b_t}$, multiplying by b_t, and transposing the quantity between parentheses in the first member of the above equation, we have

$$b_t p_t + b_p p_p + b_{p'} p_{p'} + b_{p''} p_{p''} + \cdots + b_k p_k + b_{k'} p_{k'} + b_{k''} p_{k''} + \cdots = p_b;$$

this equation is none other than the equation of the average cost of product (B) as it appears in system [4] of our equations of production (§ 199), with this restriction that, where there appear several types of services of personal faculties (P), (P'), (P''), $\cdots$, and several types of services of capital goods properly speaking (K), (K'), (K''), $\cdots$, there appears only one type of land service (T). Thus, the English theory of rent rests still on the hypothesis that there never enters more than a single type of land service in making the products. Now, this hypothesis is incorrect with respect to agricultural products as well as with respect to industrial products. Wheat, serving as an example in Ricardo's work, does not fit into the hypothesis, because in the production of wheat a raw material is used, namely manure fertilizer coming from cattle fed on meadows that are land of type other than the land for growing wheat. For this reason, and also for the reason, as we will see below, that the English School does not determine directly either wages or interest, we must complete the equation of the average cost of product (B) as follows:

$$b_t p_t + b_{t'} p_{t'} + b_{t''} p_{t''} + \cdots + b_p p_p + b_{p'} p_{p'} + b_{p''} p_{p''} + \cdots$$
$$+ b_k p_k + b_{k'} p_{k'} + b_{k''} p_{k''} + \cdots = p_b,$$

and then join it to the other equations of production to determine at the same time, as we have done, the prices of the products and those of the productive services. The production functions will serve to determine the coefficients of production. Therefore, all that remains of Ricardo's theory, after a rigorous critique, is that rent is not a part but a result of the price of products. The same thing can be said of wages and interest. Hence, rents, wages, interest, the prices of the products, and the coefficients of production are the unknowns of one and the same problem and they must be determined together and not independently of one another.

Notes

i James Anderson, *Inquiry into the Nature of the Corn Laws*, Edinburgh: Mrs Mundell, 1777.

ii Sir Edward West, *An Essay on the Application of Capital to Land*, London: Underwood, 1815.

iii Thomas Robert Malthus, *Inquiry into the Nature and Progress of Rent and the Principles by which it is regulated*, London: Murray, 1815.

iv James Mill, *Elements of Political Economy*, London: Baldwin, Cradock, and Joy, 1821.

v John Ramsey McCulloch, *The Principles of Political Economy*, Edinburgh: William and Charles Tait, 1825.

vi Mill's formulation of the theorem is: 'The rent, therefore, which any land will yield, is the excess of its produce beyond what would be returned to the same capital if employed on the worst land in cultivation.' (*Principles of Political Economy*, book II, ch. XVI, § 3, page 425.) However, Walras wrote: 'La rente est égale à la différence de revenu de la terre qui la produit et des plus mauvaises terres cultivées.' This is what we translated, but it is not the translation of a text written by Mill. Walras used the French translation (1854) of Mill's book. This translation has been supplemented by the translators with hundreds of one-sentence summaries at the beginning of each section. Here, Walras simply copied the French one-sentence summary of the relevant section.

vii At this place, Walras wrote: 'La rente est aussi la différence de revenu qui existe entre un capital et le capital employé dans les circonstances les plus défavorables.' Mill (*Principles of Political Economy*, book II, Ch. XVI, § 4, page 427.) formulated the theorem as follows: 'The rent of all land is measured by the excess of the return to the whole capital employed on it, above what is necessary to replace the capital with the ordinary rate of profit, or in other words, above what the same capital would yield if it were all employed in as disadvantageous circumstances as the least productive portion of it.' Similarly to what he did above, Walras simply copied the French one-sentence summary of the relevant section. In our opinion, Jaffé (Walras 1954, page 404, note 2 and page 405, note 4), however, apparently misconstrued Walras's presentation of the two theorems as paraphrases of Mill's formulation.

viii Walras forgot, in all editions after the first, to change 'two' into 'one', which he should have done because he combined lessons 57 and 58 of edition 1 into one lesson (lesson 32 in editions 2 and 3, and lesson 40 in editions 4 and 5).

Exposition and refutation of the English theories of wages and interest

SUMMARY: – 'To purchase produce is not to sustain[i] [*alimenter*][ii] labour.' Ambiguity of the word *sustain*: it is desired to prove that to purchase the product does not mean to demand labour, and it is proven that to purchase the product is not to furnish circulating capital. 'Wages depend on the proportion between population and capital;' *Rate*: average [wage] rate. *Capital*: circulating capital. *Population*: number of wage earners. Hence the average wage is equal to the quotient of the total amount of wages and the total number of wage earners. We have only to find the average wage; neither capital nor population are determined.

Confusion between the *interest* on capital and the *profit* of the entrepreneur. 'Rent does not really form any part of the expenses of production. Profit is the excess of the amount produced over the cost of production in terms of wages.' The English doctrine claims in this way to determine two unknowns with a single equation. J.-B. Say's definitions of *wages*, *interest*, and *rent*. Mr. Boutron's vicious circle. The system of the three markets for services, products, and capital goods constitutes the only scientific theory of the establishment of prices.

311. Concerning the English theory of wages, we refer to John Stuart Mill, not because he was the first to formulate it, but because his demonstration is the most complete one that has been given. This demonstration is constituted, in his work, of two theorems formulated in his *Principles of Political Economy*, one in Book I, Chapter V, § 9: – *To purchase produce is not to sustain labour*; and the other in Book II,

Chapter XI, § 1: *Wages depend on the proportion between population and capital goods.* We will examine them successively. What is striking immediately is the quite singular way of expressing the first of these two theorems. This first impression is not misleading, and the theorem in question is only a long and fatiguing ambiguity. What does this vague and hardly scientific word *sustain* [*alimenter*] mean?[iii] Mill himself explains it to us: 'To purchase produce is not to sustain labor,' means that 'the demand for labor is constituted by the wages which precede the production, and not by the demand which may exist for the commodities resulting from the production.' So, 'To purchase produce is not to sustain labour' means 'To purchase produce is not to demand labor.' Then why not state the theory in these terms, or rather, instead of this negative formulation, why not use a positive formulation like the one that Mill eventually furnishes? That is what an attentive study of the proposition will enable us to learn.

Mill considers a consumer and assumes that he spends his income either directly on purchasing services like, for example, having a house built, or on buying products like, for example, lace or velvet. Then he tells us that these two operations are different, and he tries to specify in what way they are different, in which effort he fails completely. He should have compared a man who has a house built with a man who buys a finished house, or a man who buys finished lace or velvet with a man who has the lace or velvet made; he would then have shown us clearly an essential difference between the direct purchase of productive services, by means of which a person provides the circulating capital needed for the manufacture of the product, and the purchase of products, by means of which he only reestablishes this circulating capital for a subsequent production. Indeed, dissatisfied, it appears, with the comparison that he gave us in his text, he presents a second one in a footnote.[iv] A rich individual, A, who spends every day a certain amount on wages or on alms that the workers and the poor persons spend on ordinary food, passes away, and he is replaced by a heir, B, who consumes the wealth himself in the form of delicacies. This example, however, is even more incoherent than the first. The author should have distinguished between the case of the alms and that of the wages, which are not at all the same; and, in adopting the latter case, he should have told us how the labor paid by the wages is employed. If it is work done by gardeners who grow delicacies for A, we have simply to do with the distinction between the purchase of productive services and the purchase of products, and with the circumstance that circulating capital is furnished in the first case and not in the second.

This suffices to show how Mill was misled by the ambiguity of the word *alimenter*. Due to a double meaning he gives to the word, he announces that he is going to demonstrate one thing and he demonstrates something quite different. He had to demonstrate that buying the product is not sustaining labor in the sense that buying a product is not the same as demanding labor; and he demonstrates, not without difficulty, that buying a product is not the same as sustaining labor in the sense that buying a product is not the same as furnishing circulating capital that is used in the manufacture of the product. Hence, we may consider the first theorem as null and void.

312. Let us now consider the second one.

Wages, then, depend mainly upon the demand and supply of labour; or as it is often expressed, on the proportion between population and capital. By population is here meant the number only of the labouring class, or rather of those who work for hire; and by capital only circulating capital, and not even the whole of that, but the part which is expended in the direct purchase of labour. To this, however, must be added all funds which, without forming a part of capital, are paid in exchange for labour, such as the wages of soldiers, domestic servants, and all other unproductive labourers. There is unfortunately no mode of expressing by one familiar term, the aggregate of what has been called the wages-fund of a country: and as the wages of productive labour form nearly the whole of that fund, it is usual to overlook the smaller and less important part, and to say that wages depend on population and capital. It will be convenient to employ this expression, remembering, however, to consider it as elliptical, and not as a literal statement of the entire truth.

With these limitations of the terms, wages not only depend upon the relative amount of capital and population, but cannot, under the rule of competition, be affected by anything else. Wages (meaning, of course, the general rate) cannot rise, but by an increase of the aggregate funds employed in hiring labourers, or a diminution in the number of the competitors for hire; nor fall, except either by a diminution of the funds devoted to paying labour, or by an increase in the number of labourers to be paid.[v]

That is a theory of wages that is more easily put into a mathematical form than is the theory of rent. The population in question does not include, we are told, idle persons, nor even all the persons who work; there is only the group of workers who earn a wage or *the number of wage earners*. Let *T* be this number. Mill explains, moreover, that the capital of which he is speaking does not include fixed capital; it is not even all the circulating capital, but only that part of the capital destined for paying wages, *the working capital spent on labor*. Let this amount be *K*. There is another point he deals with much more rapidly, but that must not escape us either. It appears that the rate to be determined is only *the average wage rate*. Let *s* be this rate. Having posited all this, to say that *the wage rate is settled by the ratio of the population to capital*, is the same as to say that $s = \dfrac{K}{T}$, namely that *the average wage rate is equal to the quotient of the total amount of wages paid and the total number of people who receive a salary*. It is undoubtedly not astonishing that a proposition of this type does not need further demonstration. Furthermore, also undoubtedly, it will not be a surprise that it cannot be of much use to us.

313. Let us first make this observation: we do not need the average wage rate, but the wages paid in the various enterprises. And this is all the more necessary given that, in the English School's system, we need the price of the productive services in order to determine the prices of the products. If these products consist of excavation works, we need the wage rate of excavation workers; if they are watches and clocks, we need the wage rates of the clockmakers. For this, the average wages, assumed to be determined by the formula, cannot be of any use to us; but is that rate really determined in that way? That would certainly be the case if we knew the capital and the population as given data; that is to say, the amount of circulating capital available to pay for labor and the number of wage earners; unfortunately, those are magnitudes that are undetermined as utterly as they are perfectly defined. And far from their ratio being able to determine the wage rate, it is they that depend on this rate.

Whether the wage rate rises or falls, it is sure that the number of wage-earners will increase or decrease with the decrease or increase of the other working classes, or even of the leisure classes; and it is equally certain that the amount of circulating capital destined for paying wages will increase or decrease with the decrease or increase of the other parts of circulating capital or even of fixed capital. It would be as impossible to distinguish the circulating capital used for wages from the circulating capital used for rent or the circulating capital used for 'profits' as to distinguish, in a tank with three outlet taps, the water destined to flow from one tap from that destined to flow from the other two. In such a container, the quantity of water passing through a tap will be determined, for each of the taps, by its width. It is exactly the same for the distribution of circulating capital in the form of wages, rent, and interest among the workers, landowners, and capitalists. If the wages were raised and the wage fund were insufficient, the fund would grow first of all at the expense of the circulating capital used for rent and the circulating capital used for 'profits'. Then it would perhaps be the circulating capital that would be insufficient. The rate of interest on this capital would be very high compared with the rate of interest on fixed capital, and savings that are being formed, instead of becoming fixed capital, would circulate. Fewer shares and bonds would be bought at the Bourse, and larger deposits would be made in the banks. And if the wages to be paid were low and the circulating capital used for payment of wages were excessive, this fund would shrink to the advantage of the circulating capital used for land services and 'profits'. Then there would perhaps be too much circulating capital. The rate of interest of this capital would be very low compared with the rate of interest on fixed capital, and savings in course of being made would become fixed capital instead of circulating capital. Deposits in the banks would be withdrawn to acquire securities in the bourse.

Therefore, instead of the wage rate being determined by the amount of circulating capital destined for payment of wages, it is rather that same amount that is determined by the wage rate. And what determines the wage rate, and the rates of rent and interest? That is, whatever Mill may say about it, the price of the things in the production of which labor, land services, and 'profits' are used; that is to say, the competition of consumers in the market for products, and not that of entrepreneurs in the market for services. It is quite true that the productive services are bought in the market for services; but it is no less true that their price is determined in the market for products. But there is no need to develop again here our theory of the determination of the price of the productive services, and it suffices that we have shown what the English theory of wages is worth.

314. The theory of interest is no less important than that of rent and that of wages. It is a point at which the socialists have frequently aimed their attacks, attacks to which economists have not replied in a convincing manner until now.

First of all, an error that overshadows the entire theory of interest, in particular in the work of the English School, is the confusion between the role of the capitalist and that of the entrepreneur. Under the pretext that, it is difficult in the real economy to be an entrepreneur without being at the same time a capitalist, they do not distinguish between the functions of the one and the other. This why the term *profit* used by them means both the *interest* on capital, and the *profit* of the enterprise. This detail must not be lost from view when their writings are read.

The confusion is regrettable. It is certainly difficult, but not impossible, however, to be in fact an entrepreneur without being a capitalist: every day, we see men, who do not possess themselves any capital, but whose intelligence, honesty, and experience are known, find funds that can be borrowed for an agricultural, industrial, commercial, or financial enterprise. In all these cases, and assuming that there are few entrepreneurs who are not capitalists, there is a great number of capitalists who are not entrepreneurs: they are holders of mortgage loans, unsecured loans, shares as a silent partner, or bonds. And finally, if the two roles were to be mixed together in practice even more often than they are now, the theory should distinguish them nonetheless.

Concerning the part of the profit that constitutes the enterprise's profit, the English School does not understand that it corresponds to a possible loss, that it is risky, that it depends on circumstances that are exceptional and not normal, and that, theoretically, it should be neglected. Concerning the part that constitutes interest on capital, the English School defines it as 'the remuneration for the abstinence by the capitalist who has saved capital'. Here we will show how it determines the one as well as the other under the name of profit. It is again from J.S. Mill that I here borrow the explanation of the English doctrine.

315. Basing itself on Ricardo's theory of rent, it starts by establishing, or, at least, it subsequently establishes that *the advances of capital consist only of wages*, or that *rent does not form a part of the cost of production of agricultural products.*

I undertook to show, (Mill writes), in the proper place, that this is an allowable supposition, and that rent does not really form any part of the expenses of production, or of the advances of the capitalist. The grounds on which this assertion was made are now apparent. It is true that all tenant farmers, and many other classes of producers, pay rent. But we have now seen, that whoever cultivates land, paying a rent for it, gets in return for his rent an instrument of superior power to other instruments of the same kind for which no rent is paid. The superiority of the instrument is in exact proportion to the rent paid for it. If a few persons had steam-engines of superior power to all others in existence, but limited by physical laws to a number short of the demand, the rent which a manufacturer would be willing to pay for one of these steam-engines could not be looked upon as an addition to his outlay, because by the use of it he would save in his other expenses the equivalent of what it cost him: without it he could not do the same quantity of work, unless at an additional expense equal to the rent. The same thing is true of land. The real expenses of production are those incurred on the worst land, or by the capital employed in the least favourable circumstances. This land or capital pays, as we have seen, no rent; but the expenses to which it is subject, cause all other land or agricultural capital to be subjected to an equivalent expense in the form of rent. Whoever does pay rent gets back its full value in extra advantages, and the rent which he pays does not place him in a worse position than, but only in the same position as, his fellow-producer who pays no rent, but whose instrument is one of inferior efficiency.[1,vi]

Rent having been eliminated in this way from the cost of production, there remains in the costs, independently of interest, only wages, the rate of which is, according to the English School, determined by the ratio of capital to population. Consequently, the interest (or, as the English say, 'the profit', combining interest properly speaking with the profit[vii] of the enterprise) is easy to determine. Mill concludes:

---

[1] J.S. Mill, *Principles of Political Economie*, L. II, Ch. XVI, § 6.

The capitalist, then, may be assumed to make all the advances, and receive all the produce. His profit consists of the excess of the produce above the advances; his *rate* of profit is the ratio which that excess bears to the amount advanced.[2,viii]

This is therefore, briefly, the English theory of the determination of the prices of productive services. The capitalists are the entrepreneurs; they compensate the landowners by paying them, in the form of rent, the excess of the products resulting from the more or less superior quality of their land, they compensate the workers by distributing among them, in the form of wages, the circulating capital used for those payments, and they remain the masters of the products. What is obtained by the entrepreneurs, after deduction of costs, represents interest on their capital plus the profit[ix] of their enterprise: this is the English School's *profit*. We still have to discuss this theory mathematically in order to see on what point it is misleading.

316. Let P be the total of the products of an enterprise; let S, I, and F be the amounts of the wages, the interest, and the rent paid by the entrepreneur during the process of production as prices for the services of the personal faculties, the capital goods, and the land. Remember here that, according to the English School, the price of the products is determined by their cost of production; that is to say, it equals their average cost in terms of productive services; thus we have the equation

$$P = S + I + F.$$

P is therefore determined; only S, I, and F have still to be determined. And, indeed, if it is the price of the services that determines the price of the products, and not the price of the products that determines the price of the productive services, we need to be told by what the price of the productive services is determined. That is just what the English economists undertake to do. To that end, they present us a theory of rent according to which rent is not included in the cost of production; this changes the above equation into the following:

---

[2] J.S. Mill, *Principles of Political Economie*, L. II, Ch. XV, § 5.

$$P = S + I.$$

After this, they determine S directly by means of the theory of wages. Then, finally, they tell us that 'the amount of interest or profit is the difference between the total price of the products and the cost of wages'; that is to say, I is determined by the equation

$$I = P - S.$$

Here it appears clearly that this determination eludes them, for one cannot, on the one hand, determine the term P by using the term I, and, on the other hand, determine the term I by using the term P. In sound mathematics, a single equation cannot be used to determine two unknowns. This is said with all reservations concerning the way in which the English School eliminates rent from the cost of production and carries out the determination of wages.

317. However, let us see in what state economics is still in as far as concerns the determination of the prices of services. J.-B. Say had said, in chapter V of book I of his *Traité d'economie politique*:

> An industrious person can lend his activity to someone who possesses only capital and land.
> The owner of some capital can lend his capital to a person who has only land and industriousness.
> The owner of a piece of land can lend it to a person who has only industriousness and some capital.
> When one lends industriousness, capital, or land, they are combined to create value; their use also has a value, and is remunerated in the ordinary way.
> The payment for borrowed industriousness is called a *wage*.
> The payment for borrowed capital is called *interest*.
> The payment for borrowed land is called *rent*.

That is a sufficiently clear and exact conception of the combination of the three productive services in the production process. The wording used is good, so we have adopted it ourselves. But there remain important gaps to be filled in. In the first place, J.-B. Say did not conceive of the distinctive role of the entrepreneur: this personage is lacking in his theory. Furthermore, Say gave an imperfect explanation of what services wages, interest, and rent are the price;

and his theory does not indicate, any more than did the Physiocrats' theory, how the price is determined. Here, it would be necessary to introduce a valid theory of value, of the mechanism of exchange, of capital and income, of the mechanism of production, the concept of the entrepreneur, and of the market for products and services; but, during fifty years, the French School of economics has not taken a single step in that direction; it has not produced any doctrine of economic theory; it still does not know how interest, wages, and rent are determined.

Here is evidence of this ignorance; I have taken it from the work of P.A. Boutron titled *Theorie de la rente foncière,*[x] awarded a prize by the Academy of Moral and Political Sciences. The author starts by stating resolutely that the price of products is determined by their average cost. Then, he defines rent as 'the excess of the price of products over their average cost in wages and interest'. If it were a question of furnishing the theory of wages, evidently he would have defined wages as 'the excess of the price of the products over their average cost in interest and rent'. And if the Academy had organized a competition for the theory of interest, he would undoubtedly have won the prize by defining interest as 'the excess of the price of the products over their average cost in rent and wages'.

318. It is in place of these inadequate systems that we substitute the one in which the three main elements are the expositions of the mechanism of free competition in exchange (effective supply and demand; price increase, price decrease, current equilibrium price), presented in part II; of the mechanism of free competition in production (land and its services, persons and labor, capital goods properly speaking and their services; landowners, workers, capitalists; entrepreneurs; profit, loss, equality of price and average cost) presented in part III; and of the mechanism of free competition in capital formation and credit (new capital goods properly speaking, excess of income over consumption; ratio of total net income of new capital goods to the total excess of income over consumption), presented in part IV. Thanks to these fundamental conceptions, we have: 1° a market for services on which the services of land, the labor of persons, and the services of capital goods properly speaking are supplied by the landowners, workers, and capitalists,

who lower prices if there is an excess supply, and are demanded by the entrepreneurs and by landowners, workers, and capitalists, who, the former group in their role as producers and the latter group in their role as consumers, raise prices if there is an excess demand; 2° a market for products in which consumable products are supplied by entrepreneurs, who lower prices if there is an excess supply, and demanded by landowners, workers, and capitalists, who raise prices if there is an excess demand; and 3° a capital goods market in which new capital goods properly speaking are supplied by entrepreneurs, who lower prices if there is an excess supply, and demanded by capitalists, who, in their role as creators of savings, raise prices if there is an excess demand. And, consequently, we have also: 1° the prices of the services, or, rent, wages, and interest; 2° the prices of products; and 3° the rate of net income, and consequently the prices of land, personal capital, and movable capital. The demand for services and the supply of consumable products and new capital goods are determined by the entrepreneurs by their consideration of the profit that can be obtained or the loss that can be avoided. The supply of the services and the demand for consumable products and newly produced capital goods are determined by the landowners, workers, and capitalists according to the criterion of the maximum satisfaction of wants.

Some people will perhaps ask me, as has indeed happened, whether it was really necessary, or even whether it was not more harmful than useful to present in mathematical form a doctrine that seems in itself simple enough and clear enough. My answer to that question will be as follows.

Asserting a theory is one thing, demonstrating it is another. I know that in economics every day so-called demonstrations are presented and received that are nothing other than gratuitous assertions. But, to be clear, I think that economics will not be a science until the day it compels itself to demonstrate that which it has practically limited itself so far to affirming without justification.. Now, to demonstrate that commodity prices, which are quantities, namely quantities of numeraire that can be exchanged for commodities, result effectively from such and such data or conditions, it is, in my opinion, absolutely indispensible: 1° to formulate, on the bases of those data and conditions, a system of equations, rigorously equal in number to the number of unknowns, of which the quantities in question are the roots, and 2° to prove that the interlinked phenomena in the real economy constitute indeed the empirical solution of this system of equations. This is what I have done successively for exchange, production, and capital formation. And the use of the mathematical language and the mathematical method did not only permit me to demonstrate thusly the laws of the establishment of the current prices in equilibrium, but it also permitted me to demonstrate, in addition, the laws of the variation in these prices, to analyze the fact of free competition, and in so doing, to put it on a sound base. Undoubtedly, the exposition of the system of free competition and its confirmation by reasoning are two distinct things that, united in my work, could, if necessary, be separated from each other. I do not oppose in any way the right of those of my readers who are economists without being mathematicians to leave aside the second of these two parts to benefit exclusively from the first. Very few among us are capable of reading Newton's *Mathematical Principles of Natural Philosophy* or Laplace's *Celestial Mechanics*; and nevertheless, we all accept, on the authority of competent men, the description given to us of the world of astronomic facts ruled by the principle of universal attraction. Why should we not accept similarly the description of the world of economic facts ruled by the principle of free competition? Nothing therefore prevents leaving aside the demonstration of the system, once it has been made, and retaining only the contents of the system for use in the study of questions in applied economics or in practical economics; but, for my part, I had to develop the theory and to demonstrate it in order to outline, as I wanted to do, a truly scientific theory of social wealth.

Notes

i Mill wrote 'employ'.

ii Walras quoted a French translation of Mill's book. The translator translated 'employ' as 'alimenter'. Walras adopted the latter word in his representation of Mill's sentence, and clearly did not consult Mill's English text. Walras then presented a critique of the French rendering of the sentence, although the operative word 'alimenter' was certainly not what Mill would have used if he had translated the book into French. Walras's critique is therefore misdirected. It is imperative, however, to present a translation of 'alimenter', rather than 'employ', because Walras's text would otherwise not make sense.

iii Walras himself seems to be misled here by the enigmatic French version of Mill's book, *Principes d'économie politique*, translated by H. Dussard and J.-G. Courcelle-Seneuil, page 94: 'Acheter le produit n'est pas alimenter le travail.' The verb 'alimenter' is the French equivalent of 'to feed', or 'to sustain'. In an ineffectual effort to salvage more or less what Walras wrote, William Jaffé, in his translation of Walras's *Éléments*, did not present Mill's wording ('to purchase produce is not to employ labour'), but translated the French translation used by Walras in this way: 'To purchase produce is not to *support* labour' (our emphasis).The following citation of the opening section of § 9 of Chapter V of Book I may be of use:

> We now pass to a fourth fundamental theorem respecting Capital, which is, perhaps, oftener overlooked or misconceived than even any of the foregoing. What supports and employs productive labour, is the capital expended in setting it to work, and not the demand of purchasers for the produce of the labour when completed. Demand for commodities is not demand for labour. The demand for commodities determines in what particular branch of production the labour and capital shall be employed; it determines the *direction* of the labour; but not the more or less of the labour itself, or of the maintenance or payment of the labour. These depend on the amount of the capital, or other funds directly devoted to the sustenance and remuneration of labour.

The confusion has been caused by the notion of the 'wage fund' and its interpretation. We remark in passing that by 'labour', Mill meant 'work', not workers, otherwise he would have written in the second sentence of the quotation above: 'what supports and employs productive labour*s*', etc.

iv J.S. Mill, *Principles of Political Economy*. Ninth edition (1885), edited by W.J. Ashley, new impression, 1923, London/New York/Toronto:Longman, Green and Co. Book I, Chapter V, § 9, pages 85–6.

v Ibid., Book II, Chapter XI, § 1, page 343.

vi Ibid., Book II, Chapter XVI, § 6, pages 433–4. The French translators, on their own authority, added to this section the following: 'la rente égalise ces deux situations.' (the rent equalizes these two situations).

vii Walras here was referring to 'bénéfice', namely revenue minus all costs, or *profit* in standard modern terminology.

viii Ibid., Book II, Chapter XV, § 6, pages 417–18. Walras erroneously said that this passage can be found in § 5.

ix Again, here Walras was referring to the conventional modern definition of profit.

x Paris: Guillaumin, 1867.

PART V

THEORY OF MONEY

LESSON 33

The problem of the value of money

SUMMARY: – The role of the numeraire; the role of circulating money and money saved. Framing the problem of the value of money. Hypothesis of a non-commodity money. The desired cash balance; the equation of circulation. The mechanism of circulation; the market for money capital; the determination of the rate of interest. The law of the direct proportionality of the price of the money commodity to its quantity, and its inverse proportionality to the desired cash balance. The hypothesis of a commodity being money; its price curve as money; its price curve as a commodity. The law of the establishment and variation of the price of the money commodity.

319. From the explanation I gave of the mechanism of free competition in matters of exchange, production, and capital formation, there follows quite evidently the necessity for having

1° A commodity in terms of which the prices of the other commodities are cried, or to the value of which the values of the other commodities are related, either in the market for services, or in the market for products, or in the capital market. This commodity then serves as the *numeraire*. As we have seen, one of the fundamental theorems of theoretical economics is the demonstration that, given m commodities (A), (B), (C), (D), $\cdots$ in a market, one can dispense with crying the $m(m - 1)$ prices of the commodities taken two by two, and cry only the prices $p_b, p_c, p_d, \cdots$ of $m - 1$ of them, (B), (C), (D), $\cdots$, in terms of the mth, (A), taken as the numeraire.

2° A commodity obtained by selling services in the market for services, and by means of which the products in the market for products are bought, and that serves as *circulating money*. In fact, we sell our services to entrepreneurs who do not make the products we need, and we buy the products we need from entrepreneurs who do not use our services. Hence the necessity for a medium of exchange.

3° A commodity in which the excess of income over consumption is formed, and in which fixed and circulating capital is lent, and that serves as *money savings*. In fact, in general we do not use our savings to buy machines, instruments, tools, raw materials, products made to be offered for sale, in order to lend them to entrepreneurs. We form our savings in money and we lend that money to entrepreneurs. Hence the necessity for the intermediation of credit.

But the designation of a commodity as circulating money and money savings has an effect, on its rareté and therefore on its value, that has to be studied.

320. In deciding that a certain commodity, gold or silver, Médoc wine or Havana cigars, will serve as money, its total quantity will be divided into two parts, one of which will be put into tills, wallets, and moneyboxes of the exchangers, while only the other part will be at the disposition of the consumers, drinkers, or smokers; consequently, its quantity as a commodity is decreased and its rareté is increased as well as its value compared with the value of the other commodities. In this way, the obscure and confusing controversy pursued without a truce and without respite between the monometallists and the bimetallists on the subject of the value of the money commodity is eliminated. According to the former, this value is owed completely to its use as a commodity, and the law that designates the money has nothing to do with it; according to the latter, this value is owed completely to its use as money, and it is the law that designates the money that creates the value: νόμος *law* νόμισμα *money*. Well, they both see only half of the real and complete problem, which is as follows: the money commodity has, by itself and as a commodity, a certain value; but the law that designates it as money adds, so to speak, to this first value a second value from which the overall and definitive value results. How is this overall and definitive value determined? And how is the total quantity of the money commodity divided into a quantity of commodity and a quantity of money? This is the problem of the value of money.

To solve it as clearly as possible, we first assume that a determinate quantity of a well-defined thing is chosen as circulating money and as money for savings, but that the thing is not useful, and that, consequently, it does not have exchange value in and of itself, like certain stones, shells, chestnuts, or even pieces of paper with certain engravings on them. Undoubtedly, there is only one commodity properly speaking that must be selected as an intermediary in exchange and credit; in other words, money must be one of the sorts of social wealth. If laws and decrees were enacted that decree arbitrarily that stones or other similar objects had value and were legal tender, it is evident that, at the first moment of trouble, the authorities having become powerless, the holders of this money would be ruined. Now, it is precisely in these circumstances that money must have the most value. This, however, is a matter of applied theory that we can put aside temporarily. In order to develop pure theory, it would evidently be advantageous for us to investigate how a thing takes on value as money before investigating how the value as money is combined with a value as a commodity.

321. Without wondering which natural circumstances can necessitate the landowners, workers, and capitalists keeping, at a certain time, a more or less considerable amount of money, with a view to making more or less considerable purchases or savings, we assume in fact, for the sake of simplicity, that the amount of that money depends not only on the situation, but also on the characteristics and the habits of each person. And, indeed, here as well as in the case of the want curves, we can and must admit that the human will has a certain influence, this influence being exercised within limits that are as wide as is wished, which does not prevent its consequences from being subject to the laws of mathematics. Now, it must be clearly understood that when a consumer or a producer wishes to keep a certain stock of gold, silver, Médoc wine, Havana cigars, stones, shells, chestnuts, or paper money, his sole consideration is not the quantity of the money, which in itself is completely indifferent to him, but the quantity of other commodities, products, services, or capital goods that he can obtain in exchange for his money. Therefore, on the conditions defined above for the equilibrium of exchange, production, and capital formation, let (U) be the item

chosen to be money; Q_u the existing quantity of that item; (A), (B), (C), (D), $\cdots$ the consumable products; (T), $\cdots$, (P), $\cdots$, (K), (K'), (K''), $\cdots$ the capital goods, land services, personal services, and the services of capital properly speaking; (M), (M'), $\cdots$ the raw materials; $p_a, p_c, p_d, \cdots, P_t, \cdots, P_p, \cdots, P_k, P_{k'}, P_{k''}, \cdots, p_t, \cdots, p_p, \cdots, p_k, p_{k'}, p_{k''}, \cdots, p_m, p_{m'}, \cdots$ the prices of these commodities in terms of (B); and i the common rate of net income and of interest. Let $a, b, c, d, \cdots T, \cdots, P, \cdots, K, K', K'', \cdots, t, \cdots, p, \cdots, k, k', k'', \cdots, m, m', \cdots$ be the quantities of these same commodities of which the exchangers want to have the equivalent in money in their till. And let

$$ap_a + b + cp_c + dp_d + \cdots + TP_t + \cdots + PP_p + \cdots + KP_k + K'P_{k'} + K''P_{k''}$$
$$+ \cdots + tp_t + \cdots + pp_p + \cdots + kp_k + k'p_{k'} + \cdots + k''p_{k''}$$
$$+ \cdots + mp_m + m'p_{m'} + \cdots = H.$$

It is evident that the existing quantity of (U), Q_u, would take a value determined by the equation

$$Q_u p_u = H.$$

If we pass from the system of prices in terms of (B) to the system of prices in terms of (U), by dividing all the prices in terms of (B) by $p_u = \dfrac{H}{Q_u}$, yielding $\pi_a, \pi_b, \pi_c, \pi_d, \cdots$, $\Pi_t, \cdots, \Pi_p, \cdots, \Pi_k, \Pi_{k'}, \Pi_{k''}, \cdots, \pi_t, \cdots, \pi_p, \cdots, \pi_k, \pi_{k'}, p_{k''}, \cdots$, $\pi_m, \pi_{m'}, \cdots$ as quotients, we would obtain

$$a\pi_a + b\pi_b + c\pi_c + d\pi_d + \cdots + T\Pi_t + \cdots + P\Pi_p + \cdots + K\Pi_k + K'\Pi_{k'}$$
$$+ K''\Pi_{k''} + \cdots + t\pi_t + \cdots + p\pi_p + \cdots + k\pi_k + k'\pi_{k'} + \cdots + k''\pi_{k''}$$
$$+ \cdots + m\pi_m + m'\pi_{m'} + \cdots = Q_u;$$

and it is evident that, this cash balance being lent at the price $Q_u i$, the equilibrium of circulation would exist together with those of production and capital formation. Indeed, in this way, we would always have the equilibrium of the exchange, because, the prices always being proportional to the raretés, the consumers would always have maximum satisfaction of their needs; we would also always have the equilibrium of production, because, the prices of the products being always equal to their average cost in terms of services, the entrepreneurs would never make profits or suffer losses; we would always have the equilibrium of capital formation, because, the net rate of revenue not having changed, the prices of the capital goods would always be proportional to the prices of the services; and, finally, we would have the equilibrium of circulation, because the exchangers would have the desired cash balance at the rate of interest that has been announced. Moreover, it is obvious that, all other things remaining unchanged, if Q_u increased or decreased, the equilibrium would maintain itself by a proportional rise or fall of all the prices, and that if H increased or decreased, it would maintain itself by a proportional fall or rise of all the prices. However, it remains to be demonstrated how this direct proportionality of the prices to the quantity of money and this indirect proportionality of the prices to the desired cash balance tend to maintain themselves in a regime of free competition. And for this it remains to define the mechanism of free competition in matters of circulation.

322. In order to reduce this mechanism to its essential elements, we will establish the identity of two circumstances.

First, supposing that fixed capital is rented partially in money and that all circulating capital is rented in money, we will not make any difference between the one and the other. In reality, these two types of capital are rented in two markets that are different but connected to each other, at two interest rates that differ but that depend on each other. We will find all these differences once again in the applied theory of credit. Here, to develop the pure theory of money, we should neglect them. We will therefore consider only one market that we will call henceforth the *market for money capital* and no longer the *market for numeraire capital*, in which the entrepreneurs enter to demand money every day to constitute, complete, or maintain their fixed capital, consisting of machines, instruments, tools, and their circulating capital, consisting of raw materials and finished products. The interest generated by the circulating capital pays for the service of money during the time it is kept, and for the stocks of raw materials and finished products, just like the interest generated by the fixed capital is the payment for the use of machines, instruments, tools. During the day, the entrepreneurs will buy, with their money, fixed and circulating capital; and the next day, the sellers bring to the market the money that they will have received, except for the part that they will need for themselves.

Then, we will no longer distinguish, from the point of view of hiring of fixed and circulating capital, between landowners, workers, and capitalists as consumers on the one hand, and, on the other hand, entrepreneurs that are producers. Furniture, clothing, objects of art and luxury, and the stocks of consumer articles provide the same services to the former as do the stocks of raw materials and finished products to the latter. In both cases, the same price is paid for these services. Hence we assume that the landowners, workers, and capitalists, just like the entrepreneurs, come to the market for money capital every day to demand the money they need to constitute, complete, or maintain their circulating and fixed capital. With their money they will buy, during the day, furniture, clothing, objects of art and luxury, and consumer goods; and the next day the sellers will also bring to the market the money they will have received.

If we join to this twofold demand for money the demand that will be effectuated by the creators of savings to buy new capital goods in order to rent them out in kind, we will have the daily demand for money in the market for money capital. And if we join the money brought by the sellers of these new capital goods to that brought, as we have said, by all the other entrepreneurs who will have received it the day before in exchange for commodities, and by the landowners, workers, and capitalists, who will have received it in exchange for their services, we will have the daily supply of money in the market for money capital, equal to the existing quantity of money, that obtains on the market for money capital. If, at the rate of interest that is cried, demand is superior to supply, the rate will be raised and the producers and consumers will reduce their desired cash balances. If supply is superior to demand, the rate will be lowered and the producers and consumers will increase their desired cash balances. The current rate of interest will be the one for which the demand for and the supply of money capital will be equal.

Such is the market that is at the same time the market for money capital and the money market. The daily demand for money that is brought to it is nothing other than the demand for that fraction of fixed and circulating capital of the society that is renewed every day, as we explained when discussing the permanent market (§ 271).

Those who borrow money in fact borrow fixed and circulating capital for which they exchange the money that same day. When they pay interest on the money borrowed, they pay the interest on the fixed and circulating capital represented by the money. It is therefore normal that the price to be cried in the market is the rate of interest on money capital. Alongside this rate, there is the rate of net income, which is always the ratio of the price of the service of new capital goods to the price of those goods themselves. And these two rates tend to equality because, according to whether the first is greater or less than the second, the creators of savings and the borrowers are equally interested in either leaving money capital in the market or in withdrawing it; however, this does not mean that the two rates are any the less distinct. Moreover, according to whether savings will be substantial or slight, the part of the desired cash balances relating to consumption will be small or large, and the one relating to production large or small, and the rate of interest low or high.

As I should have done, I have simplified as much as possible. Those of my readers who would be eager to know the varied and complex details with which this mechanism can enrich itself in reality have only to read the fine book by Walter Bagehot, *Lombard Street*.[i] Furthermore, I have assumed that the total quantity of money existing is brought every day to the market. Given this hypothesis, the transformation of money savings into circulating money, and of circulating money into money saved, is just as fast as possible because all the money brought to the market during the morning is saved money, and becomes circulating money during the afternoon when it is exchanged for fixed and circulating capital. After some reflection, one will see that this is really the ideal approached in a society in which one deposits the money from his sales in a current account at the bank, and takes from that account the money for his purchases, and in which the money in the tills, the purses, and the moneyboxes will decrease more and more. In a society in which money is kept in a cash register from the moment it is received until the day it is given as payment or until the day it is lent, money does not render much service, and those who keep it, be they producers or consumers, will unnecessarily lose the interest on the capital represented by the money. But, after all, this circumstance does not change in any respect the essential mechanism of monetary circulation and of the market for money capital. Its only consequence is that the desired cash balance is much more considerable, and that, on the one hand, the daily supply of money is diminished by the existing quantity of money that is kept in reserve, while, on the other hand, its demand is diminished by a corresponding fraction of the desired cash balance; but the current rate of interest is always determined, as we have said, by the supply and the demand that occurs in the market.

323. The market for money capital having thus been defined, let us assume that, on a certain day, after the determination of the current rate of interest equal to the rate of net income, the existing quantity Q_u of money has decreased or that the desired cash balance H, representing the utility of money, has increased. The next day, equilibrium in the market would only be established at a new, higher rate of interest and, accordingly, the desired cash balance would decrease. But, as a result of this reduction of the desired cash balance, all the prices of products, capital goods, services, and raw materials would fall; because of this fall, the desired cash balance would become again as it was before; and the day after that equilibrium would establish itself at the current rate of interest equal to the rate of net income. The contrary would take place in the case of an increase of the existing quantity of money or of a decrease in the desired cash balance. Consequently: – *If, all other things remaining unchanged, the existing quantity of money increases, or if the desired cash balance decreases, prices rise proportionally. If the existing quantity of money decreases, or if the desired cash balance increases, prices fall proportionally.* This law extends to money the principle by virtue of which value increases with utility and decreases with quantity. This is, in itself, plausible enough; and many economists have already formulated it at least as far as it concerns the ratio of the variation in the prices to the variation in the quantity of money; but I am doing something more by demonstrating it mathematically by means of all the foregoing economic theories.

324. It is therefore well established that, if money (U) is something that is not a commodity, its price in terms of (B) is given by the equation

$$Q_u p_u = H.$$

Let us now assume that we take as money a commodity (A) existing in total quantity Q_a, of which a quantity Q_a' will retain its character as a commodity, while a quantity Q_a'' will be given the form of money; in consequence of which the price of (A) will rise from p_a to P_a, and the latter price will satisfy the equation

$$Q_a'' P_a = aP_a + b + cp_c + dp_d + \cdots + TP_t + \cdots + PP_p + \cdots + KP_k + K'P_{k'}$$
$$+ K''P_{k''} + \cdots + tp_t + \cdots + pp_p + \cdots + kp_k + k'p_{k'} + k''p_{k''}$$
$$+ \cdots + mp_m + m'p_{m'} + \cdots = H + a(P_a - p_a).$$

Now, since a is very small compared to H, we may neglect the term $a(P_a - p_a)$ and consider the price of money (A) in terms of (B) as given by the equation

$$Q_a'' P_a = H.$$

Let there now be two rectangular axes (Fig. 28): a horizontal *price axis* Op, and a vertical *quantity axis* Oq.

We have just seen that the price curve of (A) as money in terms of another commodity (B) is, as a function of the quantity of (A), if we neglect an insignificant term, a rectangular hyperbola with axes as asymptotes and with equation

$$q = \frac{H}{p};$$

that is to say, a curve such that the product of its ordinates, representing quantities of (A) as money, and its abscissa, representing the price of money in terms of (A), is constant and equal to the magnitude H of the desired cash balance in terms of (B), which is assumed to be determined.

Now, we know on the other hand (§ 226) that the price curve of (A) as commodity in terms of (B), as a function of the quantity, is a curve $A_q A_p$ (Fig. 29) that has the equation

$$q = F_a(p);$$

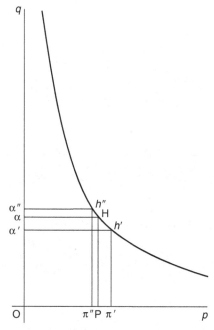

Fig. 28

that is to say, such a curve that, the quantity of (A) decreasing from a finite quantity represented by the length $\overline{OA_q}$ to zero, the price of (A) increases always from zero to a price, infinite or not, represented by the length $\overline{OA_p}$.

That having been stated, it is really easy to understand that the price curve of (A), in terms of (B), considered both as a commodity and as money, is, as a function of the quantity, a curve passing through the point G the equation of which is[ii]

$$q = F_a(p) + \frac{H}{p}$$

and that can be obtained graphically by superposing, for all the abscissas, the ordinates of the curve h″Hh′ upon the ordinates of the curve $A_q A_p$. Indeed, this construction having been made, let $\overline{OA}$ be a length representing the total quantity Q_a of (A); if we draw the horizontal line AG until it meets the superior curve, and if we

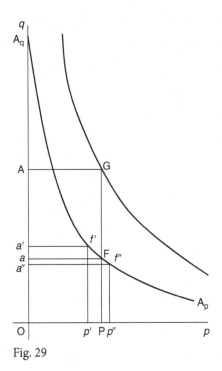

Fig. 29

draw downwards the perpendicular GP, we will get the abscissa $\overline{OP}$, the representation of the price P_a of (A), as commodity and money, corresponding to the quantity Q_a. And furthermore, we will have [in Figures 28 and 29] the lengths $\overline{Oa} = \overline{PF}$ and $\overline{aA} = \overline{O\alpha} = \overline{FG}$, representing, respectively, the quantities Q_a' and Q_a'' of (A) as a commodity and (A) as money when there will be no transformation of (A) as commodity into (A) as money nor of (A) as money into (A) as commodity.

If, instead of dividing the quantity Q_a into Q_a' and Q_a'', as we did just above, we had divided Q_a randomly into two quantities, the one represented by $\overline{Oa'} > \overline{Oa}$, and the other by $\overline{a'A} = \overline{O\alpha'} < \overline{O\alpha}$, the price of (A) as a commodity would be represented by $\overline{Op'} < \overline{OP}$ and the price of (A) as money by $\overline{O\pi'} > \overline{OP}$; commodity would then be transformed into money, which would diminish $\overline{Oa'}$, increase $\overline{O\alpha'}$, and, consequently, increase $\overline{Op'}$ and diminish $\overline{O\pi'}$. And, if we had divided randomly into two quantities, the one represented by $\overline{Oa''} < \overline{Oa}$, and the other by $\overline{a''A} = \overline{O\alpha''} > \overline{O\alpha}$, the price of (A) as a commodity would be represented by $\overline{Op''} > \overline{OP}$ and the price of (A) as money by $\overline{O\pi''} < \overline{OP}$; money would then be transformed into commodity, which would increase $\overline{Oa''}$, diminish $\overline{O\alpha''}$, and, consequently, diminish $\overline{Op''}$ and increase $\overline{O\pi''}$. So, our construction furnishes the solution of the problem of the determination of: 1° the price of the money commodity (A), 2° the quantity of (A) as a commodity, and 3° the quantity of (A) as money, just as takes place in reality by tatonnements as is shown very well by Figures 28 and 29.

Hence – *In the case of a unique monetary standard, the common and identical price in terms of any other commodity of the money commodity as a commodity and as money is determined by minting or demonetization depending on whether the price of the money is higher than the price of the commodity or the reverse.*

325. The two curves $h''Hh'$ and $A_q A_p$ and the length $\overline{OA}$ thus being the elements of the establishment of the price of the money commodity and of the respective quantities as a commodity and as money, they are also, for the same reason, the elements causing variations in that price and those quantities. Hence, it will suffice to examine the effects of shifts of the curves $h''Hh'$ and $A_q A_p$, and the effects of changes in the length $\overline{OA}$, in order to give an account of all the phenomena of variations in the price of the money commodity and of the respective quantities as a commodity and as money. For example, the curve $h''Hh'$ moves away from or approaches the origin O in accordance with the increase or decrease of the magnitude of the desired cash balance; the curve $A_q A_p$ moves away from or approaches the origin O in accordance with the increase or decrease of the utility of (A) as a commodity. Now, depending on whether the two curves move away from or approach the origin, the price of (A) increases or decreases. Hence, *this price increases or decreases with the increase or decrease of the magnitude of the desired cash balance and the utility of the commodity.* Concerning the length $\overline{OA}$, it increases or decreases with the increase or decrease of the quantity of (A). Now, according to whether this length increases or decreases, the price of (A) decreases

or increases. Hence, *this price increases or decreases with the increase or decrease of the quantity of the commodity.*

Notes

i   *Lombard Street, a Description of the Money Market,* third edition, London: H.S. King, 1873.

ii The equation that follows must then be seen as giving p implicitly as a function of q. Walras defines a price curve as q as a function of p (see, for example, in this section above and § 151), so the equation is that of a price curve. He also writes, however: 'the purchase curve has a very remarkable character: it becomes a *curve of the price* as a function of the total quantity in existence, since its abscissas give the price of the commodity as a function of the total quantity in existence represented by its ordinates' (§ 152). Walras therefore meant that the curve through G in the graph can be considered as the price curve showing q as a function of p, as well as the curve portraying p as a function of q (compare Jaffé's translation, which obscures these features (Walras 1954, p. 335)). The former is given by the equation above, whereas the price as a function of the quantity is given by solving the equation for p as a function of q. Since Walras is concerned with the division, at each price, of the total quantity of the substance (A) into the part that is used as money and the part that is used as a commodity, he shows q as the dependent variable in the graph by putting it on the vertical axis.

LESSON 34

Mathematical theory of bimetallism

SUMMARY: – In the monometallic system, there are three equations to determine the three unknowns of the problem of the value of money; in the bimetallic system, there are only five equations to determine six unknowns; a sixth equation has to be introduced. This sixth equation can be obtained by fixing a legal ratio between the value of gold money and silver money. Once that ratio is fixed, the ratio of the value of gold as a commodity to the value of silver as a commodity tends to equal to the former ratio by the transformation of each of these two metals from money into a commodity or from a commodity into money. Equation of bimetallism. Geometric solution of the equations of bimetallism. Law of the establishment of the common and identical price of the two money commodities. Increase and decrease in the quantity of each metal. Effects of a suspension or a resumption of minting silver.

326. The dispute between the monometallists and the bimetallists shows strikingly, by lack of the application of the only appropriate method of studying essentially quantitative facts, how there are left obscure and uncertain some fundamental points in these questions that it would be possible, if one so wished, to clarify with mathematical rigor.

In the preceding lesson, titled 'The problem of the value of money', I showed that, if we use one single commodity (A) as money, there are just three unknowns:

1° the quantity of (A) that remained a commodity;
2° the quantity of (A) that became money;

3° the common price of (A) as a commodity and of (A) as money in terms of any other commodity.

There are three equations, expressing:

1° that the sum of the quantities of (A) as a commodity and of (A) as money is equal to the total quantity of (A);

2° how the price of (A) as a commodity depends on the quantity of (A) as a commodity;

3° how the price of (A) as money depends on the quantity of (A) as money.

If we now employ simultaneously two commodities (A) and (O) as money, there will be six unknowns:

1° the quantity of (A) as a commodity;
2° the quantity of (A) as money;
3° the quantity of (O) as a commodity;
4° the quantity of (O) as money;
5° the price of (A) as a commodity and as money;
6° the price of (O) as a commodity and as money.

But, to determine those six unknowns, there are no more than five equations, expressing:

1° that the sum of the quantities of (A) as a commodity and of (A) as money is equal to the total quantity of (A);

2° that the sum of the quantities of (O) as a commodity and of (O) as money is equal to the total quantity of (O);

3° how the price of (A) as a commodity depends on the quantity of (A) as a commodity;

4° how the price of (O) as a commodity depends on the quantity of (O) as a commodity;

5° how the price of (A) as money and the price of (O) as money depend together on the quantities of (A) as money and of (O) as money.

If three commodities were used simultaneously as money, there would be only seven equations to determine nine unknowns.

If four commodities were used simultaneously as money, there would be only nine equations to determine twelve unknowns. And so forth.

So, in the case of a unique standard, the problem is completely determinate and is solved automatically in the market by the mechanism of free competition. The legislator has nothing to do except to designate the money commodity (A), to permit the transformation of (A) from money into commodity if the value of (A) as a commodity is greater than the value of (A) as money, and to transform, if so asked, commodity into money as soon as the value of (A) as money is greater than the value of (A) as a commodity.

On the other hand, in the case of a double standard, the problem is not completely determined, and the legislator can intervene to determine arbitrarily one of the six unknowns or introduce in one way or another a sixth equation. For example, he could determine arbitrarily the quantity of (A) as money, or the quantity of (O) as money, or the ratio of the first quantity to the second one. In the latter case, we have a bimetallism *at a fixed ratio of quantities.*[1] Alternatively, he could determine arbitrarily the price of (A) as money or the price of (O) as money, or the ratio of the first price to the second one. In this case, we have bimetallism *at a fixed ratio of values.* If he bases the arbitrary determination on quantity, the value will be determined automatically in the market. If he bases it on value, the quantities will be determined automatically in the market through the mechanism of free competition.

327. If we assume that the latter option has been chosen by fixing at 15½, as the bimetallists are demanding, the ratio of the value of gold money to the value of silver money, here is how the respective quantities of minted and unminted gold and silver will be established as a consequence. When the ratio of the value of gold as a commodity to the value as silver as a commodity is *greater* than 15½, not only all the gold extracted from the mines will be used for jewellery or utensils, but, furthermore, a part of the gold money will be transformed into a commodity, while, at the same time, all the silver extracted from the mines will be minted, and, moreover, a part of silver as a commodity will be transformed into silver money. Hence, the quantity of *gold money will diminish*, and that of *silver money will increase*. The

---

[1] In an article titled 'On Remedies for Fluctuations in Prices', in the *Contemporary Review* of March 1887, Alfred Marshall outlined a monetary system that is nothing other than bimetallism at a fixed ratio of quantities. [The article has been reprinted in *Memorials of Alfred Marshall*, edited by A.C. Pigou, London: Macmillan, 1925, pages 188–211.]

quantity of *gold as a commodity will increase*, and that of *silver as a commodity* will decrease; and that will continue until the ratio of the value of gold as a commodity to the value of silver as commodity has fallen back to 15½. When the ratio of the value of gold as a commodity to the value of silver as a commodity is *less* than 15½, the inverse phenomena will take place. The quantity of *gold money will increase*; that of *silver money will decrease*. The quantity of *gold as commodity will decrease*; that of *silver as commodity will increase*; and that will continue until the ratio of the value of gold as money to the value of silver as money has risen again to 15½.

From these explanations it follows that the monometallists are wrong when they maintain categorically that promising that the 15½ rate is irrevocable is promising the impossible. Within certain limits, that irrevocability is possible without violating free competition. But it follows also that the bimetallists themselves are wrong in thinking that the ratio 15½, being fixed as the legal ratio of the value of gold as money to the value of silver as money, will be, by this very act, imme-. diately and forever, the natural ratio of the value of gold as a commodity to the value of silver as a commodity. A single commodity can be money; in becoming money, it remains nonetheless a commodity, and as such it has nonetheless a price determined by the law of supply and demand. Exceptionally and for a moment, this price can be sometimes greater and sometimes less than the price of money, and, consequently, it can be advantageous for a miner to bring his metal sometimes to the market, sometimes to the Mint, and for the money changer sometimes to melt coins, sometimes to mint ingots. We see this every day in the system of a unique standard, as well as in the system of a double standard. Undoubtedly, in the latter case, the ratio of 15½ imposed on the two metals as money by the legislator will be imposed on these metals as commodities by the mechanism of free competition, but not immediately nor forever. *Greater* than 15½, the ratio of the value of gold as a commodity to the value of silver as a commodity can only be lowered by the *demonetization of gold*, and *as long as there is gold to be demonetized*; subsequently, the rate will maintain itself at 16, 17, 18, ⋯. *Less* than 15½, this same rate can only be raised by the *demonetization of silver*, and *as long as there is silver to be demonetized*; subsequently, the rate will maintain itself at 15, 14, 13, ⋯. The bimetallists tell us, rightly or wrongly, that the present fall of the value of silver is to be attributed to the action of the law, and not to that of nature; but they cannot seriously think they can guarantee us that the latter action will never take place. It is therefore of utmost importance to know that in the bimetallic system there can occur such an increase of the quantity of silver that a demonetization of the total quantity of gold will be brought about, and this will oblige us to make our large payments by means of very heavy sums, or there can occur such an increase of the quantity of gold that a demonetization of the total quantity of silver will be brought about, and this will oblige us to fulfill our small payments by means of extremely small coins; that is to say that the system of the double standard at the legal rate of 15½, whether *local* or *universal*, still is, after all the system of the alternative standard in which the depreciated metal has driven the appreciated metal more or less out of circulation.

This is the theory that must be developed mathematically.

328. The geometrical demonstration presented in lesson 33 corresponds with the algebraic solution of the three equations

$$Q_a = Q'_a + Q''_a,$$

$$Q'_a = F_a(P_a),$$

$$Q''_a = \frac{H}{P_a},$$

to determine the three unknowns P_a, Q'_a and Q''_a. Hence, in this case, there are indeed three equations for the determination of three unknowns.

Let now (A) and (O) be two commodities used simultaneously as money; let Q_a and Q_o be their respective total quantities, Q'_a and Q'_o the quantities that have remained commodities, Q''_a and Q''_o their quantities in the form of money. Let P_a and P_o be their prices in terms of any third commodity (B). For the determination of these six unknowns, we have the five equations:

$$Q_a = Q'_a + Q''_a, \tag{1}$$

$$Q_o = Q'_o + Q''_o, \tag{2}$$

expressing that the total quantities of (A) and (O) are equal to the sums of the quantities of (A) as a commodity and of (A) as money and the quantities of (O) as a commodity and of (O) as money;

$$Q'_a = F_a(P_a), \qquad [3]$$

$$Q'_o = F_o(P_o), \qquad [4]$$

expressing how the prices of (A) as a commodity and (O) as a commodity result from the quantities of (A) as a commodity and (O) as a commodity;

$$Q''_a P_a + Q''_o P_o = H, \qquad [5]$$

expressing that the quantity of (A) as money and the quantity of (O) as money yield together the desired cash balance.

In order to complete the determination of the problem, we can, if we wish to do so, state the following equation

$$P_o = \omega P_a, \qquad [6]^2$$

that fixes a ratio between P_a and P_o. This is what happens when the state declares that 1 of (O) and ω of (A) are equivalent as means of payment.

329. Bringing the value P_o from the equation [6] into the equations [4] and [5], and then the values of Q'_a and Q'_o taken from [3] and the modified equation [4] into the equations [1] and [2], we obtain

$$Q_a = F_a(P_a) + Q''_a,$$

$$Q_o = F_o(\omega P_a) + Q''_o,$$

---

² In bimetallism with a fixed ratio of quantities, the sixth equation would be

$$Q''_a = \alpha Q''_o,$$

and the mathematical theory of the system would be given by the solution of six equations just as that theory is going to be given for the case of bimetallism with a fixed ratio of values.

hence

$$Q_a'' = Q_a - F_a(P_a),$$

$$Q_o'' = Q_o - F_o(\omega P_a)$$

Bringing these values of Q_a'' and Q_o'' into the modified equation [5], we obtain

$$\left[Q_a - F_a(P_a)\right]P_a + \left[Q_o - F_o(\omega P_a)\right]\omega P_a = H,$$

hence

$$Q_a + \omega Q_o = F_a(p_a) + \frac{H}{P_a} + \omega F_o(\omega P_a);$$

an equation from which P_a can be deduced, and that is amenable to a very simple geometric solution.

Let there be given (Fig. 31) two rectangular axes: a *price axis*, Op, horizontal, and a *quantity axis*, Oq, vertical.

Let the curve through the point H in Figure 28 (§ 324) be a rect-angular hyperbola with the two axes as asymptotes that has the equation

$$q = \frac{H}{p};$$

let A_qA_p (Fig. 30) be the curve of price of (A) as a commodity in terms of (B), as a function of the quantity, with equation

$$q = F_a(p);$$

and let O_qO_p (Fig. 31) be the curve of the price of (O) as a commodity in terms of (B), as a function of the quantity, with equation

$$q = F_o(p).$$

I now subject this equation to the following transformation. On the horizontal axis, starting from O, I mark the abscissa 1.5, 2, 2.5, 3, $\cdots$

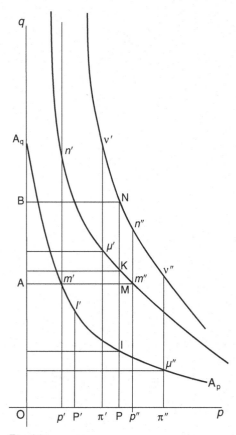

Fig. 30

equal to $\dfrac{1}{\omega}$ times the abscissa 15, 20, 25, 30, $\cdots$ (in the figure, ω is equal to 10). And on the lines parallel to the vertical axis through the first abscissa, I mark, measured from the horizontal axis, ordinates O'_q, s', s'', s''', $\cdots$ equal to ω times the ordinates r, r', r'', r''', $\cdots$. In this way, I obtain the curve $O'_q O'_p$ with equation

$$q = \omega F_o(\omega p).$$

This transformation will immediately become evident if we recognize that, in the system of the fixed ratio between the values of (A) and (O), 1 of (O) may be replaced by ω of (A) at a price that is ω times

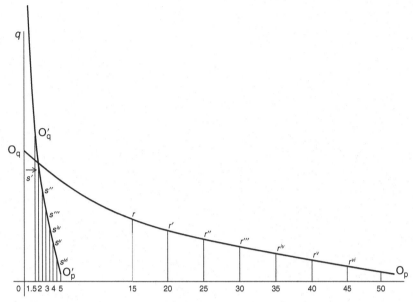

Fig. 31

less. The curve $O'_q O'_p$ is therefore, in some sense, the price curve of
(O) in the form of (A).

These preparations having been made, the geometrical solution of
the equation

$$Q_a + \omega Q_o = F_a\left(P_a\right) + \frac{H}{P_a} + \omega F_o\left(\omega P_a\right)$$

can be achieved as follows.

In Fig. 30, I superpose graphically, for all the abscissas, the ordinates of the curve passing through the point H [Fig. 28], on the ordinates of the curve $A_q A_p$, and obtain in this way the curve $\mu' Km''$
with equation

$$q = F_a\left(p\right) + \frac{H}{p}.$$

Then, I superpose graphically, for all the abscissas, the ordinates of
the curve $O'_q O'_p$ on the ordinates of the curve $\mu' Km''$, and obtain in
this way the curve $v' Nn''$ with equation

$$q = F_a(p) + \frac{H}{p} + \omega F_o(\omega P_a).$$

Now, let $\overline{OA}$ be a length representing the total quantity Q_a of (A), and $\overline{AB}$ a length representing ω times the total quantity of (O), hence ωQ_o; if we draw the horizontal line BN until it meets the uppermost curve, and if, from the point N, we draw downwards the perpendicular PN, we obtain, in the form of the abscissa $\overline{OP}$, the representation of the price p_a of (A) as a commodity and as money corresponding to the quantity Q_a. And, moreover, we get, in the form of the lengths $\overline{PI}$ and $\overline{IM}$, the representation of the respective quantities Q_a' and Q_a'' of (A) as a commodity and (A) as money, when there will be no transformation of (A) as a commodity into (A) as money, nor of (A) as money into (A) as a commodity. Furthermore, we have in the abscissa $50 = \omega \overline{OP}$ (Fig. 31) the representation of the price p_o of (O) as a commodity and as money corresponding to the quantity Q_o. Moreover, we have, in the form of the lengths $\overline{NK}$ and $\overline{KM}$ (Fig. 30), the representation of ω times the respective quantities Q_o' and Q_o'' of (O) as a commodity and (O) as money, when there will be no transformation of (O) as a commodity into (O) as money, nor of (O) as money into (O) as a commodity. Exactly as in the case of a unique standard, it can be demonstrated that, if instead of dividing the quantities Q_a and Q_o into Q_a' and Q_a'' and into Q_o' and Q_o'', as has been done above, we had divided them randomly into different quantities, there would have occurred, depending on the case, a transformation of (A) as a commodity into (A) as money or a transformation of (A) as money into (A) as a commodity, and a transformation of (O) as a commodity into (O) as money or a transformation of (O) as money into (O) as a commodity. For this, it would suffice to assume that the three parts of the length $\overline{NP}$ differ from $\overline{PI}$, $\overline{IK}$ and $\overline{IM}$ and are differently placed between the axis OP and the three curves A_qA_p, $\mu'Km''$, and $\nu'Nn''$. I abstain from repeating this demonstration for the sake of brevity and in order not to complicate the figure, which must serve for demonstrating another point.

Hence: – *In the case of two interdependent standards, just as in the case of a unique standard, the common and identical price in terms of any other commodity of each of the two money commodities as merchandise and as money is established by monetization or demonetization according to whether the price of money is greater than the price of the commodity or vice versa.*

330. The three curves H, A_qA_p, O_qO_p, the lengths $\overline{OA}$ and $\overline{AB}$, and the ratio ω, thus being the elements of the establishment of the price of the two money commodities and that of their respective quantities as a commodity and as money, are also, by this very fact, the elements of the variation in these prices and these quantities. Here again, it would suffice to examine subsequently the effects of displacements of the curves H, A_qA_p, O_qO_p, and the effects of changes in the lengths $\overline{OA}$ and $\overline{AB}$, and in the ratio ω, to see all the phenomena of variation in the price of the two money commodities as money and their respective quantities as commodities and as money. And by comparing the results of this study for the case of two interdependent standards with the results of a similar study for the case of a unique standard, one could declare, having complete knowledge of the matter, what the respective merits of monometallism and bimetallism are from the point of view of the greatest possible stability of the value of the numeraire and of money. This is what we want to do in the next lesson, but first we are going to study here the effects of changes in the lengths $\overline{OA}$ and $\overline{AB}$ corresponding with changes in the quantities Q_a and Q_o.

Let us first assume that Q_a, represented by $\overline{OA}$, remains constant, and that Q_o, represented by $\dfrac{\overline{MN}}{\omega}$, increases to a quantity represented by $\dfrac{\overline{m'n'}}{\omega}$, or decreases to a quantity represented by $\dfrac{\overline{m''n''}}{\omega}$. Figure 30 shows that, in the first case, the total quantity of silver, represented by $\overline{p'm'}$, would be a commodity, and that the monetary circulation would exclusive be served by gold, whereas, in the second case, the total quantity of gold, represented by $\dfrac{\overline{m''n''}}{\omega}$, would be a commodity, and the monetary circulation would be served by silver. The figure shows also that, if Q_o would increase to a quantity greater than $\dfrac{\overline{m'n'}}{\omega}$, or decrease to a quantity less than $\dfrac{\overline{m''n''}}{\omega}$, the price of silver would then remain equal to p' or p'', whereas the price of gold would become less than p' or greater than p''; the ratio of the value of gold as a commodity would be less than ω in the first case, and greater than ω in the second case.

We now assume that, while Q_o, represented by $\dfrac{\overline{MN}}{\omega} = \dfrac{\overline{\mu'v'}}{\omega} = \dfrac{\overline{\mu''v''}}{\omega}$, remains unchanged, Q_a, represented by $\overline{PM}$, increases to a quantity represented by $\overline{\pi'\mu'}$, or decreases to a quantity represented by $\overline{\pi''\mu''}$. The figure shows us that, in the first case, the total quantity of gold, represented by $\dfrac{\overline{\mu'v'}}{\omega}$, would become a commodity, and that the monetary circulation would be served exclusively by silver, whereas, in the second case, the total quantity of silver, represented by $\overline{\pi''\mu''}$, would become a commodity and the monetary circulation would be served exclusively by gold. The figure shows also that, if Q_o would increase to a quantity greater than $\overline{\pi'\mu'}$, or decrease to a quantity less than $\overline{\pi''\mu''}$, the price of gold would remain equal to π' or π'', while the price of silver would become less than π', or greater than π'', and the ratio of the value of gold as a commodity to the value of silver as a commodity would be greater than ω in the first case and less than ω in the second case.[i]

I have done enough, I think, to show how the question of monometallism versus bimetallism has until now been studied only superficially, and to put on the right track the persons who wish to make a more profound study of the subject. On the one hand, it is absolutely necessary that the monometallists give up answering the bimetallists in the same way, namely 'that it is just as difficult for the State to maintain a fixed ratio between the value of gold and the value of silver as it is between the value of wheat and that of rye. It is quite easy for the State to maintain a fixed ratio between the value of gold and the value of silver, and, once introduced, this ratio will tend indirectly to become the ratio of the value of gold as a commodity and the value of silver as a commodity. However, the bimetallists, too, must give up protesting 'that money can change in value by changing its form', and maintaining 'that there is a constant identity between the value of the metal in bullion, of the metal in numeraire, and of the metal in jewellery'.[3] This identity of the value of the metal as a commodity and the value as money, is far from being constant, and can only be maintained by monetization or by demonetization of metal, and ceases to exists when there is no more metal to demonetize.

331. The formulas used in the present theory, apart from the fact that they clarify the principle of bimetallism, could also furnish the means to give an explanation of the results of a practical application of this system. If the arbitrarily chosen functions or curves above are substituted, all or in part, by functions or curves with concrete coefficients, we will be able to calculate approximately the real effects of a resumption of the monetization of silver on the basis of some legal ratio between the value of gold as money and the value of silver as money. Let us assume that, in the country to which our curves correspond, an increase of the quantity of silver has taken place after the establishment of equilibrium, and that the occurrence of the natural and necessary effects of the legal ratio has been prevented by the suspension of minting silver. In this case, the quantity of silver money still being represented by $\overline{IM}$, and its price still being represented by $\overline{OP}$, the quantity of silver as a commodity will be represented by $\overline{P'I'}$, and its price by $\overline{OP'}$. If minting silver is then resumed, the effects of the legal ratio are produced by the superposition of the lengths $\overline{P'I'}$ and $\overline{IM}$ and by the placement of this total length to $\pi'v'$, between the points P and P'. It is evident that, within this framework, minting a certain quantity of silver will have as a reaction the demonetization of a certain quantity of gold, and the rise of the price of silver as a

[3] *Journal des économistes*, December 1876, page 457.

commodity from $\overline{OP'}$ to $\overline{O\pi'}$ will have as a reaction the fall of the price of silver as money from $\overline{OP}$ to $\overline{O\pi'}$ and of the price of gold as a commodity and as money from $\omega\overline{OP}$ to $\omega\overline{O\pi'}$. If concrete numbers would be useful to make the chain of phenomena understood more easily, here are some relating to our country and to our figure. In the situation of equilibrium, resulting from the ratio $\omega = 10$, the total quantity of silver, $\overline{OA} = \overline{PM} = 5$ billion demi-decagrams, is divided into $\overline{PI} = 2$ billion of silver as a commodity and $\overline{IM} = 3$ billion of silver as money; and the quantity of gold, $\dfrac{\overline{AB}}{10} = \dfrac{\overline{MN}}{10} = 433$ million

demi-decagrams, is divided into $\dfrac{\overline{MK}}{10} = 100$ million of gold as money

and $\dfrac{\overline{KN}}{10} = 333$ of gold as a commodity. The price of silver in terms of wheat is 5 pounds, that of gold is 50 pounds per demi-decagram. In other words, wheat is worth 0.20 F per pound. The total quantity of silver increases, by hypothesis by 2 billion, and, the minting of silver being suspended, the quantity of silver as a commodity would be raised from 2 to 4 billion; as a consequence of this, its price would fall from 5 to 1.66 pounds of wheat per demi-decagram. One could therefore buy 1 unit of silver as a commodity with 0.33 = 1.66/5 units of silver as money. If minting silver is resumed, 2 billion 1.66 million of silver would remain as a commodity, and 1 billion 833 million would be transformed into money; and, on the other hand, the 100 million of gold as money would be transformed into a commodity. The price of silver as a commodity would be raised from 1.66 to 4.33 pounds; conversely, the price of silver as money would diminish from 5 to 4.33 pounds, and the price of gold as a commodity and as money from 50 to 43.33 pounds of wheat per demi-decagram. In other words, wheat would then be worth $\dfrac{1\,\text{franc}}{4.33} = 0.23$ F per pound. We see that there would have been a 15 per cent rise in the prices of all commodities.

Note

i First, Walras shifts MN to the left while leaving N on the curve $v'Nn''$; M
will then follow a curve 'parallel' to $v'Nn''$; the latter curve intersects $v'Nn''$
at v'. Second, he shifts MN to the right while leaving N on the curve $v'Nn''$;
M will then again follow a curve 'parallel' to $v'Nn''$; this curve intersects
$v'Nn''$ at the point n''. Walras drew his curves in such a way that these
points of intersection do indeed exist, but that outcome is not always certain.
Therefore, it seems clear that the argument presented in this section cannot
be substantiated in general by means of Figure 30 because it is not certain that
the points v' and n'' always exist. Walras should have interchanged the roles
of gold and silver, and, therefore, should have made a new figure for this case,
in which the following function would have to be depicted:

$$Q_o + \frac{Q_a}{\omega} = F_o(P_o) + \frac{H}{P_o} + \frac{1}{\omega}F_a\left(\frac{P_a}{\omega}\right).$$

LESSON 35

Relative stability of the value of the bimetallic standard

SUMMARY: – Construction of the five curves of variation of the price in terms of wheat: 1° and 2° of the silver franc that is both a commodity and money and of the gold franc that is only a commodity on the hypothesis of the silver standard; 3° and 4° of the gold franc that is both a commodity and money and of the silver franc that is only a commodity on the hypothesis of the gold standard; 5° of the silver franc and of the gold franc each of them both a commodity and money on the hypothesis of bimetallism. Similarity of the curves of the variation of the price of the metal at the same time a commodity and money, and of the metal as only a commodity. Conditions of viable bimetallism. Intermediate position of the bimetallic curve. Transformation of bimetallism into monometallism. Limits of the compensatory action of bimetallism. Jevons's error. Seeking greater fixity of value of the standard.

332. To complete the *mathematical theory of bimetallism*, it remains for me to discuss the system of bimetallism from the point of view of the stability of the value of the monetary standard.

Let us call, in the bimetallic system, the unit of quantity of silver, 5 grams or a demi-decagram of silver 0.9 fine, a *silver franc*, and a *gold franc*, not as has been done, the unit of quantity of gold at 5 grams or a demi-decagram of gold 0.9 fine, but instead the ωth part of that unit. In our Figure 31, where ω was assumed to be equal to ten, this gold franc was half a gram. In this case, the curve $O'_q O'_p$ with equation $q = \omega F_o (\omega P_a)$ that we have substituted for the curve $O_q O_p$ with equation $q = F_o (p)$, was the curve of the price in terms of wheat of the gold franc as a commodity as a function of the quantity.

Let there now be two rectangular axes (Fig. 32): a horizontal *time axis* Ot, and a vertical *price axis* Op. On the first one, we mark equal lengths $\overline{0-1}$, $\overline{1-2}$, $\cdots$ corresponding to the unit of time or, more exactly, to the equal intervals that separate the calculations of the prices assumed to be brought about by the mathematical data. On the second axis, and on the parallels drawn from the points 1, 2, $\cdots$, we measure lengths corresponding to:

1° the price in terms of wheat of the silver franc as a commodity and as money, supposing silver only serves as money;

2° the price in terms of wheat of the gold franc as a commodity, under the same hypothesis;

3° the price in terms of wheat of the gold franc as a commodity and as money, supposing gold only serves as money;

4° the price in terms of wheat of the silver franc as a commodity, under the same hypothesis;

5° the price in terms of wheat of the silver franc and of the gold franc as a commodity and as money, supposing silver and gold both serve as money.

If we refer to our foregoing explanations and to our Figure 30, we will see that at the beginning, that is, at time zero, the first quantity, p'', represented by $\overline{Op''}$, is the root of the equation

$$q = F_a\left(p''\right) + \frac{H}{p''};$$

the second one, π', represented by $\overline{O\pi'}$, is the root of

$$\omega Q_o = \omega F_o\left(\omega\pi'\right)$$

the third one, π'', represented by $\overline{O\pi''}$, is the root of

$$\omega Q_o = \frac{H}{\pi''} + \omega F_o\left(\omega\pi''\right);$$

the fourth one, p', represented by $\overline{Op'}$, is the root of

$$Q_a = F_a\left(p'\right);$$

and, finally, the fifth, P, represented by $\overline{OP}$, is the root of

$$Q_a + \omega Q_o = F_a(P) = \frac{H}{P} + \omega F_o(\omega P).$$

Hence starting from the origin in Fig. 32, we measure the lengths $\overline{Op''}$, $\overline{O\pi'}$, $\overline{O\pi''}$, $\overline{Op'}$, and $\overline{OP}$ on the vertical axis Op.

After a first interval of time, the quantities Q_a, Q_o, and H, and the functions F_a and F_o having changed, the same magnitudes will be p_1'', π_1', π_1'', p_1', P_1, represented by the lengths $\overline{1p_1''}$, $\overline{1\pi_1'}$, $\overline{1\pi_1''}$, $\overline{1p_1'}$, $\mathbb{P}_1$ indicated on the parallel to the vertical axis passing through the point 1 of the horizontal axis.

After a second interval of time, these magnitudes will be p_2'', π_2', π_2'', p_2', P_2, represented by the lengths $\overline{2p_2''}$, $\overline{2\pi_2'}$, $\overline{2\pi_2''}$, $\overline{2p_2'}$, $\overline{2P_2}$ indicated on the parallel to the vertical axis passing through the point 2 of the horizontal axis.

And so forth. In this way, we get the following five curves:

1° The curve $p''p_1''p_2''\cdots$ of the variation of the price of the silver franc as a commodity and as money on the hypothesis of the silver standard. It results analytically from the equation

$$Q_a = F_a(p'') + \frac{H}{p''}$$

in which Q_a and H are independent variables, the function F_a varies, and p'' is a dependent variable instead of being a determined value;

2° The curve $\pi'\pi_1'\pi_2'\cdots$ of the variation of the price of the gold franc as a commodity on the same hypothesis of silver monometallism. It results analytically from the equation

$$\omega Q_o = \omega F_o(\omega\pi')$$

in which Q_o is an independent variable, the function F_o varies, and π' is a dependent variable instead of being a determined value;

3° The curve $\pi''\pi_1''\pi_2''\cdots$ of the variation of the price of the gold franc as a commodity and as money on the hypothesis of gold monometallism. It results from the equation

$$\omega Q_o = \frac{H}{\pi''} + \omega F_o\left(\omega\pi''\right)$$

in which Q_o and H are independent variables, the function F_o varies, and π'' is a dependent variable;

4° The curve $p'p_1'p_2'\cdots$ of the variation of the price of the silver franc as a commodity on the same hypothesis of gold monometallism. It results from the equation

$$Q_a = F_a\left(p'\right)$$

in which Q_a is an independent variable, the function F_a varies, and p' is a dependent variable;

5° Finally, the curve $PP_1P_2\cdots$ of the variation of the common price of the silver franc and the gold franc as a commodity and as money on the hypothesis of bimetallism. It results from the equation

$$Q_a + \omega Q_o = F_a\left(P\right) + \frac{H}{P} + \omega F_o\left(\omega P\right)$$

in which Q_a, Q_o and H are independent variables, the functions F_a and F_o vary, and P is a dependent variable.

The discussion of the curves 1, 3, and 5 will give us the conclusion we looked for on the respective advantages of monometallism and bimetallism from the point of view of the stability of the monetary standard.

For the sake of simplicity, we have made abstraction in our figure from variations in the value of H, and from changes of the functions F_a and F_o; and we have assumed variations in the quantities Q_a and ωQ_o only in the way indicated in Figure 33 by the curves A and B, where the quantities of silver money are represented by the curve AA_{45} above the horizontal axis, and the quantities of gold by BB_{45} under the axis. Our conclusions, however, will be completely independent of this restriction.

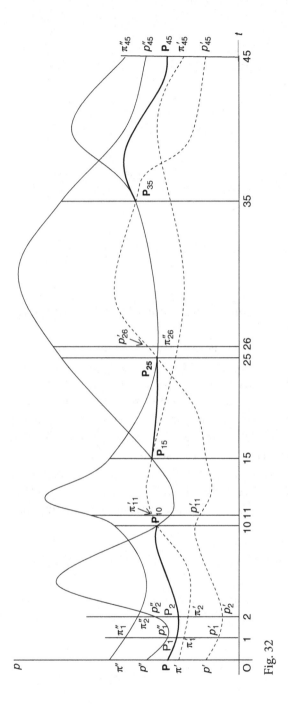

Fig. 32

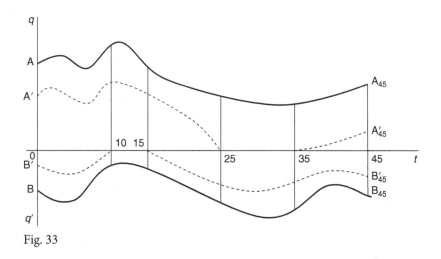

Fig. 33

333. First of all, we must point to the similarity of the two curves $p''p_1''p_2''\cdots$ and $p'p_1'p_2'\cdots$ on the one hand, and of $\pi''\pi_1''\pi_2''\cdots$ and $\pi'\pi_1'\pi_2'\cdots$ on the other hand. This similarity is understandable. The price of a metal that is at the same time a commodity and money is always greater than the price when the same metal is only a commodity since attributing to it the function of serving as money will have as a result the diminution of the quantity reserved for industrial usage and for luxury goods. Moreover, this adoption of a metal as money, which raises its price, increases also the variations in its price, without changing its nature in general. Hence the curve $p''p_1''p_2''\cdots$ is both similar to and at the same time lies above the curve $p'p_1'p_2'\cdots$, and the curve $\pi''\pi_1''\pi_2''\cdots$ is both similar to and at the same time lies above $\pi'\pi_1'\pi_2'\cdots$.

334. Having posited this, let us now return to Figure 30, and let us see why bimetallism is practicable from the outset. This is because, if only silver were money, the silver franc would take a value p'' given by the equation

$$Q_a = F_a\left(p''\right) + \frac{H}{p''},$$

and the gold franc a value π' given by the equation

$$\omega Q_o = \omega F_o \left(\omega \pi' \right);$$

and because $p'' > \pi'$, it would be advantageous to transform gold francs as a commodity into gold francs as money, which would lead to a fall of the value of the silver franc as money compared to the silver franc as a commodity and to a transformation of silver money into silver as a commodity; and because, if only gold were money, the gold franc would take a value π'' given by the equation

$$\omega Q_o = \frac{H}{\pi''} + \omega F_o \left(\omega \pi'' \right),$$

and the silver franc a value p' given by the equation

$$Q_o = F_a \left(p' \right);$$

and because $\pi'' > p'$, it would be advantageous to transform silver francs as a commodity into silver francs as money, which would lead to a fall of the value of the gold franc as money compared to the gold franc as a commodity and to a transformation of gold money into gold as a commodity.

Hence: – *Bimetallism is only practicable on the condition that the price of the silver franc as a commodity and as money is greater than the price of the gold franc that is only a commodity, and that the price of the gold franc as a commodity and as money is greater than the price of the silver franc that is only merchandise;* that is to say that the curve $p'' p_1'' p_2'' \cdots$ (Fig. 32) lies above the curve $\pi' \pi_1' \pi_2' \cdots$ and the curve $\pi'' \pi_1'' \pi_2'' \cdots$ lies above the curve $p' p_1' p_2' \cdots$. In our figure, this takes place during the first 10 time intervals, then from 15 to 25, then from 35 to 40.

335. The common price P of the silver franc both as a commodity and money and of the gold franc both as a commodity and money is given by the equation

$$Q_a + \omega Q_o = F_a \left(P \right) + \frac{H}{P} + \omega F_o \left(\omega P \right);$$

and we have, on the one hand

$$F_a(P) + \frac{H}{P} > Q_a > F_a(P),$$

and also, on the other hand,

$$\frac{H}{P} + \omega F_o(\omega P) > \omega Q_o > \omega F_o(\omega P),$$

since the total quantity Q_a of silver, and the total quantity Q_o of gold are both partly commodities, for the quantities Q_a' and Q_o', and in part money, for the quantities Q_a'' and Q_o'', the first inequality, moreover, evidently leads to the second, and vice versa.

Now, we have $Q_a = F_a(p') = F_a(p'') + \dfrac{H}{p''};$
and

$$\omega Q_o = \omega F_o(\omega \pi') = \frac{H}{\pi''} + \omega F_o(\omega \pi'').$$

We have therefore also

$$F_a(P) + \frac{H}{P} > F_a(p'') + \frac{H}{p''},$$

which assumes $p'' > P$, and

$$F_a(p') > F_a(P),$$

which assumes $P > p'$. And we have, moreover,

$$\frac{H}{P} + \omega F_o(\omega P) > \frac{H}{\pi''} + \omega F_o(\omega \pi''),$$

which assumes $\pi'' > P$, and

$$\omega F_o(\omega \pi') > \omega F_o(\omega P),$$

which assumes $P > \pi'$.

Hence: – *When bimetallism is the monetary system, the common price of the silver franc as a commodity and as money, and of the gold franc as a commodity and as money is both less than the price of the silver franc as a commodity and as money, and greater than the price of the gold franc only as a commodity, under silver monometallism; and it is also at the same time less than the price of the gold franc as a commodity and as money, and greater than the price of the silver franc only as a commodity, under gold monometallism;* that is to say that the curve $PP_1P_2 \cdots$ lies at the same time under the two curves $p''p_1''p_2'' \cdots$ and $\pi''\pi_1''\pi_2'' \cdots$ and above the two curves $\pi'\pi_1'\pi_2' \cdots$ and $p'p_1'p_2' \cdots$. This is still the case in our figure for the same time intervals as above.

336. Let us go back once more to Figure 30, and see how bimetallism changes into monometallism. It changes into silver monometallism when Q_a becomes equal to or greater than $\pi'\mu'$, or when ωQ_o becomes equal to or less than $\overline{m''n''}$. It changes into gold monometallism when ωQ_o becomes equal to or greater than $\overline{m'n'}$, or when Q_a becomes equal to or less than $\overline{\pi''\mu''}$. In the two first cases, the price p'' of the silver franc is given by the equation

$$Q_a = F_a\left(p''\right) + \frac{H}{p''},$$

and the price π' of the gold franc by

$$\omega Q_o = \omega F_o\left(\omega\pi'\right).$$

However, if p'' is equal to or less than π', there is no advantage in transforming gold as a commodity into gold as money. In the two last cases, the price π'' of the gold franc is given by the equation

$$\omega Q_o = \frac{H}{\pi''} + \omega F_o\left(\omega\pi''\right),$$

and the price p' of the silver franc by the equation

$$Q_a = F_a\left(p'\right).$$

However, if π'' is equal to or less than π', there is no advantage in transforming silver as a commodity into silver as money.

Hence: – *Bimetallism changes into silver monometallism as soon as the price of the gold franc only as a commodity becomes greater than the price of the silver franc as a commodity and as money*; that is to say when the curve $\pi'\pi'_1\pi'_2\cdots$ lies above the curve $p''p''_1p''_2\cdots$ as is the case during the 5 time intervals from 10 to 15 in Figure 32. *It changes into gold monometallism as soon as the price of the silver franc only as a commodity becomes greater than the price of the gold franc as a commodity and as money*; that is to say when the curve $p'p'_1p'_2\cdots$ lies above the curve $\pi''\pi''_1\pi''_2\cdots$ as is the case during the 10 time intervals from 25 to 35.

Furthermore, it is evident that: – *When bimetallism changes into silver monometallism or into gold monometallism, there is no longer a common price of the silver franc and the gold franc.* The curve $PP_1P_2\cdots$ will be interrupted.

337. In circumstances such as those to which our Figure 32 corresponds, the result of the substitution of bimetallism for silver monometallism during the period 0–45 would have been to substitute, in place of the curve $p''p''_1p''_2\cdots p''_{45}$, the curve $PP_1P_2\cdots P_{10}P''_{11}\cdots P_{15}\cdots P_{25}\pi''_{26}\cdots P_{35}\cdots P_{45}$ as the graph of the variation of the value in terms of corn as the numeraire and monetary standard. The result of the substitution of bimetallism by gold monometallism would have been the substitution of the same curve by the curve $\pi''\pi''_1\pi''_2\cdots \pi''_{45}$. The circumstances corresponding to our figure have undoubtedly no relation to reality, the less so because we have made abstraction of certain elements, among which are the variation in the magnitude of the desired cash balance and the changes of the utility of the precious metals considered as commodities, which would have increased or decreased the effects of the variations in their quantity; but it is no less certain that the curve $PP_1P_2\cdots$ undergoes phases of rising and of falling that are less considerable than those of the curves $p''p''_1p''_2\cdots p''_{45}$ and $\pi''\pi''_1\pi''_2\cdots \pi''_{45}$ because it always lies below these two curves and only coincides with the lower of the two as soon as the other tends to rise appreciably in relation to the lower one. This curve $PP_1P_2\cdots$ is remarkably horizontal in our example, which is caused by our hypothesis that the quantities

of silver and gold vary in general in opposite directions; nevertheless, such as it is, it enables us very well to recognize the limits of the compensating effect of bimetallism.

Let us first complete Figure 33 by means of the two curves $A'A'_{45}$ and $B'B'_{45}$, relating to the bimetallic system; the first curve divides the total quantity of silver francs into silver francs as a commodity and silver francs as money, where the former are measured by the upper part of the ordinate, between the curves A and A', and the latter on the lower part, between the curve A' and the horizontal axis. The second curve divides the total quantity of gold francs into gold francs as a commodity and gold francs as money, where the latter are measured by the upper part of the ordinate, between the horizontal axis and the curve B', and the former on the lower part, between the curves B' and B. Now, other things remaining unchanged, it may happen that, when the quantity of one of the metals increases or decreases, the quantity of the other metal decreases or increases by the same amount, in such a way that the total quantity of silver francs and gold francs remains the same, and that, moreover, the quantity of gold francs as a commodity, the quantity of silver francs as a commodity, and the total quantity of gold francs and silver francs remains also the same; thus, it is only the proportion of gold francs and of silver francs as money that changes; this takes place during the period 15–25. In this case, bimetallism is always practicable, and, consequently, the ratio of the value of gold as a commodity to the value of silver as a commodity is maintained at ω in the market. Moreover, the quantity of money neither increases nor decreases, and, consequently, the money prices of the commodities neither rise nor fall. However, first, and even in the event that one of the two metals becomes abundant or rare while the other becomes rare or abundant, it can happen that the abundant metal drives the rare metal completely out of the monetary circulation and furnishes alone more or fewer francs than were furnished before by the two metals taken together, as takes place during the period 10–15 and during the period 25–35. In this case, bimetallism changes into monometallism, and, consequently, the ratio of the value of gold as a commodity to the value of silver as a commodity rises above or decreases below ω in the market. Furthermore, the quantity of money increases or decreases, and, therefore, an increase or a fall of the money prices of the commodities will occur. Second, it can also happen that, when the quantity of one of the two metals increases or decreases, the quantity of the other metal increases or decreases at the same time, so that the two metals, gold and silver, will still function in the monetary circulation, but furnish together more or fewer francs than they did before, as happens at the beginning of the period 0–10 and at the end of the period 35–45. In this case, bimetallism is still practicable, and, therefore, the ratio of the value of gold as a commodity to the value of silver as a commodity is maintained at ω in the market, but the quantity of money increases or decreases, and, as a consequence, the money prices of the commodities rise or fall.

Hence: – *The bimetallic standard keeps a certain stability with respect to value in the cases in which the monometallic standards would have varied in opposite directions. It varies just as much as the monometallic standards when they vary in the same direction.*

To summarize, from the point of view of the stability of the monetary standard, bimetallism entrusts itself to chance, just as monometallism does; it has only somewhat more favorable chances.

338. The curve $P\,P_{10}P_{15}P_{25}P_{35}P_{45}$ has been glimpsed and pointed out in the controversies between economists on the subject of bimetallism. It is this curve that the late W. Stanley Jevons wanted to present and believed he had done so in Chapter XII, 'The battle of standards', of his *Money and the Mechanism of Exchange.*[i] Jevons's curve has often been referred to and reproduced confidently by the bimetallists. But there is, between the curve P, deduced mathematically from the condition of the value of money, and Jevons's curve D, empirically based, a noteworthy difference. The curve P sometimes differs from the two curves p'' and π'' below which it lies, as it does, for example, from P to P_{10}, from P_{15} to P_{25}, and from P_{35} to P_{45}. In certain circumstances only, will it coincide with the one or the other of those two curves: for example, it coincides with the curve p'' from P_{10} to P_{15}, and with π'' from P_{25} to P_{35}. Jevons's curve D coincides always with the one of the two curves p'' and π'' that lies below the other. In our figure, this would be a curve $p'CDP_{10}p''_{11}\cdots$. This position of Jevons's curve corresponds to the hypothesis, quite clearly expounded in his text, that the bimetallic system is essentially a system with an alternative standard in the sense that it never accepts more than one metal in

circulation: sometimes gold, sometimes silver. Now, it is certain that this is an error. Our reasoning has established and experience shows that bimetallism is practicable; and, in that case, the common and identical value of the gold franc and the silver franc is necessarily less than the value that the gold franc would have had under gold monometallism and than that of the silver franc under silver mono-metallism. This example demonstrates the importance of proceeding methodically in these questions of quantitative relationships that do not tolerate the least vagueness.

This error having been rectified, it remains none the less true, as Jevons recognized, that bimetallism certainly has a compensatory action. I do not want to return to the fact that this action results from a perpetual monetization and demonetization of metal; but I will make a final observation to the bimetallists.

339. Supposing that we undertake to introduce, in the applied theory of money, the consideration of the greater or lesser stability of the value of the monetary standard, why content ourselves with an erratic and imperfect stability and not aim at a sure and perfect stability? Let us investigate whether wheat fulfills, under certain reservations, the conditions of a commodity with a rareté and a value that are appreciably constant. Let us investigate whether the rareté and the value of money must be constant, or whether it would not be better that these magnitudes vary with the average rareté and average value of social wealth; and let us substitute in place of wheat some *multiple standard* to be determined. In all these arrangements, the bimetallic curve P would be closer to horizontality than the monometallic curves p'' and π''; but, instead of adhering to the use of the curve P, why not look for the horizontality itself by means of an action performed with full knowledge of the quantity of metal in circulation? This is what we would achieve, not by bimetallism, but by gold monometallism combined with a silver token, distinct from coins for small change, to be introduced into the circulation or withdrawn from it in such a way that the value of the multiple standard would not vary. The State, which would execute this operation, would benefit from the emission and lose on the withdrawal, and the difference between the loss and the profit would be added to or deducted from the cost of minting and demonetizing, to constitute the price the society would

pay for the stability or the regularity of the variation of the monetary standard. However, we shall return further on[ii] to these questions of applied and practical economics; for the moment, it will suffice us to have established the most important suppress points of the pure theory of money.

Notes

i   New York: D. Appleton and Co, 1876. The figure to which Walras alluded is the following (*Money and the Mechanism of Exchange*, chapter 12, end of the fifth section, titled 'Compensatory Action'):

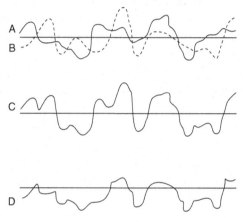

Jevons wrote:

In the first place, it does not follow that the prices of commodities follow the extreme fluctuations of value of both metals, as many writers have inconsiderately declared. Prices only depend upon the course of the metal which happens to have sunk in value below the legal ratio of 15½ to 1. Now, if in the accompanying figure we represent by the line A the variation of the value of gold as estimated in terms of some third commodity, say copper, and by the line B the corresponding variations of the value of silver; then, superposing these curves, the line C would be the curve expressing the *extreme* fluctuations of both metals. Now the standard of value always follows the metal which *falls* in value; hence the curve D really shows the course of variation of the standard of value. This line undergoes more frequent undulations than either of the curves of gold or silver, but the fluctuations do not proceed to so great an extent, a point of much greater importance. (*Money and the Mechanism of Exchange*, chapter 12, fourth section)

ii In the fourth edition, Walras changed these words into 'elsewhere', but he should have done that in the second and hence in the present edition, because in the second edition (1889) he eliminated the pertinent (very long) passage, putting it later into Chapter I of his *Études d'économie politique appliquée* (1898). The latter book has been translated into English by Jan van Daal with the title *Studies in Applied Economics*, London and New York: Routledge, 2005.

LESSON 36

Fiduciary money and offsetting claims.
Foreign exchange

SUMMARY: – Diverse means to settle exchanges without the
intervention of metallic money: *Book credit*; *Commercial paper*;
Bank notes; *Checks*. Definitive equation of monetary circulation.
Circulation of bills of exchange. Rate of currency exchange.
Exchange rate properly so called. *Parity, loss, premium*. Payments
achieved by drawing up and remittance of bills of exchange.
Determination of the rate of exchange. Limit to the loss or premium of exchange. Equation of exchange rate. General equilibrium of exchange rates. Arbitrage. Result of arbitrages.

340. It is a curious fact of the theory of money, quite worthy of being
pointed out, that using money was first considered progress, and that,
once it was introduced, doing without it was considered the next step
forward. There are, indeed, some ways of making exchanges without
the intervention of metallic money, and the importance of them is
growing from day to day. These ways are the following.

341. *Book credit.* X and Y are two traders who buy and sell commodities reciprocally on credit. At certain times, as, for example, at the
end of each semester, the total amount that X owes to Y, and the total
amount that Y owes to X are calculated, and it is seen which of the
two debts is the greater. Only the difference is paid in money; most
often, however, the difference is carried over in the books. In this
way, some rare payments in money suffice to settle a long sequence
of very considerable sales and purchases.

So, there is here a certain quantity of exchanges that have been
effectuated without the intervention of metallic money; however, the

transactions assume the invention and the existence of the numeraire and of money; and if the precious metals are absent in fact, they are always present in principle. It is thanks to the existence of the numeraire that the bookkeeping of debit and credit can be done; it is thanks to the existence of money that each trade between X and Y can be considered as a complete, definitive exchange operation needing nothing more than to be settled in detail by handing over coins, and that it was possible to consider X and Y as leaving to each other the disposal of the coins owed to each other and of which they were the owners. There is more: the units of loan could be compared, that is to say, the products of units of money lent out times the units of time during which the loan is outstanding, and take exactly into account, at the occasion of settlement, the difference between the credit granted by X to Y and that granted by Y to X; and this latter operation would always have been impossible without the intervention, not real but virtual, of the numeraire and of money.

342. *Commercial paper.* It does not always happen, it happens even quite rarely that two traders carry out business with each other that is extensive enough and frequent enough to keep such an account with each other. In that case, and when, for example, X has placed an isolated order with Y, then either at the same time, or after a certain period of book credit, the transaction will be settled as follows. If X and Y live in the same town, X will *make out* a *promissory note* to Y in these terms: 'At such and such date, I shall pay to Y, or to his order, such and such an amount, having received that value in commodities. Signed X.' If X and Y do not live in the same town, Y will *draw* a *bill of exchange* on X in these terms: 'At such and such date, pay to my order such and such an amount, having received that value in commodities. Signed Y.' This bill of exchange will be *accepted* by X in these terms: 'Accepted. Signed X.' It is certain that, at the due date, X, while paying his note or Y's draft, will pay with coins; but before that time, the following will have happened. Y, once in possession of the promissory note or the accepted bill of exchange, may have used it to settle a transaction with a third merchant Z. He may have handed over the note or the draft to Z, endorsing it in these terms: 'Pay to Z, or to his order, such or such amount, value on account. Signed Y.' Z himself may have used the paper by endorsing it in his

turn to a fourth party W for settling some transaction. So, it is possible that, from the moment of its creation to that of its expiry, the paper has served to settle two, three, four, five, ten, twenty sales and purchases of commodities. If, at the date of expiry, X did not pay, the paper would return from endorser to endorser and finally to Y; but if X does pay, everything is finished, and the twenty transactions have been settled with one single paying out of coins.

Here again the existence of the numeraire and of money is necessary, and their virtual, if not real, intervention. Each of the endorsers is assumed to leave X in the possession of the coins that belong to him (the endorser) all the time during which he keeps the paper, and each of them receives, in the form of a part of the interest paid by X, a remuneration for this service.

343. *Banknotes.* The circulation of promissory notes and bills of exchange has the disadvantage that they are payable only at the due date, that is, after a certain interval of time, and there is a risk that the maker of the draft or the acceptor becomes insolvent during that period; moreover, because they are transmissible by endorsement only, each endorser has the obligation of reimbursing the entire sum, should the necessity arise, with the possibility of not being reimbursed himself. There are institutions called *issuing banks* that then perform the following operation. They accept commercial paper payable after a fixed term and transmissible only by endorsement, and replace it by notes payable on demand, transmissible without endorsement, that are called *banknotes*. Such is the banknote: basically, it is a *bill payable at sight to the bearer*, substituted for a *bill payable at maturity*. Just because one can, if one so wishes, from one moment to another, go to the bank to exchange them for coins, and because they are transmitted without endorsement or liability, these notes circulate much more easily than commercial paper: the very fact that they are due for payment by all the holders is the reason that the holders let them pass from hand to hand. In this way, the banknote remains in circulation at least until the maturity of the commercial paper it has replaced; the bank then presents the paper for collection and receives its own banknote or, when it is lacking, coins that it keeps until the presentation of the bank note that had remained in circulation. Therefore, it suffices that the total of commercial paper in the

bank's portfolio and the coins in till are equal to the amount of bank-notes in circulation; that is to say that with a certain amount of cash, a bank can have two, three, four, five times more banknotes in circulation. In the part on *Credit*, in the applied theory of the *Production of wealth*, we will study in detail the conditions of the functioning of this phenomenon; for the time being, we accept the fact as such and from the point of view of its consequences with respect to the use and the value of the metallic currency. Now, it is evident that, if the bank's cash reserves amount to 100 million and the circulation of its banknotes to 300 million, the two-thirds of transactions settled by banknotes are made, not independently of the numeraire and money, but without actual use of precious metal and, in reality, they are achieved by means of commercial paper.

344. *Checks.* X, Y, Z, and W do not have an account the one with the other; they do not make out promissory notes to each other, nor do they furnish each other bills of exchange; they do not make use of banknotes, either; here is how they act. Each of them has a banker with whom they deposit a certain amount of money, commercial papers, or banknotes, which constitute a *reserve*. They draw upon this reserve by means of *checks*, which are receipts drawn on the banker and by means of which they pay for their various purchases. If matters were restricted to this, the reserve would soon be exhausted; but there is something else. When X, Y, Z, and W make purchases, they also make sales, and they receive checks themselves in the payments for the commodities, drawn either on their own banker, or on other bankers in the town. As and when they receive checks, they take them to their banker to be added to their reserve, and they dispose of this extra reserve by writing other checks, just as they did with respect to their original reserve. This is still not all. There is, in the town, an institution called a *clearing house* (*chambre de liquidation*) where all the bankers meet every day. There each of them hands over to the other bankers the checks that he has that are drawn on them and receives from them the checks that they have that are drawn on him. As for the difference, he pays or receives it in specie; that is to say, the excess of what he owes over what is due to him or what is due to him over what he owes. In this way, checks can be created for an amount quite superior to that of the original reserves. This means that checks

form a powerful means of settling sales and purchases without the actual use of metallic money, in particular in combination with the clearing house, which is the crowning achievement of the system. Similarly, in the clearing houses of London and New York business amounting to hundreds of millions of pounds or dollars is settled by means of the use of some thousands of pounds or dollars in specie.

345. Commercial paper and banknotes together constitute the whole of the *fiduciary* or *paper* money, in contrast to *metallic* money. We have already identified the equation of the metallic circulation (§§ 321 and 324); it is useful to complete this equation by introducing a term relating to the fiduciary money. Let F be the amount of this fiduciary money, and let us introduce this term, alongside the one representing the amount of metallic money, into the first term of the equation of the money circulation. With respect to the payment by means of book credit, transfers of specie, or with checks, it must be admitted that as and when these practices are increasingly used, the desired cash balance becomes progressively smaller, but that, at a given moment, the cash balance is what it is because of the transactions that are to be settled in money, abstraction being made from offsetting claims, or, more exactly stated, offsetting claims being taken fully into account.

As we said, the introduction of the term F into our equation yields in general

$$\left(Q_a'' + F\right) = H;$$

and it remains to be seen, if the quantity Q_a'' on the one hand, and, on the other hand, the money prices rise or fall proportionally, whether the term F would automatically increase or decrease proportionally, and whether H would remain constant. It takes only a moment of reflection about this to be convinced that those phenomena will occur. Indeed, as we have seen (§ 321), all the essential conditions of the four equilibriums, of exchange, production, capital formation, and circulation, being fulfilled, if the rise or fall of the prices are proportional to the increase or decrease of the quantity of money, then there is no reason why the entrepreneur would not bring the same quantity of capital into the circulation for an amount proportionally greater or smaller of commercial papers and banknotes, in order that the same quantities of commodities will be sold and bought for an amount that is nominally greater or smaller. So, the two facts of circulation and compensation do not undermine in the least the theorem of the proportionality of prices and the quantity of money.

Let it be clearly noted that I fully admit that, if, from one moment to another, all the data of the problem change, there will no longer be the necessary relation of proportionality between the quantity of money and prices; if, for example, the quantity of metallic money diminishes, and paper money replaces the metallic money more and more, or if offsetting claims come more and more into use, prices would remain unchanged instead of falling; but I maintain that if, at a given moment or from one moment to another and while other things remain unchanged, the quantity of money increases or decreases, prices rise or fall in proportion. If my demonstration is refuted, I will accept that; but using purely and simply the data of the offsetting claims made in the clearing houses of London and New York to conclude that 'we no longer live in the time in which there was a correlation between the quantity of the precious metals and the prices', is to show an absence of any idea of the way in which a quantity that is a function of several variables can depend on each of these variables in particular.

346. Banknotes circulate nearly exclusively within the country of their issue; the circulation of bills of exchange is much wider. From all places in Europe, East India, America, bills of exchange are drawn on Paris and London, and they pass through an endless number of hands to settle various and numerous sales and purchases before being presented at the place where they must be paid. Consequently, bills of exchange are of exceptional importance as a part of fiduciary money. The great centers of commerce and banking: London, Paris, Amsterdam, Hamburg, Genoa, Trieste, New York, each have markets where bills of exchange are bought and sold. In each of these markets, letters of exchange are quoted against all the others: this is what is called the *exchange rate* or the *exchange*. In Paris, the exchange rate on London, Amsterdam, Frankfort, Trieste are quoted: for example: – 'To-day, in Paris, the exchange rate on London is 25.15, on Amsterdam 208.25, on Frankfort 210, on Trieste 195.50.' That is

to say that 1 pound sterling payable in London is bought and sold in Paris for 25.15 Fr, that 100 guilders payable in Amsterdam, or in Frankfort, or in Trieste, are bought and sold in Paris for 208.25 Fr., 210 Fr., 195.50 Fr. From this we see that for there to be an exchange rate there must be two terms: a *certain* term that is implicit, that is 1 pound sterling, 100 guilders, and an *uncertain* term that is explicit, that is 208.25 Fr., 210 Fr., 195.50 Fr. In the above exchange rates, London, Amsterdam, Frankfort, Trieste furnish the certain term, Paris the uncertain term.

347. In the establishment of these exchange rates, there is an element due to the difference of the moneys, and there is an element due to the exchange properly speaking. Thus, 1 pound sterling contains just as much gold as there is in a piece that is 25.22 Fr. If, therefore, the exchange rate of Paris on London is 25.22, this exchange is *at par*: any amount whatsoever of gold would have the same value either in London, or in Paris. The difference between the exchange rate of 22.15 in the example above and the par of 25.22 is then the exchange properly speaking. The matter becomes simpler, and the exchange properly speaking more apparent, if the moneys are the same. So, if the exchange rate of Paris on Brussels is 101, on Genoa 95, then this means that 100 francs payable in Brussels are bought for 101 francs in Paris, that 100 Italian liras are bought for 95 francs in Paris.[i] In this case, Brussels is above par or stands at a *premium*, and Genoa is below par or stands at a *discount*.

The exchange rate is therefore generally the price at one place of an amount payable at another place. What are the causes that make an amount payable at the latter place have a higher or a lower value than at the former one? This is what we have to investigate. To do so, we will see under what conditions the trade in commercial paper takes place.

348. Payments from one place to another normally take place by means of the remittance of bills of exchange and not by sending metallic money. X, a merchant in London, has sold merchandise to Y, a merchant in Paris. On the other hand, Z, a merchant in Paris, has sold merchandise to W, a merchant in London for an amount that we may assume to be equal to the first one. Under these circumstances,

it is useless for Y to send gold or silver from Paris to X in London, and for W in London to send gold or silver to Z in Paris. The two payments can be carried out without the intervention of metallic money, by drawing and remitting two bills of exchange, and here is how this happens. Let X in London draw on Y in Paris; if W in London buys the bill of exchange, X will be paid and W will have paid. Let W remit that same bill of exchange to Z in Paris; when Z has cashed the bill of exchange with Y in Paris, Z will be paid and Y will have paid. Thus, the two debts will be cancelled and the two credit lines reimbursed.

349. That is the principle; let us go to the application, and, for the sake of simplicity, assume two places use the same currency. Various merchants in Brussels have sold merchandise to various merchants in Paris for an amount of 101,000 francs And, on the other hand, several merchants in Paris have sold merchandise to merchants in Brussels for 100,000 francs In accordance with what has been said before, it is useless for 101,000 francs in silver or gold to be sent from Paris to Brussels, and for 100,000 francs to be sent from Brussels to Paris. Assume that the creditors in Brussels furnish bills on Paris amounting to 101,000 francs and sell the entire lot for 100,000 francs to the debtors in Brussels on behalf of the debtors in Paris; or that the creditors in Paris furnish 100,000 francs in bills of exchange on Brussels and sell the entire lot for 101,000 francs to the debtors in Paris on behalf of the creditors in Brussels; or that the operation takes place partly in the first way, partly in the second, in proportional fractions, in such a manner that no debtor, whether in Brussels or in Paris, can gain an advantage by buying a draft rather than having one drawn on him. In any case, 101 francs payable in Paris is worth 100 francs payable in Brussels, and the exchange rate of Paris on Brussels will be $\frac{100}{101}$, expressed as 99.01; 100 francs payable in Brussels are worth 101 francs in Paris, and the exchange rate of Brussels on Paris will be $\frac{101}{100}$, expressed as 101. The debtors in Paris will send 1000 francs to Brussels, because their creditors have the right to be paid in full, even if this must be done by sending metallic money; moreover, they

will suffer from the discount in the exchange; the debtors in Brussels will benefit, in principle, from the premium of the corresponding exchange rate.

350. But, it will be said, if Paris owes 200,000 francs to Brussels, whereas Brussels owes only 100,000 to Paris, the respective exchange rates of Paris on Brussels and Brussels on Paris would then be $\frac{100}{200}$ and $\frac{200}{100}$; in other words, 200 francs payable in Paris would be worth 100 francs in Brussels, and 100 francs payable in Brussels would be worth 200 francs in Paris! No: that absurd consequence is not possible. There is a limit to the discount and the premium of the exchange: this limit is the total cost of the transport, risks included, of 100 francs in specie from the one place to the other. As long as the discount in the exchange does not reach this limit, the debtor prefers to buy a draft or let one be drawn on him rather than sending specie. If the limit is reached, he is indifferent between the two procedures. If the limit is exceeded, he would prefer sending specie; hence the limit cannot be exceeded.

351. In his *Recherches sur les principes mathématiques de la théorie des richesses*, Cournot devoted a special chapter to foreign exchange.[ii] I permit myself to refer the reader to this chapter for fuller details, and I will restrict myself here to borrowing the notation used by that author to furnish the general formula of exchange.

Let (1) and (2) be two centers of exchange; $m_{1,2}$ is the sum of the amounts that locality (1) owes to locality (2), $m_{2,1}$ is the sum of the amounts that locality (2) owes to locality (1), $c_{1,2}$ is the exchange rate of locality (1) on locality (2), $c_{2,1}$ is the exchange rate of locality (2) on locality (1). According to what has been said, we have, within the limits determined by the cost of the transport of money,

$$c_{1,2} = \frac{m_{2,1}}{m_{1,2}}, \qquad c_{2,1} = \frac{m_{1,2}}{m_{2,1}};$$

from this double equation, it follows also that

$$c_{1,2} c_{2,1} = 1.$$

Hence: – *The exchange rates are equal to the inverse ratios of the remittances that must be made.*

They are reciprocals of each other.

We recognize the reappearance of the ratios of the prices (§ 44), which are as they should be inasmuch as the exchange rates are, by definition, the prices in each locality of a unit or of a certain quantity of money payable in all the other places.

352. The formula

$$c_{1,2} = \frac{m_{2,1}}{m_{1,2}}$$

is applicable to two countries with the same money, gold money, for example. In this case, the merchant who has to make a remittance from place (1) on place (2), and who has at his disposal the necessary gold to carry out this remittance, buys a draft if

$$\frac{m_{2,1}}{m_{1,2}} < 1 + \gamma,$$

where γ is the cost of transport of 1 unit of gold from (2) to (1), or sends the gold if

$$\frac{m_{2,1}}{m_{1,2}} > 1 + \gamma.$$

$1 + \gamma$ is therefore the fixed limit of the exchange rate.

If the two countries have different moneys, the formula for the exchange rate of (1) on (2) becomes

$$c_{1,2} = \frac{m_{2,1}}{m_{1,2}} p_{1,2},$$

where $p_{1,2}$ is the price of the monetary unit of place (1) in the money of place (2). Normally, the exchange rate $c_{1,2}$ is stated without indicating the values of the factors $\dfrac{m_{2,1}}{m_{1,2}}$ and $p_{1,2}$ from which it results; but, theoretically and practically, in many cases, it could be important to distinguish these two factors of which one, relating to the ratio of the respective debts and claims of the two places, is the *exchange rate* properly speaking, and of which the other, relating to the ratio of the value of the two moneys, could be called the *agio*.

That having been said, if place (2) has a money that is convertible into the money of place (1), for example, silver money convertible into gold, then the merchant has silver at his disposal. He buys a bill of exchange if

$$\frac{m_{2,1}}{m_{1,2}} p_{1,2} < p_{1,2} + \gamma,$$

where γ is the cost of transporting 1 unit of silver from (2) to (1), or sends silver if

$$\frac{m_{2,1}}{m_{1,2}} p_{1,2} > p_{1,2} + \gamma.$$

There is therefore a variable limit here to the exchange rate. But if place (2) has a money that is not convertible into the money of place (1), for example, a paper money in the form of legal tender, the merchant has paper at his disposal that he cannot send in any case.

Whatever $\dfrac{m_{2,1}}{m_{1,2}}$ and $p_{1,2}$ are, he must buy either a draft or gold. Then there is no limit to the exchange.

353. Let (1), (2), (3), (4), $\cdots$ be an indefinite number of centers of exchange, $c_{2,1}$ and $c_{3,1}$ the exchanges rates of places (2) and (3) on place (1), $c_{3,2}$ the exchanges rate of place (3) on place (2); by a reasoning identical to that used in the case of the exchange of several goods among one another in a market (§ 111), it can be demonstrated that there cannot be a general equilibrium among the exchange rates unless we have, in general,

$$c_{3,2} = \frac{c_{3,1}}{c_{2,1}}.$$

Hence – *In the situation of general equilibrium, the exchange rate of any one place on another is equal to the ratio of the exchange rates between each of the two places on any third place.*

354. When general equilibrium does not exist, it will be brought about by arbitrages, carried out on bills of exchange, exactly the same as the arbitrages that we have assumed to be carried out on any types of commodities (§ 113). The bills of exchange are precisely and par excellence the commodity on which arbitrages are made. In all the centers of commerce there are bankers, specializing as *foreign exchange brokers*, who are occupied daily by studies of the rates of exchange and who bring about the general equilibrium by benefitting from the substitution of indirect purchases in place of direct purchases, or, saying it better, by the combination of an indirect purchase or sale with a direct sale or purchase. This intervention has two extremely important consequences.

355. A first result of the arbitrages is that exchange from one place on each of the others is not determined by the simple ratio of the debts of that place to its credits on each of the other places, but depends, in a more complex way, on the ratio of the debts and the credits of that place to those of all the other places. In other words, the exchange rates of a country with the foreign countries vary simultaneously and in the same direction depending on whether the general results of the exchanges of this country with the foreign countries form an excess of the total value of the exports over that of the imports or an excess of the total value of the imports over that of the exports. When a country has sold more than it has bought, the exchange rate of its paper[iii] has a tendency to rise above par; when it has bought more than it has sold, its exchange rate has a tendency to fall below par. In the former *system* known as *the balance of trade*, this was expressed by saying that the foreign trade is *for* or *against* the country in question, or that the balance is *favorable* or *unfavorable*. These expressions reflect the presumed advantage of the import of precious metals and

the disadvantage of their export. Ideas in this respect have changed notably; and yet, it is good to know that, depending on whether a country's foreign trade balance is favorable or unfavorable, it imports or it exports money; in the first case, this leads to a rise in prices and, consequently to an expansion of imports and a contraction of exports, and, in the second case, this leads to a fall in the prices and, consequently to a contraction of imports and an expansion of exports, so that in both cases, equilibrium tends to be reestablished automatically.

356. The second effect of the arbitrages made on bills of exchange, a practical result of immense importance, is that an enormous mass of international exchanges and services are settled by means of the smallest possible shipment of gold or silver. Until not long ago, the international contracts and their payments from country to country came nearly entirely from the export and import of commodities, that is to say, agricultural, industrial, and commercial products. Nowadays, a considerable number of diverse elements enters into the composition of these debits and credits. The most important of these elements are summed up by Mr. George G. Goschen in his *Theory of Foreign Exchange*;[iv] they are the following: import and export of public and industrial credit instruments, public and industrial securities, payment and collection of the arrears of these titles, payment of profits, commissions, and brokerage fees, expenditures made abroad by nationals, etc., etc. England, for example, has every year an excess of imports over exports of commodities properly speaking of several hundreds millions; it brings its balance into equilibrium by means of the charges for the freight carried by their shipping companies, the commissions and the brokerage fees on commercial and banking operations that it undertakes, incomes from the capital it possesses. This is the business settled by bills of exchange. Paris owes an excess to Brussels, but Amsterdam or Frankfort owes an excess to Paris; the first excess is paid by the means of the second. So, the universal market for exchange bills is like a vast *clearing-house* where the trades of the whole world are liquidated by the simple payments of differences. And this result is obtained by the simple working of the mechanism of free competition left to itself. This is the law of supply and demand that regulates all these exchanges of commodities, like the law of the

universal gravitation governs all the movements of the celestial bodies. Here the system of the economic world finally appears in its full extent and complexity, and is seen to be just as beautiful, that is to say, both as vast and as simple, as the system of the astronomic world.[v]

Notes

i   Note that at the time when Walras wrote his books, France, Italy, Belgium, Italy and Greece formed the so-called Latin Union, a precursor, to a degree, of the euro zone; see chapter 1 of his *Études d'économie politique appliquée* (*Studies in applied economics*) (2005).

ii Translated into English by Nathaniel T. Bacon under the title *Researches into the Mathematical Principles of the Theory of Wealth*, 1897; reprint, New York: Kelley, 1971; see chapter 3.

iii Walras wrote 'paper', meaning, in this case, bills of exchange, because he was discussing arbitrage in relation to those bills. He should, however, have meant and written 'currency' or 'money'.

iv London: Effingham Wilson, 1864, chapter 2.

v   The broad meaning in French of this word is 'L'ensemble formé par la Terre et les astres visibles, conçu comme un système organisé. ⇒ cosmos, univers. *Les Anciens plaçaient la Terre au centre du monde.*'; and by extension, 'Les systèmes comparables pouvant exister dans l'univers' (Robert 2002, p. 1659).

PART VI

PRICE FIXING, MONOPOLY, AND TAXATION

LESSON 37

Price fixing and monopoly

SUMMARY: – Various modes of economic organization of society other than free competition. Abstraction from second order effects. *Maximum* prices of productive services: the entrepreneurs cannot buy as much as they would like despite making profits; *minimum* prices of productive services: the owners of productive services cannot sell as much as they would like. *Maximum* prices of products: the entrepreneurs decline to produce; minimum prices of products: they make a profit.

Monopoly consists of the fact that there is only one provider of a productive service or a product. The price increases, the *demand*, the *output*, or *consumption* decreases. Total product increases and decreases; maximum. Fixed expenses. The entrepreneurs intervene, in the case of monopoly, to take as profit a part of the wealth that is exchanged. Principle of Cournot's analytic theory of monopoly.

Sale of various fractions of the total demand at the variety of prices that are, for each fraction, the maximum price. Partial gross products; total gross product; maximum. Partial expenses. Partial net products; total net product; maximum. The multiplicity of prices is much easier to maintain in the case of monopoly than in the case of free competition. The error in Dupuit's mathematical theory of utility: the utility is not given by the area under the demand curve.

357. All our foregoing conclusions relate to a single and unique hypothesis: that of absolute free competition in exchange, production, and capital formation. Thus, what we have learned are the

effects of free competition. But whatever economists may say, or what they seem to say, free competition is not the only possible system of economic organization; there are others: those of regulation, price fixing, special privileges, monopolies, etc. To choose between free competition and the other systems, or, if we so wish, to prefer free competition over these other systems, and to do so in full awareness of their causes, it is also necessary to know their effects. And, once again, even if there were no reason to apply that knowledge, it would still be necessary to study the natural and necessary effects of the various possible types of social organization, if only because of scientific curiosity.

358. We have now to distinguish between restrictions on *laisser faire, laisser passer* in regard to production or circulation of wealth, and State intervention in regard to the distribution of wealth. In the first category there are maximum and minimum prices, prohibitive and protective tariffs, monopolies, and the issuance of paper money; in the second are income taxes and fiscal taxes. It can be seen what a variety of subjects are included in this part of economic theory, completely neglected these days and that will be developed progressively as a full and complete knowledge of the general case makes possible the study of all kinds of exceptions. We will take up here only some principal points in order to show the way to treat these questions, or because their clarification has relevance for the elaboration of basic applied and social economics.

It is unnecessary, moreover, when it is desired to take account of the various sorts of disruptions that can be introduced into the mechanism of free competition, to trace out these effects in their last details. Abstraction can be made from the variations that compensate each other and from those that are accessory and very slight in comparison with the principal variations. In that respect, the price curves (§§ 225, 226) are very useful.

359. Let us assume that the price of a productive service or of a product is regulated. There are two cases to be distinguished: one in which it is forbidden to sell the service or a product at a price higher than a certain fixed price that is less than the price that results from free competition, which is the case of the *maximum*; and one in which

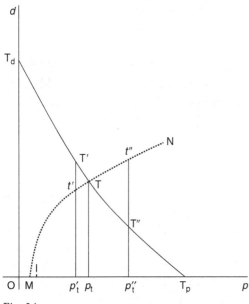

Fig. 34

it is forbidden to sell the service or a product at a price lower than a certain fixed price higher than the freely competitive price, which is the case of the *minimum*. It is, in practice, generally very difficult to enforce such prohibitions, but it is not impossible. And, furthermore, however that may be, what we have to examine here are the consequences of substituting an artificial price in place of the natural price, considered apart from the ways and means of enforcing the substitution. We will examine the effects of price fixing successively on productive services and on products.

360. Let $\delta_t(p_t)$, $\omega_t(p_t)$ be the purchase and sales functions of the productive service (T) represented by the curves $T_d T_p$ and MN (Fig. 34). The price of (T) being fixed at the maximum $p_t' < p_t$, or at the minimum $p_t'' > p_t$, the equality

$$\delta_t(p_t) = \omega_t(p_t)$$

would be replaced, in the first case, by the inequality

$$\delta_t\left(p'_t\right) > \omega_t\left(p'_t\right)$$

represented by the greater height of the ordinate $\overline{p'_t\,T'}$ in comparison with the ordinate $\overline{p'_t t'}$, so long as the rise in price that would result from the excess of effective demand over effective supply is ruled out; and, in the second case, by the inequality

$$\delta_t\left(p''_t\right) < \omega_t\left(p''_t\right),$$

represented by the lesser height of the ordinate $\overline{p'_t\,T''}$ in comparison with the ordinate $\overline{p''_t t''}$, so long as the fall in price that would result from the excess of effective supply over effective demand is ruled out. In the case of the maximum, a certain number of entrepreneurs would be unable to purchase land services, or all the entrepreneurs would be unable to buy as much land service as they would like. Furthermore, a profit would be realized on the quantity purchased as a result of the price of the products being higher than their average cost. In the case of the minimum, a certain number of landowners would be unable to sell any land services, or all the landowners would not be able to sell as much as they would like. In the same way, if, for example, a maximum interest charge were established, the entrepreneurs would not be able to borrow as much capital as they would like, in spite of the profit they would make. And similarly, finally, if the State, by legislation, or certain private organizations by the use of threats and violence, established a minimum wage, a certain number of workers would not be able to sell their labor, or all of the workers would not be able to sell as much as they would like; which, in any case, does not prejudge the question of the advantage or disadvantage that they could have in working more at a lower price, or less at a higher price. It is necessary at this point to refer to the theory of monopoly. Indeed, the theory of monopoly and that of price fixing are here related to each other: in the case of price fixing, we have just seen that the price of commodities is set arbitrarily and the volume of sales is determined in consequence; in the case of monopoly, as we shall see presently, the volume of sales is set arbitrarily and the price of commodities is determined in consequence. In either case, the goal can be set to obtain the greatest possible magnitude of the quantity sold multiplied by the price; and that could be the *Internationale*'s guiding principle, one that the adversaries of that organization have no more refuted than its partisans have successfully defended.

361. The price of the product (B) being fixed at the maximum $p_b' < p_b$, or at the minimum $p_b'' > p_b$, the equality

$$b_t p_t + b_p p_p + b_k p_k = p_b$$

would be replaced, in the first case, by the inequality

$$b_t p_t + b_p p_p + b_k p_k > p_b'$$

without there being the withdrawal of entrepreneurs that would normally result from the excess of the average cost over the price, which would lead to a rise in the price of (B); and in the second case, by the inequality

$$b_t p_t + b_p p_p + b_k p_k < p_b''$$

without there being the entry of entrepreneurs that would normally result from the excess of the price over the average cost, which would lead to a fall in the price of (B). In the case of a maximum, the entrepreneurs, rather than incur the loss $D_b'(p_b - p_b')$, represented by the area $p_b'B'b'p_b$ (Fig. 35), would completely cease production. In the case of a minimum, those entrepreneurs who would be able to sell their products would realize a profit $D_b''(p_b'' - p_b)$, represented by the area $p_b b''B''p_b''$. Thus, if a maximum were established for the price of bread, no bread would be baked; and if a minimum were established, bakers would sell at a profit. Under these conditions, there would hardly be any reason for establishing the maximum or the minimum. Matters are different if it is assumed that the State becomes an entrepreneur to make, in the case of a minimum, a profit in lieu of a tax, and to make, in the case of a maximum, a loss that it covers by some tax or other. These schemes can be more or less satisfactory, but we should not avoid criticizing them by declaring them impossible. It is easy to conceive of a country in which the State might manufacture, for example, the primary necessities of life at a loss and luxuries at a profit; and it remains to be demonstrated, by applied economics

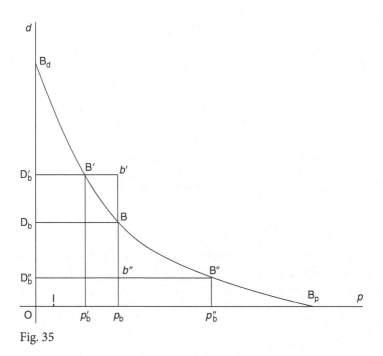

Fig. 35

and social economics, that this system would not be consistent with either public welfare or social justice.

362. The economic theory of *monopoly* has been furnished in mathematical form, which is the clearest and most precise form, by Cournot in Chapter V of his *Recherches sur les principes mathématiques de la théorie des richesses*, published in 1838, and by Dupuit in two memoirs, the first of which is titled, 'De la mesure de l'utilité des travaux publics', and the second, 'De l'influence des péages sur l'utilité des voies de communication', published in 1844 and 1849 in the *Annales des Ponts et Chaussées*. Unfortunately, economists have not thought it pertinent to learn about that theory, and have been reduced, on the subject of monopoly, to a confusion of ideas that, in their work, is perfectly expressed by a confusion of terminology. They have given the name of monopoly to economic activities that are found to be, not in the hands of one firm, but in the hands of a limited number of them. They have even given, by analogy, the name of monopoly to the ownership of certain productive services that are

limited in quantity; for example, to the ownership of land. But all productive services are limited in quantity; and if landowners have a monopoly of land, workers have a monopoly of personal faculties, and capitalists have a monopoly of capital goods. With that sort of an extension of the sense of the terms, monopoly, being everywhere, is nowhere. In fact, the word monopoly has been shifted from its original meaning and is used to express the idea of the limitation in quantity from which value and wealth result; and now there is no longer a word to express the circumstance of there being a productive service or a product that is in the hands of a single firm. Now, it is precisely that circumstance that is of great importance here, because it nullifies these two conditions of free production: that the price of each product be equal to its average cost, and that that price is the only one for the product on the market. To make clear this double result of monopoly, it is best to present an example.

363. Let us assume there is an entrepreneur who, for one reason or another, has a monopoly of some product in the sense that we have agreed to understand that word. That entrepreneur has the power to set the price of his product as he wishes. But what does not depend on him, for example, is the quantity of the product that is demanded, sold, consumed at whatever price is charged. In this respect, only one thing is certain: the dearer the product is, the less will be demanded, and the cheaper it is, the more will be demanded. It is absolutely certain for any given product that the demand for any product decreases as its price rises and increases as its price falls. The only thing that varies from one product to another is the law of the increase or decrease in demand as the price rises or falls; that is what Cournot and Dupuit call the *law of demand, of sales*, or *of the consumption* of each product. For every product there is, on the one hand, a maximum limit to price: it is the price at which the demand is zero, and, on the other hand, a maximum limit to the demand: it is the demand corresponding to a zero price, in other words, the quantity of the product that would be sold and consumed if the product were free and available in such a quantity that everyone can have as much as he wants. Let us assume that the demand for our product is zero at a price of 100 francs per unit, and that the demand corresponding to a price of zero would be 50,000 units. Let us assume, furthermore,

Price	Demand	Total gross receipts	Cost	Total net receipts
Fr.	[in units]	Fr.	Fr.	Fr.
100	0	0	0	0
50	10	500	20	480
20	50	1,000	100	900
5	1,000	5,000	2,000	3,000
3	2,500	7,500	5,000	2,500
2	5,000	10,000	10,000	0
1	12,000	12,000	24,000	−12,000
0.50	20,000	10,000	40,000	−30,000
0	50,000	0	100,000	−100,000

that at different prices ranging from 100 to 0 francs and taking the values 50, 20, 5, 3, 2, 1 and 0.50 francs, the corresponding quantity demanded ranges from 0 to 50,000 units, amounting respectively to 10, 50, 1,000, 2,500, 5,000, 12,000 and 20,000 units, in accordance with the above table.

The respective gross receipts will be, for our entrepreneur, 0, 500, 1,000, 5,000, 7,500, 10,000, 12,000, 10,000, and 0 francs. Thus the gross receipts start at zero when the price is at the maximum corresponding to a zero demand; they increase, reach a maximum, then diminish; and they return to zero at the zero price to which the maximum demand corresponds. The maximum gross receipts are realized, in our example, at the price of 1 franc to which corresponds a demand of 12,000 units. They are then 12,000 francs. If our entrepreneur had no costs of production, he would choose the price of 1 franc for his product: that is the one that would give him the greatest profit. How would he find this price? By the simplest kind of tatonnement. Adopting at first the highest prices, he would see that the demand is zero or very small, and that his receipts are also zero or very small. Then, lowering his price more and more, he would see the demand increase and his receipts along with it. In this way, he would arrive at the price of 1 franc. Continuing to lower his price, he would see that the demand continues to increase, but the receipts begin to diminish. He would immediately raise his price to 1 franc and keep it there. That operation is performed without difficulty, and businesses do it all the time.

364. Generally, however, our entrepreneur will have some costs of production. He will have general expenses[i] and special expenses or, to put it more precisely, expenses that are more or less fixed and expenses that are more or less proportional to the quantity sold; that is to say, growing either exactly in proportion to that quantity, or in a greater or smaller proportion, all that depending, naturally, on the special and particular conditions of the industry. Let us assume, for greater simplicity, that the expenses relating to the manufacture of this product are proportional, amounting to 2 francs per unit. These expenses will be, at the various assumed prices when the related quantities demanded are taken into account, respectively 0, 20, 100, 2,000, 5,000, 10,000, 24,000, 40,000, and 100,000 francs. The corresponding net receipts, equal to the excess of gross receipts over costs of production, will be 0, 480, 900, 3,000, 2,500, 0, -12,000, -30,000, and -100,000 francs. Thus, maximum net receipts are earned, in our example, at a price of 5 francs per unit to which corresponds a demand of 1,000 units. It is then 3,000 francs. The price of 5 francs would therefore be the one that the entrepreneur should set. He would find it by the same tatonnement as above.

365. For greater simplicity, we assumed that our entrepreneur had no fixed general expenses. If they were 1,000 francs, for example, it would be necessary to deduct these 1,000 francs from the net receipts obtained at each price, which would reduce the maximum net receipts by that amount, but would not change the position of this maximum, the price that maximizes profits being always the same. It is essential to note that the price that maximizes profits is completely independent of the fixed expenses.

366. Having found the price of 5 francs that gives him maximum profits, our entrepreneur would maintain it for the reason that he is the only seller of the product. If the product were not monopolized, the profits of the firm would attract competitors, the quantities sold and consumed would increase to 5,000 units, and the price would fall to 2 francs, equal to the 2 francs of expenses of production. Hence the consequence of monopoly is that, instead of having 5,000 units at a price of 2 francs, consumers have 1,000 units at a price of 5 francs. We see the difference. The principle of *laisser faire, laisser passer* applied

to an industry subjected to unlimited competition has the result that the consumers obtain the greatest possible satisfaction of their needs consistent with the condition that each product has only one price on the market, this price being equal to the average cost, and the producers making neither profit nor loss; the same rule applied to a monopolized industry has the result that the consumers obtain maximum satisfaction subject to the condition that the price is higher than the average cost and that the producers make the greatest possible profit. We shall see shortly what happens to the uniformity of prices. In the first case, the entrepreneur is an intermediary from whom we may make abstraction, and the landowners, workers, and capitalists exchange productive services for productive services with one another on the basis of equivalent values; in the second case, the entrepreneurs intervene, not only to combine the productive services and convert them into products, but to take for themselves a certain portion of the wealth exchanged.

367. We could extend the theory of the price that yields maximum profits in the case of monopoly to services as well as products. We could also give it a more abstract and scientific expression than we have done so far, sharing with Cournot the equation of quantity sold as a function of the price: $D = \mathrm{F}(p)$.

Since, he says, the function $F(p)$ is continuous, the *function pF(p)*, that expresses the total value of the quantity annually sold must be continuous also. This function would become zero if p were zero, since the consumption of a commodity is always finite, even on the hypothesis that it is absolutely free; or, in other words, it is always possible to assign to the symbol p a value small enough that the product $pF(p)$ becomes approximately zero. The function $pF(p)$ disappears also when p becomes infinite; or, in other words, a value can always be assigned to p great enough that the commodity ceases to be demanded and produced at that price. Thus, since the function $pF(p)$ at first increases with p and then finally decreases with it, there is a value of p that maximizes it and that is given by the equation

$$\mathrm{F}(p) + p\mathrm{F}'(p) = 0, \qquad [1]$$

F′ designating, according to Lagrange's notation, the differential coefficient of the function F.

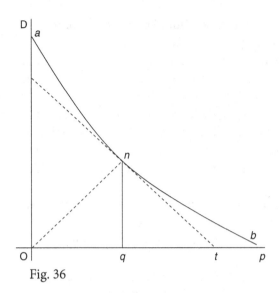

Fig. 36

If we trace the curve anb (Fig. 36) of which the abscissas $\overline{Oq}$ and the ordinates $\overline{qn}$ represent the variables p and D, the root of equation [1] will be the abscissa of the point n from which the triangle Ont, formed by the tangent nt and the vector ray On, is isosceles, so that we have $\overline{Oq} = \overline{qt}$.[1]

In fact, the maximum of a function is given by the root of the equation of the derivative. The derivative of a product like $pF(p)$ is equal to the sum of two products: the factor $F(p)$ multiplied by the derivative of p, plus the factor p multiplied by the derivative of $F(p)$. The derivative of p is equal to unity.

The equation of a tangent to the curve $D = F(p)$ at a point with co-ordinates (D, p) is

$$y - D = F'(x)(x - p).$$

If we substitute into this equation the value

$$F'(p) = \frac{-F(p)}{p}$$

[1] A. Cournot, *Recherches sur les principes mathématiques de la théorie des richesses.* Ch. IV.

from equation [1], and then seek the point of interception of the tangent with the x axis by setting $y = 0$, we get $x = 2p$.

It is on this determination of the maximum that Cournot founds his theory of monopoly. He passes from the case of a natural product to that of a manufactured product, and from maximum gross receipts to maximum net receipts; then from the case of a monopolist to that of two monopolists, and, finally, from monopoly to unlimited competition. I have preferred, for my part, to start with unlimited competition, which is the general case, and to arrive at monopoly, which is a special case; and, proceeding in this way, I have been able (§§ 152, 226) to relate the equations of exchange and of production, which are rational and rigorous, to the equation of sales as a function of the price, which is only an empirical and approximate equation.

368. We have just seen how monopoly undermines the condition that the price of a product equals its average cost; it remains for us to see how monopoly undermines the other condition, namely that there be only one price in the market.

Let us return to the example that we have used and assume, for more simplicity, that each consumer consumes only one unit of the commodity. At 50 francs a unit, 10 units would be sold; therefore, out of the 50 units that would be sold at 20 francs a unit, there would be at most 40 units for which that price is a maximum price and that, in all cases, would be sold at this price. In deducting in this way from the total quantity demanded at any given price, the total quantity demanded at the price immediately greater, we obtain the partial quantity for which the first price is a maximum and that, under all circumstances, would be sold at this price. Now, it can be assumed for a moment that in place of a single price there are several on the market, and that the partial quantity demanded is sold at each of them. In our example, on condition that all the indicated prices are maintained, and of forcing each consumer to pay the price that, for him, is a maximum, it will be possible to sell 0 units at 100 francs per unit; 10 units at 50 francs; 40 at 20 francs; 950 at 5 francs; 1,500 at 3 francs; 2,500 at 2 francs; 7,000 at 1 franc; 8,000 at 0·50 francs; and 30,000 at 0 francs, according to the following table.

These operations would respectively yield the gross receipts 0, 500, 800, 4,750, 4,500,5,000, 7,000, 4,000, and 0 francs. If only 50 and 20

Price	Partial demand	Partial gross receipts	Total gross receipts	Partial cost	Partial net receipts	Total net receipts
Fr.	[in units]	Fr.	Fr.	Fr.	Fr.	Fr.
100	0	0	0	0	0	0
50	10	500	500	20	480	480
20	40	800	1,300	80	720	1,200
5	950	4,750	6,050	1,900	2,850	4,050
3	1,500	4,500	10,550	3,000	1,500	5,500
2	2,500	5,000	15,550	5,000	0	0
1	7,000	7,000	22,550	14,000	−7,000	−1,450
0.50	8,000	4,000	26,550	16,000	−12,000	−13,450
0	30,000	0	26,550	60,000	−60,000	−73,450

francs, the first two prices at which the quantity demanded is not zero, were charged, the total gross receipts would be 1,300 francs. And if there were not only these two prices, but the third, fourth, fifth, sixth, and seventh prices at which the demand is not zero, the total gross receipts at each of these prices would be respectively 6,050, 10,550, 15,550, 22,550, and 26,550 francs. In addition, 30,000 units could be given away.

369. The expenses of production being 2 francs per unit, the partial expenses of each of the partial quantities demanded at the different prices would be respectively 0, 20, 80, 1,900, 3,000, 5,000, 14,000, 16,000, and 60,000 francs. Subtracting these partial expenses from the partial gross receipts, we obtain the net receipts: 0, 480, 720, 2,850, 1,500, 0, −7,000, −12,000, and −60,000 francs. The sixth of these figures is zero; the last three are negative and represent losses. Eliminating prices like 0, 0.50, and 1 franc, that are lower than the average cost, and retaining only the others, we arrive at the following result. If there were only two prices, 50 and 20 francs, the total net receipts would amount to 1,200 francs. And if there were not only these two prices, but also the prices 5 francs and 3 francs, there would be successively the total net receipts 4,050 francs and 5,550 francs. Thus, on the assumption that the expenses of production are 2 francs per unit, the maximum net receipts would be 5,500 francs. In addition, 2,500 units could be sold at their average cost.

370. The preceding observation does not pertain exclusively to the case of monopoly. It is clear that if an entrepreneur, even one with a product sold under conditions of free competition, can adopt the average cost as an extreme limiting price and maintain, above that limit, staggered prices, and that if he can in addition lead each consumer to pay the price among these that constitutes his maximum price, the monopolist would benefit from those very differences. In fact, these assumed conditions really obtain much more frequently in trade and commerce than is thought. There is, among manufacturers and merchants, an art of selling the same commodity at different prices, and at the highest possible price to each class of consumers; and the practice of that art is very often facilitated by the thoughtlessness, vanity, and caprice of consumers. Sometimes it suffices to use a variety of labels in order to multiply prices and to find customers at each price. More often, the commodity, while remaining fundamentally the same, is given a slightly different form. Thus, a manufacturer of chocolates, who sells his chocolate for 3 francs per pound when it is sold under the modest name 'superfine chocolate', wrapped simply in glazed paper, will sell it for 4 francs a pound when he flavors with vanilla, and sells it with the name 'the chocolate of princes', and wrapped in gilt paper. The same is true of different seats in a theater, where the different prices are in no wise proportional to the costs of production of the seats. It is readily seen, however, that, under a regime of free competition, these techniques are much more difficult to employ, for the precise reason that, the spread of prices being considerably greater than the expenses necessitated by the modification of form and the change of labels, competition tends always to reduce that spread. Alongside our chocolate producer, there will soon be another who will sell 'the chocolate of princes' at 3 francs 80 centimes, thereby compelling our original manufacturer to offer it at 3 francs 60 centimes; whereupon, since the competitor will change his price to 3 francs 40 centimes, the other producer will be forced to charge 3 francs 20 centimes. Under the regime of monopoly, on the contrary, nothing could be easier than to employ the schemes which are seen every day. Very often a publisher, exclusive owner of rights over a sensational book by a famous author, sells a first edition in octavo at 7 francs 50 centimes, then two or three editions in smaller format at 3 francs, and finally a popular edition at 1 franc. The difference in

the price of the paper and the cost of printing is insignificant. The only difference consists in the greater or lesser speed of availability of the volume. By being more or less eager readers, the buyers thereby classify themselves with respect to the maximum price they are willing to pay; and the publisher profits by this classification. That is, in regard to monopoly, the importance of the method that consists of maintaining several prices in place of a single one on the market and of leading the consumer to pay the highest possible price.

371. As we have already pointed out, Cournot was the first to present a scientific theory of the fact of the decrease of demand with the increase of the price of commodities, and of the consequences of this fact, in his formulation of the mathematical conditions of maximum gross receipts and net receipts in the case of a monopoly. In this respect, Dupuit only repeated under the name of the *law of consumption* the propositions and corollaries originally presented by Cournot under the name of the *law of sales*. Dupuit's own contribution, for example, was his observations on multiple prices for one and the same commodity. He made a very complete and ingenious study of this fact in the two memoirs that we have mentioned. We therefore limit ourselves at present to referring the reader to these two memoirs, but not, however, without drawing attention to a most serious error on a major matter.

372. Dupuit says that

The diverse considerations that we have just elaborated on utility, can be portrayed geometrically in a very simple fashion.

If we assume that, on an unbounded line OP (Fig. 37), the lengths $\overline{Op}$, $\overline{Op}$, $\overline{Op''}$ ⋯ represent the price of an article, and the perpendicular lines $\overline{pn}$, $\overline{p'n'}$, $\overline{p''n''}$,⋯ represent respectively the number of units of the article consumed corresponding to these prices, we will form in this way a curve Nnn'n''P that we will call a consumption curve. $\overline{ON}$ represents the quantity consumed when the price is zero, and $\overline{OP}$ the price at which consumption becomes zero.

Since $\overline{pn}$ represents the number of units of the article consumed at the price $\overline{Op}$, the area of the rectangle Ornp expresses the expenses of production of $\overline{np}$ units, and, according to J.-B. Say, their utility. We believe that we

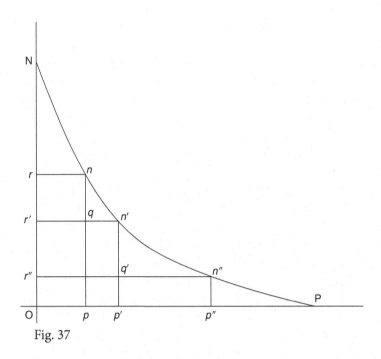

Fig. 37

have demonstrated that the utility of each of these $\overline{np}$ units is at least $\overline{Op}$, but that, for almost all, it is greater. For example, by erecting a perpendicular from p', we will have $\overline{n'p'}$ units for which the utility is at least equal to $\overline{Op'}$, because they are bought at that price. Consequently, of the $\overline{np}$ units, there are only $\overline{np} - \overline{n'p'} = \overline{nq}$ for which the utility is really no greater than $\overline{Op}$ (or rather a mean between $\overline{Op}$ and $\overline{Op'}$); for the others it is at least $\overline{Op'}$. We are thus led to conclude that, for $\overline{nq}$ units, their utility is represented by the horizontal slice rnn′r′, and that the utility of the remaining $\overline{qp}$ or $\overline{n'p'}$ units is greater than the rectangle r′n′p′O; assuming the price to be further increased by $\overline{p'p''}$ we could demonstrate that, for $\overline{n'p'} - \overline{n''p''} = \overline{n'q'}$ units, the utility is an average of $\overline{Op'}$ and $\overline{Op''}$, and is given by the area r′n′n″r″, etc., etc., and we would succeed in demonstrating that the absolute utility of these $\overline{np}$ units for the consumer is the mixtilinear trapezoid OrnP. If we want to find the relative utility, it suffices to subtract the expenses of production, i.e., the rectangle rnpO, leaving the triangle npP, which, we contend, remains for the consumers of the $\overline{np}$ units after they have paid for them. It can be seen that the area of this triangle beyond the line np has no relation to that of the rectangle to the left of it.

When it is a question of a natural product that entails no cost to acquire it, the utility is expressed by the big triangle NOP.

We see that as the price of a good increases, its utility diminishes, but less and less rapidly, and that, on the contrary, when the price decreases, the utility increases, but more and more rapidly, since it is represented by a triangle that contracts or lengthens.[2]

373. This geometric representation is, in effect, a very exact and clear expression of Dupuit's theory of utility. Instead of measuring utility, as J.-B. Say did, by the pecuniary sacrifice that the consumer actually makes when he considers the price, Dupuit measures utility by the sacrifice that the consumer is willing to make. The maximum pecuniary sacrifice that a consumer is willing to make in order to procure a unit of product being the measure of the utility of this unit of product for the consumer, it follows that the sum of the maximum pecuniary sacrifices that all consumers are willing to make to obtain the largest number of units of a product that can be sold is the measure of the utility of this product for the totality of consumers or for society. Thus, the measure of total utility is given geometrically by the area under the demand curve as a function of price, and arithmetically by the total gross receipts that we have just obtained by adding the partial gross receipts. Unfortunately, all these assertions are erroneous, and Dupuit's theory is no better than J.-B. Say's. Undoubtedly, the maximum pecuniary sacrifice that a consumer is willing to make to obtain a bottle of wine, for example, depends, in part, on the utility of the bottle of wine for the consumer; because, according as this utility increases or decreases, the maximum sacrifice in question will increase or decrease. But what Dupuit did not perceive is that this same maximum sacrifice depends also, in part, on the utility that bread, meat, clothes, and furniture have for the consumer; for, as the utility he derives from other commodities increases or decreases, the maximum sacrifice that he will be willing to make for wine will decrease or increase. And finally, what Dupuit also failed to see is that the maximum pecuniary sacrifice depends, in part, on the quantity of the wealth measured in terms of numeraire that the consumer

---

[2] *Annales des Ponts et Chaussées*, 2nd series. 1844. 2nd semester, p. 373.

possesses; for, according as this quantity is larger or smaller, the sacrifice that he will be ready to make for wine will be larger or smaller. In general, the maximum pecuniary sacrifice that a consumer is willing to make to obtain a unit of a product depends not only on the utility of the product, but also on the utility of all the other products that are in the market, and also, finally, on the consumer's means. We have already developed sufficiently the interrelations among the phenomena of utility, effective demand, effective supply, and current price, to make it unnecessary to return to the subject here. Let us just say that it is appropriate to put entirely aside all the considerations in Dupuit's two memoirs relative to the variation of utility with the prices and with the quantities demanded at these prices. It is true that these considerations are the principal subject of his study; but it is also true that he bases his considerations only on a complete confusion between the utility or want curve and the demand curve.

Note

i   'General expenses' is Walras's term for 'overhead costs'.

LESSON 38

Taxation

SUMMARY: – Role of the State. The State must be supported by either property or taxation. Hypothesis of a tax of 1 billion. The tax can be levied only on income; it can be levied on all incomes. Three sorts of direct taxes and one sort of indirect tax. Abstraction is made here from questions of rights, of economic advantageousness, and even of practical possibility.

A direct tax on wages falls on workers' incomes. A direct tax on rents falls on the landowners' capital; when all the land has changed hands, the tax is no longer paid by anyone; its elimination is then a free gift to the landowners. Its effects are attenuated in a progressive society as time passes. It is better for the State to become a proportional co-proprietor than to levy a lump sum tax on land.

A direct tax on certain types of interest is partially an indirect tax on consumption; a direct tax on all types of interest is partially levied on the income of capitalists. The case of a tax on the income from the State's bonds. An indirect tax on consumption is part of the expenses of production of products. It is levied more or less on the owners of productive services. The case of a tax on certain selected products.

374. To complete the theory of monopoly, we should show, when competition is unlimited, how the owners of services or the entrepreneurs who produce products are led to combine with each other to profit from a monopoly. We should also, if we want to complete the subject of the effects of diverse modes of organization of production and of the circulation of wealth, analyze the effects of prohibitive and protective tariffs, and of paper money. But we will find all these

questions more interesting when we treat, in the applied economics course, the exceptions to the principle of *laissez faire, laisser passer*, or its special applications: the question of combinations when we deal with the great economic monopolies such as those in mining and railways; with the question of prohibitive and protective tariffs when we deal with the freedom of foreign trade; with the question of paper money when we deal with the right to issue banknotes. At the present moment, we take up the subject of the effects of different systems of distribution of wealth.

375. In describing in the way that we have the mechanism of exchange, production, and capital formation, we have not only assumed complete freedom of competition in the markets for products, services, and capital goods; we have also abstracted from two things: first, the method of appropriation of services, whatever it may be, and, second, the role of the State, the services it provides and its needs. It is certain, however, that an economic society cannot function without the intervention of an authority charged with the duty of maintaining order and security, of rendering justice, of guaranteeing the national defense, and of performing many other services besides. The State, however, is not an entrepreneur; it does not sell its services in the market, nor according to the principle of free competition, that is, of the equality of price and average cost, nor according to the principle of monopoly, that is, of the maximization of net receipts; it often sells its services at a loss and sometimes gives them away. And we will see later that this is as it should be, for the reason that the services of the State are collectively and not individually consumed. There remain, then, two ways of providing for the needs of the State, that is, for public expenditures: the first is for the State as well as individuals to participate in the distribution of social wealth by owning *property*; the second is for it to use for its purposes a levy on the incomes of individuals taken by *taxation*. Which of these two systems is preferable? Can they not be fused into one? That is what we will examine in our course on social economics. We will see then how to work out simultaneously the theory of property and the theory of taxation. At present, we will inquire only into the natural and necessary effects of different kinds of taxes. Even if we assumed taxation to be abolished, it would still be useful, if only to know what is done and why it is

done, to know the effects of taxation. And, furthermore, that is yet another of the questions that we have a right to study in the interests of science, independently of any reasons for making practical applications. All the economists who have contributed to economic theory, like Ricardo, James Mill, and Destutt de Tracy, have devoted important chapters to it.

376. Let us reconsider the hypothetical country to which our economic table (§ 268) refers, where there are 80 billion worth of land yielding annually 2 billion in rent, 50 billion worth of personal faculties yielding 5 billion in wages, and 60 billion worth of capital properly speaking yielding 3 billion in interest. And now let us assume that there is a question in this country of raising annually, for public expenditures or for expenditures in the common interest, a sum of 1 billion annually. This figure could be discussed and considered to be too large or too small in view of the needs of the State; but such considerations are not in the domain of economic theory. The essential thing here is to come to clear conclusions by simple calculations; I therefore take the figure of 1 billion for convenience and for clarity of the analysis.

377. Now, in order to pose properly the question of taxation properly, several observations are indispensable.

The first is that capital should never be used for consumption, neither public nor private. It may be that some individuals consume their capital; they are free to do so, and this regrettable fact is compensated for by the fortunate circumstance that other individuals save out of their incomes. But the State should not systematically destroy the source of national wealth. Land, personal faculties, and capital goods properly speaking form the resources available for production. Land services, labor services, and capital good services constitute the fund available for consumption, and it is only on that fund that taxes ought to be levied.

378. There are therefore three incomes in a society: the services of land, the labor of personal faculties, and the 'profits' of capital goods properly speaking, sometimes consumed directly in the form of consumable services, sometimes combined with one another in the form

of productive services to make products, namely income goods and new capital goods properly speaking. The total value of consumption services and products is 10 billion, two-tenths of which, or 2 billion, are derived from land services, five-tenths or 5 billion from labor, and three-tenths or 3 billion from 'profits'. We must not lose sight of the fact that, among consumable services, that is, among the items of income subject to taxation, we include in particular the income from the personal faculties of persons who do not work and who lead a life of leisure, as well as the income from the land of those landowners who do not rent their land, and the income from the movable capital goods of those capitalists who do not lend their capital goods to others. We levy taxes only on incomes, but we levy them on all incomes. That is not the way of proceeding of governments and theorists in general, for they, making their classifications purely empirically, are determined to tax workers, but never think of taxing idlers as owners of personal faculties.

At the same time as we have, in our society, three productive elements, we also have three classes of consumers: landowners, workers, and capitalists, corresponding to the three factors of production. The landowners receive as rent 2 billion in the form of services or products in return for 2 billion worth of land services; the workers receive as wages 5 billion in the form of services or products in return for 5 billion worth of labor; and the capitalists receive as interest 3 billion in the form of services or products in return for 3 billion worth of 'profits'. Figures 2, 5 and 3 are the proportional amounts of consumption and of production. As for the entrepreneurs, they have no function here: no one earns his livelihood from being an entrepreneur, and it is immediately evident that the tax can only fall on them insofar as they are landowners, workers, or capitalists.

We may now observe that whatever process the State adopts to collect taxes, the various possible ways of proceeding can be classified under four headings. In fact, the State can only intervene before or after the exchange of services for consumption goods and services, or for products. In the second case, the State deals directly either with the landowners to take a part of their rents, or with workers to take a part of their wages, or with the capitalists to take a part of their interest income. This makes in all three kinds of *direct taxation*. In the first case, the State takes its part from the social income viewed not as composed of 2 billion of rent, 5 billion of wages, and 3 billion of interest, but as composed of 10 billion of consumable services and products. We have consumption goods and services. It deals with the entrepreneurs who advance it the total tax amount, with the understanding that they will reimburse themselves by adding the amount of the tax to the prices of the products that they sell to landowners, workers, and capitalists. Thus, the rents, wages, and interest are indirectly reduced. That is *indirect taxation*. Direct taxes are levied on services, and indirect taxes are levied on products. We are speaking here only of *property* taxes and not of *personal taxes*, which have neither a basis for assessment nor a traceable incidence.

379. Finally, it should be noted that we are abstracting from the right that the State can have to impose one or another of these four taxes, as well as from its interest in doing so, and similarly from the ease or difficulties that it can encounter in that operation, just as we made abstraction from the ease or difficulties of establishing maximum or minimum tariffs. In fact, the direct tax on rents is easy to establish although not without much effort and great expense; the direct tax on wages, with the exception of the one that is levied on the salaries of government employees, and the direct tax on income from capital, with the exception of the one that is levied on house rentals and on the interest paid on the public debt, are on the contrary totally impossible to impose with any accuracy, no matter how much effort or money is spent for that purpose. An indirect tax is easy to impose on certain products and hard to impose on others. But these are practical considerations that must be put aside. If we assume that the State is invested with the power to collect the three kinds of direct taxes and the indirect taxes, and that it resorts successively to these four methods, what will happen? That is specifically the subject that concerns us.

380. In our hypothetical country, the total annual wage bill amounts to 5 billion. If we assume that it is desired to impose a proportional tax of 1 billion on the income from personal faculties only, the immediate effect of such a tax would be the allocation to the State of one-fifth of the wages of each worker. Now, the price of labor is determined, as we have seen, by the supply and demand that exists regarding services

that are either consumable or productive. The imposition of the tax does not change these conditions in any way. The State acts simply as consumer of 1 billion worth of goods and services in place of the taxed workers. It is impossible to say which services or goods will be more in demand and which will be less in demand than before. It is equally impossible to say if the supply of labor will increase or decrease and even, if the supply increases or decreases, whether the total wage bill will increase or decrease. Consequently, it is necessary to abstract from these possibilities, or to assume that they compensate for one another and assume that the wage rate will be the same after the imposition of the tax as before. Thus, the workers will find it impossible to shift the tax to others by raising the price of their work. Each of them will be deprived of one-fifth of his income. Assume, for example, that a worker works 10 hours and earns 5 francs a day, it can be said of him either that the State takes from him 1 franc every day or that he works two hours every day for the benefit of the State. There is only one case in which the tax can have a different effect, and that is the case in which wages are just sufficient for the subsistence of the workers. Then the imposition of a tax has the inevitable consequence of a diminution of the working population, and the conditions of the effective supply of labor on the market for productive services will change. The supply decreases, wages rise, and the amount of the tax enters, in reality, into the cost of production of the products. Hence, it will be paid, in this case, by the consumers of the products; in all other cases, it will be paid by the workers.

381. A direct tax on rent would be a land tax, which, unlike the land taxes that have always existed and that still exist today, would fall exclusively on the income from land and not on the income from the capital goods properly speaking that are combined with land in agricultural industry. The same reasoning that has been made concerning the tax on wages would serve to establish the fact that the tax on rent would have the effect of allocating to the State a portion of the income of landowners, without their being able to find a way to pass the tax on to the consumers of products by raising the price of their land services. This was correctly stated, if not rigorously proved, by Ricardo in Chapter X of his *Principles of Political Economy and Taxation*. Taking that as his starting-point, Destutt de Tracy argued

with no less reason, in Chapter XII of his *Traité d'économie politique*, that when land is taxed in perpetuity, it is equivalent in every respect to the confiscation of a part of the land corresponding to the rate of the tax. Here is what he says, in his own words, on that matter:

As for the tax on land income, it is evident that it is he who owns the land at the time the tax is established that really pays, without being able to shift it to anyone else; for it does not give him the means of increasing his products, since it does not add anything to either the demand for the commodity or to the fertility of the land, and does not cause any decrease in the expenses of production. Everyone agrees that this is true; but what has not been sufficiently noticed is that the landowner in question ought to be considered less as having been deprived of a portion of his annual income than as having lost the part of his capital that would produce that portion of income at the current rate of interest. The proof of this is that if a farm that yields a net income of five thousand francs is worth one hundred thousand francs, the day after a perpetual tax of one-fifth of its value has been levied, if it is put on sale, will be worth, all other things being equal, only eighty thousand francs, and will be valued at only eighty thousand francs in the assets of an estate in which there are other items that have not changed in value. When, indeed, a State declares that it takes in perpetuity a fifth of the income of land, it is as if it had declared itself proprietor of a fifth of the asset, for no property is worth more than the utility that can be derived from it. That is so true that when, as a result of a new tax, the State obtains a loan for the interest of which it pledges the tax revenue, the operation is consummated. The State has really drawn upon the capital it has appropriated, and has used it up all at once instead of spending the income annually. This is like when Mr. Pitt made a once-for-all levy of the capital value of the land tax levied on the landowners. They found themselves free of the tax, and Mr. Pitt used up the capital value.

Therefore, it follows that, once all the land has changed hands after the establishment of the tax, it is not really paid by anyone. The buyers, having acquired only what remains, have lost nothing; for heirs, having received only what is in the estate, the surplus is as if their predecessor had spent it or lost it, as in actuality he lost it; and in the case of inheritances abandoned as worthless, it is the creditors who lost the capital that the State took out of the property that served as security for the loan.

It follows, also, that when the State gives up all or part of a land tax formerly established in perpetuity, it simply and purely makes a gift to the current landowners of the capital value of the income that it no longer collects. From their point of view, it is an absolutely free gift, to which they have no more right than any other citizen, because none of them had counted on that capital in the transaction by which he became a landowner.

The results would not be exactly the same if the tax had originally been established only for a given number of years. Then there would really have been taken from the landowner only that part of their capital that corresponds to the given number of *annual tax payments*. The State, furthermore, would have been able to borrow only this sum from the lenders to whom it would have given the tax in payment for their principal and their interest, and in transactions the land would have been considered as reduced in value by only that amount. In this case, when the last tax installments and the corresponding interest coupons on the loan are paid, the debt is extinguished on both sides, because it is paid off. On the whole, the principle is the same as in the cases of a perpetual tax and of a perpetual loan.

It is always true then, that when a tax is levied on the income from land, there is taken away from those that currently possess it a value equal to the capital value of the tax; and when all the land has changed hands after the tax is levied, it is, in reality, no longer paid by anyone. This observation is, indeed, unusual but important.[i]

Destutt de Tracy erroneously extends his observation to a tax on the income from buildings, and erroneously up to a certain point, as we shall see, to a tax on government bonds; but in the respects that it deals with a tax on the income from land, his observation is perfectly well founded on reasoning and confirmed by history. It has always been known that taxes on land income, whether levied by the State, feudal lords, the Church, or any religious community, affect the value of the landed capital, and do so exactly by the ratio of the amount of the tax to the amount of the rent. It has happened that the tax has sometimes completely absorbed the rent, and then the value of the land to the owner has been reduced to zero. This leads us to another observation that has also not been made and that is no less important than the preceding one.

382. The value of land and of land services rises steadily in a progressive society; this fact results mathematically from our theory of social wealth. From this, it follows, first of all, that the harm done to the first generation of landowners, at the time of the establishment of the tax, diminished as time passes, while the later landowners, who have never lost anything, benefit fully from the increasing value of the landed capital and land income. It follows, also, that it is better for the State to establish the tax on the basis of a definite proportion of the rent rather than as a lump sum, because, in the former scheme,

its proportional part will grow at the same time as that of the land-owners. The establishment of that land tax will have thus had the definitive result of associating the State with the ownership of the land or of sharing the ownership of the soil between individuals and the State. It is clearly seen now how the two questions of property and taxation are intimately related to each other.

383. If we now assume, in our hypothetical country, there is levied entirely on rents not a fixed tax of 1 billion, but rather a tax raising one half of the total of the rents, this is what will happen:

1° The landowners who own the land at the time of the establishment of the tax will, first of all, be deprived of half of their capital as well as half of their income. The State will become a co-proprietor, owning half of the land.

2° When all the land has changed hands by sale, gift or inheritance, the tax will no longer be paid by anyone.

3° As soon as economic progress has raised the total rent from 2 to 4 billion, the original owners who held on to their land will recuperate their losses completely and the new owners will see their income double.

4° The revenue of the State will itself increase from 1 to 2 billion.

It is therefore certain that it is preferable for the State to become a co-proprietor of the land than to be entitled to a rent assessed on the land, if the society is a progressive society and on the condition of attentively overseeing the increases in the value of land and of land services. We will return to this question when we deal with the cadaster.

Those are the conclusions of a study of a tax on rents. The effects of that tax are the same at first as those of a tax on wages; but they soon become intermingled with other phenomena that result from two facts: 1° that land can be bought and sold, which is not the case for personal faculties in countries that prohibit slavery, and 2° that the value of land and of land services rise constantly in a progressive society, which is a characteristic peculiar to this type of wealth.

384. Now let us assume that a tax is imposed directly on the interest charges on capital properly speaking, and ask what will happen.

I maintain in this case that if the tax is imposed on the interest charges on all kinds of capital goods without exception, all capitalists would be affected in proportion to their incomes, just as they would be by a fall in the rate of income. Moreover, a fall in the rate of income can lead either to an increase or to a decrease in savings (§ 238); therefore we cannot put aside this consequence and assume that the incidence stops there. But, that having been said, I will make an observation, applicable to a degree to taxes on land and personal faculties, but much more so to taxes on income from capital goods properly speaking, because: 1° it is difficult, if not impossible, to reach all capital goods, and 2° capital goods are products, the price of which, under normal conditions, must equal the average cost: the observation, namely, that if the tax is imposed on the interest income from only certain kinds of capital, the tax on interest would be, in part, a tax on consumption. To demonstrate this, I will show how we pass from the second situation to the first by extending the tax on a certain kind of capital good to all the kinds of capital goods successively.

Let us return to our hypothesis of a country in which there are 60 billion worth artificial capital, yielding annually 3 billion in interest, and in which it has been decided to impose exclusively the income from artificial capital by a proportional tax of 1 billion; but let us assume that we proceed by first establishing a tax of one-third of house rents. Let us single out, from all the owners, the owner of a house worth 60,000 francs yielding annually 3,000 francs in house rent. From these 3,000 francs, the tax takes 1,000 francs per annum; if this measure has only the simplest and most direct effect, the house in question would thereafter yield only 2,000 francs in income and would consequently not be worth more than 40,000 francs. But we know that the 60,000 francs correspond to the total cost of production of the house. Now, if houses cost 60,000 francs to construct but, upon completion, are not worth more than 40,000 francs, entrepreneurs will lose 20,000 francs on each house. Under these conditions, the building of houses stops at once; old houses deteriorate and fall into ruins, new ones are not built; thus, little by little, and as the effect of the laws of the market, house rents rise, and the value of houses rise in keeping with them; rents and houses recover their value; production is resumed and events resume their natural and normal course. The time will come, for our landowner, when his house will be worth 60,000 francs and will yield 4,000 francs in annual interest, from which the State will take 1,000 francs in taxes. Who then will pay the tax? The tenants. The tenants will be of two sorts. Some will rent the house in order to live in it; in technical terms, they will buy the capital service for use as a consumable service. Others will rent the house to install an industrial enterprise in it; they will buy the capital service for use as a productive service. In the first case, the tax will be paid immediately; in the second case, the tax will be included in the expenses of production of the industry and will be paid, in the final analysis, by the buyers of the products of that industry.

Hence a tax on house rent would act like a tax on consumption, at least in part; because, if we look at the matter closely, we will see that the burden falls partly on the capitalist. In fact, the capital goods previously employed in the construction of houses being transferred to all sorts of other employments, a general decline in the rate of income would result, to the detriment of all capitalists including the owners of houses, and to the advantage of all consumers including the renters of houses. It would be possible to try to discover the extent to which the consumers would recover, through the decline in the prices of other services and products, what they lost by the rise in house rents.

Having taken note of these two phenomena, it is now easy to understand that if we pass from houses to railways and then, in turn, to capital goods of all kinds without exception, the original distribution of savings among the various types of capital goods will be restored; in such a way that, finally, the number of houses, railways, and all other capital goods will become what it was before, there would remain only the general and growing fall of the rate of income and that consequently the tax would cease to weigh upon the consumers and would weigh exclusively upon the capitalists.[ii]

385. The case of a direct tax levied in perpetuity on State bonds deserves special consideration. If, after the tax has once been introduced, the State does not borrow any more, the bonds will be like natural wealth, and the owners of the bonds will lose capital at the same time as they lose income. The quotation on the securities exchange of these bonds will fall the same day as the establishment of tax. If, on the contrary, the State borrows more, the bonds become

like produced wealth, and the subscribers of the new bonds will take them only at a price corresponding to the current rate of interest. If they foresee that the State is going to impose a new tax, they will deduct another proportional amount from the subscription price; and, at the moment of the establishment of that tax, the fall in value having already been anticipated, the fall of the bond price will cease, or at least it will not be extreme.

386. Consideration of a tax on interest income leads us to a tax on products. Let us assume that, in our country, it has been decided to impose a proportional tax of 1 billion to be assessed on the 10 billion worth of products annually produced and no longer on any part of the 10 billion worth of services. The fiscal authority will then call upon the entrepreneurs and will collect the tax in proportion to the value of the products. It is evident that, in the state of general equilibrium of exchange and production, the entrepreneurs, being assumed to make neither profit nor loss, must consider the amount of the tax as an addition to their expenses of production and add it to the price of their products. If this cannot be done immediately, it will be done ultimately, by ceasing production, decreasing the quantity and raising the price of the products, as in the case of houses. Thus, sooner or later, the total amount of products will be sold to the consumers for 11 billion and the consumers will pay the tax. That is why the tax on products is also called an indirect tax on consumption. We count consumable services here among the products, considering them as products made with a single productive service, with the owner of the service being the entrepreneur.

387. But we have identified thus far only a part of the complete incidence of the consumption tax. It cannot be supposed that the price of all the services or products will rise proportionally by 10 per cent. There are, among these services or products, goods of prime necessity for which the effective demand will fall very little in consequence of such a rise in price; and there are luxury articles, for which the effective demand will fall considerably as the price increases. Hence the first effect of the tax, levied, as we have assumed, on all products in proportion to their value, would be, above all, to diminish the consumption and consequently the production of certain luxury articles. From this it results that the price of productive services that are used together in

the production of those articles would fall in the market for those services. Therefore the consumption tax results also in a decrease in the value of certain productive services. We may note that the effects of a consumption tax being therefore to restrict the demand for services or products, the yield of 1 billion would not be obtained by a tax of 10 per cent, and that it would be necessary to impose a higher tax rate.

388. In general, a consumption tax is not imposed on all products any more than a direct tax is imposed on all categories of interest income. Certain products that are widely and dependably consumed are selected to bear the tax. It is thus that, in our hypothetical country, it is possible to raise 1 billion in taxes on salt, beverages, and tobacco. In this case, the effects of the tax are those we have just described, but restricted naturally to the products on which it is imposed; that is to say that it is paid partly by the consumers of these products, and partly by the owners of the productive services that enter into their production, these latter being more or less affected according to whether the product is more or less an article of prime necessity or a luxury, and also according to whether the productive service is more or less specialized. A tax on wheat would weigh more heavily on consumers of bread and not much on landowners because bread is an article of prime necessity; a tax on wine, on the contrary, would weigh much more heavily on landowners, first, because wine is, to a certain degree, a luxury, and, second, either because the land suited for vineyards cannot be used for any other kind of agriculture, or because there would not be any advantage in changing the purpose or the use of the land as a consequence of the tax. It can be seen how complex the incidence of consumptions taxes is and how much the effects of a tax on one or another product require separate study. This is what needs to be done when it is a question of taking practical decisions; but the general principles that we have considered amply suffice us for the development of the theories of social economics and applied economics that we have in mind.

Notes

i   Antoine-Louis-Claude Destutt de Tracy, *Traité de la volonté*, Paris 1815; republished under the title *Traité d'économie politique*, Paris, 1823. The translation of the passage is ours. English translation (1817, edited by

Thomas Jefferson), *A Treatise on Political Economy*, Georgetown D.C., 1817, reprinted by Augustus M. Kelley Publishers, New York, 1970; the quoted passage can be found on pages 184–6.

ii　Walras wrote regarding the effects of a tax on houses: 'la baisse générale et croissante du taux du revenu subsisterait seule, et que, par conséquent, l'impôt cesserait de peser sur les consommateurs pour peser exclusivement sur les capitalistes.' Jaffé translated that as 'The only lasting effect will be a general and continuous decline in the rate of income. Consequently the burden of the tax will gradually cease to be borne by the consumers and will rest finally on the shoulders of the capitalists alone' (Jaffé in Walras 1954, § 400, p. 456). In fact, Walras did not write that 'there will be a general and continuous decline' but that 'there would be a general and growing fall'. He did not write that 'the tax will gradually cease⋯' but that 'the tax would cease⋯'.

APPENDIX I

Geometrical theory of the determination of prices

I THE EXCHANGE OF SEVERAL COMMODITIES FOR ONE ANOTHER

1. In my *Éléments d'économie politique pure*, passing from the theory of the exchange of two commodities to the theory of the exchange of several commodities for one another, and seeing that in that case the demand for or the supply of each of the commodities by each of the traders is a function not only of the price of that commodity but also of the prices of all the others, I believed that it was necessary to adopt exclusively the analytic method of expression and to do without the help of diagrams. But since then I have found a means, that I will describe briefly, of working out the theory in question by the method of geometrical representation.

Assume that an exchanger holds, for a certain period of time, the quantities $q_a, q_b, q_c, q_d, \cdots$ of the commodities (A), (B), (C), (D)$\cdots$, represented by the lengths $\overline{Oq_a}, \overline{Oq_b}, \overline{Oq_c}, \overline{Oq_d}, \cdots$ (Fig. 38), and has, during the same period of time, the wants for those commodities expressed by the curves $\alpha_q\alpha_r, \beta_q\beta_r, \gamma_q\gamma_r, \delta_q\delta_r, \cdots$. I must explain the nature and indicate the law of these curves that are the essential and fundamental basis of the entire mathematical theory of social wealth.[1]

---

[1] Of the three sections composing that theory, the first appears in a memoir read to the Société des ingénieurs civils de Paris on October 17, 1890, and reproduced in the January 1891 *Bulletin* of that Society, to which section I have made some modifications, one of which is quite important, with the aim of simplifying the

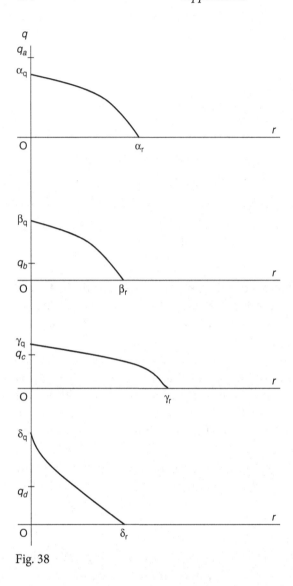

Fig. 38

fundamental demonstration of the theorem of maximum satisfaction; and the last two of which sections similarly appear, together with some modifications introduced by the first section, as part of a text written for the *Recueil inaugural* of the University of Lausanne (1892). *The Théorie géometrique de la détermination des prix* appeared in English, very nearly as it is presented in this first appendix, in the July 1892 number of the *Annals of the American Academy of Political and Social Science.*

It is permissible to say in ordinary language: 'The desire that we have for things, or the utility that the things have for us, decreases as their consumption increases. The more we eat, the less hungry we are; the more we drink, the less thirsty we are, at least in general and except for certain unfortunate exceptions; the more hats and shoes we have, the less need we have of a new hat or a new pair of shoes; the more horses we have in our stables, the less effort we make to procure one more horse, always excluding impulsive behavior, from which the theory has the right to abstract except when taking account of one or another special case.' But, in mathematical terms, we will say: 'The intensity of the last want satisfied, is a decreasing function of the quantity of commodity consumed'; and we will represent these functions by curves, the *quantities consumed* by the ordinates, and the *intensities of the last want satisfied* by the abscissas. For example, take the commodity (A), the intensity of the want for our consumer, that would be $\overline{O\alpha_r}$ at the beginning of the consumption, would be zero after the consumption of a quantity $\overline{O\alpha_q}$, the consumer having then reached satiety. I call that intensity of the last want satisfied, to be more brief, its rareté. The English call it the *Final degree of utility*, the Germans *Grenznutzen*. It is not a measurable quantity; but it is sufficient to conceive of it in order to found the demonstration of the great laws of economic theory upon the fact of its diminution.

2. For the present, let $p_b, p_c, p_d, \cdots$ be the prices of (B), (C), (D), $\cdots$ in terms of (A) cried at random in the market. The first problem that we have to solve consists of determining the quantities x, y, z, w, $\cdots$ of (A), (B), (C), (D), $\cdots$, some of the quantities positive, namely the quantities demanded, some of them negative, namely the quantities supplied, that our trader will add to the quantities $q_a, q_b, q_c, q_d, \cdots$ that he possesses, or that he will subtract from them, so as to consume the quantities $q_a + x$, $q_b + y$, $q_c + z$, $q_d + w, \cdots$ represented by the lengths $\overline{Oa}$, $\overline{Ob}$, $\overline{Oc}$, $\overline{Od}, \cdots$ [Fig. 39]. Just as we employed above the general hypothesis of an exchanger for whom the rareté decreases with the quantity consumed, so we employ here the general hypothesis of an exchanger who seeks in the exchange the greatest satisfaction of his wants. Now, the sum of the wants satisfied by a quantity Oa of commodity (A), for example, is the surface $Oa\rho_a\alpha_r$. *The effective*

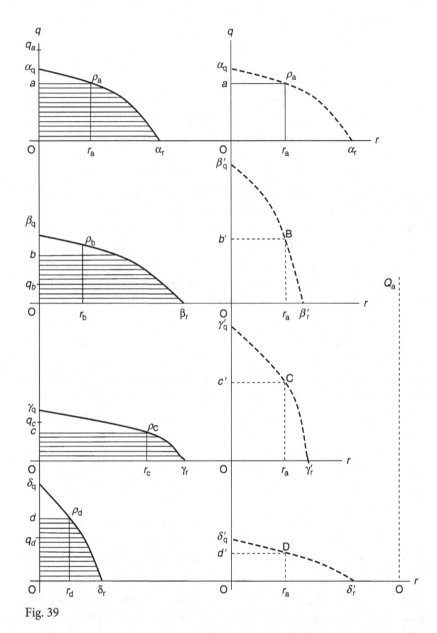

Fig. 39

utility is the definite integral of the rareté in relation to the quantity consumed. Consequently, the problem whose solution we are seeking consists precisely of determining $\overline{Oa}, \overline{Ob}, \overline{Oc}, \overline{Od}, \cdots$, subject to the condition that the sum of the shaded areas $Oa\rho_a\alpha_r$, $Ob\rho_b\beta_r$, $Oc\rho_c\gamma_r$, $Od\rho_{dr}, \cdots$ be a maximum.

In order to furnish that solution very simply in geometric form, I subject the curves of utility or want $\beta_q\beta_r, \gamma_q\gamma_r, _{qr}, \cdots$ to the following transformation. I measure off from the origin O upon the horizontal axes the new abscissas equal to $\dfrac{1}{p}$ times the old abscissas. And, on the parallels to the vertical axes drawn through the extremities of the new abscissas, I measure off from the horizontal axes the new ordinates equal to p times the old ordinates. In the figure, $p_b = 2$, $p_c = 3$, $p_d = 0.5, \cdots$. As is easily understood, the new curves $\beta_q'\beta_r', \gamma_q'\gamma_r', \delta_q'\delta_r', \cdots$ represent the utility of (A) to be spent for (B), for (C), for (D)$\cdots$, or, in other words, the want the exchanger has for (A) in order to procure some of (B), of (C), of (D)$\cdots$ Indeed, if we consider the areas $O\beta_q\beta_r, O\gamma_q\gamma_r, O\delta_q\delta_r, \cdots$ as the limits of sums of infinitely small rectangles, we may consider the surfaces $O\beta_q'\beta_r', O\gamma_q'\gamma_r', O\delta_q'\delta_r', \cdots$ as the limits of equal sums of infinitely small rectangles, each base being p times less, and each height p times greater. Now, each of the rectangles of the former sum represents the effective utility of an increment of commodity; each of the rectangles of the latter sum represents, in the same way, the equal effective utility of the p increments of (A) with which that increment of commodity is bought.

The curves $\alpha_q\alpha_r, \beta_q'\beta_r', \gamma_q'\gamma_r', \delta_q'\delta_r', \cdots$ being placed in vertical order, I take a vertical length $\overline{OQ_a}$, representing the equivalent in terms of (A) of the quantities $q_a, q_b, q_c, q_d, \cdots$ of (A), (B), (C), (D), $\cdots$ at the prices $1, p_b, p_c, p_d, \cdots$, namely $q_a + q_b p_b + q_c p_c + q_d p_d + \cdots$, and I draw it from right to left in such a way as to satisfy the varying wants in the order of their intensity, until it is sub-divided among the curves into the ordinates $r_a\rho_a = \overline{Oa}$, $r_aB = \overline{Ob'}$, $r_aC = \overline{Oc'}$, $r_aD = \overline{Od'}$, $\cdots$ corresponding to the same, particular abscissa $\overline{Or_a}$.[i] That abscissa $\overline{Or_a}$ will represent the rareté of (A) in terms of (A), of (B), of (C), of (D), $\cdots$, namely r_a, corresponding to a maximum of effective utility. The ordinates $\overline{Oa}, \overline{Ob'}, \overline{Oc'}, \overline{Od'}, \cdots$ will represent, in terms of (A), the quantities to be consumed of (A), of (B), of (C), of (D), $\cdots$, the only commodities to be consumed being those for which the intensity of the first want to be satisfied is greater than r_a. If we carry back the abscissas $\overline{Or_a} = r_a$, $\overline{Or_b} = p_b$, $\overline{Or_b} = p_b$, $\overline{Or_c} = p_c$, $\overline{Or_d} = p_d$, $\cdots$ to the curves $\alpha_q\alpha_r, \beta_q\beta_r$,

$\gamma_q \gamma_r$, $\delta_q \delta_r$, $\cdots$, we would obtain the ordinates $\overline{Oa}$, $\overline{Ob}$, $\overline{Oc}$, $\overline{Od} \cdots$, representing the quantities of (A), of (B), of (C), of (D), $\cdots$ to be consumed.[2] The exchanger will therefore offer, when all is said and done, the quantities $x, z, \cdots$ of (A), (C), $\cdots$, represented by $\overline{q_a a}$, $\overline{q_c c}$, $\cdots$, and will demand the quantities $y, w, \cdots$ of (B), (D)… represented by $\overline{q_b b}$, $\overline{q_d d}$, $\cdots$. And thus, *in a state of maximum satisfaction, the raretés are proportional to the prices*, in accordance with the equations:

$$\frac{r_a}{1} = \frac{r_b}{p_b} = \frac{r_c}{p_c} = \frac{p_c}{p_d} = \cdots$$

3. That is how, given the quantities possessed and the utilities of the commodities, we determine for an exchanger the demand for or supply of each of the commodities, at prices cried at random, that will provide the maximum satisfaction of his wants. There remains, given the demand and supply of commodities by all the parties in the exchange at prices cried at random, to determine the current prices at equilibrium, subject to the condition of the equality of the total effective demand and supply. The solution of the second problem is also amenable to being furnished geometrically.

---

[2]   We would also be able, as I did in the memoir read to the Société des ingénieurs civils, to construct a total curve by superimposing all the transformed partial utility curves of (B), (C), (D), $\cdots$ on the partial utility curve of (A) by the addition of all the ordinates corresponding to the same abscissa. It is also easy to take into account the circumstance that the total curve represents the total utility of (A) used, in terms of (A), of (B), of (C), of (D)$\cdots$, or, in other words, the total want that the exchanger would have for (A) in order to obtain some of (A), of (B), of (C), of (D), $\cdots$. Indeed, if we consider the surfaces of the partial curves as limits of sums of infinitely small rectangles, we could consider the surface of the total curve as the limit of the total sum of all these rectangles superposed one upon another in the order of their horizontal length. By putting the ordinate $\overline{OQ_a}$ into the total curve, we would obtain the abscissa $\overline{Or_a}$ representing the rareté of (A) in terms of (A), of (B), of (C), of (D), $\cdots$, corresponding to the maximum effective utility, namely r_a. That diagram, which can be constructed not only in the case of the exchange of several commodities for each other but also in the case of the exchange of products and services for each other, permits bringing to light, in a rigorous fashion, the gains of utility made in exchange and production.

Let us, for an instant, make abstraction from $p_c, p_d, \cdots$ and seek first to determine p_b provisionally. And, for that purpose, let us ask how, $p_c, p_d, \cdots$ being assumed constant, the variations of p_b influence the demand and supply of (B).

If y is positive; that is to say, if the trader is a demander of (B), an increase of p_b can only decrease y. In short, if that exchanger demands the same quantity at a higher price, he would owe a difference that he would not be able to pay except by decreasing his quantities of (A), (C), (D), $\cdots$. But he will then increase his raretés of these commodities; and, in consequence, the condition of maximum satisfaction will be approached even less. Hence, the quantity demanded y is too great for a price higher than p_b. And, in consequence, *the demand curve is decreasing.*

If y is negative; that is to say, if the exchanger is a supplier of (B), there are three possible outcomes. The exchanger, being assumed to supply an equal quantity at a higher price, is due a surplus, and by means of that difference he can increase his quantities, and consequently decrease his raretés of (A), (C), (D), $\cdots$. Then, one of three things occurs: either the surplus is insufficient to reestablish the condition of maximum satisfaction, or it is exactly sufficient, or it is more than sufficient; and, in consequence, at a price higher than p_b, the exchanger must supply a quantity of (B), either greater than, equal to, or less than y. It is certain that he will find himself in one of these three situations, depending upon the degree of increase of p_b.

Let us assume that an exchanger who, at the prices $p_b, p_c, p_d, \cdots$ of (B), (C), (D), $\cdots$ in terms of (A), is a supplier of a quantity o_b of (B) and a demander or supplier of (A), (C), (D), $\cdots$ in such a way as to obtain maximum satisfaction in conformity with the equations:

$$\frac{r_a}{1} = \frac{r_b}{p_b} = \frac{r_c}{p_c} = \frac{p_c}{p_d} = \cdots.$$

If, in this state of affairs, $p_c, p_d, \cdots$ remaining constant, p_b increases, and if our exchanger supplies always the quantity o_b of (B), using, as he should, the difference that is due him for the purchase of (A),

(C), (D), $\cdots$, the ratio $\dfrac{r_b}{p_b}$ will decrease because of the increase of the denominator p_b, while the ratios $\dfrac{r_a}{1}, \dfrac{r_c}{p_c}, \dfrac{p_c}{p_d}, \cdots$ will decrease because of the decrease of the numerators $r_a, r_c, r_d, \cdots$. Now, the first ratio [*i.e.* $\dfrac{r_b}{p_b}$] cannot become zero unless p_b becomes infinite; while, if we assume: 1° that the prices $p_c, p_d, \cdots$ are not infinite, 2° that the number of commodities in the market is not infinite, 3° that the exchanger cannot consume an infinite quantity of any of them, the latter ratios will become zero at some price of (B) that is quite high, although not infinite, so that the difference that is due permits the exchanger to have all that he wants of (A), (C), (D), $\cdots$. And, at this point, the respective ratios of the raretés at those prices being $\dfrac{0}{1}, \dfrac{r_b}{p_b}, \dfrac{0}{p_c}, \dfrac{0}{p_d}, \cdots$, the exchanger, to regain his maximum satisfaction, will have to sell quantities of (A), of (C), of (D)$\cdots$ to purchase (B); that is to say, to decrease his supply o_b of (B).

It is therefore very certain that the rise of p_b that causes the exchanger to switch from being a demander to being a supplier, makes him switch, additionally, from an increasing quantity supplied to a decreasing one; that is to say, in other words, that *the supply curve, taken positively, is successively increasing and decreasing*. Moreover, we can assume the supply o_b to be infinitely small at a certain price of (B); but it is necessary that this price be infinitely great in order that $r_a, r_c, r_d, \cdots$ become zero. Then satisfaction will be maximized by virtue of the equations:

$$\frac{0}{1} = \frac{r_b}{p_b} = \frac{0}{p_c} = \frac{0}{p_d} = \cdots; \text{ii}$$

that is to say that the supply becomes zero again at an infinitely great price, and that, in other words, *the supply curve is asymptotic to the price axis*.

The variation of p_b, from zero to infinity, therefore causes the exchanger to switch from the side of demand to the side of supply;

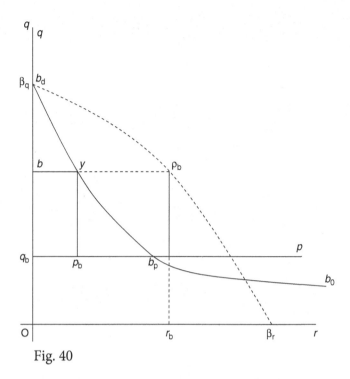

Fig. 40

then from an increasing supply to a decreasing supply. When the price is zero, the demand is equal to the excess of the quantity necessary to satiate completely the desire for the commodity over the quantity possessed; at an infinitely high price, the amount supplied is zero. In the case of the exchange of several commodities, just as in the case of the exchange of two commodities for each other, these preferences can be represented geometrically for an exchanger by a curve $b_d b_p b_o$ (Fig. 40) referred to the two axes: first, $q_b p$, *the price axis*, and, second, $b_d O$, *the axis of quantities demanded* above the origin q_b, and *the axis of quantities supplied* below that origin. Thus, at the price of zero, our exchanger would demand a quantity of (B) represented by $\overline{q_d b_d}$, at the price p_b, represented by $\overline{q_b p_b}$, he demands a quantity represented by $\overline{p_b y} = \overline{q_b b}$; at the price b_p, represented by $\overline{q_b b_p}$, he would neither demand nor supply; at higher prices, he would supply the quantities represented by the distances from the $q_b p$ axis to the curve $b_p b_o$; at an

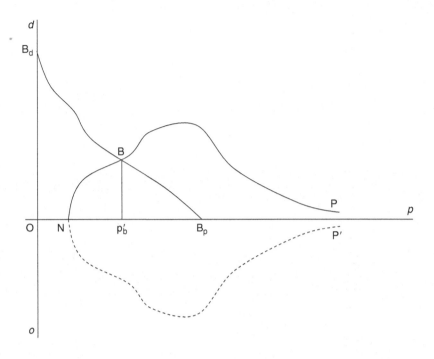

Fig. 41

infinite price, he would no longer be a supplier, the curve $b_p b_o$ being asymptotic to the $q_b p$ axis.

All the exchangers having preferences that are not the same but are similar as far as concerns the commodity (B), it is clear that all the partial demand curves can be added up to a total curve $B_d B_p$ that continually decreases (Fig. 41), and all the partial supply curves added up to a total curve NP′, successively increasing and decreasing, from zero to zero, if we take it positively and asymptotic to the price axis, and make NP′ turn around the horizontal axis so as to bring it into the position NP.[iii] The abscissa $\overline{Op_b'}$ of the point of intersection B of the two curves $B_d B_p$ and NP will provisionally be the current equilibrium price at which the total effective supply and demand for (B) will be equal. Furthermore, that intersection of the two curves, $B_d B_p$ and NP, can take place either when the second curve rises, or when it falls.

It follows from the nature of the curves that we will obtain the provisional current price of (B) by raising it in case of an excess of effective demand over effective supply, and lowering it, on the contrary, in case of an excess of effective supply over effective demand. Passing then to the determination of the current price of (C), then to the current price of (D) and so forth, we obtain them by the same means. It is certainly true that, in determining the price of (C), we may destroy the equilibrium with respect to (B); that, in determining the price of (D), we may destroy the equilibrium with respect to (B) and with respect to (C), and so on. But, inasmuch as the determination of the price of (C), of (D), of ⋯ will have, on the relation of the demand and supply of (B), effects in opposite directions, the market will probably always be closer to equilibrium after the second round of tatonnement than after the first.[iv] We enter here into the theory of tatonnement as I have expounded it in my works and in virtue of which *the equilibrium of the market is reached by raising the price of commodities whose demand is superior to the supply and lowering the price of those whose supply is superior to the demand.*

4. Thanks to the concurrent employment of analytic expression and geometric representation, we have here not only the idea but also the image of the phenomenon of the determination of prices in the market in the case of the exchange of several commodities for one another; and with this, in my opinion, we possess at last the theory. Some critics, however, have made fun of the number of pages I used to demonstrate that the current price will be reached by raising the price in the case of an excess of the demand over the supply, and lowering it in case of an excess of the supply over the demand. — 'And you,' I said once to one of them, 'how do you demonstrate it?' — 'But,' he answered, a little surprised and even quite embarrassed, 'does it need to be demonstrated? It seems to me to be evident'. — 'There is nothing evident except axioms, and this is not one. But you are implying, I assume, the reasoning that Jevons formulated explicitly in his little treatise *Political Economy*, namely that raising the price, and thereby necessarily making demand decrease and increasing supply, leads to their equality in case of there being an excess of one over the other⋯' — 'Precisely'. — 'Very well! There is an error here: the rise necessarily decreases the demand; but it does not necessarily increase the supply.

If you are a supplier of wine, it may very well be that you supply less at a million, than at a thousand francs, less at a billion than at a million, simply because you would prefer to drink your wine yourself, rather than use the superfluous commodities that you would be able to acquire by selling it for more than a certain price. The same is true of labor: we comprehend perfectly that a man who supplies ten hours per day of his time at a price of 1 franc an hour would not supply more than four at the price of 10 francs per hour, and only one at a price of 100 francs. We see, every day, in the large towns, that workers, when they earn 20 or 25 francs a day, do not work more than three or four days a week.' — 'But if that is so, how is raising the price a means of reaching the current price?' 'That is what the theory explains to you. Two individuals can meet either by walking toward each other or, if they are walking in the same direction, by one overtaking the other. Supply and demand equalize themselves, sometimes in the first manner, sometimes in the second.'

Is it not worthwhile to demonstrate rigorously the fundamental laws of a science? We count today I do not know how many schools of economics: the *deductive* school and the *historical* school; the school of *laisser faire* and the school of *State interventionism* or *academicians' socialism*, the *socialist* school properly speaking, the *Catholic* school, the *Protestant* school. For me, I recognize only two: the school of those who do not demonstrate their propositions, and the school, that I hope to see founded, of those who will demonstrate their propositions. It is through demonstrating rigorously the elementary theorems of geometry and algebra, then the theorems of the calculus and mechanics that are deduced from them, in order to apply them to experiential data, that we achieve the marvels of modern industry. Let us proceed in the same way in economics, and we shall, without doubt, succeed in acting upon reality in the economic and social order as we have done in the physical and industrial order.

II THE EXCHANGE OF PRODUCTS AND SERVICES FOR ONE ANOTHER

5. The concern at present is to extend the method of exclusively geometric demonstration that I used in sketching the theory of exchange

in the preceding section to the theory of production and the theory of capital formation. Now, in formulating the theory of exchange, it is assumed that the quantities of the commodities are given and not unknowns of the problem; to construct first of all the theory of production, the commodities must be considered as products resulting from combining productive services with each other, and, in consequence, the quantities made of products must be introduced into the problem as that number of unknowns, and adding to them, as is appropriate, an equal number of determining mathematical conditions. That is what I am going to do here, referring to my *Éléments d'économie politique pure* for definitions and notations.

6. Assume, then, that there are the landed, labor, and movable-capital services of the kinds (T), (P), (K), $\cdots$ susceptible of being utilized, either directly as consumable services or indirectly as productive services; that is to say, in the form of the products of the kinds (A), (B), (C), (D), $\cdots$. The first problem that we have to solve consists of determining, for each consumer, the supply of services and the demand for services, either in the form of consumable services or as products. But the solution of the problem is furnished us by the theory of exchange. Assume there is a consumer possessing, during a certain period, the quantities $q_t, q_p, q_k, \cdots$ of the services (T), (P), (K), $\cdots$, and having, during the same period of time, wants for these services and wants for the products, (A), (B), (C), (D), $\cdots$ expressed by the curves of utility or want giving the raretés, or the *intensities of the last wants satisfied*, by their abscissas as decreasing functions of the *quantities consumed* represented by their ordinates. And assume that $p_t, p_p, p_k, \cdots$, $\pi_b, \pi_c, \pi_d, \cdots$ are the prices of (T), (P), (K), $\cdots$ and of (B), (C), (D), $\cdots$ in terms of (A) cried at random in the market. We will transform the curves of utility or of want for services and products other than (A) into curves of utility of (A) used in (T), in (P), in (K), $\cdots$, in (B), in (C), in (D), $\cdots$, or, in other words, into curves of wants for (A) to be used in procuring some (T), some (P), some (K), $\cdots$, some (B), some (C), some (D) $\cdots$, by dividing the abscissas and multiplying the ordinates by the prices that are cried. The curve of the utility or want of (A) and the transformed curves of utility or want of (T), (P), (K), $\cdots$ (B), (C), (D), $\cdots$ being placed one under the other, we will draw a

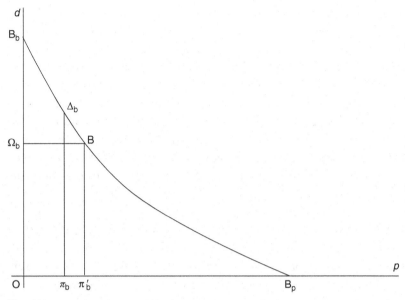

Fig. 42

vertical line $Q_a = q_t p_t + q_p p_p + q_k p_k + \cdots \left[+ q_b p_b + q_c p_c + q_d p_d + \cdots \right]^v$
in length from right to left until it is divided up among all the curves
into ordinates corresponding to the same abscissa. That abscissa will
represent the rareté or the intensity of the last want satisfied of (A)
in the form of (T), of (P), of (K), $\cdots$ of (A), of (B), of (C), of (D), $\cdots$,
namely r_a, corresponding to a maximum of effective utility. By car-
rying back the abscissas $\overline{p_t r_a}$, $\overline{p_p r_a}$, $\overline{p_k r_a}$, $\cdots$, $\overline{r_a}$, $\overline{p_b r_a}$, $\overline{p_c r_a}$, $\overline{p_d r_a}$,
$\cdots$ to the primitive curves, we obtain the ordinates representing the
quantities of services (T), (P), (K), $\cdots$ and of products (A), (B), (C),
(D), $\cdots$ to be consumed. It is evident that *in the state of maximum
satisfaction, the raretés will be proportional to the prices in accordance
with the equations*:

$$\frac{r_t}{p_t} = \frac{r_p}{p_p} = \frac{p_k}{p_k} = \cdots = \frac{r_a}{1} = \frac{r_b}{p_b} = \frac{r_c}{p_c} = \frac{p_c}{p_d} = \cdots.$$

7. Our prices $p_t, p_p, p_k, \cdots, \pi_b, \pi_c, \pi_d, \cdots$ for services and products are
assumed to be cried at random. We are now going to assume that the
random quantities $\Omega_a, \Omega_b, \Omega_c, \Omega_d, \cdots$ of (A), (B), (C), (D), $\cdots$ have

been produced, and, leaving $p_t, p_p, p_k, \cdots$ as they are, we are going to determine the prices of (B), (C), (D), $\cdots$ by the condition that the demand for the products is equal to their supply; that is to say, to the quantity produced. The solution of the second problem is also furnished to us by the theory of exchange. Assume, then, that Δ_b, represented by the ordinate $\overline{\pi_b \Delta_b}$ (Fig. 42), is the total demand for (B) at the prices cried for services and products. We know, by the theory of exchange, abstracting at first from the prices of (C), (D), $\cdots$ and seeking to determine provisionally the price of (B), that if we vary this price from zero to infinity, the demand for (B) will decrease always in accordance with the curve $B_d B_p$. Hence, there exists a price π'_b corresponding to the equality of the demand for (B) with the supply Ω_b, that is $> \pi_b$ if, at the price π_b, the demand for (B) is greater than the supply, and that is $< \pi_b$, if, at the price π_b, the supply of (B) is greater than the demand. We will likewise find a price π'_c corresponding to the equality of the demand for (C) with the supply Ω_c, a price π'_d corresponding to the equality of the demand for (D) with the supply Ω_d, and so on. After that first tatonnement, we will proceed to a second, to a third reprise, and so on, until we have obtained a series of prices $\pi''_b, \pi''_c, \pi''_d, \cdots$ at which the demands for (B), (C), (D), $\cdots$ would be equal to the supplies $\Omega_b, \Omega_c, \Omega_d, \cdots$. We state, therefore, that in the matter of production, as in the matter of exchange, *the equilibrium in the market for products is reached by raising the price of those commodities for which the demand is greater than the supply and lowering the price of those commodities for which the supply is greater than the demand.*

8. $\pi''_b, \pi''_c, \pi''_d, \cdots$ are therefore the *prices* of the quantities $\Omega_b, \Omega_c, \Omega_d,$ $\cdots$ of (B), (C), (D)$\cdots$. But, the prices $p_t, p_p, p_k, \cdots$ of the services, (T), (P), (K) $\cdots$ result in certain *average costs* $p_b, p_c, p_d, \cdots$ of the products, (B), (C), (D), $\cdots$.[3] And the differences, positive or negative, between the prices and the average costs in the production of (B), (C), (D), $\cdots$

---

[3] It is true that, in order to assume there is an average cost common to all the entrepreneurs, it is necessary to assume that the *fixed expenses* are distributed over the same quantities of products, in order to be able to put them into the same category as *proportional expenses*; that is to say, it is necessary to assume

result in the gains or losses $\Omega_b(\pi_b'' - p_b)$, $\Omega_c(\pi_c'' - p_c)$, $\Omega_d(\pi_d'' - p_d)$, $\cdots$. It is now necessary to determine the quantities produced of (B), (C), (D), $\cdots$ subject to the condition that the price and average cost be equal, so that there will be neither profit nor loss for the entrepreneurs. This third problem is the particular problem of the theory of production, and may also be solved geometrically as follows. Let $\overline{Op_b}$ (Fig. 43) be an abscissa representing the average cost p_b. And let $\overline{O\pi_b''}$ be an abscissa representing the price π_b'', and $\overline{\pi_b''B'}$ an ordinate representing the quantity Ω_b of (B) produced at random and demanded at the price π_b''. If we assume $p_t, p_p, p_k, \cdots, \pi_c'', \pi_d'', \cdots$ determined and constant, and that we vary the price of (B) from zero to infinity, it is certain that the demand for (B) will always decrease following a curve $B_d'B_p'$. Consequently, there exists a demand Ω_b', corresponding to a price equal to the average cost. Ω_b' will be $\geqq \Omega_b$ according to whether $\pi_b'' \geqq p_b$. We can also find a demand Ω_c' corresponding to a price equal to an average cost p_c, a demand Ω_d' corresponding to a price equal to an average cost p_d and so on. If we now were to substitute the produced quantities Ω_b', Ω_c', Ω_d', $\cdots$ for the produced quantities Ω_b, Ω_b, Ω_b, $\cdots$ and sell them in accordance with the mechanism of rise and fall of prices described in the preceding

that all the entrepreneurs are producing the same quantities of products. The hypothesis is no more real than that of the absence of profit and of loss, but it is as rational. If, in effect, at a given point a certain quantity of products corresponds to the absence of profit and of loss, the entrepreneurs that produce less than that amount make losses, reduce their production and end by going into liquidation, and those who produce more make profits, increase their production, and attract the customers of the failing firms. Thus, owing to the distinct nature of proportional expenses and fixed expenses, production under free competition, after taking place with a great number of small enterprises, tends to be distributed among a smaller number of medium-sized enterprises, then among a small number of large enterprises, finally ending up, first in a *monopoly selling at average cost*, then in a *monopoly selling at the price that gives maximum profit*. This statement is corroborated by the facts. But it is, during the entire period of competition and even during the period of monopoly selling at average cost, always permissible, in order to simplify the theory, to assume that the entrepreneurs produce the same quantities of products and to treat the fixed expenses as proportional expenses.

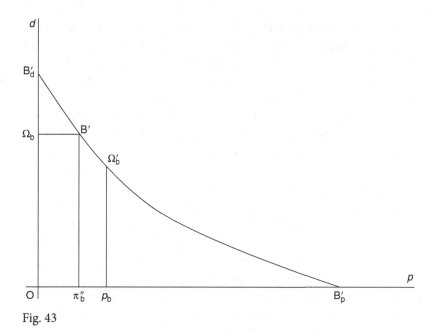

Fig. 43

sections, we would obtain new prices that would still be slightly different from $p_b, p_c, p_d, \cdots$. Proceeding after that to a second, to a third reprise of the two tatonnements... and so on, we would finally obtain certain quantities $D_b, D_c, D_d, \cdots$ of (B), (C), (D) $\cdots$ being sold at prices equal to the average costs $p_b, p_c, p_d, \cdots$. We can then enunciate this proposition that belongs specifically to the theory of production: *the equality of the price of products and their average cost in productive services is attained by increasing the quantity of products for which the price exceeds the average cost, and by decreasing the quantity of those whose average cost exceeds their price.* By this it is seen that, strictly speaking, the consideration of the expenses of production determines not the *price* but the *quantity* of the products.[4]

---

[4] Imagine that instead of saving only himself, Robinson Crusoe had been accompanied by a hundred sailors and passengers who brought with them rice, rum, etc. If all these individuals held a market on the shore in order to exchange their commodities with each other, these would have current prices perfectly

9. Our prices of services $p_t, p_p, p_k, \cdots$ are always determined at random; there remains for us a fourth and last problem to solve, which is to determine the way in which the quantities demanded and the quantities supplied are equalized. Now, at the point at which we have arrived, there are quantities supplied of (T), (P), (K), $\cdots$, $U_t, U_p, U_k, \cdots$ that are determined by the condition of maximum satisfaction, in conformity with the solution of our first problem. And, opposite these quantities supplied, there are quantities demanded that are composed of two elements: first, the quantities demanded by the consumers in the way of consumable services $u_t, u_p, u_k, \cdots$ that are also determined by the condition of maximum satisfaction; then the quantities demanded by the entrepreneurs in the way of productive services, $D_t, D_p, D_k, \cdots$ that are determined by the quantities produced of the products (A), (B), (C), (D), $\cdots$, for which the demand is equal to the supply, and the price equal to the average cost, in conformity with the solution of our second and third problems. It could be demonstrated exactly as in the theory of exchange that if, everything else remaining equal, p is made to vary from zero to infinity: 1° the demand for (T), $D_t + u_t$, will always decrease following a curve $T_d T_p$ (Fig. 44); 2° the supply of (T) will, starting from zero, increase, then decrease and return to zero following a curve QR; and that, consequently, there exists a price p'_t, at which the supply and demand of (T) are equal, which is $> p_t$ if, at the price p_t, the demand for (T) is greater than the supply, and $< p_t$ if, at the price p_t, the supply of (T) is greater than the demand. There exists, likewise, a price p'_p at which the supply and demand of (P) are equal, a price p'_k at which the supply and demand of (K) are equal, and so on. After a first series of tatonnements with the prices $p_t, p_p, p_k, \cdots$ including, of course, the

determinate and completely independent of the costs of production. This is the problem of exchange and shows how the prices depend only on the rareté, that is to say, on the utility and the quantity possessed of the commodities. But if, afterwards, these individuals, having found on the island the necessary productive services, proceeded to produce the same commodities and carried them to the market, the commodities whose price exceeds their average cost would become more numerous, and those whose average cost exceeds their price would become fewer, until the equality of price and average cost was established. That is the problem of production and it shows how the consideration of the cost of production determines the quantity and not the price of the products.

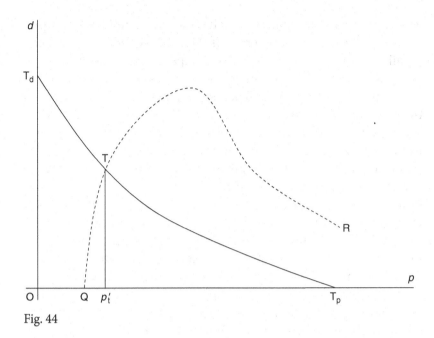

Fig. 44

tatonnements in the second and third problems, we would proceed to a second reprise on the prices $p'_t, p'_p, p'_k, \cdots$, then to a third, and so on. And, consequently, *an equilibrium of the market for services is reached, as in the one for products, by raising the price of those for which the demand is greater than the supply, and lowering the price of those whose supply is greater than the demand.*[5]

10. We must envision as taking place simultaneously all the operations that, by the requirements of the demonstration, we have had to assume occur successively; that is to say, in the market for products and in the market for services, the demanders raise the price when the demand exceeds the supply, and the suppliers lower the price when there is an excess of supply over the demand; the entrepreneurs who make products increase their production when the price exceeds the average cost and, on the contrary, reduce it when the average cost exceeds the price; and, here again, thanks to the

[5] The price of natural raw materials would be determined like that of productive services.

geometric representation, we will have an exact and complete pic-
ture of the general phenomenon of the establishment of economic
equilibrium under the rule of free competition. But, nevertheless,
the analytic form of expression would be necessary to achieve a truly
scientific idea of the matter. To achieve it, then, after having defined
the elements of the system, or, the quantities that come into play,
it would be necessary to distinguish the givens and the unknowns,
to express by equations the conditions of economic equilibrium, to
establish that these equations are exactly equal in number to that of
the unknowns, to show that, through the tatonnements, the solution is more and more closely approached, to explain the particular
conditions of equilibrium so far as concerns the numeraire product
(A), all matters of which nothing has been said here and regarding which I will take the liberty of referring the reader to part III
[above] of my *Éléments*. The present exposition is therefore only
a summary but one which, perhaps, nonetheless enables a better
perception of the general course of the theory. As is clearly seen
here, the theory of production, like that of exchange, begins with
the problem of each exchanger obtaining maximum satisfaction
of wants and ends with the problem of the establishment on the
market of the equality of supply and demand. Except that *services*
are substituted for goods. And, indeed, in the mechanism of production, we exchange services for services. But while a part of the
services that we buy is indeed services, another part is services in
the form of *products*. It is necessary therefore to introduce into the
theory the fact of the transformation of a part of the services into
products; and that is what I did in the second and third problems.
I did it in the simplest possible fashion, and almost all of the criti-
cisms that have been leveled at me have consisted in pointing out
to me various complications from which I had abstracted. My reply
is very easily conceived. The objective that I set for myself, as far
as I am concerned, was to expound and explain the mechanism
of production by reducing it to its essential elements. Economists
that come after me are free to bring into it, one by one, whatever
complications they want. They and I, I think, will thus have done
all that we should do.

III THE EXCHANGE OF SAVINGS FOR NEW
CAPITAL GOODS

11. In order to simplify, we will assume for the moment that the equilibrium prevails that was established regarding the quantities of commodities produced as well as the prices of commodities and of services, and we will abstract from the changes in this equilibrium that can result from the search for the special equilibrium of capital formation. We will similarly make abstraction from the depreciation and insurance of capital goods.

12. The elements of the equilibrium of capital formation are the quantities produced of new capital goods and the rate of income, i, from which result the prices of the capital goods in accordance with the general formula $\Pi = \dfrac{p}{i}$. Let us therefore assume that there are produced at random the quantities $D_k, D_{k'}, D_{k''}, \cdots$ of new capital goods of the types (K), (K'), (K'') $\cdots$, and that there is a rate of income i cried at random. At that rate, each exchanger determines the excess of his income over his consumption, and the total of these individual excess quantities forms a total excess quantity E, which is the quantity of numeraire offered to buy new capital goods, or, the demand for new capital goods at the rate i. On the other hand, at the current prices, assumed to be determined and constant, of their productive services $p_k, p_{k'}, p_{k''}, \cdots$, the quantities $D_k, D_{k'}, D_{k''}, \cdots$ of the capital goods (K), (K'), (K'') $\cdots$ yield a total income $D_k p_k + D_{k'} p_{k'} + D_{k''} p_{k''} + \cdots$, and have a total value

$$\frac{D_k p_k + D_{k'} p_{k'} + D_{k''} p_{k''}, \cdots}{i},$$

which is the quantity of numeraire demanded in exchange for the new capital goods or the supply of new capital goods at the rate i. If, by chance, these two quantities of numeraire were equal, the rate i would be the equilibrium rate of income; but generally they will be

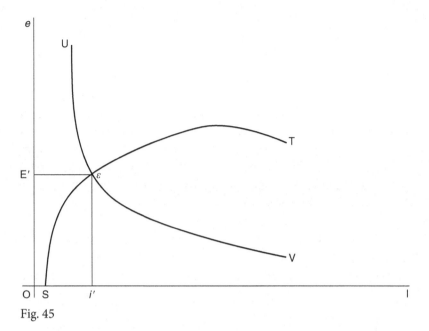

Fig. 45

unequal and it is a question of leading them to equality. Now, it can be assumed in fact that the excess of the income over consumption is at first zero at a zero rate, then it begins to grow at a positive and increasing rate, then decreases and returns to zero if the rate tends to become infinitely great; that is to say, if, with a minimum saving, it is possible to obtain an extremely large increment of income. In other words, the rate of income shown as an abscissa on the axis OI (Fig. 45), the excess of income over consumption will be the ordinate of a curve ST successively increasing and decreasing. As for the value of the new capital goods, it evidently increases or decreases according as the rate of income decreases or increases. In other words, the rate of income being an abscissa on the axis OI, the value of the new capital goods will be an ordinate of a curve UV that is always decreasing. Hence, it is immediately seen that *it is necessary to raise the price of the new capital goods by lowering the rate of income if the demand for new capital goods in numeraire is greater than the supply, and to lower the price of the new capital goods by raising the rate of income if the supply of the new capital goods in numeraire is greater than the demand.*

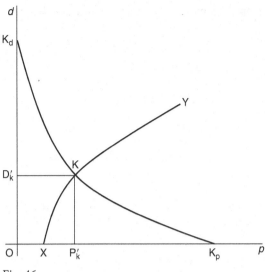

Fig. 46

13. At this point, at the prices $\Pi_k, \Pi_{k'}, \Pi_{k''}, \cdots$ of the new capital goods (K), (K'), (K''), $\cdots$ there are the average costs $P_k, P_{k'}, P_{k''}, \cdots$. And it is a question of leading them to reduce the prices and the average costs to equality, which generally does not exist between them. Now, we may regard as justified by the foregoing demonstrations that by increasing or decreasing the quantity of a capital good (K), the rareté and the price of its use are decreased or increased, and, consequently, so is the price of the capital good; that is to say, the curve of the quantity as a function of the price is a constantly decreasing curve K_dK_p (Fig. 46). And we are equally justified in stating that by increasing or decreasing the quantity of the same capital good (K), the rareté and the prices of the productive services that enter into the making of the capital good are increased or decreased, and, consequently, so is its average cost; that is to say that the curve of quantity as a function of the average cost is an increasing curve XY. Hence, it is seen immediately and without the necessity of reproducing here the exposition of the successive tatonnements on the quantities of capital goods (K), (K'), (K'')$\cdots$ and of the successive reprises of tatonnement, that it *is necessary to increase the quantity of the new capital goods whose price exceeds their average cost and to decrease the quantity of those whose average cost exceeds the price.*

14. The equilibrium of capital formation once established as has just been explained, we have:

$$P_k = \Pi_k = \frac{p_k}{i}, P_{k'} = \Pi_{k'} = \frac{p_{k'}}{i}, P_{k''} = \Pi_{k''} = \frac{p_{k''}}{i}, \cdots,$$

hence

$$\frac{p_k}{P_k} = \frac{p_{k'}}{P_{k'}} = \frac{p_{k''}}{P_{k''}} = \cdots;$$

that is to say, the rate of income is the same for all the savings that are capitalized. It can be demonstrated geometrically in a very simple manner, at least as far as concerns capital goods that produce consumable services, that *this identity of rate of income is the condition of the maximum utility of new capital goods.*

There are two problems of maximum utility relative to the services of new capital goods: the one that arises in regard to the distribution by an individual of his income among his various kinds of wants, and the one that arises in regard to the distribution by a society of the excess of its income over its consumption among the various varieties of capital goods. The first is solved, by virtue of the construction that was made in the theory of exchange and that we recalled at the beginning of the theory of production, by the proportionality of the raretés to the price of its services, in accordance with the equations:

$$\frac{r_k}{p_k} = \frac{r_{k'}}{p_{k'}} = \frac{r_{k''}}{p_{k''}} = \cdots,$$

It will be understood without difficulty that the second problem would be solved by virtue of a construction exactly similar to the former (except that instead of transforming the curves of the wants for the services by dividing the abscissas and multiplying the ordinates by the prices of the services $p_k, p_{k'}, p_{k''}, \cdots$ we would divide the one and multiply the other by the average costs $P_k, P_{k'}, P_{k''}, \cdots$ of the capital goods) by the proportionality of the raretés to these prices of the capital goods, in accordance with the equations:

$$\frac{r_k}{P_k} = \frac{r_{k'}}{P_{k'}} = \frac{r_{k''}}{P_{k''}} = \cdots,$$

or, dividing the latter system by the former, by the identity of the rate of income for all the capital goods, in accordance with the equations:

$$\frac{p_k}{P_k} = \frac{p_{k'}}{P_{k'}} = \frac{p_{k''}}{P_{k''}} = \cdots.$$

Notes

i See Walras's footnote 2 below.

ii We think that LW should have written $\dfrac{0}{1}, \dfrac{r_b}{p_b}, \dfrac{0}{p_c}, \dfrac{0}{p_d}, \cdots$.

iii Walras indicated the vertical axis of the coordinate system in which he has drawn the graph NP′ by Oo, where the symbol o means 'offre', 'supply' in English.

iv If there were no irrevocable disequilibrium transactions, there would be only one tatonnement. Virtual pricing and determination of virtual supply and demand quantities would go on until a set of general equilibrium prices is found. Then actual trade would occur, after which all markets would simultaneously reach equilibrium. However, there are disequilibrium transactions in Walras's system in the following sense. In each temporarily isolated market during the course of reaching temporary equilibrium, there are no trades at which market supply and demand are unequal, no market day disequilibrium transactions. The price in each market is changed until desired supply and demand are equal, whereupon trade occurs. However, the prices are not equilibrium ones from a general equilibrium point of view; the trades at prices temporarily equating supply and demand are disequilibrium trades. The traders learn the prices that have been temporarily settled upon in other markets, and they readjust their supply and demand quantities, thus disrupting the temporary equilibria. The new set of individual desired supply and demand functions are not the same as the ones that existed at the initial distribution of assets, so they are not equal at the set of prices that have been found at the end of the initial tatonnement. A reprise of tatonnement begins. Prices are raised or lowered again in accordance with the Walrasian rule until a new temporary equilibrium price is found.

The process is repeated with a new tatonnement on each successive 'day' in each market, tracing out a series of temporary equilibrium prices in each market. The entire set of temporary prices, Walras argued in his discussion of stability, moves progressively closer to the final set of equilibrium prices and thus to general equilibrium.

v   Presumably Walras forgot to add the terms that we have placed inside brackets.

Observations on the principle of Messrs. Auspitz's and Lieben's theory of prices[1]

1. According to Messrs. Auspitz and Lieben, the price of a commodity is determined by the slope of the vector ray Oc that is common to the two curves ON' and OA' (Fig. 47). These two curves are respectively the curves of the derivatives (abgeleiteten Kurven) of[i] ON and OA; that is to say, the vector rays of the former are parallel to the tangents of the latter. Hence, whatever the meaning of the curves ON, ON', OA, OA', it is evident that the first two can be replaced by a single curve vv' (Fig. 48) giving by its areas the values that the curve ON gives by its ordinates, and giving by its ordinates the values that the curve ON' gives by the slope coefficients of its vector rays; and the latter two by a single curve αα' giving similarly by its areas the values that the curve OA gives by its ordinates, and by its ordinates giving the values that the curve OA' gives by the slope coefficients of its vector rays. Thus, divested of their disguises, the two curves vv' and αα' immediately appear to us as Cournot's[2] and Mangoldt's[3] curves of demand and supply that have been used by a number of English

---

[1] Reprinted from the *Revue d'économie politique*, May–June, 1890. The principle under discussion was expounded in the first chapter (pp. 1–24) and in the corresponding appendix (pp. 431–5) of the *Untersuchungen über die Theorie des Preises* [*Researches into the Theory of Prices*], by Rudolf Auspitz and Richard Lieben, Leipzig, Verlag von Duncker & Humblot, 1889.

[2] *Recherches sur les principes mathématiques de la théorie des richesses* (1838) [translated into English by Nathaniel T. Bacon under the title *Researches into the Mathematical Principles of the Theory of Wealth*, (1897), reprint, New York: Kelley 1971], chapters IV and VIII.

[3] *Grundriss der Volkswirtschaftslehre* [An Outline of Economic Theory], 1st ed., Stuttgart, Engelhorn (1863), sections 62 to 67. It should be noted that, in the second edition of this work, that was published after the death of the author, the editor Friedrich Kleinwachter thought it appropriate to omit the curves.

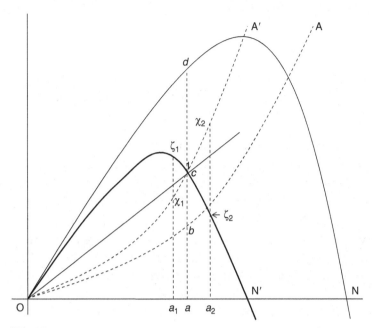

Fig. 47

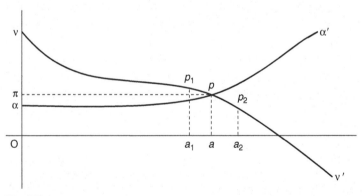

Fig. 48

economists, following the lead of Mr. Marshall of Cambridge. The curve vv' gives the demand by its abscissas as a function of the price, which is represented by its ordinates; the other, $\alpha\alpha'$, gives the average cost by its ordinates as a function of the *supply*, which is represented by its abscissas. From this it follows that the abscissa Oa of the point of intersection p gives the demand equal to the supply, and that the ordinate Oπ of the same point gives the price equal to the average cost.

2. The first observation to be made on the subject of these curves is that, since their ordinates represent prices in money, the use of a *numeraire* is assumed implicitly in specifying them, the introduction of which without a prior analysis is not good scientific method.

3. The *demand curve* vv', or, the curve representing the *quantity sold* as a function of the *price*, cannot be accepted as being a rigorously exact curve. The quantity sold of a product is a function not only of its own price, but also of the prices of all other products and the prices of all productive services. Messrs. Auspitz and Lieben assume that the prices of other products and the prices of productive services do not vary while the price of the product under consideration varies. Theoretically, they have no right to do this. The prices of products and the prices of productive services depend on each other. In varying the price of a product, the prices of the productive services are changed, and consequently the prices of the other commodities also. It is strange that those authors have wrongly taken me to task, in their preface, for an error that I have good reason here to accuse them of committing, namely that of treating demands that are functions of several variables as functions of a single variable.

4. The definite integral of the demand function does not represent the total utility; and, consequently, if the curve ON' (Fig. 47) is a *demand curve (Nachfragekurve)*, then the curve ON is not a *total utility curve (Gesammtnützlichkeitskurve)*. Here Messrs. Auspitz and Lieben fall into Dupuit's error, to which I called attention in lesson 37 of my *Éléments d'économie politique pure*. It follows that the *consumers' surplus (Nutzen der Konsumtion)* is not measured by the expression that they give.

5. The *supply curve* αα' or *average cost* curve as a function of the *quantity of output*, is not acceptable either. The average cost of a product is a function of the prices of the productive services employed in the production of the product; and it is because the prices of

the productive services increase or decrease that the average cost increases or decreases with the quantity produced. But, as the prices of the productive services increase or decrease, the average costs of all the products in the production of which those services are used will also increase or decrease; and the economic equilibrium will be completely disturbed. It is, therefore, theoretically impossible to construct an average cost curve for a product as a function of the quantity produced of the product on the supposition that economic equilibrium will maintain itself with respect to the average costs and with respect to the quantities produced of other products.

6. The definite integral of the supply function does not represent the total cost of production of the quantity manufactured. In the system of free competition, every unit in the quantity Oa (Fig. 48) must be considered as having the same average cost *ap*, whence it follows that the total cost is represented not by the area O*apa*, but by the area O*πpa*. Consequently, if the curve OA' (Fig. 47) is a *supply curve* (*Angebotskurve*), the curve OA is not a *total cost of production curve* (*Gesammtherstellungskostenkurve*). Therefore, there is no such thing as a *producers' surplus* (*Nutzen der Produktion*) that would be measured by the given expression.[ii]

7. It remains to examine the construction on the supposition that it is being proposed as an approximate construction. Now, by referring back to the equations of production (*Éléments*, §§ 198, 199), we will become convinced that the construction is needlessly contradictory and complex.

In order to construct the demand curve for (B), we must take from system [2] the equation

$$D_b = F_b\left(p_t, p_p, p_k, \cdots, p_b, p_c, p_d, \cdots\right)$$

It is assumed that $p_t, p_p, p_k, \cdots, p_c, p_d, \cdots$ are determined and constant. All possible values are given to p_b and all the corresponding values of D_b are obtained from the equation. In order to construct the supply curve, it would be necessary to take all the equations of systems [1] and [3], and eliminate $O_t, O_p, O_k, \cdots$, to obtain

$$a_t D_a + b_t D_b + c_t D_c + d_t D_b + \cdots = F_t\left(p_t, p_p, p_k, \cdots, p_b, p_c, p_d, \cdots\right),$$

$$a_p D_a + b_p D_b + c_p D_c + d_p D_b + \cdots = F_p\left(p_t, p_p, p_k, \cdots, p_b, p_c, p_d, \cdots\right),$$

$$a_k D_a + b_k D_b + c_k D_c + d_k D_b + \cdots = F_t\left(p_t, p_p, p_k, \cdots, p_b, p_c, p_d, \cdots\right),$$

$$\vdots$$

and to take from system [4] the equation

$$b_t p_t + b_p p_p + b_k p_k + \cdots = p_b$$

and substitute it into the above equations. It would then be assumed that $D_a, D_c, D_d, \cdots p_c, p_d, \cdots$ are determined and constant. All possible values would be assigned to D_b, from the modified equations we take p_t, p_p, p_k, and thus we obtain all the corresponding values of p_b.[4]

The intersection of the two curves of demand and supply would give the value of D_b at which the price is equal to the cost of production.

Now, on the one hand, it is evident that, in the second operation, $p_t, p_p, p_k, \cdots$ are varied, and so consequently are $p_c, p_d, \cdots$, which are assumed to be determined and constant in the first operation. And, on the other hand, as soon as $p_t, p_p, p_k, \cdots$ are assumed to be determined and constant, it suffices to deduce p_b from them and to substitute this value of p_b into the equation of the demand curve to obtain D_b.

Let $p_b = \overline{O\pi} = \overline{ap}$. If the quantity $\overline{Oa_1} < \overline{Oa}$ is produced, the price will be $\overline{a_1 p_1} > \overline{O\pi}$; there will be a profit and output will increase. If the quantity $\overline{Oa_2} > \overline{Oa}$ is produced, the price will be $\overline{a_2 p_1} < \overline{O\pi}$; there will be a loss and output will decrease.

Moreover, this curve of demand as a function of the average cost is also a curve of the price as a function of the quantity supplied.

Let $\overline{Oa}$ be that quantity. If the price $\overline{a_1 p_1} > \overline{ap}$ is cried, the demand will be $\overline{Oa_1} < \overline{Oa}$, and it will be necessary to lower the price. If the

---

[4]   The abscissas of the curve would be successively increasing and decreasing as its ordinates progressively increased, and would be asymptotic, not to a line parallel to the price axis as Messrs. Auspitz and Lieben believe, but to that axis itself.

price $\overline{a_2 p_2} < \overline{ap}$ is cried, the demand will be $\overline{Oa_2} < \overline{ap}$, and it will be necessary to raise the price.

Conceived of in this way, the demand curve has served me in the construction of the pure and applied theory of money.[5] I would not wish to maintain that, in one or another question, it would not be advantageous also to use the supply curve. But I assert adamantly that those two curves cannot serve as the starting-point of a complete and rigorous theory of the determination of prices.

Notes

i   Walras should have inserted at this point the words 'the functions whose graphs are, respectively'.

ii Walras could have criticized purely mathematical aspects of the nonsensical figure. The derivative of ON is initially positive and then everywhere decreasing and so cannot be increasing and then decreasing. ON' cannot be the derivative of ON. The derivative of OA is certainly not OA'. The derivative of the former would lie much closer to the vertical axis.

---

[5] As soon as it is assumed that the market is in a complete state of equilibrium, except in regard to product (B), the curve vv' represents the two curves $B_d B_p$ (Fig. 42) and $B'_d B'_p$ (Fig. 43) of Appendix I conflated into a single curve of which the abscissas represent the quantities and the ordinates the prices. That is my *price curve*.

Note on Mr. Wicksteed's refutation of the English theory of rent[1]

1. The exposition and refutation of the English theory of rent that forms the subject of lesson 31 of my *Éléments d'économie politique pure* is one of the problems of mathematical economics that has given me the greatest trouble and that has thus far had the fewest readers. It was, however, an attempt to formulate a rigorous critique in mathematical language of one of the theories about which the confused and sterile discussion in ordinary language has engendered such a volume of writings that just listing them would fill a book; and I have always been convinced that an attempt at a formulation would attract the attention and excite the zeal of mathematical economists when they had had enough of the vacuity that currently constitutes the critique of economic theory. That is why I read attentively Mr. Wicksteed's short treatise on this subject, and found with the liveliest satisfaction that his work reached, by the same methods, exactly the same conclusion as mine.

2. System [4] of my *Production equations* is a system of m equations stating that 'the prices of the products are equal to the average cost of the productive services employed in their production', and having the form

$$b_t p_t + \cdots + b_p p_p + \cdots + b_k p_k + \cdots = p_b$$

---

[1] Reprinted [except for the postscript] from the *Recueil publié par la Faculté de Droit de l'Université de Lausanne* (1896). — This refutation was published in a book entitled *An Essay on the Coordination of the Laws of Distribution*, by Philip H. Wicksteed, author of *The Alphabet of Economic Science*. London, Macmillan & Co., 1894.

(*Elements*, § 199), and therefore becoming, when multiplied by the quantity produced D_b

$$D_b b_t p_t + \cdots + D_b b_p p_p + \cdots + D_b b_k p_k + \cdots = D_b p_b.$$

This system is completed by adding the system of equations expressing the relation between the coefficients of production (§ 274) and having the form

$$\phi\left(b_t, \cdots, b_p, \cdots, b_k, \cdots\right) = 0$$

Mr. Wicksteed writes the equation

$$P = F(A, B, C, \cdots)$$

subject to the condition

$$mP = F(mA, mB, mC, \cdots)$$

(*Essay*, Prefatory Note and § 6); and deduces from it

$$P = \frac{dP}{dA} A + \frac{dP}{dB} B + \frac{dP}{dC} C + \cdots$$

(*Essay*, § 6). He calls *P* 'the product', and *A*, *B*, *C* 'the factors of production'; and writes the former as a 'function' of the latter. That way of expressing matters is ambiguous by design: the author reserves the right to interpret *P* *ad libitum* as either a quantity or a value. But this is a minor matter. If $P = D_b$ and is the quantity of output, his

$$\frac{dP}{dA}, \frac{dP}{dB}, \frac{dP}{dC}, \cdots$$

correspond respectively to my

$$\frac{p_t}{p_b}, \cdots, \frac{p_p}{p_b}, \cdots, \frac{p_k}{p_b}, \cdots.$$

If $P = D_b$ and is the *value of the product*, his

$$\frac{dP}{dA}, \frac{dP}{dB}, \frac{dP}{dC}, \cdots$$

correspond respectively to my $p_t, \cdots, p_p, \cdots, p_k, \cdots$. In the two cases, $A = D_b b_t$, $B = D_b b_p$, $C = D_b b_k$, $\cdots$ always subject to the condition

$$\phi\left(b_t, \cdots, b_p, \cdots, b_k, \cdots\right) = 0,$$

and his equation does not differ from mine (if it really differs at all) except by being more general in form.[i]

3. Having posited this equation, Mr. Wicksteed makes a detailed criticism of the English theory of rent (*Essay*, § 5) that is identical to the one I made (*Éléments*, lesson 31).

I modify the English theory in such a way as to express it in a formula

$$p_t = F(x) - xF'(x)$$

that I recognize as being the same statement as the equation

$$b_t p_t + \cdots + b_p p_p + \cdots + b_k p_k + \cdots = p_b.$$

Mr. Wicksteed starts with his equation

$$P = \frac{dP}{dA} A + \frac{dP}{dB} B + \frac{dP}{dC} C + \cdots$$

and derives from it a formula expressing the modified English theory

$$p_t = F(c) - cF'(c).$$

For exacting readers, I will note that Mr. Wicksteed and I each make a slightly different modification to the English theory.

In my formulation, the variable x is 'the total, in numeraire, of the different kinds of personal and movable capital (P), (P′), (P″), $\cdots$, (K), (K′), (K″), $\cdots$ applied to the land (T)', in accordance with the equation

$$x = H\left(b_p P_p + \cdots + b_k P_k + \cdots\right) = \frac{H}{i}\left(b_p p_p + \cdots + b_k p_k + \cdots\right),$$

$H = \dfrac{1}{b_t}\dfrac{1}{\vartheta(b_p,\ldots,b_k\ldots)}$ being the number of units of product obtained

per unit of land (§ 306). From this it follows that my $\mathrm{F}\left(x\right) = H p_b$, that my $\mathrm{F}'\left(x\right) = i$, that my $x\mathrm{F}'\left(x\right) = H(b_p p_p + \cdots + b_k p_k + \cdots)$, and, finally, that my $p_t = H p_b - H(b_p p_p + \cdots + b_k p_k + \cdots)$.

In Mr. Wicksteed's formulation, the variable c would be, in a notation like mine, 'the number of units of *capital* + *labour* (K) applied to land (T)', in accordance with the equation

$$c = H b_k$$

(*Essay*, p. 24). From this it would follow that his $\mathrm{F}\left(c\right) = H p_b$, that his $\mathrm{F}'\left(c\right) = p_k$, that his $c\mathrm{F}'\left(c\right) = H b_k p_k$, and, finally, that his $\mathrm{p}_1 = H p_b - H b_k p_k$.

For Mr. Wicksteed as well as for myself, the total area under the curve, representing $\mathrm{F}(x)$ or $\mathrm{F}(c)$ is, therefore, 'the total amount of units of output in numeraire', and the upper area, representing $\mathrm{F}\left(x\right) - x\mathrm{F}'(x)$ or $\mathrm{F}\left(c\right) - c\mathrm{F}'(c)$, is 'the amount of rent measured in numeraire' and not in *units of product* as in the English theory. But the fact that, advancing matters further than Ricardo and Jevons along the same path, I take as my abscissa the *total in terms of numeraire of the personal and movable capital applied to land*, and as my ordinate the *rate of net income in numeraire*, permits me to assume any number of services; and the fact that Mr. Wicksteed takes as his abscissa the *number of units of capital + labor applied to land*, and as his ordinate the *price of the service*, compels him not only to reduce all the different varieties of personal capital to a single category and all the different varieties of movable capital to a single category, but to lump those two categories together into a single one. That way of proceeding is explained by his intention: 1° to represent the law of the variation of rent geometrically, and 2° to invert the situation of the two factors *land* and *capital + labor* in order to construct for their situation a geometrical theory symmetrical to the geometrical theory of the aforementioned law. But whatever intrinsic merit this arrangement may have, it nevertheless constitutes only a difference of form; and the substance of his criticism consists, as I have said, in deducing the formula of the English theory of rent from an equation similar to my average cost equation, just as I reduce the formula of the English theory of rent to my average cost of production equation.

4. Whether we proceed in one direction or the other, the aim of the operation is the same. We see immediately, once the operation has been finished, that my equation or Mr. Wicksteed's, to which the formula of the English theory of rent is reduced, cannot be specially applicable to the determination of the price of land services (p_t or $\frac{dP}{dA}$) to the exclusion of the determination of the prices of the services of personal faculties (p_p or $\frac{dP}{dB}$) and of capital goods (p_k or $\frac{dP}{dC}$). This is what I meant by saying: 'Thus all that remains of Ricardo's theory after a rigorous critique is that rent is not an element, but a result, of the price of products. Now, the same thing can be said of wages and interest' (*Éléments*, § 310). That is what Mr. Wicksteed means when he writes: 'Rent is not the cause but the effect of the exchange value of the product' we read in our books. Precisely so, and since the law of rent is also the law of wages and the law of interest, it is equally true that "*wages* are not the cause but the effect of the exchange value of the product". And so too with interest'. (*Essay*, p. 47). I could cite in this respect several other passages in the *Essay* (p. 18, line 14; ibid., line 6), that, like the preceding passage, seem to be translated from the *Éléments* (p. 367, line 18; p. 369, line 18) and that the author could, in a pinch, have put in quotation marks while using this opportunity to mention my work.

5. There are, however, several differences between the book in which I have endeavored, since 1874–77, 'to make clear how a certain

distribution of products results from a given distribution of services' (*Elements*, § 219) and Mr. Wicksteed's *Essay on the Coordination of the Laws of Distribution* that he published in 1894.

After noting that what can be said about rent can also be said about wages and interest, I add: 'Consequently, rent, wages, interest, the prices of products, and the coefficients of production are all in the same problem, and must be determined all together and not independently of one another' (*Éléments*, § 310). And, in consequence, I combine my system of equations expressing *equality between price and average cost* with the system of equations expressing *equality between the demand and supply of services*, and with the systems of equations of the *supply of services* and of the *demand for products*; and I show how free competition, by solving all these equations, determines all their unknowns. Mr. Wicksteed has done nothing like that. As I said, earlier, he leaves his equation

$$P = F(A, B, C)$$

in a form capable of expressing either the quantity, or the value of the product, or, as he puts it, either a 'physical product' or a 'commercial product'; he shows up to what point, in each case, the function is equal to the sum of the products of the partial differential coefficients multiplied by the variables; how, consequently, the rate of remuneration of each factor is the differential coefficient of the product with respect to the quantity of that factor; and he furnishes a geometrical theory of the rate of remuneration of the service capital + labor that is perfectly symmetrical with the theory of rent he disproves. It is not my intention to evaluate that part of Mr. Wicksteed's work; however interesting it may be, I doubt if it authorizes his declaring that: 'I am not aware that any satisfactory attempt has been made to state what may be called the new theory of Distribution in its entirety; and *still less have its relations to the old theory been defined*'(*Essay*, p. 3),[ii] and offering us his opuscule to fill that gap.

September 1894.

P.S. That doubt was well founded. In a note that has just been communicated to me, Enrico Barone has assessed the part of Mr. Wicksteed's work on which I had reserved judgment; and the following is my understanding of that critique.

Mr. Wicksteed rigorously demonstrates his proposition for the case in which his equation is homogeneous and linear and identical to mine. In this case, in fact, the differentials are respectively proportional to their variables; and since we have

$$dP = \left(\frac{dP}{dA}\right)dA + \left(\frac{dP}{dB}\right)dB + \left(\frac{dP}{dC}\right)dC + \cdots$$

we also have

$$P = \left(\frac{dP}{dA}\right)A + \left(\frac{dP}{dB}\right)B + \left(\frac{dP}{dC}\right)C + \cdots$$

But he has not demonstrated it for the case in which his equation is neither homogeneous nor linear; that is to say, for the case in which the coefficients of production vary with the quantity produced. Mr. Barone, on the other hand, has demonstrated it in this case by means of my equation

$$D_b p_b = D_b b_t p_t + \cdots + D_b b_p p_p + \cdots + D_b b_k p_k + \cdots.$$

that is

$$P\pi = Ap_a + Bp_b + Cp_c, \tag{1}$$

and of my equation

$$\phi\left(b_t, \cdots, b_p, \cdots, b_k, \cdots\right) = 0$$

which, already modified by Mr. Pareto by the introduction of D_b, becomes

$$\phi\left(b_t, \cdots, b_p, \cdots, b_k, \cdots, D_b\right) = 0$$

and which Mr. Barone puts into the form

$$D_b = \phi\left(D_b b_t, \cdots, D_b b_p, \cdots, D_b b_k, \cdots\right)$$

that is,

$$P = \phi\left(A, B, C, \cdots\right), \tag{2}$$

which is Mr. Wicksteed's equation that may be assumed to be non-homogeneous and non-linear and in which P is a quantity and not a value of the product.

Differentiating equations (1) and (2) to minimize the cost of production, he obtains

$$\frac{d\phi}{dA} = \frac{p_a}{\pi}, \frac{d\phi}{dB} = \frac{p_b}{\pi}, \frac{d\phi}{dC} = \frac{p_c}{\pi}, \cdots \tag{3}$$

Now, the entrepreneur who is undertaking tatonnements adds to or subtracts from the quantity of each productive service according as the value of the increment of this service is less than or greater than the value of the increment of the product that this increment of service produces, in such a manner as to arrive at the equalities

$$\Delta A p_a = \frac{d\phi}{dA} \Delta A \pi, \quad \Delta B p_b = \frac{d\phi}{dB} \Delta B \pi, \quad \Delta C p_a = \frac{d\phi}{dC} \Delta C \pi, \cdots$$

that is, as given above

$$\frac{d\phi}{dA} = \frac{p_a}{\pi}, \frac{d\phi}{dB} = \frac{p_b}{\pi}, \frac{d\phi}{dC} = \frac{p_c}{\pi}, \cdots \tag{3²}$$

[2]   The meaning of the differentiation and the agreement of practice with the theory is made apparent by saying, following the course of the demonstration of which I made use for the theorem of maximum satisfaction of new capital goods, that: *in the state of equilibrium, the minimum average cost is equal to the price* when the partial differential increments of cost pertaining to each of the productive services are: 1° equal to one another, otherwise, it would be profitable for the entrepreneur to substitute certain services for others; and 2° equal to the partial differential increments of receipts relative to each service, otherwise the entrepreneur would have occasion either to increase or decrease his output; that is to say, when

$$\pi = \Delta P = p_a \Delta A = p_b \Delta B = p_c \Delta C = \cdots$$

that is, when

$$\frac{d\phi}{dA} = \frac{p_a}{\pi}, \frac{d\phi}{dB} = \frac{p_b}{\pi}, \frac{d\phi}{dC} = \frac{p_c}{\pi}, \cdots$$

or when, finally, *the marginal productivities are equal to the rates of remuneration.*

From equations (1) and (3) we obtain

$$P = \frac{d\phi}{dA}A + \frac{d\phi}{dB}B + \frac{d\phi}{dC}C + \cdots \qquad (4)$$

Therefore: 1° *Free competition leads to minimum average cost*; 2° *Under that regime, the rate of remuneration of each service is equal to the partial derivative of the production function, that is, to its marginal productivity*, in accordance with equations (3); 3° *The total quantity of the output is distributed among the productive services*, in accordance with equation (4).

That triple proposition constitutes the 'theory of marginal productivity',[3] a very important theory, first, because it introduces into the problem of production system (3) of equations in which the latter are equal in number to the number of coefficients of production and in which those coefficients figure as unknowns; and, second, because it thereby makes possible a critique and definitive refutation of the English theory of rent, by showing that the consideration of marginal productivity is applicable to the determination of the coefficients of production, but not to the determination of the prices of services, precisely as I said in lesson 31, Mr. Barone deduced that very rigorously from my theory of economic equilibrium; and Mr. Wicksteed, who did not succeed in establishing it for the more general case, would have been better inspired if he had not exerted himself to appear ignorant of the work of his predecessors.[iii]
October 1895

Notes

i Walras does not make clear whether he regarded his equation or Wicksteed's as the more general one.
ii Walras's italics.

3 This theory has been taken up on several occasions in the *Quarterly Journal of Economics*, published by Harvard University, and in the publications of the American Economic Association by various American economists, notably by Messrs. Wood, Hobson, and Clark. As for Barone's note, it will appear, in more developed form, in the *Giornale degli Economisti*.

iii Walras wrote the following section [Fonds Walras, V 1] for this appendix, with three alternative constructions that we have put in brackets, but he deleted it before settling on the final version:

Thus, assuming that the coordination of the laws of distribution depends essentially on the theory of marginal productivity, that coordination would have been, if not accomplished, at least well on the way to being accomplished before the efforts of Mr. Wicksteed, who did not perfect it; and he would have been better inspired to render more justice to those who had preceded him. But did the coordination of the laws of distribution depend on the theory of marginal productivity? I leave the discussion of that question to others. In my opinion, the truth is rather the contrary. The theory of marginal productivity once having been elucidated [developed correctly], as it is in substance in Mr. Barone's note [translated by Walras as 'Sur un livre récent de Wicksteed', 1895, in Walras 1965, vol. 2, pp. 644–8], it is immediately seen that it introduces simultaneously into the body of the theory of production, a certain number of unknowns that are the coefficients of production $b_t, \cdots, b_p, \cdots, b_k, \cdots$, assumed to be variable and that depend not only on each other but also on the quantity produced, and an equal number of equations: the equations of marginal productivity, which are none other than the equations of minimum average cost that I indicated but did not furnish (*Éléments*, §§ 200, 274). As for the unknowns, which are the prices of the services $p_t, \cdots, p_p, \cdots, p_k, \cdots$, and as for the equations that serve to determine them, they are the subject of another part of the theory of production. Now, this other part can be developed, abstraction being made from the determination of the coefficients of production; while that determination, on the contrary, assumes that the prices of the services are determined, since it rests upon the differentiation of the equation of average cost. The more I think about it, the more I am persuaded that fundamentally Mr. Wicksteed, in giving us the theory of marginal productivity having in mind the purpose of the coordination of the laws of distribution, tries (without at all succeeding) to furnish us the equations of minimum average cost having in mind the determination of the prices of the services, a confusion thanks to which he still has one foot in the theory of Ricardo's from which he believes he is completely free. But see what has happened! He tries especially to solve the problem that I have already solved; and that is why he has only half solved the one that still remained to be solved. Messrs. Pareto and Barone proceed differently: they [are the first that] do not claim to refute me by proving that I have not all by myself completed mathematical economic theory, and they do not set themselves the task of redoing what I have done. They take the science as it is at the point to which I have brought it and left it, and propose to continue on with it after me; and hence they arrive at results that are important and new, complete and definitive.

Index

Printed in the United States
By Bookmasters